D1334716

New
Gardening
Year

READER'S DIGEST NEW GARDENING YEAR
was revised, edited and designed by
Tucker Slingsby Limited, London

First edition copyright © 1968
New revised edition copyright © 1997 The Reader's Digest Association Limited,
11 Westferry Circus, Canary Wharf, London E14 4HE
www.readersdigest.co.uk

We are committed both to the quality of our products and the service we provide to our
customers. We value your comments, so please feel free to contact us on 08705 113366,
or by email at cust_service@readersdigest.co.uk

If you have any comments about the content of our books, you can contact us at
gbeditorial@readersdigest.co.uk

Copyright © 1997 Reader's Digest Association Far East Limited
Philippines Copyright © 1997 Reader's Digest Association Far East Limited

Paperback edition 2001

® Reader's Digest, The Digest and the Pegasus logo
are registered trademarks of
The Reader's Digest Association, Inc., of
Pleasantville, New York, USA

All rights reserved. No part of this book may be reproduced, stored in a retrieval system, or transmitted in
any form or by any means, electronic, electrostatic, magnetic tape, mechanical, photocopying, recording
or otherwise, without permission in writing from the publishers.

A CIP catalogue record for this book is available from the British Library

ISBN 0 276 42569 3

Printed and bound in Italy by Milanostampa

New Gardening Year

Reader's
Digest

PUBLISHED BY THE READER'S DIGEST ASSOCIATION LIMITED
LONDON • NEW YORK • SYDNEY • CAPE TOWN • MONTREAL

NEW GARDENING YEAR

The publishers wish to thank the following people for their contribution in preparing this revised edition:

Horticultural consultant: Peter McHoy.

Writers: David Bates, John Bishop, Peter Blackburne-Maze, Leo Boullemier, William Davidson, Dilys Davies, Brian Davis, Liz Dobbs, Jenny Hendy, Sophie Hughes, Janet James, Michael Jefferson-Brown, John Mattock, Peter Maynard, Peter McHoy, David Small, Philip Swindells, Rosemary Titterington, Michael Upward, Ray Waite.

Artists: David Baxter; Leonora Box; Wendy Bramall, Wildlife Art Agency; Lyn Chadwick, Illustration Agency; Ian Garrard; Sally Goodden, Wildlife Art Agency; Ron Hayward, Hayward Art Group; Richard Lewington; Bob Mathias; Carol Merryman, Wildlife Art Agency; Sean Milne; Thea Nockels; Liz Pepperell, Illustration Agency; David Threlfall, Bernard Thornton Artists.

Editorial: Antony Atha, Caroline Ball, Deirdre Clark, Marion Dent, Julia Forrest, Barbara Haynes, Stella Martin, Deirdre Mitchell, Rick Morris.

Design: Bob Mathias, Helen Mathias, Ruth Prentice, Steve Rowling.

Photographs: All the photographs in this book were provided by Peter McHoy or by The Reader's Digest Photographic Library with the exception of the following: Liz Eddison 107, 139tl; John Glover 102, 139tl, 139b, 228l, 228r, 229bl, 229tr; Clive Nichols, pages 4-5 Little Bowden, Berkshire, 8-9 Red Gables, Worcestershire, 14-15, 32-33 Wollerton Old Hall, Shropshire, 50, 52-53 Kew Gardens, London, 74, 84, 86-87, 116, 118-119, 144-145 Mottisfont Abbey, Hampshire, 164bl, 165r, 206l Red Gables, Worcestershire, 206r White Windows, Hampshire, 207t, The Priory, Kemerton, Hereford & Worcester, 207bl Red Gables, Worcestershire, 166-167, 190-191 Little Bowden, Berkshire, 209-210 Waterperry Gardens, Oxfordshire, 230-231, 252-3, 272-3 Brook Cottage, Oxfordshire.

Index: Robert Hood.

Typesetting and text film output: Mega Typesetting Ltd, London W1.
Additional typesetting: Vicki Collinson.

Origination: Studio One Origination Ltd, London WC1.

ABOUT THIS BOOK

The *New Gardening Year* is divided into three sections: GARDENING MONTH BY MONTH, PLANTS FOR YOUR GARDEN and GARDEN BASICS.

SECTION ONE: GARDENING MONTH BY MONTH runs from January to December. Each month opens with an introduction to set the gardening scene. This is followed by a table listing the essential 'jobs that won't wait' for that month; a list to which all gardeners should give priority.

Thereafter each month is broken down into 26 topics which reflect popular gardening interests. These are arranged in alphabetical order, beginning with annuals and biennials and ending with water plants and pools. Each month, for every one of the 26 topics, the work to be tackled and exactly how to do it is clearly explained, with step-by-step colour diagrams for additional clarity where necessary.

Every month closes with a feature on a subject of particular gardening interest or an important gardening project, for instance *Winter Colour* in January, *Creating a New Lawn* in March and *Making a Pond* in April.

SECTION TWO: PLANTS FOR YOUR GARDEN is divided into the 26 gardening topics featured in Section One. It has two purposes: it is a visual directory to over 400 of the best and most widely available garden plants and, with 26 'Year at a Glance' charts, it provides an instant reminder, summarising all the tasks to be carried out each month. With each full-colour photograph there is a description of the plant and details of its ultimate size – an important consideration when planning a new bed or border, or when planting containers.

SECTION THREE: GARDEN BASICS covers the fundamentals of gardening: soils and fertilisers – discussing soil structure, and how and why various manures and fertilisers can be used to help your plants achieve their full potential; the recognition and control of weeds, pests and diseases – offering chemical and cultural remedies; pruning; propagation; tools and equipment; and, finally, greenhouses, frames and cloches.

The book ends with a glossary, highlighting many gardening terms, and a comprehensive index.

Contents

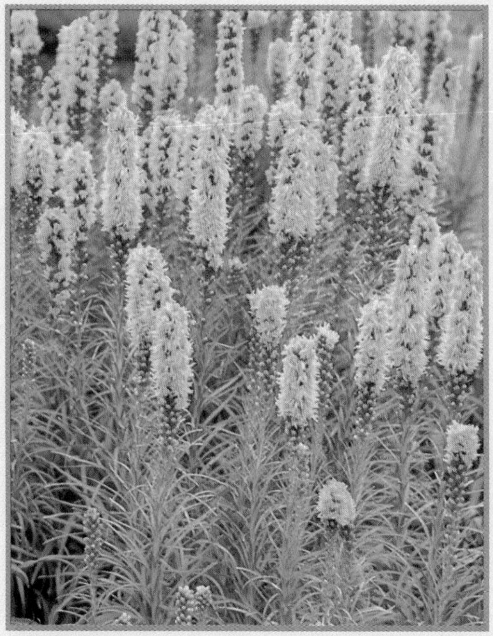

SECTION THREE

Garden Basics

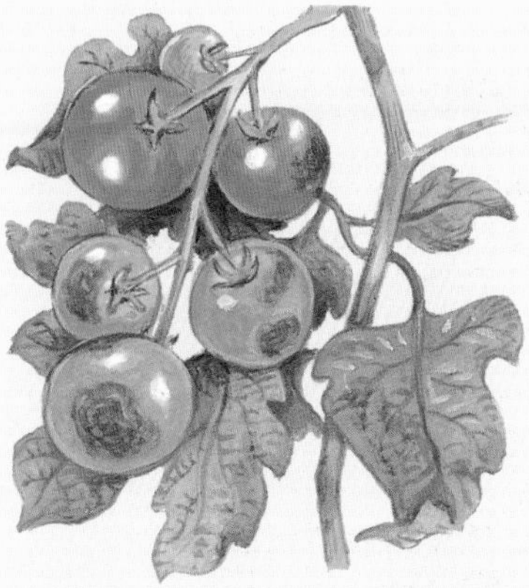

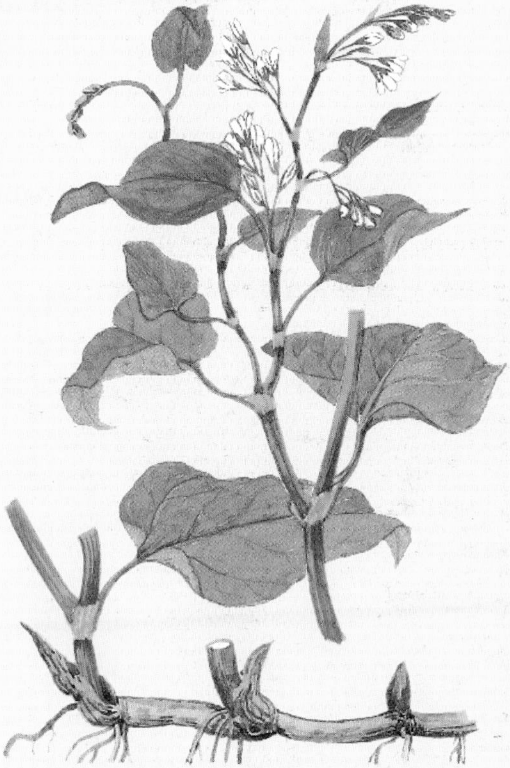

Introduction

Welcome to Reader's Digest New Gardening Year. *This is a completely revised edition of one of the most popular gardening books ever published. Since the original edition appeared nearly thirty years ago, over a million and a half copies have been sold and a generation of gardeners have successfully relied on its invaluable, practical advice.*

This new edition has been rewritten and redesigned for a new generation. It is packed with essential, up-to-date gardening information – whether you have a small patio or a large plot to look after and whether you want to learn new skills or remind yourself of the essentials. Written by a panel of leading gardening authorities, each one a specialist in his or her own area, it is illustrated throughout with detailed photographs and step-by-step colour diagrams demonstrating all the basic gardening techniques from planting bulbs to building a pond.

The New Gardening Year *is a comprehensive and indispensable manual that follows the seasons month by month. This ensures you will find the advice you really need at the time you really need it.*

Happy Gardening!

MONTH BY MONTH

Section One: Introduction

In this section the information given each month is divided into 26 topics which are organised alphabetically. These topics cover all the plants you will want to grow: annuals and biennials; border perennials; bulbs, corms and tubers; carnations and pinks; chrysanthemums; climbers and wall shrubs; dahlias; fruit; fuchsias; heathers; herbs; house and conservatory plants; irises; lilies; pelargoniums; rhododendrons and azaleas; rock plants; roses; sweet peas; trees, shrubs and hedges; vegetables; and water plants. In addition, there are individual entries giving all the information you need on container gardening, lawn care, garden maintenance and growing under glass in greenhouses, cold frames and cloches.

Each month opens with an introduction highlighting what to expect and what to do in the garden that month. A list highlights the priority jobs that won't wait. These are the tasks that should be attended to before anything else.

Garden basics

For all of the plants included in this section comprehensive, practical advice is given each month on care and propagation. In addition, as many gardening techniques are common to a variety of plants, cross references to the third section of the book, *Garden Basics,* are included throughout. *Garden Basics* is an invaluable reference section; it contains all the essential gardening information you will need including how to get the best from the soil in your garden, the control of pests, diseases and weeds, successful propagation and pruning techniques, and the right equipment to buy to get the job done efficiently and speedily.

Section One is also cross-referenced between months so you can benefit from the advice in the *New Gardening Year* at any time. There is no need to start in January! Tasks are cross-referenced back to earlier months or forward to later months as appropriate so you won't miss any of the valuable information in the book whenever you start using it.

Features

At the end of each month there is a special feature covering a particular gardening topic in greater depth. While the month-by-month text ensures you can tackle all the routine gardening tasks successfully, these features show you how to add extra interest and beauty to your garden all round the year. Features include planting for winter colour, building a pond, creating a new lawn, making the most of herbs and planning beautiful borders.

Weather wise

The *New Gardening Year*'s unique month-by-month approach means you get a realistic idea of what needs doing and what to enjoy in your garden each month. Even so, regional variations must be taken into account. Terms such as 'cold areas' and 'mild areas' have been used throughout rather than named regions. This has been done to reflect the considerable variations that can occur even within a tiny area. For example, inland regions are often colder than coastal ones a few miles away; gardens on high ground are usually colder and more likely to suffer from damaging winds than those in a valley close by; and temperatures are usually a degree or so warmer in large cities than in rural areas. These local variations mean that quite tender plants may survive in a sheltered northern garden but die in an exposed garden much further south.

It is important to be able to interpret your own local conditions, so keep the following criteria in mind. If severe frosts are uncommon and seldom prolonged and spring comes early (with daffodils out in February) as in many parts of the South West and the Isles of Scilly for example, this can be considered a mild area. If there are normally prolonged periods of severe frosts and exposure to biting winds with frost not uncommon in early June, this can be regarded as a cold region.

Tender test

To decide how to categorise your garden take note of how well plants of borderline hardiness survive the winter cold. If the top growth of *Fuchsia magellanica*, for example, lives through the winter, you are gardening in a mild spot. If the top growth is killed but the roots come through the winter unscathed without being given extra protection, the area is neither exceptionally mild nor cold. If the plant is killed outright you are gardening in an area that can certainly be classified as cold.

Changeable conditions

As well as testing whether your garden is in a generally cold or mild area, bear in mind that our weather is notoriously fickle. In some years April and May may be mild and balmy, in others there will be cold winds and sharp frosts at night. Most plants will suffer a check in growth if subjected to sharp frosts in April and May so it is always wise to delay sowing and planting until all danger of frosts has passed in the area in which you live.

After some years you will learn by experience but, if you are in need of immediate help, look around at the gardens in your area, check what other gardeners are doing, and look out for the activities of the local parks department; they have years of experience of local weather conditions and their activities are a good guide to what should be done when. In particular, follow their example as to when it is safe to plant out summer bedding.

Plants and plantings

To increase your stock, full details of the appropriate times for sowing seeds, taking cuttings and dividing plants are given under the relevant entries within this section. However, if you want to acquire new plants for your garden, you can browse through Section Two where you will find photographs of over 400 plant varieties that are widely available. Each photograph is accompanied by information which will enable you to select plants that will thrive in your garden.

TWELVE TIPS FOR EVERY GARDENER

- Plan your garden to suit your lifestyle. For low maintenance, you should consider raised beds and paving instead of a lawn. If you a require a garden suitable for children, plan for a large lawn and play area.

- Be guided by the weather: sow seeds and put plants out in the garden when all danger of frost is passed. Be especially careful if the weather is unseasonably cold. Seeds that are sown later will usually catch up.

- Look after the soil in your garden and feed all your plants, including the lawn, shrubs and fruit trees, every spring and throughout the year if necessary.

- Control weeds before they set seed and deal with infestations by pests such as greenfly and blackfly straightaway. You will then have fewer weeds and pests to deal with over the years.

- Grow plants that suit your soil. It is always a struggle to grow plants in an environment they do not relish. If you particularly want to grow plants not suited to your soil it is best to grow them in containers.

- Check which plants are growing happily and look attractive in your neighbours' gardens. Don't be too proud to choose the same plants – or to ask for cuttings!

- Remember that pruning is easy. A good rule of thumb is to prune most shrubs after flowering. More detailed advice for pruning particular plants is given throughout this book.

- Save money by shopping around when buying plants, and by asking for cuttings and divisions of plants from gardening friends.

- Take cuttings of tender plants to overwinter in the greenhouse, cold frame or on a windowsill. Then if the plants do not survive in the garden you will have replacements ready.

- Keep a garden diary recording the plants you have bought and where you have planted them. Be disciplined about labelling and recording the names of your plants.

- Be realistic in your expectations of house plants. Some of the tougher ones may be happy for years but many of the more delicate ones which originated in tropical rainforests will not survive indefinitely however careful you are.

- Make time to sit and enjoy the results of all your labours in the garden.

JANUARY

Bare stems and branches have a beauty of their own, proving colour and interest can still be found in the garden even in the dark, cold days of January.

January

In the middle of winter, thoughts of gardening may still seem a distant dream – rather like the summer holidays. But this is the turning point of the year when you can increasingly start to enjoy gardening again. Much cold weather lies ahead, but often the first spring bulbs are poking through the ground, the buds on many shrubs and trees are beginning to swell and the days are starting to grow longer – albeit almost imperceptibly.

There are not many outdoor jobs that can be done, but planning, buying, and starting off the season in the greenhouse are all pleasant tasks to undertake now. And they all satisfy the urge to be doing something constructive for the gardening year ahead.

The weather in January

The coldest nights of the year often occur during January, with the worst affected areas being inland, well away from the coast. The western coastal regions can be surprisingly mild in some years and gardens in inner cities are usually a degree or two warmer than those in more exposed country areas.

There are often wide temperature variations between different parts of the country. Although sheltered areas in the south and west may still not have received very severe and damaging frosts, Scotland and other northern areas will almost certainly have been affected.

Snow is almost certain to be a problem for short periods this month, except in milder areas such as the Isle of Man, the extreme south-west of England and coastal areas of southern Ireland. Light falls of snow cause little damage and require no action, but heavy falls can break or damage branches on shrubs and trees and the snow should be knocked off the branches before damage occurs.

Heavy snow can also damage fruit cages if the top nets have been left on, so it is a good idea to remove and store the nets if you have not already done so.

Providing winter protection

Shrubs that are not totally hardy are more likely to be killed by a combination of low temperatures and cold winds than by very low temperatures on their own. This effect is known as wind-chill and it can be particularly devastating for evergreens. Winter protection, in the form of a windbreak, is an excellent idea.

All types of winter protection should have been put in place in late autumn or early winter, but if you have not done this, and you do have vulnerable shrubs, it is still worth taking the trouble to wrap them up if severe weather is forecast. Hessian, perhaps with straw packed inside, will be enough to protect most shrubs. Alternatively, you can make a frame from canes and create a 'tent' using several layers of environmental netting or horticultural fleece or bubble plastic. Make sure air can circulate, and ensure that light can penetrate if the plant is an evergreen.

While thinking about protection, do not overlook those plants that are tough enough to flower this early in the year but whose blooms are sometimes damaged by a very heavy frost. The Christmas rose (*Helleborus niger*) and Algerian iris (*Iris unguicularis*) are likely to be in bloom in many parts of the country. The flowers on both these plants are delightful, and look lovely in flower arrangements. If you want unblemished blooms to bring indoors, put a cloche over them, or protect them with a supported pane of glass.

Winter digging

Whether you are preparing a new bed or border for spring, clearing land for a new garden, or getting your vegetable plot ready, digging is an ideal job if you want some warming physical exercise on a cold winter's day – provided the soil is not waterlogged or frozen. If the ground is very wet or is frozen hard, digging will not only be a dauntingly heavy task it may also do more harm than good. On frozen ground it will disturb the coldest top layer of soil and move it lower down into the ground. The soil will warm up more quickly if you leave it undisturbed.

Clean and tidy

Most gardens look rather drab at this time of the year even if a number of plants, such as laurustinus (*Viburnum tinus*) and wintersweet (*Chimonanthus praecox*), are being grown for winter flowers and scent. A visually unexciting garden may be unavoidable in January but the garden will look much better if it is kept tidy.

An untidy garden is more obvious in the middle of winter because, when the leaves have fallen from shrubs and trees and herbaceous plants have died down, some previously hidden garden eyesores will be exposed. This is a good time to go round the garden and tidy everything up: repair broken fences and trellis; cut or tie back plants that are overhanging paths or the lawn; remove canes and other supports left standing in beds; clear away containers and windowboxes standing empty or full of dead plants.

Choose a dry day and hoe the soil to loosen the surface compacted by winter rains; this will give the garden a cultivated look, and make an enormous difference to its appearance. This job is physical enough to keep you warm!

Mulches also improve the appearance of bare soil, although they are best applied for the first time in spring when the soil has warmed up but is still moist. Existing mulches that have worn thin, or become disturbed by animals and birds rummaging for food, can be raked over and topped up if necessary. Wait until there is a mild day – don't mulch over frozen soil.

Work indoors

There will be many days when the weather is just too unpleasant to work outdoors however keen you are to progress work in the garden. Fortunately there are many things that can be done in the comfort of your sitting room or kitchen, and even more activities if you have a heated greenhouse to work in.

Go through the seed and summer bulb catalogues and place your orders now. This will mean there is one less job to do during the busy spring period and early ordering means you are more likely to receive your preferred choice of seeds and bulbs before stocks run out. This is also a good time to order plants and seedlings by post. They probably won't be delivered until spring, but the closing date for orders is much earlier.

Getting seed trays and pots ready (wash and disinfect old ones or buy new ones), and purchasing the potting and seed compost, all give a much-needed psychological boost, acting as a reminder that the growing season is about to start. Early January may be too soon to sow the majority of your seeds, but at least you can write the labels in anticipation. That, too, will ease the pressure later if you want to sow and transplant a lot of seeds and seedlings.

Don't start sowing too early, especially if you only have a couple of windowsills to raise the plants on. Seeds sown now may suffer from lack of light as well as space. If you have a warm greenhouse, however, there are a number of seeds, such as fibrous-rooted begonias and pelargoniums, which can be sown, and cuttings, such as chrysanthemums, to be taken.

Now is also the time to think about how your garden can be improved in the year ahead. If you don't already keep a garden notebook, the beginning of a new year is a good time to start. Use it to write down your ideas and work out detailed plans. You can then take it along on buying trips. A garden notebook or diary is also invaluable for recording details of plants purchased, any special care required and the position you have planted them in the garden.

JOBS THAT WON'T WAIT

- Order seeds to be sown in January or February – you may have to wait some weeks for delivery.
- Protect vulnerable plants from frost and wind damage.
- Firm in any autumn-planted shrubs and border plants lifted by frost.
- Knock snow off branches, especially on conifers and hedges, if they are bending under the weight.
- Check stakes and ties on newly planted trees; make sure they are secure and not rubbing.
- Keep an area of water ice free if you have fish in the pond.
- Check on bulbs being forced for indoor display every week so that you don't miss flowering.

ANNUALS & BIENNIALS

● Sowing slow-maturing bedding

Some half-hardy annuals and other bedding plants take a long time to flower from seed and must be sown in January or February if they are to bloom by early summer. To be successful in this, you will need a heated propagator to germinate some of the seeds and a warm, light position to grow them on once they have been pricked out (*see* Propagation, page 427). Indoors, good light is critical to avoid plants becoming pale and drawn, but seedlings and young plants must be shaded from strong, direct sunlight. Plants for early sowing include antirrhinums, African marigolds, *Begonia semperflorens*, gazanias, pelargoniums and lobelias (*see* March, page 57). If you do not have the facilities for early germination, consider buying plants as ready-to-prick-out seedlings (*see* February, page 36).

● Damping off

Seedlings started off so early in the year are especially vulnerable to the fungal disease damping off, which causes seedlings and young plants to collapse at soil level (*see* Diseases, page 407).

Always clean used seed trays and pots thoroughly and sterilise them with a garden disinfectant. Sow seeds thinly, avoid overwatering and provide newly germinated seedlings with the best growing conditions you can (*see* Propagation, pages 424–427).

● Preparing new beds

Take advantage of any periods of dry, mild weather to dig new flower beds ready for sowing and planting in spring. Leave the final raking and levelling until later, as weed seeds are bound to germinate and can be removed in spring.

BORDER PERENNIALS

● Tidying borders

Clear borders of weeds and debris, to keep them neat and to prevent a build-up of garden pests and diseases. Some weeds will continue to grow and seed in mild winters, while others, such as creeping buttercup, are more easily seen when the ground is cleared. Avoid compacting the soil, particularly in wet winters, by using short pieces of board to walk on. Fork over the soil when the job is finished.

● Ground preparation

Dig any heavy clay soil that was left unturned in the autumn. Frosts will help to break the soil down, creating a finer tilth. Dig in annual weeds, provided they are not seeding, but remove and destroy the roots of all perennial weeds.

BORDER PERENNIALS – TIDYING BORDERS

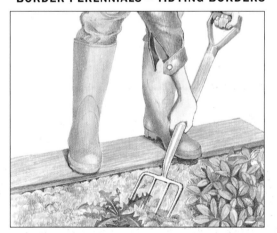

Tidy borders by removing overwintering weeds. You can remove dead stems and leaves from plants at the same time. This improves their appearance and reduces the risk of them sheltering pests and perpetuating diseases.

● Sowing

Some border perennials will bloom in their first season if the seed is sown in warmth under glass over the next two months. Consult seed catalogues to see which varieties are likely to be successful (though all make better plants in their second year). Among the plants to try are alchemillas, campanulas, poppies and violas.

Generally, seeds of hardy perennials should be sown in the appropriate compost and the pots and trays placed outdoors. Cover them with netting to protect them from birds and cats. Many seeds, such as hellebores and peonies, require frost to trigger germination. When the first shoots appear, move the pots into a cold frame or unheated greenhouse. Leave sowing until February if this shelter is not available.

● Frost and wind protection

Check that half-hardy perennials are protected against frost. Plantings from last autumn may also require some protection if the weather turns very cold. Use covers such as cloches, netting, plastic sheeting, newspaper or even old woollens. Natural materials, such as dead bracken, straw, mulches and conifer branches, can also be used. Ashes and cinders from fires must be weathered before use, as they may contain harmful chemicals. Remove all damp coverings as soon as the danger of frost passes since waterlogged materials may cause mildew. Provide permanent or temporary shelter against wind damage. Shrubs, trees and hedges will help break the force of the wind.

Check that slightly tender perennials, such as *Lobelia cardinalis* and osteospermums, have adequate winter protection in cold frames and greenhouses. Close and cover cold frames in frosty weather but open them in milder weather to prevent mildew.

BULBS, CORMS & TUBERS

● Summer-flowering bulbs

Order new summer-flowering bulbs and tubers, such as begonias, galtonias, tigridias and gladiolus corms, in good time from a reputable supplier. When they arrive unpack and examine them. They should be firm and dry – discard any which have a soft base. Those which are sprouting will grow, but they may be slower to put on growth when they are planted out. Store the bulbs in shallow boxes or trays or return them to their bags after cutting holes for air circulation. Keep in a dry, frost-proof place.

The theory that the largest gladiolus corms are best is quite erroneous. A young, plump, high-necked corm with a small root-base is preferable to a larger, flatter corm with a broad root-base.

● Stored bulbs

Check bulbs, corms and tubers that have been stored over winter and remove any that are soft or diseased.

● Forced bulbs

Continue to bring bulbs in bowls and pots into the warmth and light for indoor flowering as they become ready (*see* November, page 256). Apply a half-strength liquid feed, such as a tomato or rose fertiliser, every three weeks. Deadhead the bulbs as the flowers fade and continue to water regularly.

These bulbs can be planted in the garden when flowering has finished, but do not plant them out until the weather and soil conditions are favourable (*see* March, page 59).

● Hippeastrums

Water the bulbs planted last month, and keep them warm and moist as growth accelerates.

CARNATIONS & PINKS

● Improving soil condition

Test the pH of your soil with a kit or meter (*see* The soil in your garden, page 387). Carnations like a pH of at least 6.5. Garden lime can be used to increase the pH; peat or sulphur to decrease it. Carnations also dislike waterlogged conditions (*see* August, page 195), so if weather permits, dig over any poorly drained sites, incorporating grit and well-rotted manure or garden compost.

● Planning ahead

Order plants and seeds for spring planting. Bear in mind the impact that silver-grey dianthus foliage has when combined with other plants and plan future plant associations into your garden design.

Sow seeds of annual carnations. Space the seeds 5 mm (¼ in) apart in trays and cover them with a fine layer of compost. Cover with glass or plastic sheeting and keep them at a constant temperature of 13–15°C (55–60°F).

PERPETUAL-FLOWERING
● Maintaining healthy conditions

Ensure that the temperature does not drop below 7°C (45°F) for perpetual-flowering carnations in the greenhouse and make sure there is some ventilation at all times. Water and feed sparingly (*see* April, page 92), cutting blooms and disbudding flower stems as necessary (*see* September, page 214).

● Controlling pests and diseases

Watch out for aphids and carnation rust (*see* March, page 60) and, if necessary, use dusts in preference to sprays in winter so that the atmosphere in the greenhouse does not become too humid.

● Increasing stock under glass

Continue to propagate perpetual-flowering carnations by cuttings (*see* December, page 276). Pot up rooted cuttings into 5 cm (2 in) pots. Start sowing seeds.

● Ordering new plants

Order new plants now from reputable nurseries for spring delivery.

CHRYSANTHEMUMS

● Ordering new plants

January is the ideal time to order new plants for spring planting.

EARLY-FLOWERING (GARDEN)
● Overwintering

Examine the soil around outdoor-flowering varieties which have been left to overwinter in sheltered, mild gardens. If the soil seems to be waterlogged, pierce the ground around each plant several times with a fork inserted to its full depth. Tread any ground loosened by frost to refirm it around the roots.

Ventilate dormant clumps bedded in cold frames when it is not freezing or windy, but protect them from frost with sacks or matting. Water dormant clumps sparingly.

● Soil preparation

Complete digging on heavy ground and work bulky organic matter into the top 15 cm (6 in) of soil. Test for alkalinity. Chrysanthemums do best in soil with a pH of 6.5 (*see* November, page 257).

LATE-FLOWERING (GREENHOUSE)
● Controlling pests

Treat chrysanthemums under glass affected by

aphids and leaf miners (*see* Pests and Diseases, pages 395 and 401). Keep the maximum temperature in the greenhouse at 10°C (50°F).

● Taking cuttings

Take cuttings of large exhibition varieties (*see* March, page 61). Even if you don't plan to take cuttings now, cut back any shoots longer than 8 cm (3 in). This will keep the plants in good condition for propagation, which you can then carry out during March and April.

Flowers of very late-flowering varieties will carry on well into this month in a cool, dry greenhouse. Take cuttings from these plants now, provided the shoots are strong and healthy.

● Potting up

Towards the end of the month pot up rooted cuttings of large exhibition varieties growing in the greenhouse into 9 cm (3½ in) pots.

CLIMBERS & WALL SHRUBS

● Supports for climbers

Check on trellis, pergolas, arches and all other structures supporting climbers, and carry out any repairs that are needed (*see* November, page 261). If necessary, untie the plants and remove them from their supports – a task which is much easier to do while the plants are dormant.

● Renewing plant ties

Before plants start growing actively, check on the ties that secure them to their supports. Replace any ties which have rotted and add extra ties if these are required – a large climber in full leaf can be very heavy.

TIES AND TYING

It is important to tie climbing plants correctly to supports using the right materials, as otherwise they may be severely damaged by constriction or wind.

Use ties made from non-preservative-treated twine, or any product that will stretch, or rot within a year. Do not use ties made from wire, plastic string or bailer twine, as these will chafe and damage the plant as it rocks in the wind.

The figure-of-eight is one of the best knots to secure climbers and wall shrubs to canes, wires or

trellis. To stop the tie and plant slipping sideways, pass the twine twice around the cane, wire or bar

of the trellis, then cross it over, passing it around the front of the plant. Secure it with a reef knot.

● Pruning

If you have climbers, such as Virginia creeper (*Parthenocissus quinquefolia*), ivy (*Hedera* spp.) and climbing hydrangea (*Hydrangea petiolaris*), growing on the house cut them back by at least 45 cm (18 in) from all windows and door frames. Then the plants can regrow without obscuring these.

● Hardwood cuttings

If the weather permits, take hardwood cuttings of hardy climbers now to save time in the spring (*see* March, page 63).

● Fan training

A few ornamental wall shrubs, pyracantha and the Japanese apricot (*Prunus mume*) are good examples, respond best to being trained in a fan. This ensures that the branches are well spaced out and get an even amount of light and air. The shape of a fan is

CLIMBERS – FAN TRAINING

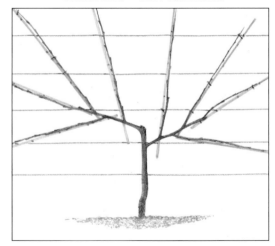

Stretch horizontal wires along a wall at 30 cm (12 in) intervals. Tie bamboo canes to the wires in the desired fan shape, then tie suitable branches to the canes. The tips of the branches should be about 30–45 cm (12–18 in) apart.

established during the first few years of the plant's life. Select the branches to form the fan and tie them on to the canes. Prune out any unwanted shoots flush with the stem.

CONTAINER GARDENING

● Moving containers under cover

January often brings the first hard frosts of winter and plants in pots and baskets are especially vulnerable. Move them to a more protected area or greenhouse if possible until milder weather returns.

● Avoiding snow damage

If heavy snowfalls build up on specimen conifers, there is a risk that some branches may get pulled out of position or break. To prevent this happening,

CONTAINER GARDENING – CONIFERS

Conifers are vulnerable to damage by a heavy snowfall which can break branches and spoil the shape of the tree. If heavy snow is likely, bind the main shoots of conical specimens together by winding string around the tree.

either regularly shake off loose snow or tie loops of soft garden twine down the length of the plant to hold the branches in place. Large evergreen shrubs such as Mexican orange blossom (*Choisya ternata*) are also vulnerable to snow damage, as the weight of snow causes the branches to tear and fall outwards, leaving a hollow centre. Support with a criss-cross of twine running through the middle of the plant.

● Planting trees and shrubs

If the weather is suitable you can continue to plant deciduous shrubs and trees in containers. Once planted, move to a sheltered spot to avoid wind-rock and desiccation (*see* November, page 258).

● Tidying winter containers

Pick off fading flowers and foliage and trim back any frost-damaged shoots. Replace any dead plants and check the compost is not too dry.

DAHLIAS

● Inspection of tubers

Examine stored tubers every few weeks during the winter and, if they are shrivelling, plunge them in a bucket of tepid water for a night (under cover if it is a cold night) to plump them up again. Dry the tubers thoroughly and replace in their boxes.

If stored tubers are showing any signs of rotting, such as dampness on the stems, cut away any portions of the tubers that are damaged and treat the cuts with a sulphur dust. Ensure the labels remain tightly attached to the tubers.

● Ground preparation

Dahlias prefer a position in full sun and do not grow as well if they are planted in a mixed border of herbaceous plants as they do in a bed on their own. If you want to grow top-quality blooms, whether for cutting, for exhibition, or for colour in the garden, try to find a place for them where they will not have to compete with other plants.

Start to dig the dahlia bed as early in the year as possible to permit frost to act on the soil. Dahlias will thrive in any soil that is neither too acid nor too alkaline, but they are gross feeders and require considerable amounts of moisture during the year. To help provide this, incorporate as much compost or well-rotted manure as possible.

FRUIT

Spray fruit trees and bushes with a winter wash if pests were a problem last year. This should only be done if it is essential since it kills as many beneficial insects as it does pests (*see* December, page 277).

Fruit trees and bushes can be planted if the soil conditions are suitable. If not, keep any container-grown plants in a frost-free place or heel them in (*see* November, page 259).

Apply a general fertiliser, such as Growmore or blood, fish and bone, to all fruit trees over 4.5 m (15 ft) high, following the manufacturer's instructions.

CONTROLLING VIGOUR

If an established fruit tree is growing strongly but not fruiting, there are several possible ways to cure the problem. First, stop feeding the tree or switch from a high-nitrogen feed to a high-potash feed. Second, sow grass under the tree to take up some of the moisture, since wet conditions encourage leafy growth. As a last resort, consider root pruning (*see* Pruning, page 423) or bark ringing. Both these operations should be undertaken with caution because if carried out incorrectly they could kill the tree.

Applying now will allow ample time for the fertiliser to be dissolved and carried deep into the root systems. When the trees are growing in grass, use a fertiliser higher in nitrogen to compensate for the nitrogen that will be taken up by the grass.

Inspect ties regularly during the winter and replace any that are tight or broken. Replace broken stakes only if the tree still needs support, as hammering in a new stake may damage the root system (*see* October, page 247).

● Apples and pears

Continue pruning apples and pears (*see* November, page 259) except when the temperature is below freezing. If possible shred the prunings and add the shreddings to the garden compost. This is a valuable raw material and the shreddings will help to aerate your compost heap or bin.

Check all apples and pears that you have stored over the winter and throw away any that have rotted before they spoil the sound fruit.

● Peaches and nectarines

Feed all large fan-trained trees with a balanced fertiliser, such as Growmore or blood, fish and bone; follow the manufacturer's instructions. This will ensure that plenty of new shoots are formed.

● Plums and cherries

Plums and other stone fruit should only be pruned during the growing season – not at this time of year. This reduces the risk of infection by silver leaf fungus (*see* June, page 152).

● Cane fruits

Cut down newly planted canes of raspberries, blackberries and any hybrids, such as loganberries and tayberries, to within 25–30 cm (10–12 in) of the ground. These stumps will produce shoots and, possibly, some fruit in the summer but their main purpose is to sustain the new root systems.

● Gooseberries and currants

Prune newly planted bushes of gooseberries and red and white currants by cutting back strong new shoots by half their length to form the main branches. Cut weak and misplaced shoots right out. On cordons, cut back leading shoots (those on the ends of branches) by a third.

Cut back newly planted blackcurrant bushes to about 2.5 cm (1 in) after planting to encourage strong new shoots to come from below the ground. Although it is later than recommended for propagating (*see* November, page 260), well-ripened shoots can still be used for taking cuttings.

FUCHSIAS

TENDER AND HALF-HARDY

● Dormant plants

Check that plants packed away in peat for the winter and those remaining leafless and dormant in their pots do not become completely dry.

Spray with tepid water any early growth on plants in the light to soften the wood. Do this sparingly as the inactive roots cannot cope with heavy watering.

● Overwintering plants in green leaf

Ensure plants kept in green leaf get as much light as possible and are not becoming pale and leggy. Keep the greenhouse well ventilated even in cold weather, as condensation may encourage grey mould (botrytis) (*see* Diseases, page 407).

● Pruning

Towards the end of the month, watch for the first pink 'eyes' (embryo shoots) appearing on the stems. This indicates that the earliest plants are ready for pruning (*see* February, page 40).

● Vine weevil

Inspect plants in pots for vine weevil larvae (*see* Pests, page 404). These white, crescent-shaped grubs lodge in the rootball and, if undetected, will eat away entire root systems. Gently knock each plant out of its pot and pick off any weevils by hand. Alternatively, dust the soil with a suitable pesticide or use a biological control.

HARDY

In severe winter conditions ensure the crown and base get some extra protection with a layer of garden compost or fine gravel.

GARDEN MAINTENANCE

● Tool maintenance

To save time in the busy spring period, use the winter months to maintain your garden tools. The blades of cutting tools should be wiped with an oily rag after each use, but once a year use wire wool to remove any rust or dried sap, then oil them lightly. Tighten the blade tension of garden shears to improve their cutting. Remove and sharpen the blades of other pruning tools, or replace them if damaged. Service mowers and cultivators and check electrical equipment as many plugs, sockets and leads deteriorate with use in the garden. Replace damaged leads rather than repairing them with tape and ensure that all the connections and fittings are suitable for outdoor use.

● Disposing of unwanted chemicals

Dispose of old chemicals, particularly those for which the instructions have been lost. Dilute dregs and pour them away on unused ground; never down drains. Wrap solid chemicals or empty containers in newspaper and put them in the dustbin. If you are in any doubt, or have large amounts of chemicals to dispose of, take them to a local authority waste disposal site where staff can dispose of them safely.

● Repairing fences and trellis

Check fences, trellis, pergolas and arches and make any necessary repairs while the plants are still dormant (*see* November, page 261).

GREENHOUSES & FRAMES

● Checking insulation and heating

Insulation benefits both greenhouses and frames and can be done simply with plastic bubblewrap. If not already done, make the time to do it now (*see* Greenhouses, pages 444–445). Check the heaters.

● Watering

Water the plants only when the soil in the pots shows signs of drying out. Avoid overwatering annuals in pots and any other young plants in the greenhouse, or the roots may be damaged. Take care not to splash the flowers or leave water lodging in the crowns of the plants. Try to water as early in the day as possible, especially in a cold or cool greenhouse, so that surfaces are dry before nightfall.

● Controlling pests and diseases

Remove any leaves showing signs of grey mould (botrytis), and discard any cuttings which have diseased stems. Check for pests such as vine weevil and take action if necessary (*see* Pests and Diseases, pages 404 and 407). Where possible use dusts rather than sprays in winter to avoid increasing the humidity in the greenhouse.

● Sowing seeds

If you have a heated propagator available which can maintain a temperature of 16–18°C (61–65°F) during germination, you can start sowing seeds towards the end of the month. Without the extra boost of a heated propagator, delay sowing for another month. Sow greenhouse plants, such as begonias, gloxinias and streptocarpus, and also plants for the garden, including pelargoniums, half-hardy annuals, lilies, perennials and sweet peas.

● Lilies for forcing

If you want to force lilies to produce early flowers pot up the bulbs now (*see* Lilies, page 26).

● Vines

Complete the pruning of vines in the greenhouse while they are still completely dormant (*see* December, page 279). Peel or rub any loose bark from the stems of mature vines as this can harbour pests over the winter, but do not pull off so much bark that green shows underneath.

HEATHERS

● Preparing new beds

If you want to plant a bed of heathers, new planting areas can be prepared now during suitable weather. Mix copious amounts of sphagnum moss peat (or peat substitute), sand, pea grit or perlite into heavy clay soils to improve the texture. Light sandy soils

GREENHOUSES – VINES

The loose bark on old vine stems provides an ideal hiding place for overwintering greenhouse pests so be sure to rub it off and, if possible, burn it. Do not strip too much bark from the vine. Wear gloves to protect your hands.

can also be improved by the addition of sphagnum moss peat (do not use sedge peat for this). For summer-flowering heathers avoid spent mushroom compost as this contains lime and, if the pH of the soil is above 6.5, add flowers of sulphur to acidify the bed (*see* The soil in your garden, page 387).

Dig in the peat and any other additives, mixing thoroughly with the original soil, to a full spade's depth. The addition of fertilisers is not necessary.

● Autumn-planted heathers

Examine heathers planted last autumn, remove any weeds around them and gently firm into place any plants which have been partially lifted by frost.

HERBS

● Preparing the site

The dormant period of winter is the ideal time to prepare the ground for your herb garden. Many herbs like hot, dry conditions and need to be planted in a sunny, south-facing position with some protection from north and east winds.

A sloping plot of ground facing south is ideal, and provides a choice of locations which will suit different herbs.

● Ordering seeds and plants

When you have decided on the shape and size of the herb garden (*see* July, pages 188–189) order seeds and plants in readiness for the spring. While many herbs will grow true to type from seed, others will not, and should be purchased as plants from a reputable herb nursery or garden centre to ensure that you obtain the correct varieties.

HOUSE & CONSERVATORY PLANTS

● Protection and light

Plants are vulnerable to cold, draughts and overwet compost at this time of year. Keep tender plants at or above their minimum temperatures. Remove plants from cold windowsills at night, but keep them near a window during the day so they get as much light as possible. Artificial light is beneficial, but keep foliage away from direct heat and avoid the hot, dry air of centrally heated houses.

When the compost is consistently too wet, the roots will rot. If this happens, tip the plant out of its pot and wrap its rootball in several layers of newspaper or absorbent paper for a day or two. Change the paper when it is saturated. When the compost has dried out slightly, replace the plant in its pot.

Try to provide a minimum temperature of 7°C (45°F) in the conservatory. Insulation can help to reduce heating costs (*see* Greenhouses, page 444).

HOUSE PLANTS – OVERWATERING

Most house plants will collapse if overwatered. You may be able to save an affected plant by wrapping the rootball in absorbent paper for a day or two. Cover the roots and change the paper if it gets too saturated.

● Feeding

Only feed house plants if they are growing strongly or are in flower.

● Flowering plants

Keep flowering plants purchased at Christmas in a cool room and deadhead azaleas and primulas regularly to extend their period of flowering. Modern poinsettias last a long time in flower. After flowering cut back their stems to 15 cm (6 in) from the bases. Keep the compost almost dry until May.

Bring pots of polyanthus which were potted up in the summer (*see* July, page 181) indoors and keep them in a cool room at a temperature of no more than 10°C (50°F) until they are about to flower.

HERBS TO GROW FROM SEED

anise
sweet basil
borage
– (*self-seeding biennial*)
caraway
– (*biennial*)
German chamomile
chervil
chives – (*perennial*)
coriander
dill
fennel – (*perennial*)
lovage – (*perennial*)
sweet/knotted marjoram
purslane
salad rocket

Fennel

HERBS TO BUY AS PLANTS

lemon balm
bay
bergamot
garlic chives
curry plant
hyssop
lavender
cotton lavender
pot marjoram
mints
rosemary
rue
sage
French sorrel
southernwood
French tarragon

Sage

Sow seeds of gloxinias and streptocarpus in a propagator (*see* Propagation, page 424) over the next two months so that they will make plants large enough for display by late summer.

● Indoor bulbs and corms

Increase watering of hippeastrums planted up last month and keep them warm and moist.

Keep cyclamen and lachenalias in a cool room; deadhead regularly to extend the flowering period.

Bring pots of forced bulbs still in light, cool positions into the warmth when they are ready to flower. Keep the compost moist and deadhead when blooms fade. Feed with half-strength tomato feed if you want to keep them to plant out.

● Bromeliads

Keep these in bright light at a minimum winter temperature of 15°C (60°F). Bromeliads such as the urn plant (*Aechmea fasciata*) and billbergia will survive at 7°C (45°F) but will become dormant.

Mist air plants once or twice a week, holding a hand-held mister about 30 cm (12 in) away from the plants. Mist lightly; do not make them too wet.

● Cacti and other succulents

Rest these over winter at a temperature between 7 and 10°C (45 and 50°F). See that the plants get plenty of light but keep them dry or barely moist.

● Orchids

Water sparingly unless they are in active growth but don't let the compost dry out completely. Keep any growing plants at their optimum winter temperature, and dormant plants just above their minimum. A number of popular orchids can be overwintered successfully at a temperature as low as 10°C (50°F).

IRISES

● Dwarf irises under glass

Check pots of winter-flowering bulbous irises under glass, such as *Iris reticulata, I. histrioides* and *I. danfordiae*, for signs of drying out. If necessary, water the compost to keep it moist. Feed every fortnight with a weak liquid feed, such as tomato or rose fertiliser, at half strength.

● Cold weather protection

Winter-flowering bulbous irises may begin flowering outside in very sheltered gardens, so protect them from adverse weather.

IRISES – COLD WEATHER PROTECTION

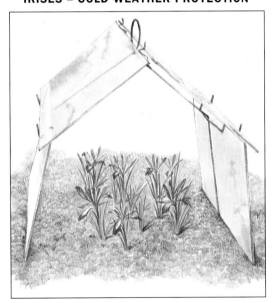

Early-flowering winter bulbous irises may show signs of buds by the end of the month. Covering the plants with a cloche may encourage them to flower earlier. Close the ends of the cloche in severe weather.

● Controlling diseases

Dig out and destroy immediately any bulbs that have stunted growth or yellow-streaked leaves. This indicates that they have been attacked by a virus (*see* Diseases, page 411).

LAWNS

Grass will not be growing at this time of the year and the best treatment is to stay off it. Take especial care not to damage the grass by walking on it when the ground is frozen or waterlogged. Any areas of rough grass, such as an orchard or wild-flower meadow, can be mown if the weather is dry and fine.

● Lawnmower maintenance

Service your lawnmower either by using the manufacturer's service manual, or take it to a service agent. Get several quotes if you can as prices vary greatly. Check blades, cables and all connections on electrical mowers and lawn tools (*see* Tools & Equipment, page 439.)

LILIES

● Sowing seeds

January and February are excellent months for sowing seed under glass. Sow lily seeds not more than 1 cm (½ in) deep in pots or boxes.

The seeds of some lilies, such as *Lilium candidum* and *L. lancifolium* (syn. *L. tigrinum*), germinate and appear above ground within a month of sowing, usually as little green loops rather similar to onion seedlings. Others, such as *L. martagon*, start by producing a tiny bulb. Nothing further emerges until possibly a year after sowing, when a small lance-shaped leaf appears on the surface.

● Forcing bulbs

Bring pots of lilies inside for forcing (*see* October, page 244). Keep them at a temperature of 7–10°C (45–50°F) until growth is well started, then raise it gradually to 15–20°C (60–70°F). The lilies should bloom 12 to 13 weeks later – in time for Easter.

Lift any surplus strong lilies from the garden for gentle forcing under glass. Use a good soil-based compost such as John Innes No. 1 with added peat (or peat substitute) and grit to keep the texture open. An added handful of leafmould is beneficial.

● Planting new bulbs

Lilies can be planted at any time until the end of March, provided both soil and weather allow (*see* October, page 244). Otherwise, temporarily pot up the bulbs to keep them in good condition until the weather improves (*see* November, page 265).

PELARGONIUMS

● Taking cuttings

Pelargoniums are never dormant so if you can provide warm compost by using a propagator (without the lid) or a soil-warming cable, cuttings can be taken in any month of the year. Any good seed and cutting compost will be suitable and the cutting should be well rooted in about three weeks, depending on how warm the compost is and how good the light conditions are. Do not let the compost dry out and never cover the plants. The cuttings like being dry and will rot if they are kept in humid conditions, so keep them in a light, airy place.

● Potting on

Regal and zonal pelargoniums to be grown as large specimens, which were rooted as cuttings in the

PELARGONIUMS – TAKING CUTTINGS

1 Choose a healthy shoot and cut it away from the plant above a node (leaf joint). The cutting does not need to be very long – about 8 cm (3 in) is the ideal length. You can take several cuttings from one plant.

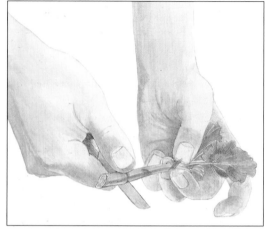

2 Trim the cutting to just below a node. Break off any sideshoots where they join the main stem and remove all but a few of the leaves. If you can, take cuttings from non-flowering shoots. If you can't, remove any flower buds.

3 Dip the cutting in a hormone rooting powder. This helps it to develop a good fibrous root system. Generally pelargoniums will root without rooting powder, providing they are kept reasonably dry and are not overwatered.

4 Insert the cuttings into moist compost in holes about 2.5 cm (1 in) deep. Firm the compost round them. Water from below after one week and again a week later. When new leaves appear, the cuttings have rooted.

autumn, will need to be potted on to larger pots. Give them plenty of room to grow and remove all dead or damaged leaves. Turn the pots regularly and shape the plants by stopping (*see* February, page 45).

● Sowing seeds

Seeds of pelargoniums ideally need to be raised in a constant soil temperature of 20–24°C (70–75°F). Given these conditions, germination will take only a few days. If the soil temperature is not maintained germination can be erratic, so do not give up on the seeds until several weeks have passed. Plant them about 5 mm (¼ in) deep and do not let the compost either dry out or become waterlogged. Covering is not essential, but if you put the seeds in the dark, check every day to see if any have germinated as seedlings will rapidly become spindly if they are not given good light conditions.

RHODODENDRONS & AZALEAS

● Protecting from the weather

The flower buds of many rhododendrons (especially dwarf varieties) and evergreen azaleas can be damaged by cold weather and harsh winds. Erect a netting screen on the north and east sides of the plants to reduce the damage in severe weather (*see* November, page 268 and December, page 281). In very cold weather cover the plants with woven fibre frost-protection fleece or a similar lightweight material. Remove it during mild periods. If flower buds do become damaged, pinch them out to prevent the development and spread of fungal diseases.

● Controlling coral spot

This is a good month to look for traces of the fungus disease, coral spot (*see* Diseases, page 407),

particularly on weak or dead branches. Although this fungal disease does not normally kill plants, it can spread from dead growth to live growth under certain conditions. Cut any trees and shrubs that are affected back to healthy wood and then dispose of the prunings. Don't put them on the compost heap.

● Removing suckers

A particular problem with rhododendrons is the development of suckers from the base of grafted plants (*see* Pruning, page 422). Cut back all suckers at their point of origin, as soon as you notice them.

ROCK PLANTS

● Maintaining the beds

Remove any dead leaves and work over the soil between plants with a hand fork.

● Sowing seeds

Sow remaining seeds that need frost to germinate (*see* December, page 281).

● Ordering new plants

This is a good month to study plant catalogues and order plants for the spring. Remember when ordering that you will need up to 12 slow-growing rock plants to fill 1 m² (10 sq ft), but only four or five of the more vigorous kinds.

ROSES

● Caring for greenhouse roses

Roses which are being forced in pots in the greenhouse for early flowers and cuttings will benefit from a little heat during cold spells – aim to keep the greenhouse at 5°C (41°F). Close the

ventilators at night, but open them on sunny days. Water to keep the soil moist, but do not soak.

SWEET PEAS

● Top dressing seedlings

Prick over the top of the compost of plants sown in pots in October. Use a piece of stick or an old kitchen fork to aerate the compost. A light dressing of fresh compost acts as a tonic for the plants.

● Sowing seeds under glass

Seeds can now be sown in slight heat, about 4°C (40°F), following the method outlined for autumn sowing (*see* October, page 246). Many sweet pea growers consider sowing this month preferable to sowing in the autumn and it is certainly more suitable for the compact types.

● Dressing with lime or sulphur

The most suitable pH for sweet peas is around 6.5, which is very slightly acid. If the pH of your soil is below this, apply lime to increase alkalinity; if above, add sulphur to acidify the soil.

KNOW YOUR SWEET PEAS

For exhibition or cut flowers with long, straight stems, choose a Spencer type, and grow the flowers up canes, training them using the cordon system (*see* June, page 161). For ordinary garden display, sweet peas grow well up wigwams or other supports. You may find Multiflora varieties particularly pleasing grown like this for general garden decoration. There are various dwarf mixtures – some as low as 30 cm (1 ft) – which are suitable as an edging for a bed. Intermediate varieties, that grow to about 90 cm (3 ft), are useful for a patio or confined space. The stems of these mixtures are not long so they are less useful for cutting.

TREES, SHRUBS & HEDGES

● Pruning

Check for broken, diseased or dead branches on established trees and shrubs. Using a pair of secateurs or a pruning saw, carefully remove affected branches, leaving a clean cut that will heal quickly (*see* Pruning, page 423). Also remove any crossing or rubbing branches that are causing obstruction. Avoid pruning members of the *Prunus* family (ornamental cherries and plums). These should only be pruned in the summer as they are prone to attack from silver leaf (*see* June, page 152).

● Planting and overwintering

Provided the soil is not frozen or waterlogged, container-grown and bare-root deciduous hardy shrubs and trees can be planted. Dig the soil well (*see* September, page 225) and add liberal amounts of organic material, such as well-rotted manure, garden compost or a peat substitute, to ensure good root development. Add bonemeal, according to the manufacturer's instructions, to give the plant all the nutrients it needs when growth starts in the spring.

When the weather is unsuitable for planting, dig a shallow trench in a sheltered spot and heel in any plants that arrive from the nursery. Alternatively, store new plants in an unheated, frost-free area and place moist material around the roots of bare-root plants, planting out when weather improves.

Ensure that stakes are inserted properly, are of a suitable size and that the tree or shrub is correctly tied to the stake (*see* October, page 247).

HEDGES

Bare-root plants for hedges may arrive when the soil is frozen or waterlogged. If they have been packed in

TREES & SHRUBS – HEELING IN

If you are unable to plant bare-root trees or shrubs immediately, place the roots in a shallow, sloping trench, firming the soil around them. Leave until the weather improves and you can plant them in the final position.

bundles, open them out to allow air to circulate and prevent rotting. Cover roots with straw, hay or similar material and store in an open, rodent-free place. Keep just moist to avoid dehydration.

Stand container-grown plants in a sheltered corner, but not under protection. Normally, these do not require watering but keep a careful watch on evergreens if planting is delayed for long. Plant out once the soil is workable. The establishment and successful development of hedges depend on well-prepared soil (*see* September, page 226).

● Hardwood cuttings

Take hardwood cuttings and insert them in a prepared trench if the weather is mild (*see* November, page 268).

VEGETABLES

Prepare for early sowings by choosing a part of the vegetable patch which is sheltered from wind and gets the most sun. Lay down clear plastic sheeting or cloches over this patch three to four weeks before sowing to warm and dry the soil. Continue to harvest winter vegetables if weather permits.

● Potatoes

Home-grown potatoes taste far better than shop-bought ones so they are well worth growing. Buy some seed potatoes from a garden centre or, if you want a specific variety not usually found in shops, order from a mail order specialist. Do not risk using your own or supermarket potatoes as they are more likely to become diseased.

Many gardeners concentrate on growing early varieties as these are the ones which taste so good when they are home-grown. To get early potatoes off to a good start, you can sprout (chit) them from the end of January; in colder areas wait until next month. To do this, put the potatoes upright in seed trays and keep them in the light in a cool, but frost-free place; a windowsill in a spare room with the central heating turned down is ideal. When the seed potatoes have sprouted, select two or three fat shoots to grow on and rub out all the rest.

● Salad crops

Harvest chicory forced indoors after three to four weeks (*see* November, page 269).

VEGETABLES – CHITTING POTATOES

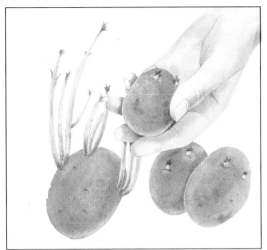

VEGETABLES – FORCING RHUBARB

1 Sprout seed potatoes in trays to get them off to a good start. Stand them upright with the end with the most eyes uppermost. Keep them in a cool, light place so that the developing shoots grow strong.

2 Shoots that are long and thin like those on the left indicate insufficient light. They will probably be damaged when you plant the tuber. Shoots should be short and sturdy. Rub out some to leave two or three on a tuber.

Force established crowns of rhubarb by covering them with a lightproof container such as a dustbin or a purpose-made rhubarb pot. Pack straw or bracken (shown here in cutaway diagram) inside the container and weight it down if needed.

PERENNIAL VEGETABLES

● **Jerusalem artichokes**

Continue to harvest tubers as they are required for the kitchen (*see* October, page 249).

● **Rhubarb**

Force established outdoor rhubarb by packing straw or leaves around a clump and then covering it with an old bucket or bin with some ventilation holes in. You may have to weight or rope the bin down to prevent it being blown away. Only force strong clumps of plants that are at least three years old. The plants should not normally need watering and the blanched shoots should be ready for pulling by the beginning of March or a little earlier.

Harvest any rhubarb that has been forced indoors (*see* December, page 283). Pull sticks about four to six weeks after forcing. Pick every few days to reduce the risk of grey mould (botrytis) developing and throw the plants away when harvesting has finished.

WATER PLANTS & POOLS

● **Creating ice-free areas**

Continue to keep an area of water free of ice to release noxious gases. Use a pool heater or place a saucepan full of hot water on the ice and allow it to melt through (*see* December, page 283). Do not break thick ice in the pool, because of possible harm to the fish. Rubber balls, or large logs, floating on the

water's surface will absorb the pressure of ice in any concrete pool, such as an ornamental pond, which can otherwise expand so much that it can crack the perimeter.

● **Pumps in winter**

Pumps not removed in the autumn (*see* November, page 269) can usually be operated throughout the winter. They must be positioned well below the ice-line to avoid mixing the colder, upper layer of water with the lower, relatively warmer, zone.

This may mean raising the pump intake and the return flow to a higher level than normal, but take care that the pump is still below the likely depth of any ice. Check if you have a really hard frost.

Winter Colour

The garden can be a beautiful place in winter: small, dainty, often fragrant flowers stud bare branches, and variegated evergreens gleam in the watery sunshine. In summer such subtleties would be lost, overwhelmed by massed foliage and bigger, brighter blossoms.

Witch-hazels are among the most enchanting and colourful of winter-flowering shrubs. They tolerate shade well and look stunning against a dark background. The spidery, fragrant flowers are usually yellow, although there are varieties with reddish or orange flowers. Also fragrant are some of the fine deciduous viburnums such as *V. × bodnantense*, whose pink flowers are produced throughout winter. *Viburnum tinus* is evergreen and reliably produces clusters of pinkish-white flowers from November through to spring. For sunshine-yellow flowers, look to *Mahonia lomariifolia* and the hybrid *M.× media* 'Charity'. The large flower heads and bold, rather spiny, evergreen foliage, often tinged with red, make them eye-catching.

USE WALLS WISELY

Walls offer protection and shelter to shrubs such as the silk-tassel bush, *Garrya elliptica*, with its long pendant catkins of silvery grey and glossy evergreen foliage. Winter jasmine, *Jasminum nudiflorum*, has lax green stems which are smothered with yellow

▲ *Frost sprinkles a special magic over evergreens, and the garden can often look especially beautiful on a crisp, cold day. This is Oregon grape* (Mahonia aquifolium), *an evergreen with large, bold leaves which often turn red or purple in winter.*

▲ *The Christmas rose* (Helleborus niger) *braves the worst of the weather and produces stunning white flowers in the depths of winter.*

flowers in winter. It will need tying in, but can also be supported by other plants such as pyracanthas.

Pyracanthas also have beauty at this time of year, with evergreen foliage and persistent red, orange or even yellow berries. This paragon among wall shrubs tolerates hard pruning and can be trained close to house walls. Japanese quinces (*Chaenomeles*), are also ideal for growing near walls.

They lose their leaves in winter but will usually flower in February, or even January in mild areas.

There are some climbers which you can plant to brighten winter days. The most reliable are the tough ivies, which carry berries in winter. Look for ones with variegated foliage. A few take on richer tints in winter. *Clematis cirrhosa* is evergreen and produces clusters of dainty, pale yellow flowers. Position it on a south or south-west facing wall.

ON THE GROUND

Prostrate evergreen *Cotoneaster dammeri* provides pleasant green ground cover. Later in the year it will be smothered with bee-attracting flowers followed by berries. For something brighter, try a variegated euonymus such as *Euonymus fortunei* 'Emerald 'n' Gold' or the winter-flowering heather, *Erica carnea*, and its many varieties. Unlike most heathers, *E. carnea* tolerates alkaline soil. Smothered in bloom from November to May, varieties come with flowers of white and all shades of pink. There are others with handsome bronze-tinted or golden foliage that will further enrich the winter garden.

Bulbs are obvious candidates for winter colour and snowdrops are the earliest to flower. Following on in February come the cheery yellow winter aconites and the first of the crocuses, including *Crocus tommasinianus*. Like all crocuses, it flowers best in sun, so choose an open or very lightly shaded position.

No discussion of winter flowers would be complete without mentioning the hellebores. Earliest to flower is the white Christmas rose, *Helleborus niger*, but only slightly later comes the Lenten rose, *H. orientalis*. Its flowers come in a fascinating range of colours: from creams and greens to pinks and purples. Hellebores delight in shady, moist, woodland conditions and are best left to flourish undisturbed.

COLOURFUL BARK

After leaf fall the stems and bark of a number of woody plants come into their own. Silver birch stems are well known, but look to the maples for richer colours. The snake-bark maples and the peeling, reddish-brown bark of *Acer griseum* can be best appreciated once the foliage has gone. Arbutus are evergreen but their cinnamon-coloured bark and elegant form make them striking in winter.

The bright bark colour of some shrubs can be encouraged by coppicing or hard annual pruning in spring. The red-stemmed dogwoods are the most popular and look particularly good if planted

▲ *Trees with colourful bark, like* Arbutus × andrachnoides *with a peeling, reddish-brown trunk, are especially appreciated in winter when they can become a focal point.*

in combination with the yellowish-green stems of another dogwood, *Cornus stolonifera* 'Flaviramea'. The willow *Salix alba vitellina* 'Britzensis' has orange stems and can be coppiced in a similar way.

▲ *Snowdrops are one of the most welcome sights this month, though in severe winters or cold areas they may not flower until later. They continue flowering until early spring.*

▲ *Hollies are at their best in winter, and in most years the berries on female plants should still be in good condition in January; in hard winters the birds may strip them early.*

FEBRUARY

Frost and ice bring their own beauty to the winter garden and, as bulbs begin to appear above ground, there are the first welcome signs of spring to enjoy as well.

February

In February the garden begins to stir from its winter slumber. Winter aconites and the first snowdrops and crocuses are in bloom, and by the end of the month primroses and early daffodils such as 'February Gold' may be making an appearance. The early-flowering shrubs, including chaenomeles and daphnes, will be flowering freely in mild areas and, by the end of the month, will be showing colour even in the colder parts of the country.

This can be a time of considerable activity if you have a greenhouse, especially if it is maintained at a temperature warm enough for propagation. Don't be in too much of a hurry to sow summer bedding plants however, unless the plants need a long period of growth. Even then it may be more economical to start them off on the windowsill for a few weeks before moving them into the greenhouse. It is much easier to maintain higher temperatures in the greenhouse in March, and seeds sown then often catch up with earlier sowings, thereby saving on heating costs.

Even if you delay most of the greenhouse propagation until March, stock up this month with compost, pots and seed trays, and check that the seeds ordered earlier have arrived.

The weather in February

Although described as late winter, February can be the coldest month of the year. It is also a period of rapid change. The month often starts with bitter cold, and heavy snowfalls and severe frosts are not uncommon. Yet there are usually many bright and sunny days too, and by the end of the month there may be a mild spell that deludes you into thinking that spring is just around the corner.

Do not be lulled into a false sense of security by these mild spells. Sowing and planting too early can soon lead to disappointment as the weather turns cold again. Winter nearly always returns for a spell in March and biting cold winds will then set back young plants that have been started too soon.

Test the temperature

Both past experience and specific advice in books and magazines can be misleading or inappropriate in an exceptional year. Do not sow or plant just because the instructions tell you that February is a good time, unless you can see that the ground and weather are suitable. Even if you have covered the soil in the kitchen garden with cloches or plastic sheeting, you cannot be sure the soil is warm enough for sowing unless you test it with a soil thermometer. A soil thermometer is not expensive, and if used properly, can make a considerable difference to the number of seeds you germinate successfully. The temperature of the soil responds more slowly than the air temperature to changes in the weather, and a soil thermometer is the only accurate way to tell if conditions are right for sowing.

Whether you are sowing vegetables or early hardy annuals, it is a wise precaution not to sow anything until the soil temperature has remained above 7°C (45°F) for a week. (Less hardy plants require warmer soil than this, but they should not be sown until later in the year in any case.) In open ground, without the protection of cloches or protective sheets, a suitable soil temperature is unlikely to be reached before the beginning of March.

Planting in February

Trees and shrubs can usually be planted successfully in February. However, it is best to delay planting evergreens, as the soil will not be warm enough for them to form new roots readily and, as a result, their moisture uptake from the soil will be slow. Cold winds may cause an evergreen to lose more moisture through its leaves than it can absorb through its roots – the recipe for a dead plant.

If the weather is still very cold, or the ground is frozen, it is not worth buying or planting shrubs that are of borderline hardiness; let the nursery or garden centre bear the winter losses. Buy in March or April when the worst of the weather is over and you can ensure that new growth is alive before making a purchase.

Pruning

February is a good month to start pruning the trees, roses, climbers and shrubs that should be cut back in late winter and early spring. New buds are usually clearly visible by the end of the month and it is best to finish winter pruning before the spring growth really gets under way.

Not all shrubs need pruning, and many

ornamentals are pruned after flowering, so check before you go to work with the secateurs.

Think ahead

If you haven't already done so, order your plants now. Sometimes you *can* buy the exact plants you want from a garden centre but they rarely have such a wide choice as is available from a mail order specialist nursery. This is the last chance to order young bedding plants – there is often a cut-off ordering date of the end of February for mail order purchases even though delivery may still be a month or two away. Don't miss the chance to order the plants you really want.

Take time to plan not only which summer bedding plants and bulbs you need, but also how many. This will help you to calculate how many seeds to sow and how many plants or bulbs to buy, thus minimising waste.

If you buy on impulse you are likely to have too many or too few. Planning will not ensure you always get it exactly right, but it is better than buying without a clear idea of how you intend to use the plants. It is also a very pleasurable task for a cold day!

Continue to prepare the ground for planting during the next couple of months. Winter dig the vegetable garden if this has not been done, and prepare the ground if you are planning to sow or turf a new lawn. This will give the ground time to settle, and for you to firm it and weed it again if necessary.

February is a good time to test your soil to see whether the pH needs adjusting or if the soil is deficient in any major nutrients. It is advisable to make any necessary corrections before the main growing season, although nitrogen, which is easily washed out of the soil, should be applied during the growing season when plants are best able to make use of it.

Regular maintenance

Continue to refirm any young plants lifted by frost. Established plants that have rooted into the surrounding soil will not be affected, but more recent additions to the garden, such as trees and shrubs planted in the autumn, may not yet have grown out from their rootball. This means the rootball can be pushed out slightly as the ground freezes and expands. Lack of adequate contact with the surrounding soil may then lead to it drying out.

Make sure that winter protection around plants of borderline hardiness is kept in place. Winds can dislodge such protection and it is too early to lower your guard.

Pests, especially aphids such as greenfly and blackfly, can already be a problem in the greenhouse and outdoors in mild parts of the country. Be vigilant, as small infestations can easily be controlled cutting down the risk of a much bigger problem later on. Continue to remove rubbish and debris wherever you find it in the garden. In the course of doing so you will almost certainly come across slugs and snails. Deal with them now to reduce the problems they cause later in the year.

JOBS THAT WON'T WAIT

- Knock heavy snow from trees and shrubs and keep an area of the pond ice-free.

- Protect vulnerable plants from frost and wind damage and firm in plants lifted by frost or windrock.

- Sow slow-maturing bedding plants such as antirrhinums and African marigolds.

- Sow quick-growing perennials such as campanulas and poppies to flower this year.

- Make a regular check on pots of bulbs being forced for indoor flowering.

- Order or buy summer-flowering bulbs, corms and tubers, especially if you are planning to grow any that need starting off indoors, such as tuberous begonias.

- The closing date for ordering young bedding plants by post is often at the end of February; order them now.

- Pot autumn-rooted fuchsia cuttings into small, individual pots.

- Put cloches in position to warm the soil for early sowings of vegetables in March. They should be in place for at least three weeks for the soil to benefit.

- Make any necessary repairs to wooden structures supporting plants before the plants begin to grow.

ANNUALS & BIENNIALS

● Sowing slow-maturing bedding

Sow slow-growing annuals (*see* January, page 18) as soon as possible this month to avoid late flowering. In addition, sow bedding calceolarias, cinerarias and bedding dahlias. In mild regions, you can begin sowing most half-hardy annuals under glass this month for pricking out towards the end of March (*see* March, page 57).

● Sowing climbers

Begin sowing Chilean glory flower (*Eccremocarpus scaber*), cup-and-saucer vine (*Cobaea scandens*) and morning glory (*Ipomoea* spp.). Soak the seeds of cup-and-saucer vine and morning glory for 24 hours prior to sowing. Check the seed packet for the germination temperature required, generally a temperature of 15–18°C (60–65°F) is sufficient.

● Buying seedlings

During this month garden centres stock a range of seedlings which are ready to prick out. These include plants which need an early start such as antirrhinums and ones which are difficult to sow and germinate such as *Begonia semperflorens*, busy lizzies and lobelias. This is an economical way to buy bedding plants as the cost of heating, seed and compost is included in the price and there is little or no wastage from seeds failing to germinate. To help prevent damping off (*see* January, page 18), water pricked-out seedlings with a fungicidal solution.

● Preparing seed beds

Free-draining sandy soil should be dry enough to cultivate now. Delay cultivation on sticky, wet clay until March or April unless the soil has been covered with black plastic sheeting or cloches. To prepare seed beds for sowing hardy annuals next month, lightly fork over the surface, breaking down large lumps, then rake the soil to a fine tilth.

● Ordering young plants

Order from mail order nurseries the young plants that you require to grow on in the spring.

BORDER PERENNIALS

● Feeding

As plants begin to grow in spring they are able to utilise fertilisers more readily. Apply a controlled-release fertiliser or a slow-acting one, such as hoof and horn, to the soil in established borders, avoiding the new foliage. Any possible damage is minimised if fertiliser is applied shortly before rain. Different soil conditions need different nutrients (*see* The soil in your garden, pages 386–390).

● Sowing

Continue to sow seeds for outdoor germination in pots or trays using a suitable compost, and protect them from birds or other animals if necessary. Sow any quick-growing perennials that may flower this year without delay and raise them in warmth (*see* January, page 18).

● Frost and wind protection

Continue to check on the frost protection for all susceptible half-hardy and slightly tender perennials and any new plantings. If heavy frosts or biting winds are forecast, provide added protection with whatever materials you have available. Any protection can be removed once the temperature rises (*see* January, page 18).

BULBS, CORMS & TUBERS

● Soil preparation

If the ground has not been prepared for gladiolus planting, do this at the first opportunity (*see* November, page 256).

● Sprouting gladioli

Gladioli will flower earlier if sprouted before planting. Place single layers of corms in trays and place in full light in a greenhouse or on a window-sill. Maintain a temperature of around 10°C (50°F). Young shoots will soon appear, but watch out for signs of aphids (*see* Pests, pages 395–396).

● Checking for disease

Check bulbs, corms and tubers that you have stored, and discard any that are soft or diseased.

● Planting begonias

Plant begonia tubers in pots of soilless potting compost. Keep the tubers just damp until the first shoots begin to show.

● Forced bulbs

Continue to bring in bulbs for indoor flowering as they become ready for extra warmth (*see* November, page 256). Water and deadhead plants when the blooms fade. Give the leaves of all plants a foliar feed to build up the bulb. Do not replant them outdoors until weather and soil conditions are favourable (*see* March, page 59). You can put the bulbs in a greenhouse or cold frame if you have one.

● Hippeastrums

Continue to keep hippeastrums moist and feed them occasionally.

● **Protecting early rockery bulbs**

Cover dwarf winter-flowering irises with sheets of glass, plastic or cloches if there is prolonged cold or wet weather.

● **Ordering bulbs and corms**

Order or buy summer-flowering bulbs and corms, if you have not already done so.

CARNATIONS & PINKS

● **Soil conditions**

Test or retest soil where you intend to grow carnations or pinks for lime content (*see* The soil in your garden, page 387) and add lime if the reading is below pH 6.5. Continue to improve soil texture by digging in compost, and improve the drainage by adding gravel (*see* August, page 195). Carnations and pinks, raised in the greenhouse, can be planted out into well-drained, open sites next month.

● **Ordering new plants**

Order plants of old-fashioned and modern pinks, and of border carnations.

● **Growing annuals from seed**

Make further sowings of annual carnations under glass (*see* January, page 19). Prick out the seedlings once they have four leaves and gradually acclimatise them to cooler greenhouse temperatures. Pinch out the growing tips to encourage bushy sideshoots.

PERPETUAL-FLOWERING
● **Cultivation and propagation**

Maintain a healthy environment and general care (*see* January, page 19) and continue to take cuttings (*see* December, page 276).

● **Stopping rooted cuttings**

Pot on new plants when their roots fill their containers, and stop all young rooted cuttings when they have made nine or ten pairs of fully developed leaves. This will encourage the development of sideshoots. If perpetual-flowering carnations are not stopped they are likely to produce only one flowering stem. To stop carnations hold the stem firmly at the seventh joint and bend the top of the plant sideways to break off the tip. If it does not snap off cleanly, cut it just above the seventh joint.

● **Sowing seed under glass**

Continue to sow seeds of annual carnations and prick out the young plants when they are ready.

CHRYSANTHEMUMS

EARLY-FLOWERING (GARDEN)
● **Overwintering**

Continue to check plants left in the ground and keep those bedded in cold frames just moist, avoiding overwatering (*see* January, page 19).

● **Controlling weeds**

Keep beds clear of weeds. Groundsel and chickweed in particular should be removed from around growing chrysanthemums, as they are host plants for the chrysanthemum eelworm.

LATE-FLOWERING (GREENHOUSE)

Maintain a cool, ventilated greenhouse.

● **Propagation**

Take cuttings of any varieties which have strong shoots throughout the month, but leave the single and anemone-flowered varieties until the end of the month (*see* March, page 61). Ensure that exhibition varieties potted up last month are kept moist. Check regularly as the pots will dry out quickly on sunny days. Pot up any rooted cuttings that remain.

CLIMBERS & WALL SHRUBS

● **Preparing a planting site**

Careful preparation of the soil when planting climbers and wall shrubs is very important. Many climbers reach substantial heights and cover large areas, so their roots range widely in search of food and moisture. The planting area may be restricted, but make sure the site is at least 45 cm (18 in) away from the wall or fence. Ideally the minimum prepared planting area should be 1m² (1 sq yd).

When working close to buildings, always check where the drains, gas, water and electricity services are located. If working near paths or patios, take care not to undermine their stability when digging under or next to them.

Dig the planting hole to a minimum depth of 45 cm (18 in), and ensure that there is at least 20 cm (8 in) of good topsoil. Bring in new soil to supplement what is there if necessary.

● **Planting hardy climbers**

Plant hardy climbers this month (*see* page 38) if the soil is not frozen or waterlogged. It is important to keep new climbers and wall shrubs well watered, and to keep a careful watch for signs of drying out. Do not overwater if the ground is wet.

● **Hardwood cuttings**

Weather permitting, take hardwood cuttings of hardy climbers now to save time later in the spring (*see* March, page 63).

CLIMBERS – PLANTING

The soil close to a wall or fence is usually very dry so prepare the planting hole thoroughly and add plenty of well-rotted organic material and a handful of a general fertiliser such as Growmore. Place the roots about 45 cm (18 in) away from the wall, angling the main stem back towards the support. Clematis (as shown above) should be planted with about 5 cm (2 in) of soil covering the top of the compost the plant has been grown in, but other shrubs should be planted at their original depth. Water in well.

● **Annual climbers**

Sow seeds of annual climbers such as Chilean glory vine (*Eccremocarpus scaber*), cup-and-saucer vine (*Cobaea scandens*) and morning glory (*Ipomoea* spp.) (*see* Annuals and Biennials, page 36).

● **Pruning**

If you have overgrown climbers and wall shrubs start rejuvenation pruning using the one-third system (*see* Pruning, page 421). It is now time to carry out the first year's pruning which will help the plants regrow more strongly. However, in the second year, revert to pruning immediately after flowering.

In sheltered warm gardens, prune tender climbers and wall shrubs that are already showing signs of strong growth. This will encourage good growth and foliage (*see* April, page 94).

Complete winter pruning of wisteria if this was not done in November (*see* November, page 258).

Cut back self-clinging climbers, such as ivies, Virginia creeper (*Parthenocissus*) and *Hydrangea petiolaris*, to keep them within bounds, if this has not already been done (*see* January, page 20).

● **Frost protection**

Frost protection screens (*see* December, page 277) should not be removed until next month even if the temperature rises.

CONTAINER GARDENING

● **Protecting plants**

In a mild spring, some deciduous trees and shrubs will already have started into growth. New shoots are particularly vulnerable to frost and wind damage so keep the containers in a sheltered spot.

Severe conditions in February can take their toll of winter and spring bedding plants in containers. Whenever possible, move the containers under glass or to a more sheltered spot, close to the house walls for example, when hard frost is forecast.

● **Maintaining a winter display**

Check plants regularly, removing faded flowers and foliage. If plants are badly damaged or die off, replace them – garden centres will have plenty of suitable plants. Look for pots of dwarf, early-flowering bulbs such as scillas and daffodils. Pansies and other bedding plants often have a break from flowering at this time of year, but don't discard them; they will shoot back into growth next month.

● **Pruning shrubs**

By the end of February, most deciduous shrubs and trees should be starting to bud which makes it easy to distinguish living from dead wood. This is a good time to carry out any necessary pruning jobs, but never prune without checking on the appropriate treatment for a particular plant or you risk pruning out this year's flowers (*see* Pruning, pages 420–423). The aim is to produce a natural and attractive shape, in proportion to the size of the container, and to keep the plant healthy and free-flowering.

In cold areas leave hard pruning until next month as pruning stimulates growth and any resulting young leaves may be damaged by frost.

● **Summer-flowering bulbs**

Many summer-flowering bulbs prefer well-drained soil and plenty of sunshine. They make ideal container plants, especially in gardens where heavy clay soil or slugs are a problem. The majority are tender, so wait until the weather improves before planting (*see* April, page 91 and May, page 124).

DAHLIAS

● Inspecting tubers

Continue to examine stored tubers every few weeks during the winter for any signs of shrivelling or rotting (*see* January, page 21). Make sure the labels remain tightly attached to the tubers or you will not know which dahlia is which when you come to plant them out.

● Taking cuttings from tubers

Stock of specific dahlia varieties can only be increased by taking cuttings, or dividing tubers (*see* April, page 96), since they are hybrids and do not grow true from seed. If you have a heated greenhouse, put the tubers into boxes with a good seed or cutting compost containing extra sand or grit for drainage. Keep them at a temperature of 15–18°C (60–65°F). Alternatively, if you have the appropriate equipment, put the boxes on a heated propagating bench or into a heated propagator. Spray the compost with tepid water (preferably every day). This encourages the growth of new shoots which will provide the cuttings.

Make sure that the cuttings are labelled clearly, water them in and keep them shaded and watered, or sprayed, until they have begun to root. Harden them off in May and plant out in June.

FRUIT

Continue to plant fruit trees and bushes if soil conditions are suitable; otherwise, heel the plants in or put them, still wrapped, in a frost-free shed (*see* November, page 259).

Apply a general fertiliser to medium-sized fruit trees up to about 4.5 m (15 ft) tall. Less time is needed for the dissolved nutrients to reach their roots than those of large trees (*see* January, page 21).

● Apples and pears

Carry on pruning apples and pears except when the temperature is below freezing. Burn or shred the prunings (*see* January, page 22).

● Peaches and nectarines

Prune newly planted fan-trained trees by cutting back the shoots that are to be retained for the main branches to 30–45 cm (12–18 in).

Peach leaf curl disease is an extremely disfiguring fungus disease. Soon after they appear the young leaves become distorted and turn red. This gets progressively worse throughout the growing season until the leaves are completely useless and drop off.

DAHLIAS – TAKING CUTTINGS FROM TUBERS

1 Start off your dahlia tubers in trays or boxes of moist seed or cutting compost with extra grit or sand. They do not have to be completely covered.

2 Keep the boxes in a warm, light place, and use the new shoots as cuttings when they are about 8–10 cm (3–4 in) long. There should be several shoots on each plant.

3 Trim the base of the cutting with a sharp knife or blade, immediately below a joint. Remove any leaves which would be below the compost.

4 Dip the base in a rooting hormone, then insert 2.5 cm (1 in) deep in seed or cutting compost with extra sand or grit. Place the pot in a propagator if possible.

FRUIT – PEACHES & NECTARINES

Peach leaf curl disease on wall-trained peaches and nectarines can be controlled by making a plastic shield for the tree as shown above. This greatly reduces the risk of infection.

The fungus spores spread the disease and by late summer the tree can be almost completely leafless. This weakens the tree which, after a few years, will stop fruiting, then cease to grow and possibly die.

Spray peaches and nectarines with fungicide as soon as the buds start to swell, and again a fortnight later. Repeat at leaf-fall in the autumn. In late winter, wall-trained trees can be protected with plastic sheeting stretched over an open-sided wooden frame. This will keep the foliage dry which will help to stop the fungus from spreading.

BLUEBERRIES

These are related to the wild, moorland bilberries or blaeberries but are much better cropping and form bushes rather than low, straggly plants. They are lime-hating plants for which acid soil with a pH of between 4–5.5 is absolutely essential. The ground must be well drained but with adequate moisture in the summer. Late autumn to early spring is the best planting time as the plants are deciduous, but container-grown bushes can be planted at any time when the soil is workable.

Blueberries take a while to start fruiting, but by about the fifth year a bush can produce up to 2.5 kg (5 lb) a year from mid summer to mid autumn, depending on the variety.

The best fruit is produced on branches 2–3 years old, so prune to encourage new growth by removing the oldest branch systems once the bush is 3–4 years old. It is best to prune in early spring when the buds are just coming to life.

Good varieties include 'Bluecrop' (mid season), 'Bluetta' (early) and 'Coville' (late). 'Herbert' is perhaps the best flavoured of all.

Blueberries need well-drained, acid soil.

● Cane fruit

In mild years, autumn raspberries may already show signs of new growth. Prune old canes down to the ground as soon as new growth appears.

● Strawberries

Start forcing maiden plants (those propagated last summer and which have not fruited yet). Plants growing in pots or other containers can be brought into the greenhouse straight away. With little or no heat, you can harvest strawberries from these by late May. Outdoor, first-year plants can also be brought forward simply by covering them with cloches or a plastic sheeting tunnel. These strawberries will be ready two weeks or so ahead of those in the open.

FUCHSIAS

TENDER AND HALF-HARDY
● Pruning

Prune half-hardy fuchsias being kept under cover as soon as the pink 'eyes' (embryo shoots) appear on the branches. This will help shape the plants and encourage the new growth on which flowers are produced. Prune standards and trailing varieties to one pair of eyes to encourage tighter growth.

● Repotting

Two weeks after pruning, sufficient young growth will have developed for repotting to be necessary. Contrary to expectation, this means potting back

FUCHSIAS – PRUNING

1 Prune fuchsias when they start into growth and pink buds (eyes) appear on the branches. Start by removing dead and spindly stems.

2 Prune back last year's growth by about two-thirds. You can be even more drastic if you prefer, as new shoots will be produced freely.

3 The buds grow in alternate pairs. Cut back all sideshoots to leave one pair of buds on standards and trailing varieties and two pairs on other types.

into smaller pots. Remove all the old soil without damaging the new white roots. Lightly prune large old roots or ones that are damaged, and pot back from 13 cm (5 in) into 9 cm (3½ in) pots.

● Potting up cuttings

Transfer cuttings taken in the autumn (*see* November, page 261) into 5 cm (2 in) pots. Newly potted cuttings will need regular spraying but avoid heavy watering as the root systems are not yet fully established and cannot cope with too much water.

● Overwintered plants

Spray overwintered plants with tepid water on sunny days and keep the greenhouse well ventilated.

Towards the end of the month, if the temperature remains above freezing at night, unearth winter-stored plants (*see* November, page 261) ready for pruning in March.

● Ordering new plants

Order new plants from nurseries this month. Garden centres will also be stocking up, but beware of buying too early if you cannot provide the light and warmth the young plants require.

HARDY

Firm in any plants loosened by windrock as gaps around the roots could allow frost to penetrate. If the long bare stems are unsightly, they can be trimmed, but do not prune them right back yet.

GARDEN MAINTENANCE

● Tool maintenance

Clean and oil the blades of all cutting tools, service mowers and cultivators and remove the blades for sharpening. Check your electrical equipment if you have not already done so (*see* January, page 22).

● Unwanted chemicals

Dispose of old and unwanted chemicals, as necessary (*see* January, page 23).

● Repairs and plant care

Check round the garden and repair fences, trellis, pergolas and arches, as necessary (*see* November, page 261). Check that all tree ties are secure and firm in plants lifted by frost.

GREENHOUSES & FRAMES

● Overwintering plants

Move dormant fuchsias, heliotropes, hydrangeas and other pot plants on to the greenhouse staging. The ideal is a warm spot where a temperature of 10°C (50°F) can be maintained. Spray the plants with water on sunny days, and give them increasing amounts of water as growth becomes active. Remove dead and discoloured foliage.

Start dahlia tubers into growth (*see* Dahlias, page 39) and pot up lilies (*see* Lilies, page 45).

● Potting on

Check young plants and rooted cuttings regularly and pot them on into larger pots as soon as their roots fill the pot they are in.

● Sowing

Sow seeds of greenhouse plants such as coleus, gloxinias, tuberous and fibrous begonias, abutilon and streptocarpus in seed trays in a heated propagator. When the seedlings are large enough to handle, prick them out into pots or trays filled with soilless potting compost and grow them on in warmth (*see* Propagation, pages 424–425).

Also sow early vegetables, shrubs, perpetual

carnations, annual climbers, parsley and further half-hardy annuals.

● Tomatoes

To raise tomatoes in a cool greenhouse, sow the seeds this month at a temperature of 15–20°C (60–70°F) (*see* March, page 82).

● Vines

It is essential that vines are properly chilled in winter, so keep the greenhouse well ventilated until growth starts. Once growing, a vine needs as much light and heat as possible, so reduce the ventilation and apply a coat of white paint on the wall of a lean-to greenhouse to increase the intensity of the light.

HEATHERS

● Preparing new beds

Complete digging over new beds in preparation for planting, incorporating garden compost and sphagnum moss, peat or peat substitute plus, on heavy soils, sand, grit or perlite. Adjust the pH if necessary (*see* January, page 23).

● Autumn-planted heathers

Examine heathers planted last autumn, remove any weeds and gently firm into place any plants which have been lifted by frost.

HERBS

● Preparing a new herb garden

Cultivate the soil to about a spade's depth. Lighten heavy soil by incorporating wood ash, leafmould or garden compost at the rate of two buckets per m² (sq yd). Many herbs grow best in warm, still air; if there is a prevailing wind a hedge of lavender, sage or roses will provide shelter. Rosemary will make a good hedge in favourable climates, but leaves can brown in prolonged frost followed by drying winds.

● Sowing parsley in pots

Sow parsley in pots indoors or outdoors under glass, sieving a light covering of compost over the seeds (*see* Propagation, pages 424–426).

● Propagating mint

Mint may be increased by the long, rooted runners which form immediately below the soil surface. Uproot them, select and separate healthy runners from the parent plant, and plant them out on their own in rich, moist soil. Mint is very invasive and it is advisable to contain it by planting in an old bucket or pot sunk into the ground.

HERBS – PROPAGATING MINT

Mint is easily propagated from the long runners that it forms beneath the ground. To increase your stock of mint, lift a plant, separate out some runners, then pot or plant them up individually.

HOUSE & CONSERVATORY PLANTS

● Protection and light

Protect plants, especially tender ones, from extremes of temperature and moisture, and continue to provide as much light as possible during the day (*see* January, page 24).

● Watering and feeding

Water sparingly, letting the compost dry out slightly, until new growth begins. Plants kept in a centrally heated room may continue to grow slowly, so these should be watered more frequently. Take care not to overwater plants kept in a cool room as this will cause the roots to rot and the plant will die. Only feed plants that are growing strongly or in flower.

● Maintaining healthy foliage

Remove dead leaves as soon as they fall to prevent grey mould (botrytis) (*see* Diseases, page 407) from attacking the plants.

Spray or wipe a proprietary leaf shine on upper leaf surfaces of glossy-leaved plants (but follow the manufacturer's instructions as some plants are not suited to this treatment) or just use water. Clean hairy-leaved plants with a soft, dry brush.

Remove dead or discoloured fronds from ferns. Cut old fronds from maidenhair ferns (*Adiantum* spp.) to allow new growth. Repot ferns with cramped roots into larger pots, using a good potting compost. To increase stock, remove vigorous portions of crowns from the outside of old ferns and pot up the divisions separately into 8 cm (3 in) pots.

HOUSE PLANTS – HEALTHY LEAVES

Dust on house plants can reduce the amount of light the leaves receive, and cause them to lose their sparkle. Use a proprietary leaf shine or moist cloth to remove dust from glossy-leaved plants.

HOUSE PLANTS – PRUNING PASSION FLOWERS AND PLUMBAGOS

The passion flower is a vigorous climber and should not be confined to the hoops provided when the plant is purchased. Train it against a conservatory wall. Prune it down to within two buds of where last year's growth started.

Plumbago is best tied to a support such as a trellis fixed against a conservatory wall. Shorten shoots by at least two-thirds in early spring. If space is restricted, prune back to within one or two buds of last summer's growth.

● Flowering plants

Carefully remove any discoloured or dead flowers or dead buds from azaleas. Indoor azaleas in flower should be kept in humid conditions.

Buy clivias in bud this month: they are easy plants to grow and spectacular when in flower.

Continue to sow seeds of streptocarpus and gloxinias in pots in a propagator. When the seedlings are large enough to handle, prick them out into seed trays filled with soilless potting compost and keep them at a temperature above 13°C (55°F).

● Indoor bulbs and corms

Start an early batch of achimenes into growth by placing the scaly rhizomes in shallow trays of moist peat, maintaining a temperature of 13–15°C (55–60°F). When the shoots are about 2.5 cm (1 in)

high, pot into 13 cm (5 in) pots containing John Innes No 2 or soilless potting compost.

Continue to keep hippeastrums moist and feed occasionally. Restart growth of overwintering gloriosas by keeping them warm and watering sparingly.

Continue to keep pots of lachenalias and cyclamen cool and just moist, to prolong flowering. Remove faded flowers from cyclamen and pull yellowing leaves gently from the base, taking care not to cut the leaf stalks, which can lead to rotting.

Remember to bring in pots of forced bulbs for indoor flowering. Water, deadhead and feed all bulbs to rebuild their strength before planting out (*see* January, page 19).

● Flowering climbers

Give bougainvilleas their first watering. Tie in

spreading growth to a trellis fan inserted into the compost. Keep bougainvilleas in pots, as they can become invasive if they are planted in a border under glass without any root restriction.

Prune plumbagos and passion flowers to within one or two buds of last summer's growth, water sparingly and ventilate well on mild days.

● Bromeliads

Keep in bright light, and maintain a minimum temperature of 15°C (60°F).

Mist air plants once or twice a week with a hand-held mister, but do not make them too wet.

● Cacti and other succulents

Continue to keep them cool during their resting period (*see* November, page 264).

● Orchids

Water regularly so that the compost, which is very open and free draining, is moist but not soaking wet. Immerse the container in water for a few minutes, then allow it to drain well. Repeat this about once a week – more often in the growing season, less often when the plants are resting.

Buy easy-to-grow orchids such as cambrian hybrids (in flower between now and summer), cymbidiums and moth orchids (*Phalaenopsis*). They will provide a succession of blooms over several months. These orchids need plenty of indirect light and to be kept at a temperature of 10–20°C (50–70°F). Cymbidiums can be kept a little cooler but most indoor orchids thrive in a warm, humid kitchen or, better still, a bathroom.

IRISES

● Cold weather protection

Winter-flowering bulbous irises, such as *Iris reticulata* vars., *I. histrioides* and *I. danfordiae*, are now flowering under glass and in the garden. Cover outside irises with a sheet of glass, plastic or a cloche to protect the flowers during prolonged cold or extremely wet weather (*see* January, page 25).

LAWNS

It is best to keep off the grass as much as possible during winter. In particular try to avoid walking on the lawn when it is very wet and waterlogged or after a severe frost as the grass can be damaged.

● Mending lawn edges

Lawn edges can be repaired during the winter if the ground is not frozen or waterlogged.

LILIES

● Purchasing bulbs

When selecting bulbs, choose plump, healthy-looking ones. Avoid dried-up specimens, any with very advanced shoots and any that show evidence of brown rot around the base. Bulbs that look limp and dry may be revived by planting them in moist soil or by laying them on a bed of moist sand or compost in a frost-proof place. They can recover within a day or so and be potted up prior to planting outside (*see* November, page 265).

LAWNS – MENDING EDGES

1 A lawn edge that has become trampled or damaged is easy to repair. First cut out a rectangle of grass with a half-moon edger, using a straight edge as a guide.

2 Use a spade to undercut the turf, then slide it out sufficiently to cut a neat edge. Use a straight-edged plank as a guide.

3 Fill the gap left with garden soil, preferably sifted to a fine tilth. Firm and level it to make sure it is flush with the surrounding grass.

4 Sow grass seed, water well, and cover with clear plastic sheeting until the seeds have germinated. This will help retain moisture and discourage birds.

● Planting outdoors

Lilies can be planted outside if the weather is fine and the soil suitable (*see* October, page 244).

In an unusually mild winter a few lilies may already be coming through in the garden. These very early shoots should be protected by covering them with a layer of shredded bark, compost or cloches; they will also need protection from slugs (*see* Pests, page 403).

● Controlling basal rot

Various fungi can cause rotting around the flat piece of tissue between the scales and the roots of the lily bulb. Called the basal plate, this is actually a greatly compressed stem. Rot can spread quickly and kill the plant but if you cut away the affected tissue before the rot becomes too extensive you may save the bulb. Dip or dust the bulb well with a fungicide and then plant up. Keep a sharp eye on nearby bulbs so that any trouble can be checked quickly before it spreads.

● Cultivating lilies as pot plants

Most of the lily bulbs now on sale make splendid pot plants. Use a good quality compost, such as John Innes No. 1, with an equal amount of peat or peat substitute. Ericaceous compost will be needed for lime-hating Oriental hybrids. Ensure good drainage by adding extra grit.

A 15 cm (6 in) pot will hold three small lilies such as *Lilium pumilum* (syn. *L. tenuifolium*) or one Asiatic hybrid such as 'Enchantment'. Tall trumpet kinds such as 'Pink Perfection', which can reach a height of 1–1.5 m (3–5 ft) or more, need a larger pot or even a half-tub to make sure that they do not get blown over when in flower.

The bulbs should be covered with 5–10 cm (2–4 in) of compost, more if possible for taller-growing varieties and stem-rooting types such as *L. bulbiferum*, as these will send out roots from the lower part of the stem to help anchor the plant firmly in the soil.

● Sowing seeds

Sow seeds under glass (*see* January, page 25). Lily seedlings raised from this sowing should make good headway through the year and will be ready for planting out or potting up by the end of the growing season in the autumn.

● Feeding forced bulbs

When flower buds appear on forced lilies, raise the temperature to 18–20°C (65–70°F) and feed with a diluted tomato or other high-potash fertiliser every week. Flowers should open six to seven weeks after the buds first appear.

PELARGONIUMS

● Cuttings

Take cuttings of ivy-leaved pelargoniums for hanging baskets and tubs. They can be rooted in a propagator (*see* January, page 26). Continue to propagate zonal pelargoniums and pot up cuttings that were taken last month.

● Pricking out

Seedlings that were sown in January will need to be pricked out or potted individually into 5–8 cm (2–3 in) pots, preferably in a good peat-based or soilless compost. Pelargoniums like a dry atmosphere, so the seedlings can be kept on windowsills in the house, but the ideal place is a frost-free greenhouse or conservatory.

SHAPING PELARGONIUMS

For a well-grown plant it is essential to provide good light and ensure it is never crowded. Aim for lots of flowers, even growth all the way round and foliage that extends down to the pot.

Once a young cutting or seedling is established, 'stop' the plant to encourage bushy growth. This is done by pinching out the growing tip – the plant will respond by sending out several new shoots lower down the stem. As the young plant develops stop any shoots that are growing out of line.

As the plant grows, turn it regularly so that it develops evenly on all sides.

Space and light are essential for a well-shaped plant.

RHODODENDRONS & AZALEAS

● Preparing for spring planting

Rhododendrons and azaleas, because of their woodland origin, require more organic material in the soil than many other plants. They also require an acid soil. Test your soil with a soil testing kit (*see* The soil in your garden, page 387). Rhododendrons and azaleas will not survive for more than a few years on soils with a pH higher than 5.5. They only live that long because their fibrous rootball does not root in the soil that surrounds it but survives independently. This deprives the plant of moisture and nutrients and it very slowly dies.

If conditions in your garden are not ideal, grow rhododendrons and azaleas in containers, using a lime-free compost (*see* March, page 74).

Drainage is also important. An excess of water can damage the plant just as surely as drought, particularly when it is newly planted. Both the evergreen foliage and the fibrous roots will be affected, and in severe cases the plant will die.

Rhododendrons are happiest in dappled shade and only the most vigorous types do well in full sun, although azaleas do better than rhododendrons in a sunny position. For varieties which flower early in the season, avoid positions that are exposed to the early morning sun.

Dig the soil to a depth of at least 45 cm (18 in). Add a general fertiliser with a high acid content in powder or granule form. If the soil is low in organic material, add generous quantities of leafmould or well-rotted garden compost.

ROCK PLANTS

● Looking after mail order plants

Unwrap plants received through the post and stand them in a sheltered place, watering if necessary. If there is prolonged bad weather, pack damp compost around them and keep under cover until the weather is suitable for planting out.

● Applying top dressing

Adding a top dressing of gravel or chippings will enhance the appearance of the rock garden, suppress weed seedlings and help drainage round the plant.

● Slugs

In a mild winter keep a constant check on the slug population (*see* Pests, page 403), especially around early bulbs, whose flowers seem particularly attractive to slugs at this time of year.

● Root cuttings

The dormant period is a good time to take root cuttings (*see* Propagation, page 431). Rock plants from which root cuttings can be taken include *Morisia monanthos*, *Primula denticulata*, *Pulsatilla vulgaris* and dwarf verbascums, such as 'Letitia'.

ROSES

● Maintaining supports

Check all wooden structures, arches, trellises and pergolas, including standard stakes and rose ties (*see* November, page 261).

● Applying fertiliser

To create a greater resistance to disease and encourage healthier plants, apply sulphate of potash at a rate of 15–35 g per m² (½–1 oz per sq yd) wherever roses are growing.

● Pruning

In very mild winters and in warmer parts of the country begin pruning roses by the end of this month (*see* March, page 75).

SWEET PEAS

● Preparing ground for planting

When the weather permits, fork over the area where sweet peas are to be planted. Break up any clods and work the soil to obtain a good tilth. Treading will

help to provide a firm, settled structure beneficial to root establishment. Apply a balanced fertiliser such as Growmore to the soil at the rate recommended by the manufacturer.

● Erecting supports for cordons

To grow plants on the cordon system (*see* March, page 78), erect the supporting framework of wooden or metal posts and cross-pieces, with stout

SWEET PEAS – CORDONS

Sweet peas grown to exhibition standard are trained as cordons. To do this you need a framework, such as the one shown above, against which to secure the tall canes which are then used to support the plants. The basic framework must be strong enough to withstand strong winds.

strands of wire connecting them. Though design details are usually determined by the materials available, the structure must be sufficiently firm and rigid to withstand strong winds. Make sure you have adequate canes to support the plants. Bamboo canes 2.5 m (8 ft) long are ideal.

● Sowing seeds outdoors

Towards the end of the month, in mild areas and with soil and weather conditions permitting, sow seeds outdoors in their flowering positions, following the method outlined for autumn sowing (*see* October, page 246). Protect the seeds and seedlings against birds, rodents and slugs (*see* Pests, pages 394–405).

● Potting on January seedlings

Prick out and pot on seedlings sown last month. These potted-on plants should be kept in the greenhouse and placed as near the glass as possible. This will gradually harden them off before moving them to a cold frame outside.

To encourage sideshoots to develop as early as possible, pinch out the tips, or growing points, of the seedlings after the formation of the first or second pair of leaves.

TREES, SHRUBS & HEDGES

● Planting

Continue to plant new trees and shrubs into well-prepared soil when the weather is favourable. Mulch, stake and tie those that require it (*see* September, page 225).

● Controlling pests and diseases

If necessary, spray with a tar oil winter wash to remove lichen, moss and overwintering eggs or spores of pests and diseases from established ornamental trees and large shrubs. Spray only if the problem is serious, as the wash will also kill the eggs and larvae of beneficial insects.

Cover the area below shrubs and trees being sprayed with a large piece of plastic sheeting or with old newspapers to prevent the wash from contaminating the soil or damaging any underplanting. Protect your clothes and eyes when spraying and apply the wash following the manufacturer's instructions.

● Replanting suckers

Some shrubs, such as the coloured-bark dogwoods (*Cornus alba* and *C. stolonifera* varieties), *Kerria japonica*, *Rhus typhina* and a number of trees, produce suckers from the base of the plant or along the roots. These can be removed and planted up in pots or a nursery bed as new plants.

After replanting, reduce the length of any sideshoots on the suckers from shrubs by at least 50 per cent; this will encourage a bushy habit. However, shoots from trees are not normally reduced, and are allowed to grow away freely.

● Taking hardwood cuttings

Continue to take hardwood cuttings in mild weather (*see* Propagation, page 429).

● Propagating from seed

The seeds of many ornamental shrubs, including those seeds that have a dry nature or have been stratified to remove their fleshy outer coat (*see* Propagation, page 424), can be sown now. Germinate in a heated propagator at 13–18°C (55–65°F) and pot on into suitable sized pots when the seedlings are large enough to handle. The seeds of many shrubs are slow to germinate and develop, so may not reach the potting-on stage for many months.

● Pruning

Use the one-third method (*see* Pruning, page 420), to prune all shrubs, such as winter-flowering viburnums, which have just finished flowering.

Remove the end foliage rosettes on young, tall-growing mahonias, such as *Mahonia japonica* and *M. 'Charity'*, when they have finished flowering. This will encourage branching.

HEDGES

Continue to plant both bare-root and container-grown hedging plants (*see* September, page 226), but delay planting evergreens until next month.

Clear weeds and rubbish from around the base of established hedges. Cut back and reshape overgrown deciduous hedges (*see* March, page 80).

VEGETABLES

Continue to harvest winter vegetables such as Brussels sprouts, kale and spinach. Start planning spring sowing. Do not sow too early or the seedlings will struggle in the cold and be vulnerable to soil pests and diseases. As a general guide, in mild areas early sowings can be made directly into the ground towards the end of this month. In cold areas cover seed beds with clear plastic sheeting or cloches for three or four weeks prior to sowing to warm the soil.

In practice, each year is different and you should be guided by the soil temperature. Use a soil thermometer to check the temperature of the soil in the morning. Push the thermometer 5–10 cm (2–4 in) down into the soil. Once the temperature remains above 7°C (45°F) for a week you can start to sow

VEGETABLES – SOIL TEMPERATURE

Sow when the soil temperature remains above 7°C (45°F) for at least a week. Take the temperature at a depth of 5–10 cm (2–4 in) in the mornings.

VEGETABLES – SECOND CROP OF SPRING CABBAGE

1 It is possible to get a second crop from spring cabbages. Make a cross-cut in the stump after you have cut the head. Hoe in fertiliser around the plant and water well.

2 After a month or two there should be four mini-cabbages on top of the stump, which you can harvest for additional spring greens.

the early vegetables in prepared seed beds.

Wait until the soil is dry enough to be workable then prepare a seed bed using a garden fork to dig the soil. Break down any large clods of soil remaining from the winter and rake the surface thoroughly to level it, picking out any stones, weeds or other debris as you go along. The finished seed bed should be flat with a fine, crumbly surface.

● Beans

Broad beans are very easy to grow and are one of the earliest vegetables to crop. Sow individual seeds in small pots in a cold frame or greenhouse. These will produce seedlings ready to be planted out in March by which time the soil should be warm and workable. Check on broad beans sown under cloches the previous November.

● Brassicas

Cut spring cabbages as spring greens, taking alternate plants along the row. The plants that are left will produce a good heart by late spring. To get a second crop from the cabbages you have cut, leave the stumps in the ground and cut a cross in the top. After five or six weeks there should be four mini-cabbages growing on the stump. These can be cut and cooked in the same way as spring greens.

● Carrots

In mild areas, if the soil is workable, make a first sowing of a quick-growing variety of carrot such as 'Early Nantes'. Sow carrots thinly in rows 15 cm (6 in) apart, aiming for a seed every 2.5 cm (1 in). Sowing thinly minimises the need for thinning out later on. Repeat sow at fortnightly intervals.

● Other roots and swollen stems

Celeriac tastes like celery but is easier to grow. Start seeds off in pots under glass in a heated greenhouse from late February to mid March. Do not cover the seeds with compost. They need a minimum temperature of 15°C (60°F) to germinate.

● Peas

Sow early peas, such as 'Kelvedon Wonder' or 'Early Onward', about 2.5 cm (1 in) deep and 5 cm (2 in) apart in single rows. Allow 60 cm (2 ft) between rows. You can overcome cold, wet soils by starting off early peas in sections of plastic guttering. When the peas have germinated slide the entire contents of the guttering into shallow trenches. As for carrots, repeat sowing at fortnightly intervals will provide a succession of crops through the year.

VEGETABLES – SOWING PEAS IN GUTTERING

1 For extra-early peas, sow an early variety in a length of plastic guttering filled with compost. Sow the seeds and keep in a greenhouse or frame to germinate.

2 When the peas are a few centimetres tall, cut out a shallow trench in the soil and slide the peas out of the guttering, into the trench. Cover with a cloche if necessary.

● Potatoes

Sprout (chit) early potatoes (*see* January, page 29). In cold areas, wait until the end of the month.

For a very early crop, early varieties can be planted from late February onwards in mild areas if you are prepared to protect them from late frosts.

● Salad crops

Sow a quick-growing lettuce such as 'Little Gem' in rows 15 cm (6 in) apart. Sow seed thinly, 1–2 cm (½–¾ in) deep and thin the plants out to their final spacing of 20 cm (8 in) after the the first true leaves have appeared.

Sow radishes and spring onions thinly in shallow drills, 1–2 cm (½–¾ in) deep and 10–15 cm (4–6 in) apart, for early crops.

Harvest forced chicory.

PERENNIAL VEGETABLES

● Asparagus

Asparagus produces separate male and female plants. Males are preferable, because although the female plants give bigger spears they also produce self-sown asparagus. The newer 'all-male' varieties are worth trying but have to be ordered from a specialist grower. Buy one-year-old crowns, which establish more quickly than two or three-year-old crowns. Allow them plenty of space (*see* March, page 82).

● Globe artichokes

Globe artichokes are an attractive perennial vegetable but they do take up a lot of room in the garden. They need a sunny, sheltered site and, as they make handsome plants, could be planted among flowering perennials in a border. They are often grown in company with other grey and silver-leaved plants.

Sow the seed in pots under glass and keep at 10–15°C (50–60°F).

● Jerusalem artichokes

This perennial vegetable can reach 2 m (6½ft), but is worth trying if you have an area of poor soil that is partly shaded. If the soil is workable, tubers can be planted between February and April. Plant them 10–15 cm (4–6 in) deep, 30 cm (12 in) apart.

● Rhubarb

Continue to harvest rhubarb which you have forced indoors (*see* January, page 29).

WATER PLANTS & POOLS

● Keeping ice-free areas

Use a pool heater to keep an area of water ice-free; this will prevent the build up of noxious gases in the water. Alternatively, place a saucepan full of hot water on the ice and allow it to melt through (*see* December, page 283).

● Sowing bog plants

The seeds of moisture-loving primulas and similar bog garden plants germinate better after freezing. Sow in seed trays filled to within 1 cm (½ in) of the top with John Innes seed compost. Stand the trays outside on a level site in light shade and allow them to freeze, but cover them against heavy rain.

A well-ventilated cold frame is useful for raising the plants once they have germinated.

● Servicing pumps

If you think your pump needs servicing or repairing, this is a good time to have it done.

Choosing a Hedge

Hedges are much more than boundary markers. A hedge is part of the creative planting that forms the backbone of the garden and provides a backdrop for other plants. Useful for dividing up a garden into smaller areas, internal hedges offer more scope for using flowering shrubs than do boundary hedges. Shrubby roses and berberis will form a prickly barrier, while lavender is suitable for low hedges bordering beds or terraces. As a boundary hedge, deciduous plants, although attractive, rarely offer total screening in winter. February is a good time to think about creating a hedge, or if you've already planned, now is the time to put in bare root plants.

THE CHOICES

Start by deciding what you want from your hedge. If you are planting a hedge for privacy, or to block an unsightly view, an evergreen is more suitable than a deciduous plant. Height is also an important consideration. The taller the hedge the less you are overlooked but the more work is entailed in keeping it in trim. You will need to use a step ladder to reach the top of a hedge higher than 1.8 m (6 ft). Also bear in mind that a tall hedge will cast long shadows which may shade too much of your garden. Low hedges are easier to maintain, but give less privacy.

A formal hedge looks very smart but will need to be clipped several times a year to keep it neat. Yew is the classic choice for a tall, formal hedge, while slow-growing box is favoured for formal dwarf hedges. The ubiquitous privet hedge should not be discounted; it need not be boring. Like box and yew it can be clipped to a regular outline and the profile can be neatly tapered or rounded at the top, or perhaps castellated. A flat-topped hedge can be made more interesting by allowing some shoots to grow long and training them into topiary shapes.

Where formality is less important, flowering shrubs such as potentillas and forsythias can be used. Both will make an attractive dense hedge. In general, informal hedges can be kept in shape with an annual trim.

To make choosing a hedge easier, the table opposite lists a selection of plants arranged by height and formal or informal appearance. The heights given are the most usual for each plant, but bear in mind that some will grow much taller if they are left untrimmed or conditions are particularly favourable. For example, privet is usually kept at 1.2–1.8 m (4–6 ft), but can reach 3 m (10 ft) or more and beech can become a large tree.

PLANTING AND AFTERCARE

The soil plays its part in how vigorously a hedge will grow. A hedge is a very long-term garden feature, so it is important to prepare the soil well before planting. Remove all traces of perennial weeds and incorporate plenty of organic matter as you dig over the ground. Dig bonemeal or slow-release, general purpose fertiliser into the soil.

Mark the position of the hedge with a taut line and dig a trench deep enough to accommodate the roots of the plants. Space the plants evenly along the row at the recommended distance. If you want a particularly wide, dense hedge, put the plants in a double, staggered row. Firm the soil well around the roots of each plant as you backfill.

Once planted, a hedge needs to be well-maintained. This means regular trimming and keeping the area round the base weed-free and watered in periods of drought. A generous mulch of garden compost or other organic material each spring will help to control weeds and conserve soil moisture. An annual feed of balanced fertiliser will also help to keep your hedge growing well.

◀ *A tall, well-sculpted hedge of Leyland cypress (× Cupressocyparis leylandii) sets off the bright blooms of this lively herbaceous border. The undulating hedge has been trimmed to form a gateway into the garden.*

PLANTS FOR HEDGES

NAME	DESCRIPTION	PLANTING DISTANCE	BEST HEIGHT	WHEN TO PRUNE
Formal evergreen foliage hedges – low				
Buxus sempervirens 'Suffruticosa' (box)	Classic hedging plant with small evergreen leaves; formal; slow-growing.	25 cm (10 in)	30–100 cm (1–3 ft)	June and August
Lonicera nitida (Chinese honeysuckle)	Small evergreen leaves (gold in 'Baggessen's Gold'); frequent trimming essential.	30 cm (12 in)	60–120 cm (2–4 ft)	Monthly, May–August
Formal evergreen foliage hedges – tall				
Chamaecyparis lawsoniana (Lawson's cypress)	Widely planted conifer; many varieties with foliage in shades of green, blue and gold; fast-growing.	60 cm (2 ft)	1.5–3 m (5–10 ft)	August
Euonymus japonicus (Japanese spindle)	Medium-sized, glossy green or variegated leaves.	50 cm (20 in)	1–2.5 m (3–8 ft)	June
Griselinia littoralis	Shiny, pale green leaves; best in mild areas.	60 cm (2 ft)	1–2.5 m (3–8 ft)	July or August
Ilex (holly)	Stiff dense growth with spiny, green or variegated leaves.	60 cm (2 ft)	1.5–3 m (5–10 ft)	August
Ligustrum (privet)	Green, gold or variegated foliage: regular trimming essential.	50 cm (20 in)	1–2.5 m (3–8 ft)	Monthly, May–August
Prunus laurocerasus (common laurel)	Very large glossy green leaves; makes a dense hedge; evergreen.	60 cm (2 ft)	1.5–3 m (5–10 ft)	July or August
Prunus lusitanica (Portugal laurel)	Pointed dark green leaves with red stems; evergreen.	60 cm (2 ft)	1.5–3 m (5–10 ft)	July or August
Taxus baccata (yew)	Classic formal hedging plant; fairly slow-growing conifer; can be trimmed to a crisp outline; good on chalk.	60 cm (2 ft)	1.2–2.5 m (4–8 ft)	August
Thuja plicata (western red cedar)	Conifer with drooping sprays of aromatic foliage; fast-growing; needs lime-free soil.	60 cm (2 ft)	1.5–3 m (5–10 ft)	August
Deciduous foliage hedges – tall				
Berberis thunbergii 'Atropurpurea'	Bronze-purple leaves, red in autumn; spiny; deciduous.	45 cm (18 in)	1–1.2 m (3–4 ft)	After leaf-fall
Carpinus betulus (hornbeam)	Forms a solid hedge similar to beech, but better choice for wet, heavy soils; dead foliage retained over winter.	45 cm (18 in)	1.2–3 m (4–10 ft)	August
Fagus sylvatica (beech)	Pale green leaves in spring; dead foliage retained over winter.	45 cm (18 in)	1.2–3 m (4–10 ft)	August
Hippophae rhamnoides (sea buckthorn)	Grey willow-like leaves; orange berries; good for coastal gardens.	60 cm (2 ft)	1.5–3 m (5–10 ft)	July or August
Prunus × cistena	Coppery red foliage; deciduous; pink flowers in spring; thorny; tolerates poor soil.	45 cm (18 in)	1–1.5 m (3–5 ft)	July or August
Informal flowering hedges – low				
Berberis × stenophylla	Arching sprays of small yellow flowers in spring; evergreen; spiny.	45 cm (18 in)	1–1.2 m (3–4 ft)	Once as flowers fade
Fuchsia magellanica	Colourful hedge for mild and coastal areas; may be killed back in winter but will reshoot.	45 cm (18 in)	60–120 cm (2–4 ft)	March or October
Lavandula augustifolia (lavender)	Grey-green aromatic foliage; evergreen; flowers in various shades of blue; sunny position; trim off faded flowers.	30 cm (12 in)	60–90 cm (2–3 ft)	Shape in April
Potentilla fruticosa	Yellow or white flowers in summer; deciduous.	45 cm (18 in)	1–1.2 m (3–4 ft)	Once in March
Rosa (rose)	Choose tall floribundas (cluster-flowered) or *R. rugosa* which makes a dense screen and bears large hips in autumn.	60 cm (2 ft)	1–1.2 m (3–4 ft)	
Rosmarinus officinalis (rosemary)	Aromatic evergreen herb; blue flowers; greyish foliage.	45 cm (18 in)	1–1.2 m (3–4 ft)	When flowers fade
Spiraea × arguta	Arching sprays of white flowers in spring; deciduous.	45 cm (18 in)	1–1.2 m (3–4 ft)	When flowers fade
Informal flowering hedges – tall				
Escallonia macrantha	Small, glossy evergreen leaves; red or pink flowers in summer.	60 cm (2 ft)	1.2–2.5 m (4–8 ft)	Once as flowers fade
Forsythia × intermedia	Yellow flowers in spring; deciduous.	60 cm (2 ft)	1–2.5 m (3–8 ft)	Once as flowers fade
Ribes sanguineum (flowering currant)	Pink or red flowers in spring; deciduous.	60 cm (2 ft)	1.2–1.5 m (4–5 ft)	After flowering

MARCH

Crocuses open their flowers
to the strengthening sun,
early shrubs are covered
in flowers, the grass
is growing again – suddenly
spring is here.

March

March is the month that brings fair-weather gardeners out of hibernation. By now the early spring bulbs are flowering prolifically and by the end of the month, in mild areas or after a favourable winter, the main spring-flowering shrubs such as forsythia will be in bloom.

Warmth can now be felt in the strengthening sun, and many seeds germinate readily if they are sown outside. Weed seedlings also germinate freely at this time, and plants such as nettles that die down to ground level in the autumn start to produce fresh new growth. It is impossible not to be aware suddenly that there are all kinds of jobs that need to be done in the garden. Fortunately the better weather makes most of these jobs a pleasure.

The weather in March

This is a month when extreme swings in temperature and weather conditions can be expected, both from day to day and from one part of the country to another. In mild areas it can be perfect warm spring weather for much of the month, but in cold, northern parts gardens will be still in the grip of winter with rain, frost and snow. Furthermore, the weather varies enormously across the country from year to year. For these reasons it is important to treat with caution any advice about when to sow and plant. Be guided by where you live and the temperature and rainfall in that year, as much as by the calendar. Wherever you live, remember that the increasing hours of daylight benefit the plants as much as the increasing warmth.

Weeding and mulching

It is a good idea to attack weeds while they are young. Hoe any weed seedlings before they become established and set seed themselves. Even perennial weeds are easier to control when the young leaves emerge from the old rootstock. If weeding is neglected now, it will become a more difficult chore later.

Once the ground has been cleared – whether by hoe, hand or spray – it is much easier to keep it clear. One of the best ways to control weeds over a large area is with ground-cover plants. These take time to establish but are attractive in their own right as well as being useful in keeping weeds at bay.

Mulching beds and borders is an immediate and effective way to control weeds. March is a good time to apply a mulch or to renew or replenish old ones. Although some mulches, such as chipped bark, rot down very slowly, all mulches require a top-up after a year or two.

If you can mulch your border plants (and shrubs if you have enough mulch to go round) with well-rotted manure or garden compost, they will also derive nutritional benefit.

Wait until the ground is moist or water well before mulching. An application of mulch to dry ground will make it difficult for moisture to penetrate when it does rain.

Modern path weedkillers will keep paths free from weeds for most of the year and the garden will look tidier as a result. Apply an appropriate weedkiller taking care to ensure there is no run off on to borders and beds.

Protecting tender plants

Most shrubs of borderline hardiness protected for the winter can be 'unveiled' this month. But don't rush this if you live in a cold area, or if the spring is unseasonably late arriving.

Seedlings and cuttings in the greenhouse or on windowsills may require some shade on very hot days when the sun's rays are intensified by the glass. Temperatures can also plummet, especially at night, so be prepared to give seedlings and cuttings extra protection from cold if necessary. If you can't boost the heat, make sure the insulation over the glass is good, and cover the plants – even those on windowsills – at night with horticultural fleece if sharp falls in temperature are forecast.

Low temperatures may not kill a tender plant, provided the temperature remains above freezing, but they may check its growth and the plant may find it hard to recover.

Sowing hardy annuals

The instructions on the seed packets for many hardy annuals recommend sowing from March onwards, but in most areas this means from late March unless you are sowing under cloches or another form of protection.

Do not rush to sow annuals. If the soil is too cold, too wet or too dry, germination will probably be poor. Moreover cold, windy weather or the unexpected return of night frosts will kill vulnerable seedlings and check the growth of others. If you wait for a few weeks you will get better plants in the long run.

Controlling pests and diseases

Pests such as greenfly will now be multiplying rapidly so keep a watch for early signs of infestation. If you take action now to control and eradicate pests you may not need to take more drastic measures later.

Pests and diseases can become rampant in the warm and humid environment of a greenhouse. Plan a strategy for keeping the greenhouse free from such problems. Consider using biological controls such as bacteria, insects or nematodes that either eat or parasitise and kill specific pests. Biological controls are advertised in seed catalogues and gardening magazines and sent to you by post.

Pond precautions

Fish become more active in early spring, and soon many of them will be breeding. This increased activity means that the water quality in your pond may begin to deteriorate, especially when you start feeding the fish after the winter. If the pump and filter have been turned off, get them working again as soon as possible; the filter will take several weeks to become recolonised by beneficial bacteria and work efficiently again.

Start feeding your fish in moderation when the water temperature stabilises at 7°C (45°F) for about a week. Don't start feeding regularly until the water temperature stabilises at 10°C (50°C) or more. This is likely to be in April but in some years, especially in mild areas, it might be by the end of March.

JOBS THAT WON'T WAIT

- Feed seedlings before nutrients in the compost become exhausted.
- Mulch beds and borders while soil is moist to reduce watering and weeding later in the year.
- Sow seeds of summer bedding plants, annual climbers, herbs, sweet peas, tomatoes and many vegetables this month. Some seeds can be sown directly into open ground but most benefit from being started off in pots or trays with protection from bad weather and pests.
- Prick out seedlings before they become overcrowded, otherwise they will make poor plants.
- Thin hardy annuals and vegetables sown in the open ground before they become crowded and compete with each other for light and nutrients.
- Pot up or space out in seed trays in the greenhouse young bedding plants and tender perennials ordered by post as soon as possible after they arrive.
- Divide congested clumps of border perennials before they make a lot of new growth.
- Take hardwood cuttings of any shrubs you wish to propagate. Soon new growth will make this kind of cutting inappropriate.
- Take root cuttings; they are more likely to root if taken from dormant plants.
- Prune roses as soon as possible, ideally before this year's new growth is well developed.
- Complete planting of bare-root fruit trees and bushes and bare-root roses and other shrubs this month to give them time to establish before dry summer weather.
- Start spraying fruit such as apples and pears if you have had problems with pests and diseases in previous years. The timing for some sprays is critical and depends on the state of buds or flowers to avoid harming bees and other beneficial insects.
- Be strict about pest control in the greenhouse. Warm March days under glass can encourage a population explosion of many greenhouse pests and early control is important.
- Remove the pool heater if you used one over the winter and replace it with the pump.

ANNUALS & BIENNIALS

● Sowing climbers

Complete the sowing of annual climbers early this month to allow the maximum growing time (*see* February, page 36). As well as those listed last month, also sow purple bell vine (*Rhodochiton atrosanguineum*) which, although a perennial, can be treated as an annual; black-eyed Susan (*Thunbergia alata*); and canary creeper (*Tropaeolum canariense*, syn. *T. peregrinum*).

Soak the seeds of the black-eyed Susan and canary creeper overnight before sowing to help the seeds absorb water and germinate faster.

● Preparing seed beds

Continue to prepare seed beds for outdoor sowing, provided the soil is dry enough. Cover with netting to prevent cats fouling the area.

● Transplanting hardy annuals

Once the milder weather arrives, remove cloches from overwintered hardy annuals and start to move the plants to their final flowering positions in the garden. When transplanting, thoroughly water the plants in and protect vulnerable specimens from slugs and snails (*see* Pests, page 403).

● Sowing bedding plants

Most bedding plants should be sown this month, either in a heated propagator in the greenhouse or on a warm windowsill. Exceptions are slow-maturing plants which need to be sown earlier (*see* January, page 18 and February, page 36), and fast-maturing plants which can be left until May. Follow instructions for sowing fine seed (*see* Propagation, pages 425) for busy lizzies, mimulus, petunias and

ANNUALS & BIENNIALS – TRANSPLANTING HARDY ANNUALS

1 Hardy annuals overwintered under cloches or in frames can now be transplanted into their flowering positions. Water, then lift with a hand fork or trowel.

2 Replant with as little delay as possible, making a hole large enough to take the rootball with minimal disturbance. Firm in well to remove large pockets of air.

3 Water thoroughly. This will help to settle the soil around the roots as well as prevent wilting. Water as often as necessary until the plants are growing well again.

nicotiana. Some seeds, such as nemesias, pansies, mesembryanthemums and verbenas, germinate best in darkness, so cover the containers in which they have been sown with brown paper or foil. Always look on the seed packet to check the conditions required for germination.

Instructions on seed packets may give a range of sowing times spread over several months. You should only sow during the earliest months if you can maintain suitable warmth for the germination of the seeds and if you can provide a light position for the seedlings afterwards. The later months are more appropriate if you do not have a greenhouse and cannot provide ideal conditions.

● Pricking out seedlings

As soon as seedlings produce their first true leaves (these tend to look quite different from the seed leaves), they can be pricked out into trays of compost. Handle each seedling very gently by one of the seed leaves, not by the stem. Ease the roots out using a dibber or the sharp end of a pencil and make a small hole in the compost to accommodate the root. If the seedlings have become slightly leggy, plant them a little deeper than they were growing originally. Firm them in lightly and water with a fungicidal solution, if damping off has been a problem (*see* Diseases, page 407).

Tiny seedlings, such as lobelia, are best pricked out in small clumps to prevent damage; they can remain in clumps when planted out in the garden, to give a better display.

Grow seedlings on in warm, light conditions, but protect them from strong, direct sunlight. Apply shading to the greenhouse glass if necessary. Indoors, make sure that the seed trays get as much light as possible and turn them daily to encourage the seedlings to produce even growth.

WHICH ANNUALS TO SOW WHEN				
	HALF-HARDY Sow in frame or greenhouse at 18°C (65°F)	HALF-HARDY Sow in frame or greenhouse at 10°C (50°F)	HALF-HARDY Sow in cold greenhouse, frame or cloche	HARDY Sow direct in flowering position
Ageratum	Apr	Mar–Apr		
Alyssum	Apr	Mar–Apr	Apr	Apr–May/Sep
Amaranthus		Mar–Apr		Apr–May
Antirrhinum	Jan–Mar	Feb–Mar		
Aster, bedding	Apr	Mar–Apr	Mar	Apr–May
Begonia semperflorens	Jan–Feb	Jan–Feb		
Brachycome		Mar–Apr		Apr–May
Calendula		Apr	Mar	Mar–May/Sep
Candytuft				Mar–May/Sep
Clarkia				Mar–Apr
Cornflower		Apr	Mar	Mar–Apr/Sep
Dahlia, annual	Feb–Apr	Mar–Apr	Apr	
Dimorphotheca	Apr	Mar–Apr	Apr	Apr–May
Eschscholzia				Mar–Apr/Sep
Gazania	Jan–Mar	Mar		
Godetia				Mar–Apr/Sep
Larkspur				Mar–May/Sep
Lavatera				Mar–May
Lobelia	Jan–Mar	Feb–Mar		
Love-in-a-mist				Mar–Apr/Sep
Marigold, African	Jan–Apr	Mar–Apr		Apr–May
Marigold, French	Apr	Mar–Apr		Apr–May
Mesembryanthemum	Apr	Mar–Apr		Apr–May
Mimulus	Apr	Mar–Apr		
Morning glory	Feb–Apr	Apr	Apr	June
Nasturtium				Apr–May
Nemesia	Apr	Mar–Apr	Apr	May
Nicotiana	Apr	Mar–Apr		
Pansy	Feb–Mar	Mar–Apr	Apr-May	
Pelargonium	Jan–Feb	Feb–Mar		
Petunia	Mar–Apr	Mar–Apr		
Rudbeckia	Mar–Apr	Feb–Mar		
Salvia	Mar	Feb–Mar		
Stock	Mar–Apr	Mar	Apr	
Sunflower				Apr–May
Verbena	Mar–Apr	Mar		
Zinnia	Apr	Mar–Apr	Apr	Apr–May

● **Sowing hardy annuals**

Most hardy annuals produce stronger plants if they are sown in pots and trays under glass rather than directly in the soil. Use an unheated greenhouse or sheltered cold frame. Young plants can be used either to fill any gaps in the border or for growing in containers. Good plants to grow in this way are alyssum; calendula such as 'Fiesta Gitana'; star-of-the-veldt (*Dimorphotheca*); clary (*Salvia viridis*) and nasturtium, especially 'Alaska'.

To avoid root disturbance at planting time, prick out the seedlings into small pots or cells in a modular tray.

BORDER PERENNIALS

● **Filling gaps**

Check borders for plant losses and plan to fill any gaps. Some perennials however, such as *Arisaema candidissimum* and *Incarvillea delavayi*, are late arrivals above ground. Mark their whereabouts with a label, or plant crocuses or other small bulbs with them. This will act as a reminder and will help you to avoid overplanting or damaging them by disturbing the sites (*see* September, page 213).

It is not always easy to tell why a plant has died, but if you suspect that the position or the type of soil may be to blame, try a different type of plant in that position. Bear in mind that some perennials, including anchusas, many verbascums, the thistly eryngiums and blue flax (*Linum narbonense*), are short-lived by nature.

● **Controlling slugs and snails**

Be vigilant this month in controlling slugs, snails and other pests to protect the tender new foliage of plants such as hostas and delphiniums.

BORDER PERENNIALS – DIVISION

Large clumps of perennials with fine or fibrous roots, such as Michaelmas daisies, can be divided into smaller pieces. Lift the clump, then prise it apart using two forks held back-to-back as levers. Some plants can be pulled apart by hand.

● Control of invasive plants

Prune any overhanging hedges, trees or shrubs that are encroaching on borders. A dense leaf canopy will cast too much shade for most plants beneath.

Invasive shrub or tree roots will rob the soil of nutrients and moisture. Remove or cut across them, or in severe cases take out the whole shrub or tree.

● Dividing border perennials

The centres of many plants which form congested large clumps eventually exhaust the soil. There is little space for new roots to develop and the plants will produce poor flowers. Divide large clumps and replant vigorous outer pieces in fresh soil, or in the previous site with added manure, garden compost or fertiliser. Spare sideshoots may be grown on as extra stock. The inner, woody material should be discarded (*see* Propagation, page 431-432).

Some perennials, such as Michaelmas daisies and the autumn-flowering heleniums, need frequent dividing to keep them growing well. Others resent the disturbance and may take some time to settle down. Peonies are among these, as are plants with long taproots, such as globe thistles (*Echinops*), *Gypsophila paniculata* and *Crambe cordifolia*.

Clumps of plants that are infested with weeds can be treated in the same way. Dig up the clumps, clean out and dispose of all the weeds, then replant.

● Planting out cuttings and seedlings

Check the progress of cuttings and seedlings in cold frames or greenhouses for planting out as soon as the weather is mild. Increased height of shoots and roots appearing through the base of the containers show plants are ready to be moved. Young plants that have been completely protected under glass will need hardening off first. Lift the lights off frames during the daytime then, as the weather improves, remove the glass completely. Plants from a greenhouse can be moved to a cold frame temporarily.

Wait until the soil temperature has begun to rise and the soil is moist before finally planting outside.

Root cuttings should now have produced small plants. Pot these up individually and put them in a cold frame or a sheltered place outside, covered with horticultural fleece, for a few weeks.

BULBS, CORMS & TUBERS

While spring-flowering bulbs are at their best, take time to visit gardens noted for their spring displays.

● Planting hippeastrums

Plant in pots for late spring flowering. Keep in a warm humid atmosphere and water sparingly until the buds appear.

● Deadheading daffodils

Remove flower heads from daffodils after flowering, to conserve the strength of the bulbs. Do not tie or bundle the leaves in an attempt to make them look tidy but allow them to die back naturally.

BUYING PLANTS

When buying plants from a garden centre or nursery, choose plants that show healthy top growth and are clearly labelled. Avoid plants with damaged or dying leaves, and those in moss-covered containers or with loose or dried-out compost.

Although most nurseries and garden centres sell the majority of their plants in containers all year round, spring and autumn are still the best times for planting. Soil temperatures and rainfall are generally more favourable at these times and plants have a better chance to establish themselves than in the cold winter or hot, dry summer months. If, for some reason, you do buy plants in containers when it is not possible to put them straight into the ground, put the containers in a sheltered corner of the garden until conditions improve.

Some nurseries stock field-grown perennials (that is plants grown in open ground rather than in containers), which are best purchased when the weather is suitable for immediate replanting. If you cannot do this, heel the plants into trenches or place them in boxes of damp soil, first moistening the roots of any plant that has dried out.

Unpack any mailorder plants as soon as possible after arrival. Keep them in a sheltered, light, airy place with adequate water to the roots (but not leaves) until conditions are suitable for planting.

For advice on planting, see April, page 90.

● **Planting out pot-grown bulbs**

The last of the pot-grown bulbs, such as daffodils, narcissi, hyacinths, crocuses and some smaller irises, will finish flowering this month. Plant them out at once, removing intact both the bulbs and the fibre or compost in which they were grown, to encourage growth that will replenish the bulbs for future flowering. These bulbs are unsuitable for forcing again, so plant them in clumps between shrubs or herbaceous plants, depending on the bulbs' size. They will flower again in two years' time and thereafter in subsequent springs.

Tulips are less likely to succeed using this method, but may well flower again for a year or two.

● **Snowdrops and aconites**

If snowdrops and winter aconites are crowded and need replanting, lift them before the leaves die down. Separate the bulbs or tubers and replant them at their original depth.

● **Summer-flowering bulbs and tubers**

Plant 'De Caen' and 'Saint Brigid' anemones for flowering during the summer. Plant lilies in their permanent positions (*see* Lilies, page 73). Divide any large canna roots and pot these into 20 cm (8 in) pots using John Innes No. 3 potting compost. Plant begonia tubers into pots of soilless compost if you did not do this last month.

If you have a lot of summer-flowering bulbs or corms of one type, you can plant them at fortnightly intervals during the next month or two. This will extend the flowering period throughout the summer.

● **Planting out gladioli**

Plant gladiolus corms in the second half of this month if the weather is warm and the soil frost-free and not waterlogged. Wait until April in cold areas.

In a mixed border, plant the corms 10–15 cm (4–6 in) apart in groups. To provide cut blooms for flower arrangements, plant them in rows 30–40 cm (12–16 in) apart. For exhibition purposes, plant the corms sprouted for earlier flowering (*see* February, page 36) in either single or double rows. Allow 45–60 cm (1½–2 ft) between single rows. Space double rows 30 cm (1 ft) apart, with a 60–90 cm (2–3 ft) gap between each pair of rows.

Plant corms a good 5 cm (2 in) deep. If you do not plant deeply enough the flower spikes may well collapse. The base of each corm must rest firmly on the soil in the base of the hole or drill.

Plant cormlets saved from last year 2.5 cm (1 in)

NATURALISED BULBS

Growing bulbs in the lawn or rough grass is a popular alternative to planting them in borders or containers. However, some bulbs are more suited to this than others. Choose early-flowering, robust varieties that do not grow too tall (unless they are to grow in long grass). Check bulb catalogues for types that are recommended for naturalising.

For an easy method of planting in grass, *see* September, page 213.

Some gardeners feed naturalised bulbs, but it is difficult to feed bulbs in grass satisfactorily without creating vigorously growing grass which then competes with the bulbs. Usually, the bulbs are left to depend upon the organic matter which accumulates from mowing the grass to provide much of their nutrition.

After flowering, allow at least six weeks for the leaves to die down naturally before mowing.

It is mostly spring-flowering bulbs, such as the 'De Caen' anemones shown here, that are naturalised in a lawn because of the need to mow the grass in summer. However, some summer-flowering bulbs can be naturalised very successfully in areas of long grass such as an orchard or wildlife garden. These bulbs include many alliums, such as *Allium moly*, and lilies. The former are normally planted in the autumn, but lilies can be planted in March.

Bulbs can also be naturalised in the front of a shrub border or in a woodland garden. Dwarf autumn-flowering cyclamen such as *Cyclamen hederifolium* are ideal for

'De Caen' anemones naturalised in grass.

naturalising beneath trees, and these bulbs can also be planted in March.

When choosing a site for naturalised bulbs bear in mind that the object is to get the bulbs to multiply freely and to grow undisturbed over a period of years.

deep in rows 10–15 cm (4–6 in) apart. They can be set so that they are almost touching one another.

CARNATIONS & PINKS

● Planting outdoors
Sturdy container-grown pinks and border carnations can be planted out now in staggered rows, at intervals of about 25 cm (10 in), incorporating bone-meal into the soil.

● Stopping and staking
Stop pinks which are running to flower without making bushy side growths by snapping off or cutting out top growth above the tenth joint – tops snap off cleanly in the early morning when the plants are crisp. This treatment may be used for all types of border pink, of any age, if the plants look leggy. Border carnations, however, are bushy by nature and should not be stopped. If border carnations grow too tall and start falling over they should be discreetly staked.

● Controlling pests
The chief pests of pinks and border carnations are aphids, thrips, caterpillars and carnation flies. Slugs may also be a problem during warm, damp spells. (*See* Pests, pages 395–405).

● Rust, leaf spot and other diseases
Check regularly for any signs of the diseases to which the dianthus family is vulnerable. Most modern hardy carnations and pinks are resistant to rust, though older varieties are often susceptible to this fungal disease. Rust usually starts near the base of the plant and is recognisable by small yellow blisters which burst to release a reddish-brown

CARNATIONS & PINKS – STOPPING BORDER PINKS

1 Some border pinks produce flowers on the initial upright stem without making bushy plants. To encourage more sideshoots, snap out the top of the stem after ten joints have developed.

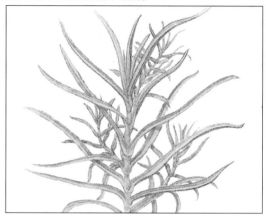

2 Side shoots will soon form once the growing tip has been removed, and this will mean more flowers to enjoy. Only stop pinks; border carnations should not be stopped.

powder. Poor air circulation helps to spread this type of fungal disease.

Leaf spot diseases show first on older leaves as brownish-purple patches and can be treated with a fungicide. While unattractive, these diseases are rarely fatal and plants otherwise thriving will usually overcome them. If they do not, take cuttings from healthy growth (*see* June, page 150) and start again, or replace with fresh stock.

Some diseases are incurable, including stem-rot at ground level, which results from over-deep planting or poor drainage, and wilt disease, characterised by yellowing of the top growth followed by the total collapse of the plant. Lift any affected plants, including the roots, and dispose of them. Avoid using the site for any dianthus species for two seasons. (*See* Diseases, pages 405–411.)

● Sowing and pricking out
Continue pricking out seedlings of annual carnations under glass, and sowing seeds of all dianthus species and varieties (*see* January, page 19).

PERPETUAL-FLOWERING
● Healthy environment
Maintain a minimum temperature of 7°C (45°F) in the greenhouse. You will need to increase the ventilation in warm weather.

Keep a careful watch for pests and diseases, and act quickly if necessary. Destroy any plants infected with wilt or debilitating virus disease and maintain good greenhouse hygiene at all times. Damp down the floor and staging if the atmosphere becomes too hot and dry. This will discourage infestations of red spider mite (*see* Pests, page 402).

● **Potting on and stopping**

Continue to pot on new plants as their roots fill their containers and stop young rooted cuttings (*see* February, page 37). Cut any blooms and disbud flower stems as necessary (*see* September, page 214).

● **Buying new plants**

Order new plants for delivery next month.

CHRYSANTHEMUMS

EARLY-FLOWERING (GARDEN)
● **Preparing the soil**

On light, sandy soil continue to dig, incorporating well-rotted manure or garden compost into the top 15 cm (6 in) of soil. Test the soil for alkalinity if this has not been done (*see* November, page 257).

● **Starting off overwintered stools**

Pot up chrysanthemums which have been over-wintered under cover, or bed them out in cold frames. Firm the soil in the base of the frame and cover it completely with a piece of plastic sheeting. Then spread an 8 cm (3 in) layer of compost on top, pack it down lightly, and plant the stools about 10 cm (4 in) apart. This method gives better results when the plants are lifted to put in their final positions outdoors as they are easier to move and the roots extend readily into the soil.

LATE-FLOWERING (GREENHOUSE)
● **Moving plants to a cold frame**

In milder areas, move plants in small pots from the greenhouse to a cold frame as soon as possible to harden them off. Protect them from slugs and snails and cover frames with mats or sacking at night if the weather turns cold and frost threatens.

CHRYSANTHEMUMS – TAKING CUTTINGS

1 Select shoots about 3–5 cm (1½–2 in) long, with evenly spaced leaves of good colour. Ensure they are free from insects and obvious disease. Shoots chosen for cuttings must not be tough or wiry.

2 Remove the lowest leaves, and trim off the stem below the lowest leaf joint. Root in a moist cuttings compost with one-third perlite or washed sharp sand added. Keep in a humid atmosphere at about 13°C (55°F) until rooted.

VERY LATE-FLOWERING VARIETIES
● **Cuttings for later propagation**

Pot up cuttings of very late-flowering varieties rooted in February, putting five or six in a 23 cm (9 in) pot. As soon as they become established, pinch out the tips so that sideshoots are produced.

These cuttings are not left to grow on and flower but are used to take further cuttings in the summer (*see* June, page 151). This method produces suitable shoots at the right time: shoots that have been growing for several months by the summer would be unsuitably large and woody, while cuttings taken in March would flower too early.

● **Propagating chrysanthemums**

All chrysanthemums are best grown from cuttings; plants increased by division will be inferior.

March is the main month for the propagation of chrysanthemums, although large exhibition varieties should have been propagated in January and February. Some of the early-flowering and very late-flowering varieties should be left until April or May. You can also take cuttings of mid season and late varieties grown in the greenhouse now as these will provide stock plants for further cuttings for rooting in June or July.

Generally the best cuttings come from shoots some way away from the old stem. During sunny weather shade the cuttings and spray them lightly with clean water twice a day, morning and early afternoon. At the beginning of the rooting period the cuttings will appear limp. Eventually they will look greener and show signs of growth; when this happens, but not before, water the compost again.

● **Potting on**

When the roots have formed all round the base of the stem and grown to about 2.5 cm (1 in) long, it is time to pot up the cuttings. Take care when doing this not to press the tender roots too firmly into the compost or they will be damaged.

Bury the roots without covering any part of the main stem, leaving the top 1 cm (½ in) of the pot unfilled. Water in well by filling the pot to the brim then letting it drain. A good soaking will keep the compost moist for several days. Plastic pots, being non-porous, need less frequent watering.

Label each pot with the plant's name and the dates of rooting and potting. Stand them on a free-draining base where they will get plenty of light and air, but protect from draughts. Maintain an average temperature of 7°C (45°F).

Pot on cuttings of large exhibition varieties rooted in January and early February as soon as the roots have become well established, since their growth will suffer if they are left too long in small pots. It is always important to keep exhibition varieties of chrysanthemums growing steadily all the time.

CLIMBERS & WALL SHRUBS

● **Choosing plants**

When the most severe weather has passed you can start planting all hardy climbers and wall shrubs. Wait another month for less hardy types.

Choosing the right plant for the right position needs careful thought to avoid disappointment. Check on the plant's ultimate size – not only its height and spread, but also the space it needs to flower to its full potential. Also consider whether a plant will interfere with doors and windows when it has reached its ultimate size.

CLIMBERS & WALL SHRUBS – PRUNING MID-SUMMER FLOWERING CLEMATIS

1 Clematis that flower from mid summer onwards, on shoots produced this year, should be pruned annually – in late winter or early spring. Cut all the shoots back to about 23–60 cm (9–24 in) above the ground.

2 Cut back to just above a pair of buds – the exact position is not critical. Try to ensure this is done before the new leaves are fully opened, in the first half of March, if not before. New shoots will soon be produced.

North and east-facing walls and fences that are exposed to frost and cold winds require plants that can tolerate such conditions. There are a good number of shrubs and climbers, including roses, that will flourish on north and east-facing walls and, conversely, a number that require the extra warmth and shelter that a south-west or south-facing wall provides. Suggestions for the best climbing plants to suit different conditions and situations are given on the next page.

● **Providing plant supports**

If not already done, fix additional trellis or support wires in place, and tie new stems to them as climbing plants grow (*see* January, page 20).

● **Feeding**

It is important to feed climbers and wall shrubs as they need to cover large areas of space quickly. Apply a balanced, slow-acting, general fertiliser in the spring around all established plants, and also when planting any new shrub or climber (*see* February, page 38).

● **Frost protection**

Continue to protect any tender climber or wall shrub in case of damaging spring frosts at night (particularly when a frost warning has been given). On more hardy plants it may now be safe to remove any frost protection that you have in place unless there is a sudden drop in temperature.

● **Annual climbers**

Sow seeds of annual climbers if not already done (*see* February, page 38).

● **Hardwood cuttings**

Cuttings of hardy climbers such as climbing bitter-sweet (*Celastrus orbiculatus*), jasmine, honeysuckle and Russian vine (*Polygonum baldschuanicum*, syn. *Fallopia baldschuanica*) usually do well if they are taken this month. Choose stems from wood grown the previous year (*see* Propagation, page 429).

● **Layering**

Dig up layers made last summer (*see* August, page 196), which should now be well rooted, and cut them away from the parent plant. Pot the new plants into 15 cm (6 in) pots to grow on until the autumn or plant them out in their final growing positions. Prepare the ground well.

● **Pruning clematis**

Early-summer flowering clematis only require a light trimming over. Remove shoots now that show no live buds. Cutting away too much live growth will mean cutting away future flowers.

Clematis which bloom from July to August onwards produce their flowers on new growth. These should be cut back hard to within 8–15 cm (3–6 in) of last year's growth. This may leave little more than a stump. Prune before the leaves develop fully, but do not worry about cutting away fat leaf buds – plants will easily grow to 2.5 m (8 ft) or more in a season (*see* May, pages 126–127).

● **Pruning other climbers**

Treat old shoots of golden hop (*Humulus lupulus* 'Aureus') in the same way as late-flowering clematis

---

CHOOSING A CLIMBER

Climbers for a north or east-facing wall

Clematis Most clematis will grow in shade, and those with delicate colouring, such as the popular *Nelly Moser*, generally look better in a shady spot as the flowers tend to fade in strong sun.

Hedera (ivy) All ivies do well, and there are many forms of the common *H. helix*, but try the attractively variegated large-leaved *H. colchica* 'Dentata Variegata' too. Ivies have the added bonus of being evergreen.

Hydrangea petiolaris (climbing hydrangea) This self-clinging climber can be grown up a tree or against a wall. The white flower heads appear in June and July.

Lonicera japonica (Japanese honeysuckle) Grow the variety 'Halliana' for its scent and profuse whitish yellow flowers. *L. japonica*. 'Aureoreticulata' has yellow-veined netted leaves. Evergreen or semi-evergreen.

Parthenocissus The Boston ivy (*P. tricuspidata*) and Virginia creeper (*P. quinquefolia*) grow very tall. *P. henryana* is less vigorous and ideal for a shady wall. All have good autumn colour.

Vitis (ornamental vine) Grow these for foliage effect. *V. vinifera* 'Purpurea' has purple-claret leaves, turning wine-purple later. *V. coignetiae* has much larger leaves, with good autumn colour.

Climbers for a south or west-facing wall

Actinidia kolomikta (kolomikta vine) Large, heart-shaped leaves splashed cream and pink.

Aristolochia macrophylla (syn. *A. durior*) (Dutchman's pipe) Vigorous twiner with large green leaves and flowers.

Campsis radicans (trumpet vine) Woody-stemmed root climber with red to orange trumpet-shaped flowers.

Clematis These popular plants like their roots in shade. The flowers tolerate full sun although some may lose colour.

Lonicera x brownii 'Dropmore Scarlet' (scarlet trumpet honeysuckle) Produces tubular scarlet flowers in mid summer.

Passiflora caerulea (passion flower) Fascinating blue flowers, but needs a sheltered position.

Vitis (ornamental vine) Grown for its ornamental leaves, those of *V. coignetiae* being particularly large.

Wisteria Popular twining climbers with long racemes of lilac to purple flowers. There are also white forms.

Climbers for a pergola

Clematis Some large-flowered varieties will cover pillars, but choose a suitable species such as *C. montana* if you want cover across the top of a pergola too.

Jasminum officinale (jasmine) A twiner with fragrant white flowers in summer.

Lonicera periclymenum (honeysuckle) Very fragrant. 'Belgica' flowers early, 'Serotina' late, 'Graham Thomas' is also widely available and flowers profusely. *L. japonica* varieties are suitable too.

Roses Climbing, rambler and pillar roses are all suitable, and there are many varieties.

Vitis (ornamental vine) Foliage plants with sometimes spectacular autumn colour.

Self-clinging climbers for a wall

Hedera (ivy) Will reach to the top of very tall walls in time, but can be pruned back to size. Evergreen.

Hydrangea petiolaris (climbing hydrangea) Naturally grows up trees, but will cover a wall.

Parthenocissus (Boston ivy, Virginia creeper) Foliage plants for high walls. Good autumn colour.

to induce strong new basal growth – it can grow more than 5.5 m (18 ft) in a season and produce good foliage and flowers.

Wall shrubs and tender perennial climbers that flower on new wood should be cut back hard as soon as strong growth begins (*see* April, page 94).

● Watering and mulching

If climbers and wall plants show signs of drying out, give them a thorough watering and mulch them.

CONTAINER GARDENING

● Removing insulation

In most parts of the country, the severest winter weather will have passed by mid March and vulnerable pots and tender shrubs can be unwrapped from their insulation. You can also untie the anti-snow damage bindings on conifers and other shrubs. Do be guided by the weather; if it is still very cold and frosty then delay this for another week or two.

● Planting and pruning trees and shrubs

Try to get all planting of new deciduous trees and shrubs completed before the leaves open out. Finish pruning and shaping deciduous shrubs that are normally pruned when dormant. It should be easy to spot any dead wood now as buds on living shoots will have started to swell and expand (*see* February, page 38). Don't prune those shrubs that flower on the wood produced the previous year – these should be pruned when they have finished flowering.

● Bulbs and tubers

Buy summer-flowering bulbs before stocks run out for planting in April and May. Start begonia tubers into growth (*see* February, page 36).

● Replanting and top dressing

When a pot becomes full of roots, it is time to replant. Choose a container which is just one or two sizes larger, and cover the drainage hole with crocks, stone chippings or similar. Put in a little fresh compost. Remove the plant from its existing pot and, if possible, tease out a few of the roots at the bottom. Put it in the new pot with some fresh compost on top. Leave about 2.5 cm (1 in) of space at the top to allow for watering. Next, fill in down the sides with compost and firm this in. Water thoroughly to settle the compost in the pot.

Repotted plants will continue to grow larger, but when a shrub reaches a particular size and you do not want it to get any bigger, top dress instead of repotting it. Do this by removing about 2.5 cm (1 in) of compost and replacing it with fresh compost. Add a slow-release fertiliser to feed the plant through the rest of the season.

To rejuvenate an old pot-grown shrub, remove it from its pot and tease off all loose soil from the rootball. Trim the roots lightly and replant, working new compost well in to fill any gaps. Trim back shoots to compensate for the reduced root area.

● Buying early for summer

Young plants in plugs, or net pots, come into garden centres very early on. If you have somewhere warm and light to keep them, such as a kitchen windowsill, heated greenhouse or conservatory, you can get a head start by growing them to a larger size so that they make an instant display when planted out in May or June. However the roots of these tiny plants are very prone to drying out, so either pot them on straight away or plant them directly into hanging baskets (*see* April, page 94) – there is no need to remove the net pots first.

DAHLIAS

● Ground preparation

Continue to prepare beds for dahlias. Although planting time is not until the end of May or June, fertilise the ground now with a slow-acting feed.

● Taking cuttings

To obtain new plants of specific dahlia varieties, you will need to take cuttings or divide old tubers.

Take cuttings from new shoots on tubers (*see* February page 39). The cuttings will root more quickly in a cool greenhouse if the pots are placed in a large box covered by a pane of glass, or a transparent plastic bag, to conserve warmth and moisture. On hot days place brown paper or newspaper over the glass to shade the cuttings.

If you have no greenhouse, increase your stock by dividing clumps of tubers (*see* April, page 96).

● Potting up early cuttings

Check on the cuttings taken in February and, if they have rooted, pot them on singly into a good potting compost in 8 cm (3 in) pots.

● Sowing seed

If you do not require specific varieties, you can raise dahlias from seed. Near the end of the month sow home-saved and commercial seed of bedding, cactus, decorative and pompon varieties in pans or trays filled with fresh seed compost. Scatter the seeds thinly and cover with a further 5 mm (¼ in) of compost. Place the containers in plastic bags or cover with glass and stand them in a greenhouse or propagator heated to 18°C (65°F). Remove the covering as soon as the seeds germinate. Prick out the seedlings into trays when they are large enough to handle.

● **Inspecting tubers**

Continue to check on any tubers remaining in storage (*see* January, page 21).

FRUIT

This is the last month for planting bare-root trees and bushes and other soft fruit, so complete this as soon as soil and other conditions allow. Firm in earlier plantings if necessary. Within reason, container-grown plants may be planted all year round.

Feed shallow-rooted small or trained trees, bush and cane fruits and perpetual (autumn) strawberries in the first half of the month. Use a general fertiliser, such as Growmore or blood, fish and bone, at the rate recommended by the manufacturer. Soft fruit, in particular, will benefit from a mulch of garden compost or well-rotted farmyard manure.

Be ready to protect early-flowering tree fruits

FRUIT – POLLINATING PEACHES

Peaches and nectarines flower early and may need help with pollination. Use an artist's soft paint brush to transfer the pollen from the male stamens of one flower to the female stigmas of another. This is best done in sunny weather.

from frost by draping horticultural fleece over all that you can reach.

● **Apples and pears**

Finish pruning established trees as soon as you can and, in any case, before the buds start to open.

Spray against apple and pear scab and powdery mildew, and also pests such as capsid bug, greenfly and winter moth caterpillar with an appropriate fungicide or insecticide (*see* Pests and Diseases, pages 395–411). Check the manufacturer's instructions for the most suitable time. If the trees were winter washed (*see* December, page 277), only the scab and mildew spray should be necessary.

● **Peaches and nectarines**

These flower so early in the year that there are seldom enough insects around to pollinate the flowers. All the trees therefore, in the greenhouse or outside, will benefit from hand pollination.

Spray trees against peach leaf curl if the season is a late one and the leaves are only now opening (*see* February, page 39).

● **Plums and cherries**

Once plums have started into growth, pruning can be carried out with much less risk of silver leaf disease infecting them (*see* June, page 152). This is a good time to prune an overgrown tree as it is much easier to see the main structure of the tree before the leaves develop. Don't worry if it oozes sap.

Cut back the shoots chosen to be the main branches on newly planted bush trees by half their length. Cut out surplus shoots completely.

If there is any sign of pests such as greenfly, winter moth caterpillar and cherry moth caterpillar, spray with an appropriate insecticide (*see* Pests,

pages 395–405). Where only aphids have to be controlled, choose an insecticide that will not harm beneficial insects such as bees or ladybirds.

● **Blueberries**

Complete planting of blueberry bushes this month (*see* February, page 40).

Prune bushes over three years old by removing fruited branches.

● **Cane fruits**

Raspberries can still be planted this month. Prune them back hard afterwards. Cut all the canes of autumn raspberries down to the ground at the first sign of growth.

Loganberries and tayberries that were tied in bundles for winter protection can now be freed and tied to the permanent wire support system. Cut back any that have been damaged.

● **Figs**

Figs require a sunny and sheltered site and are best fan-trained against a wall. Their roots need to be severely restricted and they should be planted in a hole about 1 m² (1 yd²) and 60 cm (2 ft) deep. Line the hole with planks, paving slabs or corrugated iron and fill with a mixture of soil and brick rubble.

● **Gooseberries and currants**

Cut back to undamaged buds any shoots that have been attacked by bullfinches or tits in the winter (they often feed on the buds). Remove weak shoots from newly planted bushes of gooseberries and red or white currants and shorten the remainder by a third. Feed with a general fertiliser.

Prune back any recently planted blackcurrant bushes hard by removing weak shoots and shortening

KIWI FRUIT (CHINESE GOOSEBERRY)

Kiwis should be grown in a sheltered position, facing south to west, in a rich, moisture-retentive soil with a pH of about 6–7. Protection should be given from spring frosts and in very cold winters. Normally, male and female plants are needed but there is now a self-fertile variety, 'Issai', which has smaller but more reliably produced fruits. One male plant is enough to pollinate up to eight females. 'Hayward' (female) and 'Tomuri' (male) are two recommended varieties.

The Guyot system of training vines is suitable for kiwi fruit outdoors and under glass (*see* Pruning vines, opposite). Plant in the spring, pushing a cane in behind each plant and cutting the stem back to just below the bottom wire. When growth starts, keep only three strong shoots; pinch out all the others. Tie the middle shoot to the cane, and train the other two laterally along the bottom wire. When the upright shoot reaches the second wire repeat the process until all the wires are occupied. When the laterals reach about 1 m (3 ft) long, nip out the tips to encourage sideshoots (sub-laterals) which will develop into the fruiting shoots. Pinch back the sub-laterals to five leaves to form the fruiting spurs. Any shoots growing from them are stopped at seven leaves. In the winter, after fruiting, cut back all the spurs to just two buds beyond where the last fruit was formed.

Kiwi fruit need a sheltered position to produce fruit.

the remainder to the first or second bud above the ground. Feed with a general fertiliser.

● **Strawberries**

Remove the flower buds to prevent fruiting on summer-fruiting varieties that have just been planted.

Autumn strawberries are actually perpetual-fruiting varieties such as 'Aromel' or 'Ostara' but, by removing the flower buds until the end of May, fruiting is delayed until August. These may also be planted now. Dig plenty of well-rotted manure or garden compost into the soil before planting.

Feed perpetual strawberries now but do not feed summer varieties. Don't overwater strawberries grown under glass and when the fruit is setting, feed the plants fortnightly with normal strength tomato feed. Keep plants frost free.

● **Vines**

There are many methods of pruning and training outdoor vines. The Guyot method is one of the simplest. Train a new plant by cutting it back to about 30 cm (12 in) and training two strong new shoots horizontally, with a third shortened to three buds. To prune an established plant, cut off all the stems except the three central ones. Cut the central vertical stem to three buds and bend the other two to a horizontal position. Pruning must be finished early in the month, before there are any signs of growth. Pruning after growth starts can result in 'bleeding', which will weaken the vine.

FUCHSIAS

TENDER AND HALF-HARDY
● **Pruning**

Prune half-hardy fuchsias kept under glass as soon

FRUIT – PRUNING ESTABLISHED VINES

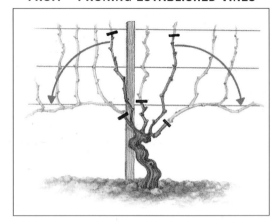

If using the Guyot method of pruning, cut off all the stems except the three central ones. Cut back the central vertical stem to three buds, then bend down the other two to the horizontal position.

as the plants start producing little pink 'eyes' on the bare branches (*see* February, page 40). A little heat, about 7°C (45°F), will encourage early growth.

● **Potting back**

Pot back last year's plants if not done last month (*see* February, page 40). Some plants are late starters and only now will have made sufficient growth.

● **Potting on**

Young plants grown from cuttings will need repotting regularly so that growth is not checked.

Always use fresh potting compost and clean pots. Any good quality compost is suitable, but John Innes No. 1 is particularly good for this purpose. Keep pot size increase to a minimum – too much compost unoccupied by roots can turn the soil sour.

When potting, check for signs of winter-laid vine weevil grubs which, left undisturbed, would devour entire root systems (*see* Pests, page 404).

Autumn cuttings should now be ready to pot on into 9 cm (3½ in) pots.

● Taking cuttings

Take cuttings from new growth. Normally, a cutting consists of a shoot with three or four pairs of leaves as shown here, but small tip cuttings, taking the tip of the shoot with one pair of leaves, also work successfully for fuchsias. Insert the cuttings in potting compost in seed trays or shallow pots. Firm well, leaving no air pockets.

Water in the cuttings or mist them, and keep them in warm but not over-humid conditions with sufficient moisture to prevent them wilting. With heat, the cuttings will usually root in about 10 to 14 days; without heat they may take up to four weeks.

● Stopping

Stop any plants which have made sufficient growth (usually once they have two pairs of leaves). This means pinching out the central growing tip of each shoot. This will encourage the plant to produce sideshoots and promotes bushy growth. You can use the tips you have removed for further cuttings.

● Planting up hanging baskets

Mid March is an ideal time for planting up hanging baskets as long as they can be kept under cover until all fear of frost has passed; otherwise wait until next month (*see* April, page 95). If you want the best results from all-fuchsia baskets, fill each basket with the same variety rather than a mixture. A 38 cm(15 in) basket will hold five fuchsias but a 30 cm (12 in) basket will look full with only three plants.

FUCHSIAS – TAKING CUTTINGS

1 There are various ways to take fuchsia cuttings. One of the easiest is to cut off lengths of new shoots with three to four pairs of leaves.

2 Trim the stem with a sharp knife. Pull off the lowest leaves that would otherwise be buried by the compost.

3 Fill a pot with potting compost. Making a hole with a dibber or pencil, insert each cutting. Firm well to ensure there are no air pockets.

● Feeding

Start feeding now, with a high-nitrogen feed. Follow the manufacturer's instructions for a weak dilution: it is better to give frequent weak feeds than strong feeds less often.

● Providing shade and humidity

Shade new growth on plants under glass from direct sun and spray with water almost daily, but allow time for the foliage to dry before the evening. If necessary, damp down the greenhouse floor to reduce temperatures and maintain humidity.

HARDY

Weed round fuchsias carefully, as they have a shallow root system which can easily be damaged. In milder areas strong new growth will appear at the base and you can then cut them back. More often this will be next month (*see* April, page 99).

GARDEN MAINTENANCE

● Checking plant ties

Go round the garden and check that all plant ties are secure but not constricting the stem growth. Loosen any ties that require it in preparation for the growing season ahead (*see* January, page 20).

● Mulching

Covering the surface of beds and borders now with a 5 cm (2 in) layer of organic matter or a sheet of black plastic helps to reduce watering and weeding later in the season. An organic mulch also adds nutrients to the soil. In an ornamental bed or border a mulch of chipped bark, leafmould or cocoa shells looks attractive, but on the vegetable plot, where appearance is less important, use black plastic sheeting as a mulch, cutting slits in it for planting (*see* The soil in your garden, pages 392–393).

GREENHOUSES & FRAMES

As the weather in March becomes warmer, more use can be made of the greenhouse; seeds can be sown, bulbs planted and cuttings taken. Unless the spring is very cold, you can now remove the winter insulation from the glass.

● Controlling pests and diseases

Higher temperatures bring an increase in insect activity, so watch out for aphids, red spider mites and whitefly (*see* Pests, pages 395, 402 and 405).

● Watering and feeding

Increase watering: do not let pots or seed trays dry out. Apply liquid feed to plants in pots on a regular basis as they start into growth.

● Sowing seeds

The seeds of many plants can be sown this month. Sow everything listed in February (*see* pages 41–42). Also sow dahlias, lilies, annual carnations, herbs, hardy annuals and any flowering plants that you plan to grow in pots. Prick out seedlings as soon as they are large enough to handle.

● Potting on

Annuals such as schizanthus and nemesias that have been overwintered in 8 cm (3 in) pots (*see* September, page 218) grow rapidly at this time of year. Pot them on into 15 cm (6 in) pots containing John Innes No. 2 potting compost. Insert supporting stakes for the taller plants and tie them in as it becomes necessary. Move these plants into the house or conservatory when they start flowering.

At the end of the month, pot on gloxinias and begonias into 9 cm (3½ in) pots containing John Innes potting compost No. 2 with peat added at the rate of one part peat to nine parts compost.

Pot on fuchsias and chrysanthemums as required.

● Cuttings

Take cuttings of dahlias, fuchsias, pelargoniums, chrysanthemums, some shrubs, and indoor plants, such as abutilons, inserting them in a free-draining compost, preferably in a heated propagator.

● Peppers and aubergines

Sow peppers two seeds to a pot at a temperature of 18–20°C (65–70°F) and remove the weaker of the two seedlings when they germinate.

Sow aubergines at the same temperature, 5 mm (¼ in) deep in pots.

● Tomatoes

Indoor tomato plants sown in February will now need extra space to prevent them becoming drawn and spindly. Where practicable, stand the pots on the greenhouse border where they will be planted. Otherwise, space them out on the staging.

If you wish to plant tomatoes in an unheated greenhouse in May, or outdoors, and have a heated propagator or a warm windowsill, sow the seeds this month at a temperature of 15–20°C (60–70°F), covering them with a thin layer of sifted compost. Pot the seedlings individually into 8 cm (3 in) pots of John Innes No. 2 potting compost as soon as the seed leaves are fully developed.

If you have a cool greenhouse, prepare the border for planting tomatoes next month. Dig in plenty of well-rotted manure or compost and apply a balanced fertiliser. Alternatively, you can buy grow-ing bags or use the ring culture method. To prepare the border for ring culture dig out a trench at least 20 cm (8 in) deep and line it with plastic sheeting. Fill the trench with a layer of pea gravel 15 cm (6 in) deep. Tomato plants are then grown in purpose-designed bottomless pots which can be sunk into the gravel. The plants are watered via the gravel but fed via the pot.

● Vines

Once growth begins ensure vines get as much light and heat as possible.

HEATHERS

● Pruning summer-flowering heathers

Cut off the dead flower spikes which have protected the summer-flowering heathers throughout the winter. Pruning too early risks damage from late frosts, too late delays flowering and can cause the heathers not to flower at all. If you do not prune,

HEATHERS – PRUNING

Prune heathers by removing the dead flower heads without cutting back into old, hard wood. Secateurs or even scissors can be used to prune a small number of plants. For a large bed it is best to use shears.

the plants become straggly and unsightly and the life of the heather bed is shortened.

Use secateurs, scissors or shears, whichever is most convenient, and cut off stems at the base of the flowers without cutting into old wood. As the plants become older, take less off the top. Also check the varieties with coloured foliage for any stems which have reverted to green. Cut these stems out completely otherwise the green foliage will take over and the plant will revert totally.

Prune young tree heathers by cutting off half of last year's growth; this ensures a shapely plant in future years. Once they are three or four years old, confine pruning to shaping after flowering. Pruning causes a two or three-week delay in flowering, so prune the whole bed not just individual plants.

● Checking heather layers

Check that shoots you have layered (*see* July, page 179) are well rooted by gently lifting the stem. If resistance is felt, cut these stems at ground level near the parent plant, but leave the layered stems undisturbed. They should be replanted next month (*see* April, page 101).

● Last summer's cuttings

Using an ericaceous compost, plant the rooted cuttings deeply in pots, burying any bare stems, so that the lower foliage rests on the compost surface. Firm well to stop the cuttings rocking in the wind. Place the pots outside in a sheltered area.

● Watering

Potted-up plants will dry out very quickly in dry weather, keep them moist and water daily if necessary. Rainwater is best, but if none is available, use tap water. Never use domestic softened water.

PRUNING TIMETABLE FOR HEATHERS		
Name	Pruning time	Comments
Calluna vulgaris	Feb–Mar	Prune long flowering spikes every year. Trim off all flower heads.
Bruckenthalia Daboecia	Feb–Mar	Trim off dead flowers and seed pods every year.
Erica ciliaris E. tetralix	Mar–May	Lightly trim every year.
E. cinerea	Feb–Mar	Trim every year, particularly long flowering spikes.
E. arborea E. australis E. scoparia E. terminalis E. x veitchii	After flowering	Trim half of previous year's growth for the first four years to encourage bushy plants. Trim off broken branches. Stake for support.
E. manipuliflora E. vagans	Mar	Leave flower heads on for russet colours during winter. Trim every year. Do not be afraid of limiting growth.
E. x watsonii E. x williamsii	Mar	Trim hard every other year.

HERBS

● Cultivating established beds

Clear away any remaining rubbish and dead growth, then fork the bed over to loosen up the soil; be careful not to disturb roots or damage dormant plants. Remove any weeds and scatter a light top dressing of bonemeal around the herbs. Mulch with good garden compost if the soil has warmed up, to prevent new weed growth and retain moisture. Do not mulch frosted or really cold soil.

● Sowing seed

As soon as the air temperature is high enough to warm up the soil, make a seed bed (*see* Propagation, page 426). Sow small amounts of herbs to be used when young at monthly or six-weekly intervals. Continue throughout the summer to maintain a succession of fresh leaves and flowers. In cold areas delay the first sowing until the end of the month or early April. Herbs that can be sown in this way for use as salad flavourings include coriander, chervil, chives, dill, nasturtium, pot marigold, purslane, salad rocket, sorrel and sweet marjoram.

If you are planning to grow herbs for drying and storing, then sow more than the amount you think you need – it takes a considerable bulk of fresh herbs to provide an adequate amount when dried.

Very fine seed may become lost if sown outdoors. It is better to sow small quantities in trays indoors or in the greenhouse (*see* Propagation, page 427).

● Sowing basil

Basil requires warmth, water and plenty of root space if it is to make a really prolific, healthy showing of leaves. Use a fine seed compost, water and allow it to drain, then sow three seeds of basil on the top of each pot. Do not cover the seeds with compost. If possible, place the pots in a heated propagator indoors or in the greenhouse. Cover the pots with glass and brown paper or newspaper and keep them out of direct sunlight. Remove the covering as soon as the seeds start to germinate.

As the plants grow, remove the two weakest seedlings to leave one strong plant. Pinch out the top of the plant when three pairs of leaves have developed from the main stem. This will encourage sideshoots to form at an early stage.

● Sowing parsley

Sow parsley in shallow drills 25 cm (10 in) apart, in a damp, shady position. Sow a few radish seeds in the rows of parsley. These will act as a marker crop, for while parsley may appear after two to three weeks, it can sometimes take as long as nine or ten weeks to germinate and very often gets forgotten. Pouring boiling water along the drill before sowing seems to work well for many gardeners, as this warms and moistens the soil while, hopefully, deterring any germinating weed seeds.

● Dividing large clumps of herbs

As soon as the shoots show above the ground, lift large (four to five-year-old) clumps of bergamot, chives, comfrey, fennel and sorrel that were not dealt with in the autumn. Divide the roots (*see* Propagation, page 431), then replant in groups of three or five plants, with each group 30 cm (12 in) apart in a new position in rich, moist soil and full sun. If you cannot provide a new position, dig over the old soil and add compost and fertiliser.

Older herbaceous herbs, such as bergamot and marjoram, can develop small rooted sections which can be detached from the main plant and replanted.

HERBS – DIVIDING CHIVES

Established clumps of chives are easy to divide and if you have lots of plants they can be used to form an attractive edging. Lift them, gently pull the clump apart, then replant the divided sections about 30 cm (12 in) apart.

● Planting hedges for shelter

Small hedges of plants such as box, germander and lavender have been traditionally used in herb and knot gardens for centuries. They are generally aromatic and help to shelter the plants within their boundaries. Permanent hedges of these herbs may be planted now in mild areas, but leave this until April if the soil is cold and wet.

Use a string line to mark out the hedge's position, then dig a narrow trench. Make sure the soil is well dug and free of perennial weeds. Scatter bonemeal in the trench. Space plants 25 cm (10 in) apart. Firm soil around roots, water in, then lightly trim the plants so that new growth will be even.

● Pruning

Shrubby herbs such as artemisias and hyssops are improved by cutting them back to just above the start of last year's growth. This produces a vigorous rounded bush of aromatic new shoots and leaves.

HOUSE & CONSERVATORY PLANTS

● Watering

As plants start to grow, increase watering gradually but let the compost dry out slightly between waterings. If the compost feels moist to the touch then watering is not necessary, but if it feels dry, then water. Use a watering can with a long spout, fill the plant container with water and let it drain away, but do not put water on the top of any plant as the foliage and crown may rot.

● Feeding

Feed plants if they are growing actively. For healthy foliage add a slow-release fertiliser or a high-nitrogen liquid feed when the compost is damp.

● Light and aspect

Move plants from south-facing windowsills in sunny weather or they will get too hot and dry. As the days get longer move plants in flower, such as African violets, to west-facing windowsills.

● Maintaining healthy foliage

Cut back neglected plants (except palms) to healthy buds to encourage fresh foliage. Cut back ferns to their crowns, water well and leave them in light shade. They should soon produce fresh new fronds.

Wipe glossy-leaved plants with a leaf shine and remove dead leaves (*see* February, page 42).

● Flowering plants

Feed with either a high-potash feed formulated specifically to promote flowering in house plants or, as a good, cheap alternative, tomato fertiliser. Give azaleas and camellias an ericaceous feed designed especially for acid-loving plants.

Take cuttings of abutilons and *Tibouchina semidecandra* from now until September. Insert the young shoots in sandy compost and keep them at a temperature of about 20°C (70°F) until rooted.

● Indoor bulbs and corms

Keep gloriosas warm and increase watering as growth restarts. Provide trellis or stakes for the new shoots to grow up.

Plant out pot-grown bulbs as soon as they finish flowering this month (*see* Bulbs, page 59).

Plant hippeastrums for late spring flowering in pots. Keep them in a warm humid atmosphere and water sparingly until the buds appear.

● Climbers and feature plants

Cut out weak or diseased shoots, tie in any growth that needs support and clear away dead leaves from the surface of the compost. Cut abutilons back hard (you can use the prunings for cuttings) but do not prune bottle brushes (*Callistemon*).

● Bromeliads

Water freely with rainwater if possible, but let the compost dry between waterings. Avoid wetting the neck of the plant as this can encourage rotting. Put water in the 'urn' formed by the rosette leaves, but change the water now and then. Feed with a liquid feed, diluted to a quarter or third the normal strength, once a month.

Mist air plants with a foliar feed once a month, and continue to mist with water only, once or twice a week (*see* January, page 25).

● Cacti and other succulents

Stand forest succulents, such as Christmas and Easter cacti, on a tray of moist pea gravel, to provide extra humidity if they are in a dry room.

Towards the end of March move cacti and

HOUSE & CONSERVATORY PLANTS – REPOTTING CACTI

1 Repotting cacti can be painful, but this technique makes it less so. Ensure the rootball is loose by pushing a pencil through the drainage hole.

2 Make a 'handle' from a strip of thin card and lift the plant from the pot. Loosen the compost around the roots if it is compacted.

3 Repot the cactus in a pot one size larger. Trickle in cactus compost around the edge. Tap the pot on a hard surface to settle compost round the roots.

succulents kept dry over winter to a warm room, and water them. Fill the pots to the brim with water and repeat, until water flows from the drainage holes. Let the compost dry out before watering again.

Pot on cacti if they begin to look too large for the pot or growth is poor or slow for that species. For advice on handling prickly cacti, see page 71.

● Orchids

Water so that the compost is moist but not soaking wet. Keep orchids without swellings at the base of their leaves (pseudobulbs), such as moth orchids (*Phalaenopsis*) and slipper orchids (*Paphiopedilum*), constantly moist but not waterlogged. Orchids with pseudobulbs, such as cambrian hybrids, cymbidiums and cattleyas, are more drought tolerant and can be allowed to dry out slightly between waterings.

Purchase flowering cambrian hybrids and cymbidiums if not yet done (see February, page 44). It is best to buy orchids from a specialist nursery.

IRISES

● Controlling diseases

Examine bearded irises, pulling off any dead leaves and cutting out brown leaf tips and spots. Check the rhizomes and cut out any areas affected with a disease such as soft rot. Disinfect your knife after cutting each rhizome to avoid the infection spreading from plant to plant. Dust cut surfaces of rhizomes with a fungicide.

Dig out and destroy any bulbous irises showing symptoms of fungus disease or virus attack (see January, page 25).

● Weeding and feeding

Weed growth around bearded irises can be a particular nuisance because these irises form a tight clump. Take special care when loosening the soil around the rhizomes to get at weeds as the rhizomes' roots are very near the surface.

Feed with a general fertiliser and mulch *Iris sibirica* and water-loving irises such as *I. ensata* and the Japanese hybrids to conserve moisture (see The soil in your garden, pages 392–393).

Apply a top dressing of sulphate of potash to early-flowering bulbous irises after flowering and when their leaves have started to lengthen; this will benefit next year's flowers.

● Cold weather protection

In warmer areas dwarf bearded irises may begin flowering and need protection (see February, page 44).

LAWNS

● Planning a new lawn

If you are planning a new lawn then work can start as soon as conditions are suitable (see pages 84–85).

● Reseeding worn areas

Towards the end of March, reseed worn areas and any bare patches, but wait until April to do this if the weather is cold and the ground very wet.

Level any depressions in the soil and rake to remove debris and create a seed bed. Sow grass seed at 35 g per m² (1 oz per sq yd), rake in and water with a watering can fitted with a fine rose. Cover with plastic sheeting or horticultural fleece until the first seedlings emerge, then remove the protection. If the whole lawn looks thin, with lots of bare earth, try oversowing it with grass seed of a similar type. To do this, first scarify (rake) the lawn to remove any debris. Sow seed at a rate of 25 g per m² (¾ oz per sq yd) and

rake in well. Cut no closer than 2.5 cm (1 in) until the new grass is established.

● Fertilisers and weedkillers

If the spring has been mild and the lawn is already growing actively, start applying spring fertilisers and weedkillers, but in most years it is better to wait until April. Save time by using a combined weed and feed which also contains a mosskiller (see April, pages 105–106).

● Moss problems

The appearance of moss is a sign that the growing conditions for the grass are not right. In the short term, apply a mosskiller and feed the lawn but the real cure is to tackle the underlying cause of moss, which may be poor drainage, too much shade, an infertile soil or a combination of factors.

● Scarifying

Thatch (layers of dead grass and moss building up on the soil surface) must be removed to maintain healthy grass. There are two methods of removing thatch. One is to remove it little and often using a spring-tined rake. Do this monthly from March through to August, except during periods of drought. The other method is to do a single, vigorous scarifying, ideally in autumn, using a power lawnrake (see Tools and Equipment page 440).

Scarifying by hand is hard work. Press down on the rake so the tines pull up the dead grass. There is little chance of damaging the grass by overscarifying with a hand rake. However, if you are using a machine, take care not to damage the living grass; the base of the shoots must be left intact. Apply mosskiller to the lawn a week or two before scarifying so dead moss can be removed at the same time.

The first spring cut

Cut the grass for the first time when it is 8 cm (3 in) high. Check the mower blades are sharp and set them high; reduce the cutting height in stages as the season progresses. Delay the first cut if the weather is very wet or frosty. Do not leave any grass clippings on the lawn at this time of year.

Repairing lawn edges

Repair any lawn edges that have crumbled if this was not done last month (*see* February, page 44).

Wormcasts

If you are troubled by wormcasts, flick them off the lawn with a stiff broom or besom before starting to mow. Don't use chemicals to kill earthworms as they are beneficial in a garden and help to keep the soil healthy. If the problem persists, apply acidic fertilisers such as sulphate of iron or sulphate of ammonia (*see* Fertilisers, page 388). If you remove clippings and leaves from the lawn this helps to discourage earthworms.

Fusarium patch

Fusarium patches on lawns are a common problem in damp periods, particularly spring and autumn. Look out for small orange or brown spots which get larger and then join up. Similar-looking patches can have other causes, such as cat or dog urine, but white fungal growth in damp weather is a tell-tale indicator. Some mosskillers will control it but to prevent fusarium you need to improve the drainage and reduce shade. Regular mowing and removing all the lawn clippings also helps.

Damping off

Damping off on newly sown lawns is a fungal disease and can be recognised by the appearance of red and yellow patches of collapsed grass. It is difficult to control, but you can help to prevent it by preparing a free-draining seed bed, sowing the grass seed thinly and evenly, and taking care not to sow too early in the year.

LILIES

Protecting young shoots

March is probably the month when you first see shoots beginning to break through the soil surface. Apply a light mulch of well-rotted compost, manure, or chipped bark on top of the clumps of established lilies. Use cloches or loose litter (straw, bracken, chipped bark or compost) to protect the young shoots against frost damage at night.

Sowing seeds

In warmer areas sow seeds outdoors in a cold frame, 2.5 cm (1 in) apart and 1 cm (½ in) deep, in boxes 15–20 cm (6–8 in) deep. In cold districts wait till weather warms up in April before sowing.

Seed trays sown earlier can go into a cold frame if greenhouse space is restricted, but do not allow the compost to dry out.

Planting outdoor bulbs

March is an excellent month to plant lilies outside, especially stem-rooting types (*see* September, page 222). Aim to complete all the main planting before the end of the month.

Check for basal rot before planting (*see* February, page 45). Set each bulb two and a half times deeper than the bulb's height. Lilies thrive in well-drained, deeply cultivated soil which contains plenty of humus. They do not like poor soil or fresh manure.

It is best to prepare the beds in advance adding plenty of leafmould or well-rotted compost. Dig the beds to a depth of 45 cm (18 in).

If you garden on heavy clay or badly drained ground and want to grow lilies, it is best to prepare a raised bed by adding topsoil enriched with plenty of leafmould or well-rotted garden compost to 25–40 cm (10–16 in) above the surrounding soil.

Forced bulbs

Plant any lilies you have purchased especially for growing in pots (*see* February, page 45).

When forced lilies are about to open reduce the temperature to around 13°C (55°F) to prolong their flowering. Feeding should also stop at this stage.

PELARGONIUMS

Potting up

Pot up rooted cuttings or young seedlings into 8–9 cm (3–3½ in) pots in a good seed or potting compost. Position the plants where they will receive good light – never crowd them together so that the light does not reach the lower leaves. Keep them moist at the roots, but never waterlogged, and maintain a dry atmosphere. Pelargoniums do not like high humidity, and are inclined to rot in a moist atmosphere.

Pot up plants as soon as they look too large for the pot. Tap the plant out of its pot to see how the roots are developing; if they are filling the pot, then it is time for a move. Plants remaining in the same pot without access to fresh compost will need feeding as they soon exhaust the nutrients in their potting compost. It is important to feed as soon as possible if the leaves begin to look paler than normal or growth is stunted.

● Feeding

Give young plants a balanced liquid feed but, as they mature, change to one which is higher in potash, such as a feed formulated for tomatoes. If plants receive too much nitrogen they will grow large leaves to the detriment of their flowers.

● Shaping

Keep turning plants so that they do not grow 'one-sided'. This is especially important for any plants on windowsills which receive light from only one direction. Pinch out the growing tip to encourage a bushy shape (*see* February, page 45).

● Stopping

If you are going to exhibit your plants they should now be receiving their last stopping (*see* September, page 223). This is a matter of judgement, but leaving it too late could delay the flowering too long.

● Cuttings

Continue to propagate pelargoniums, including scented-leaved varieties, from cuttings in a heated propagator (*see* January, page 26).

RHODODENDRONS & AZALEAS

● Planting new shrubs

Continue to prepare the soil (*see* February, page 45) and start planting when warm weather arrives.

Unlike some shrubs, it is quite usual to buy rhododendrons and azaleas in flower. Between them azalea and rhododendron flowers cover almost every colour in the spectrum so you should be able to find the colour you want for your garden. There is also a huge range of varieties available, from dwarfs to types which, in time, grow into multi-stemmed

trees. When choosing and planting rhododendrons and azaleas, take into account the ultimate height and spread of the varieties chosen, so that the plants do not become too crowded later on.

Care needs to be taken when watering and whenever possible, use rainwater. Newly planted rhododendrons and azaleas are very slow to root into the surrounding soil, so make sure that both the rootball and ground are soaked before planting and check new plantings regularly to see if they need watering.

RHODODENDRONS & AZALEAS – GROWING IN CONTAINERS

If you want to grow rhododendrons or azaleas but have alkaline soil, growing them in a container is often the most satisfactory solution. Both make good container plants. Even large specimens can be kept in good condition for a number of years, but there are also many dwarf hybrids that are excellent if you are short of room. Choose a permanent container at least 15 cm (6 in) in diameter larger than the rootball or the pot the plant is supplied in. Add a good quantity of crocks or stones for drainage and fill the container with lime-free (ericaceous) compost.

Position the plant carefully at its original level and firm the compost round the rootball. Water well with rainwater if available and feed with a sequestrene-based fertiliser. Keep the compost moist.

If you are growing a large specimen you may need to top dress the plant each year; smaller plants can be repotted into containers one size larger.

Rhododendrons grow successfully in pots.

● Layering

Assess which established rhododendrons would be suitable for propagation. If you want to propagate by layering, prune some lower branches now to encourage fresh shoots suitably placed for layering in 18 months' time (*see* August, page 202).

● Semi-ripe cuttings of azaleas

Pot up semi-ripe azalea cuttings taken last year into individual pots and grow on until the autumn (*see* May, page 136).

ROCK PLANTS

● Controlling weeds

As the surface of the soil becomes drier, hoe lightly and carefully round the plants to remove newly germinated weed seedlings, taking care not to disturb any bulbs that may be emerging. An onion hoe or a three-tined cultivator is ideal (*see* Tools and Equipment, pages 435–436). Replenish any top dressing disturbed during this work with fresh stone chippings or gravel (*see* February, page 46). Fork out weeds, such as annual grasses and groundsel, and shake off any excess soil. Carefully remove any perennial weeds, such as dandelion, ground elder, and creeping buttercup, either with a hand fork or a trowel, ensuring that all the roots are removed.

● Germinating seeds

Watch carefully early in the month for signs of germination in trays of seed placed outside for weathering (*see* December, page 281). Replace any of the top dressing that has been washed away with sand or fine chippings. Once signs of growth appear, move the choicer or slower growing plants to a cold frame or unheated greenhouse before pricking out. Take care at this stage not to allow trays to dry out, but do not overwater.

● Planting

Plant rock plants from the nursery or garden centre as soon as possible after purchase. If they have come by post and the weather is cold, pot them up and store them in an unheated greenhouse or cold frame.

Add leafmould or garden compost mixed with a general fertiliser or bonemeal to the planting area at the rate recommended by the manufacturer. A nutrient-enriched peat or peat substitute eliminates the need for any additional fertiliser. Monitor the spread of plants so that slow-growing rock plants are not crowded out by quick-growing neighbours.

● Division

Dividing clumps of plants (*see* Propagation, pages 431–432) is a good way of increasing stock and rejuvenating those which have become old and woody in the centre. It is also a way of saving live portions of plants which have suffered from dieback in wintry weather. Carpeting plants which root as they travel along, such as androsaces, campanulas, raoulias, and some saxifrages and sedums, respond well to this treatment, as do some other taller plants. With early-flowering plants it is better to wait until after flowering before dividing.

Lift the plants out of the soil, trim them and cut out dead or unhealthy parts. Then pull the clump gently apart into portions about 2.5–5 cm (1–2 in) across. Dig over the soil where the old plants were and add bonemeal and leafmould before replanting the divided portions.

Gentiana sino-ornata, one of the most beautiful of the alpine rock plants, should be divided every other spring. Prise the root thongs apart and replant them in a moist, humus-rich soil.

● Potting up root cuttings

Check root cuttings taken in February that have been growing over the past month. Plant these up into small pots using John Innes No. 1 potting compost when they have produced a few leaves and have a well-developed root system.

● Lewisias

Start watering lewisias that have been kept in dry conditions over winter.

● Controlling pests

Check rock plants in pots for vine weevil and treat as necessary (*see* Pests, page 404).

ROSES

● Planting bare-root roses

Planting bare-root roses (*see* November, page 266) must be completed by the middle of the month, or by the end of the month in cold areas. As with any planting in whatever season, the site must be properly prepared beforehand and you should add at least one large forkful of well-rotted garden compost or manure per plant.

If you are replacing a plant damaged during winter, the soil in the immediate vicinity must be replaced for much the same reason that vegetable crops are rotated. The soil can suffer from 'rose sickness'; when it becomes exhausted from supporting roses. Remove the soil to a depth of 45 cm (18 in) and replace with fresh soil taken from a part of the garden where roses have not grown for five years.

All newly planted roses must be trodden in very firmly and, if the weather has been frosty, refirm plants that were planted or transplanted during the autumn and winter.

● Pruning

March is the traditional month for pruning most types of rose. In mild areas late February is not too soon and by the end of March pruning should be completed even in the coldest regions.

In theory, all stems that produced flowers the previous season are now obsolete and must be removed. In practice this is not possible as the bush must be allowed to build up a framework of branches. Whether the rose is a hybrid tea (large-flowered),

ROSES – PRUNING

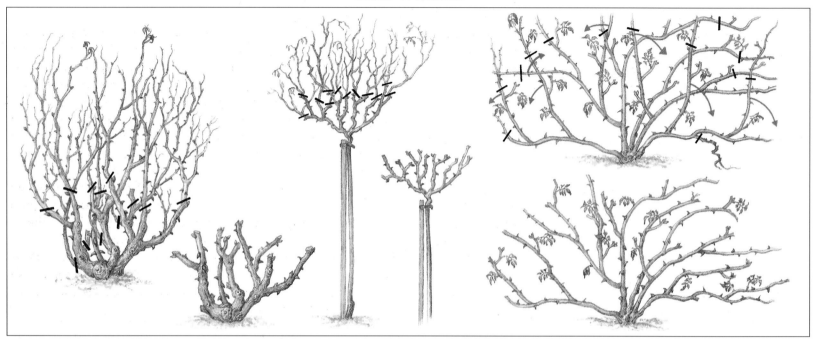

Established hybrid tea (large-flowered) and floribunda (cluster-flowered) roses benefit from strong shoots being cut back by about two-thirds. Cut out very old stumps, dead, diseased and damaged wood, and any spindly shoots, completely.

Prune ordinary standard roses (not weeping standards) by cutting out very old or damaged wood, then reducing the rest of the shoots by about two-thirds, being careful to retain an even shape.

Only established repeat-flowering climbers (those that bloom from mid summer to mid autumn) should be pruned now. Cut out any dead or diseased wood, and shorten the sideshoots that flowered last year by about half.

floribunda (cluster-flowered), patio, miniature or re-current-flowering shrub, the procedure is the same.

First, identify the three categories of wood that constitute the fabric of all roses. They are the old and decaying stumps, small twiggy growth and the good, strong, healthy growth.

The old stumps should be removed in their entirety, although in practice this is sometimes difficult because they are inaccessible. Any dead or decaying wood must be eliminated as this is the

source of much disease. Long-armed pruners or a pruning saw are ideal for this purpose; never use good sharp secateurs on this type of wood as they are not strong enough and you will damage them (*see* Tools and Equipment, pages 437–438).

Next, all very thin spindly wood must be cut out. This is the type of wood that does not have the potential to support new, strong growth to encourage new shoots. Then shorten the strong shoots by two-thirds to an outward-facing bud.

BUSH ROSES

These include hybrid tea (large-flowered) and floribunda (cluster-flowered) roses, as well as miniature and the small patio types. A bush rose is one which is not trained into a special shape and does not have a sprawling or climbing habit.

Cut down newly planted roses to about 15 cm (6 in), and see that they are trodden in firmly. On established bushes, cut out old stumps and diseased wood and remove twiggy growth (miniatures, in particular, develop a tangle of thin branches in the centre of the bush). Cut back strong shoots by about two-thirds to an outward-facing bud.

SUMMER-FLOWERING SHRUB ROSES

Old garden roses which include gallicas, damask, albas, centifolias and moss roses, are pruned in the same way as most shrubs, for rejuvenation rather than size of bloom.

Newly planted shrubs will not require pruning. Apart from cutting out dead and damaged wood on established shrubs, the chief criterion is to cut back old flowering wood by a third to a half with an emphasis on giving a good shape to the plant. If a shrub is getting too leggy, reduce the number of stems by cutting down one or two to about 15 cm (6 in), encouraging new shoots to break from the base.

CLIMBERS AND RAMBLERS

Only repeat-flowering climbers are pruned in the spring; climbers and ramblers which flower once only in the summer are cut back in autumn (*see* October, page 246). Newly planted climbers and ramblers do not require any pruning. Check with an expert to find out the type of rose you are dealing with if you are not sure.

Remove all damaged wood and non-productive stems on established repeat-flowering plants. Reduce the previous year's flowering growth by half, taking out some sideshoots completely. Cut all the old ties and rearrange the rose to give a good spread over the wall or fence. Tie in using soft string rather than plastic ties (*see* January, page 20).

GROUND COVER ROSES

This type of rose must be allowed to grow naturally and cutting back will encourage inappropriate growth.

STANDARDS

Prune back main stems of the top growth of newly planted roses to 15–20 cm (6–8 in), preferably to an outward-pointing bud. On established standard forms of hybrid tea (large-flowered) and floribunda (cluster-flowered) roses remove old and damaged wood and reduce the main fabric of the plant by two-thirds, taking care to maintain a neat, even head.

Weeping standards are created by budding ramblers on to an upright stem, and so should be treated as other ramblers by lightly pruning back in the autumn (*see* October, page 246).

● After pruning

Check all stakes and ties. Do not leave prunings lying around. Dispose of them or shred before composting. Spray all plants and the surrounding soil with a systemic fungicide and mulch the soil.

SWEET PEAS

● Planting out

As soon as soil and weather conditions permit, plant autumn-sown seedlings which have overwintered in pots or trays. Spread the roots out well in the holes and plant them firmly. Discard all plants which have a brown collar on the white part of the stem above the seed. If planted, these invariably collapse prematurely. Loosely tie the seedlings to stakes, or place small supporting twigs around each plant to prevent damage from windrock.

Plant in pairs with 15 cm (6 in) between each pair in single rows wherever practicable. To support the growing plants, use 1.8 m (6 ft) bushy sticks or branches, bamboo canes or wire netting.

Sweet peas planted in 30 cm (12 in) or 45 cm (18 in) circles at the back of the border look

SWEET PEAS – SUPPORT SYSTEMS

Twiggy sticks make a natural-looking support for sweet peas if you are growing them in a border. Use small sticks for dwarf varieties and taller ones for the larger upright kinds.

If you are growing sweet peas in rows to provide cut flowers then netting stretched between stout posts is a convenient way to support a large number of plants. Alternatively grow them up bamboo canes.

especially attractive. The old-fashioned varieties are particularly suitable for natural culture. Support dwarf sweet peas with tent-shaped lengths of wire netting placed over the rows. This has a double value, as it also keeps off birds while the plants are young. The 'Snoopea' and 'Supersnoop' types which have no tendrils will not need support. They can also be grown in containers and hanging baskets.

Protect the new plants immediately from birds and slugs and consider applying a mulch to conserve water (*see* The soil in your garden, page 392–3).

Planting for growing as cordons

To grow exhibition-quality blooms on the cordon system, set the plants out in double rows spaced at least 30 cm (12 in) apart with a pathway at least 1 m (3 ft) wide between each pair of rows. Allow 20 cm (8 in) between plants (*see* February, page 46). Insert a 2.5 m (8 ft) cane alongside each plant and attach the canes to the support framework by tying them in or using cane clips to hold them steady.

Sowing seeds

Soil and weather conditions permitting, sow seeds outdoors in their flowering positions, following the method outlined for autumn sowing (*see* October, page 246). Make spring sowings under glass as early in the month as possible.

TREES, SHRUBS & HEDGES

Planting new trees and shrubs

As long as the soil is not frozen or waterlogged, continue to plant shrubs and all types of hedges (*see* September, page 225). Complete the planting of bare-root specimens by the end of this month so that they will be established before the summer.

Feeding

Apply a general fertiliser such as Growmore to all trees and shrubs according to the manufacturer's instructions (*see* Fertilisers, page 390).

Protection from late frost

When sharp frosts are forecast, protect new leaves, shoots and flower buds of susceptible varieties of shrubs and trees from damage by wrapping them in horticultural fleece or netting. The shrubs most at risk are the silver or grey-leaved plants, such as cistus, halimium, caryopteris and the Californian poppy (*Romneya coulteri*), and those whose native habitat is sheltered woodland, for example Japanese maples, hydrangeas, camellias, crinodendrons and pieris.

Many of the most ornamental trees and large decorative shrubs which have become increasingly popular in gardens originated in warmer climates and need some cosseting. These include *Cytisus battandieri*, ceanothus, foxglove tree (*Paulownia*) and eucryphia.

Layering

Many shrubs with low branches can be layered now either into pots or directly into the soil at the base of the parent plant (*see* Propagation, page 432–3).

Choose low-growing shoots from the previous season's growth. If you are layering the branch directly into the ground, prepare the soil by forking it over. Dig in some garden compost to help retain moisture and add a handful of bonemeal.

With many species, wounding the stem slightly encourages rooting. Remove a very thin layer of bark from the reverse side of one of the buds on the shoot that is to be layered and apply a little rooting hormone to the wounded area. Bury the layer, peg it down and water occasionally. By October the new

plant can be removed from its parent and potted up or planted in its final growing position.

Hardwood cuttings

Most hardy shrubs will still propagate well from hardwood cuttings taken this month (*see* Propagation, page 429). Insert these cuttings in a trench in the garden and leave them undisturbed, apart from the occasional watering in dry weather, until the autumn.

Increasing ground cover

Dig up, divide and replant the self-rooted shoots of quick-spreading shrubs and sub-shrubs, such as rose of sharon (*Hypericum calycinum*) and periwinkle (*Vinca*), to increase the amount of ground cover.

Propagating from seed

Continue to sow seeds of shrubs and trees into pots of seed compost, including seeds that are of a dry nature or have been stratified over winter. Germinate at a soil temperature of 13–18°C (55–65°F) in a heated propagator (*see* February, page 47).

Pot on seedlings sown last summer which have been overwintered in frost-free conditions.

Semi-ripe cuttings

By the end of the month, semi-ripe cuttings taken last spring and summer should have developed good roots. Pot these on into individual pots. Don't worry if the leaves have dropped off (even from evergreens) as new shoots will form from the buds at the base of the cutting.

Leaf bud cuttings

Camellias can be increased by leaf bud cuttings (*see* Propagation, page 430). Keep the cuttings moist,

GROWING TREES AND SHRUBS FROM SEED

Some trees and shrubs grow relatively quickly from seed. Listed below is a selection of interesting or fast-growing species for which seeds should be widely available. Specialist suppliers will be able to provide a larger range. Always read the instructions on the seed packet or in the catalogue before planting as some tree and shrub seeds need warmth for rapid germination, while others require a cold spell. Seeds also vary considerably in how quickly they germinate, so don't be in a hurry to discard the pots.

Latin name	Common name	Tree/shrub	Comments
Buddleja davidii	Butterfly bush	Shrub	Self-sown seedlings grow on derelict sites showing how easy this plant is to grow from seed, but don't expect strong colours.
Cercis siliquastrum	Judas tree	Tree	Often slow to germinate and growth not fast.
Chimonanthus	Wintersweet	Shrub	Germinates best if seeds have been subjected to a cold period.
Cistus	Rock rose	Shrub	Can flower in 18 months from sowing.
Cryptomeria japonica	Japanese cedar	Tree	Conifer, quick-growing in early years.
Cytisus	Broom	Shrub	Chip and soak the seeds first. May flower the next year if sown in spring.
Eucalyptus (hardy)	Gum tree	Tree	Germinates and grows quickly.
Genista aetnensis	Mount Etna broom	Shrub	Germinates and grows quickly.
Ginkgo biloba	Maidenhair tree	Tree	Deciduous conifer. Grows rapidly from seed.
Kolkwitzia amabilis	Beauty bush	Shrub	Germinates best if seeds have been subjected to a cold period.
Lavandula	Lavender	Shrub	Germinates best if seeds have been subjected to a cold period. Easy and quick to grow.
Liquidambar styraciflua	Sweet gum	Tree	May be slow to germinate.
Parthenocissus quinquefolia	Virginia creeper	Climber	Quick-growing, vigorous climber.
Passiflora caerulea	Passion flower	Climber	May flower within two years.
Robinia pseudoacacia	Common acacia	Tree	Chip and soak the seeds first.
Santolina chamaecyparissus	Lavender cotton	Shrub	Germinates quickly in warmth.
Ulex europaeus	Gorse	Shrub	Germinates easily and grows quickly.

warm and shaded and they will normally be rooted and ready to pot on by late summer.

● Root cuttings

Shrubs such as *Romneya coulteri* can be increased by taking root cuttings (*see* Propagation, page 431). When new growth appears, remove the cuttings, pot on and keep them watered in a sheltered part of the garden for planting out next spring.

Last spring's root cuttings will have matured into new plants by now. Plant these out in their final growing positions.

● Pruning

Start to prune spring-flowering shrubs over three years old, as they finish flowering, using the one-third method (*see* Pruning, page 420).

Early in the month prune the shrubs that produce their best show on vigorous new wood. Cut them hard back to within a few inches of the main framework. This hard pruning is best done just as the leaves begin to open, but before they are fully formed. It is most successful if done annually to prevent the plants from becoming hard and woody.

Shrubs that respond especially well to this method are *Buddleja davidii*, caryopteris, ceratostigma, *Hydrangea paniculata*, lavatera, leycesteria, perovskia, santolina and senecio.

Shrubs grown for their decorative stems, such as *Cornus alba* and *C. stolonifera* varieties and certain eucalyptus species, should be hard pruned in the same way (*see* Pruning, page 421).

● Frost damage

Remove the ends of shoots on shrubs damaged by frost, even if they should not be pruned now. This prevents the spread of disease and further dieback.

HEDGES

● Planting and feeding

Continue to plant bare-root and container-grown hedging plants, including evergreens (*see* September, page 226), and feed both newly planted and established hedges with Growmore, following the manufacturer's instructions.

● Cutting back

Cut back newly planted deciduous hedges of leggy plants, such as hawthorn and privet, to 15 cm (6 in) from the ground. In their second winter cut them back hard again by half of the previous season's growth. This hard pruning promotes good bushy growth at the base.

Hedging plants that are naturally bushy at the base, such as beech and hornbeam, should be cut back by one-third. Conifer hedges are trimmed in late summer (*see* August, pages 203–204).

Reshape overgrown laurel and privet by the three-year method used for yew hedges (*see* July, page 185).

● Removing seedlings

Watch for brambles, ash, holly and sycamore that have been self-sown by birds using the hedge as a roost or resting place, and dig them out.

VEGETABLES

This is the month when many vegetables are sown. Prepare seed beds if this has not been done already (*see* February, page 48).

Apply fertilisers according to the fertility of your soil and the crops you intend to grow. If you add well-rotted organic matter, such as farmyard manure or spent mushroom compost, to the soil every year then you may not need to add any additional fertiliser. Most garden soils contain plenty of nutrients, apart from nitrogen which is easily leached out of the soil. For the majority of leafy crops you can use a straight nitrogen fertiliser to counteract this. For root and fruiting crops it is better to use a balanced fertiliser (*see* The soil in your garden, pages 388–392).

Put down black plastic mulches to suppress weeds (*see* The soil in your garden, page 393). This technique works well for widely spaced crops such as courgettes, marrows, cabbages, cauliflowers and Brussels sprouts. Rake the soil into a slight mound and bury both edges of the plastic sheeting in slit trenches on either side of the bed. Use a knife to cut holes through the sheet and plant seedlings with a dibber or trowel as usual.

Protect plants from slugs and snails if the weather is mild and damp.

Consider starting seeds off in 8 cm (3 in) pots in a greenhouse rather than sowing direct into open ground. If you do not have a greenhouse, you can use a cold frame for pots of the hardier vegetables such as lettuces. Tender crops, such as French beans, tomatoes and sweetcorn, can be started off on a windowsill indoors.

Sowing in pots means you can more easily protect young plants from bad weather and soil pests. Most pot-grown crops can be planted out or potted on within four weeks of sowing. To harden them off put the pots outside during the day for a couple of weeks, bringing them in at night. Then plant out the seedlings in their final growing position in a prepared bed.

The advantages of this early start are twofold: first there will be no need to thin the crop and secondly crops are ready up to two weeks earlier than if directly sown into seed beds.

● Beans

Sow broad beans in pots if they have not been sown earlier (*see* February, page 48). Plant out those sown last month. Broad beans can be grown in double rows with plants 20 cm (8 in) apart each way, in single rows 45 cm (18 in) apart, or in blocks with plants 20–30 cm (8–12 in) apart.

● Brassicas

Give overwintered brassicas a high-nitrogen feed at the start of the growing season, by adding a suitable nitrogenous top dressing (*see* Fertilisers, page 388).

Summer cabbages, cauliflowers and Brussels sprouts are best started off in pots under glass. If you grow a few like this in succession you avoid a glut at harvest time. Sow two or three seeds in each 8 cm (3 in) pot and if more than one grows, pull out all but the strongest. The alternative is to sow in rows in a seed bed and transplant the young plants to their final positions in late May or early June. Sow 2.5 cm (1 in) deep in rows 15 cm (6 in) apart.

Make the first sowing of an early calabrese variety. Sow a couple of seeds per pot, germinate at 15°C (60°F), then keep well watered and frost free. They should be ready for planting out under cloches in six to eight weeks from sowing.

Cut the first spears of early sprouting broccoli and the heads of winter cauliflower, planted the previous summer (*see* May, page 138).

● Carrots and parsnips

In mild areas, sow short rows of an early carrot such as 'Early Nantes' for a succession of baby carrots in the summer (*see* February, page 48). Later in the month start sowing maincrop carrot varieties such as 'Autumn King' in rows 15 cm (6 in) apart. Thin the seedlings later to one about every 5 cm (2 in).

Parsnips can be sown now in mild areas, but in most places they are better sown later in April or May (*see* April, page 113).

● Celery

Celery is one of the hardest vegetables to grow well; self-blanching types are easier than the traditional trench celery. To germinate, celery seed must have light and a minimum temperature of 15°C (60°F). Sow seeds thinly on a tray of compost in late March. Do not cover them and keep the compost moist. It may take a month for the seeds to germinate. If you cannot provide these conditions, buy in young plants.

● Onions and leeks

Give overwintered (Japanese) onions a high-nitrogen feed at the start of the growing season.

Onions can be grown from seed or from sets (small onions). Sets are the easiest option but there is a greater choice of varieties from seed. Onions raised from seed are also less likely to bolt and generally store better. Sow seeds in pots in a cool greenhouse and harden off before planting out in April. Seeds can also be sown outside, with or without a cloche. Sow 2 cm (¾ in) deep, with 30 cm (12 in) between the rows. Thin the seedlings to 3 cm (1½ in) apart.

Plant onion sets from early March onwards. Push them gently into the soil, spacing them 5 cm (2 in) apart in rows 25 cm (10 in) apart. Plant shallots 15–20 cm (6–8 in) apart, with 30 cm (12 in) between the rows. Leave just the tips of the onions and shallots exposed and cover them with fleece or netting to prevent birds from pulling them out.

Sow leek seeds under glass, 2.5 cm (1 in) apart. Prick out the seedlings to about 3 cm (1½ in) each way when they are large enough to handle. Start to harden off the seedlings up to a month before planting outside. You can also sow direct outdoors but cloches or fleece may be needed in cold areas. Sow the seeds 2 cm (¾ in) deep, with 15 cm (6 in) between the rows. Then thin out to 3 cm (1½ in).

● Other roots and swollen stems

In mild areas, start to sow beetroots little and often for a succession of tender baby beets throughout the summer. Sow beetroot about 2 cm (¾ in) deep; each seed capsule will usually produce up to four seedlings. Thin to about 5 cm (2 in) between plants and allow 15 cm (6 in) between rows.

Sow celeriac seeds if not done last month (*see* February, page 48). Prick out celeriac seedlings sown last month.

Kohlrabi is a member of the brassica family that produces swollen stems instead of roots. They are

---

VEGETABLES – ONION SETS

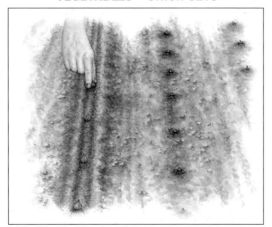

Plant onion sets in shallow drills in loose, well-prepared ground. Press the sets gently into the soil, then pull back the soil to leave just the tips of the bulbs exposed. This reduces the risk of the new roots pushing them out of the soil.

---

grown and used in the same way as turnips. Sow a succession, leaving 30 cm (12 in) between rows and 25 cm (10 in) between plants.

● Peas

Make the first successional sowings of peas if not done already (*see* February, page 48). An alternative is to sow an early variety and a main crop like 'Hurst Green Shaft' at the same time to spread the harvest.

Mangetout peas and snap peas are worth trying. As you eat the pods whole, this saves time and preparation when cooking. Both are grown like ordinary garden peas. Taller varieties of peas need support in the form of canes and string, netting or twiggy brushwood, the traditional pea sticks.

● Potatoes

Chit maincrop potatoes (*see* January, page 29).

Plant sprouted tubers of early varieties 10–15 cm (4–6 in) deep. Space them 40 cm (16 in) apart in rows 45 cm (18 in) apart. Draw the soil around them from either side to form a flat-topped ridge up to 30 cm (12 in) high. Do this in several stages as the plants grow. An alternative is to plant the tubers in a trench and then cover with a thick mulch of well-rotted organic matter or old straw. Some gardeners add grass clippings to the trench when planting to keep the tubers clean. Protect the foliage if frost threatens with a double layer of horticultural fleece. Soak the soil every week during dry spells.

● Salad crops

In mild areas, start to make sowings of salad crops such as lettuces, radishes and spring onions. To prevent a glut, sow them at intervals so that the harvest is staggered – crops such as these are best harvested little and often.

Sow lettuces 2 cm (¾ in) deep; if the soil is dry, water the bottom of the seed drill before sowing. A mature lettuce needs a space up to 30 cm (12 in) in diameter. If sowing in rows, allow the following space between rows and plants: 20 cm (8 in) for small lettuces such as 'Little Gem'; 30 cm (12 in) for butterhead, cos and salad bowl types; and 40 cm (16 in) for crispheads. In cold areas, start lettuces off in pots under glass.

Sow non-forcing chicory and curly endive outdoors. Non-forcing or 'Sugar Loaf' chicory forms a tight head in the autumn, so the heart is blanched and can be used in winter salads. Curly endives are related to chicory and look like loose-leaved lettuces but are bitter, though they can be blanched (*see* August, page 205). Sow both in the same way as lettuces from March onwards.

VEGETABLES – PLANTING POTATOES

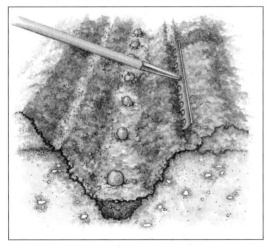

Dig a shallow trench with a spade. Plant the tubers with the shooting eyes uppermost at the spacings recommended for the variety. Add compost or grass clippings if you wish. Cover by pulling earth over them with a rake or draw hoe.

● Spinach and spinach beet

In mild areas, make the first sowings of spinach and spinach beet for a succession of crops. Avoid a glut by sowing small amounts at regular intervals so that the harvest is staggered throughout the summer.

Sow spinach and spinach beet about 2 cm (¾ in) deep, in rows 30 cm (12 in) apart, thin the young seedlings to 10–15 cm (4–6 in). In cold areas start spinach and spinach beet off in pots under glass.

● Tomatoes, peppers and aubergines

In most parts of the country, greenhouse tomatoes are more reliable than outdoor varieties. In milder areas cordon types can be grown successfully outdoors, but bush varieties are earlier and easier to grow in most places. 'Tumbler' is good for container growing. Sow outdoor varieties in a heated propagator at 15–20°C (60–70°F). Seedlings should appear in seven to ten days. When they are large enough to handle, prick out individually into 8 cm (3 in) pots of multi-purpose compost and grow on in the greenhouse. If you do not have a propagator use a warm windowsill or buy plants from a garden centre in late April or May.

Peppers require similar conditions to tomatoes. Grow them in the greenhouse or, in mild areas, under a cloche when young. Sow two seeds to each pot and keep in a propagator at 18–20°C (65–70°F) until germination, then remove the weakest seedling.

Aubergines are worth trying in milder areas. Growing under cloches will increase the chance of fruit ripening. Sow seed 5 mm (¼ in) deep in pots in a propagator set to 18–20°C (65–70°F).

● Turnips and swedes

Sow turnips 2.5 cm (1 in) deep; if you want to harvest baby turnips make the rows 25 cm (10 in) apart with 15 cm (6 in) between plants. Sow turnips for storage with 30 cm (12 in) between rows and 25 cm (10 in) between plants.

Sow swedes 2.5 cm (1 in) deep, in rows 40 cm (16 in) apart with 25 cm (10 in) between plants.

PERENNIAL VEGETABLES
● Asparagus

Prepare an asparagus bed by digging the soil over and removing every bit of perennial weed you can find. Add plenty of organic matter, such as spent mushroom compost, before planting. Allow 1 m (3 ft) between each row and 45 cm (18 in) between plants when planning the bed.

● Jerusalem artichokes

Plant tubers if not yet done (*see* February, page 49).

● Rhubarb

Blanched shoots should be ready outdoors in the first half of March (*see* January, page 29).

WATER PLANTS & POOLS

● Cleaning and repairs

Once established, a pond should not need regular cleaning; never clean out a pond for the sake of it. However, if there is a large accumulation of organic debris (leaves) in the water, or if the water is bluish in colour and smells unpleasant, then early spring is a good time to clean thoroughly. Even if the pond does not need cleaning, tidy by removing any faded overwintered foliage from marginal plants.

Net out the fish and keep them in a large bucket or container filled with pool water, not fresh tap water. Their temporary home need not be very large, but it is vital that they are kept somewhere cool and

HOW TO MAKE A BOG GARDEN

Bog plants won't thrive if you plant them in ordinary soil next to a lined pond. The ground there will be as dry as the rest of the garden, and bog plants require the constant moisture that occurs at the edge of natural pools. To grow bog plants well you must try to re-create these conditions. This is most easily done by using offcuts or spare pieces of pond liner to contain your bog garden. Excavate the area to a depth of 30–45 cm (12–18 in), and line the hole with rubber or plastic sheeting. Make slits or drainage holes about 90 cm (3 ft) apart so that surplus water can drain away slowly. Alternatively,

build the soil up on the finished bog so that the crowns are above any standing water.

Your plants will grow better if you fill the bog area with a mix of equal parts soil and sphagnum peat, peat-substitute or leafmould, rather than ordinary garden soil. Rake in a balanced slow-release fertiliser or a seaweed fertiliser at the manufacturer's recommended rate. Early spring is the ideal time to make and plant a bog garden.

Keep the bog garden moist. The ideal way is to use a seep hose or other irrigation system. Otherwise flood it with a hose periodically whenever the weather is dry.

Pick of the bog plants

Some bog plants demand a lot of space, others can be rampant. Those listed here are suitable for bog gardens large or small.

Astilbes – There are several good hybrids, their feathery plumes resembling large red, pink or white feather dusters from a distance. Most grow no more than about 60 cm (2 ft) tall, and start to flower in early summer.

Hemerocallis – Individual blooms are short-lived, but a succession of them will span the summer. There are many hybrids with trumpet-like flowers in shades of yellow, orange and red. Tall ones grow to 1.2 m (4 ft), but there are dwarfs half this height.

Hostas – Popular foliage plants, ranging from dwarfs to large varieties of 90 cm (3 ft).

Houttuynia cordata – A versatile plant that will grow in water, in a border or in a bog garden. 'Chameleon' is best used as a foliage plant as the small white flowers are no match for the red, green and yellow variegation. Grows to about 30 cm (12 in).

Iris ensata – The Japanese iris may also be sold under its old name of *Iris kaempferi*. The large, flattened flowers, looking almost like clematis, bloom in mid summer.

Lobelia cardinalis – This and the similar *L. fulgens* are grown for their dark-red foliage and spikes of red flowers about 90 cm (3 ft) tall in mid and late summer.

Lysichiton – Popularly known as the skunk cabbage, the arum-like spring flowers of *L. americanum* are yellow, those of *L. camtschatcensis* are white.

Lythrum salicaria – The purple loosestrife, grown for its tall spikes of pinkish purple flowers that reach 1.2–1.5 m (4–5 ft), flowers from mid summer to early autumn.

Matteuccia struthiopteris – The ostrich feather fern is one of the most attractive ferns for the pondside, looking almost like a large shuttlecock.

Primula, candelabra – There are many types, but *P. japonica* is a popular one with whorls of flowers up the 60 cm (2 ft) stems in late spring and early summer.

Rodgersia aesculifolia – Large, green to bronze leaves that resemble horse chestnut foliage in shape. White flowers top the 90 cm (3 ft) plants in summer.

Schizostylis – The Kaffir lily flowers in mid and late autumn, the pink or red flower spikes bringing very welcome colour at that time.

Trollius – The yellow or orange flowers, like large, globular buttercups, are at their best in late spring and early summer. The plants grow to about 60 cm (2 ft).

out of the sun, such as a garage or outhouse. Check on them every day.

You can empty the pond with a bucket or, if you have somewhere lower than the pond to which the water can be drained, by siphoning or with a pump. Keep back some pond water to return to the pond when you refill it. This introduces beneficial organisms into the pond and helps the fish to re-acclimatise. Once the debris and sludge have been cleared, refill the pond. Leave for several days to allow the effects of the chlorine to wear off before

reintroducing the fish, or better still use a proprietary dechlorinator.

The pond will also need to be drained and cleared if there are repairs required to the liner. If the damage is not too great, liners can be patched by using special repair kits. Hairline cracks in a concrete pool can be sealed with a quick-drying sealant and then painted with waterproof paint.

● **Replacing heater with pump**

Remove the pool heater if you used one during the

winter and, if you removed the pump, replace that. Start the UV water clarifier if you have one.

● **Herons**

You may well have to protect your fish against herons. One way is to push short stakes about 15 cm (6 in) into the ground about 30 cm (12 in) from the edge of the pond and 1 m (3 ft) apart. Attach strong fishing line to these stakes to create a low barrier which surrounds the pond. Otherwise you will have to cover the pond with netting.

Creating a New Lawn

Spring and autumn are the best times to create a new lawn. Whether you intend to use turf or seed, the ground needs to be well prepared, preferably a month or so in advance. This will allow the soil to settle and weeds to be cleared. A firm level surface is essential for a good lawn.

PREPARING THE SOIL

It is best to prepare the ground late the previous autumn if you are planning to plant a new lawn in the spring. Choose a fine day and begin by clearing the site of existing grass, plants and perennial weeds. Fork over or rotovate the area and leave the soil to settle over winter.

In spring, check that the soil surface is fairly dry before preparing a bed for lawn seed or turf. First trample the earth and break up clods with a rake, removing weeds or large stones as you go. Aim to achieve as level a site as possible. Firm the ground by taking small overlapping steps, with your weight on your heels. Rake the soil several times in different directions to produce a crumbly but even surface.

◀ *A lawn is the most dominant feature in many gardens. When creating a new lawn it is important to prepare the site well; you may be looking at the result for many years!*

SOWING A NEW LAWN

1 Clear the site and leave over winter if possible. Break up any clods and rake the soil to a crumbly and even surface, removing any weeds and large stones.

2 To ensure an even distribution of seed across the lawn, and therefore an even growth of new grass, peg out strings 1 m (3 ft) apart over the site.

3 Place two bamboo canes across the strings to form an area 1 m² (9 sq ft) and sprinkle the recommended amount of seed evenly across the square.

4 Hang bird scarers over the new lawn. Water during dry spells; do so carefully so as not to wash away the seed which should germinate in three weeks or less.

GRASS SEED

Grass seed mixtures are available to suit different situations and uses. There are mixtures for shady or dry sites, hard-wearing mixtures for family lawns or fine-grass mixtures to give a 'bowling green' effect. The disadvantages of a lawn grown from seed is that you may have to wait up to six months before it is usable, and birds and cats can disturb the seed bed.

CHOOSING TURF

Turf provides an instant lawn, although the lawn should not be used extensively for the first month after laying. Against this convenience, turves are expensive and laying them is heavy work.

It is important to plan delivery and laying of turves with care. For a domestic lawn, there is a choice of ornamental or wear-tolerant turf. Ornamental turf consists of narrow-leaved grasses that grow densely and low, and respond well to frequent, close cutting. The drawbacks, apart from lack of wear-tolerance, are the cost and the regular care needed to keep the lawn looking its best. Wear-tolerant turf has a mixture of narrow-leaved and coarse grasses, making it easier to look after.

Cheaper meadowland turf may grow quickly but can contain agricultural ryegrasses and weeds which form a patchy, coarse lawn. This patchiness makes the turves more likely to fall apart when handled. To combat this they are often cut more thickly than cultivated turves, making them harder to move around and lay. As cultivated turf is sown with selected grass seed, it is easier to handle and contains fewer weeds than meadowland turf.

Inspect a sample of turf before buying. Avoid turves that tear or fall apart when handled or where the grass is starting to turn yellow or has a white mould on it. The grass should form a thick, even cover, be cleanly cut and no more than 4 cm (1½ in)

high. Look at the turf soil: a sandy or loamy base is better than a heavy clay which can lead to moss and poor drainage. Check the sample for weeds, avoiding coarse grass weeds such as Yorkshire fog and cocksfoot, dandelion and all types of thistle.

Turf is normally supplied in rolls measuring 30 x 90 cm (1 x 3 ft). Most suppliers will deliver, but they may charge for this service. Turf should be laid within 24 hours of delivery. If this is not possible, unroll it in a shaded area and water lightly.

LAYING A NEW LAWN USING TURVES

1 Create a level bed of soil with a fine tilth, then lay the first turves against a straight edge such as a plank.

2 Lay alternate courses of turves in staggered rows. Work from a board to protect the soil.

3 When the turves are in place, closely butted up to one another, brush fine topsoil into the cracks. Repeat if more cracks open later. Water the turves in, if the soil is dry.

4 If you want to shape the edge of your lawn, it is best to wait until the turves have taken. Then clearly mark out the shape and use an edger to cut the lawn.

APRIL

Showers bring the garden to
life and shrubs and border
plants are now in full growth.
Leaves are fresh and green
and new flowers open
every day.

April

For many gardeners April is their favourite month. Spring flowers are often at their best, summer bedding plants are on sale, and plants in the herbaceous border seem to grow by the day. The longer days not only benefit the plants, they also provide more opportunities for the gardener to work in and enjoy the garden.

The rapid plant growth this month means it is one of the busiest months of the year in the garden. If you grow your own bedding plants, these may well need daily watering and feeding while they are still in their trays and pots. Many established plants in the borders also require attention: staking, tying in and sometimes pruning; while in the kitchen garden vegetable sowing is usually at its peak.

The lawn now requires regular mowing, often twice a week if the grass is growing really strongly, and April is also a very busy time if you concentrate on growing any of the specialist plants such as chrysanthemums, dahlias, sweet peas, fuchsias or pelargoniums.

The weather in April

There are still wide regional variations in the weather. In the south, south-west, and other favourable areas, the month is usually mild, but in the north-east, Scotland, and other cold areas, it may be little warmer than March. Snow is not unusual in April, though it seldom lasts for long.

April is traditionally associated with showers, and in most parts of the country there is usually adequate rainfall to germinate any seeds sown outdoors, and to keep new plants well watered. However, dry areas, such as East Anglia, may have a deficit of water and there can be dry spells in any part of the country.

Watering and mulching

Be prepared to water regularly if you have sown seeds or planted new shrubs and rain is not forecast. The germination failure of most seeds sown outdoors can usually be put down to lack of moisture.

Always water seed drills before and after sowing, and keep the ground moist until the seeds have germinated. Most seeds are sown in shallow drills and as the surface soil dries out first, the seed bed can quickly become too dry for seeds, even though established plants in the garden show no signs of stress.

Seeds remain vulnerable to water shortage even after germination. Seedlings will die or be severely checked if the surface inch or so of soil is allowed to dry out – especially if cold drying winds increase the moisture loss from the leaves.

Established trees and shrubs are unlikely to suffer from drought this month, but be sure to water any that have just been planted – and also those planted last autumn if they do not appear to be growing vigorously.

Mulching helps to conserve moisture in the ground, and organic materials, such as garden compost or rotted manure, also contribute nutrients and help to improve the soil structure as they decompose and are worked into the earth by worms and other organisms. Make sure mulches are applied only to moist soil and that they are in place before the dry weather arrives. Water before mulching if necessary and don't forget to check whether existing mulches require replenishing.

Controlling pests and diseases

Unfortunately, the warmer moist days that encourage plant growth are also ideal for the proliferation of many pests and diseases. Be alert to potential problems.

Make it a routine to walk round the garden at least once a week looking for problems. You will often find something which needs attention, especially if you make a point of turning over a few leaves on the plants that you pass. If you inspect regularly, the trouble can often be cut off, or nipped out, before it spreads. Pick off or squash any pests you see. Some gardeners like to have ready one hand sprayer containing a ready-mixed general-purpose insecticide, and another containing a fungicide. A small squirt may result in fewer chemicals being applied in the long term.

Slugs and snails are a year-round problem, but they can do a disproportionate amount of damage at this time. A seedling can be eliminated with a bite, whereas an established plant may just be disfigured. Hostas, in particular, can be spoilt for the season if slugs and snails eat through several layers as the leaves unfurl, whereas later in the year the damage caused may be restricted to holes in a few leaves.

Make a determined effort to control slugs and snails by baiting, trapping or hand picking them. Clear away any rubbish and debris in the garden to expose these pests and to eliminate some of their hiding places.

Pay special attention to protecting vulnerable plants by placing physical anti-slug barriers around them. A circle of grit or a plastic collar cut from a bottle helps to keep slugs at bay.

War on weeds
Weeds appear everywhere at this time – in beds and borders, between paving stones and in paths, and especially in freshly cultivated soil. Hoe regularly; this will gradually eliminate most of the weeds in beds and borders, though an appropriate weedkiller may be needed for long-established difficult perennials. Hand weeding paths and patios can be a tedious job, and you can use weedkillers that will suppress weed growth for most of the season.

The key to keeping down weeds is to keep hoeing them persistently for the first season or two. After that deal with new weeds as soon as they appear. That way your garden will usually look weed-free with just the occasional hoeing.

Make haste slowly
Bedding plants may be on sale in some shops and nurseries, but do not buy them unless you can keep them in a greenhouse or frost-free frame. If you have a greenhouse, it is worth buying bedding plant seedlings to grow on if you missed sowing your own earlier.

JOBS THAT WON'T WAIT

- Sow seeds of summer bedding, herbs, lilies, trees, shrubs and many vegetables this month. Some seeds can be sown directly into open ground but many benefit from being started off under glass.

- Prick out and pot up young seedlings and cuttings before they become overcrowded.

- Start hardening off bedding plants but put plants under cover if frost threatens.

- Control pests and diseases especially slugs and snails.

- Ventilate cold frames and greenhouses whenever possible. This encourages sturdy plant growth. Remove winter insulation from greenhouse and put on shading.

- Place supports in position around border perennials that require staking. If the supports are put in position early, the plants will grow through them and hide them.

- Stop chrysanthemums as close as possible to the ideal date for the type you are growing.

- Plant hanging baskets and keep them in a greenhouse or frost-free conservatory or porch.

- Apply a general slow-release fertiliser to containers; applied as a surface dressing in spring it should last plants in containers for the whole growing season.

- Start removing sideshoots and pinching out tendrils if growing sweet peas on the cordon system.

- Feed shrubs, trees, new hedges and fruit bushes as necessary.

- Hard prune shrubs, such as buddleja, that produce their best show on vigorous new wood. Prune spring-flowering shrubs that are over three years old once they have finished flowering.

- Protect brassicas, such as cabbages and cauliflowers, with brassica collars against cabbage root fly, and erect plastic screens in the vegetable garden to deter carrot fly.

- Earth up early potatoes to protect them from light and frost.

- Begin mowing the lawn regularly. Frequent mowing encourages dense growth.

- Feed fish when they become active again after the winter.

ANNUALS & BIENNIALS

● Sowing summer bedding

To give the plants a good start, continue to sow plants required for bedding under glass (*see* March, page 56), especially in cold, exposed regions. Shade the greenhouse with blinds or a shading wash to keep temperatures down and prevent scorching young leaves (*see* May, page 130).

● Pricking out seedlings

There will be lots of seedlings to prick out this month and you are likely to need extra space to accommodate all the trays. If you do not have a greenhouse, and windowsill space is limited, a cold frame is an extremely useful place for growing on seedlings. Shade the glass and ventilate during warm, sunny days, closing the vents at night. If frost is forecast, cover the frame with bubble plastic or a piece of old carpet or blanket.

● Hardening off

Begin to harden off young plants raised from early sowings, as well as plants overwintered as cuttings, ready for planting out in their final position this month. If you have a cold frame, gradually increase the ventilation during the day for a week, closing the vents again at night. During the second week, take the vents off altogether during the day and re-place them at night. Cover the frame with insulation material if frost is forecast.

If you do not have a cold frame, find a sheltered spot outdoors and place the trays on the ground for a few hours each day, bringing them back indoors at night. Build up exposure time gradually, until the plants are being left out all night. Cover the plants with fleece or newspaper if frost is forecast.

ANNUALS – COTTAGE GARDEN STYLE

1 Hardy annuals look particularly attractive if grown in irregular blocks. Mark out the areas with a stick or cane.

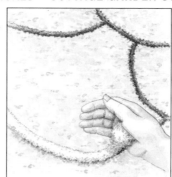

2 When you are satisfied with the design you have drawn, use sand to mark the outlines of the separate blocks more clearly.

3 Within each block sow seeds in lines to make weeding and thinning easier. Change the direction of the lines from one block to another.

● Sowing outside

Hardy annuals are the best plants for providing colour quickly and cheaply in a new garden and on areas of bare soil. In sheltered parts of the garden, on prepared soil which has warmed up sufficiently, you can start to sow hardy annuals direct from the middle of April. Complete this sowing by the end of the first week in May.

In exposed gardens, and areas notorious as frost pockets, leave this outdoor sowing until next month. In the coldest parts of the country, where the growing season is short, it is best to sow all annuals in an unheated greenhouse or cold frame as this will give the plants a head start. Sown outside they may not flower until late summer.

Before sowing, water the bed thoroughly if the soil is dry (*see* Propagation, page 426). Many hardy annuals do well in poor soil, so you should not have to add fertilisers unless the soil is very impoverished.

BORDER PERENNIALS

● Planting

Spring or autumn are good times for planting hardy perennials, and April and September are generally the best months. In wet or cold parts of the country April is usually preferable: new plants will not have to struggle for survival over winter in waterlogged or compacted soil. In southern and eastern districts, where dry summers are becoming more evident, planting may be more successful in the autumn months, when there is likely to be sufficient rain for the plants to do well (*see* September, page 212).

If you are planting this month, choose a day when the soil is moist and it is not too cold. If you can, avoid exposing the plants to cold winds. In dry or stony ground it is particularly important to make sure that all new plantings are kept well watered until they are established.

BORDER PERENNIALS – STAKING

Twiggy sticks are ideal supports for many herbaceous border plants – they are hardly visible once the plants have grown up through them.

Tall plants such as delphiniums benefit from tall canes, but you must keep tying the plants to the supports as they grow.

Proprietary metal stakes are very effective and come in various shapes and sizes. Position them early so the plants can grow through them.

● Planting out young plants

Plant out any plants you have raised from root cuttings or seeds that have been hardened off in a cold frame or sheltered position outside. To help them get off to a good start, cover them with horticultural fleece for a couple of weeks.

● Staking

Stake plants sooner rather than later to avoid wind damage. It is also easier to support a small plant rather than one that has grown and started to flop. Use materials such as pea sticks, brushwood, bamboo stakes, metal hoops or large-mesh netting. Good staking should be unobtrusive, designed to support the plant rather than fence it in.

● Filling gaps

Newly planted beds and borders often look sparse because of the space needed to allow for growth: a clump of goat's beard (*Aruncus dioicus*) or a large red-hot poker (*Kniphofia* spp.) will spread to about 1.2 m (4 ft) across when mature. To avoid a bare look at the beginning, you can either plant closer together (bearing in mind the extra expense and that the excess plants will need to be found new homes in a year or two), or fill the gaps with 'short-term' plants such as annuals, herbs or cheap and cheerful lupins. Although border perennials can increase in size considerably even in their first year, you still may have bare patches remaining by early summer. These can be filled with summer bulbs, tender perennials or annuals (*see* June, page 149).

BULBS, CORMS & TUBERS

● Deadheading

Remove the faded flowers from daffodils and other early-flowering bulbs to prevent them wasting their energy producing seed. It also makes the plants look much tidier. Leave the flowers on bulbs such as snowdrops, crocuses, scillas and muscari. They will then seed themselves and spread.

● Summer-flowering bulbs

Plant bulbs such as acidantheras and tigridias 5–8 cm (2–3 in) deep and 10–15 cm (4–6 in) apart in a sunny, well-drained position.

● Gladioli

Commence regular, shallow hoeing around gladioli once the young shoots appear through the soil. This will check the growth of weeds and keep the soil aerated and moist.

There is no need to water gladioli until the secondary roots have formed, which should be by the end of this month.

Continue planting gladiolus corms in mixed borders or for cutting (*see* March, page 59).

● Arum lilies

Plant out arum lilies (*Zantedeschia aethiopica*) in very mild areas (*see* May, page 125).

● Begonias

When shoots appear on begonia tubers planted in February or March, thin them to leave only the strongest. You can use the shoots you have removed as stem cuttings (*see* Propagation, page 429). Put them in 13 cm (5 in) pots containing a mixture of equal parts peat and perlite. Water freely.

● Hippeastrums

Hippeastrums planted last month will need watering more frequently, as growth accelerates. Keep them warm and moist through the growing season.

● **Tuberoses and gloriosas**

Pot up tuberoses and gloriosas for flowering under glass (*see* House & conservatory plants, page 103).

CARNATIONS & PINKS

● **Planting outdoors**

Apply a general fertiliser to growing and mature plants. Continue planting border carnations and pinks up to the middle of the month. Stop pinks that have become leggy (*see* March, page 60).

● **Supporting pinks**

If necessary, stake tall-growing pinks by pushing branching twigs into the ground around the plants. The plants will then grow up and through them. Proprietary metal supports are very efficient, but are more obtrusive than twigs when used with bushy and leafy plants in a border.

● **Pests and diseases**

Take action at the first signs of pests or disease (*see* March, page 60) and, in particular, watch for slugs as the weather warms up. They find the young growth of pinks irresistible and can remove all the buds from low-growing varieties overnight at this time of the year. You may need to use slug pellets to control them.

● **Sowing and potting up**

Make further sowings of carnations, pinks and all dianthus species and varieties in cold frames or an unheated greenhouse (*see* January, page 19). Continue to pot up young seedlings already germinated, and plant out hardy forms when the roots have filled a 5–8 cm (2–3 in) pot, and the top growth is bushy and vigorous.

PERPETUAL-FLOWERING
● **Growing conditions**

Perpetual-flowering carnation plants are delivered by nurseries this month and next. They require a greenhouse with full light and plenty of ventilation, and in winter will need a minimum temperature of 7°C (45°F). Shade the glass throughout the summer during the warmest part of the day, keeping the atmosphere humid yet well ventilated. Aim to keep plants growing steadily. Newly purchased plants, generally grown in 8 cm (3 in) pots, will already have had their first stopping and will have made side-shoots. Plants that you have propagated at home should be at the same stage.

Perpetual-flowering carnations may grow up to 1.2–1.5 m (4–5 ft) tall in their second year, so set their pots on slatted staging a little way from the ground, to ensure free movement of air around them. Support the stems with canes and wire rings, being

---

PERPETUAL CARNATIONS – SUPPORTING

Carnation stems can be brittle, and those on pot-grown plants are often long. Canes or split canes make ideal supports, and soft garden twine or split rings can be used to fix the stems to the support.

careful to damage neither roots nor shoots while handling them. Third-year plants are too big for most greenhouses, but can be planted out for the summer in warm, sheltered situations and may continue to flower until early autumn.

● **Potting on**

Put the plants into 10 cm (4 in), then 15 cm (6 in), containers as soon as the roots reach the sides of the pot. Use a loam or fibre-based compost. The first flowers will be produced when they are in 15 cm (6 in) pots. During April and May pot second-year plants into 20 cm (8 in) pots.

● **Stopping sideshoots**

The sideshoots produced as a result of the first stopping will themselves normally require stopping, and the timing determines the development of the flowers. Stopping up to the middle of June produces autumn flowers. Stopping from then until the middle of July produces winter flowers. Stopping from mid July to the end of August produces early spring flowers. After the second stopping, cutting blooms acts as a further natural stopping. Side-shoots are ready for stopping when they are 18 cm (7 in) long.

● **Watering and feeding**

Container-grown carnations should not be kept saturated. Wait until the soil ball is nearly dry, then water thoroughly. When watering, feed mature plants with a weak, high-potash fertiliser every fortnight during the warmer months and once a month during the rest of the year. During hot spells give the plants an overhead spray of water about once a fortnight, avoiding any blooms that are open or about to open.

Sowing seed

Finish sowing annuals early this month (*see* January, page 19).

CHRYSANTHEMUMS

● Buying new plants

Start to buy new plants this month, but not too early unless you have adequate space to keep them before hardening off.

● Hardening off

Remove cold frame tops at every opportunity to harden off both outdoor and greenhouse-flowering varieties, but protect at night if frost threatens.

Move out of the greenhouse pots of any outdoor-flowering varieties you plan to plant out in a few weeks' time. Keep them in a sheltered position, protect from frost and cold winds, and bring them inside again if the weather turns cold.

● Controlling pests

Aphids are often troublesome at this time and leaf miners may start to tunnel through the leaves this month (*see* Pests, pages 395 and 401). Spray with a suitable insecticide or squash larvae at the end of the tunnel between your finger and thumb. Remove and destroy any 'mined' leaves with their network of white tunnels.

● Watering

Water pots outdoors as early as possible in the day. Take care not to overwater newly potted plants.

● Breaking and stopping

Left to their own devices, most chrysanthemums will grow long unbranched stems and only send out side-

CHRYSANTHEMUMS – BREAKING AND STOPPING

1 Remove the growing tip of large-flowered chrysanthemums in April to induce more sideshoots, and therefore flowers, to form.

2 When the sideshoots are about 8 cm (3 in) long, pinch out surplus shoots if you want to produce fewer, larger blooms.

Some varieties are stopped twice. With these, remove the growing tip from the sideshoots. This encourages more flowering sideshoots.

shoots from the leaf axils very late in the season. This means lanky plants with very few flowers: only one on the end of each long stem.

To encourage a bushier shape, as well as more and larger flowers, the growing tip needs to be pinched out. This stimulates the dormant side growths into action. However, this also has the effect of delaying flowering; different types are set back by a different number of days.

Gardeners growing for exhibition or to meet specific showing times, should note the stopping dates, as this will influence the time of flowering. Stopping is carried out one or two weeks earlier in cold areas than in mild ones. Catalogues from specialist nurseries usually include stopping guidelines.

When a plant is stopped once, it sends out several shoots each with a single (first) crown bud. When a plant is stopped twice, each of these original shoots sends out further shoots and these also have (second) crown buds.

● Stopping this month

There needs to be a balance between gaining extra flowering shoots and leaving enough time for plants to come into flower before the frosts:

ANEMONE-FLOWERED: first stop in mid April.

SINGLES: first stop in mid April.

INCURVED: if a second crown bud is wanted, make the first stop in mid April (however, if only one stop is needed, then wait until next month).

EARLY-FLOWERING (GARDEN)
● Preparing the soil for planting

Break down the ground dug earlier in the year. Rake in a balanced general fertiliser at the rate recommended by the manufacturer.

LATE-FLOWERING (GREENHOUSE)

● **Preparing standing ground**

Greenhouse chrysanthemums will grow soft and sappy if they remain in the greenhouse all year, as well as taking up valuable space, so from May until early September they are better off outside. Don't stand them on soil as worms will enter the pots.

● **Potting up**

Pot up the rooted cuttings taken last month into 8 cm (3 in) pots.

Pot several rooted cuttings of indoor spray varieties into 23 cm (9 in) pots in the greenhouse for late flowering. Remove the tips when they have been established for ten days.

VERY LATE-FLOWERING

● **Taking basal cuttings**

If very late-flowering varieties have started sprouting this month, take basal cuttings (*see* Propagation, page 429), and then discard the old plant.

CLIMBERS & WALL SHRUBS

● **Feeding and watering**

This is the last month in which to feed climbers efficiently. Use Growmore or other general inorganic fertiliser. Water climbers and wall shrubs regularly. Plants growing against a wall receive less rain and are particularly vulnerable in dry weather.

● **Controlling pests and diseases**

Watch out for aphids and for powdery mildew and treat accordingly (*see* Pests and Diseases, pages 395 and 410). Honeysuckle is one of the prime plants to suffer from both these problems so check this plant carefully and treat if necessary.

CHRYSANTHEMUMS – STANDING GROUND

Greenhouse chrysanthemums should be taken outdoors for the summer to strengthen them. Stand the pots on gravel or boards rather than on soil, and provide supports for the growing stems. Two stout posts and wire strands are ample.

● **Tieing in**

Tie in new shoots regularly to protect against wind damage and to help training (*see* January, page 20).

● **Potting on annual climbers**

Pot on into individual pots previously sown seedlings of annual climbers.

● **Pruning**

Tender climbers and wall shrubs which have been dormant throughout the winter should now begin to show signs of life. Like less hardy shrubs in the open garden, they benefit from being pruned back hard before the leaves open fully. This encourages plenty of fresh growth from the base and stops the plants from becoming straggly.

CONTAINER GARDENING

● **Planting hanging baskets**

Although you will not be able to hang baskets outdoors until the risk of frost has passed, plant them up towards the end of March (*see* page 67) or in April so that the plants will have filled out and begun to flower by the time they are put out into the garden. You will need somewhere light and warm to hang them, such as a greenhouse, porch or conservatory, until it is safe to put them outside.

Choose as large a basket as possible, one of 40 cm (16 in) diameter suits most plants and positions. Some wire baskets allow planting through the sides, but you will need to use a thick lining of sphagnum moss or similar material to keep the compost from washing out. Alternatively, use ready-made or pre-formed liners, or black plastic sheeting and plant in the top only or through slits in the plastic. Self-watering baskets are available which have a reservoir of water in the base. These are useful if you can only water once a day.

Don't forget that a half basket may be more appropriate against a wall than a full basket.

CONTAINER GARDENING – HOW TO PLANT A HANGING BASKET

◁ **1**

2 ▷

3 ▷

◁ **4**

5 ▷

(1) Sit the hanging basket on a bucket or large pot to keep it stable. Line with moist sphagnum moss packed in tightly. (2) Put in some soilless or multi-purpose compost and plant the sides of the basket. Water the plants well before putting them into the basket. (3) Add more moss and compost, firming the soil around the plants. (4) Plant around the edge of the rim, setting the plants at an angle. (5) Put upright plants in the centre, adding more soil if necessary. Firm the soil and water well.

● **Planting evergreens and hardy climbers**

April is a good month for planting evergreen shrubs in containers, especially the more tender Mediterranean types and silver-leaved herbs such as lavender and artemisia. These all achieve the best results when given an uninterrupted growing season in which to establish themselves. If you live in a very cold, exposed part of the country, delay planting until next month.

As well as growing climbers against a wall, you can also grow them in free-standing pots. Erect a wigwam of canes for support and cover the wigwam with the green netting sold for supporting peas and beans. For large, formal, square tubs you can buy trellis-covered obelisk kits to fit inside them.

● **Applying slow-release fertilisers**

Use a general slow-release fertiliser with trace elements; this will save both time and effort. If it is applied as a surface dressing in spring it should last plants in containers for the whole growing season. The fertiliser is gradually released when the plants are watered. Apply according to the manufacturer's instructions. For seasonal containers you can also get granules of slow-release fertiliser to mix in with the potting compost, and tablets which are pushed in around the roots of plants.

● **Mulching**

Mulching permanent containers with a 3–5 cm (1–2 in) layer of gravel, cocoa shells, or medium-grade bark chippings not only looks attractive, it cuts down moisture loss and prevents soil eroding from around surface roots when the pot is watered.

● **Planting summer-flowering bulbs and tubers**

Plant dormant dahlia tubers but leave this until next

month in very cold areas (*see* Dahlias below). Plant other bulbs such as ranunculus, tigridia, nerine and large-flowered anemones. Bring begonia tubers into growth if these have not been started earlier (*see* Bulbs and Corms, page 91).

● Pruning topiary

To keep shapes looking neat, topiary shrubs should receive their first trim now. If they are trimmed at regular intervals throughout the summer the shape is easy to maintain. Don't trim after early autumn.

● Controlling pests and diseases

Search flower buds and shoot tips regularly for signs of greenfly. If you have only a small infestation, rub off the colony with your fingers or spray off with a sharp jet of water. Otherwise, a ready-to-spray insecticide hand gun is a useful thing to carry round the garden for instant treatment of small areas.

Other pests, such as leafhoppers and red spider mite, are harder to spot and control. Both cause a pale mottling on the surface of leaves. Large, ragged holes in the leaf edges are most likely to have been caused by caterpillars – they sometimes roll leaves over for camouflage as well.

Regular removal of dead plant material reduces the risk of slugs and disease but also check for signs of fungal attack, especially as the season progresses. At first sign, either remove affected plants or cut off diseased parts and spray with a systemic fungicide to help prevent the disease from spreading.

DAHLIAS

● Preparing the ground

Complete digging of the dahlia bed, and apply a slow-acting fertiliser such as bonemeal.

● Dividing tubers

It is a good idea to divide up large clumps of dahlia tubers, otherwise they develop into very large plants which become a thicket of growth unless the shoots are thinned drastically. Pull the clumps apart. Ideally start the tubers into growth before you do this to ensure that each portion has a live shoot (*see* Propagation, page 433).

● Planting tubers

In mild areas plant out healthy dormant tubers towards the end of the month. Tubers that are completely shrivelled or have rotted around the crown will be useless. Prepare the soil as for young plants, and plant the tubers so that the crowns are 8–10 cm (3–4 in) below the surface of the soil. They should be 75–90 cm (2½–3 ft) apart. If shoots appear above ground and spring frosts are forecast draw some soil over them as you would with potatoes,

DAHLIAS – DIVIDING TUBERS

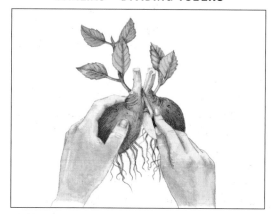

Dahlia tubers can be divided, and this is an easy way to increase your stock of plants. It is important to divide them so that each tuber has a piece of old stem and a shoot or a bud attached otherwise the tuber will not produce shoots.

or protect them with a double layer of horticultural fleece. In colder areas you should delay planting tubers until mid May after late frosts.

● Cuttings under glass

Pot up rooted cuttings and take more as needed (*see* February, page 39).

Rooted cuttings and seedlings should be hardened off in a cold frame at the end of April or in early May. Protect them from slugs (*see* Pests, page 403). Ventilate the frame during the day by partially opening the lights.

● Sowing seed

Continue to sow seed (*see* March, page 64). This will require less heat than earlier sowings.

FRUIT

Pears, plums, cherries and early apples will all be flowering in April. Only five to ten per cent of the flowers need to set fruit for there to be an adequate crop, but there must be a good show of blossom to start with. Honey bees are the main pollinators of fruit blossom but bees work best at temperatures of 15°C (60°F) and above, so if possible plant new trees where they will be sheltered from the wind. You can protect small trees and bushes from frost by covering them with horticultural fleece.

Newly planted fruit trees and bushes can be damaged by shortage of water, so check all new plantings regularly in dry weather: dry soil needs a good soak, 25 litres per m² (5 gallons per sq yd) at a time. Mulch fruit planted since the autumn, to conserve moisture and discourage weeds. Well-rotted manure or garden compost is best as this adds organic matter to the soil, but perforated black plastic sheeting or woven mulching sheet is just as effective (*see* The soil in your garden, pages 392–393).

Keep a sharp eye open for pests and diseases and treat immediately. Never spray fruit trees at blossom time when the flowers are open, as bees are killed by most insecticides. Always check the instructions on the spray carefully.

● Apples and pears

Spray (provided blossom is not open) against aphids, and also apple and pear scab and powdery mildew (*see* March, page 65). Scab is worse than mildew in a wet season; vice versa in a dry one.

● Peaches and nectarines

Protect the tiny fruitlets from late frosts. Pick off any caterpillars when you see them.

● Plums and cherries

Treat at the first sign of greenfly or blackfly.

FRUIT – PRUNING CHERRIES

To maintain an attractive shape for fan-trained cherries, remove shoots growing towards or away from the wall or fence. This can be done while the shoots are still young by rubbing them off with your thumb.

Prune cherries now. Keep the tree open by removing branches that are causing overcrowding. For fan-trained trees, remove any shoots that are growing straight towards or away from the wall to retain the shape and avoid crowding.

● Figs

Apply a high-potash fertiliser, such as one recommended for tomatoes or roses, every other year.

Prune by cutting back any frost-damaged shoots to their point of origin. Cut back some young shoots to one bud to stimulate replacement growth, and cut back one or two of the oldest branches to within one bud of the point of origin to stimulate new growth and keep the plant rejuvenated. On fan-trained figs carefully tie in new shoots so that they are well spaced over the fan.

● Gooseberries

From the middle of April look out for the small, black-spotted caterpillars of the gooseberry sawfly (*see* Pests, page 403). These will quickly reduce leaves to skeletons and eventually strip the whole plant. They are usually first seen in the centre of the bush.

● Strawberries

Make sure that those under cloches or in the greenhouse are given adequate ventilation. This keeps them cool and allows bees and other pollinating insects to get to the flowers. Liquid feed them weekly from now on (*see* March, page 66).

Remove flower buds on perpetual (autumn-fruiting) varieties to stop them fruiting too early. Give a general foliar feed if the plants are slow to start into growth. Watch out for greenfly but be very careful with the use of insecticides that may affect pollinating insects.

● Vines

Treat powdery mildew (*see* Diseases, page 410).

FUCHSIAS

TENDER AND HALF-HARDY
● Potting on

All plants will need regular potting on since pot-bound plants will flower prematurely and deteriorate early. When a definite root system is established, move into the next sized pot, increasing the pot size by 2–3 cm (¾–1½ in) each time. Potting straight from 8 cm (3 in) into 13 cm (5 in) pot checks the growth and the plant then produces a large amount of foliage at the expense of flowers.

● Pruning

Complete pruning of later fuchsias as they start into growth (*see* February, pages 40–41).

● Taking cuttings

Take further cuttings (*see* February, page 41). Any taken later than April will not flower this year.

● Planting hanging baskets

Complete planting of hanging baskets.

● Training fuchsias

Fuchsias are often trained into different shapes, from simple bushes to large pillars, fans and espaliers. Bushes and standards are the easiest to train; the others need more skill and patience. All are created by encouraging the development of some stems at the expense of others and by pinching out growing tips at specific times.

At each stage, all shoots should be stopped at the same time to ensure even growth. Maintain the symmetry of the plant by giving each plant a half turn every third day to ensure the whole plant receives an equal amount of light.

BUSHES

Bush plants start from a vigorous variety raised from a cutting. When the plant has developed three pairs of leaves, remove the growing tip to encourage sideshoots to develop in each leaf axil (first stop). Pinch out these shoots when they in turn have produced two pairs of leaves (second stop). This is sufficient for an attractive display, but for really bushy plants stop a third time – flowering will be delayed a little but there will be more blooms.

STANDARDS

Most vigorous uprights make good standards, and 'Lena', 'Marinka' and 'Pink Marshmallow' make good weeping standards. 'Shelford', 'Derby Imp' and 'Tom Thumb' excel as miniatures. Miniatures can be trained and brought into flower in one season, but larger standards will need overwintering, and training is completed in the second year.

Standards are trained by making the young plant produce a single stem without any sideshoots. Feed with a high-nitrogen fertiliser to obtain rapid height and pot the plant on regularly – fast, unchecked growth is vital. The young plant (whip) must never become pot-bound.

At this stage all sideshoots in the leaf axils except for the topmost two or three should be removed, but do not remove any leaves on the main stem.

● Growing conditions

Continue to feed with a weak nitrogenous fertiliser and ensure conditions are kept humid but well ventilated (*see* March, page 67). Space out plants so

FUCHSIAS – TYPES OF TRAINED FUCHSIA

◁ **Pillar**

▽ **Fan**

▽ **Espalier**

△ **Bush**

◁ **Standard**

Fuchsias can be trained into many shapes, simply by pinching out the appropriate shoots at the right time. Bushes and standards are the easiest for beginners – fans and espaliers are more demanding.

FUCHSIAS – TRAINING A BUSH FUCHSIA

◁ **First stop**

Second stop ▷

▽ **Third stop**

Train a bush by pinching out the growing tip when a cutting has three pairs of leaves (first stop). Repeat when the new shoots have produced two pairs of leaves (second stop). Repeat again for an even bushier plant (third stop).

FUCHSIAS – TRAINING A STANDARD

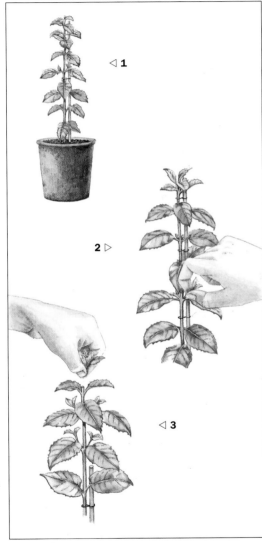

◁ **1**

2 ▷

◁ **3**

(1) To grow a standard fuchsia, train a single stem, supporting it with a cane. (2) Remove all sideshoots except the top two or three. (3) Continue this until the stem has reached the required height, then pinch out the growing tip.

that the leaves do not overlap one another. Plants that grow in shadow will become soft and leggy as they search for light.

● Controlling pests

Red spider mites flourish in hot, dry conditions, so a humid atmosphere will help to keep them at bay as well as keeping the plants healthy and therefore better able to withstand pests and diseases. An insecticide or an insecticidal soap solution applied early in the season will help to prevent any pests present from increasing and becoming a problem later.

HARDY

Cut back almost to soil level as strong new basal growth appears. Weed and tidy round the base of plants and gently fork in a general fertiliser, being careful not to damage the shallow roots.

Prepare new planting sites in a well-drained border by digging over and incorporating liberal amounts of garden compost, peat or peat substitute.

GARDEN MAINTENANCE

● Weeding hard surfaces

Remove isolated weeds in paths, drives and patios with an old knife or by spraying with a spot weeder. For more persistent widespread weeds, use a path weedkiller to eliminate existing weeds and prevent new ones from growing (*see* Weed Control, page 415). Keep a sprayer or watering can fitted with a dribble bar specifically for this purpose.

● Neglected areas of the garden

Parts of the garden left vacant for a season or more will be full of weeds; pull out those that are starting to self-seed and cut down the rest. Alternatively,

you can clear the ground quickly by applying a total weedkiller (*see* Weed Control, page 415). Deep-rooted perennial weeds, such as bindweed and horsetail, may need several applications. Once the ground is clear of weeds, cover it with a sheet of black plastic or old carpet to keep weeds at bay until planting begins.

GREENHOUSES & FRAMES

● Shading and ventilating

The changeable weather in April can cause violent temperature fluctuations in the greenhouse. Remove winter insulation if you have not done this already. Shade young seedlings and newly potted plants from the sun with horticultural fleece or sheets of newspaper. Keep the greenhouse well ventilated, but only open those lights facing away from the wind if there is any risk of hailstorms.

● Watering and feeding plants

Give increasing amounts of water to all plants in pots or containers, which should now be established and growing rapidly. Continue to feed established plants such as zonal and regal pelargoniums, annuals in pots, fuchsias and other summer-flowering plants. Apply liquid fertiliser at ten-day intervals.

● Hardening off half-hardy plants

Move any half-hardy plants into a cold frame for hardening off. This will also provide space for sowing melons and cucumbers at the end of the month or in early May. Plants in frames require regular watering and the lights propped open on sunny days to give them extra ventilation. Move tall plants to the back of the frame so that they do not touch the glass. Protect plants from slugs and snails.

● Controlling pests and diseases

Introduce *Phytoseiulus persimilis* as a biological control if red spider mite is a problem – chemical controls are often less effective (*see* Pests, page 402).

● Sowing seeds

Make further sowings of dahlias, dianthus, annuals, lilies, shrubs and vegetables (*see* individual sections, March and April). Sow winter cherry (*Solanum capsicastrum* and *S. pseudocapsicum*) at about 15°C (60°F). Prick out the seedlings when they are large enough to handle.

● Potting cuttings

Pot up rooted cuttings, and pot on cuttings and young plants which have made good growth and produced a mass of roots.

● Cucumbers and melons

Cucumbers are a worthwhile greenhouse crop, and a single plant will be sufficient for most households. 'Butcher's Disease Resisting' is an excellent variety. Melons of the cantaloupe type are usually grown in a cold frame or under cloches.

Sow melons and cucumbers in a temperature of 15–18°C (60–65°F). In each case sow the seeds individually about 3 cm (1½ in) deep in 8 cm (3 in) pots of John Innes No. 1 potting compost.

Where a single cucumber plant is being grown, plant it on a mound. Add John Innes base fertiliser or a slow-release fertiliser at the rate recommended by the manufacturer. Female types will not require lateral training as they only fruit on the main stem.

● Peppers and aubergines

Prick out into individual pots when the seed leaves are fully expanded.

GREENHOUSES & FRAMES – PLANTING AND TRAINING CUCUMBERS

Single plants of bush cucumbers can be grown on a mound of prepared soil. Use one part well-rotted manure to two parts good sifted soil, enriched with a balanced fertiliser. Pinch back surplus growth. Water little and often.

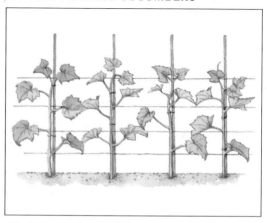

Climbing cucumbers should be grown up canes, and the lateral shoots which carry most of the fruit should be trained along horizontal wires 30 cm (12 in) apart. Pinch out growing tip and sideshoots two leaves beyond a female flower.

● Tomatoes

In a cool greenhouse plant tomatoes in the bed prepared last month, allowing 35 cm (14 in) between plants; alternatively use growing bags. Water the tomato plant before planting.

If you are growing plants by the ring culture system (*see* March, page 68), use John Innes No. 3 potting compost and bottomless containers which are 20 cm (8 in) deep and 20–25 cm (8–10 in) in diameter. Keep the gravel base moist after planting, watering the plants in the pots just sufficiently to keep them growing. Once the roots have penetrated into the gravel, no further watering via the containers will be needed, except when the plants are fed.

Train tomato plants up tall canes or up strings. You can hang these from wires on glazing bars down to hooks of thick wire pushed into the soil alongside the plants. If you are growing tomatoes in a growing bag, take care not to push the canes through the bottom.

From the time the first tomato flowers open, spray the plants lightly at about midday during sunny weather. During dull weather, dust the flowers with a feather duster or a paint brush; or give the supporting string or cane a sharp rap with a stick, to dislodge the pollen and help to set the trusses. Remove all sideshoots of cordon tomatoes from the axils of the leaves when they are 2.5 cm (1 in) long. Leave the sideshoots on bush varieties.

● Vines

Ensure vines get as much light and heat as possible once growth begins but try to maintain adequate ventilation to assist pollination.

GREENHOUSES – RING CULTURE TOMATOES

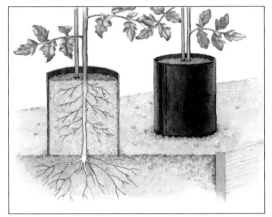

Ring culture is a method of growing tomatoes (and some other plants) in bottomless pots that hold compost for the feeding roots, above a gravel or an aggregate bed which holds water for the water roots.

HEATHERS

● Pruning

Complete pruning of summer-flowering heathers, cutting back to the base of dead flower heads (*see* March, page 68).

If winter-flowering species are to be pruned, this should be carried out as soon as possible after the flowers start to fade. If this is delayed, there is danger that the plants will be blind the following year. Pruning delays flowering by two to three weeks, so to ensure an even display, prune all plants of a particular variety at the same time.

Cut back just enough to retain shape. Vigorous varieties of *Erica carnea* will certainly require pruning every other year, including a little off the top. *E. x darleyensis* will need trimming each year; do not

GREENHOUSES – TOMATO SIDESHOOTS

Most greenhouse varieties of tomato are best grown up a cane on a single stem. Remove sideshoots while they are still small, and tie the new growth to the cane for support. This ensures more nutrients go to the fruit.

be afraid of limiting growth. To encourage bushy plants of *E. erigena*, cut back half of the previous year's growth for the first three years and take off any broken branches.

● Layers and cuttings

Dig up the rooted layers started last summer and, using an ericaceous compost, plant the young plants deeply. Bury any bare stems, so that the lower foliage rests on the soil surface. Firm well to stop the cuttings rocking in the wind. Cut back all shoots to 5 cm (2 in).

If you are planting the layers in pots instead of open ground, place the pots outside on a well-drained surface in a sheltered part of the garden.

Pot up last summer's cuttings in the same way if you have not already done this. Grow them on in a

cold frame or sheltered position in the garden until they are large enough to plant out in position.

● Watering

More heathers die from drought than from all other causes added together. To make matters worse, they give no indication of distress but suddenly go brown. Potted-up plants will dry out very quickly indeed in dry weather so keep them well irrigated, watering daily if necessary. Newly planted heathers must be kept well watered during their first spring and summer. After a week without rain, start watering daily, preferably with rainwater. If none is available use tap water, even hard tap water, but never use domestic softened water.

HERBS

● Sowing outdoors

Sow further small amounts of culinary and salad herbs (*see* March, page 70). Thin seedlings sown in March to 15 cm (6 in) apart, and hoe regularly between the rows to keep the weeds to a minimum.

● Sowing and potting on

Continue to sow seeds under glass (*see* March, page 70). Seedlings making strong growth should be potted on into larger pots to establish good root systems. Pinch out the tips of branches of bushy herbs such as basil once three pairs of leaves have formed. Harden them off gradually as the weather improves, ready for planting outside in May.

● Rooted cuttings

Cuttings taken last summer of bay, hyssop, lavender, mint, rosemary, rue and sage should now be well rooted and ready to plant out into their permanent positions. Plant sage and hyssop 30 cm (12 in) apart in light, dry soil if they are to form a hedge. Otherwise, plant in groups of three, five or seven to make irregular groups in the border. Bay may be planted into a container, or into its final position in the garden.

SKIN IRRITATION

The sap of some plants is an irritant and can cause a painful rash or blistering when it comes into contact with the skin, especially in the presence of sunlight. Parents with young children should plant rue, in particular, well away from play areas and paths. Euphorbia is another plant with harmful sap.

● Shelter and hedging plants

Finish planting these if not completed last month (*see* March, page 70). Water them in thoroughly, then only as necessary during the next few weeks; this will encourage their roots to establish properly.

● Pruning straggly shoots

Cut back any weak or damaged shoots on established herbs to encourage new, strong growth. Wear gloves and long sleeves, particularly when handling plants, such as rue, in strong sunshine.

● Supporting large plants

Many herbs make rapid spring growth and these plants will need support to prevent them from being blown around, or flattened by heavy showers of rain. Such plants include angelica, comfrey, dyer's chamomile and lovage. Carefully placed supports will become almost invisible as the plants grow.

● Planting up a new herb garden

If you have planned a new herb garden you can start

HERBS – HANGING BASKETS

Hanging baskets, lined with moss or dyed coir, look most attractive when planted with herbs – either on their own or among ornamentals. Suitable herbs include chives, nasturtiums, hyssop, marigold, parsley, green, purple or golden sage, savory and trailing or variegated thyme. Use a good multi-purpose compost and plant thickly. Keep the basket under glass, to encourage rapid rooting and growth, before hardening off at the end of the month ready for hanging outside.

Here, a variegated sage has been grown in the top of an attractive hanging basket which includes vegetables and ornamentals.

planting this out now unless the weather is very inclement. Draw up a design on paper in advance (*see* July, pages 188–189).

HOUSE & CONSERVATORY PLANTS

● Maintaining healthy leaves

Remove dead and dying foliage from plants. When removing debris, examine each plant, including shoot tips and undersides of leaves, for pests and diseases and treat them as necessary.

If the weather is warm enough, the quickest way to clean many plants is to group them outside and spray with tepid water from a watering can with a fine rose. If there are just a few, clean with a damp sponge or cloth, using a leaf shine on glossy-leaved plants (*see* February, page 42).

● Shaping plants

Pinch back long or tall shoots on any plants, such as busy lizzies and ivies, that have become straggly because of poor light levels in winter. Plants produce fresh shoots readily at this time of year, and by frequent pinching back you can usually achieve larger bushy plants.

● Repotting

Check to see if any plants that look overcrowded need transferring into a larger pot to give them more room to grow. To judge this, tip the plant out of its pot and examine the roots. If the roots are taking up nearly all the space, it is time for a slightly larger pot. Water the plant before transferring it, giving it time to drain before putting it in the larger pot. Water again when it is firmed in. When repotting cacti (*see* March, page 71), use a gritty, soil-based specialist cactus compost.

HOUSE PLANTS – REPOTTING

1 When a plant outgrows its pot, move it into one a size or two larger, using a similar compost to fill the gap. An easy method of repotting is to use the existing pot, or one of the same size, to form a 'mould' in the new compost.

2 Water the plant well, let it drain, then knock it out of its existing pot. Tease out a few of the largest roots at the base if they are tightly wound around the rootball.

3 Insert the plant into the hole already made in the new pot. Firm in with your fingers to make sure the compost makes good contact and that there are no air pockets. Water in well.

● Temperature, light and humidity

Many house plants come from the tropics where humidity is high and they can therefore suffer in dry, centrally heated homes even if they are getting enough light and warmth.

To remedy this, place a bowl of water beside plants or mist them regularly with a hand-held spray. Alternatively, plunge the pots into a larger container packed with damp sand or grit or put them on a tray of pebbles or clay granules, and keep the bases moist. Water vapour will then be given off to the surrounding plants.

Similarly a conservatory can become extremely hot even this early in the year, so ensure it is well ventilated and shaded.

Turn plants on windowsills a quarter turn every two or three days to ensure even growth.

● Watering and feeding

Increase watering and feeding as plants grow, especially plants repotted last month (*see* March, page 71).

● Increasing your plant stock

Divide established plants that produce stems from below the surface of the compost, such as maidenhair ferns, calatheas and aspidistras. Alternatively, detach offsets from the parent plant and pot up.

Take cuttings from ivies, philodendrons, busy lizzies, pileas and tradescantias (*see* Propagation, pages 428). Five or six cuttings can be rooted indoors on a warm windowsill in an 8 cm (3 in) pot.

● Flowering plants

Some plants, such as clivia and gardenia, flower better if their roots are restricted in a small pot, so only pot on to a larger size if the plant deteriorates. Make sure that gardenias are always planted in an ericaceous compost.

Keep hydrangeas at a temperature of 10°C (50°F) and spray with water every day. Water the pots as required and feed with liquid fertiliser every ten days. To increase stock, take cuttings of non-flowering shoots when they are 8–10 cm (3–4 in) long and root them in a propagating frame at a temperature of 15°C (60°F).

Pot on gloxinias into 13 cm (5 in) pots filled with a good potting compost.

● Planting bulbs and corms

Pot up a few tuberoses (*Polianthes tuberosa*) for flowering during June and July. Plant 2.5 cm (1 in) deep in John Innes No. 1 potting compost, one tuber to a 15 cm (6 in) pot, and stake. Water well and then do not water again until the new shoots are well established.

Pot up new gloriosas, one tuber to a 15 cm (6 in) pot or three to a 25 cm (10 in) pot containing John Innes No. 2 potting compost. Add stakes or a trellis to support the plants once they start to grow.

Water hippeastrums, planted last month, more frequently as growth accelerates and keep them warm and moist through the growing season.

Water lachenalias more generously as the flower spikes start to appear.

Once cyclamen have finished flowering, move to a cooler position – a spare room or cold frame – reduce watering and feed them with a balanced liquid fertiliser.

● Climbers and feature plants

Pinch out the growing tips of abutilons and trailing plants, such as tradescantias, regularly throughout the growing season to encourage more leaves and a bushier appearance.

Climbers benefit from a supporting framework which can be trellis, a hoop of wire or a moss pole. Insert the support when repotting and tie in any unruly growth. Attach plants with more upright growth to canes using metal clips or soft string.

To keep *Jasminum polyanthum* down to a manageable size, cut back two-thirds of the previous year's growth after the plant has finished flowering.

● Bromeliads

Water them freely, mist air plants and feed once a month (*see* March, page 71).

● Cacti and other succulents

Move cacti and succulents to a warm room and start watering by early April if not yet done (*see* March page 71). Most will now be growing actively.

Check for mealy bugs and pick them off with a small stick (*see* Pests, page 401).

Feed with a high-potash liquid feed, such as a tomato feed at half strength, once a month.

To propagate, take cuttings from stem and leaf sections and leave the fleshy cuts to dry for several days before inserting them into compost. This helps to prevent rot. Alternatively, propagate by removing offsets, pot them up and keep on the dry side until they have rooted.

Keep Christmas and Easter cacti humid and in subdued light, away from direct sun, or the leaves may scorch and become unattractive.

CACTI – PROPAGATION

Cacti with jointed leaf-like stems, such as the Christmas and Easter cacti, can be propagated from the leaf pads. After cutting, leave them exposed to the air for a couple of days before inserting in compost for rooting in a propagator.

● Orchids

Water so that the compost is moist but not soaking wet and start to feed with a high-nitrogen feed at half strength every other watering.

Repot only when the orchid pushes itself out of its pot. Use a compost formulated for orchids as they need very light, free-draining compost with plenty of air spaces. Repot when not in flower as the flower stems break easily. Trim off dead roots and old pseudobulbs. After repotting, wait for six weeks before feeding.

IRISES

● Planting herbaceous irises

If you live in a colder area you can now plant all irises without bulbs or rhizomes, such as *Iris sibirica*, *I. spuria* and water irises. If you live in a warmer part of the country these can still be planted, but keep them moist until they are established. It is better to plant in autumn (*see* September, page 221).

● Controlling pests and diseases

Before flowering begins, treat bearded irises to control aphids and prevent leaf spot and rusts (*see* Pests and Diseases, pages 395, 408 and 410).

● After flowering

The bearded dwarf hybrids, and species such as *I. lutescens*, will begin flowering in sheltered gardens this month. After flowering, cut off the flower stems close to the rhizome. Never allow seed pods to form on hybrid irises unless needed for propagating.

● Replanting bulbs

Take winter-flowering bulbous irises, such as *I. reticulata* and *I. histrioides*, or their varieties, out of their pots as leaves are dying down, and plant any good-sized bulbs in the rock garden if required.

LAWNS

● Sowing grass seed and laying turf

If you are planning a new lawn, sow seed or lay turf this month if this has not been done (*see* March, page 72). Do this as soon as conditions are suitable.

● Mowing a new lawn

Make sure the mower blades are sharp or the seedlings may be pulled up rather than cut. Start cutting an ornamental lawn when grass is 3–5 cm (1½–2 in) long, setting the blades so they remove the top 1 cm (½ in). Start cutting a wear-tolerant, ordinary lawn when the grass is 6–8 cm (2½–3 in) long, setting the blades so they remove the top 1–3 cm (½–1½ in). If necessary, mow twice a week.

● Mowing an established lawn

To maintain a grass height of 2.5 cm (1 in), cut when the grass reaches 3 cm (1½ in). As a guide, this may be once a week for an ordinary family lawn and twice a week for a fine-grassed ornamental lawn. Frequent mowing encourages dense growth. Lower the blades at each successive cut, down to 2.5 cm (1 in) for a family lawn and 1 cm (½ in) for an ornamental lawn. Do not allow the grass to grow

LAWNS – APPLYING WEEDKILLERS & FERTILISERS

▽ Spreading by hand

△ Fertiliser spreader

△ Applying with a watering can

The best time to apply lawn-care products is when the weather is warm but not windy or wet. Wait at least three days after mowing before applying, then leave three more days before mowing again. It is very important to apply the correct dose evenly over the lawn. Grass will scorch if too much fertiliser or weedkiller is applied. To prevent this, divide the lawn into sections using canes or string, and apply the fertiliser as recommended by the manufacturer. For a small lawn weigh out the correct

amount into a container and divide it between the number of squares or strips of lawn you need to cover.

On larger lawns, a wheeled fertiliser spreader is more convenient. How much product is dispensed depends on your walking speed and the machine's settings. Settings are usually only approximate, so calibrate them yourself. When pushing the machine over the lawn, treat two strips at each side, then apply at right angles to the first strips. As you push the machine, overlap the wheel

tracks of the neighbouring strip to ensure even coverage.

Water the entire lawn if there is no rain within two days of applying a dry lawn-care product.

A number of selective weedkillers and fertilisers can be applied in liquid form which many gardeners find easier. Apply with a watering can fitted with a fine rose or dribble bar, but be sure to keep a separate can, preferably in a different colour from your usual one, to prevent accidents with weedkillers.

very long and then cut it very short. This weakens the grass and encourages weeds.

Remove all the grass clippings from ornamental lawns, preferably using a mower fitted with a grass box or by raking them up afterwards. However, on ordinary family lawns, small quantities of clippings left on the lawn will protect it against drought and will add nutrients. Remove all clippings if there are problems with weeds or moss (*see* Weed Control, pages 418–419), wormcasts or poor drainage.

● Feeding an established lawn

A lawn needs regular feeding to produce the dense turf that will prevent moss and weeds getting a foothold. When the lawn is growing actively in spring and summer, it needs plenty of nitrogen for leaf growth and a good green colour. Nitrogen tends to get washed away over winter and is used up quickly, so apply a nitrogen fertiliser each spring (*see* Fertilisers, page 388). A slow-acting fertiliser may last all season, but most are quick-acting so you may need more than one application.

Lawns will also benefit from phosphates and potash applied once a season, either in spring or autumn. The easiest way to apply these nutrients is to use a compound fertiliser such as a general-purpose fertiliser for use all round the garden (*see* Fertilisers, page 390). Apply at the rate recommended by the manufacturer, according to the fertility of the soil. Proprietary lawn fertilisers are also available as feed and weed preparations. Some of these include mosskiller.

● Weed control

Apply selective weedkillers to the lawn when the grass and weeds are growing actively (usually from April to September), but not during a dry spell. Use

LAWNS – CORRECTING HUMPS AND HOLLOWS

1 Small humps and hollows in your lawn are easy to rectify. First make an H-shaped cut over the affected area using a half-moon edger against a straight-edge. Slice under the flaps and roll them back.

2 If you are correcting a hump, remove some soil from the high area. If correcting a hollow, add fine sifted soil to bring it level. Refirm, check the level, then fold back the grass and sift soil into the cracks. Water thoroughly.

a combined weed and feed, a straight weedkiller or a weed and feed with a mosskiller (*see* Weed Control, pages 418–419). Usually, more than one application is needed to kill off all the weeds.

● Scarifying

Use a spring-tined rake and lightly scarify if thatch or dead moss is a problem (*see* March, page 72).

● Lawn edges

Use long-handled shears or mechanical edgers to trim the edges of the lawn. If the lawn's edges crumble easily, insert an edging of wood or plastic set below grass level. It is often difficult or impossible to trim grass under shrubs, along fences or on steep slopes

with a lawnmower. If you have many such areas invest in lawn shears or an electric trimmer (*see* Tools and Equipment, pages 439–440).

● Fusarium patch

If the problem of fusarium patch occurs on your lawn treat it as required (*see* March, page 73).

LILIES

● Planting seeds and bulbs

Hurry to sow any lily seeds that you have remaining (*see* January, page 25).

All lily bulbs should be planted by now, though those temporarily potted up can wait until May.

● Controlling pests and diseases

In humid weather control grey mould (botrytis) with a fungicide if necessary. Also check for and control possible virus-carrying aphids and lily beetles (*see* Pests, pages 395 and 401).

● Watering pots

As the lilies grow, more water will be required. Capillary matting placed underneath the pots and kept wet will help.

● Forced bulbs

It is unwise to use the same bulbs for forcing two years in succession so plant them outside after flowering. Lilies in pots that have not been forced can remain in the same container for two years. Renew the topsoil for the second season.

PELARGONIUMS

● Planting hanging baskets

Now is the time to plant up hanging baskets with pelargoniums if you have somewhere to hang them in good light and out of all danger from frost (*see* Container Gardening, page 94). If not, continue growing your plants in 9 cm (3½ in) pots, so that they are ready to plant up outside next month. A 40 cm (16 in) basket will hold five plants and a 30 cm (12 in) basket three plants.

● Controlling pests

Keep an eye out for greenfly and whitefly at this time of year, especially on regals and scented-leaved varieties. If the weather is warm, an adult whitefly can start laying eggs three days from hatching and, as the eggs and pupae are wax coated, it is only the adults that are easily killed by an insecticide.

PELARGONIUMS – PLANTING IN CONTAINERS

Ivy-leaved pelargoniums come in a wide range of colours and, as they tend to trail down, they are ideal for hanging baskets, tubs and windowboxes. They can be raised from seeds or cuttings (*see* January, page 26) and will develop rapidly in the spring. When the main shoot is 8–10 cm (3–4 in) long, remove the growing tip. The plant will then produce more shoots from lower down from which, in turn, flowers will develop. They should bloom constantly throughout the summer.

The cascade ivy-leaved pelargoniums, so popular in Austria and Switzerland, branch naturally, so they do not need to be stopped in this way, and they produce such a mass of blooms that it is not necessary to deadhead them. Always allow room for rapid, spreading growth if planting these varieties in a hanging basket. Like all pelargoniums, they appreciate being fed throughout the growing season with a high potash feed: tomato fertiliser is a convenient feed to apply.

Cascade ivy-leaved pelargoniums are ideal for windowboxes and flower throughout the summer.

● **Potting up seedlings and cuttings**

Prick out seedlings when they are large enough to handle and pot both seedlings and cuttings on into individual pots when they have developed a good root system. Keep turning them so they get an even amount of light.

● **Specimen plants and regals**

Specimen plants and regal pelargoniums should by now be quite large and may need potting on. It is essential to keep them fed and turned regularly. Do not give too much nitrogen as this creates large leaves. Apply a liquid feed that is high in potash, such as a tomato feed.

RHODODENDRONS & AZALEAS

● **Completing spring planting**

Complete planting (*see* March, page 74) by the end of the month to ensure that the plants grow well throughout the summer.

● **Transplanting established plants**

April is a good month to transplant rhododendrons and azaleas that need to be relocated. Rhododendrons can be moved without damage because of their fibrous rootball. If you dig a large hole around the plant it should be possible to ensure that the rootball is not disturbed. Prepare the new planting site thoroughly (*see* February, page 46).

● **Watering and feeding**

In dry conditions continue watering newly planted rhododendrons through April into the late spring and throughout the summer. Ensure the rootball is always moist. Once a week, add a high-nitrogen liquid fertiliser to the water. The strain and demands on their roots at this time of year can be excessive, particularly with new plantings. Spray the foliage regularly as the plants absorb moisture through their leaves. Do this in the evening – or at least out of strong sunlight – to prevent leaf scorch, particularly on new foliage.

● **Deadheading**

Remove as many dead flowers as possible, so that the plant's energy is not wasted producing seed but is directed into forming flower buds for next spring.

● **Controlling vine weevils**

Vine weevil can be a serious pest problem for both rhododendrons and azaleas (*see* Pests, page 404). The grubs attack the roots and stems below ground, and the adults attack the foliage and sometimes the flowers. A succession of mild winters helps these pests to multiply and they may reach infestation level in the garden. Chemical control is possible but is not always effective. The best way to deal with vine weevil is to introduce a biological control system of predators.

● **Rejuvenation pruning**

Rhododendrons and azaleas that are over 20 years old may become bare and unattractive at the base, and benefit from rejuvenation. This is best done just after flowering, so begin the process this month on early-flowering varieties (*see* Pruning, page 421).

ROCK PLANTS

● **Dealing with frost damage**

Replace any plants where the damage is deep-seated, such as loss of vigour, partial loss of foliage, discoloured leaves and dead patches. It is always sensible to propagate spare plants for replacements as any surplus can be given away or sold. If the damage is not too severe, the plants can be divided and healthy portions replanted. With spring-flowering plants it is better to wait until after flowering before dividing them. In a dry spell, water the ground well before digging up the plant and again after replanting.

PLANTING AN ALPINE TROUGH

Stone troughs and sinks are traditional containers for creating miniature alpine gardens. Genuine stone sinks are difficult to obtain and expensive to buy, but good reproductions are readily available. Once planted they make an interesting feature on a sunny patio.

To ensure adequate drainage, cover the holes in the bottom of the container with fine-mesh metal or plastic gauze, then broken crocks followed by about 10 mm (½ in) of gravel. Fill the container with a soil-based potting compost, mixed with some coarse sand or grit to give it an open texture.

Position the alpines with sufficient space between the plants to allow them to develop their shape without overlapping, and choose compact, slow-growing plants with similar requirements.

Many alpines are spring-flowering, but for best results try to choose plants with varying habits and a spread of flowering periods. This will make your container look interesting all the year round. Do not overlook the importance of foliage varieties.

A sink or trough will look much more appealing if 'landscaped' with a few rocks or large stones. These add height and make the feature interesting even when no plants are in flower. Use pieces of stone in proportion to the size of the container – several small pieces usually look more convincing than one large one. Always bury part of the rock, preferably at an angle so that it looks like an outcrop. If using several pieces, make sure they all lie with any strata in the rock sloping in the same direction.

Rocks need not limit the planting space. Small

Take care not to damage any self-sown seedlings that you want to keep, when you are pulling out old plants, or weeding generally.

● Root cuttings

Pot on root cuttings (*see* March, page 75) once they have produced a few leaves.

● Seedlings under glass

Begin to prick out seedlings raised from seed sown in the winter. Pot the seedlings that have three or four leaves into John Innes No. 1 potting compost and move the pots outdoors from the middle of the month onwards. Remember that seed from rock plants can take several years to germinate, so do not discard pots that are apparently barren for at least three years. Make sure they are clearly labelled.

● Dividing plants

Divide any earlier flowering rock plants, such as *Primula allionii*, being kept in a cold greenhouse.

ROSES

● Pruning

Complete all pruning by the beginning of this month (*see* March, pages 75–77).

● Feeding and pest and disease control

Apply rose fertiliser and gently hoe in around the plants; this will promote strong growth. As the weather gets warmer, treat roses regularly for pests, such as greenfly, and fungus problems such as black spot (*see* Pests & Diseases, pages 396 and 405).

● Applying mulches

Rose beds benefit from the application of an even layer of a mulch, primarily to feed but also to keep down weeds and conserve moisture through the summer (*see* The soil in your garden, pages 392–393). Apply evenly to a depth of at least 5 cm (2 in) on a moist surface. An ideal mulch for roses is equal parts organic material, such as garden compost or rotted manure, and peat, or a peat substitute.

● Choosing roses

Garden centres are now full of container-grown roses. Care must be taken to select only the best. Look for good, sound plants with at least two strong basal growths and a multitude of sideshoots. Avoid plants with moss on the surface of the soil.

Container-grown plants must be repotted or

Above: with suitable pieces of rock and tiny plants, it is possible to create a miniature alpine landscape.

Right: alpine troughs look more effective if raised slightly.

alpines can be planted in crevices in the stone or between two adjacent rocks, especially if they are arranged to provide planting pockets where a small amount of potting soil can be inserted.

Apply a layer of fine stone chippings or gravel over the surface of the finished container. This helps to prevent water standing around the necks of the plants, which many alpines do not like, and greatly improves the appearance of the finished sink or trough.

Avoid the temptation to plant rampant and spreading plants such as aubrieta. They will take over the whole trough and swamp weaker plants.

Many dianthus make attractive sink garden plants, but choose carefully. Some are tiny and compact, others taller and spreading: not all alpine dianthus are suitable. Sempervivums (houseleeks) and many of the smaller saxifrages are especially effective, but there are many other choice plants that can be used.

replanted immediately after purchase. Prepare the site and planting mixture in exactly the same way as for planting bare-root roses (*see* November, page 266): water the container well before planting; do not disturb the root system when taking the plants out of their pots and water again after planting. Roses do not require regular watering apart from those transplanted from containers.

● Temperatures under glass

Plants in the greenhouse being grown for their early flowers will now be coming into bud and will soon be flowering. This means that they will be very susceptible to variations in temperature. Maintain a constant flow of fresh air through the greenhouse and keep a minimum night temperature of 10°C

(50°F) and a maximum day temperature of 22°C (72°F). In sunny weather, shading the glass to lower the temperature will improve the quality of the blooms. Put the containers outside after flowering. Water constantly and control greenfly and powdery mildew (*see* Pests & Diseases, pages 396 and 410).

SWEET PEAS

● Planting out seedlings

When March-sown seedlings are growing strongly and hardened off, plant out in prepared ground (*see* February, page 46). Water and feed young plants from now until they finish flowering.

Sweet peas sown outdoors in October can now have their protection removed.

● Training plants on cordons

Start restricting growth if you wish to grow sweet peas on the cordon system.

TREES, SHRUBS & HEDGES

● Planting

Bare-root trees and shrubs should not be planted between April and September as they will not have time to establish themselves before the hot, dry weather of summer. Container-grown trees and shrubs can be planted during April in well-prepared soil. Add a balanced general fertiliser following the manufacturer's instructions and mulch well.

Water all newly planted trees and shrubs, particularly those that were container-grown. Ensure that

SWEET PEAS – TRAINING YOUNG PLANTS ON CORDONS

1 To produce flowers with long, straight stems, grow sweet peas up a cane and remove the sideshoots – known as the cordon system. When each plant is about 25 cm (10 in) tall, select the strongest shoot and cut out the others.

2 The selected stem must be tied to its support as it grows. Split metal rings are sometimes used, but you can use raffia or soft string instead. Always allow space for the stem to thicken with age.

3 Pinch out the tendrils (the thread-like growths that normally cling to the support) and sideshoots as they form. Also remove flower stems which have fewer than four buds. Allow the others to flower.

the rootball is kept moist until the shrub is well established. Water thoroughly – a light sprinkling may not wet the rootball sufficiently.

● Feeding

Feed established trees and shrubs, if not done last month, with a balanced fertiliser (*see* Fertilisers, page 388–391), according to manufacturer's instructions.

Apply a dressing of dried blood, dry tomato fertiliser or acidifying fertiliser to any trees or shrubs that need a pick-me-up, particularly any showing signs of chlorosis (yellowing of leaves). This usually applies to acid-loving shrubs growing on an alkaline soil. Apply a dressing of dried blood to all conifers except yew to improve their foliage and colour.

● Propagating by seed

Sow any remaining seeds of trees and shrubs (*see* February, page 47).

● Layering

Prepare and peg in place layers of suitable shrubs, such as chaenomeles, fothergilla and kalmia, either into pots containing a moist potting compost or directly into well-prepared soil at the base of the parent plant (*see* Propagation, page 432).

● Taking hardwood cuttings of evergreens

April is a good month to take hardwood cuttings of evergreen shrubs and trees. Prepare them in the same way as other hardwood cuttings (*see* Propagation, page 429). Trim the top half off large leaves to reduce the amount of moisture lost.

Shrubs and trees suitable for hardwood cuttings include aucuba, box, large-leaved varieties of cotoneaster, escallonia, holly, *Prunus laurocerasus* and *P. lusitanica*, pyracantha, senecio and *Viburnum tinus*.

● Pruning deciduous shrubs

Hard prune selected shrubs (*see* March, page 79) as new growth becomes evident. If this is not done now, these plants will become very woody in habit, with drastic reduction of foliage and flower size.

After flowering, prune spring-flowering shrubs, such as forsythia, that are over three years old by the one-third method (*see* Pruning, page 420).

● Pruning broad-leaved evergreens

Shorten last year's growth on all evergreens by half to encourage a bushy habit and fresh new foliage. This method is one of the lesser-known techniques, but it will give good, long-term growth and foliage, and only temporarily reduce the overall height and spread of the shrub. Avoid cutting through leaves when you prune as this makes them go brown.

TREES FOR SMALL GARDENS

These trees are a cross-section of flowering, fruiting and foliage trees suitable for a small or medium-sized garden. The heights are those likely about 15 years from planting, but this will be affected by soil and local climate. In favourable conditions some of these may grow much larger.

Acer griseum (paperbark maple) Small yellow flowers in spring, good autumn colour, brown peeling bark. Height: 4.5 m (15 ft).

Amelanchier lamarckii (snowy mespilus) Masses of white flowers in spring, good autumn colour. Can be grown as a large shrub or small tree. Height: 3 m (10 ft).

Betula pendula 'Youngii' (Young's weeping birch) Small, dome-shaped weeping tree with cascading branches. Silvery bark. Height: 4.5 m (15 ft).

Catalpa bignonioides 'Aurea' (golden Indian bean tree) Large, golden leaves retain colour well throughout summer. Height: 4.5 m (15 ft).

Cotoneaster 'Hybridus Pendulus' Now more correctly *C. salicifolius* 'Pendulus'. Semi-evergreen, small weeping tree with white flowers in early summer and red autumn berries. Height: 2.5 m (8 ft).

Crataegus laevigata (syn. C. oxyacantha) (hawthorn) Red, pink or white flowers in late spring and early summer. Red fruits in autumn. Height: 4.5 m (15 ft).

Laburnum x watereri 'Vossii' (golden chain tree) Long, drooping tassels of yellow flowers in late spring or early summer. Height: 4.5 m (15 ft).

Malus 'John Downie' (crab apple) Pinkish white blossom in spring, large red and yellow crab apples in autumn. Height: 4.5 m (15 ft).

Malus floribunda (flowering crab) Masses of pink and white blossom in spring. Height: 4.5 m (15 ft).

Malus tschonoskii (bonfire tree) Narrow, upright growth, white flowers in spring, small crab apples in autumn, plus excellent autumn colour. Height: 7.5 m (25 ft).

Prunus 'Amanogawa' (flagpole cherry) Narrow, upright growth. Pale pink flowers in spring, autumn colour. Height: 4.5 m (15 ft).

Prunus cerasifera 'Pissardii' (purple-leaved plum) Pink buds open to white flowers in early spring. Purple foliage. Height: 4.5 m (15 ft).

Prunus x subhirtella 'Autumnalis' (winter-flowering cherry) Small white or pink flowers in autumn and into winter during mild spells. Autumn colour. Height: 4.5 m (15 ft).

Pyrus salicifolia 'Pendula' (weeping willow-leaved pear) Small weeping tree with silver-grey foliage. Height: 3 m (10 ft).

Robinia pseudoacacia 'Frisia' (golden acacia) Golden foliage, retaining its colour all summer. Height: 6 m (20 ft).

Salix matsudana 'Tortuosa' (corkscrew willow) Now more correctly *S. babylonica pekinensis* 'Tortuosa'. The contorted and twisted stems are especially attractive when bare in winter. Height: 6 m (20 ft).

Sorbus 'Joseph Rock' White flowers in late spring or early summer, yellow berries in autumn, excellent autumn colour. Height: 4.5 m (15 ft).

● **Trimming and shaping conifers**

To improve the foliage and shape of upright conifers, remove 3–5 cm (1½–2 in) of last year's growth. Do this by stroking the outer surface with a very sharp knife. Also remove any protruding shoots without damaging the conifer's overall shape. Tie in larger branches with suitable plastic-covered wire, ensuring that the main stems are not restricted. Encasing the wire in a length of plastic garden hose helps to prevent any potential damage.

If a conifer has more than one leader – the top central shoot – remove the weaker. This stops the development of two strong leaders, which eventually will spoil the conifer's overall shape.

On spreading conifers shorten all the shoots produced last year by half. This helps to maintain a good shape on the tree and improves the foliage colour. Use secateurs to remove the leading growth. The shoots will then branch out.

With very large spreading conifers you can reduce the overall size by removing whole stems or branches. Lift the canopy to identify major branches that you can remove to reduce the spread. This also allows the upper branches to grow nearer the ground. Use care when cutting large branches.

HEDGES

Continue planting hedges with container-grown plants, including evergreens and conifers. Water at least three times a week in dry conditions and spray foliage and stems in the late evening.

Check that all newly planted specimens are firmly in the soil and refirm them if they have been dislodged by frost or wind.

Feed newly planted and established hedges, as you would individual specimens (*see* page 111). Feeding now will get hedges off to a good start.

VEGETABLES

Dig in any green manure planted last year if this has not been done before (*see* September, page 226).

Protect young plants from slugs and snails, and keep the vegetable garden tidy as slugs are encouraged by dead leaves, weeds and debris.

A sharp hoe is most effective for weeding between rows of closely spaced vegetables. Try to hoe on a warm, windy day when the exposed weeds will shrivel and die quickly. Weeds within rows will need to be hand picked until the vegetables can shade them out. Mulching will suppress weeds and is especially useful for sweetcorn, whose roots can be damaged by hoeing, and for other widely spaced crops such as brassicas and marrows. Paths and areas surrounding the plot can be kept weed-free by putting down old carpet or woven polypropylene.

● **Beans**

Broad beans can now be sown directly into the ground. Plant out broad beans started in pots (*see* March, page 80). Pinch out the top 10 cm (4 in) of each plant when they are in full flower. This makes bushier plants, encourages pods to form and reduces blackfly damage. Support taller varieties if necessary.

In mild areas sow French and runner beans in 8 cm (3 in) pots in a greenhouse or on a sunny windowsill for planting out next month.

● **Brassicas**

Fit collars around the stems of cabbages, cauliflowers and Brussels sprouts to prevent cabbage root flies from laying their eggs (*see* Pests, page 397). Cover all brassicas with fine netting supported on hoops. This deters many other pests, including aphids, cabbage white butterflies and root fly.

Continue sowing summer cauliflower and calabrese in pots under glass for a succession of crops (*see* March, page 80). Transplant those sown earlier when they have four true leaves. Water well.

Sow autumn cauliflowers in an outdoor seed bed from the middle of the month onwards. Sow in drills 2.5 cm (1 in) deep and 8 cm (3 in) apart with 15 cm (6 in) between rows.

Sow sprouting broccoli, which crops from March to May the following spring, from the middle of the month onwards. As broccoli transplants easily, you can start the plants off in an outdoor seed bed. Cloches should not needed unless it is an exceptionally cold spring. Sow 1 cm (½ in) deep, 15 cm (6 in) apart with 10 cm (4 in) between the rows. Trickle water into the bottom of the seed drill before sowing if the soil is dry.

VEGETABLES – BRASSICA COLLARS

Brassica collars – which you can make or buy – are a simple means of controlling cabbage root fly larvae on cabbages, cauliflowers and Brussels sprouts. Just slip them round the base of a young plant.

Kale gives a better yield if not transplanted from open ground, so sow the seed where the plants will grow. Alternatively start off in pots, so that the roots are less likely to be damaged when planted out.

Sow Brussels sprouts and summer cabbage if not yet done (*see* March, page 80).

● Carrots and parsnips

Continue sowing early carrots in short rows every fortnight. This avoids a glut and gives you young tender roots all summer. Sow maincrop carrots and parsnips if not yet done (*see* March, pages 80–81).

For large parsnip roots, sow 15 cm (6 in) apart in seed drills 30 cm (12 in) apart. For smaller roots, sow 8 cm (3 in) apart in seed drills 20 cm (8 in) apart. Sow groups of three or four seeds at each position and pull out all but the strongest. Thin out any sowings made last month if necessary.

Prevent carrot fly reaching your carrots by erecting

VEGETABLES – PROTECTING CARROTS

Carrot fly can be deterred without chemical means by erecting a barrier of plastic sheeting about 45 cm (18 in) high around the bed. Make a frame of wood or canes and attach the sheeting to this.

a physical barrier of plastic sheeting. Growing carrots under fleece or fine netting also helps.

● Marrows, courgettes and squashes

In mild areas sow seeds of all these crops in 8 cm (3 in) pots in a propagator or on a sunny window-sill. Sow seeds one to a pot 1 cm (½ in) deep and on their narrow sides so the water does not sit on them. They need a minimum temperature of 18°C (65°F).

● Onions and shallots

Continue to plant onions and shallots raised from seed or as sets (*see* March, page 81).

● Other roots and swollen stems

Continue sowing beetroot to produce a succession of crops. In cold parts of the country sow the first kohlrabi (*see* March, page 81).

● Peas

Continue sowing peas for a succession of crops.

● Potatoes

Earth up early potatoes and protect from frost (*see* March, page 81). Plant out maincrop varieties 10–15 cm (4–6 in) deep and 40 cm (16 in) apart in rows 75 cm (30 in) apart. Earth up.

● Salad crops

Continue sowing lettuces, radishes and spring onions for a succession of crops; sow lettuces in pots under glass in cold areas (*see* March, page 82). Transplant those sown earlier when they have four true leaves. Water all vegetables thoroughly after transplanting, especially if the soil is dry.

Sow a forcing variety of chicory towards the end of this month. Choose a modern variety such as

VEGETABLES – EARTHING UP POTATOES

Earth up potatoes by drawing soil up around the stems into a ridge. This protects the developing tubers from light, which would make them green and inedible. Keep earthing up potatoes in stages as the plants grow.

'Normato' or try a red one if you want radicchio. Sow them where they are to grow – chicory resents being transplanted – in rows 30 cm (12 in) apart and thin to 15 cm (6 in).

Harvest the first non-forced chicory.

● Spinach and spinach beet

Continue sowings of spinach and spinach beet in short rows in succession to avoid a glut (*see* March, page 82). Harvest overwintered spinach beet by picking young leaves from the base as they regrow.

● Sweetcorn

Start sweetcorn off in mild areas. Sow two seeds per 8 cm (3 in) pot. Cover with 3 cm (1½ in) of compost and keep them at 15–20°C (60°–70°F) in a propagator or on a sunny windowsill. If both seeds germinate, pull out the weaker one.

● Tomatoes, peppers and aubergines

Prick out outdoor tomato seedlings into individual pots when they are large enough to handle if this was not done last month (*see* March, page 82). Peppers and aubergines are slower growing – prick them out when the seed leaves are fully expanded. Once all seedlings are well established, start to harden them off in cooler conditions.

● Turnips and swedes

Sow main crop swedes if not yet done (*see* March, page 82). Thin out any sowings made last month.

Continue successional sowings of turnips (*see* March, page 82).

PERENNIAL VEGETABLES

● Asparagus

Plant new crowns early this month. Dig a trench wide enough to take the crowns with their roots spread out and 20–25 cm (8–10 in) deep. Lay the

VEGETABLES – PLANTING ASPARAGUS

Asparagus is best planted on a slight ridge in a trench, with the roots of the crown over the mound of soil. Space the crowns about 38 cm (15 in) apart, and cover the roots with about 5 cm (2 in) of soil.

crowns on a small ridge about 10 cm (4 in) high in the bottom of the trench. Cover the roots with about 5 cm (2 in) of soil and then fill in the trench as the plants grow. When weeding established plants, draw up more soil to make a ridge. This will encourage longer and stronger blanched stems, improve drainage and make harvesting easier. Ridge the asparagus the spring before the first cut. Rebuild the ridges each spring if necessary.

Control weeds, either by applying a mulch, by hoeing – do this with great care round the plants – or with a suitable weedkiller (*see* Weed Control, page 414–416). Apply a general fertiliser (*see* Fertilisers, page 390) to established beds before the first asparagus spears appear.

Take the first spears from beds at least two years old. Cut 5 cm (2 in) below the soil surface when the spears are 12–15 cm (5–6 in) tall.

● Globe artichokes

Sow globe artichokes in a seed bed where they will grow slowly for a year.

Transplant those sown last spring into their permanent homes. This is also the last month to transplant artichokes sown under glass in February. They need a sunny, sheltered site and plenty of well-rotted organic matter incorporated into the planting hole. Space them 75–90 cm (2½–3 ft) apart.

● Rhubarb

Harvest the first non-forced sticks this month.

WATER PLANTS & POOLS

● Feeding fish

As the fish become active they should be fed regularly from April to October with a proprietary fish food.

Place as much food as the fish can eat in 20 minutes on the surface of the water. Take out with a net any food that remains after 20 minutes to prevent it decomposing. Feed the fish about three times a week. Introduce new fish by placing the bag in which they were transported on to the surface of the water. Allow the temperature in the bag to adjust to that of the pool before emptying the fish out.

● Planting aquatics

You can start to plant in the pond towards the end of the month if the weather is warm. Plant in lattice aquatic baskets or crates sold for the purpose. Baskets help to keep water plants under control, but tall plants in baskets may blow over in strong winds. If you have at least 10–15 cm (4–6 in) of soil in the bottom of your pool you can plant directly into that, firming the plants in well.

Special aquatic planting soil is available for use in baskets. Avoid using nutrient-rich soil which will encourage algae. All soils used in pools should have ground chalk added. Heavy soil, even clay, is normally better than light soil. Avoid fibrous materials, peat and strawy manure, and very soluble fertilisers.

Release into the pond any winter buds (turions) gathered in September and kept in a jar over winter.

● Waterlilies

When purchasing waterlilies from a garden centre, choose established plants in a container. Only buy bare-root plants from a specialist nursery and check that the rootstock is firm with no soft spots.

Set the rootstocks with the growing point or crown just below the surface of the soil and firm in.

Spread out the roots of plants which will grow in the shallow margins of the pool and push them downwards into the soil.

WATER PLANTS & POOLS – DIVIDING AND PLANTING WATERLILIES

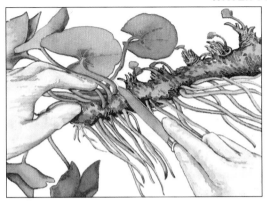

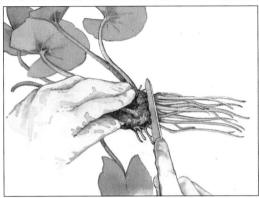

1 *When waterlily foliage becomes congested, lift the tuber, divide and replant it. Sever the healthy end sections of the tuber about 15 cm (6 in) from the growing tip. The discarded section can be used to propagate more plants.*

2 *Cut off the long anchor roots from the new plant to within 5 cm (2 in) of the rootstock but do not cut or damage the smaller, whiter roots as these will be needed to sustain the new plant. Trim off dead or damaged leaves.*

3 *Prepare a large planting basket or solid-sided container by filling it with aquatic soil. You can use ordinary garden soil provided it does not contain fertilisers. Insert the new plant then cover the surface with gravel.*

CHOOSING THE RIGHT WATERLILY

Small waterlilies growing in 30–45 cm (12–18 in) of water will reach 60–90 cm (2–3 ft) across in two or three seasons. Waterlilies suitable for growing in 45–60 cm (18–24 in) of water will reach 1–1.2 m (3–4 ft) across, while the very strong ones will extend to over 1.5 m (5 ft).

Waterlilies will only grow well in still water. They require several hours of sunshine each day to flower at their best and will not flourish in the shade of a tree. You should choose varieties that have been bred to grow in the depth of water you can offer them otherwise your pool may become swamped in foliage with few flowers.

Species plants are also prone to take over a small pool, so select one of the many beautifully coloured, named hybrids which have been developed specifically for garden ponds. These are available in a range of colours, including white, yellow, pink and red, and some are fragrant.

● Marginals and oxygenators

Ensure that the rhizomes of plants such as irises and callas (bog arums) are more or less horizontal.

Push the lower ends of the stems of submerged oxygenating plants (usually supplied as small bunches of unrooted cuttings with a lead weight on the base) about 2.5 cm (1 in) into the soil.

● Transplanting seedlings

Replant self-sown seedlings of water hawthorn (*Aponogeton distachyos*) and the young plants of the water fringe (*Nymphoides peltata*) which are produced on stolons.

● Sowing seeds

Sow seeds of waterside primulas in a cold frame for planting out in August or later. Sow mimulus now in a cold frame to produce flowers as soon as July.

● Dividing aquatics

Lift and divide any overgrown waterlilies and other aquatics. Select the healthiest portions for new plants and, using a sharp knife, sever them about 15 cm (6 in) from the crown or growing tip. Cut the long anchor roots from underneath, leaving the young whiter roots. Trim off any dead or damaged leaves and replant the severed portion without delay.

Most waterlilies can also be propagated by growing on individual 'eyes' (*see* May, page 141).

● Top dressing

Add a top dressing of pea gravel to newly planted containers and, if possible, to exposed areas of soil within the pool. Covering the exposed soil with gravel helps to prevent fish from stirring up the soil in the water when they are searching for food at the bottom of the pond.

Making a Pond

Spring is the ideal time to construct a garden pond. A wide range of water plants will be available at garden and aquatic centres and it is also the safest time to introduce new fish. However, provided the ground is not frozen or too wet, a pond can be dug at most times of the year.

POSITIONING YOUR POND

Before you do anything else, decide on the best place in your garden for a pond. The position may also dictate its size and shape. The ideal site is an open one, in full sun for at least eight hours a day if you want aquatic plants, especially waterlilies, to flower well. Falling leaves can cause problems in the autumn which may lead to water pollution, so avoid building a pond near deciduous trees.

If you want to install a filter, fountain or lights, the pool should be near to a power supply. A power supply is essential for an efficient filter and UV water clarifier, although you can buy solar-powered pumps for fountains. Low-voltage pumps can be used for fountains and filters; these allow the transformer to be kept indoors with only safe voltage being taken outside. It is best to consult a qualified electrician at the planning stage if you require powerful equipment and an external pump.

You have more flexibility when siting a wildlife pond. Fountains and cascades are not suited to this type of pool and, as ornamental fish are not in keeping either, a filter is not essential. Some fish may be needed to keep down mosquitoes but keep the number low or frogs and newts may disappear.

PREFORMED OR FLEXIBLE?

Preformed shells enable you to visualise what the final pond will look like. You are, however, limited to the shapes and sizes offered by manufacturers. A flexible liner offers much more scope for individual design and almost always looks more natural.

▲ A pond should be a very attractive feature in the garden so take time to plan the position and design.

Preformed ponds are made from plastic or glass fibre. In general, the latter gives a better quality and longer-lasting pond, but is more expensive. High-quality plastics are reasonably thick and rigid and should last as long as the cheapest flexible liners.

The thickness and quality of flexible liners vary according to the material. The best quality liners are those made from either rubber (sometimes described as EPDM) or butyl rubber. These can be significantly more expensive than liners made of PVC or low-density polyethylene but can last for over 30 years. PVC is strong and comes in a wider range of colours than most of the alternatives, although black is the recommended colour for

most ponds, as it tends to look better and last longer. Reinforced versions are available. Good quality low-density polyethylene can have a life expectancy and guarantee of over 15 years. Do not dismiss this material if you want a pond liner at a reasonable cost.

SIZE AND SHAPE

Within reason, the larger the pond the better, as it will suffer less from extremes of temperature and will be able to support a greater variety of plant and animal life. Once you have decided on the position and material for your pond, you can work out the size and shape. Mark out the shape on the ground with a hosepipe or length of rope and assess it from various vantage points, including from both upstairs and downstairs windows. Experiment with the shape until it looks right.

The deepest part of the pond should be at least 38 cm (15 in). Aim for 60 cm (2 ft) if you are planning to stock the pond with ornamental fish. You can increase the depth to 75 cm (2½ ft) for a pool of over 9 m² (100 sq ft), but making it any deeper will only create unnecessary work.

It is important to incorporate 'shelves' to accommodate marginal plants which prefer to grow in shallow water. Make the shelf around 20–30 cm (8–12 in) below the surface of the water. A shelf can be continuous or interrupted, but should extend around one-third to three-quarters of the perimeter in total. This will enable you to grow a wide range of plants in baskets or planted in the soil around the water's edge.

An area of shallow, shelving beach covered with small pebbles will encourage garden birds and other wildlife to visit your pond.

HOW TO INSTALL A FLEXIBLE POND LINER

1 Mark out the edge of your new pond with something flexible such as a hosepipe or a length of rope.

2 Dig out to the required depth, creating shelves around the edges for plants. Check levels as you go.

3 Line with moist sand or polyester sheeting sold for the purpose. Lay the liner loosely in place on top.

THE AMOUNT OF LINER YOU WILL NEED

Overall length of pool + twice maximum depth
= length of liner.
Overall width of pool + twice maximum depth
= width of liner.
For example:
A pool 3 m (10 ft) long, 2.4 m (8 ft) wide and 45 cm (18 in) deep would need a liner:
3 + (2 x 0.45) by 2.4 + (2 x 0.45) = 3.90 by 3.30 m
(10 + (2 x 1½) by 8 + (2 x 1½) = 13 by 11 ft)

4 For a good finished effect, fold the liner carefully round the curves. Do not trim the liner yet.

5 Hold liner in place with bricks and fill the pond. Trim liner to 15 cm (6 in) and mask with paving or grass.

HOW TO INSTALL A PREFORMED POND

1 To establish the shape you need to dig, first push canes into the ground around the edge of the preformed shell.

2 Remove the soil to the depth of the marginal shelf. Place the shell in the hole and press to mark the deeper part.

3 Excavate the deeper area, then try the shell for size. Adjust the depth if necessary. Line with sand or fine soil.

4 Put in the shell checking it is level and fill with water. Backfill with soil around the edge as the pond fills.

MAY

As spring changes to summer, and the days lengthen, the garden is both a hive of industry and the perfect place to relax on a sunny day.

May

May is a lovely time of the year. Signs of summer are everywhere, days are warmer and longer and more flowers are in bloom, adding colour and scent to the garden. Summer bedding plants are available from shops and garden centres and, if you have grown your own bedding plants, you will be anxious to get them planted outdoors – both to make space in the greenhouse and to reduce the amount of time you spend watering and feeding them.

You should, however, resist the temptation to plant out tender annuals during a spell of fine, summer-like weather at the beginning of the month. Be guided by past experience as to the likelihood of late frosts in your area. In favourable parts of the country, such as the south and south-west, it may be reasonable to take the risk and plant out at the beginning of the month. But even in those mild areas, the middle of the month is a safer choice. In cold regions wait until the end of the month or even delay planting out until the beginning of June. If you are in any doubt as to when to plant out, and you live in a town, be guided by the local parks – and plant out summer bedding when they do. They will be basing their timing on many years of local experience.

The weather in May

The weather is more consistent in May than April although it can still be changeable and erratic as the days progress towards summer. Throughout May the weather usually improves steadily, and there are often long sunny spells and many warm days. But beware of late frosts. These are the bane of all gardeners and they are most likely when night skies are clear – usually after a warm, sunny day!

The difference between the timing of the seasons between north and south is now starting to close, but many parts of the country will be a week or two later than the south-west, while cold parts of northern Scotland will be four weeks or more behind.

Protecting plants

If your bedding plants are still hardening off in pots or trays, in a cold frame or standing outside, take them under cover if a frost is forecast. If you have already planted them out, you have no choice but to cover them.

Late frosts and cold winds are both killers of newly planted summer bedding. You can often save your plants simply by covering them with layers of newspaper. A double layer of horticultural fleece also provides excellent protection. Weight the newspapers or fleece down with large stones or peg them down with wire or canes to stop them blowing away. Remember to remove the protection as soon as the danger of frost or cold winds is passed.

Watering and weeding

Water newly planted bedding plants thoroughly whenever the weather is dry – preferably with a sprinkler so that the water really penetrates the soil. If you do this regularly for the first few weeks, the plants will root down well and be much better able to withstand dry weather later in the summer.

Continue to water trees, shrubs and border plants that you have planted this spring, unless the weather is wet. They will all look after themselves once established, but neglecting watering at this time can lead to losses.

Unfortunately watering encourages weeds. They will be easy to control if you hoe them off while they are still seedlings, but more difficult if you leave them to grow, flower and set seed. Time the hoeing mid-way between waterings, as it is most effective if done when the surface of the soil is dry. The chopped-off weeds will wither in the air more quickly and are less likely to re-root. Watering too soon after hoeing can undo your good work as it can help weeds to survive by washing them into the soil where they may re-root.

Mulching

Most mulches will already be in place, but it is never too late to add one. Summer bedding is not normally mulched, but herbaceous and shrub borders benefit greatly if they are covered with a layer of organic mulch.

This is particularly important if you have planted new shrubs. Fork in a general fertiliser and water the ground round them thoroughly before adding the mulch.

Loose mulches (as opposed to sheet mulches such as plastics) should be at least 5 cm (2 in) thick. If necessary, top up existing mulches to ensure they remain effective.

Controlling pests

In a greenhouse many pests can successfully be controlled biologically by importing natural predators such as insects or nematodes (*see* Pests, page 394), but if you don't use these be vigilant and spray with an appropriate chemical before the pest population builds up.

Outdoors, aphids, slugs and snails are ever-present in most gardens. You may prefer to spray aphids only if they become a major problem or spoil prized plants, but bear in mind that they can spread virus diseases from one plant to another. For that reason alone, you should always take them seriously, especially if you grow plants such as dahlias and lilies that are susceptible to viruses. Slugs and snails can usually be controlled by hand picking or with traps or pellets. Bear in mind that slug pellets may harm other creatures in the garden.

Staking

Ensure that tall or floppy plants in herbaceous borders are staked before they grow too tall. Stake dahlias early, particularly any that have been raised from cuttings which have not yet formed large tubers. Dahlia stems are brittle and can break relatively easily if they are exposed to strong winds.

Spring-flowering bulbs

Most spring-flowering bulbs have finished blooming by May. Deadheading them will make the garden look tidier, but if possible allow all the foliage to die down naturally.

JOBS THAT WON'T WAIT

- Sow fast-maturing and late-flowering annuals, herbs and vegetables including parsnips, early carrots and runner beans.

- Harden off summer bedding plants and plant out. Check the weather forecast regularly and be prepared to provide temporary protection, with newspapers or horticultural fleece, if frost is forecast.

- Thin out hardy annual, vegetable and other seedlings sown outdoors.

- Maintain a programme of weeding and checking for pests and diseases.

- Water and feed plants as necessary. Pay particular attention to seedlings, plants in containers and newly planted trees and shrubs.

- Take basal cuttings of border plants, such as lupins and delphiniums, before they develop hollow or pithy stems, at which point it is too late for successful cuttings.

- Stake and support chrysanthemums except compact varieties and dwarf bedding. Stop incurved and large exhibition chrysanthemums this month.

- Prune spring-flowering clematis after flowering.

- Finish planting of permanent containers so plants have the summer to establish themselves.

- Pinch out the growing tips of bush fuchsias while the plants are still small, and check all types of tender fuchsias for pests – these plants are particularly vulnerable at this time.

- Make sure the greenhouse has adequate shading and ventilation to prevent overheating. Train greenhouse cucumbers and tomatoes. Remove male flowers from cucumbers.

- Prune winter-flowering heathers. Any not pruned by the end of May should be left till next year.

- Plant onion sets as soon as possible.

- Earth up early and maincrop potatoes; protect foliage if frost is forecast.

- Cut lawns with naturalised bulbs growing in them. Keep mower blades high.

ANNUALS & BIENNIALS

● Sowing fast-maturing annuals

For a succession of blooms throughout the summer months continue to sow the seeds of annuals such as calendulas, candytuft, clarkias and godetias every two weeks till the middle of June. In cold areas, however, complete sowing by the end of the first week of May as even quick-maturing annuals may not have sufficient growing time to flower well if sown later in the month.

Although at this time of year hardy annuals will germinate if sown directly into seed beds outdoors, you will usually get better results by sowing them under glass and then pricking them out into pots or divided seed trays. You will then need to harden off the seedlings (*see* April, page 90). If you adopt this method, strong, weather-resistant plants should result. Moreover there is no need for thinning and the root disturbance when planting out is minimal.

Annuals for late flowering include ageratums, love-lies-bleeding or tassel flowers (*Amaranthus caudatus*), nicotianas, nasturtiums, zinnias, annual lavateras such as 'Silver Cup' or 'Mont Blanc', ten-week stocks and annual rudbeckias including 'Rustic Dwarfs' and 'Marmalade'. If sown now, these annuals will flower from August until the first frosts arrive. They make perfect gap fillers for the mixed border, especially as they come into flower as many early-flowering herbaceous perennials are over. Sow some in containers; these can then be moved around the garden to create interest.

● Transplanting overwintered annuals

Move any hardy annuals, which were sown in rows and overwintered (*see* September, page 212), to their final flowering position in the garden.

● Feeding young plants

There is only a certain amount of fertiliser in compost and, when it runs out, seedlings and young plants can show signs of starvation. Such signs include poor growth, pale, yellowing foliage and red and purple leaf tints. This is a particular problem for plants sown early in the year which cannot be planted outside until the risk of frost has passed. Water them with a balanced liquid feed, applied according to the manufacturer's instructions.

● Clearing spring bedding

Once displays of spring flowers start to fade, or if you need the space for planting out summer bedding, you can begin to clear the beds. Most plants can be discarded, but bulbs, such as tulips, should be moved to a trench in a spare part of the garden to finish building up reserves for next year's flowering (*see* Bulbs, page 124).

● Planting out

Check on the last likely frost date for your area. In milder regions it should be possible to plant out half-hardy plants around the end of the month. Plants sown during February or March should now be ready to harden off (*see* April, page 90). Do this two weeks before you intend planting them out. Hardy annuals sown in pots and trays during March and early April can also be planted outside in their flowering position once they are hardened off.

● Sowing biennials

In mild areas, towards the end of the month, you can start to sow biennials for flowering next spring. Sow the seeds in straight rows in prepared seed beds. Space the seeds out well to cut down on the need for thinning. Sow double daisies (*Bellis perennis*), forget-me-nots, polyanthus, wallflowers and sweet williams now, but leave Brompton stocks till June or July.

● Thinning out

It is very difficult to sow hardy annuals sparsely enough to avoid overcrowding. Thinning may seem wasteful, but it is better to thin out the plants than to keep seedlings crowded together. Overcrowded seedlings will grow tall and leggy instead of developing into bushy, weather-resistant plants.

Pinch out the tips of annuals, such as salvias, which can be induced into a bushy habit. This will delay flowering but produce better plants.

● Controlling pests

Plants are often infested soon after being planted out and, if unchecked, foliage and flowers can become unsightly. Watch particularly for aphids such as greenfly (*see* Pests, pages 395–396).

ANNUALS & BIENNIALS – THINNING

Annuals and biennials sown in the open ground should be thinned before they become overcrowded. Pull out the surplus seedlings. Keep the soil round the adjacent plants firm with your other hand while you do this.

BIENNIALS: GUIDE TO SOWING AND PLANTING

	Colours	Flowering period	Situation	Uses (see note [1] below)	Sow in greenhouse, frame or cloche	Sow in open ground	Space in nursery rows	Space in flowering position
Bellis perennis (double daisy)	Red, pink, white	May–July	Sun or partial shade	D	June	May–June	8 cm (3 in)	15 cm (6 in)
Campanula medium (Canterbury bell)	Blue, pink, purple, white	June–July	Sun or partial shade	B,T	June	May–June	15 cm (6 in)	23–30 cm (9–12 in)
Cheiranthus x allionii (Siberian wallflower) [2]	Orange, yellow	May–June	Sun or partial shade	M	June–July	June	10 cm (4 in)	23–30 cm (9–12 in)
Cheiranthus cheiri (wallflower) [2]	Wide range	April–May	Sun or partial shade	M	June–July	May–June	10 cm (4in)	23–30 cm (9–12in)
Cynoglossum (hound's tongue)	Blue	May–June	Sun or partial shade	M	June–July	June–July	15 cm (6 in)	23 cm (9 in)
Dianthus barbatus (sweet william)	Red and pink shades	June–July	Sun or partial shade	B,M T	June–July	June–July	15 cm (6 in)	23–30 cm (9–12 in)
Digitalis (foxglove)	Purple, pink, white shades	June–July	Partial shade	B	June	May–June	15 cm (6 in)	30–45 cm (12–18 in)
Lunaria annua [3] (honesty)	Purple, white	May–July	Sun or partial shade	B	June	May	10 cm (4 in)	30 cm (12 in)
Matthiola (Brompton stock)	Wide range	June–July	Sun or partial shade	T	June–July	June–July	15 cm (6 in)	23 cm (9 in)
Myosotis (forget-me-not)	Blue, pink	April–May	Sun or partial shade	D,M	June	May–June	10 cm (4 in)	15–20 cm (6–8 in)
Papaver nudicaule (Iceland poppy)	Wide range	June	Sun	B,T	June–July	June–July	10 cm (4 in)	23–30 cm (9–12 in)
Primula (hybrids) (polyanthus)	Wide range	April–May	Sun or shade	M	April–May	March–May	15 cm (6 in)	15–20 cm (6–8 in)
Viola x wittrockiana (pansy)	Wide range	March–Aug	Sun or shade	D	June–July	June–July	10 cm (4 in)	15 cm (6 in)

Notes:

[1] B: best grown in a herbaceous or mixed border. D: suitable for dwarf bedding to about 23 cm (9 in): M: suitable for medium bedding, 23–45 cm (9–18 in). T: suitable for tall bedding, 45–90 cm (18–36 in).

[2] *Cheiranthus* are now more correctly called *Erysimum*, but this name is seldom used in seed catalogues.

[3] *Lunaria annua* may sometimes be listed under its older name of *Lunaria biennis*.

BORDER PERENNIALS

● Planting

Continue planting border perennials, including any that are semi-tender and slow-growing, as well as seedlings and cuttings. If the soil is impoverished add a slow-acting fertiliser, garden compost or well-rotted manure before planting. You should mix it thoroughly into the soil (*see* The soil in your garden, pages 386–393). Water the new plants well in, especially in dry weather.

● Filling in gaps

Fill in any unsightly empty spaces between border perennials. To fill gaps it is not too late to sow the seeds of some hardy annuals straight into their flowering positions. Once frost no longer threatens, sow half-hardy annuals or tender annuals in pots for sinking into the soil later in the summer. Summer-flowering bulbs, tender perennials and foliage plants in pots will also add interest and colour.

● Basal cuttings

Take basal cuttings (*see* Propagation, page 429–30) from plants, such as lupins and delphiniums, which later develop hollow or pithy stems. Keep cuttings out of direct sun. Pot up individually when rooted.

BULBS, CORMS & TUBERS

● Deadheading

Continue to remove dead blooms from daffodils, tulips and hyacinths as they finish flowering.

● Lifting bulbs

Most bulbs, such as tulips or daffodils, have finished flowering by now, and it may be necessary to lift

BULBS, CORMS & TUBERS – LIFTING AND HEELING IN

1 Provided the flowers have died you can lift spring-flowering bulbs and corms to release the space for other plants. Lift them carefully with a fork, keeping as much soil around the roots as possible.

2 Place the bulbs at a slight angle in a shallow trench so the foliage is above ground. Put netting in the bottom to make it easier to retrieve the bulbs later. Cover the bulbs with soil. Lift and store when the foliage has died down.

them from the beds or borders to make way for summer bedding. Heel in the bulbs in another part of the garden so that they can die down naturally.

● Cleaning and storing bulbs

Clean the bulbs of early tulips and daffodils that have had time to die back and store them in shallow trays in a cool, airy shed for replanting in October. Destroy any diseased tulip bulbs that are soft or have prominent brown or grey marks or scars on the body of the bulbs. If they are placed on a compost heap they may carry disease to fresh plantings.

● Watering and feeding

Water all plants thoroughly in dry spells. Daffodils in a light, sandy soil will particularly benefit from this.

Give gladioli and summer-flowering bulbs a general liquid feed (*see* Fertilisers, page 390).

● Hippeastrums

After hippeastrums have finished flowering allow the foliage to die back. Cut off any leaves cleanly above the neck and store the bulbs in their pots in a cool place until next spring.

● Crinums

Plant crinum bulbs 15–20 cm (6–8 in) deep in a south-facing border. Alternatively, if you live in a cold area, plant them in tubs which can be moved under cover during the winter.

● Arum lilies

Arum lilies (*Zantedeschia aethiopica*) are often grown in pots in the greenhouse for protection and early flowers but, except in cold areas, they also flourish in the open. Plant them out when all danger of frost has passed, either in moist soil or up to 30 cm (12 in) deep in a pool to grow as water plants.

● Gladioli

Continue to plant gladiolus corms for a succession of flowers (*see* March, page 59). Try to finish planting by the middle of the month.

● Small alpine bulbs

Gradually reduce the watering of dwarf bulbs which you are growing in a bulb frame or greenhouse as the leaves start to turn brown.

● Perennial nasturtiums

Plant out tubers of *Tropaeolum speciosum* and *T. tuberosum* (*see* Climbers, page 126).

CARNATIONS & PINKS

● Planting out

Dianthus grown as half-hardy annuals may now be planted out in mild areas. Young plants get off to the best start if they are already big enough to fill a 5 cm (2 in) pot. Water in new plants, and keep the soil around any earlier plantings moist if the weather is windy and dry to avoid a check to growth.

PERPETUAL-FLOWERING

Continue to pot on perpetual-flowering carnations and maintain healthy conditions in the greenhouse. Take any necessary action against pests and diseases (*see* March, page 60).

CHRYSANTHEMUMS

● Stopping this month

Continue the programme of stopping as required:
INCURVED: if not stopped last month to produce a second crown, then stop once between mid May and mid June.
LARGE EXHIBITION: these types usually break naturally, but if not stop by the last week of May (*see* April, page 93).

● Staking and supporting

Most chrysanthemums, except the smaller bushy varieties such as Charms, will need some sort of support. To stake plants in the garden insert stout canes or stakes close to the plants. Pass raffia or soft twine gently around the plant, and then around the cane, then tie the plants loosely to the canes.

When growing flowers in a separate bed or in rows for cutting, the most convenient way to support them

CHRYSANTHEMUMS – SUPPORTING

This is one method of supporting chrysanthemums grown in a block. Lay 20 cm (8 in) wire mesh on the ground and insert four stout stakes. Plant the chrysanthemums in alternate squares and raise the mesh as the plants grow.

is with welded wire mesh secured to stakes. To support chrysanthemums in pots, insert three 1.5 m (5 ft) canes, equally spaced, into each pot. Tie the main stem of the plant loosely to one cane. Alternatively, place one cane in the centre of the pot and tie in the flowering stems.

EARLY-FLOWERING (GARDEN)

● Planting

Weather permitting, plant outdoors in the first week of May in mild areas, but a little later in cold areas.

Chrysanthemums are prone to attack from several pests and diseases, so spray them with suitable fungicide a few days before planting out. Rake the bed prepared over the last two months. Set the plants in the ground at the same depth as they were in the pots or frame; any deeper and growth will be adversely affected. Firm in the plants enough to keep them upright, but do not damage the tender young roots.

Plant pompons and Koreans 30–45 cm (12–18 in) apart in each direction and stake them. Water each plant thoroughly on planting. Over the next few days spray plants lightly to prevent drying out.

● Overwintered plants

Check on stools which have remained in the open all winter. Discard any damaged by pests or the weather.

Lightly fork the ground around each plant, then sprinkle some general fertiliser, and water it in.

If the stools have a large number of new ground shoots, retain the six best shoots, cutting the remainder off at ground level before staking. This will improve the size and quality of the flowers.

● Taking cuttings

Take cuttings of both early-flowering and very late-flowering varieties (*see* March, page 61).

LATE-FLOWERING (GREENHOUSE)

● **Potting on**

Except in cold areas, pot on late-flowering varieties into 20–23 cm (8–9 in) pots. Insert 1.5 m (5 ft) canes and water well. Fill the pot to the top with water and allow it to drain through. Do not water again for seven to ten days, but during warm weather spray the plants with clean water.

After seven to ten days, set out pots 20–30 cm (8–12 in) apart on their summer standing ground (*see* April, page 94) in mild areas, but in cold areas wait until June. When moving the plants, take care not to damage the developing sideshoots.

● **Caring for stock plants**

Continue to water, stake and treat for pests those later-flowering varieties which will provide cuttings for autumn and winter-flowering plants.

CLIMBERS & WALL SHRUBS

● **Taking softwood cuttings**

These are taken from new shoots produced in March and April and, as their name implies, should be firm enough to handle but not at all rigid (*see* Propagation, page 428). Climbers to propagate this way include honeysuckle, jasmine and pyracantha.

● **Taking cuttings of clematis**

Where shoots of spring-flowering clematis have grown well and become firm, softwood cuttings can be taken this month. These cuttings, called internodal cuttings (*see* Propagation, page 429), need only be just over 5 cm (2 in) long.

Trim about 5 mm (¼ in) above a node (joint on the stem where leaves and buds emerge) and 5 cm (2 in) below it. Remove one of the leaf stems. Dip

CLIMBERS & WALL SHRUBS – TAKING CUTTINGS OF CLEMATIS

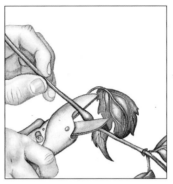  

1 Cut shoots about 5 mm (¼ in) above the buds at a leaf joint (node) and 5 cm (2 in) below. You can take several cuttings from one stem.

2 Remove one of the leaf stems. Dip the bottom of the cutting into a rooting hormone.

3 Insert into pots or trays filled with a rooting compost. Keep warm and humid. Rooting takes about three weeks in a propagator.

the cutting in hormone rooting powder, plant in rooting compost and keep in a propagator, or under a sheet of glass, at a temperature of 15°C (60°F). Rooting should take about three weeks and is indicated by new growth emerging from the node.

Pot on in the autumn (*see* September, page 215).

● **Planting out annual climbers**

Plant out annual climbers, such as morning glory and black-eyed Susan (*Thunbergia alata*), once all danger of frost has passed. Provide sufficient trellis support, as many of these annuals are very fast-growing, and can easily grow 3 m (10 ft) in a season.

● **Planting out tuberous climbers**

Plant out the tubers of perennial climbers such as *Tropaeolum tuberosum* and *T. speciosum* once all danger of frost has passed. They are not fussy, but prefer a well-drained soil and light shade. Plant tubers horizontally about 5 cm (2 in) deep in well-prepared soil with plenty of humus.

● **Pruning spring-flowering clematis**

After flowering, cut back all last year's growth of spring-flowering clematis, such as *Clematis alpina* and *C. macropetala* varieties, to 25–30 cm (10–12 in) from its point of origin. This encourages new growth and the plant will flower better next spring – if this pruning is not done the flowers will be fewer and the plant may well die within two or three years.

When over five years old and if they have become too large for their position, cut back all sideshoots on plants of *C. montana* varieties to within 5–8 cm (2–3 in) of the central skeleton framework or main shoots, after flowering. *C. montana* is very vigorous and difficult to prune and this will help to control its size. Tie in main branches to encourage new strong growth for abundant and healthy flowers.

CLIMBERS & WALL SHRUBS – PRUNING SPRING-FLOWERING CLEMATIS

1 Spring-flowering clematis such as C. montana *require pruning only when they are over five years old and have become too large for their site, or their shape needs to be controlled. Prune, if necessary, as soon as flowering is over.*

2 Decide which framework shoots you wish to retain to form the basic shape required, then cut back to these shoots any growth that has outgrown its space. Vigorous new shoots will soon fill the spaces and should flower next spring.

CONTAINER GARDENING

● Planting and sowing

Try to finish the planting of permanent containers by early May so that the plants have the long summer period ahead in which to establish themselves. If tender evergreens were not planted last month, plant these now. Finish sowing hardy annuals directly in pots or liners for flowering by the end of June or early July (*see* April, page 90).

● Hanging baskets

Harden off hanging baskets by sitting them in a large pot in a sheltered corner during the day. Return them to the greenhouse, conservatory or porch at night. Do not expose them to possible wind damage or the plants may not recover.

● Remedying winter damage

Evergreen shrubs which have been severely damaged by frost drop their leaves and often look dead. Don't discard any plants unless you are positive there are no signs of life; test by scratching the bark to see if there is any green pith showing. Some will not revive until June, when they may regrow from the base or shoot again from the branches. When this happens, prune out any dead material and reshape the shrub to make a pleasing outline.

● Sprucing up windowboxes

By the end of May, most spring flowers in containers will have started to fade and look unsightly. If you have used cheap containers inside an ornamental windowbox it is a simple matter to lift them out and replace them with ones ready-filled with plants for the summer. Throw away the faded annuals but salvage ivies and other evergreens such as periwinkle (*Vinca*) and euonymus, which can either be planted out in the garden or potted up and used again in containers later in the year.

● Feeding

Soilless composts contain sufficient fertiliser to keep plants fed for several weeks after planting (check the information on the compost bag). After that, unless you have already applied a slow-release fertiliser, you will need to feed plants in seasonal displays regularly. It is best to use a general-purpose liquid fertiliser recommended for flowering plants and bedding. Follow the manufacturer's instructions and do not be tempted to use at a higher rate than the recommended concentration, as this can harm the plants. Plants in coir-based composts may need more frequent feeding and watering than those in peat-based composts. Lush, leafy growth at the expense of flowers is usually an indication of overfeeding or too high a proportion of nitrogen in the fertiliser.

● Watering

As the weather warms up, watering becomes a daily exercise, especially for hanging baskets and plants in small pots which quickly dry out. Use a watering can without a rose to direct water on to the soil rather than the foliage, otherwise it can be wasted. Grouping pots together on the patio can cut down on the time spent watering, as can hosepipe attachments such as hand-operated spray guns and long lances for reaching up into hanging baskets.

If the compost in a hanging basket dries out too much, it can be difficult to rewet. Try taking the basket down and leaving it soaking in a sink or bowl of water until the plants have revived.

● Protecting against slugs and snails

Check regularly for slug and snail damage. Vulnerable plants that are often grown in containers include pansies, petunias and hostas. Slugs and snails will climb up walls, so do not assume that plants in ground floor windowboxes are safe.

Check for other pests and diseases and treat as necessary (*see* April, page 96 and Pests and Diseases, pages 394–413).

DAHLIAS

● Staking

A fully grown dahlia plant (except bedding varieties) will grow to around 1.4 m (4½ ft) tall and 75 cm (2½ ft) across, so it needs extra support to avoid wind damage. Stake the plants of non-bedding varieties either with 1.5 m (5 ft) stakes driven 30 cm (1 ft) into the ground, or with three bamboo canes. Put the supports in position before planting as this avoids damaging the roots. Loosely tie the plants to the stake with soft string.

● Planting out

Young dahlias grown in pots can be planted out now in mild areas when all danger of frost is past. The plants should be about 20–25 cm (8–10 in) high, and should be planted 60–90 cm (2–3 ft) apart, depending on the variety of dahlia (typically, the larger the flower, the further apart). Before planting, spray the plants with a systemic insecticide, and make sure they are well watered. Dig out a hole big enough to take the rootball comfortably. If the soil is heavy, place two or three handfuls of garden compost or leafmould into the planting hole to improve the soil's moisture-holding capacity and help the plants to become established. Plant firmly,

---

DAHLIAS – STAKING

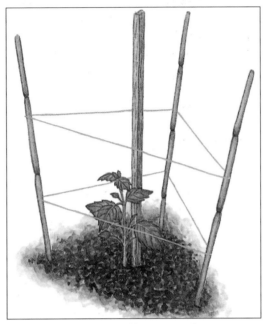

Non-bedding varieties of dahlia require staking. Position the supports before planting. Use either one central 1.5 m (5 ft) stake or three bamboo canes. Loop string around the canes as the plant grows. Both options are shown here.

---

leaving a saucer-shaped depression around the plant to collect any rainwater; the depression also helps the water get to the roots. Water thoroughly in dry weather with a hose or watering can.

● Caring for cuttings

Make sure that any pots of rooted cuttings being kept in cold frames are well watered, and feed them once a week with liquid fertiliser as the supply in the compost is used up. Examine all plants regularly for aphids and other pests.

FRUIT

Spring frosts can still be very damaging to blossom, especially inland and in colder districts.

Be careful that plants, including trees, do not run short of water. It is vital, when the fruit is setting and immediately afterwards, that there is enough for the fruitlets. If there is not, they are often shed.

Weed control is very important, especially around bush and cane fruits and strawberries. Mulch where possible (*see* April, page 96).

● Apples and pears

Trees planted for less than two years should not be allowed to carry crops or it will stunt their growth. Limit the potential crop by rubbing out flower clusters or removing the fruitlets by hand.

Prune new shoots that are not needed on espaliers, cordons and fans while they are still soft, green and short. Start codling moth control in apples and, to a lesser extent, pears (*see* Pests, page 399). In the average garden, where there are just a few trees, pheromone traps will help to control the moth population without spraying.

● Plums and cherries

Carry out the same procedure for controlling red plum maggot (plum fruit moth) as for codling moth (*see* Apples and Pears), but with a different trap. Watch out for aphids, especially the leaf-curling plum aphid and the mealy plum aphid. Both prefer the ends of shoots. They make the leaves curl downwards and exude honeydew which falls on to lower leaves, encouraging a sooty mould to form. Spray with a suitable insecticide.

Cut out any unwanted new shoots on fan-trained cherries while they are still soft and green.

FRUIT – THINNING YOUNG APPLES

Do not let young apple trees bear a heavy crop of fruit too early. Limit the potential crop by thinning the number of developing fruits at an early stage. Older trees are usually thinned later when the fruits are larger.

● Peaches and nectarines

When the fruitlets on fan-trained trees are about the size of a hazelnut, single and thin them, if necessary, to leave one fruitlet every 10 cm (4 in). If they are any closer, the size will suffer (*see* June, page 152).

Watch out for attacks of red spider mite near the end of the month and greenfly at any time (*see* Pests, pages 396 and 402).

Prune shoots on fan-trained trees so that they develop the desired shape.

● Cane fruits

Tie in new canes as they grow from the stools (clump of roots) of blackberries and hybrid cane fruits. This year's fruiting canes will have been trained along horizontal wires above the stool either last summer or earlier this spring. Tie the new year's canes in

vertically above the stool to the same wires. This keeps them largely separate from the fruiting canes and less likely to be infected by any diseases that may affect the plant.

Maintain weed control round raspberries by either hoeing or applying a suitable weedkiller. Do both with care (*see* Weed Control, pages 414–416) as raspberries are shallow-rooting.

● Gooseberries

To encourage large fruits on dessert varieties remove alternate berries towards the end of the month. These early fruits can be used for pies or stewing. Watch for sawfly larvae and control powdery mildew (*see* Pests and Diseases, pages 403 and 410).

● Strawberries

Cover the ground under the plants with straw, or a proprietary equivalent, such as strawberry mats, before the fruit trusses begin to bend with the weight of the fruit. This stops the berries being mud-splashed and helps to discourage slugs.

Once the first white petals form take steps to deter grey mould (botrytis) (*see* Diseases, page 407).

Remove the flower buds from perpetual (autumn-fruiting) varieties until the end of the month. This will delay fruiting until August or even later into the autumn.

Plants being forced under glass will be fruiting towards the end of the month. Continue to feed and water them (*see* March, page 66).

● Vines

Stop the tips of fruiting shoots once they have produced two leaves beyond the flower truss. Tie these shoots to the training wires. Stop non-fruiting shoots at just one leaf.

FRUIT – VINES

When a lateral fruiting shoot of a vine has produced a satisfactory flower truss, stop the growing tip two leaves beyond the truss. This will keep the growth compact and stop the vine producing excessive foliage.

Guard against powdery mildew on vines in the greenhouse (*see* Diseases, page 410).

FUCHSIAS

TENDER AND HALF-HARDY
● Feeding and watering

Feed now, at each watering, with very weak, high-nitrogen fertiliser – fuchsias are heavy feeders.

● Potting on

Pot on fuchsias when new roots protrude through drainage holes. Different varieties have considerably different rates of growth: 'Countess of Aberdeen' and 'Chang', for example, may be happy in 9 cm (3½ in) pots, but a more vigorous variety such as 'Celia Smedley' may require a 15 cm (6 in) pot.

Routine care

Check plants every other day to see if they need watering and continue spraying with water until bud stage. Check for pests also. Turn pots regularly to keep the plants growing symmetrically.

Keep the greenhouse well ventilated and damp down regularly. To grow fuchsias successfully under glass you need a warm, humid environment. Take care to shade young growth from direct sun.

Triphylla hybrids

The *Triphylla* hybrids, which have clusters of long-tubed flowers, resent excessive moisture, so keep these plants on the dry side. They also need a longer period of growth after their final stopping, so allow at least 12 weeks from final stopping to the time the flowers will be at their best and most prolific.

Stopping and training

Pinch out bush plants when the new shoots each have two pairs of leaves (*see* April, page 98). This will produce a sturdy well-shaped plant with the maximum number of flowers.

Stopping fuchsias delays the flowering: singles will be at their best 60 days after the final stopping; semi-doubles 70 days and doubles 80 days.

Young standards will now be growing rapidly; make sure they are properly staked, the cane should always be higher than the top growth. The main stem will probably now be tall enough to make a miniature standard, so you can start pinching out to form the head (*see* June, page 154).

Hardening off

Gradually harden off hanging baskets and any fuchsias that will be planted outdoors in beds or containers before moving them outside next month.

HARDY

Feed newly shooting plants with a nitrogenous fertiliser and keep the base free of weeds.

Plant out new hardy varieties in mild areas, but wait until June in most areas (*see* June, page 154).

GARDEN MAINTENANCE

Maintaining paving and brickwork

Remove general dirt and grime by scrubbing with washing powder (wear gloves) and hosing down with water. Hire a high-pressure hose to remove moss and algae. Wear goggles and do not direct the hose at any loose mortar or you will dislodge it. Alternatively, use a mosskiller without added fertiliser to remove moss, algae and lichen.

GREENHOUSES & FRAMES

Shading, humidity and ventilation

On warm, sunny days provide shade for plants, seedlings and cuttings.

Increase the humidity by damping down the staging and floor. Provide adequate ventilation, but do not open side or top ventilators on the windward side of the greenhouse on windy days.

Watering and feeding

Give the plants plenty of water, and feed vigorous plants weekly with liquid plant food.

Controlling pests and diseases

As weather conditions improve, introduce the predator *Encarsia formosa* to control whitefly (*see* Pests, page 405). You may need to make two introductions to build up its numbers sufficiently to keep the whitefly population under control.

GREENHOUSE SHADING

In winter and early spring, you need as much light as possible in the greenhouse, but from late spring and throughout the summer, shading is the most important consideration. Shading helps prevent the delicate leaves of seedlings from being scorched and stops the greenhouse from overheating.

The best form of shading is provided by external automatic blinds that roll up or down as necessary. These give variable control, and work more efficiently because they cut down the sun's heat before it has a chance to be intensified through the glass. They are more expensive than manual ones.

Shading nets, which let plenty of light through but have a filtering effect, are relatively inexpensive and can be fixed inside the glass (like winter insulation), or draped over the outside and anchored in position. They are not so good at reducing temperature.

Shading washes are inexpensive and easy to paint on to the outside of the glass. Some become more translucent when wet, allowing extra light through on rainy days. A further application of wash may be necessary as the season progresses.

Sowing cinerarias

Towards the end of the month sow cineraria seeds. This will produce plants that will flower indoors from December onwards. Sow the seeds thinly in pans of John Innes seed compost, cover lightly with compost, and germinate at a temperature of 10–13°C (50–55°F). Prick out the seedlings into a seed tray as soon as they are large enough to handle and keep them watered and shaded.

Planting out

In mild areas plant out any vegetables raised in the greenhouse once they have been hardened-off. Half-hardy bedding plants can also be planted out; many will be suitable for hanging baskets and containers.

GREENHOUSES & FRAMES – STOPPING CUCUMBERS

1 Pinch out the male flowers on those cucumbers that produce male and female flowers. Females (shown left) have an embryo fruit behind the bloom. Pollination adversely affects the flavour.

2 Cucumbers with male and female flowers should also have the growing tips of sub-laterals (sideshoots off the sideshoots) pinched out two leaves beyond their first fruit.

STOPPING MELONS

Pinch out the growing tip of a young melon plant when it has formed four or five leaves. This will encourage it to produce more shoots and help to form a compact plant.

Move outside roses that have been forced in containers when they have finished flowering.

● Taking softwood cuttings

Take softwood cuttings of suitable herbs, shrubs and perennials; take semi-ripe cuttings of clematis.

● Cucumbers

Sow seed as soon as possible if this has not been done (*see* April, page 100). Stop laterals growing from the main stems of cucumbers at two leaves beyond the first or second fruit, unless they are the much preferred all-female flowered type which do not make laterals and which fruit on the main stem. Cucumbers with male and female flowers will also need subsequent sub-laterals pinched out as soon as they have made two leaves beyond their first fruit. Remove all male flowers (those without an embryo fruit) and tendrils.

● Melons

Sow seed as soon as possible if this has not already been done (*see* April, page 100).

Plant out any melons raised from seed sown in April into cold frames, one plant to each frame light. Set each plant on a mound of soil mixed with well-rotted compost. Pinch out the growing point when the plant has developed four or five leaves. Avoid splashing or damaging the main stem at soil level, or damping off may occur.

● Peppers and aubergines

Transplant young plants into their final positions when they are 10 cm (4 in) tall: a greenhouse border, growing bags or 20 cm (8 in) pots are all suitable sites. Pinch out the growing tips to encourage a bushy habit. Stake tall varieties. Water in and damp down the greenhouse floor to keep the humidity high.

● Tomatoes

Twist the stems of cordon tomato plants round the supporting strings, or tie them to the canes, and remove sideshoots regularly. Feed the plants every week or ten days from the time the fruits on the first trusses begin to swell, using a high-potash fertiliser.

In a cold greenhouse, plant tomatoes in the border, in growing bags, or in bottomless containers on a gravel base using the ring culture method (*see* April, pages 100 and 101).

● Vines

Continue to guard against powdery mildew throughout the growing season (*see* Diseases, page 410). Thin and train in new shoots (*see* page 132).

HEATHERS

● Mulching

For maximum effect, a mulch on the heather bed should be at least 2.5 cm (1 in) deep and be applied when the soil is damp (*see* The soil in your garden, page 392–393). Use sphagnum moss peat, peat substitute, cocoa shells or fine composted bark chippings. Very large chippings look out of place with heathers, so use small, 10 mm (½ in), chippings if possible. Black plastic sheeting is also a good mulch as it prevents evaporation and inhibits weed germination. To make it look more acceptable, cover the sheeting with a thin layer of soil. Avoid mulching with stones or grit as these reflect too much heat which does not suit heathers.

● Weeding heather beds

Heathers will smother annual weeds but perennial weeds must be removed to ensure a low-maintenance heather bed. Hand weed the bed thoroughly or use

GREENHOUSES – TRAINING CORDON VINES

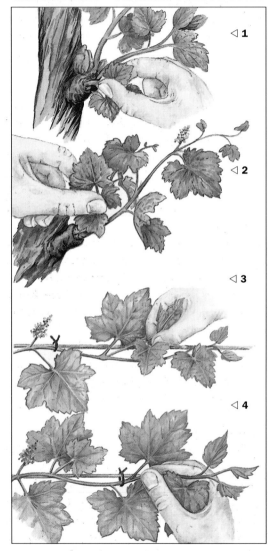

(1) Thin new shoots in stages, first to two shoots. (2)Then thin to one, leaving the strongest. (3) Train this shoot to the wire. (4) Pinch out the growing tip two leaves beyond the first bunch of flowers. Pinch out the tips of sideshoots.

a systemic spot weedkiller on individual weeds (*see* Weed Control, page 415).

● Pruning winter-flowering heathers

Complete pruning of winter-flowering heathers: those not pruned by the end of this month should be left until next year to avoid the loss of winter flowers (*see* April, page 101).

● Watering and feeding

Continue to water young plantings regularly and potted-up plants daily if necessary. Use rainwater if possible (*see* April, page 101). Heathers may be fed once this month with a liquid tomato fertiliser at half the rate recommended for tomatoes.

● Treating alkaline soils

If heathers start to show abnormal yellowing of the foliage this is an indication that the soil is too alkaline (*see* December, page 279). Test the pH of the soil and water the heathers with chelated iron (sequestrene), following the manufacturer's instructions.

HERBS

● Sowing seeds outdoors

Make further sowings of salad herbs (*see* March, page 70). At this time of year chervil, coriander and parsley are best sown in semi-shade and damp soil to produce a succession of tender leaves. A hot, dry place in the garden will encourage the plants to bolt.

Thin out seedlings of herbs sown in April to allow room for the plants to develop.

● Planting out young herbs

Small plants from early indoor sowings may be hardened off and planted out if the weather is suitable (*see* March, page 70). Make certain that the soil is moist, and water frequently until the plants are established. Protect if late frosts are forecast.

● Layering thyme

Thyme is available in an immense range of useful and beautiful varieties. It rarely grows true from seed, so the best way to increase your stock is by taking softwood cuttings in the spring, semi-ripe or hardwood cuttings with a heel in the summer or by layering (*see* Propagation, pages 428–433).

Layer the stems of creeping thyme by burying the runners in fine soil; the tiny roots at each joint will quickly establish themselves and the stems can then be separated from the parent plant.

● Taking softwood cuttings

In late May and early June it is possible to take cuttings 8–10 cm (3–4 in) long from the new season's soft growth of many of the perennial herbs such as bergamot, hyssop, oregano, pot marjoram, rosemary, sage, southernwood, tansy and thyme. Insert the cuttings round the edge of a pot filled with gritty compost or under cloches in open, sandy soil outside (*see* Propagation, page 428). Inspect daily, to ensure that they are not drying out at the roots. Spray with water if the leaves begin to droop.

● Supporting large herbs

Support the soft-topped growth of tall plants with twigs or brushwood (*see* April, page 102).

● Harvesting salad herbs

Harvest the young shoots of herbs such as chives, coriander, fennel and dill. Cut them off with sharp scissors, even if you are not going to use them, as this will encourage new, tender growth.

● Encouraging insect predators

Some herbs encourage predators, such as hoverflies and lacewings, which feed on and reduce the greenfly population. The more decorative of the herbs which have this property, such as chives, marjoram and comfrey, are well worth planting in flower borders as a form of natural pest control. They are also worth planting close to vegetables, such as broad beans, which are vulnerable to blackfly. Both chives and marjoram make attractive edgings for a vegetable bed. They attract many butterflies too – the desirable ones whose caterpillars feed on nettles and other weeds rather than those whose caterpillars feed on cabbages and related vegetables.

● Caring for herbs in containers

Loosen and aerate with a small fork the soil in tubs, pots and windowboxes filled with established plants. Work in a little balanced fertiliser, then top dress with compost or gravel to improve the appearance and conserve moisture on hot days.

Clump-forming herbs that have been in the same container for several years may require dividing. Shrubby plants that have outgrown their pots or tubs may benefit from repotting into larger pots.

Hanging baskets of herbs should now be hardened off outside (*see* Containers, page 127). Plant up new baskets if this was not done in April.

● Basil

Basil should now be growing rapidly. Pot on into large pots of rich compost. If the weather is hot give a light overhead spray of water during the day, but ensure that the leaves are dry by nightfall. Remove flowers as they appear, and trim off the ends of the sideshoots for use in the kitchen. Feed once a week with a weak solution of liquid fertiliser.

HOUSE & CONSERVATORY PLANTS

● Watering and feeding

Increase watering and feed as plants start into vigorous growth. Water weekly or daily depending on the weather and the amount of water the plants need. Give plants a weekly liquid feed, unless you used a slow-release fertiliser earlier in the year.

● Shading, ventilation and humidity

Ensure the conservatory is well ventilated and shaded at all times, especially when it is sunny. Roller blinds are visually more acceptable than a shading wash for a conservatory, and they are also easily adjusted to suit the light intensity.

To increase the humidity, set out some shallow trays of water in inconspicuous spots.

● Moving plants outdoors

Temperatures inside a conservatory often get very high during the summer and many plants will grow and flower better if they are placed outside over the summer months. A sheltered spot on a patio is ideal for many plants, otherwise find a sheltered part of the garden. Remember to water and feed them regularly and check for pests and diseases. Remove plants from south-facing windowsills until the end of summer, as the conditions will be too hot for most plants except desert cacti and other succulents.

● Healthy leaves

Remove dead leaves. Clean remaining leaves (*see* February, pages 42–43) and check for sun scorch, which occurs when the sun's rays are magnified through unshaded glass. This is particularly likely with some kinds of patterned glass where the pattern concentrates the rays.

● Supporting plants

Tie in tips of plants such as rhoicissus. Wherever tall, single-stemmed plants, such as ficus or fatshedera, outgrow their supporting canes, remove the canes and replace with taller ones.

● Controlling pests and diseases

Check frequently for the presence of aphids, whitefly, red spider mite and scale insects. A daily misting will help prevent red spider mite infestation.

If plants are infested with leaf mealy bugs, pick the bugs off by hand. If root mealy bugs are a problem, tip the plant out of its pot, wash away the compost, remove the affected roots and repot the plant in fresh compost.

Check for vine weevil. Tip plants out of their pots regularly, squash any grubs you find and repot. Also check newly purchased plants for grubs.

To deter sciarid fly or fungus gnat, keep the top of the compost dry by covering it with a layer of fine gravel or perlite.

Pick off and destroy leaves affected by mildew, grey mould (botrytis) or leaf spots, reduce the humidity slightly, and use a house plant fungicide if necessary. (*See* Pests and Diseases, pages 394–411.)

● Flowering plants

Remove dead leaves and flowers from azaleas, taking care not to damage the shoots beneath the dead flowers, as they will bear next season's blooms. Azaleas bought as house plants for Christmas or Easter may be pot-bound now, so water well, then repot them into slightly larger pots, using an ericaceous compost. Keep them in a conservatory or cold greenhouse for a few weeks, then move them to a lightly shaded spot in the garden and plunge the pots in holes filled with grit or sand. Water them

PROPAGATING FERNS FROM BULBILS

The fern Asplenium bulbiferum *produces small plantlets from bulbils that form on mature leaves. These will root into the compost if the leaves are pegged down flat. Pot each plant up individually once it is well rooted.*

daily to start with and don't let the soil dry out.

Repot poinsettias after their rest period, water and, once growth has started, feed weekly with a liquid feed (*see* Fertilisers, page 390).

● Propagating from bulbils
The fern, *Asplenium bulbiferum,* produces small bulb-like growths (bulbils) on its leaves. To propagate from these, peg the leaf down on to a tray of compost into which they can root. Pot up individually into 8 cm (3 in) pots once they have rooted.

● Indoor bulbs and corms
Continue to water plants in flower such as lachenalias

and vallotas and apply a liquid fertiliser as necessary. Cyclamen will die back and then require less water.

After hippeastrums have finished flowering and the foliage has died back, cut off any remaining leaves cleanly above the neck and store the bulbs in their pots in a cool room until next spring.

● Climbers and feature plants
Add a supporting framework as plants grow, and tie in unruly growth (*see* April, page 104).

● Bromeliads
Water freely, give them a foliar feed monthly and mist air plants daily (*see* March, page 71).

Shade forest bromeliads from direct sunlight or they will be scorched. Most bromeliads need good light to produce the best leaf markings.

● Cacti and other succulents
Take cuttings when there is plenty of new growth (*see* April, page 104).

Water well in the growing season, allowing the compost to dry out between waterings. Apply a tomato feed at half strength once a month.

Keep Christmas and Easter cacti away from direct sunlight.

● Orchids
Water so the compost is moist but not soaking wet. Feed with a high-nitrogen feed at half strength every other watering.

To increase humidity during dry, bright spells, spray orchids with clean tepid water using a hand-held mister. Stand slipper orchids (*Paphiopedilum*) and moth orchids (*Phalaenopsis*) on a gravel tray and keep the gravel moist to provide them with extra humidity.

IRISES

Standard, dwarf and intermediate bearded irises, and Dutch and Spanish irises, will flower this month, followed by Pacific Coast (Californian hybrid) irises and tall bearded irises at the end of the month.

● After flowering
Pinch out the dead flowers from intermediate and tall bearded irises to allow the new buds to open fully. When flowering is over, cut off the flowering stems of all bearded irises close to rhizome level, otherwise ants may use the base of old stem leaves to 'farm' their aphids, which suck the sap from the plant and carry viruses. Dust the cut surface of the rhizome with a suitable fungicide if the weather is damp, but if it is warm and sunny let the rhizome dry naturally in the sun.

● Controlling pests and diseases
Check bearded irises for leaf spots or rusts during wet weather. Check also for ants' nests in clumps of *Iris sibirica* and similar species with underground rhizomes, as the nests will separate the roots from the soil and damage the plants. Watch for aphids on the base of leaf fans (*see* Pests, page 395).

● Staking
In windy, exposed gardens, tall varieties of irises may need supporting. To protect a large clump, insert bamboo canes around the group and link the canes with soft garden twine. An alternative is to use plastic-covered linking stakes. When inserting supports be careful not to damage the roots.

If particular plants are vulnerable, or individual flowers are required for a show, tie single flower stems to canes.

LAWNS

● Raking and scarifying

Where thatch or dead moss are a continuing problem, scarify the lawn lightly using a spring-tined rake (*see* March, page 72).

● Controlling weeds

Treat large-leaved weeds, such as dandelions and plantains, with a stick touch weeder or dig them out by hand. If hand weeding, use one of the specialised weeding tools or a knife to get the roots out (*see* Tools and Equipment, page 436). Remove all pieces of taproots, as many weeds regrow from small pieces left in the ground. Fill any holes with sifted soil or compost. You can treat small patches of weed with a spot weeder without using chemicals over the whole lawn.

Patches of coarse grass will spoil the look of the lawn but cannot be eradicated with selective lawn weedkillers. You can weaken these coarse grasses if you keep cutting out the clump with a knife. In severe cases, it is best to kill that patch of lawn completely with a total systemic weedkiller and then reseed it (*see* March, page 72 and Weed Control, pages 418–419).

● Controlling red thread

Red thread is common in summer and autumn on lawns that lack nitrogen. It shows as patches of mottled, light brown grass and, on closer inspection, you will see pink or red threads of the fungus. Apply a lawn fungicide if conditions are not too dry, or a lawn fertiliser to promote lawn growth.

● Mowing

Continue to mow once or twice a week. If you have a powered machine, change the direction of mowing occasionally to prevent a ripple effect (washboarding) on the lawn. Vary the point on the lawn edge at which you turn the mower, as always turning in the same place will damage the grass.

● Mowing lawns with naturalised bulbs

Begin to cut grass containing naturalised bulbs about six weeks later than other grass, to allow the bulb leaves enough time to build up their reserves for flowering next year. This is essential if you want naturalised bulbs to continue to multiply and flower well in future years.

The first cut on grass where naturalised bulbs have been grown should be high and the height reduced gradually as the season progresses. As the grass is likely to be long, a nylon line trimmer may work more efficiently than a mower for the first cut.

LILIES

● Planting outdoors

Plant out lilies which were temporarily potted up for the winter (*see* November, page 264). Try to avoid too much root disturbance. Water well into their new site. Also plant out any remaining forced bulbs (*see* April, page 107).

● Controlling pests and diseases

Check for lily disease which is worst in still, humid weather (*see* July, page 182). Also watch for lily beetles (*see* Pests, page 401) and other pests, especially on lilies kept under glass.

● Preparing ground for autumn planting

Sites for autumn bulb planting can be prepared any time between now and August. Cultivate the soil deeply, ensure good drainage and try to establish an open-textured, humus-rich soil with some grit incorporated. If you prepare the site early, then you can fill it with annuals which will provide colour before the bulbs are planted out in the autumn.

● Watering lilies in containers

Continue to water well all lilies you are growing in containers and pots.

PELARGONIUMS

● Hardening off

Before planting out, harden off the plants by putting them out during the day, and bringing them in at night when temperatures of 7°C (45°F) or less are forecast. Pelargoniums will only die if they actually freeze, but if they get too cold this retards their growth and may cause discoloration of the leaves.

● Feeding

Plants that are being kept in 9 cm (3½ in) pots either for planting out, or for putting into hanging baskets, need to be fed regularly with a liquid tomato feed. They will now be growing well and soon starve if they are not fed.

● Shading

Protect coloured-leaved and regal varieties from strong sunshine. Some pelargoniums have tricoloured leaves which are particularly delicate as they do not contain much chlorophyll. These varieties can be scorched easily under glass.

● Controlling pests

Check regularly for insect damage, especially that of aphids and whitefly (*see* Pests, pages 395 and 405).

RHODODENDRONS & AZALEAS

● Mulching

Rhododendrons and azaleas, particularly those which have just been planted, benefit from mulching. Add a 5 cm (2 in) deep layer of lime-free organic material, such as leafmould, garden compost or well-rotted manure, around the plants.

● Taking semi-ripe cuttings of azaleas

New azaleas can be propagated by semi-ripe cuttings taken during May, June and early July (*see* Propagation, page 428).

● Rejuvenation pruning

When old rhododendrons and azaleas finish flowering this month, continue the rejuvenation pruning procedure (*see* Pruning, page 421).

● Watering and feeding

In dry conditions, water both newly planted and established plants, spray the foliage and feed once a week with a liquid, high-nitrogen fertiliser (*see* April, page 108).

● Deadheading

Continue to remove dead flowers as more varieties finish flowering (*see* April, page 108).

● Buying plants in flower

The last of the spring flush of flowering takes place in May, although there are a few varieties that flower later in the summer. So there are still rewards from visits to national gardens, garden centres and nurseries. It is important to take extra care when planting new acquisitions so late in the season; keep all plants well watered (*see* March, page 74).

ROCK PLANTS

May is a good month for visiting other gardens, nurseries and garden centres to see what is in flower and to get inspiration for your own garden.

● Controlling weeds

Both rock plants and weeds are growing vigorously now. Remove weeds with a hand fork or small trowel as using a hoe in the rock garden at this time of year may damage the plants.

● Cutting back aubrieta

Cut all aubrieta back hard to promote strong growth. If you don't cut back it will become lanky.

● Dead heading

Cut off dead flowers from any rock plants on a regular basis to encourage a second flowering.

● Feeding and applying top dressing

Some rosette-forming rock plants, such as saxifrages and sedums, will benefit from a feed. Sprinkle a mixture of fine soil, sharp sand and fertiliser, or a simple mixture of John Innes No. 2 potting compost plus sharp sand, between the rosettes, to encourage root growth and thus a tighter cushion.

Add a top dressing which will improve both the nutritional content and the physical make-up of the soil by spreading discarded potting compost plus sharp sand or grit thinly over the ground.

● Cuttings

Check on the development of root cuttings and plant them out in their final positions once they are large enough. Alternatively, grow them on in spare ground and plant out in the autumn or next spring.

● Feeding plants under glass

Feed plants kept in pots in a cold greenhouse every fortnight with a liquid fertiliser such as a high-potash feed recommended for tomatoes. This should be diluted to half strength.

ROSES

● Watering

Container-grown roses can still be planted but they must be kept well watered after planting. Occasionally, bare-root roses (particularly climbers) planted during the winter, will appear to be dormant or dead; a single heavy watering should encourage them into growth.

● Controlling pests

Keep aphids under control as they multiply quickly in the warmer weather. Damage caused by the leaf-rolling sawfly (leaves curling lengthways) may appear on some roses, particularly in old gardens; this is more unsightly than damaging (*see* Pests, pages 395 and 403).

● Roses grown under glass

Move plants outside immediately after flowering.

SWEET PEAS

● Training cordons

Complete restricting the growth on cordon-grown plants as early as possible this month and continue to tie the stems in to their canes as they grow, using raffia, garden twine or galvanised wire rings 3 cm (1½ in) diameter (*see* April, page 110).

Continue to pinch out sideshoots and tendrils as they appear, remembering to leave the top sideshoot.

Pinch out the first few flower stems while they are tiny, but leave the little stems, bearing four buds, which will soon appear.

TREES, SHRUBS & HEDGES

● Completing spring planting

Try to finish planting all your shrubs this month. Small numbers may still be planted throughout the summer if the weather is not too hot and dry and if plants are watered regularly, but it is now preferable to wait until the wetter weather in September.

Continue to water newly planted trees and shrubs. In addition, spray new foliage each evening to prevent it drying out.

● Softwood cuttings

Softwood cuttings are those taken from new shoots produced in mid to late spring. They should be firm enough to handle, but not yet fully ripe (*see* Propagation, page 428).

If the leaves are larger than about 2.5 cm (1 in) long, remove all but the top two leaves to reduce moisture loss. If the cuttings are taken in late spring and are woody at the base, dip them in a rooting hormone to help break down the outer skin and stimulate root development.

Rooting in a propagator should take about two to three weeks. Once roots are well developed, shoots will emerge from the upper two leaf buds. Pot up the rooted cuttings into individual 8 cm (3 in) pots containing a general potting compost. Over the next two weeks or so, shorten the new young sideshoots by half to encourage a bushy branching habit in the new plant.

It is worth trying to propagate many different shrubs in this way: hebes, helianthemums and lavateras are particularly successful, as are many of the grey-leaved Mediterranean shrubs, such as phlomis, Russian sage (*Perovskia atriplicifolia*) and santolina, and the decorative versions of shrubby herbs such as artemisias and sages.

HEDGES
● Completing spring planting

Finish planting all container-grown hedging plants. Water newly planted hedges in hot, dry weather, concentrating on the rootball of each plant.

● Hedge trimming

Start to clip hedges of privet and *Lonicera nitida*. This should be done regularly every one or two months from now until late summer.

HEDGES – SHAPING

▽ 1 ▽ 2 ▽ 3 ▽ 4

(1) The second winter after planting, cut back the summer's growth by half, and shape. (2) The following summer cut the new growth back several times to encourage the plants to shoot from the bottom. Taper the sides towards the top.

(3) In succeeding years, keep the sides trimmed but allow the height to increase gradually until the hedge finally reaches the height you want. Then trim the top. (4) From then on trim both the top and sides as necessary.

VEGETABLES

It is by no means essential to grow all vegetables from seed. If you want only a couple of tomato plants or a few lettuces, then buy plants from a garden centre rather than raise lots of unwanted plants. Tomatoes, courgettes and marrows are usually sold singly in pots, brassicas and lettuces in trays or strips. Look for fresh, healthy plants but don't buy tender vegetables too early unless you can keep them somewhere frost-free.

Give the ground a good soaking a day or two before planting out your own or purchased seedlings and water the young plants in their pots before transplanting. In very hot spells, plant in the late afternoon when it is cooler.

VEGETABLES – SUPPORTING BEANS

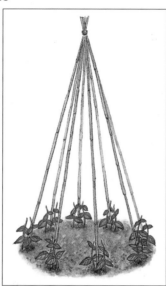

This is the traditional method of supporting runner or climbing French beans grown in the kitchen garden or on an allotment.

A wigwam of canes may be more appropriate if you only want to grow a few plants or wish to grow them at the back of a flower border.

This alternative wigwam will accommodate more plants, but growth can become very congested as the plants reach the tops of the canes.

● Beans

Continue to sow and plant out broad beans (*see* April, page 112). In mild areas plant out the first dwarf French and runner beans 15 cm (6 in) apart, after hardening them off. Alternatively sow directly outdoors, planting two seeds every 15 cm (6 in). Remove the weaker one if both survive. Dwarf French beans should not need support but you can use small twigs or canes and string to hold the plants upright and help keep the pods off the ground. In colder areas, sow French and runner beans in pots in a propagator early this month.

Erect supports for all climbing runner beans.

● Brassicas

Plant out summer brassicas started in pots, once they have been hardened off (*see* April, page 112).

Continue to sow calabrese and summer cauliflower for a succession of crops throughout the summer. Sow autumn/winter cabbage directly into the ground, and sprouting broccoli, kale and autumn cauliflower in pots if this was not done last month (*see* March, page 80).

In very mild areas, winter cauliflowers are worth trying. These are sown this month, transplanted four to six weeks later, and will produce heads from March to May next year.

If you are planting quick-growing crops, such as lettuces, radishes and turnips, in between the slow-growing main crop of winter brassicas, space the brassicas slightly wider apart and water the vegetable patch more than usual in dry spells.

● Sowing carrots and parsnips

Continue sowing early carrots to harvest when young through the summer (*see* February, page 48). This is the last month to sow parsnips (*see* March, page 81).

● Celery

Prick out seedlings of self-blanching celery into individual pots and grow on at 13–15°C (55–60°F). Give an occasional liquid feed and keep them moist. Gradually harden them off in a cold frame. When the seedlings have five or six leaves, they are ready for planting out. Grow self-blanching celery in a block of at least 16 plants, spaced 25 cm (10 in) apart. Water plants and apply a liquid feed regularly.

VEGETABLES – CELERY

Ordinary celery varieties are usually grown in rows, but self-blanching kinds should be planted in blocks so that plants help shield each other from the light as they mature. This helps to keep the stems pale.

GROWING VEGETABLES IN CONTAINERS

You don't need an allotment or vegetable patch to grow your own vegetables. Growing vegetables in containers on the patio or other paved area gives all gardeners the opportunity to harvest fresh, home-grown produce even where space is limited.

Another benefit of growing vegetables in containers is that it reduces any potential problems with soil-borne pests and diseases or with impoverished soil. For example, outdoor cucumbers need a well-drained, rich soil; raising them in growing bags saves having to prepare this. However, it must be stressed that all vegetables grown in containers will need watering and feeding regularly if you are to get reasonable yields.

The larger the container you use to grow vegetables in the better. A 25 cm (10 in) pot is the minimum size and it must have drainage holes. Cover these with old crocks or stones. Filling large containers with compost can be expensive. Use growing bags as a cheap source of compost; they can be used for tomatoes and cucumbers as a first crop followed by a second crop of lettuces or radishes.

Tall vegetable crops, including most tomatoes and trailing varieties of cucumber, will need support, so grow them next to a wall, fence or trellis.

If the containers are on a patio, make the planting as attractive as possible by growing plants with coloured leaves and stems such as ruby chard or red lettuce.

Opt for dwarf varieties (sometimes called 'mini-veg' in the seed catalogues) and quick-growing crops such as radishes, spring onions and lettuce.

Most plants are best started off in small pots. You can then plant out the best seedlings into the containers and keep a few spares for filling in the gaps.

Vegetables in containers can be planted much closer than generally recommended as liquid feeding will supply the extra nutrients and the crops will be picked young, before they compete too much with each other for light. Use a balanced liquid feed for leafy crops and a high-potash tomato feed for fruiting crops.

Above: It is surprising what can be grown in containers – here loose-leaf lettuces and mini tomatoes grow in a hanging basket!

Above right: Be prepared to improvise with containers – this tub holds plenty of compost to support vigorous runner beans.

Right: Where the appearance does not matter, put old, plastic containers not suitable for flower displays to good use.

● **Marrows, courgettes, squashes and pumpkins**

Harden off courgettes, marrows, pumpkins and squashes grown from seed sown last month, before planting them outside. Make sure that all danger of frost has passed before putting them outdoors.

Dig a hole for each plant about 30 cm (12 in) wide and deep. Fill with a mixture of soil and well-rotted organic matter. Use any spare soil to form a mound; this will direct water away from the stem and prevents stem rot. Allow 1 m (3 ft) between plants in each direction for the bush types, 1.2 m (4 ft) for trailing types; pumpkins require up to 3 m (10 ft). Protect young plants from cold winds for the first couple of days by covering them with a bottomless bucket or box and putting a sheet of glass over the top. Do not let the soil in the planting hole become dry, but do not water too much early on as this just encourages leafy growth. Soak the plants once a week when they start flowering.

In colder areas, start courgettes, marrows, pumpkins and squashes off in pots in a propagator (*see* April, page 113). Sow them four weeks before the anticipated date of the last frost.

● **Onions**

Plant onion sets if this has not yet been done (*see* March, page 81).

● **Other roots and swollen stems**

Continue sowing beetroot to provide crops throughout the summer (*see* March, page 81).

Prick out seedlings of celeriac and treat them as you would celery seedlings (*see* page 138).

Continue sowing kohlrabi if you want a succession during the summer (*see* March, page 81). Harvest the first kohlrabi, pull the swollen stems as required before they reach tennis-ball size.

● **Peas**

Continue sowing peas for a succession of crops throughout the summer (*see* February, page 48).

● **Potatoes**

Continue to earth up early and maincrop potatoes; cover foliage if frost threatens (*see* March, page 81). Give early potatoes a soaking once a week for good yields. Plant maincrop potatoes (*see* April, page 113).

● **Salad crops**

Plant out lettuces started in pots, once they have been hardened off (*see* March, page 82). Continue sowing lettuces (*see* March, page 82), radishes and spring onions (*see* February, page 49) for fresh vegetables through the summer.

Continue to sow chicory (*see* April, page 113).

● **Spinach and spinach beet**

Continue sowing of spinach and spinach beet for crops throughout the summer (*see* March, page 82).

● **Sweetcorn**

In mild areas plant out sweetcorn started in pots. Harden them off thoroughly and plant out after all danger of frost has passed. Plant sweetcorn in blocks of at least a dozen plants to ensure even pollination of the cobs. Space out the plants about 40 cm (16 in) apart each way. In colder areas, sow sweetcorn in pots in a propagator (*see* April, page 113). Sow the seeds four weeks before the last expected frost date.

● **Tomatoes, peppers and aubergines**

Harden off aubergines, peppers and tomato plants. Plant out from late May onwards or when all danger of frost has passed. Start them off under cloches, or wait until mid June in colder parts of the country.

VEGETABLES – SWEETCORN

Sweetcorn is wind-pollinated so the plants are best set out in blocks rather than rows. This increases the chance of pollen landing on female flowers which in turn means an increase in the yield.

● **Turnips and swedes**

Continue sowing turnips and swedes for a succession of crops (*see* March, page 82).

PERENNIAL VEGETABLES

● **Asparagus**

Continue cutting asparagus; if this is the first year of cutting, stop by the end of May.

● **Globe artichokes**

Plant out globe artichokes. Allow a square metre (square yard) for each plant and dig in plenty of well-rotted organic matter.

WATER PLANTS & POOLS

● **Planting aquatics**

Continue to plant all types of water plants this month (*see* April, page 114). In most seasons, tender, floating plants such as water hyacinth (*Eichhornia crassipes*) and water chestnut (*Trapa natans*) will not be available until the middle of the month. Do not plant out until the water is warm and there is no danger of frost. In cold areas, wait until early June.

● Feeding

Feed established aquatic plants either with a sachet of properly prepared aquatic fertiliser or a slow-release fertiliser tablet. Push the tablet well down into the compost next to the plant, so that the roots can easily take up nourishment and the fertiliser does not leach into the water.

● Spreading algae

Until the leaves of waterlilies are sufficiently large and numerous, and the floating plants have grown and multiplied, most of the water surface will be exposed to full light conditions and algae will probably become a nuisance. Free-floating, single-celled algae will turn the water an opaque green colour, while blanketweed produces masses of fine filaments that restrict the growth of other plants underwater by shading them out.

Remove as much blanketweed as possible with a net, roughened stick or by hand. Algicides, sold for pond use, control both green water-discolouring algae and filamentous growths. Remove the algae masses as soon as they turn brown, to prevent them from blanketing other plants and also to prevent any oxygen deficiency in the water. A pool with a suitable complement of submerged oxygenating plants and water surface shade, provided by waterlily and floating plant foliage, is the best way to resolve algal problems permanently, although they may still be a temporary problem in spring. Adding barley straw (available from aquatic centres) to the pond, is

another excellent way to control algae and keep the water clear. Although it is sometimes recommended, never use straight chemicals such as potassium permanganate in garden pools.

● Water evaporation

Warm weather results in considerable water loss by evaporation. Top up the pool using a hosepipe from the tap. Fill little and often, so that wide temperature fluctuations do not occur in the water.

● Waterlily propagation

Propagate waterlilies from 'eyes' (dormant buds) which occur with varying frequency along the root-stocks of mature waterlilies. Remove the eyes with a sharp knife, and dress the cut ends with flowers of sulphur. Insert the eyes individually into small pots of good garden soil or aquatic planting compost. Place the pots in a bowl with the water level just covering the eyes. They will produce young plants which will flower in two or three years.

Waterlilies can also be divided. This is the easiest way to propagate them if you want to raise a small number of plants (*see* April, page 115).

● Propagating marginal plants

Many water plants can be increased from cuttings taken this month (*see* Propagation, page 428). These include brooklime (*Veronica beccabunga*) and water mint (*Mentha aquatica*). Put the cuttings in pots of mud and place in a bowl. Fill the bowl with water so that it just covers the surface of the pots. The cuttings will root very quickly.

Clumps of established plants, such as pickerel weed (*Pontederia cordata*), flowering rush (*Butomus umbellatus*) and cotton grass (*Eriophorum angusti-folium*) are easily increased by division now

WATER PLANTS – WATERLILIES

To pot up the buds that form along waterlily rhizomes, first cut them off with a sharp knife and then dip the cut ends in flowers of sulphur. Place them in pots filled with garden soil or aquatic compost and cover the pots with water.

(*see* Propagation, page 431). Select the youngest and most vigorous outer portions for replanting.

● Floating plants

Place new and overwintered hardy floating plants on the surface of the water.

● Bog garden

Prick out seedlings of spring-sown bog plants, such as primulas, into seed trays using a good potting compost. Place the pricked-out seedlings in a light, airy place out of direct sunlight. Weed the bog garden regularly throughout this month.

Containers for Your Garden

Containers can add so much to your garden. They can be used to brighten the smallest paved yard or to create a focal point on a large expanse of lawn. Choose, plant and position them with care and they will be a centre of colour and interest throughout the year.

BUYING NEW CONTAINERS

There is an enormous range of pots and planters from which to choose, but before you buy, it is important to think about how you will be using the container. Pots for outdoor use need drainage holes (it is easy to drill through plastic; terracotta needs more care and a masonry bit). The larger the container the more compost it will hold, giving plants greater protection against drying out in summer or freezing solid in winter. However, once planted, a large container is heavy to move.

Containers with narrow necks are not recommended for permanent plantings, as the only way to repot an overgrown plant will be by breaking the pot. However, a plastic pot filled with trailing plants can be lodged in the top of a narrow-necked container and replaced each season. Many large 'Ali Baba' style pots look good as a feature in their own right without plants inside. Avoid pots with a narrow base as these tend to be unstable and can be knocked or blown over.

Always check whether terracotta pots are guaranteed frost proof. Many are imported from Mediterranean countries where frost damage is not a problem. Left out in a British winter, they may flake and crack. Glazed clay pots are more resilient than terracotta. Reject any pots with hairline cracks, chips or bubbles in the glaze, as this is where frost will get in and cause damage.

Matt plastic reproductions of terracotta pots provide excellent lightweight alternatives. They are easier to move around when planted and less vulnerable to frost and drying out. Make sure plastic pots are resistant to ultraviolet damage. Thin-walled plastic pots will become brittle in time, especially if exposed to strong sunlight.

WOODEN CONTAINERS

Wooden containers have the advantage of insulating plant roots against extremes of heat and cold. They range from half-barrels to elegant Versailles boxes. Wood needs more maintenance than other materials and, if left untreated, will rot. Therefore check over wooden containers before planting up and, if necessary, repaint using exterior quality microporous paint or varnish, or treat with a plant-friendly preservative stain (never creosote which will harm the plants). Their life expectancy will be further increased if you paint the inside with a waterproofing agent or line them with plastic sheeting. Pull the plastic through the drainage hole and cut it to allow water to drain away.

All containers, and wooden containers in particular, must be raised slightly off the ground to facilitate drainage. If they do not have integral feet, use bricks or purpose-made clay feet.

HANGING BASKETS AND WINDOWBOXES

Consider safety and convenience when siting a hanging basket. The weight of a basket full of plants and wet compost is considerable. Ensure brackets are the correct size to hold a fully laden basket and fix them securely into brick walls (not the mortar) using wall plugs and long screws. Hang baskets in a sheltered position, out of the wind, and where they will not be a nuisance. Remember trailing plants can grow very long. If you have to hang the basket up high, consider using a pulley system for easy watering.

The same considerations apply to windowboxes. Make sure a sill is strong enough to bear the weight of the container. As an added safety measure, choose a lightweight box made of plastic or wood, rather than terracotta or stone. Fill it with a soilless compost, with polystyrene chips providing the

▶ *Attractive Grecian style containers like this were once carved from stone but nowadays they are usually cast from concrete or reconstituted stone.*

▼ *A terracotta strawberry pot can be planted with strawberries, herbs, or trailing plants. It is an interesting shape and is designed to be featured on a patio.*

drainage layer at the bottom. Boxes above ground floor level should be secured to the wall with bolts or heavy gauge wire.

A drip tray will protect brickwork and masonry, as well as people passing below during watering. Alternatively, do not make drainage holes but line the windowbox with plastic sheeting and place a generous layer of coarse gravel or polystyrene chips on top to provide free drainage.

Even without windowledges, you can still have windowboxes. Fix two or three strong metal brackets to the outside brickwork to support the drip tray that will hold the windowbox. Look for specially designed wall brackets with an upward facing safety lip.

TIPS FOR SUCCESS

- Containers must be clean before you begin planting. If they have been used before, scrub them out and rinse well.
- Soak unglazed terracotta containers for several hours before planting and line them with plastic sheeting. Puncture the bottom of the sheeting so that water can drain through.
- Soilless, multi-purpose composts are ideal for bedding plants, bulbs and other container plantings where the compost is changed regularly. Permanent container plants do best in soil-based composts, unless ericaceous.
- To look good, all containers and hanging baskets must be packed full of plants. If any gaps do appear, fill them immediately with backups kept in reserve, or buy spares from the garden centre.
- Once planting is completed, water the plants and place the container or hanging basket in a shady place out of the wind for a few days to let the plants settle in.
- Never let containers dry out. In hot weather, daily watering is necessary, sometimes twice daily for hanging baskets and small pots. In summer, water in the cool of the early morning or evening, not when the sun is beating down.
- Feeding is essential. Use a slow-release fertiliser or liquid feed regularly. Foliar feeding is also beneficial.
- Deadhead frequently to keep your flowering display going for as long as possible.
- Check plants regularly for any sign of pests or disease and take prompt action.
- In hot, dry spells, mist container plants frequently with water to help prevent red spider mite infestations.

▶ *Old terracotta chimney pots, scrubbed clean, make a great setting for bright flowers. Plastic copies are now widely available.*

▼ *A trough like this, made of genuine or reconstituted stone, makes a perfect miniature rock garden when planted up with a small selection of alpines.*

▼ *The shape of this terracotta urn, with a neck narrower than its body, means it is best used for seasonal displays or as an unplanted ornament.*

▼ *This plastic shrub tub is light and holds plenty of compost. It is subtle enough not to detract from the plant and could be positioned anywhere in the garden.*

▼ *A wooden Versailles box such as this has traditionally been used for orange trees in conservatories, but it would also suit conifers or bay trees. Use a plastic liner to protect the wood.*

JUNE

Gardeners reap the rewards of
their labours this month with
the first vegetables of summer
ready to harvest and the flower
garden in full bloom.

June

Early summer brings the first opportunity for the gardener to relax and enjoy the garden and all its beauty without the danger of a late frost. Most of the hard work of sowing, thinning, pricking out and planting will have been completed by the end of May. Although there are still plenty of routine jobs to be done over the next few months, it is now time to enjoy the sunshine, the flowers and the long evenings.

At the beginning of June, leaves on trees and shrubs still look fresh. The dry, hot days of summer have not yet taken their toll, though prolonged fine weather can often transform gardens and countryside by the end of the month. Lawns, in particular, often start to fade and go brown and, unless you water them copiously which may not always be possible, they will remain parched for the rest of the summer. This should not be a cause for particular concern as lawns recover very quickly when autumn rains arrive.

The weather in June

Although periods of rain are common in June, they are usually followed by bright and sunny days, and temperatures of 26°C (80°F) are not unusual. In many parts of the country, this is often the sunniest month of the year.

June is also a month for thunderstorms which can bring dry spells to an abrupt and violent end. Storms help to keep the garden green and rarely do too much damage to fruit and flowers.

The sun is now quite strong so, with a few exceptions, plants under glass, whether in the greenhouse or on the windowsill indoors, need shading, and in the greenhouse or conservatory good ventilation is important.

Controlling pests and diseases

In the warm, dry weather many pests proliferate. The ever-present pests, such as greenfly and blackfly, breed rapidly, and red spider mite and whitefly can be especially troublesome.

In the greenhouse a combination of biological controls and good gardening practice may alleviate some of the problems. If you are using chemical controls, prompt action, as soon as the first symptoms appear, is the most efficient way to control most pests.

Slugs and snails are difficult to eliminate, but the population can usually be limited by baits and traps, and by picking them off by hand. Be especially vigilant at dusk or after a shower of rain. Biological control is another possibility although it is expensive, has to be repeated and won't eliminate them altogether.

Concentrate your slug and snail control efforts around plants such as hostas and daturas which are most likely to be severely damaged or disfigured.

Diseases are best tackled by a combination of fungicides and good garden hygiene. Pick off and destroy affected leaves as soon as you notice them, assuming there are just one or two, then give the rest of the plant a preventative spray. In this way you may control an outbreak before it becomes established.

Staking

Most border plants should have been staked earlier, so that they are now growing through the supports and hiding them, but plants that need individual canes or stakes, such as delphiniums, may still require staking.

Remember to keep tying individual plants to their canes regularly, or the supports will serve little purpose. This may need to be done weekly during this period of rapid growth.

Keeping weeds at bay

If you applied a thick mulch earlier in the year, weeds should not be too much of a problem but where mulch was not applied there will almost certainly be weeds to control. Pernicious perennial weeds, such as bindweed, may require an application of a chemical weedkiller, but most weed seedlings can be controlled by regular hoeing.

Hoe while the seedlings are still small. If you allow the weeds to become large, they will compete with your plants for light and nutrients, and some (shepherd's purse and groundsel, for example) will flower and shed ripe seed depressingly quickly.

Ground cover

One of the best and most attractive methods of weed control is to plant ground cover. There is a wide choice of flowering and foliage plants that will grow to cover the ground like a carpet and prevent new weeds from germinating by blocking out the light.

Low-growing evergreens, such as bergenias and *Pachysandra terminalis* 'Variegata', do this very effectively; pachysandra is especially useful in shade. Heathers, too, make attractive ground-cover plants for a sunny position but prefer acid soil. Ivies and periwinkles grow well under difficult conditions and are ideal for a large area in a wild or woodland part of the garden.

If you want the colour and beauty that come with herbaceous plants, you can grow a carpet of plants such as lady's mantle (*Alchemilla mollis*), *Geranium endressii* or *G. sylvaticum*. All these have attractive flowers and spreading foliage which will smother most annual weeds when they are likely to be a problem.

Deadheading plants

Deadheading is a tedious task, but some plants repay the effort with prolonged flowering. Pansies, for example, can have a disappointingly short season in the summer if you fail to dead-head them, while regular attention to this task will keep them blooming over many months.

Most plants look better after deadheading. Roses don't always die gracefully and it is better to remove the flowers as the petals drop. The spent flowers of African marigolds, which have large and full blooms, also look unattractive and may become diseased. This detracts from the beauty of the remaining blooms.

It is not practical to remove the dead flower heads from every plant. Those with tiny flowers, such as lobelia, are impractical to deadhead. But if you get into the habit of deadheading as many flowers as possible (unless you want to collect the seeds) you will prolong the display in the garden and this makes the effort worthwhile.

Automatic watering

If you don't have an automatic system for the parts of the garden that need regular watering, this is a good time to install one. Your plants will benefit from it throughout the summer and some systems can be programmed to take care of the watering while you are on holiday. There are many different kinds available, so it is worth looking around several garden centres to find one to suit your needs.

Buying and ordering new plants

June is a good time to visit garden centres. There are usually interesting summer bedding and patio plants to be discovered – either new plants or new varieties of old favourites. Try one or two new plants every summer – an element of experimentation makes your gardening that much more interesting.

Towards the end of June summer bedding plants are often sold off cheaply. These can be bargains if they are still in good condition but if the plants look starved and yellow, or elongated and weedy, they can be a false economy.

Autumn bulb catalogues may be advertised later this month. Send for them now so that you can get your order in early. This will give you the best chance of obtaining the particular varieties that you want.

JOBS THAT WON'T WAIT

- Check regularly to see if plants need water. Hanging baskets and small containers may need watering every day.

- Maintain a programme of weeding and of pest and disease control.

- Sow seeds of fast-maturing annuals, spring-flowering biennials, herbs and vegetables.

- Plant out summer bedding and other seedlings and cuttings. Protect from frost.

- Thin hardy annuals and vegetables sown in the open ground.

- Feed plants in borders if not already done.

- Deadhead flowers unless required for seed.

- Stop chrysanthemums as required.

- Disbud border carnations for larger blooms.

- Ensure the greenhouse and conservatory have adequate shading and ventilation.

- Cut back aubrieta and alyssum in the rock garden immediately after flowering.

- Put nets on the fruit cages over soft fruit. Harvest fruit and vegetable crops as they come into season.

- Complete planting of aquatics this month if you want a display this season.

The Fragrant Year

A successful garden is not just a matter of good design, careful choice of colours and regular care. Vital though these factors are, it is those extra 'finishing touches' that can transform your garden into an enchanting, memorable place. So, whatever your style of gardening, always try to include some plants that will add fragrance to the pleasures of your garden.

You will achieve the most intense fragrance if you grow plants in a warm, sheltered position. Honeysuckles and lilies will have a more intoxicating scent within an arbour or sheltered patio than if they are isolated and exposed to winds. Warm, still air will also enable you to enjoy those delicate scents that you might otherwise miss.

Position fragrant plants where they will be most appreciated. Close by a front door they will welcome visitors. Planted below a window, the scent of tobacco plants or night-scented stocks will waft indoors on warm summer evenings. The following suggestions are just a few of the plants that can make your garden fragrant all year round.

▲ *Ribes odoratum*

▲ *Viburnum carlesii* 'Aurora'

WINTER DELIGHTS

If you have space for a couple of large shrubs, include a witch-hazel (*Hamamelis mollis*), because its spidery yellow flowers are beautiful and wonderfully sweet-scented. Winter sweet (*Chimonanthus fragrans*) also has superbly scented, yellow flowers on bare branches. This plant benefits from the protection of a wall.

One of the very best plants for winter fragrance is a small, compact evergreen which will fit into almost any garden. You will probably smell the small whitish flowers of Christmas box (*Sarcococca humilis*) before you notice them. This modest plant, often reaching no more than 1 m (3 ft) in height, is the honeysuckle of winter.

For a small garden consider some of the scented

▲ *Hamamelis × intermedia* 'Orange Beauty'

▲ *Lonicera periclymenum*

viburnums. *V. × bodnantense* and its varieties have clusters of pink or white flowers, while the white flowers of *V. farreri* are smaller but even more deliciously scented. The large sprays of lemon-yellow flowers of *Mahonia* 'Charity' are striking, even from a distance, and delightfully fragrant too.

SPRING CHARMERS

The scented shrubs of spring are usually ornamental and there are examples to suit gardens both large and small. Many rhododendrons and azaleas are fragrant but others lack scent, so always check before you buy. Lilacs (*Syringa vulgaris*) are outstanding for their perfume, but can become rather tall and straggly unless carefully pruned.

Daphnes are compact enough for most gardens, as bushes seldom grow more than 90 cm (3 ft) tall. The mezereon (*D. mezereum*) is one of the easier species to grow and a particular favourite for spanning the gap between mid-winter and early spring when its purple-red flowers are freely produced.

Many spring-flowering viburnums are fragrant, among them the deciduous *Viburnum. carlesii* and *V. juddii*, and the evergreen *V. × burkwoodii*. For something a little different, try the yellow flowering currant *Ribes odoratum* (syn. *R. aureum*).

Few spring flowers can surpass lily-of-the-valley. Shade-loving, it prefers a moist soil. Another dainty, shade-tolerant plant of spring is the sweet violet, *Viola odorata*, which can be found in flower from winter to the end of spring.

Do not overlook seed-raised plants. The scent of the familiar biennial wallflower is surprisingly strong, especially when in a massed display.

SUMMER SCENTS

Among the woody plants, pride of place has to go to roses and honeysuckles. However, choose them with care; while some are outstanding, others lack

▲ *Phlox paniculata* 'Flamingo'

scent altogether. Among the honeysuckles, all varieties of *Lonicera periclymenum* will please.

Sweet peas are popular summer flowers with an unmistakable scent – again, some varieties are better than others. Scented summer bedding has long included old-fashioned mignonettes, night-scented stocks and ornamental tobacco plants.

Dianthus have much to offer in the way of scent, for this genus contains the pinks, border carnations and sweet williams, many of which are scented. Preferring a more moist soil than dianthus are the border phlox, *Phlox paniculata* and its many varieties. It flowers from mid summer to autumn when its perfume is especially welcome.

There are many plants with aromatic foliage. Lavender and lemon verbena come immediately to mind, as do many herbs: thyme, rosemary, sage, basil, mint. Different mints have different smells; peppermint is familiar, but there is also spearmint, and apple mint.

Like the mints, the aromas of scented-leaved pelargoniums also vary. These may have less showy flowers than their bedding cousins but their foliage can smell variously of lemon, rose, apple and pine, and is often crinkled, cut and variegated.

AUTUMN DAYS

Some of the fragrant plants of summer will continue into autumn for a few weeks, or even a month or two in the case of some roses. However, as the days get shorter, so the scented flowers become smaller and more insignificant than those of high summer.

Of the foliage shrubs the variegated *Elaeagnus pungens* 'Maculata' and *E × ebbingei* 'Gold Edge' are easy to grow and bright to look at. Fragrant small white flowers appear on mature plants.

Vigorous and sometimes evergreen, *Abelia × grandiflora* has pinkish-white flowers from late summer through to November in favourable years, although it lacks the strong fragrance of many summer shrubs. Common myrtle (*Myrtus*

▲ *Choisya* 'Aztec Pearl'

communis), with a similar flowering season, is one of several shrubs with aromatic evergreen foliage which come into their own in the autumn. Others include rosemary, cotton lavender (*Santolina chamaecyparissus*) and Mexican orange blossom (*Choisya ternata*).

JULY

In the heat of summer a shady spot outdoors is the best place to be. A herb garden makes a particularly delightful resting place as the scent of summer herbs drifts through the air.

July

It is high summer and the garden is now full of colour. Summer bedding is often at its best at this time, but if the year is dry the lawn may start to look parched and brown and the leaves on the trees and shrubs no longer look as fresh and green as they did in May and early June.

July can often be hot, too hot to do much physical work during the day, and watering and deadheading will be as much as most people want to do until the cool of the evening.

It is the time of the year when there are fewer jobs needing to be done and many people simply want to relax and enjoy their garden. Try to find time to sit in or walk round your garden to look at the flowers and shrubs, appreciate the foliage, and study the wildlife that a garden always attracts.

This is not the time of year to undertake heavy construction jobs, but if you spend time in the garden you will often get new ideas and can make plans for the future.

You will have more time to relax if you install an automatic watering system. Many are available in kit form from garden centres or by mail order and these are simple to install and can usually be tailored to individual gardens. The initial outlay may seem high but the system should continue working and benefit your garden for many years.

The weather in July

This is often the month that produces the hottest days of the year. It is also unpredictable. In some years, July is very wet, in others you will need to water constantly – assuming there are no watering restrictions – if you want to keep your plants growing well.

Pest and disease problems

In a wet year the combination of high temperatures and moist air can encourage the rapid spread of plant pests and diseases, so you need to keep a careful watch.

Aphids, particularly greenfly and blackfly, multiply rapidly and you can be sure that at any time during the summer there is at least one pest attempting to establish a colony somewhere in your garden.

In a well-planted garden, large enough for plant diversity and with plenty of wildlife, including natural predators, you can often afford to be relaxed about some pests that are not causing too much damage. However, if you grow dahlias or other plants that are susceptible to viruses, you must control aphids and other sap-sucking insects promptly to minimise the risk of diseases being spread.

Other pests, in particular lily beetles and vine weevils, can be a major problem. If your garden is attacked by troublesome pests like these, it is a good idea to use preventative pesticides as a precaution and, in the case of vine weevils, use biological controls as well.

For pest control to work effectively, you need to know exactly which pests are already in your garden, the ones that are likely to occur and the plants that are most vulnerable. You can then take preventative measures. Caring for roses is a good example. They are among the plants often sprayed routinely to avoid pests and diseases from spreading.

Weeding and mulching

If the weather is dry, weed seedlings are unlikely to be a major problem, but in moist, warm spells they can appear almost overnight. Regular hoeing is an efficient way to deal with them, but if you find this a chore, or your garden is large, use a weed-suppressing mulch.

Most plants benefit from a thick organic mulch – or even a sheet mulch – as this helps to conserve moisture. Mulching also improves the look of your beds, for dry soil is often unattractively pale and on clay soil large cracks usually appear as the surface dries out. Chipped bark or a similar decorative mulch, such as cocoa shell, looks much more attractive.

Staking and deadheading

Continue to stake and tie all your plants as it becomes necessary. Both annual climbers and wall shrubs grow at an amazing rate at this time of year, and you will find them much easier to deal with if you tie in new growth on a regular basis. If you make a habit of walking round the garden with a ball of string and a knife in your pocket this task becomes a simple routine rather than a bore.

Most staking should already have been done but inevitably you will find some plants that require a little extra help and support.

Deadheading is easy enough with large

flowers, such as roses, but don't neglect the smaller flowers: pansies and mimulus are among the many plants that will flower for longer if you remove the seed heads before they develop and ripen. Many plants with larger flowers also look much tidier if the dead and dying flowers are removed.

Feeding

By the middle of the summer many plants will need additional nutrients. Even if you added fertiliser to the soil in winter or spring, it is a good idea to feed the garden again at this time of the year, including the shrubs and border plants as well as the so-called 'hungry' plants such as dahlias, sweet peas and roses. Many plants will grow perfectly well without being fed but it is astonishing the difference an application of a general foliar feed or fertiliser can make to your garden.

If feeding is important for plants growing in the soil, it is almost essential if you want your plants growing in containers to flourish, especially if their soil is peat-based or a peat-substitute compost.

If you added slow-release fertilisers to the compost in spring, additional feeding may not be required. Otherwise feed regularly from now on if you have not already been doing so. The reserves of nutrients in many potting composts can be very much depleted within a month or so of planting and, without any supplementary feeding, the plants will grow poorly and probably die earlier.

Garden visiting

Visiting other gardens makes a pleasant trip out and you will always see new planting schemes and bring back ideas to adapt for your own garden. New flowers and plants can be discovered and often purchased.

Water features

Water features in the garden are attractive at any time, but never more so than on a hot summer's day. Bear in mind that a substantial amount of water may be lost from your pond through evaporation, particularly on hot days, so check the level every day or two to ensure the pump is still covered with water. This is especially important with small water features that have a modest reservoir.

If you do not already have a pond, now is a good time to plan the introduction of water features to your garden for the next year. July is not a good month to start building work, as the ground will be hard and dry. Construction can begin once the cooler weather arrives.

You can, however, still enjoy the sight and sound of water instantly by buying a self-contained water feature such as a wall fountain or a patio pond. There is a wide choice available from garden and aquatic centres, or you can order them by mail order from specialist suppliers. Most self-contained water features come as a kit, complete with a pump and any fittings that you require. You should be able to fix a wall fountain or assemble a raised patio pool made from resin in a day.

JOBS THAT WON'T WAIT

- Check regularly to see if plants need water. New plantings, seedlings and plants in containers are all particularly vulnerable and may need water every day. In the vegetable garden leafy plants such as lettuces and spinach, fruiting crops such as tomatoes and marrows, and peas and beans as their pods begin to swell, will all suffer if they don't get enough water.

- Weed and deadhead regularly, checking for pests and diseases at the same time.

- Sow biennials, herbs and vegetables. Plant autumn-flowering bulbs.

- Plant out seedlings and rooted cuttings.

- Disbud appropriate plants for larger blooms.

- Harvest seeds as soon as they are ripe.

- Harvest fruit, vegetables and herbs while they are in prime condition. Freeze, store or give away produce if you cannot use it all immediately.

- Plant Madonna lilies (*Lilium candidum*) as soon as possible.

- Trim and reshape hedges.

- Top up the water in ponds and aerate it if you see fish gasping for oxygen in hot weather, or if fish sensitive to low oxygen levels – such as orfe – start to die.

ANNUALS & BIENNIALS

Constant maintenance of annuals and bedding plants is vital if displays are to remain fresh-looking and continue flowering through to the autumn.

● Watering

Annuals planted or transplanted last month will still need to be watered to help them get established, especially in periods of dry, sunny weather. Water thoroughly so that the moisture penetrates the soil, otherwise surface rooting may occur which will make young plants even more vulnerable to drought.

● Biennials

If you live in a cold part of the country make sure that you have sown biennials for spring flowering by mid July. These include Brompton stocks, forget-me-nots, winter-flowering pansies and polyanthus. Also sow biennials for summer flowering such as honesty (*Lunaria annua*), evening primroses (*Oenothera biennis*) and foxgloves (*Digitalis purpurea*) (*see* June, page 148).

Plants raised in the cold frame last month will be ready to plant out in their flowering positions this month. Thin out overcrowded seedlings in nursery beds or transplant thinnings to grow on elsewhere.

● Encouraging repeat flowering

Plants which produce one main flowering stem, such as antirrhinums, can be encouraged to flower again by removing this stem after flowering. Cut just above the base where sideshoots are developing. Pansies and petunias, which often become rather straggly by July, can be rejuvenated by cutting them right back to the bushier growth at the base. Feed and water well to encourage regrowth.

BORDER PERENNIALS

When the summer flowers reach their peak, enjoy those which have been a success and note down the ones that have proved disappointing or have died. Also look at the plant combinations which have been particularly attractive.

● Planning new beds and borders

Now is the time to decide on the site and size of any new beds, and which and how many plants are required to fill the space. Plot the new area on paper, using scale drawings, and then transfer the drawing to the garden to get a better idea of how it will look in reality. Laying hosepipe on the ground is an excellent way of marking out ground plans.

Preparation can start if the work will not spoil the look of the summer garden. First clear grass and weeds: use black plastic sheeting to exclude light, or apply a systemic weedkiller. Both methods are most effective during active plant growth. If you lift the turf, stack it to rot down or use it in other areas.

After the top growth has been cleared, rotovate the ground or better still dig it by hand. The soil can be left rough for winter frosts to break it down, or can be prepared for autumn planting by digging in well-rotted manure, garden compost or slow-release fertilisers (*see* The soil in your garden, page 387–392). Try to remove all perennial weed roots, especially couch grass and bindweed.

● Harvesting seed

Many seed heads will be ripe and ready for gathering. Choose a dry day as seed may become mildewed if stored when damp. Store dry, cleaned seed in small packages in a sealed box in a refrigerator.

BORDER PERENNIALS – HARVESTING SEED

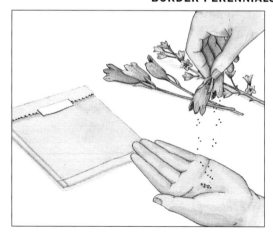

1 Pick seed heads on a dry day and put them in paper bags clearly labelled with the name of the plant. Store the bags in a dry place until the seeds are ready to be shed. Then shake the seeds out ready for cleaning.

2 Use a kitchen sieve or strainer to separate the seeds from any dirt and chaff. Repack the seeds in labelled bags and put them in a sealed box. Store this box in the refrigerator or other cool place until the seeds are to be sown.

Alternatively, seed can be sown straight away in a suitable compost. Many perennials germinate quickly and this gives the seeds a long growing period before winter sets in.

● Staking and deadheading

Cut back old stems and remove supports from plants that have finished flowering. If you are working in a thickly planted, staked area of perennials take care not to disturb nearby plants. Deadhead plants when flowering is over unless you want to save the seeds.

● Watering and feeding

Check any plants not yet established and water them well in dry weather, especially if you garden on light soil. Most perennials need at least one growing season to become established.

Hoe in a quick-acting fertiliser around late-flowering plants such as Michaelmas daisies. These plants may not have benefited from earlier dressings, particularly if they were late starting into growth.

Cut back, water and apply a liquid fertiliser to any plants that produce a second flush of flowers such as lupins and phlox. Long-flowering perennials, such as diascias, will also benefit from this.

● Planting

Container-grown plants, established cuttings and seedlings may still be planted in the garden provided the soil and weather are suitable. Water plants in thoroughly and add fertilisers if needed. Continue to water until the plants are showing new growth.

● Taking cuttings

Continue to take softwood and semi-ripe cuttings of all suitable plants (*see* June, page 149).

BULBS, CORMS & TUBERS

● Lifting and dividing

This is the best month for lifting and dividing spring-flowering bulbs, now that their foliage has shrivelled and turned yellow. Tulips and bedding hyacinths need to be lifted annually, daffodils – grown for cutting – every two or three years. Most other bulbs require dividing and replanting in fresh soil much less frequently, unless you are aiming for show-quality flowers or if the plants have become so crowded that they produce only masses of leaves.

Dig up the bulbs with a spade or fork, inserting it far enough away and deeply enough to get right under the clump. To lift bulbs heeled in earlier (*see* May, page 124), take one end of the netting and give a good sharp tug to bring them all up at once.

Spread the bulbs out to dry in shallow boxes and keep them in a well-ventilated shed.

When the bulbs have dried out thoroughly, remove the dead skin, and cut off the roots and shrivelled leaves. Discard the smallest bulbs, unless you wish to increase your stock. To ensure any diseases present are destroyed, burn or otherwise dispose of rotten or damaged bulbs and the dried debris. Put the dried and cleaned bulbs in trays or boxes, with no more than three or four layers of bulbs in each box. Store them in a cool, dry shed.

Some bulbs, such as narcissi, multiply by offsets (small bulblets which form around the parent bulb). Store these separately, planting them later in a nursery bed until they reach flowering size which will be in two or three years' time.

● Controlling daffodil pests

Eelworms (nematodes) and the grubs of narcissus flies are serious threats to daffodils. If bulbs feel slightly soft, show concentric rings of brown and

BULBS – LIFTING AND STORING

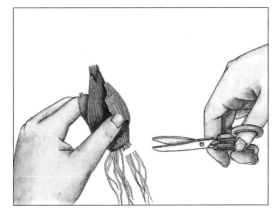

Spring-flowering bulbs can now be lifted and cleaned. When the bulbs are completely dry, rub away the old, dead skin and trim off the roots and any dead leaves with a pair of scissors. Store in trays or boxes in a cool, dry place.

BULBS – DIVIDING

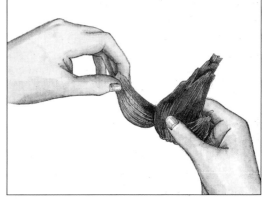

Some bulbs form offsets (small bulblets) around the parent bulb. Remove these and store separately. After planting, it will be two or three years before these flower so, if you have room, put them in a nursery bed for a couple of years.

paler tissue when cut across, with a woolly substance at the base, then eelworms are present (*see* Pests, page 400). Narcissus fly grubs eat away the centres of the bulbs, leaving them soft and rotten.

Commercially, immersing bulbs in hot water controls both these pests, but special equipment is needed. If a few of your bulbs are diseased you can remove and discard them, but if a lot are affected it is better to destroy the entire stock, order replacements and plant in new ground.

Frequent cultivation of the soil around the bulbs will help to prevent attacks.

● Begonias

When flower buds appear on begonias, remove all buds that have winged embryo seed pods behind them – these will be small, single, female flowers. In the greenhouse, shade plants during sunny weather and provide good ventilation to encourage prolonged flowering.

● Planting autumn-flowering bulbs

Plant autumn-flowering bulbs this month. They will provide a splash of colour among shrubs and trees later in the year.

Amaryllis belladonna should be planted with the tops of the bulbs about 10 cm (4 in) below the surface of the soil. In cold areas the plants will benefit from the extra protection of being planted up to 15 cm (6 in) deep. Plant them near a south-facing wall, where they will be sheltered from the coldest weather and where they can dry out and ripen during the summer.

Of the lovely South African nerines only *Nerine bowdenii* and its varieties are hardy enough to grow outside, and then only in a warm, sunny position. Plant them with the tops of the bulbs just covered

with soil. The leaves of both amaryllis and nerine follow the flowers and will probably need protection during the winter.

Colchicums (popularly but incorrectly known as autumn crocuses because they have crocus-like flowers in pinkish mauve and white) have large, broad leaves which may be out of place in a neat lawn or small flower bed. Plant them in rough grass or in small groups near the front of shrub borders, where the flowers can be seen in the autumn and the leaves will not be too obtrusive in the spring.

Autumn crocuses, such as *Crocus speciosus*, bloom from late September almost to Christmas. Plant them 5–8 cm (2–3 in) deep in soil which is not going to be disturbed by cultivation, or in rough grass which can be cut after planting the corms in July–August, and then not again until the leaves have died down in the following May–June.

Sternbergia lutea has a yellow flower rather similar to that of the crocus, but has leaves which grow at the same time as the flowers, so the grass can be cut in the spring.

Before planting bulbs, prepare the soil well by digging deeply, removing all weeds and breaking up any clods. Feed planted bulbs with a fertiliser containing potash (*see* Fertilisers, page 389).

● Controlling gladiolus thrips

Watch for signs of gladiolus thrips, which cause a brown and silver chequerboard pattern on the foliage. In severe attacks the buds shrivel and fail to open (*see* Pests, page 404).

● Ordering bulbs for autumn planting

Give priority to ordering daffodils, as they benefit from early planting. They should be planted in position no later than September.

SUMMER BULBS AS CUT FLOWERS

Most summer-flowering bulbs are grown for garden display, but many of them also make excellent cut flowers for indoors. If your garden is not large enough to devote an area specifically to flowers for cutting, you can still plant a few extra bulbs in a mixed border. If you grow them in clumps, the odd flower cut here and there will not be missed.

Lilies make excellent cut flowers (be careful when picking and handling, as the pollen may stain), and gladioli sometimes look more attractive cut than standing like soldiers in a border. It is not just the tall, large-flowered varieties that cut well, the smaller butterfly and primulinus types also look good in flower arrangements.

Dutch irises are popular with florists, less so with gardeners. But they make a bright display in early summer if planted in a bold drift, and again a few stems taken for the house won't be missed. For a succession of iris blooms plant English irises as well. These follow on a little later than the Dutch irises.

Some of the ornamental onions (alliums) can make striking cut flowers, and not all have a strong smell. The charming *Allium cowanii*, with its pure white flowers on small stems, has a pleasant, mild scent.

Many of the border alliums have attractive heads

CARNATIONS & PINKS

● Layering

Propagate border carnations by layering from established plants. Choose vigorous shoots, slit at a leaf joint and peg down into prepared soil. Water with a fine spray, and make sure that the soil does not dry out during rooting. The layers should root in about six weeks and be ready for lifting in September.

● Encouraging blooms

Continue to disbud border carnations (*see* June, page 150), deadhead pinks and cut back leggy even when flowering is over, and these can be used to enhance dried arrangements or to add drama to a group of fresh flowers. Among the best for this purpose are *A. giganteum* and *A. cristophii*, which is still widely grown under its older name of *A. albopilosum*.

Ixiolirion pallasii (syn. *I. tataricum*), which has clusters of tubular flowers on stiff but slender stems, makes an unusual and attractive cut flower in early summer.

The chincherinchee or *Ornithogalum thyrsoides* is widely grown for cutting, and also makes a lovely garden plant if you are prepared to lift the bulbs and store them over the winter. The cut flowers give good value, lasting for up to three weeks in water.

Florists' anemones can be enjoyed in the garden and provide attractive cut flowers for the house. Their season in the garden is short – from late spring to early summer.

Persian or Asiatic ranunculus with their double flowers, mainly in shades of red, orange and yellow, make brilliant plants for the flower border, and they are also ideal cut flowers.

A striking addition to a flower arrangement is the foxtail lily (*Eremurus* spp.). The rocket-like flower heads can be 1.5–1.8 m (5–6 ft) tall. These are not true bulbs, but are often sold by bulb suppliers.

plants as this will keep them flowering over the longest possible period.

● **Propagation**

Take further cuttings of pinks (*see* June, page 150), and harden off those cuttings which have already rooted for planting out in September. If the stock is in poor health, order new plants rather than taking cuttings.

PERPETUAL-FLOWERING

Continue second stoppings until the middle of the month for winter flowers (*see* April, page 92).

CARNATIONS – LAYERING BORDER CARNATIONS

1 Choose a vigorous young shoot and prepare it for layering by removing the lower leaves, leaving four to six developed leaves at the tip.

2 Make an upward slit part-way through the stem with a thin knife or safety razor, cutting into a leaf joint.

3 Peg the shoot down with a piece of bent wire into prepared soil enriched with soilless compost and sharp sand. Keep moist.

Cut the blooms and disbud flower stems (*see* September, page 214).

CHRYSANTHEMUMS

● **Reducing shoots**

Outdoor-flowering plants make very rapid growth this month, often producing too many shoots. Where large flowers are required, reduce the number of stems to four for incurved, intermediate and reflexed varieties, but to only two for large exhibition plants. This is not necessary for pompon and spray varieties.

EARLY-FLOWERING (GARDEN)

About mid July, apply a balanced fertiliser in liquid or solid form (*see* Fertilisers, page 390), according to the manufacturer's instructions. Keep dry fertiliser off the foliage. If plants appear soft and delicate, water with a solution of sulphate of potash (*see* Fertilisers, page 389). If the weather is dry, water the plants both before and after the application.

Towards the end of July, disbud any very early-flowering outdoor varieties which are showing their buds (*see* August, page 195).

VERY LATE-FLOWERING

Lightly dig and rake greenhouse borders, then plant the young plants of mid-season and late varieties which were propagated last month. Alternatively, pot up the rooted cuttings, three to a 23 cm (9 in) pot, and stand them out of doors.

Pinch out the tips of both varieties after 10 to 14 days. This encourages sideshoots to form.

Continue to take cuttings of mid-season and late varieties that were not propagated last month.

CLIMBERS & WALL SHRUBS

Potting on

Once they have rooted strongly, pot on any cuttings taken in June into individual pots. You can tell rooting has taken place when new growth emerges from the upper buds on the cuttings. Do not wait too long to repot them for climbers grow quickly and soon use up the nutrients and moisture in the compost. Once potted, tie new shoots to a 60–90 cm (2–3 ft) bamboo cane to stop the plants becoming a tangled mass of shoots. Place a cane-cap on top of the cane for eye protection.

Pruning wisteria

Reduce the long tendrils on wisteria by half or to five buds. Wisteria are pruned twice (see November, pages 257–258). This summer pruning slows down the rate of growth and encourages the formation of flower buds for next year.

Pruning other climbers

As flowering finishes, prune many climbers by the one-third method (see June, page 151).

CONTAINER GARDENING

Regular care

Continue to water, feed and deadhead plants in containers regularly (see May, page 127).

Trimming back plants

Left unchecked, some plants can swamp others. Cut out or trim overlong branches, especially of vigorous plants such as helichrysums and bidens. Towards the end of the month some plants, such as petunias and pansies, may be starting to look rather weak and leggy. Cut back to the bushier growth at the base and feed and water to encourage regrowth.

Powdery mildew

Any white, dust-like coating on leaves and stems during hot, dry weather is most likely to be caused by powdery mildew. This affects verbenas, trailing nepetas, cornflowers and nigellas (see Diseases, page 410). Keep containers well watered as this lessens the likelihood of attack. Continue to check for, and treat, other pests and diseases (see April, page 96).

DAHLIAS

Feeding and watering

Feed young plants fortnightly, particularly if slow growing, with an all-purpose liquid fertiliser or foliar feed. Dahlias are growing strongly now and must not be allowed to dry out. Tie in new growth.

Increasing flower size

Left to their own devices dahlias produce flowering stems with short 'footstalks' (the technical term for the stem between the top leaf and the flower bud). They also flower intermittently over a period of time. These flowers are not usually suitable for floral arrangements or shows and the plants can be improved by disbudding. A normal shoot has a central terminal bud and two side buds at the first pair of leaves below it. Pinch out the two side buds; this allows the central stem to grow longer and produce a larger flower. For even better blooms for shows, the sideshoots in the next lower pair of leaves should also be removed.

To produce top quality blooms for showing at the end of August and early September, you have to restrict the number of blooms produced at that time.

DAHLIAS – INCREASING FLOWER SIZE

You can increase the size of dahlia blooms by removing the two side buds that form below the main terminal bud while they are still young. Do not do this with any dahlias you are growing for a mass of blooms.

This is done by reducing the number of sideshoots on the plant at the end of July. The number of shoots varies according to the variety, but in general terms leave three on a giant, five on a large, seven on a medium, nine on a small, and as many as possible on miniatures and pompons. Once the showing season is over, the plants can be allowed to produce as many shoots as they can until frost cuts them down.

Controlling pests and diseases

Continue to check the plants for pests and diseases. (see June, page 152).

Deadheading

Dahlias will provide large quantities of flowers until the first frost if flowers are removed as they fade.

CONTAINERS – HOLIDAY ARRANGEMENTS

If there is no one to water your containers while you are away, cluster pots together in a sheltered, shady place that is open to the rain, and feed and water them thoroughly just before leaving.

Take down hanging baskets and sit them directly into a depression in the soil surface in a cool, shady spot. Drench with water so that the soil underneath is also wet. Protect them from slugs.

You can also set up a simple automatic watering system using an upturned bottle full of water set into the container – the water is slowly released as the compost dries. Alternatively, use strips of capillary matting tucked into the compost at one end and a bowl of water at the other (*see* Tools and Equipment, page 443). Test that the system is working for a few days before leaving.

Remove all flowers from plants in containers, not just the faded ones. That way you should have a fresh-looking display of new blooms when you return.

If you are growing fruit or vegetables in containers (*see* May, page 139), pick any that will not keep until your return. Give away or freeze the surplus.

Cluster containers together and remove flowers.

FRUIT

Most soft fruit will be ripening this month, as well as early plums, there may be some peaches and perhaps early apples. Remember to pick all ripe fruits, even if there are more than you want at the time. Most soft fruit can be frozen.

In a good year developing fruit can weigh down, and even break, branches of trees, especially apples, pears and plums. Prop up any that are overladen.

Birds and squirrels are particularly troublesome among bush and cane fruits. Plums may also be attacked. Most fruit can be protected from birds by nets thrown over the bushes, but the best protection is a fruit cage. Apple and pear cordons may be grown inside these.

Aphids may still require controlling but take care when spraying ripe fruit to follow carefully the manufacturer's instructions.

● Apples and pears

Ensure trees, especially young ones, are not suffering from a shortage of water. Small trees are the most susceptible to drought.

Check for bronzed leaves which indicate red spider mite damage. Biological remedies are not very effective this late in the season but it indicates that control measures will be needed earlier next year. The same applies to fruitlets with, usually, just one brown hole in them. They are probably victims of codling moth caterpillars (*see* June, page 152). The white woolly covering produced by woolly aphids becomes thicker as the year advances. Treat any outbreaks of aphid infestation as soon as you notice them (*see* Pests, page 395).

Trained apple and pear trees, such as cordons and espaliers, may be ready for summer pruning but their stage of growth is more important than the date (*see* August, page 196).

Shoots and branches will have grown a lot in the last few months so check all ties for tightness as any constriction can be damaging.

The so-called 'June drop', when apples spontaneously drop some of their half-formed fruit, does not usually occur until July. Delay any additional hand thinning until this is over, then assess whether further thinning is required. The aim is to leave one fruit every 10–15 cm (4–6 in) on dessert varieties and one per 15–20 cm (6–8 in) on large cookers such as 'Bramley's Seedling'.

To thin, first gently agitate a cluster of fruit with a finger to dislodge any that are loose. Then remove fruitlets which are damaged, misshapen or lop-sided, smaller than average and those with poor colour. Along with these, the 'king' fruit should be removed; this is the one in the centre of a cluster. It is larger than the rest and has a shorter, thicker stalk.

In a good year pears may also need thinning in the same way.

● Plums and cherries

Harvest cherries. Prune any trees that need it (*see* June, page 152) and treat cuts with a wound paint.

● **Peaches and nectarines**

Protect the ripening fruit from birds, earwigs and early wasps. Muslin or rolls of special mesh are useful for protecting trees growing against walls.

Peaches and nectarines fruit on shoots made the previous summer so cut out unwanted shoots at the earliest opportunity if this has not been done before (*see* June, page 152). Prune fan-trained peaches and nectarines after harvesting (*see* August, page 197).

● **Cane fruits**

Tie in new canes of blackberries and hybrid berries separately from the fruiting canes, so that they do not blow about and damage the fruiting canes or get damaged themselves (*see* May, page 129).

Treat raspberries for raspberry beetle early in the month (*see* Pests, page 402). Control weeds and pull up any suckers that have come up away from the row. Support autumn-fruiting varieties by running a length of twine down each side of the row.

● **Figs**

Tie in new growths to form a fan shape. Remove fruitlets formed earlier.

● **Gooseberries and currants**

Pick the fruit as it ripens and freeze any surplus.

Keep an eye open for late attacks of sawfly on gooseberries and check for signs of powdery mildew (*see* Pests and Diseases, pages 403 and 410).

It is possible, though far from essential, to prune blackcurrants when they have finished fruiting. They fruit best on new shoots formed the previous year, and as the strongest new growth comes from below ground, give priority to these shoots. Cut out about a third of the old branches completely.

Reversion virus disease on blackcurrants is clearly

FESTOONING PLUMS

Plums normally make large trees and take many years to become fruitful. They can be made to fruit more quickly – in as little as three years – by growing them on a dwarfing rootstock, such as 'Pixy', and training them as a festoon.

A festooned tree looks odd, but it is very fruitful and takes up far less room than a conventional one.

To train to this shape you need to start with a young tree. Bend down the main stems and tie the ends to the trunk. In time they will 'set' into an arching shape, when they can be untied. When this has happened, cut back the stems by one-third to a half, ideally in summer, and remove entirely any surplus shoots that make the tree congested.

With the framework established, prune routinely in the same way

as for cordon apples (*see* August, page 197). In late summer prune back new shoots growing directly from the main branches to three

leaves above a basal cluster, and those that grow from previously pruned spurs back to one leaf above the basal cluster.

seen at this time of the year. Apart from the enlarged buds that are obvious in the winter, the leaves on infected bushes are coarse with few serrations round the edges. There is no cure so dig up and burn, or dispose of, diseased bushes.

● **Strawberries**

Protect any fruit that remains from slugs and harvest when ripe. Destroy fruit with grey mould (botrytis).

Peg down runners on healthy plants which you want to propagate (*see* June, page 153).

Most varieties are pulled up when they have carried three crops. Fruit size deteriorates after that, and it is wise to grow strawberries on a three-year rotation, replacing a third of your plants each year

with healthy young runners. Cut off foliage, stalks and runners on the plants you are keeping, leaving only the stump of the stem. This removes a fair number of pests, limits the spread of disease and encourages the plants to produce healthy new foliage. Burn or compost the rubbish and any straw ground covering.

Feed summer-fruiting strawberries with a balanced feed. Apply it at the recommended rate and water it in if the ground is dry.

● **Vines**

Continue to stop unwanted shoots at one leaf but allow the replacement shoots to grow to their full length. Stop any sideshoots on them at one leaf.

FUCHSIAS

TENDER AND HALF-HARDY
● Cuttings
Pot on cuttings taken last month for early flowering next year. Keep them outside in a sheltered place until autumn, and prevent them from flowering by continually pinching off the flower buds.

● Training standards
On all but miniature standards, pinch out the three or four shoots which are now beginning to form the head once they have two pairs of leaves. Miniature standards which are now in their final 13 cm (5 in) pots can be left to flower.

● Water and humidity
Continue to check plants daily for dryness; they will

FRUIT – TIDYING UP STRAWBERRIES

When strawberry plants have finished fruiting shear off the leaves, stalks and runners from those you are keeping. This will help to control pests and diseases and will also encourage fresh, healthy foliage to grow.

need frequent watering, preferably before midday, but do not allow them to get sodden. Plunge or soak hanging baskets as often as possible.

Keep a humid atmosphere around any plants still under glass by standing their pots in trays of gravel and keeping the gravel moist.

● Feeding
Switch from a high-nitrogen to a high-potash feed and apply at low strength each time you are watering. Keep plants being trained as standards on a high-nitrogen feed to encourage rapid leaf growth.

● Pests
Continue to guard against pests in the greenhouse, especially aphids and vine weevil (*see* Pests, pages 395 and 404). Be careful not to use sprays that will mark the flowers.

HARDY
Complete planting hardy varieties to give the plants time to establish before winter. Water regularly, and feed with a nitrogenous fertiliser.

Continue to take semi-ripe cuttings (*see* Propagation, page 428).

GARDEN MAINTENANCE

● Before going on holiday
Cut the lawn and trim the edges. Ask neighbours to pick sweet peas, French beans and courgettes, which will continue to crop if they are picked regularly.

Take precautions against theft. Lock any outbuildings which contain tools and equipment. Ideally locks should be on the inside of the door with the key kept in the house, as external padlocks can be levered off. Outside lighting will discourage thieves,

so install a time switch. Record the serial numbers of all your power tools and mark items with a security marking pen.

Cement valuable garden ornaments in position, and have your name engraved on them. Take photographs so that you have a visual record should they be stolen.

● Planting record
Keep a record in a garden diary of any planting carried out during the year. Also make a note of when you feed, prune or propagate plants – recording the successes and the failures! This will be an invaluable source of reference to look back on in future years and will help you to decide what and when to plant.

GREENHOUSES & FRAMES

● Watering
Damp down the borders, paths and staging at least once a day during warm weather, but do not spray overhead as water droplets may mark the flowers of plants such as carnations and pelargoniums.

Unless the plants are standing on a capillary bench which provides water automatically (*see* Tools and Equipment, page 443), most will require watering daily and possibly two or three times a day during hot weather.

To determine whether a plant needs water, press the compost lightly with your fingertips. Moist compost is soft and resilient, but dry compost feels hard and gritty. With a little experience, the water content of a pot can be gauged by lifting it to determine its weight. It is important not to withhold water until plants are actually flagging, but to attend to watering each day.

● Shading and ventilation

Shade plants during warm, sunny weather and give them ample ventilation, especially in the early morning when a delay in opening the side ventilators may cause excessively high temperatures in the greenhouse.

Except during unusually cold or windy weather, leave the roof ventilators slightly open throughout the night. Open them on the side away from the wind to avoid damaging draughts.

● Controlling pests

Continue to introduce biological controls if insect pest populations begin to increase (*see* Pests, page 394). Yellow sticky traps hung inside the greenhouse will give a good indication of the current level of infestation and help you to decide whether the biological control is effective.

● Sowing and potting

Continue to sow late-flowering pot plants, such as cinerarias and calceolarias. Prick out the seedlings when they are large enough to be handled and pot on young plants when necessary.

● Taking cuttings

Take semi-ripe cuttings of hydrangeas for use as pot plants (*see* Propagation, page 428). Choose well-ripened, greenish-brown, non-flowering shoots of medium thickness; unripe shoots are light green. Insert the cuttings individually into 8 cm (3 in) pots. These later hydrangea cuttings are grown on without pinching out to produce a single head.

Similarly, take semi-ripe cuttings of carnations, chrysanthemums, herbs, pelargoniums, rock plants and shrubs. Details for these plants are given in the individual sections in June and July.

● Cucumbers

Cucumbers should be in full production by now; continue to pick the fruits when they are about 30 cm (12 in) long, and remove all the male flowers as soon as they appear. When a mass of white roots appears on the surface of the bed, apply a 5 cm (2 in) top dressing of well-rotted manure, fibrous loam or a mixture of the two.

● Peppers and aubergines

Water regularly and give a liquid feed every fortnight. Watch for red spider mite and whitefly (*see* Pests and Diseases, pages 402 and 405).

● Tomatoes

Pick tomatoes daily as they ripen. Twist the stems round the supporting strings, or tie them to the canes, and remove sideshoots regularly from all cordon varieties. Feed tomatoes with an appropriate liquid fertiliser every week to ten days.

● Vines

Thin bunches by removing any small, diseased or otherwise imperfect fruitlets, together with any grapes that are obviously causing overcrowding.

Continue to water generously, and try to maintain a balance between temperature and atmosphere (*see* June, page 156).

HEATHERS

● Choosing new plants

Heathers can give a colourful display throughout the year, require little maintenance and last a lifetime, so it is worth spending time considering which varieties to buy for your garden. All heathers prefer acid soil but there are a number of winter and spring-flowering heathers, notably *Erica carnea* and *E.* × *darleyensis* and their varieties, and a few summer-flowering species, which will tolerate some lime in the soil if you cannot offer them ideal acid conditions.

Never buy heathers if they look dry or if the soil has shrunk away from the sides of the pot. If there are signs of wilting or browning of leaves in the centre of the plant, it can mean the onset of disease. Also avoid old, tired-looking plants, particularly if they are badly pot-bound, as these will take a long time to establish, if they ever do.

Do not be tempted by plants in full bud or flower, particularly in the case of the winter-flowering heathers, which may consist of only three or four stems heavily laden with buds. Look instead for plants that are bushy, fill the pot and are well balanced, even if it means sacrificing some flowers in the first year. If in doubt, go to a specialist nursery for assistance in your choice of heathers.

GREENHOUSES – VINES

If you want a large bunch of well-shaped and plump grapes, cut out the smallest fruits from the bunches as the grapes start to swell. Use long, pointed scissors. It is not usually worth doing this with outdoor grapes.

● Taking cuttings

Heathers are best propagated from cuttings although layering is also possible. Varieties cannot be grown from seed. For winter-flowering species, take heel cuttings from this year's growth (*see* Propagation, page 429), avoiding shoots that have already set buds if possible.

The easiest heathers to root are *Calluna vulgaris* varieties, followed by *Erica × darleyensis*, *E. tetralix*, *E. cinerea* and *Daboecia* spp. *E. carnea* varieties usually take a long time; the white-flowered varieties are the best to try.

To take cuttings this month from heathers in flower, cut a 5 cm (2 in) length of stem, just below the flowers, on shoots where the leaves are closely grouped together.

Make a propagating compost from three parts sphagnum moss peat to one part perlite, sieved bark or acid sand. Composts that are not peat based work for some species but not for others. *Calluna* and *Daboecia* spp. particularly require acid conditions. Do not add fertiliser, and do not use rooting hormones as most are too strong for heathers. Insert the cuttings 2.5 cm (1 in) apart in trays without firming in.

After planting the cuttings, water the tray until the soil swims. This seals the holes. Drain for 20 minutes, cover with an inflated plastic bag without holes in and put the tray in a cool, shady place. Check every week that the bag is 'fogged' with condensation, if not, rewater, wait 20 minutes and reseal the bag over the tray.

The cuttings should be rooted in a couple of months but their progress can be monitored by tugging them gently. If rooting has started, some resistance will be felt. If any come out easily, check the stem. If you can see a slight swelling on the stem, replace the cutting, but remove any where the stem has rotted. Although the cuttings should be rooted by late September, leave them over the winter and pot on next spring.

● Layering

Propagating by this method does not produce such good plants as cuttings, but it is easy to do and is useful if you want just one or two extra plants.

There is no need, as with some other shrubs, to bruise the bark or cut into the wood to encourage rooting; simply peg down the chosen branch, and partly cover it with a little soil and peat mixture (*see* Propagation, page 432).

● Deadheading

The flowering season and the general appearance of all daboecias can be improved by deadheading regularly as the flowers fade.

● Controlling weeds

Continue to keep heather beds free of weeds. Check the sites of future heather beds you have prepared for any weed regrowth (*see* May, page 131).

● Watering and feeding

Continue to water young plantings regularly and potted-up plants daily if necessary. Use rainwater if possible (*see* April, page 101). Heathers may be fed once this month with a liquid tomato fertiliser at half the rate recommended for tomatoes.

● Treating alkaline soil

Water any heathers showing abnormal yellowing of foliage (chlorosis) with chelated iron (sequestrene), following the manufacturer's instructions, to correct this condition (*see* May, page 132).

HERBS

● Making further sowings

Sow more salad herbs if you need them for the end of the summer (*see* March, page 70). Start sowing land cress, lamb's lettuce and winter purslane for winter crops. Spare seeds may be sown now but remember to thin out and hoe between earlier sowings.

● Sowing angelica

Angelica seeds do not store well, so gather and sow them as soon as they are pale biscuit brown and start to drop off the plant. This is the best way to propagate angelica. Sow directly where you intend the plants to grow or in a nursery bed. Young plants can be moved to permanent positions in the autumn.

● Taking semi-ripe cuttings

Semi-ripe cuttings of many herbs can be taken this month (*see* Propagation, page 428). Among them are bay, cotton lavender, germander, hyssop, lavender, mint, rosemary, rue, sage, thyme and winter savory. Insert the cuttings into gritty, sandy soil in a shady part of the garden. For the first two weeks protect the cuttings from the sun and wind with a cloche, and water in the evenings until roots have formed. Alternatively, put the cuttings in a pot filled with gritty, sandy soil in a cold frame, or insert them directly into similar soil in the frame itself.

● Garlic

When the main outer leaves of garlic start to wither and turn brown, dig deeply under the bulbs and lift them gently to prevent bruising. The garlic should be loosely bunched (tie by the tops of the leaves), and hung in a dry, airy place to allow the stems to dry and the sap to drain down to swell the bulbs.

HARVESTING LAVENDER

Lavender flowers may be ready for harvesting this month. Cut the whole stalk when the flowers are showing colour, but are not fully opened. Tie the stalks in loose bundles and hang them up in a greenhouse or warm shed to dry, or spread them on trays in the airing cupboard for a few days. When completely dry you can either use the stalks as they are in flower arrangements or rub the flower buds free of the stalks. The sweet-smelling flowers can then be used to make lavender bags or pot-pourri.

Above: Lavender is easy to grow and simple to dry. Cut the stems when the flowers are showing colour, and tie in bundles to dry in a warm place.

Left: Lavandula angustifolia *'Imperial Gem', is just one of many superb lavenders that are highly decorative as well as aromatic. It is ideal for planting close to a path at the front of a border.*

● Flowers and aromatic leaves for pot-pourri

Gather and dry the flowers of colourful herbs such as marigold, hyssop, chamomile and dill, as well as the traditional lavender. These add scent, colour and interest to home-produced or purchased pot-pourri.

● Harvesting herbs

Cut culinary herbs for immediate use in the kitchen, or they can be frozen or dried for later use (*see* pages 188–189).

HOUSE & CONSERVATORY PLANTS

● Plant care

Continue to water and feed plants. Keep leaves clean and remove dead leaves (*see* February, pages 42–43).

● Potting up cuttings

Pot up cuttings taken last month into 8 cm (3 in) pots. Water carefully, as overwatering can make the young roots rot.

● Heat and light

Protect all plants that are indoors from strong, direct sunlight. Ensure that the conservatory is well ventilated and shaded. Move plants from south-facing windowsills except those, such as cacti and sansevieria, which can tolerate hot, dry conditions. Keep the humidity high on dry days.

● Controlling pests

Look for signs of red spider mite on the undersides of leaves and on soft top growth (*see* Pests, page 402). Discard severely infested plants as they can spread the pests to other plants.

● Holiday arrangements

If you will only be away from home for a week or less, water your house plants well and ensure they are out of direct sunlight. They will survive without further attention until you return.

Any plants in a peat-based compost that has dried out while you are away can be revived by soaking the pots in a sink full of water, with a few drops of washing-up liquid added. This helps re-wet the compost. When soaked through lift the pots out and allow to drain well.

If you are often away from home, try growing plants in self-watering containers which have a reservoir holding up to a month's supply of water. The water is drawn along a wick to the compost by capillary action.

● Flowering plants

Remove flowers just as they fade and before they set seed; this will help plants to produce more flowers.

Take cuttings of regal pelargoniums and of hydrangeas kept in pots as house plants (*see* Greenhouses, page 178).

Modern strains of polyanthus and primroses make admirable pot plants for indoor flowering. When planting out young plants grown for the garden, pot a few strong specimens into 8 cm (3 in) pots of soilless potting compost. Stand them in partial shade and keep well watered throughout the summer. If you bring them indoors in early January they will flower in February.

● Indoor bulbs and corms

Continue to keep indoor plants which are in flower, such as tuberoses, gloriosas and vallotas, well watered until their flowering period is over. Feed them as necessary.

● Climber and feature plants

Pinch out the growing tips of *Jasminum polyanthum* to encourage bushy growth.

● Bromeliads

Water these freely, mist air plants and feed them once a month (*see* March, page 71).

● Cacti and other succulents

Water well during the growing season but allow the compost to dry out between waterings. Feed monthly with a tomato feed at half strength.

Keep species such as Christmas and Easter cacti away from direct sunlight during the summer to prevent the leaves from being scorched.

● Orchids

Move cymbidiums outdoors to a shady spot if this has not already been done (*see* June, page 157).

Water so the compost is moist but not soaking wet and give them a high-nitrogen feed at half strength every alternate watering. Increase the humidity in the greenhouse around moth and slipper orchids (*see* May, page 134).

IRISES

English bulbous irises and Japanese water irises flower this month. Remember to order new bulbs now for planting in October.

● Replanting rhizomes

In cooler areas lift and divide four-year-old plantings of bearded irises. Replant and secure the best rhizomes in sites prepared last month, keeping them moist until established. In warm, dry areas wait until early autumn to divide plants (*see* September, page 221). Plant new intermediate and standard dwarf bearded irises in the same way, cutting down the leaves to half length before planting.

IRISES – REPLANTING RHIZOMES OF BEARDED IRISES

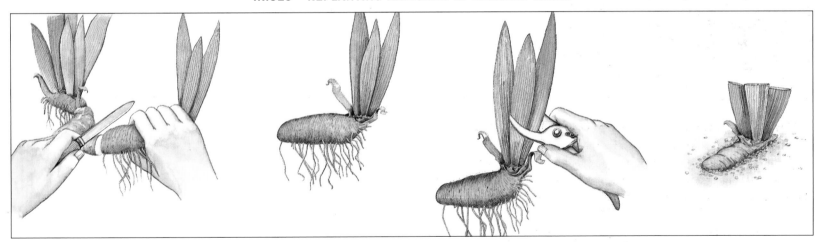

1 If clumps of bearded irises are large and congested, divide and replant them when flowering has finished. Lift the clump, split it up and cut off the young rhizomes.

2 Shorten the leaves on the young rhizomes to about 10 cm (4 in) long. This reduces water loss and prevents windrock. Discard the old rhizomes and any without leaves.

3 Replant the selected rhizomes in a sunny position. Firm soil gently round the roots but don't cover the rhizome with soil. Water and keep moist until established.

● Bulbous irises

Lift any crowded clumps of winter-flowering bulbous irises, separate the bulbs and replant them in fresh soil in the rockery or raised beds. Lift bulbs of Dutch and Spanish irises and store them in a warm, dry place to ripen until September.

● After flowering

Continue to remove stems as late irises finish flowering (*see* May, page 134).

Cut back the leaves on congested clumps of *Iris unguicularis*, particularly if flowering was poor. This will allow the sun to ripen the rhizomes. Otherwise remove dead leaves only from younger plants. Use gloves to protect your hands as the leaves have very sharp edges.

● Controlling pests and diseases

Sawfly larvae may appear on waterside irises and will destroy the leaves. The larvae are best picked off by hand (*see* Pests, page 403), but if you are spraying keep the spray well away from the surface of the water as insecticides (whether natural or synthetic) can kill pond life.

LAWNS

● Preparing a new site

If you are planning to sow a new lawn this year start preparing the ground now; make sure it is weed-free and level (*see* March, pages 84–85).

● Lawn care

Mow once or twice a week, and raise the cutting height slightly in prolonged dry weather. Keep edges clipped. Continue to scarify lightly except in drought conditions, and water both new and established lawns in dry weather. A thorough soaking once a week will do more good than a sprinkling every day (*see* June, page 158).

● Controlling red thread

Control red thread if necessary by using a fungicide (*see* May, page 135).

LILIES

● Deadheading

This is one of the peak months of the lily display. Cut flowers for the house as required. Pick off the dead flower heads unless you want the seeds.

● Producing seed

If you want to save any seed, hand pollinate the flowers by brushing the anthers with the pollen, covering all the sticky stigma surfaces.

● Controlling lily disease

Botrytis elliptica, or lily disease, is a disabling fungus disease. While not necessarily fatal in itself, it weakens the plants and therefore makes them prone to other diseases. Symptoms are small, brownish red spots, patches of grey mould (botrytis) or, sometimes, both. In severe cases leaves shrivel and the stems can be left almost bare.

Still, moist air aids the fungus. To control or prevent the disease grow lilies in airy, well-ventilated conditions. Use fungicide sprays if necessary. Infected foliage should be collected and burnt or otherwise disposed of away from the garden.

The spores overwinter on the soil surface or on the winter leaves of *Lilium candidum*. It is unusual for the disease to cause really serious problems.

● Watering

Outdoor lilies should be watered only in times of

LILIES – PROPAGATING FROM BULBILS

1 Tiger lilies, L. sargentiae *and a number of Asiatic hybrids, produce bulbils where their leaves join their stems. These bulbils can be gathered when they are ready to fall and used to provide new plants.*

2 Grow on the bulbils in pots or trays filled with compost or horticultural grit. Press them gently into the surface, then cover with more compost or grit. Grow them on in a cold frame for the first year.

severe drought and then really thoroughly, avoiding stems and foliage. Continue to water freely indoors.

● Ordering lilies

Now is the time to order new bulbs. Do not attempt to grow lime-haters, such as most Oriental hybrids, in an alkaline soil, though they make good plants for pots, tubs and other deep containers if you use a neutral or acid compost. Most Asiatic hybrids, such as 'Enchantment', and the Trumpet hybrids, such as 'Pink Perfection', are tolerant of some lime, but all lilies enjoy plenty of humus.

● Planting Madonna lilies

Try to plant *L. candidum* (Madonna lily) as soon as possible, with not more than 5 cm (2 in) of soil above each bulb. Pick a sunny spot where they can be left undisturbed for several years.

● Propagating from bulbils

Tiger lilies (*L. lancifolium*, syn. *L. tigrinum*), *L. sargentiae* and a number of Asiatic hybrids produce bulbils (baby bulbs) between the leaves and the stem. Gather these when they are loose and ready to fall. Plant then in pots or trays filled with compost or horticultural grit. Well-grown larger bulbils can produce a flower the following season.

PELARGONIUMS

● Feeding and watering

Feed any pelargoniums grown in tubs, window-boxes and hanging baskets regularly with a liquid tomato feed, and do not allow them either to dry out or become waterlogged.

Plants that are bedded out will also benefit from being watered in very dry weather. Any plants under glass will need protection from very strong sunlight and very high temperatures, both of which will cause stress to the plants.

● Cutting back regals

When regal pelargoniums have stopped flowering, cut them back hard and remove all the old leaves. This will encourage new shoots to grow for new cuttings in September, and whitefly will not be able to settle on the old leaves to lay their eggs. Whitefly may also be a problem on scented-leaved varieties (*see* Pests, page 405).

● Taking cuttings of zonals

To grow large specimen plants next year, take cuttings of zonal pelargoniums now. These will root readily at this time of year. Choose a healthy shoot and cut it away from the plant above a leaf joint. Trim the cutting to just below a leaf joint and remove any sideshoots. Dip it in hormone rooting powder and then plant in moist compost. Keep the cuttings in good light but avoid direct sunlight. When new leaves appear, the cuttings have rooted (*see* January, page 26).

● Deadheading

Keep deadheading blooms from zonals and ivy-leaved varieties, as this will bring on the new buds and keep the plants looking good.

RHODODENDRONS & AZALEAS

● Stimulating new growth

Large rhododendrons and azaleas which are undergoing rejuvenation pruning (*see* Pruning, page 421), may be slow in starting new growth. To stimulate new shoots, spray the plants with a seaweed growth supplement fortified with iron. This helps to activate the dormant buds.

Take semi-ripe cuttings (*see* May, page 136).

● Hot weather protection

When the weather becomes hot, continue to water rhododendrons. Keep the rootball moist and spray the foliage. Once a week add a liquid high-nitrogen fertiliser to the water. Provide temporary shade to newly planted shrubs (*see* June, page 159).

● Pests and diseases

Continue to watch for and control attacks of Japanese lacewing, whitefly and leaf hopper, which begins to hatch this month. Also check for bud blast and destroy infected buds (*see* June, page 159).

ROCK PLANTS

The display in many rock gardens is now past its peak, although campanulas and dianthus provide continued colour. Visit other gardens and flower shows for inspiration on plants that provide late summer colour and make notes of any plants you would like to buy.

● Routine tasks

Inspect cushion and carpeting plants to see if they need further top dressing (*see* May, page 136). Continue to take cuttings and to trim back any trailing plants (*see* June, page 159).

● Collecting and storing seed

Save the seeds of any rock plants which have set seed. Keep these either for personal use or pass them on to other gardeners. Cut the seed heads carefully, holding the flowering stem over a paper bag to ensure the seeds fall straight into it and are not lost when the stem is cut.

Sow seeds of the Primulaceae family (primulas, cyclamen, dodecatheons, androsaces and dionysias) as soon as they are ripe, since they are fertile for only a short period. Keep other seeds for sowing later (*see* December, page 281).

Remember to label the bags and keep them in a cool, dry place until they are needed.

ROSES

● Deadheading

Roses are now in full bloom and the priority is to maintain continuing colour. This can be achieved by deadheading. Remove not only the flower heads but cut back well below the old blooms to include at least three 'eyes' or buds. This will encourage a rapid resurgence of new flowering wood.

Do not, however, deadhead wild, or species, roses which will usually produce very decorative hips in the autumn.

● Feeding

Now is the last time to give an additional feed to roses to encourage the production of more flowering wood; use a specific rose fertiliser or one high in potash. Feeding after this month produces very late growth which is prone to frost damage.

● Watering

Roses do not normally require constant watering. However, if container-grown ones were planted late in the season they will need watering until well into the summer to help them get established.

Continue to water any roses in permanent containers, such as patio varieties.

SWEET PEAS

● Feeding

With flowering at its height, a liquid feed may be necessary every fortnight, even if the ground was carefully prepared in the first place. Use a proprietary liquid fertiliser with high potash content (*see* Fertilisers, page 389). It is important not to overfeed sweet peas.

● Watering and mulching

In hot, dry conditions continue misting plants either in the late evening or early morning and water copiously when required. Avoid using cold water. Top up mulch if applied earlier in the season.

● Protecting from birds and insects

In some areas sparrows and tits can be troublesome, attacking the flower buds for moisture. Protect against birds by using netting or bird scarers (*see* Pests, pages 396).

Continue to control aphids (*see* Pests, page 395). If spraying, avoid wetting the flowers directly as this may mark them.

● Routine care of cordons

Maintain the routine removal of tendrils and side-shoots on cordons, tying in and cutting flowers. If flowers are left to fade and set seed, future flower production will be adversely affected.

TREES, SHRUBS & HEDGES

● Feeding and watering

Use a high-nitrogen liquid fertiliser to feed any trees and shrubs that are performing badly. This will help to increase their vigour.

Continue to keep an eye on trees and shrubs planted earlier in the year, and water as necessary.

● Controlling pests and diseases

Many diseases, such as mildew and coral spot, and pests, such as red spider, aphids, whitefly and vine weevil, attack during the summer. Always keep on the lookout for them so that a build-up does not reach epidemic proportions.

Choose a suitable treatment for each pest and disease (*see* Pests and Diseases, page 394–411).

● Taking semi-ripe cuttings

Many new shoots on shrubs, such as heathers, box (*Buxus sempervirens*) and lavender, become firm during early July and root very well if cuttings are taken at this time (*see* Propagation, page 428).

Shrubs that are difficult to raise from cuttings, such as hibiscus, kalmia and magnolia and most conifers, usually root better if the cutting is taken with a 'heel' – a sliver of the main stem – at the base (*see* Propagation, page 429).

The sticky resin produced by many conifers can prevent rooting taking place unless the growth cells just below the skin are exposed. Cut away a sliver of the skin, approximately 2.5 cm (1 in) long, along one side of the bottom end of the prepared cutting.

Just as large leaves on other types of cuttings are reduced in size to limit moisture loss through transpiration, the same is done by slicing across the leaf spray of conifers. Then treat them as you would any other semi-ripe cuttings.

● Softwood cuttings

Plant out potted-up softwood cuttings taken in May in their final planting position and pot up softwood cuttings taken in June.

● Pruning

After flowering finishes, use the one-third pruning method on all shrubs that flowered in June and have been established in the garden for over three years (*see* Pruning, page 420).

HEDGES

● General care

Keep the base weed-free and feed with a general purpose liquid fertiliser (*see* Fertilisers, page 390), if the hedge looks undernourished. Continue to keep new hedges well watered in dry weather.

● Semi-ripe cuttings

Cuttings are an economical, although slower, way of creating a new hedge rather than buying hedging plants. Semi-ripe cuttings taken now will root well (*see* Propagation, page 428).

TREES & SHRUBS – RESHAPING YEW HEDGES

1 Reshape an overgrown yew hedge stage-by-stage over two or three years. Cut back just one side severely the first year. Trim the other side.

2 In the second year trim the new growth from last year's pruning only lightly, but cut the other side back severely.

3 If the height of the hedge also has to be reduced, do this in the third year. After this treatment an annual clipping should be sufficient.

TREES & SHRUBS – TAKING CUTTINGS FROM CONIFERS

1 Many conifers root well at this time of year. Take the cutting with a 'heel' – a small sliver of the older wood of the main stem.

2 Cut away a sliver of bark from the base of the cutting to expose the pithy green centre of the stem which contains the growth cells.

3 Although many conifer cuttings root without it, slicing across the leaf spray will cut down water loss and may improve the success rate.

● Reshaping overgrown yew hedges

Overgrown yew hedges can be brought under control, but the process is slow and can take three or four years to complete.

In the first year cut back all shoots on one side to within a few centimetres of the main stems. Normally these shoots will regrow fast the following spring, but if they do not, feed the hedge well and delay any further action for a year. The following year, cut back the opposite side in the same way and, in the year after that, reduce the top in height.

● Hedge trimming

Continue to clip hedges of green and golden privet and *Lonicera nitida* every one to two months.

Trim and reshape other types of hedge, such as beech and hawthorn, but leave conifer hedges until next month.

VEGETABLES

After harvesting early summer crops such as broad beans, shallots and early potatoes, fill the spaces with follow-on crops such as endives or cabbages. Alternatively you can use the space for vegetables for winter and early spring, such as sprouting broccoli, kale, winter cauliflowers, spring cabbages and leeks.

Ensure crops get adequate water regularly when it is most important for their development. This keeps them growing evenly. In dry spells soak the soil thoroughly once a week rather than giving the plants a daily sprinkle. Vegetables in containers will need soaking every day.

Concentrate on watering crops that will benefit the most from regular watering, i.e. 20 litres per m² (4 gallons per sq yd) a week. These include leafy vegetables such as summer cabbages, calabrese, cauliflowers, celery, lettuces, spinach and leaf beet. Fruiting crops such as courgettes, marrows, runner beans and tomatoes, as well as early potatoes, also benefit from regular watering.

You also need to water certain crops at crucial stages. These include broad beans, French beans and peas when the pods start to swell, maincrop potatoes which should be watered regularly when in flower, and sweetcorn when the tassels first appear.

All young plants should be watered in well to help them establish; in particular Brussels sprouts need watering for three weeks after planting.

● Beans

Continue to sow short rows of dwarf French beans until the end of this month for a succession of crops (*see* May, page 138).

Harvest the first dwarf French beans and runner beans when they are young and tender.

● Brassicas

Complete the planting of sprouting broccoli and other winter brassicas (*see* June, page 162).

Continue to pick off cabbage white caterpillars. Watch out for severe attacks of mealy cabbage aphid (*see* Pests, page 396).

Start off the first spring cabbages. The sowing time is critical as the plants need to be at the right stage to get through the winter. Aim to have them well established before the first frosts but not too large or they may bolt. Sow seed in the last week of July if you live in a cold part of the country; wait until the first two weeks in August in mild places. If you have space it is worth making several sowings and using the best batch. Sow in a moist seed bed 1 cm (½ in) deep, with 15 cm (6 in) between rows and thin out to 3 cm (1½ in). Raise them in pots in a cold frame if you want only a few plants.

VEGETABLES – POLLINATING MARROWS

To increase the number of fruits that form, pollinate the female flowers by hand. To do this, remove a male flower and peel back the petals. Push the male flower into the female one to transfer the pollen.

Chinese cabbages need a rich soil with plenty of organic matter. Sow them now or in August in pots or in drills 1 cm (½ in) deep. Thin the seedlings to 30–35 cm (12–14 in) apart. Water well and protect from slugs at all times.

Harvest the first calabrese and summer cauliflowers when the heads are full sized and firm and before they start to loosen and bolt. Freeze any surplus. Summer cabbages will stand for several weeks and can be cut as required.

● Carrots

Continue sowing early carrots for a succession of crops into the autumn.

● Celery

Harvest the first self-blanching celery.

● Marrows, courgettes and squashes

Remove the growing tips from the trailing stems of pumpkins and squashes when they are about 60 cm (2 ft) long. Male and female flowers are produced separately and pollination is necessary if fruit is to form. Insects will do this but you can pollinate by hand. Pick a male flower with ripe yellow pollen, peel back the petals and push it in to the female flowers – these have a swelling behind the petals. Water the plants well in dry periods and feed once a week with a tomato feed.

Harvest the first courgettes. Pick the fruit twice a week as it reaches 10–15 cm (4–6 in) long. This encourages more fruit to form.

● Onions, shallots and leeks

Lift and dry Japanese onions and shallots when the tops start to fall over.

Complete planting leeks (*see* June, page 162).

● Other roots and swollen stems

You can continue sowing beetroots and kohlrabi for crops into the autumn until the end of this month. After the end of July there will not be time for the crop to mature before winter (*see* March, page 81).

You can harvest the first beetroots when they reach about 2.5 cm (1 in) diameter and eat them as 'baby beets', or you can leave them to grow bigger.

Sow Florence fennel if you have not already done this (*see* June, page 163). Thin seedlings sown last month and plant out 30 cm (12 in) apart when the plants have two true leaves. Keep them well watered and free from weeds.

● Peas

Continue successional sowings of peas until the end of the month (*see* February, page 48). Use an 'early' quick-maturing variety for the last sowings, to be certain of a crop before the cold weather.

● Potatoes

Continue to protect against blight (*see* Diseases, page 409). Harvest early potatoes.

● Salad crops

Continue to sow lettuces, radishes and spring onions until the end of the month for cropping in the autumn (*see* February, page 49).

Sow broad-leaved endive and make a further sowing of curly endive. Sow in trays and transplant or sow direct in drills 1 cm (½ in) deep and thin to 30 cm (12 in) each way.

● Spinach and spinach beet

Sow spinach and spinach beet for a succession of crops. Any plants left to overwinter should produce a crop early next spring.

● Sweetcorn

Check to see if sweetcorn is ready to harvest towards the end of the month (*see* August, page 205).

● Tomatoes, peppers and aubergines

Traditional outdoor or bush varieties of tomatoes crop well without you having to support the plant or pinch out the sideshoots. The only disadvantage is that the bush habit makes picking and disease control harder. Bush varieties, such as 'Red Alert', crop earlier and produce less leaf than the older varieties. Bush tomatoes may need support for the trusses to keep the fruit off the soil and some varieties, such as 'Gardener's Delight', can be trained as cordons. To do this pinch out all the sideshoots to produce a single upright stem; tie this to a cane.

Feed tomato plants, especially those in containers, with a tomato feed. Once plenty of fruits have set, use a high-potash feed. Continue to protect outdoor tomatoes from blight (*see* Diseases, page 410).

Peppers may need support to keep the fruits off the ground, but they do not need training.

Limit the number of fruits on each aubergine plant to about four.

● Turnips

Begin to harvest and continue sowings of turnips until the end of the month (*see* March, page 82).

PERENNIAL VEGETABLES

● Globe artichokes

Continue to harvest (*see* June, page 163).

WATER PLANTS & POOLS

● Water evaporation

In warm weather top up the pool with fresh water to replace water lost through evaporation. Use a spray attachment on the hose to aerate the pool.

● Tidying up

Remove faded flower heads from marginal aquatic plants and cut back any excess growth. Continue to weed the bog garden regularly.

● Thinning water plants

Thin out crowded leaves on waterlilies and remove any excess growth from submerged oxygenating plants. Remove blanketweed by inserting a rough stick into the pond and winding the weed round and round. When thinning out water plants take care not to remove any young fish with the plant growth.

WATER PLANTS – THINNING OUT

Water plants often grow rampantly in summer. If necessary, thin them out. Canadian pondweed (Elodea canadensis) is a submerged oxygenating plant best dragged out with a rake. Cut back other plants with secateurs or shears.

Making the Most of Herbs

No garden is too small for a herb patch. Herbs can be grown in containers and hanging baskets, in specially designed gardens or with other plants in beds and borders. Herbs are easy to grow and are rarely troubled by pests or diseases. They prefer a sunny spot and a light, well-drained but fertile soil; for better results if your soil is heavy, dig in some grit to improve drainage. Poor soils can be improved by adding organic matter and a slow-release fertiliser.

Raise your own plants from seeds and from cuttings or by division. Many herbs self-seed freely, so look out for seedlings in spring and either thin them out or carefully dig them up, complete with soil ball, and use them to replace tired old plants. There are many specialist herb nurseries and these are worth visiting not only to buy plants, but also for ideas, as they often have superb model gardens.

PLANNING A HERB GARDEN

The most convenient place for a herb garden or a group of herbs in pots is near the kitchen. In the garden, a small collection of herbs can be planted in a cartwheel pattern, each segment planted with a different herb. Use gravel or bricks to represent the spokes of the wheel, if an actual cartwheel is not obtainable. On a larger scale, a round bed divided into wedge-shaped segments, each for a different herb, can be planted with a dwarf hedge to define the edges. A particularly charming and traditional edging can be made by planting violets 10 cm (4 in) apart round your herb garden.

Another attractive and simple pattern is made by planting out herbs in a chess-board arrangement, each square containing one species. Alternate squares are either paved, or filled with gravel or granite chippings. This allows you to walk easily between plants while you work and gather.

More ambitious designs, such as an Elizabethan knot garden, must be carefully drawn to scale on graph paper before you start. Once you are satisfied with your design, prepare the soil for planting, rake it smooth and draw out the shape with a cane. Each separate section is then filled with a herb of contrasting leaf texture. You will need plenty of plants to complete such a scheme so it is worth raising your own from cuttings. This type of design is traditionally outlined by a low hedging of box or other small evergreen.

When planting herbs together in borders, place the tallest at the back, so they do not shade out the lower growing kinds. Angelica grows up to 2 m (over 6 ft) and will self-seed freely. Mint and lemon balm tend to be invasive and will crowd out less vigorous plants unless their roots are confined.

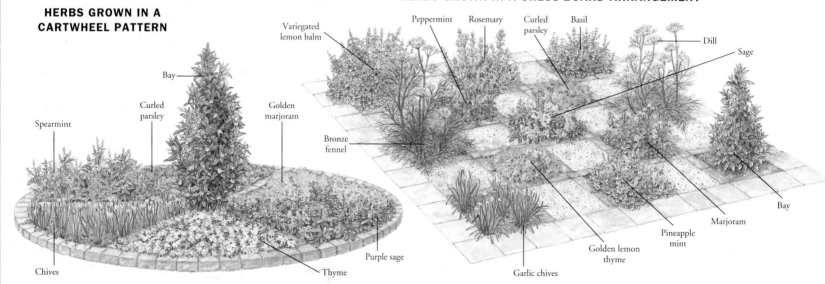

HERBS GROWN IN A CARTWHEEL PATTERN

Bay

Curled parsley

Golden marjoram

Spearmint

Purple sage

Thyme

Chives

HERBS GROWN IN A CHESS-BOARD ARRANGEMENT

Variegated lemon balm

Peppermint   Rosemary   Curled parsley   Basil

Dill

Sage

Bronze fennel

Bay

Marjoram

Pineapple mint

Golden lemon thyme

Garlic chives

PRESERVING HERBS

Harvesting herbs for the winter must be done at the right time in order to retain as much flavour and aroma as possible. Choose herbs in good condition. In general, the best time is during a dry spell, just before the plant comes into full bloom. Pick only a small quantity at a time as herbs soon wilt and deteriorate if heaped together.

Freezing

Soft-leaved plants, such as chervil, chives, coriander, dill, fennel, mint and parsley keep well when frozen. Cut small sprigs from the plants and wash the leaves. Put the herbs in a colander and immerse in salt water for 15 to 30 minutes to clean them thoroughly. Rinse under running water and shake well. Pat dry with kitchen paper or a clean tea towel. Chives should be chopped up before sprinkling on a tray or plate to open freeze, then packed into small cartons. Other herbs can be frozen in freezer bags, removed while still frozen and crunched up, then stored in labelled containers. Crunch them up as quickly as possible, as herbs defrost rapidly. Frozen herbs are good for flavouring soups and cooked dishes.

Drying

The simplest method is to dry each kind of herb in a separate bunch. Tie by the stems and hang them up in a shaded, dry, airy place such as an attic, spare room or clean shed. The leaves are properly dried when they snap easily between finger and thumb. If stems are slow to dry, strip off and store the dried leaves.

Quicker results are achieved by spreading sprigs evenly over trays, box lids or drying frames. The leaves can be stripped from large-leaved

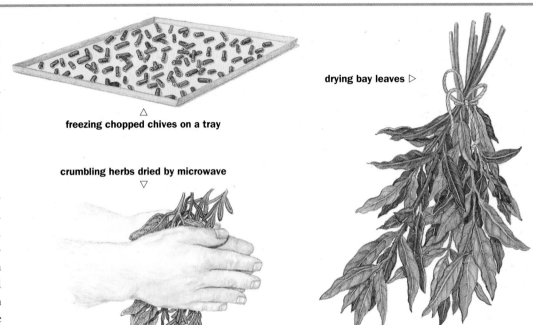

freezing chopped chives on a tray

crumbling herbs dried by microwave

drying bay leaves ▷

herbs such as lovage and comfrey and the stems discarded before drying. Place the trays in a warm, dry place with good ventilation, such as an airing cupboard. Do not dry the herbs in direct sun. Turn the herbs over by hand several times during the first two days.

Microwaving

A microwave oven will dry plant materials in minutes rather than days. Cover the turntable or plate with a piece of kitchen paper and arrange the herbs in a single layer so no two sprigs are touching. Turn the oven on low power for about three minutes. The time taken will vary according to the wattage of the microwave and the volume and density of plant material. Check after the first minute and again every 30 seconds. Remove the herbs as soon as they become crisp and papery.

Storing

Allow the herbs to cool after drying them. Rub them between your hands, discarding the stems and other chaff. Dried herbs must be stored immediately in small, air-tight containers to prevent them taking up moisture from the air. Label the jars or bags. Wooden pots or dark glass jars with tight-fitting lids are ideal containers. Store them in the dark, as nothing will destroy the quality of a herb quicker at this stage than exposure to light.

Oil or butter

Basil leaves can be washed, dried and layered in oil for later use. Make sure there are no air bubbles in the jar and that the leaves are completely submerged. Chopped basil, oregano and garlic chives can be blended into unsalted butter. Wrap in small portions and freeze for later use.

AUGUST

This is the month for holidays, when serious gardening pauses and the most important task is to sit back and enjoy the results of earlier efforts.

August

In August, the garden usually looks after itself, and you can take time out for a holiday. If you arrange for a neighbour to pick crops that will spoil, such as runner beans, courgettes and lettuces, and organise watering for the house and container plants, there should be few problems on your return. In a wet year the grass may need an urgent trim if it hasn't been cut for a week or two, but in a dry summer, with a period of drought, there may be little or no growth.

Now is the time to relax and enjoy your garden. Although there is still work to be done, the jobs are generally light and undemanding and, with a few exceptions, they can wait until early September if necessary.

The weather in August

August weather is similar to that of July. In a poor summer both months can be wet, but in some years there will be long, hot, dry spells which may last for several weeks.

Hot days and dry spells often end in thunderstorms. Heavy rain may damage some of the flowers but it generally improves the look of the garden, cleaning the leaves on the trees and bringing back a green flush to the lawn.

The daylight hours are already beginning to shorten noticeably, and the nights at the end of the month are often surprisingly cold. Strong winds are not uncommon, and they bring with them a foretaste of autumn. In exposed parts of the country, particularly in northern regions, August can be much colder than in the south.

Pest and disease problems

In a damp summer, diseases can be rampant, and in a hot, dry one, pests such as aphids and red spider mite multiply prolifically. Nobody likes looking for trouble, but early remedial action often means that only limited amounts of chemicals are needed.

It is a good idea to take a regular walk around the garden once or twice a week to inspect your plants. This is perhaps the only way to be sure of detecting the early signs of disease or infestation by insects.

Make a habit of turning over any leaves of any suspect plant as you pass by, and keep an eye on the soft growing tips of the shoots. Sometimes just pinching out stems or pulling off leaves covered with pests will contain the problem. If not, localised spraying now may avoid the need to spray the whole plant later.

Pay particular attention to vulnerable plants: blackfly are attracted to nasturtiums; canary creeper is often attacked by caterpillars; lilies are prone to lily beetles. If you find that certain plants are particularly pest and disease-prone in your garden, you may decide not to grow them another year.

Watering and weeding

The irony about watering is that when you need to water most often – during drought – this essential commodity may be rationed. Even if there is actually no hosepipe ban, there is nowadays considerable environmental pressure to economise on the use of water.

It is usually safe to use washing-up water and bath water. Arrange to siphon it through a hosepipe to a water butt or containers in the garden. Concentrate your watering on plants in containers, and on trees and shrubs planted this year and not yet established. Don't worry about more mature trees or shrubs, or the lawn, as these will usually survive.

Keep an eye on the water level in ponds – after weeks of hot weather a lot of water can be lost through evaporation. The oxygen level may also drop if the water is not aerated by a fountain or cascade. Top up the pond with fresh water using a garden hose; a spray attachment on the hose will help aerate the pool. Hosepipe bans do not usually apply to topping up your pond if you have fish, as livestock is regarded as a special case (check with your water company if in doubt).

If you mulched the borders, shrubs and kitchen garden earlier in the year then the loss of water through evaporation from the soil will have been reduced. If you failed to do this earlier, don't despair; it is not too late to add a new mulch or top up an old one, but only do this when the soil is moist.

Weeds not only use up valuable nutrients that would otherwise be available to the garden plants, but they also compete for water. Mulching suppresses weeds, while regular hoeing is needed to keep exposed ground weed-free. Hand weeding is useful too, especially among bedding plants where hoeing is difficult. Pull out the weeds as you deadhead.

Disbudding and deadheading

The vast majority of garden flowers will bloom prolifically without disbudding. Even those that are sometimes disbudded to encourage bigger or better blooms, such as dahlias and hybrid tea (large-flowered) roses, will give a good garden display if you just let them grow naturally. But if you are in search of the best blooms, this simple task does not take many minutes and you really will see the difference in the size of the flowers.

Deadheading is beneficial to a far greater number of plants. Flowering shrubs are sometimes deadheaded just to make them look tidier, but deadheading summer bedding plants can have far greater benefits by ensuring many flower for a long period. It may not be practical to deadhead all your bedding plants, so concentrate on those in hanging baskets, windowboxes and other containers. In the open garden give priority to plants that benefit most, pansies for instance. Don't waste time on plants such as antirrhinums (most varieties of which will not produce any fresh flower spikes now) unless you simply want to tidy them up.

Borrow ideas

Visit other people's gardens if you can. Many small gardens are open to the public under various schemes and these can be inspirational, with many ideas that can be adapted for your own garden. Even good ideas seen in large gardens can often be scaled down, and there are always new plants to discover.

JOBS THAT WON'T WAIT

- Organise basic care for your garden if you are going to be away on holiday. Watering and harvesting are the tasks that will most need attention if you are away for more than a few days.

- Check watering requirements daily. In hot, dry weather plants in containers may need watering more than once a day. Even if it does rain many containers in sheltered positions, windowboxes and hanging baskets in particular, may not receive sufficient water to keep them flourishing. If there is a drought, concentrate on providing water for trees and shrubs planted this year. These are usually expensive plants to buy and if they dry out before rooting into the surrounding soil they may die.

- Harvest fruit and vegetables when they are ripe. Don't forget to harvest culinary herbs as well to freeze or dry for winter use.

- Maintain a regular programme of weeding and checking for pests and diseases.

- Feed those plants that require it.

- Deadhead regularly to encourage more flowers unless you want seeds to form. If you are saving seed from your own plants, check regularly to make sure that you harvest when the seeds are ripe but before they begin to shed.

- Disbud according to the requirements of the plants you are growing. Chrysanthemums and dahlias may need attention this month.

- Pinch out the growing tips of wallflowers. The sooner you do this, the bushier the plants will be by the time they have to be moved to their flowering positions.

- Remove the growing tips from greenhouse tomatoes by the middle of the month, to encourage the fruit to develop more rapidly.

- Take the last crop of cuttings this year from pinks.

- Pinch out the growing tips of fuchsias to increase the number of shoots available for cuttings.

- Plant strawberries as soon as possible so the plants become well established before next year.

- Sow Japanese onions to overwinter. Timing is critical for this crop.

ANNUALS & BIENNIALS

● Regular care

Regular deadheading, feeding and watering will ensure that bedding plants keep on flowering well into the autumn.

● Pinching out growing tips

Take out the growing tips of wallflowers to encourage the production of sideshoots. The plants will then develop into bushier, sturdier specimens. The more sideshoots a wallflower has, the more flowers will be produced.

● Collecting seed

Many hardy annuals produce copious seed towards the end of summer which can be harvested and saved for sowing the following year. F1 hybrids and named varieties do not come true from seed but species do, and their seed is well worth collecting. Try Swan River daisies (*Brachycome iberidifolia*), calendulas, *Eschscholzia californica*, love-in-a-mist (*Nigella damascena*) and nasturtiums. Cut off the ripe seed heads, place them in paper bags and hang the bags in a warm, dry place for a few days to dry. Break open the capsules and separate the seeds from the debris. Pack seeds in labelled envelopes in a sealed container. Store in a cool, dry place.

● Controlling pests and diseases

Watch out for pest damage and signs of disease and treat immediately. Plants that are under stress from drought and overcrowding are particularly susceptible to diseases such as powdery mildew, which leaves a fine white coating on shoots and leaves (*see* Diseases, page 410). Verbenas, cornflowers and trailing nepetas are likely to succumb quickly.

BORDER PERENNIALS

● Ground preparation

Towards the end of the month clear and dig over borders which are to be renovated or replanted, removing roots and perennial weeds. Add fertilisers, garden compost or well-rotted manure at the same time. This ground can be left over the winter for frost to break down the clods to finer particles.

● Planning new borders

Design new borders for planting in the autumn, drawing up plans on paper, preferably to scale. Assess the plants you will need, bearing in mind the height and spread of the plants when mature; most perennials will provide a more effective display if they are planted in groups rather than singly. List the plants you have already and those that have to be obtained and decide which can be safely planted in the autumn and which need to be reserved until the spring. Budget for extras such as fertilisers and stakes, as well as the plants themselves, and estimate how much labour will be involved in creating the new scheme (*see* pages 206–207).

● New purchases

If you visit other gardens and nurseries you often find yourself seduced into buying plants that are not completely hardy and which may succumb to winter cold and wet. Examine such plants for pests and general health before placing them in a sheltered area or cold frame until next spring, when they may be planted out with more chance of success.

● Taking stem cuttings

Take stem cuttings (*see* Propagation, page 429) of plants that do not divide easily or if more new plants are required than will be provided by division. Penstemons and osteospermums are among the border plants most commonly propagated in this way. Pot up into individual 10 cm (4 in) pots when rooted, then place in a cold frame for the winter.

● Feeding

After cutting back old stems to encourage new foliage and secondary flowering, feed plants using a liquid feed or a fertiliser and water in well.

● Deadheading and collecting seeds

Cut off faded flowers unless collecting the seeds. Collect ripe seed heads and clean, store or sow the seeds as appropriate (*see* July, page 170).

BULBS, CORMS & TUBERS

● Spring-flowering bulbs

Finish ordering spring-flowering bulbs which are to be planted this autumn. Hyacinths, small irises, dwarf early tulips, crocuses, chionodoxas, scillas, snowdrops and miniature daffodils can all be grown in bowls or pots for flowering indoors in winter. Order tulips, hyacinths and daffodils for spring bedding or cutting. Bulbs suitable for planting in borders and rock gardens include alliums, hardy cyclamen, eranthis, erythroniums, muscari and ornithogalums.

● Planting daffodils

Plant daffodils by the end of the month, unless they are to be planted in beds which cannot be cleared of summer annuals until September or later. Daffodils recommence their root growth in late summer, so they need to be planted into soil from which they can draw moisture and food. Plant all but the smallest bulbs 15 cm (6 in) deep.

● Christmas-flowering bulbs

Plant prepared hyacinths and 'Paper White' narcissi in bowls for Christmas flowering indoors. Put the pots in a cool position outdoors or in a shed to produce strong root systems (*see* September, page 214).

● Cutting gladioli

Cut gladioli for indoor decoration as soon as the first flowers on the spike are open. For exhibition plants, timing depends on variety. When cutting a flower spike leave at least four or five leaves on the plant, otherwise the corm will be deprived of its source of nourishment. To cut a flower spike without damaging the plant, insert a sharp knife low down on the stem, give the spike a gentle jerk each way and twist. The stem will snap and can then be withdrawn from its sheath of leaves.

● Gladiolus thrips

Watch for signs of gladiolus thrips. These first show as holes in the leaves (*see* Pests, page 404).

● Begonias

When flower buds appear on begonias, remove those with winged embryo seed pods behind them, as they are single female flowers.

CARNATIONS & PINKS

● Planning and preparing beds

Choose sunny, open sites away from the shade and drip of trees and buildings. Dig the sites well, turning over the soil to a spade's depth, and incorporate plenty of well-rotted manure or garden compost, together with grit or coarse gravel if you are gardening on heavy clay. If the drainage in your garden is suspect, test by digging a hole 45 cm (18 in) deep.

If water remains in the hole less than 30 cm (12 in) from the surface over the winter, you will need to improve the drainage or consider raising the surface of the bed.

Test the acidity of the soil with a proprietary kit, and add lime if the reading is less than pH 6.5 (*see* The soil in your garden, page 387). Hoe bonemeal into the soil and incorporate bonfire ash, if desired, from now until the end of the winter, weather permitting. Store some dry soil under cover; this can be used when planting border carnations and pinks in the autumn when the garden soil may be too wet (*see* October, page 236).

● Propagation

Continue to layer border carnations (*see* July, page 173) and check the progress of those which were layered last month. It is important not to let them dry out at any time.

Take the last crop of cuttings from pinks for the year (*see* June, page 150).

PERPETUAL-FLOWERING

Continue to maintain a healthy environment; and water, feed and spray plants regularly.

CHRYSANTHEMUMS

● Watering and feeding

In dry weather, water plants that have been disbudded for larger blooms once a week and apply a general fertiliser to help fatten the remaining buds.

For very late-flowering varieties, grown either in pots or in the greenhouse border, water and feed with a balanced fertiliser every 10 to 14 days to keep the rate of growth steady and even (*see* Fertilisers, page 390).

● Controlling earwigs

Prevent earwigs from eating the opening florets by smearing a 1 cm (½ in) ring of petroleum jelly around the stem below the flower.

● Disbudding

Buds will form very rapidly during this month on outdoor-flowering varieties. If large blooms are required, reduce the buds to one per stem. As well as disbudding this is sometimes called 'securing the bud' or 'taking the bud'.

Look for the sideshoots which grow from where each leaf joins the stem; they appear at the same time as a bud forms at the tip of the stem. Allow the sideshoots to grow about 1 cm (½ in) long before removing them, otherwise you may damage the main stem and this will cause malformation of the flower when it opens. Budded shoots can form right down the stem, so be sure to remove them all using a sharp sideways pull to do this.

Complete the disbudding of outdoor-flowering varieties by the third week of August; they will then bloom before autumn is too far advanced.

Disbud large exhibition and October-flowering varieties towards the end of the month; varieties which form their buds earlier than this must be 'run on'. This means removing the buds at the tips of the stems and allowing the best sideshoots to grow on in their place. This delays flowering by about 14 days and prevents the flowers from opening with hard, green centres.

VERY LATE-FLOWERING

Plant out cuttings of mid-season and late chrysanthemums, taken in July, into greenhouse borders or growing bags, or singly into 15 cm (6 in) pots. No stopping will be required.

For cuttings taken in June of mid-season and late varieties, this is the month to reduce the long side-shoots to four per plant for spray varieties and just two per plant for all other types.

CLIMBERS & WALL SHRUBS

● Supporting plants
As autumn storms approach, ensure that all plants, in particular tall-growing, heavy wall shrubs, are securely fixed and tied to their anchorage points (*see* January, page 20). Adjust straps on shrubs and trees to stop any restriction and damage to the stems.

● Layering
Many climbing plants naturally layer themselves in the garden, often rooting some way from the parent plant, so it is now time to encourage any you wish to propagate (*see* Propagation, page 432). Plants to try include ivy, jasmine, honeysuckle, Virginia creeper and wisteria. Any rooted layers can be dug up and potted on next March before replanting.

● Pruning
When flowering finishes, prune shrubs over three years old, using the one-third pruning method (*see* Pruning, page 420).

CONTAINER GARDENING

● Regular care
Continue to water, feed and deadhead plants in containers regularly. Many containers will need watering every day (*see* May, page 127).

● Maintaining topiary
Give topiary plants their final trim to keep them in the shape you have planned. Use a pair of small, sharp shears. Don't trim after the end of August otherwise the new growth will be too soft to withstand the winter cold.

● Feeding perennial plants
Finish feeding plants which will be left outside all winter by the end of the month. The soft, sappy growth produced by feeding beyond this date may not be hardy enough to survive the winter.

● Holiday arrangements
Remember to make arrangements to have plants in pots watered while you are away (*see* July, page 175).

DAHLIAS

● Feeding and care
Continue to feed with liquid fertiliser but, from early in the month, change over to a high-potash feed to improve flower colour, strengthen the stems and improve tuber production. Keep the plants well watered and tie in new growth to the stakes.

● Exhibition flowers
Continue to disbud and remove sideshoots if you require larger blooms (*see* July, page 174). As the colour starts to develop in flowers for showing, they need some protection from the sun and the rain.

● Controlling pests and diseases
The flowers will be starting to show by now, but spraying against pests must continue. Only spray the foliage, as moisture on the flowers will cause marking on the florets which will spoil their beauty.

Continue to check for signs of virus infection and destroy any affected plants (*see* June, page 152).

● Deadheading
Remove the faded flowers regularly as this promotes further flowering.

FRUIT

Early varieties of apples and plums will now be ripening. There are still flushes of soft fruit to harvest and this is worth doing as most soft fruit freezes well even if it cannot be used immediately.

Pick off and destroy any fruits showing signs of rot, especially 'brown rot' in plums, apples and pears.

● Apples and pears
The fruit is swelling fast now so ensure that water does not run short. Small trees are the most susceptible to drought.

Prune espalier and cordon-grown trees. Summer pruning allows more light and air to reach the tree and improves fruit quality. It should be done when the current season's new shoots are becoming woody at the base and the tip (terminal) bud has formed. This coincides with the end of growth, usually in early August.

Prune away only this year's shoots which are not needed either to extend existing branches or to form new ones. Shorten any shoots arising from permanent branches to three leaves and shorten those arising from established spurs to one leaf. Leave all immature, weak and thin shoots to be reassessed in September.

All fruit should be picked as it ripens. Test for ripeness by lifting it and gently twisting. If it parts readily from the tree, it is ready to eat.

Protect ripening fruit from squirrels, birds and wasps. Wrapping branches in horticultural fleece until the fruit is ready to pick may help.

FRUIT – PRUNING CORDONS

1 *Once the base of the summer's growth begins to turn woody, prune any shoots growing from the main stem back to three leaves, but ignore any basal cluster of leaves close to the main stem.*

2 *Some shoots growing from the main stem will have been pruned previously, leaving a stump from which other new shoots have grown. Prune these back to one leaf above their basal cluster of leaves.*

● Plums and cherries

Keep a lookout for a late attack of greenfly on plums. Continue pruning if any is required, preferably after picking the fruit (*see* June, page 152).

Keep a watchful eye for signs of bacterial canker in cherries (*see* Diseases, page 406).

● Peaches and nectarines

Fruit is only carried on one-year-old shoots, so fruited shoots on fan-trained trees should be removed once the fruit has been picked. Some need to be cut back to replacement shoots at their base, which are then tied to the wires in their place. Other fruited shoots need to be removed without leaving any replacements. This depends entirely on the amount of room available (*see* June, page 152).

● Cane fruits

Harvest remaining fruit then cut out at ground level all canes that have finished fruiting. This removes many pests and diseases and allows the new canes to ripen properly. Remove weak, damaged, diseased and overcrowded new canes at the same time. Tie new summer raspberry canes to the wires, spacing them about 10 cm (4 in) apart. Blackberries and their hybrids are treated the same way, except that the canes of hybrids may be bundled together after harvesting for winter protection. Protect autumn-fruiting raspberries against birds and wasps.

● Figs

Remove small fruitlets to allow more to form which will be at a more suitable stage of development to overwinter and ripen next year.

● Gooseberries and currants

Leaf spot can affect plants (*see* Diseases, page 408). Collect and burn as many infected leaves as possible.

● Strawberries

Plant new summer varieties. Certified healthy plants

FRUIT – PLANTING STRAWBERRIES

August is a good time to plant strawberries. Spread the roots out over a slight mound of soil within the planting hole. Firm the rest of the soil around the roots before watering.

are the best but home-raised ones are acceptable if the parent plants are completely free from disease. Plant them 38–45 cm (15–18 in) apart with 75–90 cm (30–36 in) between rows, according to the vigour of the variety. Never let them dry out. If they are planted after mid September, cropping the following year will be lighter. New plants that are to be potted on into larger pots or other containers can be left till later.

Keep existing plants watered and weed-free.

● Vines

Protect the grapes from birds and spray against powdery mildew if necessary (*see* Diseases, page 410).

FUCHSIAS

TENDER AND HALF-HARDY
● Deadheading

Start removing all faded flowers, spent seed pods

and leaves. Fuchsia flowers last approximately 10 days and if the seed pods are left on, the energy of the plant will be diverted into reproduction and it will stop flowering.

● Feeding

Feed all plants frequently with a high-potash fertiliser to maintain continuous flowering.

● Watering and shading

Water regularly, but always check the compost to be sure that it is necessary; it is better for the plants to be underwatered than overwatered. Sometimes fuchsias in pots wilt because their root system is saturated with too much water. Further water at this stage is usually fatal. If you do accidentally overwater, place the plants in a cool place and spray the leaves with water. If the plants are allowed to dry out slowly they should recover.

Pots kept in full sun will put the foliage and root systems under strain, so ensure roots are kept cool.

Under glass maintain cool, humid conditions to prolong the flowering of fuchsias; a further light application of greenhouse shading will help.

● Preparing to take cuttings

Pinch out established plants from which you plan to take cuttings during late September and October. This will encourage them to make extra new shoots, providing plenty of material for the cuttings.

● Trained shapes

Continue to pinch out the shoots on the heads of standards (see June, page 154).

HARDY

Maintain a regular high-potash feed as established

plants approach the peak of their flowering season, and weed around them frequently.

Keep newly planted fuchsias well watered. They still have small root systems and are vulnerable during hot dry spells.

GARDEN MAINTENANCE

● Greenhouse

Check on the state of repair of the greenhouse before it is needed for the autumn and winter.

● Holiday arrangements

Prepare and protect the garden before going on holiday (see July, page 175). Check automatic watering systems are working properly.

GREENHOUSES & FRAMES

● Repairing, cleaning and disinfecting

Prepare the greenhouse for autumn and winter use by making any necessary repairs, such as replacing broken glass and renewing rotten wood. Then set aside time to give the greenhouse a thorough clean and fumigation. This will help to prevent problems from pests and diseases over the winter.

Before cleaning the inside, remove all the plants (apart from those growing in borders), turn off the electricity and protect any sockets with clear plastic.

Clean out all the pots, boxes and trays, and scrub containers before storage or re-use. Remove plant debris and other rubbish.

Thoroughly clean the inside glass with a hose-pipe and brush. To remove dirt trapped between overlapping panes, first dislodge the particles with a plastic plant label or a similar flat, flexible implement, then thoroughly rinse it off with water.

Use a greenhouse disinfectant to clean the glazing bars, staging and floor; wear protective clothing while doing this. If your greenhouse has removable staging it is usually easier to dismantle it and clean it outside in the garden.

When cleaning is completed, put the plants back in the greenhouse, close all the vents and fumigate everything with a smoke cone.

● Controlling pests

All the usual greenhouse pests will remain active and breed rapidly in the warm weather. Biological controls are very effective in a greenhouse, but be careful not to destroy them with insecticides.

● Taking cuttings

Take cuttings of perennial plants, herbs, carnations, pelargoniums, shrubs and rock plants that you want to propagate. Pinch out fuchsias to encourage shoots for cuttings (see Fuchsias, page 198).

GREENHOUSES – CLEANING GLASS

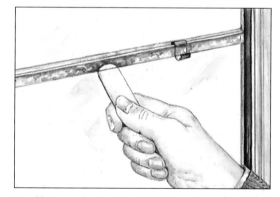

In addition to cleaning the glass inside and out, clean the area where the panes overlap and dirt and algae accumulate. Use a thin flexible label or similar implement to dislodge it, and wash away with a jet of water.

GARDEN MAINTENANCE –
GREENHOUSES & FRAMES

Greenhouse and frame maintenance should be carried out at least a couple of times a year if possible, and August is a good time to tackle the job as it is still warm enough to move the plants outside if you require full access.

- Make sure the glass fits snugly to the frame and replace any broken panes. In an aluminium greenhouse the glass is held in by glazing strips which can be unhooked, but in a wooden greenhouse they may be fixed with beading, glazing bars or putty. Wear gloves when handling glass.
- Cure any stubborn leaks around the edge of panes by covering glazing bars with mastic tape.
- Clean out debris from guttering and check that the brackets are sound and firmly attached. Check for leaks – a leaking gutter is a common cause of rotting frames in a wooden greenhouse. Small leaks can be repaired with mastic, but for larger leaks fit new gutters and downpipes.
- Check the wood on frames and staging. Cut back any rotten wood to where the wood is sound and replace with naturally durable wood, such as western red cedar or pressure-impregnated timber.
- Rub down new bare wood with steel wool. Seal knots with shellac knotting, then paint with an exterior wood stain or primer and gloss paint. Strip off the old paint if necessary (remove nearby glass if using a blow torch), then rub down.
- Clean glass thoroughly, but be prepared to reapply shading if the summer is hot and sunny.
- Replace broken or cracked panes – this will look better and reduce the risk of further damage in high winds. Cold draughts will also be reduced.
- Pay particular attention to gaps between the panes, where dirt and algae can accumulate. Clean these out by pushing a thin label between the panes, then use a jet of water from a hose or compression sprayer to remove the loosened dirt.
- Take the opportunity to disinfect staging and fumigate as appropriate.

Sow herbs in large pots for winter (*see* Herbs, page 199). Sow seeds of lilies and propagate by planting bulbils (*see* July, page 182).

● Potting up

Pot up seedlings sown last month and move cuttings into individual pots when rooted.

● Peppers and aubergines

Harvest the first fruits. Continue to water, but reduce the amount towards the end of the month.

● Tomatoes

Remove the growing tips of tomato plants by the middle of the month to encourage rapid development of the fruits on the top trusses. At the end of the month discontinue feeding and reduce watering. This helps to prevent the fruit splitting. If the nights turn chilly, close the ventilators early in the evening.

● Vines

Continue to water and feed regularly, reducing the watering as the fruit starts to ripen. Splitting fruit, a common problem, is usually caused by allowing the soil to become bone dry between drenchings. Remove any fruit and leaves affected by mildew to stop it spreading (*see* Diseases, pages 407 and 410).

HEATHERS

● Regular care

Continue to hand weed heather beds and replace mulch as necessary.

● Preserving heathers

Cut stems of heather are often used for buttonholes or as lucky charms, but they also make long-lasting table decorations. Pick double-flowered *Calluna vulgaris* in the morning, pack it in plastic wrapping and store it in the freezer. It can be thawed later when it will appear as fresh as the day it was picked.

● Deadheading daboecia

Continue to deadhead daboecia as the flowers fade (*see* July, page 179).

● New plants

Continue to acquire plants from nurseries or garden centres and increase stock by layering or cuttings (*see* July, page 179).

● Watering and feeding

Continue to water young heather plantings regularly and potted-up plants daily if necessary. Use rainwater whenever possible (*see* April, page 101). If feeding is needed, do this monthly using a tomato fertiliser applied at half the rate recommended for tomatoes.

HERBS

● Sowing herbs for winter

Sow parsley and chervil under glass in large pots for winter use inside. Lamb's lettuce, land cress and winter purslane may be sown in drills directly in the vegetable garden (*see* March, page 70).

● Harvesting seeds

Collect and dry seeds of dill, fennel, chives, sweet cicely and other herbs as they ripen. They may be resown at once in seed drills 5–10 mm (¼–½ in) deep, if required to expand the stock in the herb garden. If not needed for sowing, the seeds are useful for flavouring or adding to pot-pourri. Deadhead flowers to prolong the flowering season, if they are not required for seed. Put dried seeds in labelled paper bags and store inside a sealed container in a cool, dry place protected from insects and mice.

● Lifting and drying garlic bulbs

When the stems of garlic are dry and papery, the bulbs should be dressed for storage (*see* July, page 179). Clean off the outer skins, leaving sufficient skin to hold the cloves together. Plait the garlic into a string, or store without their leaves in a net.

● Harvesting herbs

Continue to pick leaves and seeds, storing or preserving any excess (*see* July, page 189).

● Taking semi-ripe cuttings

Take cuttings of shrubby herbs if this has not yet been done (*see* Propagation, page 428).

HOUSE & CONSERVATORY PLANTS

● Plant care

Continue to water, feed, clean the foliage and remove any dead leaves (*see* February, pages 42–43).

Ensure the conservatory is well ventilated and shaded and keep the humidity high on hot, dry days. If necessary, spray plants with tepid water using a hand-held mister.

Make arrangements to keep plants watered while you go on holiday (*see* July, page 175).

● Layering

Check on any plants layered earlier in the year (*see* June, page 157). If the roots have developed well and there is new growth, cut the new plant away from the parent and pot it up.

● Flowering plants

Gardenias are often sold in summer. Keep them in constant warmth at a temperature of 15°C (60°F) and high humidity. Hard water will turn the foliage yellow, so use rainwater or distilled water.

African violets (*Saintpaulia ionantha*) and begonias propagated earlier (*see* June, page 156) should now have rooted. Pot up the cuttings and water them.

Continue to remove any dead flower heads to prolong flowering.

● Indoor bulbs and corms

Buy cyclamen in flower from now until Christmas and feed with liquid high-potash fertiliser every 10 days. Pot up and water those resting from last year (*see* June, page 157).

Pot lachenalia bulbs, six or seven in a 13 cm (5 in) pot containing John Innes No. 1 potting compost. Water and keep cool until the cold weather comes in the autumn.

Plant prepared hyacinths and 'Paper White' narcissi for flowering indoors at Christmas, placing the pots in a cool position so that the plants produce strong roots. Order forced bulbs for winter flowering indoors (*see* Bulbs, page 195).

● Climbers and feature plants

Liquid feed jasmine (*Jasminum polyanthum*) every two weeks from now until the end of the year.

● Bromeliads

Continue to water freely, mist air plants, and feed once a month (*see* March, page 71). If you are going on holiday, put air plants in clear plastic bags.

● Cacti and other succulents

Continue to water well during the growing season,

HOUSE PLANTS – FREESIAS

Freesias, with their brightly coloured, fragrant blossoms and grassy leaves, are popular flowers. Corms are available in shops from late summer right through until April. When they flower depends on when you plant them. If planted in August, they should flower by late autumn, so by planting freesias in several stages, you will get a succession of flowers from the autumn through to spring. They can grow to 60 cm (2 ft) high, so may need a little unobtrusive support.

Plant the corms in pots of free-draining, gritty compost, just covering them. Keep them cool, and provide as much light as possible to ensure a neat, compact development. Place in the garden, preferably in a cold frame, until you can count about seven leaves to each corm, then bring them indoors. Display in a cool room.

Freesias can fill a room with fragrance.

letting the compost dry out between waterings, and feed monthly with a tomato feed at half strength. Keep species such as Christmas and Easter cacti away from direct sunlight in case the leaves scorch.

● Orchids

Move cymbidiums outdoors to a shady spot for the summer if not already done (*see* June, page 157).

Increase the humidity around moth orchids and slipper orchids (*see* May, page 134).

Water so the compost is moist but not soaking wet and feed with a high-nitrogen fertiliser at half strength every other watering (*see* April, page 104).

IRISES

● Planting rhizomes and bulbs

Continue planting or replanting bearded irises (*see* July, page 181) provided the ground is not very dry.

At the end of this month begin planting winter-flowering, dwarf bulbous irises such as *Iris histrioides*, *I. danfordiae* and *I. reticulata* in sunny, well-drained sites. There are many named varieties and hybrids available, which are often more vigorous than the species plants.

Before planting, dip the bulbs into a systemic fungicide to guard against ink spot fungus. Plant 5–10 cm (2–4 in) deep. Dwarf bulbous irises look particularly attractive planted in rock gardens.

LAWNS

● Sowing a new lawn

Continue to prepare the ground for a new lawn. Make sure it is weed-free and level. Apply a general fertiliser a week before you sow the grass seed. When the seed is sown, rake it over, water in dry weather and protect from birds. The seed should germinate within a week (*see* March, pages 84–85).

● Lawn care

If debris has built up over the summer, lightly scarify the grass from August onwards unless there is a drought and the grass is brown.

In dry weather, give the lawn a weekly soaking if there are no water restrictions (*see* June, page 158).

Continue to weed the lawn but apply weedkillers only if the grass is growing. If needed, apply fungicides to control disease (*see* May, page 135). You may find small mounds of loose earth on the lawn at this time of year indicating there is an ants' nest under the grass. Eliminate these with a proprietary antkiller or, alternately, by pouring boiling water over the nest.

● Inspecting the lawn

Late summer is a good time to judge which areas of the lawn are worn and will need renovating later in the autumn.

LILIES

● Ordering bulbs

Order lily bulbs for autumn planting if not done last month.

● Saving seed

As one pod usually contains a great many seeds, you need only save one or two pods of *Lilium pumilum* or *L. regale* for sowing. When they are ripe, the seed capsules will have swollen almost to the size of a walnut; they will then begin to turn fawn-coloured and crack open at the top.

The seed can be sown when harvested or stored in a cool, dry place for sowing early next year. Sow the seeds 1–2 cm (½–1 in) apart and 5–10 mm (¼–½ in) deep in seed compost in pots or deep trays. Some types are best sown now, including *L. regale*. These start by producing a tiny bulb but nothing appears on the surface for some months. Ultimately a small lance-shaped leaf emerges from the bulb.

Seeds sown in trays immediately after harvesting should be kept at about 10–15°C (50–60°F) for two or three months. Move into a cold frame for about six weeks during the winter. Return them to the warmth and the first leaf should appear. The seedlings can then be potted up. It is worth keeping the seed trays for as long as a year as the seeds may take that long to germinate.

PELARGONIUMS

● Taking cuttings of zonals

Take cuttings now for next year's specimen plants (*see* July, page 183), first having decided how many you have room to overwinter. There is always a temptation to grow too many and if you want good, strong plants you must limit yourself according to the amount of time and space available.

● Controlling pelargonium rust

Pelargonium rust is a fungal infection that appears as brown powdery rings on the underside of the leaves. Check for its presence, and at the first sign of disease, remove any infected leaves and dispose of them where they cannot continue to shed spores. Rust will be even more prevalent during a damp summer than a dry one (*see* Diseases, page 410).

● Deadheading

Continue to deadhead faded flowers.

RHODODENDRONS & AZALEAS

● Layering

Rhododendrons and azaleas that are difficult to root can be propagated by layering. If bushes are old, suitable young shoots will need to be encouraged; this can be done by pruning a shoot in March of the previous year (*see* March, page 74). After 18 months, these young shoots will be ready to be layered. Rhododendrons do not root quickly and it may take a further year or more for a layer to root properly. Rejuvenation pruning, if carried out the previous year, should result in new shoots suitable for layering (*see* Pruning, page 421).

● Air layering

Large-leaved varieties of rhododendrons, in particular, can be propagated by air layering (*see* Propagation, page 433). A young shoot from this year's growth should be selected, a leaf removed and a slither of bark, about 2.5 cm (1 in) long, taken off from behind the leaf joint. By the autumn of the following year roots will have formed.

● Stimulating new growth

If ageing rhododendrons and azaleas which have been pruned for rejuvenation are still showing no signs of new growth, spray with a seaweed growth supplement fortified with iron to encourage development of dormant buds.

● Hot weather protection

Continue to water all plants during dry spells, making sure the rootball is getting really wet; add a liquid high-nitrogen fertiliser to the water once a week. Spray the foliage and shade especially vulnerable plants from the sun (*see* June, page 159).

RHODODENDRONS & AZALEAS – LAYERING

1 Choose a flexible young rhododendron shoot that can be bent down to soil level. Strip the leaves from an area about 10–15 cm (4–6 in) back from the tip.

2 Wound the side in contact with the soil, making a small sloping cut almost halfway through the stem. Peg the shoot down in a shallow depression, using a piece of bent wire.

3 Firm moisture-holding ericaceous potting compost around the stem, mounding it slightly. Insert a cane and secure the stem to it. This will keep the tip upright.

● Controlling pests and diseases

Check the plants for Japanese lacewing, whitefly, bud blast and leafhoppers (*see* June, page 159).

ROCK PLANTS

● Ordering bulbs

Order spring-flowering bulbs for the rock garden (*see* Bulbs, corms and tubers, page 194).

● Taking cuttings

August is one of the busiest months for taking cuttings. If they have been trimmed back after flowering, many plants such as dianthus, achilleas, mossy saxifrages, dwarf phloxes and a number of the sub-shrubs such as helianthemums will, by now, have produced plenty of suitable shoots.

Place the cuttings in a mist propagator, if you have one available, or use an undersoil warming element. The objective is to create an enclosed humid environment. *Anchusa cespitosa*, aubrieta, *Gypsophila repens*, *Phlox douglasii*, *P. subulata* and *Silene acaulis* all root successfully from softwood tip cuttings, while some heathers, hebes and helianthemums are better taken as heel cuttings with a sliver of old wood. Rock plants that can be propagated from basal cuttings include *Gentiana acaulis*, *Primula auricula*, *P. marginata*, *Veronica peduncularis* and *Viola cornuta*. (*See* Propagation, pages 428–430.)

Cuttings require daily spraying during hot weather and should be kept shaded. After six to eight weeks test to see if they have rooted by tugging them gently. If there is resistance, then the roots are now established. Once rooted, increase ventilation and remove the cover when they begin to grow.

ROSES

● **Deadheading**

Deadhead regularly except for roses grown for their display of hips in the autumn.

● **Checking supports and tying in**

Freak wind conditions can sometimes occur at this time of year which can be disastrous to the heads of well-developed standard roses; check that all stakes, ties and straps are firm and in place.

Gently tie in the new long, soft shoots of climbers and ramblers to prevent damage in high winds (*see* January, page 20).

● **Controlling rust**

This is the time of the year when the ravages of rust become apparent. Rust can be identified by a discoloration of the leaves, and the tiny, bright red spots which appear on the underside of the leaves (*see* Diseases, page 410).

SWEET PEAS

● **Feeding, watering and mulching**

To prolong flowering, supplement any mulch applied earlier in the season and continue to water and feed as necessary (*see* July, page 184). If no mulch has been applied, hoe regularly.

● **Layering cordons**

Cordon-grown plants will need layering for the second time when they are 2–2.5 m (6½–8 ft) tall (*see* June, page 160).

● **Maintaining flowering**

Cut the flowers regularly as they bloom. This will prevent the formation of seed pods. Keep removing the sideshoots and tendrils on cordons. Tie in mature stems.

TREES, SHRUBS & HEDGES

● **Staking and tying**

Check stakes and ties. Remove and clean the ties to displace egg, pupa and adult stages of pests which otherwise may survive over the winter. Replace the cleaned ties and renew any rotten or damaged ones.

Check stem and branch growth for signs of rubbing and damage which can cause infection or allow water to enter the tree's tissue. If necessary cut back to prevent further damage.

Newly planted trees and other small trees will require staking for the first time, if they were not staked when first planted (*see* October, page 247).

● **Watering**

Drought can strike during the summer or autumn and many trees that are surface rooting such as maples, birches and ornamental pears, and shrubs such as deutzias, elaeagnus and weigelas, can be severely damaged. Water all new plantings regularly to counteract the effects of any drought. Established plants will also benefit from water, if it is available, but give priority to new plantings.

● **Taking semi-ripe cuttings**

Take the last semi-ripe cuttings of shrubs now, providing the selected shoots are not too firm (*see* Propagation, page 428).

● **Leaf bud cuttings**

Once leaf bud cuttings of camellias taken in March are well rooted, pot them up singly into a lime-free potting compost to grow on until they are 25–30 cm (10–12 in) high. They can then be planted out, usually in the spring, into their final growing position (*see* March, page 78).

● **Pot on spring-sown seedlings**

Pot on spring-sown seedlings that are large enough into individual 8–10 cm (3–4 in) pots, using a good quality potting compost.

● **Pruning**

Using the one-third pruning method, prune all July-flowering shrubs over three years old that have finished flowering (*see* Pruning, page 420).

REVERSION OF VARIEGATED PLANTS

Many variegated shrubs and trees suffering from drought or lack of food may revert some of their foliage from variegated to all-green colouring. These all-green growths are more vigorous and will outgrow the variegated foliage and spoil the plants. Cut out completely any green-leaved shoots as soon as they appear. Any gaps will soon be filled with new growth.

HEDGES

● **Annual trimming**

Complete the trimming of all hedges this month. This allows new growth to ripen before winter.

Conifer hedges, such as x *Cupressocyparis leylandii*, *Chamaecyparis lawsoniana* and western red cedar (*Thuja plicata*), should receive their annual trim now to prevent them from becoming overgrown. Again this leaves time for new growth to ripen before winter. Prune individual leaf sprays with secateurs, rather than with a hedge trimmer or shears, as cutting across the leaf spray on conifers will turn the remaining ends brown.

HEDGES – TRIMMING CONIFERS

Although very large conifer hedges may have to be pruned with hedge trimmers, where practical always prune conifer hedges with secateurs. Avoid cutting across the leaf sprays as the cut sprays can turn brown.

On conifer hedges planted this spring, reduce the leading and sideshoots by one-third now and repeat this for the first three years after planting. This will make a thicker, more robust hedge in the long term.

● **Weeding**

Keep the base of hedges free from weeds.

VEGETABLES

There will be a variety of crops to harvest this month including summer cabbages and cauliflowers, carrots, peas, turnips, beetroot and globe artichokes.

● **Beans**

Continue to harvest broad, French and runner beans. If you go on holiday pick all the runner beans, even the smallest, before you leave. This will ensure a continuing crop on your return.

● **Brassicas**

Sow spring cabbages in mild areas. Plant out Chinese cabbages if sown already; if not sow these now (*see* July, page 186).

● **Celery**

Water and feed celery regularly; harvest when ready.

● **Marrows, courgettes and squashes**

Continue to harvest courgettes regularly while they are still small; this helps to encourage the plants to produce more fruit for a continuing supply.

The first marrows, pumpkins and squashes should be ready for harvesting. Slip tiles or straw under the developing fruits to prevent soil or soil-borne diseases from spoiling them. Once the fruits start to ripen, remove any leaves that shade them. Cut pumpkins and winter squashes now. If you want to store them, they can be left on the plant to develop their flavour and harden their skins, but they must be harvested before the first frosts. Store the harvested fruit by hanging them up individually in nets in a cool, frost-free and well-ventilated environment.

● **Onions**

Sow overwintering onions, such as Japanese varieties, for harvesting early next summer before ordinary onions are ready. The timing of this sowing is critical as the plants need to be 15–20 cm (6–8 in) tall by October; plants larger than this may bolt, but smaller ones may not survive the winter. Sow in early to mid August if you live in a cold area, mid to late August in mild areas.

Choose a well-drained spot; neutral soil is best so add lime if your soil is acid (*see* The soil in your garden, page 392). Rake in a general fertiliser such as Growmore. Sow in rows 30 cm (12 in) apart with seed spaced 2.5 cm (1 in) apart within the rows. Water the soil if it is dry. An alternative is to wait until October or November and plant autumn sets.

Harvest the first of the ordinary onions choosing a time when there is no rain forecast if possible.

● **Other roots and swollen stems**

Feed and water celeriac regularly. Remove the lower leaves to expose the top of the 'root'.

Harvest the bulb-like leaf bases of Florence fennel when they are about the size of a tennis ball (usually 10–11 weeks after planting).

Make the last sowing of kohlrabi for this year (*see* March, page 81).

VEGETABLES – MARROWS

Reduce the risk of your marrows rotting, and help to expose them to the sun, by raising them off the soil on a tile supported on bricks. Cut away any leaves that shade the fruit from the sun.

VEGETABLES – HARVESTING ONIONS

  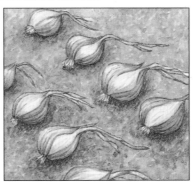 

1 Onions are ready to harvest when the foliage collapses. The old leaves at the neck of the onion should feel dry and thin, not soft and sappy.

2 Use a fork to release the roots from the ground – do not pull onions up by the leaves, or you may damage the bulb and encourage disease spores to enter.

3 Leave the onions on the surface of the soil to dry off and ripen more fully. This is important if they are to store well.

4 If the weather turns wet after you have lifted the bulbs, make certain they are dry and protected. Take them into the greenhouse or cover them with a cloche.

● Potatoes

Complete harvesting early potatoes and start to dig up the first maincrop potatoes.

● Salad crops

Sow the last spring onions, lettuces and radishes (*see* February, page 49) and continue to harvest.

Red-leaved chicory can still be sown in August (*see* April, page 113). The young plants can be cut when large enough and the stumps will re-sprout.

Blanching curly endive makes it taste less bitter. Make sure the leaves are dry, then cover them with a large plate. Harvest after a week and immediately before you want to eat the leaves.

● Spinach and spinach beet

Sow spinach beet or true spinach (choose a winter variety) now until early September and you should be able to pick leaves from November until spring.

Rake a general fertiliser into a prepared seed bed (*see* Fertilisers, page 390). Sow thinly in drills 30 cm (12 in) apart and 1 cm (½ in) deep. Thin to 10–15 cm (4–6 in) apart. Cover with a cloche during winter.

● Sweetcorn

When the sweetcorn 'silks' turn brown and wither and the cobs hang away from the stalks, peel back the sheath of leaves to check if the sweetcorn is ready for picking. Press individual kernels with a fingernail; they are at their peak when a creamy liquid is released.

● Tomatoes and aubergines

Start to pick the first ripe tomatoes and aubergines.

● Turnips

Sow the last turnips of the year to provide a crop this autumn (*see* March, page 82).

WATER PLANTS & POOLS

● Planting out

The young plants of waterside primulas (such as *Primula florindae* and hybrids) raised from spring-sown seed, should now be planted out.

● Water evaporation

Continue topping up the pool with fresh water using a garden hose. Using a spray attachment on the hose will help aerate the pool.

● Tidying up

Continue to remove the faded flower heads from marginal aquatic plants and cut off or pull away any excess growth. Thin crowded leaves on waterlilies and remove any excessive growth from submerged oxygenating plants, taking care not to remove any young fish with the plant growth.

Beautiful Borders

A border is usually planted with herbs, flowers or shrubs and adjoins a lawn or a path. Mixed borders of shrubs and herbaceous perennials are easier to look after than the traditional herbaceous border, and are brighter and more interesting than those composed entirely of shrubs. Choose your plants carefully and you can have flowers in bloom every month of the year.

◄ *Borders look best when densely planted. Although it makes mowing the lawn more difficult, plants tumbling over the edge of a lawn create a lovely natural effect.*

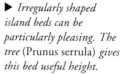

► *Irregularly shaped island beds can be particularly pleasing. The tree* (Prunus serrula) *gives this bed useful height.*

To make the most of borders in your garden, choose plants which suit the aspect of the border and your soil. There are plants for every situation so, however unpromising you think your garden is, something can always be done. Poor sandy soil should be enriched with generous applications of organic material; heavy soil can be improved by digging in rotted farmyard manure or garden compost and grit. There are lovely plants to suit limy soils and acid soils. Shady situations invite lush foliage plants, ferns and many of the lilies. Dry spots in full sun can be filled with silver foliage,

aromatic herbs and spiky phormiums and yuccas. Most nursery catalogues are helpful, providing lists of good plants for problem areas.

Once you have assessed the conditions in your own garden, look at other gardens in your area to get an idea of which plants grow well. Garden visits are helpful. In addition to the great gardens, many private gardens are also opened to the public on occasions and these are a rich source of inspiration. Always take a notebook and pencil and jot down any particular combination of plants that appeals to you – or take a photograph as a reminder.

PLANNING THE SITE

When planning a new border make sure it is in harmony with the rest of the garden. Decide what kind of bed or border you wish to make, bearing in mind that the shape, size or aspect of your garden may limit your choice. For instance, a one-sided border is not always easy to maintain as access to the rear is difficult. The backing wall or fence often restricts light and air, leading to soft lanky growth. A backing hedge may starve plants of nutrients, so leave a gap of about 45 cm (18 in) between hedge and border. An island bed has the advantage of being seen from all sides. Simple shapes look best and are easier to edge and maintain. Regular shapes, based on rectangles or circles, suit formal-style gardens, while less formal outlines with undulating edges work better with natural-style gardens.

CHOOSING YOUR PLANTS

It is as well to plan your border on paper before you order or buy plants. As you plan, think about colours and achieving a continuous display with both foliage and flowers, as well as constantly bearing in mind sun, shade and other local conditions.

The planning of a border must also take account of the height and form of each plant you want to grow. As a general rule, place the tallest plants at the rear of a one-sided border but towards the centre of an island bed. Interest is added by punctuating plants of low or more rounded habit with the occasional spiky subject such as a bright-leaved phormium or group of red-hot pokers in a sunny border, or a clump of hostas or astilbes where conditions are more moist and shady.

Separate out plants of especially rapid or slow growth, so that they don't swamp others or get lost. Consider planting small shrubs and herbaceous plants in groups of three or more. The effect will be far more striking than having single plants dotted here and there.

Height is all-important in a boundary border, whether to break up an expanse of hedge or fence, or for increased privacy. In small gardens it is not advisable to plant tall trees or vigorous shrubs, but climbing plants can be trained up wigwams of poles or purpose-built tripods. Clematis, evergreen honeysuckles and climbing or rambling roses are delightful when used in this way. Annual climbers, such as sweet peas and nasturtiums, can also be grown to provide stunning pillars of colour. If your border is backed by a wall or fence you can train

▲ *Colour themed borders, like this red one, can be very striking. They are more appropriate for a large garden as they can be too dominating in a small area.*

climbing plants along wires or through trellis. This is particularly appropriate for small gardens where shrubs take up too much space.

COLOUR THEMES

Colour is a matter of personal preference, but lovely borders can be created by limiting the number of colours. Single-colour borders, utilising all the different shades, also appeal to many gardeners but can be limiting in a small garden. It is often more effective to create pockets of colour. Try, for instance, yellow antirrhinums and argyranthemums in front of a golden-leaved shrub such as *Choisya ternata* 'Sundance' for summer cheer, with daffodils, yellow tulips and crocuses in spring.

Colour can also be used to create illusions. White and pale colours stand out at night. Shades of blue and mauve appear more distant than bright

reds, yellows and oranges. If you plant these hotter colours nearer the house, with misty blue flowers further away, your border will appear longer than it really is and make the garden look bigger.

CONTINUOUS DISPLAY

Try to aim for a continuous display, so there is always something of interest in your border whatever the time of year. If too many plants flower at the same time, this will inevitably cause the bed to look bare at other times. Devote areas of the border to different seasons of the year. Pockets of seasonal colour will have more impact than flowers thinly spread throughout the border.

Clumps of bulbs, especially those that flower in spring and autumn, are particularly useful for extending the season. Any bare patches, such as those occupied by spring bulbs, can be filled in summer with annuals. Another way of filling gaps and introducing colour is to plunge pots of bedding plants or tender perennials into gaps in the border. Once past their best they can be replaced by others held in reserve.

▲ *A mixed border, with shrubs and herbaceous plants together, will provide a long period of interest with its changing colours and foliage.*

SEPTEMBER

Bright colours in the border
accompany the harvest as the
apples, pears and plums ripen
and the kitchen garden provides
potatoes, carrots and onions
for the winter.

September

After the lull of activity at the end of summer, suddenly there are lots of jobs to be done in the garden, some of them urgent. The summer bedding will now be past its best, and it is time to think about replanting for a spring display. If there are early frosts, the transition between summer and autumn can seem abrupt, yet in some years fine weather can continue through to the end of the month. In September, you need to be especially alert to changing weather conditions to get one step ahead, so that everything that needs to be completed before the first frosts arrive is achieved.

Finish taking late cuttings as soon as possible this month and sow appropriate seeds while there is still residual warmth in the soil. Autumn is the best time to plant trees and shrubs, so plan your new plantings, organise ordering and buying and start planting as soon as there has been enough rain to make watering unnecessary. In some years this may not be until October.

The weather in September
This is a month of transition. Although it is the first month of autumn, September can provide spells of warm, dry weather and in the south it can then seem more like a continuation of summer. Generally, however, the effects of the shortening days are noticeable, and the sun has considerably less warmth than it had just a few weeks before. In colder northern regions, in an unfavourable year, it may almost seem as though winter has arrived early. There the grass and the bracken turn brown, frosts are almost certain and in some years there will be snow on the hills by the end of the month. Everywhere in the country the reliability and warmth of August disappears, yet really bad weather is unlikely, unless you garden in the far north.

Differences between north and south are much more pronounced than in August, and the advice given for this month must be read with that in mind. Certain tasks may need to be tackled several weeks earlier in cold, northern regions than in the milder southern areas. Summers also seem shorter in gardens in exposed positions or at high altitudes. Never be complacent, wherever you live, as there may well be a September frost even in the milder regions of the south.

Strong winds are likely too, particularly at the time of the equinoctial gales at the end of the month, so it is important that stakes and ties are secure.

Pests and diseases
There is a temptation to be more relaxed about pest and disease control at the end of the season. It is easy to convince yourself that it doesn't matter if leaves succumb to disease as they will fall soon anyway, and you may as well ignore those greenfly because you plan to pull the plant up soon. However, if you fail to control pests and diseases now, you may be storing up problems that will lie dormant until next year.

Diseased leaves don't have to be sprayed if you want to minimise the use of chemicals, but cut them off or prune out affected parts and burn or otherwise dispose of them so that over-wintering spores won't survive until next year. Never put infected leaves on the compost heap or leave them on the soil – the spores released could overwinter there to cause a new round of infection next spring.

Continue to watch for and control insect pests. Bear in mind that many biological controls become less reliable when the temperature drops as the predatory insects which are the control then multiply more slowly. One simple measure you can take is to prune off shoots on herbaceous plants or annuals which are infested with greenfly and burn or otherwise dispose of them.

Slug damage is less noticeable at this time as holes in old leaves are never as conspicuous as they are in young ones. But don't ease up on slug control, and check garden rubbish and uncleared areas, which give slugs shelter.

Weed control
Weeds tend to be overlooked at the end of the season, especially if beds and borders are scheduled for clearing and digging over, perhaps in preparation for spring bedding plants. But if weeds are allowed to set and shed their seeds in autumn, the seeds will be in the soil ready to germinate next year, so use the hoe now to save yourself more work in the future. The way to a weed-free garden is to reduce the number of weed seeds in the soil.

While the ground is still warm and moist it

is a good time to mulch any areas that have not been covered already and to replenish old mulches. If the soil is dry, soak it first. Be sure to weed thoroughly before you mulch.

Other jobs to remember

Two routine jobs – deadheading and watering – are often top of the maintenance list in summer, but may be overlooked now as the rains come and autumn approaches. Deadheading won't extend the flowering season for much longer, but it may help to keep summer bedding plants flowering for an extra week or so, which shortens the time in the garden without colourful flowers. Just as important at this time of year, deadheading makes the plants look neat and tidy.

The lawn probably won't need regular watering now, and if the weather is wet even newly planted trees, shrubs and herbaceous plants can be left to fend for themselves. But don't let the soil become dry, as these new plantings will not yet have rooted into the surrounding soil.

Make the most of mild weather

September is an excellent month for doing those garden maintenance jobs that you have been putting off during the warm, lazy days of summer, and for construction work such as laying a path or patio. The weather now is not too hot for physical work, and not too cold for time spent in the garden to be uncomfortable. It is also easier to work in lighter clothes, rather than in cold weather gear.

In addition, pond maintenance is less unpleasant now than later when the water becomes too cold for comfort. This is a good time of the year to clear out the pond, and even routine chores, such as cleaning pots and canes before storing them away for the winter and tidying the greenhouse, are easy and pleasant tasks for the beginning of autumn.

JOBS THAT WON'T WAIT

- Harvest fruit and vegetables when ripe. Store apples and pears for use over the winter.

- Sow hardy annuals to be overwintered outdoors as soon as possible in cold areas. They will probably require protecting over the winter with cloches or horticultural fleece.

- Sow parsley and chervil to provide leaves for winter and spring use. Put herbs in pots to force for early shoots next year. Harvest all basil since the leaves soon deteriorate as nights get colder.

- Plant out spring-flowering biennials including wallflowers and forget-me-nots in their flowering positions to give them time to establish before the winter.

- Plant prepared bulbs in containers for indoor display to ensure you have blooms over Christmas.

- Plant bulbs for spring-flowering in the garden. Give priority to daffodils as they begin their root growth earlier than most bulbs.

- Before the first frost lift tender or slightly tender perennials, such as argyranthemums, fuchsias and pelargoniums, to be overwintered under protection. If you do not have room to house many plants under cover, take cuttings of tender perennials to keep over the winter in case the parent plant dies.

- Move late-flowering chrysanthemums in pots into the greenhouse before the first frost.

- Bring in house plants that have been standing outdoors for the summer before the evenings become cold. Don't wait until the first frost is forecast.

- Cover summer bedding with several layers of horticultural fleece if it is still blooming well and frost is forecast. This protection may be sufficient to prolong the display for a little longer.

- Maintain pest and disease control so that you are not storing up problems for next year. Continue to remove weeds so that they do not shed seeds which will remain in the soil over the winter.

ANNUALS & BIENNIALS

● Planting annuals and biennials

It is important, especially in cold areas, to plant out spring-flowering annuals and biennials in their flowering positions to give the plants as much time as possible to establish themselves before the winter.

● Regular care

Hard frosts may not occur until November or even December, so it is worth continuing a regular programme of care: deadheading, watering, feeding and pest control. This helps to prolong summer bedding displays. If frost is forecast and the summer bedding is still blooming well, try covering it with several layers of horticultural fleece to prolong the display. Once the frost has spoiled summer bedding it should be cleared.

● Sowing hardy annuals

In all but the coldest regions, make use of unheated greenhouses and cold frames by sowing hardy annuals such as clarkia, godetia, larkspurs and poppies to overwinter as seedlings. Prick out into trays or individual pots when the first true leaves appear or when plants are large enough to handle.

Overwinter the seedlings under glass and plant out next spring. In mild areas they should survive the winter without supplementary heating, but it is wise to maintain a cool, frost-free environment. This brings the flowering time forward and plants are stronger and bushier. Ensure the seedlings get as much light as possible (*see* Greenhouses, page 218).

In mild areas hardy annuals can also be sown outside in prepared seed beds. Sow them in rows and protect with cloches or horticultural fleece if necessary until March. You can then transfer the plants to their flowering positions during May.

BORDER PERENNIALS

● Buying plants

Check which new plants can be planted in autumn and which are best left until the spring. List those available for propagating and those to be bought. Visit garden centres and nurseries and study mail order catalogues, ordering plants where necessary.

When buying, choose good, healthy stock with firm crowns and foliage. Containers should be well packed with firm compost and plants should be carefully labelled. Field-grown plants (*see* March, page 58) can be assessed by their top growth.

● Preparing and planting

In dry areas it is advisable to plant in the autumn, as the rainfall over the winter months will keep plants in good health. September is the best month for this, so finish preparing the ground as soon as possible (*see* August, page 194). Make sure that added fertiliser or manure is thoroughly mixed into the soil before planting.

Choose days for planting when the soil is moist and the weather is not too cold or windy. Water the plants in and, if a dry spell follows, continue to check that they have sufficient water at the roots until they are well established.

BORDER PERENNIALS – PLANTING OUT

1 Plant so that the crown of each plant is level with the surface of the soil. If plants are bare-rooted be careful not to damage the roots.

2 For plants in pots, check that the hole is the correct size, remove the plant from the pot and gently spread out the rootball. Place the plant in the hole and fill with soil.

3 Always firm in well. If the plant is small and the hole shallow, you can do this with your hands, otherwise tread the soil carefully to remove pockets of air.

4 If in doubt about whether the plant has been planted firmly enough, tug it gently. It should not move in the soil. Water in, and keep well watered until established.

● Planting spring bulbs

Plant spring-flowering bulbs such as daffodils and crown imperials (*Fritillaria imperialis*) to give early colour and to fill gaps between plants. If you are using early bulbs to mark late-flowering perennials (*see* March, page 57), choose small varieties and plant around, rather than immediately over, the dormant plants, otherwise when the dormant plants emerge, they may dislodge the early bulbs.

● Winter protection

Frosts in September are not often as severe or long-lasting as in later autumn, but care is still needed. Cover tender or young plants with cloches, netting, newspaper, old woollens or similar materials if frosts are forecast. Remove when the temperature rises.

Make preparations to overwinter tender perennials under cover in pots or as cuttings (*see* pages 228–229).

● Deadheading and collecting seeds

Keep the border tidy by cutting back flowered stems and deadheading unless seeds are required. Later-flowering plants may now have set seed, so collect these, ensuring that the seeds are dry before storing (*see* July, page 170).

BULBS, CORMS & TUBERS

When summer bedding is spoiled by frost remove it and replace it with bulbs for spring flowering.

● Planting spring-flowering bulbs

Daffodils and hyacinths are best for an early display, tulips for a later one. Plant the bulbs on their own or between plants such as wallflowers, forget-me-nots, winter pansies and polyanthus. Spring-flowering bulbs can also be planted in tubs and windowboxes (*see* Container Gardening, page 215), and dwarf irises and squills in informal groups in the rock garden (*see* Rock Plants, page 224).

Bulbs are remarkably tolerant in the first year, but whether they thrive after that depends on how well they are suited to their position. Those that come from the Mediterranean and the Near East, such as alliums, tulips and crocuses, prefer drier conditions, where they can get full sun in the summer. Woodland plants, such as bluebells and winter aconites (*Eranthis hyemalis*), will do best in deep, leafy soil that doesn't dry out too much.

When planting a bed devoted to bulbs, first plan the layout. Start planting in the centre and work outwards to the edges allowing about 15 cm (6 in) between bulbs in each direction.

If you are planting bulbs in a mixed border, plant the perennials and shrubs first and then position the bulbs between them. Allow more space between bulbs when planting them in this way.

As a rough guide to planting depth, bury each bulb twice as deep as its height. For example, cover a 5 cm (2 in) daffodil bulb with 10 cm (4 in) of soil.

If you have a great many bulbs to plant, or the weather is bad, plant the daffodils first. They begin their root growth earlier than most bulbs.

EASY PLANTING METHOD

If you want an instant display on a lawn or in rough grass, an easy method for planting small bulbs, such as crocuses, snowdrops and scillas, is to make holes 8–10 cm (3–4 in) deep with a crowbar or dibber in an irregular pattern. Fill the bottoms of the holes with peat, peat substitute or fine soil, place a bulb in each, then fill to the surface with peat, peat substitute or sand. The grass will soon cover the tiny patches, and you can mow through the autumn until the bulbs start to grow at the end of winter.

You have to allow all the leaves to die down to build up the strength of the bulbs before you start mowing again next spring, but if you want to start

BULBS – PLANTING OUTDOORS

◁ 1

2 ▽

Except where bulbs are grown as bedding plants, irregular, informal groups of bulbs look better than regularly spaced arrangements.
(1) To achieve an informal grouping, scatter between 6 and 20 bulbs on the ground and plant each where it falls.
(2) Use a trowel for planting small bulbs and a bulb-planting tool (shown here) or a small spade for planting larger ones.

mowing early in the year and you are prepared to sacrifice the bulbs, choose early-flowering varieties and replant with fresh bulbs each autumn.

● Winter-flowering arum lilies

Repot arum lilies (*Zantedeschia aethiopica*) for winter flowering under glass, using John Innes No. 3 potting compost. Place one plant in each 13–15 cm (5–6 in) pot, or three in a 20–23 cm (8–9 in) pot. Store in the greenhouse or indoors.

● Gladioli

Cut gladiolus flower spikes regularly, leaving at least four leaves on each plant (*see* August, page 195).

CARNATIONS & PINKS

Pinks, with their neat grey foliage, make a satisfying edging for flower beds and also combine well in mixed plantings. The older and species types are particularly suitable for soil pockets on tops of walls.

● Planting out cuttings

Some cuttings of pinks taken in June should now be vigorous enough for planting out. Take care not to bury plants deeper than the soil level in the pots, and for best effect space them about 20–25 cm (8–10 in) apart in groups of one variety.

Any cuttings which are not large enough to be planted out should be put in cold frames or an unheated greenhouse to overwinter. Reduce watering until growth resumes in March.

● Stopping bushy plants

Keep a watch on young plants which may be showing signs of running to flower prematurely without establishing bushy sideshoots. Shoots elongating to beyond ten joints should be stopped at the seventh joint. Hold the stem firmly with one hand and then bend the top sideways to snap it off. This is best done in early morning when the plant tissue is crisp. Alternatively, you can cut the shoots off just above the seventh joint.

● Preparing beds

Continue to prepare beds for border carnations and pinks (*see* August, page 195).

● Layers

Check on layers taken in July and August. Sever layers which have rooted and pot up those which were severed last month and have established themselves independently of the parent plant.

PERPETUAL-FLOWERING

Disbud each flower stem when the small buds surrounding the top (crown) bud and the buds lower down the stem reach 5 mm (¼ in) in length. Gently rub away all the buds except the top one.

Young plants stopped earlier will be coming into flower for the first time. Take care not to let water fall on the opening blooms as this may mark them. If the calyces (the tubular sheaths surrounding the petals) show signs of splitting, fix a split ring of thin wire, a proprietary cardboard collar or a rubber band around them.

For indoor use cut blooms with long stems, making the cut just above the sideshoots at the base. Stand the cut blooms up to their necks in water in a cool place for 12 hours before arranging them.

Continue to feed the carnations (*see* April, page 92) and adjust the shading and ventilation in the greenhouse as necessary.

PLANTING BULBS FOR INDOOR DISPLAY

Plant up bowls of bulbs now to flower from Christmas until Easter. Use bulbs specially prepared for indoor flowering if possible as these are more likely to give good results. Planting the bulbs in containers without drainage holes means the bowls can be stood on furniture without damaging the surface. Put some broken tiles or similar and a thick layer of coarse peat or moss in the bottom of the pot to prevent stagnant water from accumulating. Planting in specially prepared bulb fibre encourages root growth and allows moisture to be retained without excluding air, but any good potting compost can be used.

As a general rule small bulbs should be planted with their tops about 2.5 cm (1 in) below the rim of the container. They should then be covered with more compost or fibre until the surface is about 1 cm (½ in) below the rim. Hyacinths should be planted with the crown of the bulbs just visible on the surface. Fill the container to the rim when watering.

With all indoor bulbs the aim is to produce a mass of colour, so pack in as many bulbs as the container will hold and as closely together as possible. To obtain a spectacular show of daffodils or tulips, plant the bulbs in two layers in a 25 cm (10 in) pot. Place one layer of bulbs halfway down the pot, almost covering them with fibre. Then put another layer in the spaces on top. This method cannot be used for hyacinths.

With all indoor bulbs it is necessary for the bulbs to fill the bowl or pot with roots before the leaves and flower stems start to grow. This takes 10 to 14 weeks and is best achieved in moist, dark, cool conditions. After planting and watering, wrap the bowls in sheets of newspaper and put them in the coolest available shed or room. Alternatively, place them outdoors against a north wall. Protect with newspapers to keep them clean then cover with 15 cm (6 in) of composted bark, sand or soil. This procedure is known as plunging.

CARNATIONS – AVOIDING A SPLIT CALYX

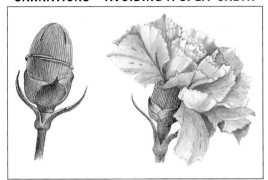

The calyces of large-flowered carnations may split, spoiling the bloom. You can prevent this from happening by slipping a split wire ring, a proprietary collar or a rubber band around the buds as soon as they show signs of colour.

CHRYSANTHEMUMS

EARLY-FLOWERING (GARDEN)

Outdoor varieties of all types will be in full flower this month. Select the best and label them clearly for propagating next year (*see* March, page 61).

● **Flowers for cutting**

Allow flowers for cutting to become well developed on the plants first. When cut, stand the blooms in 25–30 cm (10–12 in) of water in a cool place before arranging them, first stripping all leaves from the lower 30 cm (12 in) of stems.

To protect flowers for exhibition, cover blooms with greaseproof bags and protect them against earwigs (*see* Pests, page 400).

LATE-FLOWERING (GREENHOUSE)

Bring pot-grown varieties into the greenhouse for

flowering by the middle of the month, before the first frosts. Before moving them inside, clean the greenhouse glass so that the plants will get as much light as possible. Clean the pots and remove all dead or damaged leaves. Check the plants thoroughly for signs of pests or diseases such as powdery mildew (*see* Pests and Diseases, page 410), and water the day before bringing them in. Carry large plants into the greenhouse pot end first, to lessen risk of damage. Make sure that each pot stands firm and level, allowing at least 30 cm (12 in) between them.

Keep ventilators and, if possible, the doors open day and night for the first week to ten days. Keep the floor clean and dry, and the greenhouse cool.

If you are growing chrysanthemums in the greenhouse border, keep the night temperature at around 13°C (55°F) at the end of the month while the buds are forming.

● **Feeding**

Mid and late-flowering varieties will still benefit from applications of a balanced fertiliser (*see* Fertilisers, page 390) until the buds show colour. At this stage you should discontinue feeding.

VERY LATE-FLOWERING VARIETIES

Continue to disbud these as necessary (*see* August, page 195).

CLIMBERS & WALL SHRUBS

● **Buying new plants**

Garden centres and nurseries normally have a wide choice of hardy climbers and wall shrubs in stock now, so September is a good month to select new plants. Consider the size, preferred aspect, and the flowers and foliage that different plants can offer

(*see* March, page 63). Climbers add height and interest to a garden, even in narrow planting sites, but remember to allow a good-sized area for the new plant's roots. Prepare the soil before planting (*see* February, page 37).

● **Tidying up**

Remove any rubbish that has built up at the bases of climbers and wall shrubs during the summer. This allows winter rain to reach the soil below, giving the plants much needed moisture.

● **Pruning**

As soon as flowering finishes, continue the one-third pruning method on shrubs over three years old (*see* Pruning, page 420).

● **Clematis cuttings**

Any clematis cuttings propagated under glass in the spring (*see* May, page 126) should now be established and can be planted out in their growing positions.

CONTAINER GARDENING

● **Regular care and feeding**

Plants in containers can provide colour right up to the first frosts, so don't give up on routine care including watering and feeding (*see* May, page 127).

● **Planting up containers for spring**

Now is a good time to buy and plant bulbs and other spring-flowering plants for container displays. Dwarf bulbs look best as they are usually more in scale with the container – try planting scillas, chionodoxas, early crocuses (*Crocus chrysanthus* varieties), dwarf daffodils, such as 'Tête-à-Tête', and dwarf tulips. You can delay planting tulips until

October or November if you are planting them on their own but plant them now if they are to form part of a mixed display of bulbs.

If the summer displays in your main containers are still looking good and you don't want to remove them yet, plant bulbs in cheap plastic pots and sink them into the containers later when the summer flowers have died down.

For additional early colour choose small spring flowers such as dwarf wallflowers, forget-me-nots, polyanthus and hardy primrose hybrids. Evergreen alpines such as aubrieta and alyssum are useful for trailing over the edges of containers.

● Winter displays

The sooner you plant up containers for winter show, the better the result will be. Plants need time to grow and establish themselves before the really bad weather sets in. Try cyclamen, winter-flowering heathers and pansies for colour. They can be planted together with small container-grown shrubs, such as the small-leafed hebes, and with trailing ivies. Ornamental cabbages and kale bring a touch of humour to winter containers.

● Overwintering tender perennials

Lifting all the tender perennials such as osteospermums, argyranthemums, fuchsias and pelargoniums for overwintering, can cause problems if you do not have the space to house them, but save as many as you can (*see* pages 228–229).

DAHLIAS

September is the best time for dahlia shows and displays. Visit local flower shows and gardens to identify new varieties you would like to grow.

● Checking supports

By now dahlias are quite large and becoming top heavy. Any strong winds at this time of year will blow down plants that are not properly staked or protected. Check all ties and stakes or canes, adding more where needed. Do not place the extra stakes and canes too close to the dahlia stems as they will damage the developing tubers and root systems.

● Plants for propagating

Now that the plants are flowering well, mark the best ones of each variety so that they can be propagated for next year.

● Saving seeds

To produce some seeds of your own to sow next spring, allow a few blooms to develop fully and leave them on the plants until the seed heads have ripened. When they are swollen, but before the first frosts, cut them off and leave them to dry in a cool place. However, as plants grown from seed do not come true to variety, most are likely to be inferior to their parents. It is probably not worth sowing dahlia seeds unless you have a large area of ground where you can grow them on to see if any are worth propagating vegetatively in future years.

FRUIT

Pick all fruit as it ripens. Order new trees, bushes or cane fruits; some varieties may not be available later. Remember that gardens in valleys or those surrounded by hedges can be liable to damaging spring frosts. If this describes your garden, choose late-flowering and frost-resistant varieties. Bear in mind the space you have available and the ultimate size of trees and bushes.

● Apples and pears

Varieties suitable for keeping will not be ready for picking until the second half of this month and throughout October. The earlier maturing varieties should either be left on the trees to ripen or eaten within two weeks or so of picking. Dessert and cooking apples for storing should be picked at the right time for the variety.

Pick early dessert pears when still hard and ripen them indoors. Pick cooking pears as these are required and cook them while still hard.

Treat all fruit gently as damage to apples and pears before, during or after picking ruins them for storage. The best time to pick is when the fruit has reached its maximum size but before it has ripened.

Suitable storage places include garages, cellars, brick outhouses and even unheated rooms. A low and even temperature is the main requirement. The ideal

---

APPLES THAT STORE WELL

Early-maturing apples will not keep but those ripening after October can be picked immature and stored until they ripen. New varieties are always being developed but dependable ones are:

Dessert	Pick	Ready
Egremont Russet	late Sept	Oct–Nov
Greensleeves	mid Sept	Oct–Nov
Kidd's Orange Red	early Oct	Nov–Jan
Laxton's Superb	early Oct	Nov–Jan
Sturmer Pippin	mid Oct	Jan–Apr
Sunset	late Sept	Oct–Dec

Cooking		
Annie Elizabeth	late Sept	Nov–Apr
Bramley's Seedling	mid Oct	Dec–Mar
Lane's Prince Albert	late Sept	Dec–Mar
Lord Derby	late Sept	Oct–Dec
Newton Wonder	mid Oct	Nov–Mar

FRUIT – STORING APPLES & PEARS

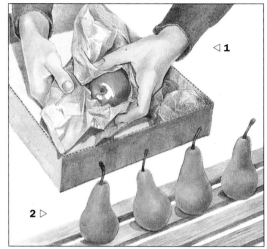

(1) Store large crops of apples individually wrapped in newspaper or tissue paper and packed in boxes. Small quantities of apples can be stored in unsealed plastic bags. (2) Pears shouldn't be wrapped but stood on trays or shelves.

storage temperature for apples and pears is between 4°C (39°F) and freezing.

Prune shoots on all espalier and cordon-trained trees that were immature in early August if they are now ready (*see* August, page 196).

Apply or renew greasebands on the trunks to catch winter moths as they climb up the trunk for the winter. The caterpillars from their eggs feed on the blossom in spring (*see* October, page 239).

● Plums and cherries

Protect ripening fruit from birds and squirrels if you can. Pick the fruit as it becomes ripe but beware of wasps when picking.

Cut back dead, diseased or broken branches after picking. Paint all saw cuts with wound paint (*see* Pruning, page 423). Do not delay pruning beyond the end of the month (*see* June, page 152).

Spray cherry trees against bacterial canker if this is necessary (*see* Diseases, page 406).

● Peaches and nectarines

Finish cutting out fruited shoots and tying in the replacements on fan-trained trees.

Protect late varieties from birds, wasps and the cold by covering them with horticultural fleece.

● Cane fruits

Pick autumn-fruiting varieties of raspberries and other cane fruits regularly and often. Cover them with horticultural fleece once the weather turns cold at night. This will keep them fruiting and will protect the berries. Guard ripening fruit from birds and wasps using netting or wasp traps.

Cut down any remaining fruited canes of summer raspberries and tie in the new ones. Autumn varieties are not pruned until next spring.

Do the same with the fruited canes of blackberries and hybrid canes. Loosely tie hybrid canes together for mutual winter protection.

● Strawberries

Finish planting summer-fruiting varieties of strawberries by the middle of the month.

Cover the rows of perpetual (autumn) varieties with cloches or horticultural fleece at night when it becomes cold. This will help them to ripen.

Protect fruiting plants from slugs, birds and wasps.

FUCHSIAS

TENDER AND HALF-HARDY
● Watering and feeding

Continue to water regularly, but always check the dampness of the soil in pots and containers, as overwatering can do more harm than underwatering at this time of the year (*see* August, page 198).

Continue to feed with a high-potash fertiliser to help the growth to ripen in preparation for winter.

FRUIT – PRUNING AND TRAINING SUMMER-FRUITING RASPBERRIES

  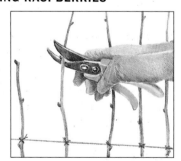

1 Cut down the stems of summer raspberries that have fruited this year to just above the ground. (Do not prune autumn-fruiting raspberries now.)

2 In their place, tie in, about 10 cm (4 in) apart on the wires, the new canes that have grown this year. These will carry next year's fruit.

3 Once the leaves have fallen, shorten long canes to about 15 cm (6 in) above the top wire. This can be done at any time until late winter.

● **Deadheading**

Continue to remove faded flower heads to encourage plants to produce a second or even a third flush of flowers, rather than the plants putting all their energy into seed production.

● **Controlling pests and diseases**

Continue to control infestations of aphids and white-fly. Discourage diseases such as grey mould (botrytis) by clearing away fallen flowers and leaves; this helps to maintain a high standard of hygiene (*see* Pests and Diseases, pages 395–411).

● **Preparing for autumn**

Move under cover before the first frost any plants raised for early flowering next year. Make sure the greenhouse is clean before bringing the plants in.

GARDEN MAINTENANCE

● **Major construction work**

Try to complete major construction jobs, especially those that involve concreting and repainting, before the first frosts.

● **Maintaining the greenhouse**

Check the greenhouse for repairs which may need to be carried out before cold weather sets in if you have not already done this (*see* August, page 198–199). Ensure the greenhouse heater is safe and in good working order. Protect all electrical fitments in the greenhouse with a residual current device (RCD) (*see* Tools and Equipment, page 439), and, if you already have an RCD, check it for signs of heat stress such as melting plastic. Also check that the leads are not damaged and that all electrical fittings are waterproof.

If you use a paraffin heater, remember to buy the fuel before the first frosts arrive. Store it safely.

● **Water butts**

It is an excellent idea to install water butts but make sure they have lids otherwise they attract insects and accumulate debris. September is a good time to clean butts out to prevent contamination of the water and blocked taps. Empty the water butts then fill them up with diluted garden disinfectant and scrub them down. Use a hosepipe to clear down-pipes of any debris, then cover the end with a piece of chicken wire. Drain away the dirty water and rinse out the inside with clean water.

GREENHOUSES & FRAMES

● **Heating**

In this transitional period of the year, as summer changes into autumn, a little artificial heat regulated by a greenhouse thermostat may be beneficial to your plants.

● **Shading**

Towards the end of the month remove the shading wash from the glass if you have not done this before. If the weather becomes hot and sunny you can always provide local shading for young and tender seedlings and cuttings, using paper, butter muslin or horticultural fleece.

● **Cleaning**

Clean and disinfect the greenhouse now if this was not carried out last month (*see* August, page 198).

● **Pests and diseases**

By the end of the month the atmosphere in the greenhouse is likely to be damper and cooler, so be alert to signs of grey mould (botrytis).

● **Bringing in tender plants**

Before the nights turn too cold, bring into the green-house any young or tender plants that have been outside in frames or in the garden during the summer. Discard any plants of indifferent quality and check carefully for signs of pests or disease.

● **Sowing annuals**

Annuals, such as cornflowers, calendulas, nemesias and godetias, sown in early September and grown as pot plants in a cool greenhouse, will make a colour-ful display during spring and early summer next year. Schizanthus is another excellent plant to grow in this way. Plant the seeds in trays of seed compost, and keep at a temperature of 13–15°C (55–60°F), and prick out the seedlings into 8 cm (3 in) pots of potting compost as soon as they are large enough to handle. Plant one seedling per pot. Keep the plants over the winter on a shelf near the glass (*see* November, page 262).

● **Taking cuttings**

If you have not already done so, it is still possible to take cuttings of a number of plants which can be overwintered under cover. These include tender per-ennials, such as osteospermums and penstemons, herbs, shrubs, fuchsias, pelargoniums and house plants (*see* pages 228–229).

● **Vines**

Reduce ventilation and watering as the grapes ripen and stop feeding as soon as the grapes start to colour. Remove leaves which are covering the grapes. This will assist ripening. Pick bunches as they ripen and remove any mildewed fruit and leaves at the same time. This helps to reduce the spread of the fungus.

● Tomatoes, peppers, cucumbers

Harvest before the first frost if the greenhouse is not heated. It is not normally economical to heat a greenhouse sufficiently to continue growing tomatoes. Once quality deteriorates, strip most of the leaves from tomatoes and peppers to encourage ripening of any remaining fruit.

HEATHERS

● Planting out new beds

Take any heathers you have grown in pots and, keeping them in the pots, arrange them in their proposed flowering positions. Place *Calluna vulgaris, Erica carnea, E. ciliaris, E. cinerea* and *E. tetralix* varieties 30–40 cm (12–16 in) apart; *E.* × *darleyensis* and *E. vagans* about 40–50 cm (16–20 in) apart; *E. erigena* 60–75 cm (2–2½ ft) apart and tree heathers 1 m (3 ft) apart.

View the bed from several angles ensuring that the plants are not in straight lines. Move the pots until you are satisfied with the overall design, then plant the heathers.

Make sure the plants are well soaked, and plant them deeply, with the lower leaves resting on the soil surface or even slightly buried. In the case of *E. carnea*, plant so that any trailing branches are bunched together in an upright position to ensure compact plants in the future.

If the bed has been prepared properly (*see* January, page 23), there is no need to add extra peat. Never plant heathers in pockets of pure peat; this is the most common cause of early failure.

● Watering

Continue to water young plantings regularly and potted-up plants daily if necessary. Use rainwater if possible (*see* April, page 101).

● Deadheading and cutting for the house

Continue to deadhead daboecia as the flowers fade (*see* July, page 179). In a late year you can continue to cut double-flowered *Calluna vulgaris* for flower arranging or freezing (*see* August, page 199).

HERBS

● Sowing seeds to overwinter

Sow parsley and chervil in a sunny, well-drained position. They will be ready for use by late winter or early spring (*see* March, page 70).

● Culinary herbs for winter use

Lift large clumps of three to four-year-old chives and separate them carefully into manageable segments, taking care that each segment retains a number of roots. Plant them in large pots, water well to settle the roots and leave the pots outside in an exposed position so that the cold induces a dormant state. In December they can be brought inside to produce early shoots next year. French tarragon, mint and sorrel may also be forced in this way.

Some basils may be brought inside on to a well-lit windowsill. The small-leaved Greek basils are best for this. Pick the rest as soon as possible, since basil leaves soon deteriorate as the nights get colder and the days start to shorten.

● Thinning seedlings

Thin earlier sowings of lamb's lettuce, land cress and winter purslane to give them room to develop.

● Trimming herbs

Lightly trim aromatic plants to tidy them up for winter. Stalks and top growth from lavender, cotton lavender, sage or thyme may be dried and tied in bundles to burn on winter fires. The stems of this season's growth of artemisia may be bound into circles for festive wreaths. Rosemary, bay, thyme and sage should not be cut until just before use.

● Garlic

Garlic can be planted outdoors in favourable areas. It grows best in light, well-dug soil; heavy soil may affect the keeping qualities. Apply sulphate of potash (*see* Fertilisers, page 390) and fork it in well.

Split the garlic bulb into cloves and plant them, root down, about 5 cm (2 in) deep and 15 cm (6 in) apart. Much of the large root growth is made during the cold season. In February green shoots will make rapid growth into a mature plant about 60 cm (2 ft) tall with long, dark green leaves by late spring.

HERBS – PLANTING GARLIC CLOVES

Garlic likes a long growing season and can be planted outdoors now in mild parts of the country. In cold areas or where the soil is heavy, start off in modular trays. Plant each clove separately and cover with compost. Keep them in a cold frame over the winter and plant out in spring.

● **Dividing perennial herbs**

Lift and divide four to five-year-old clumps of perennial herbs such as bergamot, lovage, lemon balm, tansy and soapwort. Discard the old, woody centres and replant in new positions in groups of three to five (*see* Propagation, pages 431–432).

● **Tidying beds**

Remove dead leaves, broken shoots or stems and continue to weed around herbs.

● **Cuttings**

Bay, curry plant, lavender, sage, thyme, winter savory and rue can still be increased by cuttings inserted round the rim of a pot filled with gritty compost (*see* July, page 179). Protect these cuttings under a cloche or in a cold frame.

HOUSE & CONSERVATORY PLANTS

● **Watering, feeding and cleaning**

Reduce watering and feeding towards the end of the month as growth slows down and flowering stops. Many plants rest over the winter so need very little water and no food.

Remove dead leaves and clean the remaining ones (*see* February, page 42).

● **Preparing plants for winter**

Bring in plants from their outside summer quarters. Clean and inspect pots and plants for pests (*see* May, page 133). Pick off any damaged or yellowing leaves. Remove the top layer of compost and replace with fresh compost. Clear any blocked drainage holes with a sharp stick.

Transfer plants that need plenty of light in winter from west-facing to south-facing windows.

● **Repotting and pruning**

This is generally the last month for repotting or pruning before growth slows down for the winter.

● **Layering**

Check on any plants propagated by layering earlier in the year. If the roots have developed well, cut the new plant away from the parent and pot up.

● **Flowering plants**

Stop feeding and reduce watering African violets (*Saintpaulia ionantha*) once flowering stops. Move any that have not flowered to a bright position. To develop flower buds, they need at least 12 hours of good light every day.

Bring azaleas back indoors before the first frosts and place in a cool position.

Poinsettias which have been cut back in the spring and kept growing through the summer should have their day length shortened if they are to produce

---

BRINGING COLOUR BACK TO POINSETTIAS

Poinsettias that have been kept through the summer are unlikely to flower for Christmas unless the amount of light they receive is reduced and artificial light eliminated for a couple of months. The bracts will eventually colour, but probably not until nearer spring. This is because the plants are sensitive to day length and need at least 14 hours of darkness each day to stimulate the production of flowers.

Turning on artificial light will interrupt the dark period and delay flowering, so each evening cover the plants with a thick, black plastic tent to eliminate the light, and leave in place for 14 hours. Be sure to remove the blackout in the morning so that the plants receive good light during the day.

After eight weeks the treatment can be discontinued and the plants treated normally.

---

colourful bracts for Christmas. Cover them each evening so they are in total darkness for 14 hours each night. Continue this for eight weeks.

Keep gardenias humid and at a minimum temperature of 15°C (60°F). Water with rainwater or distilled water.

Repot arum lilies (*Zantedeschia aethiopica*) for winter flowering (*see* Bulbs, page 214).

Many flowering house plants, including busy lizzies, will propagate readily from cuttings taken now. Insert several cuttings round the edge of a pot containing multipurpose or special seed or cutting compost. The cuttings will generally root satisfactorily if given a light position, but better results are obtained in a heated propagator. Pot up into individual pots once roots have developed.

● **Indoor bulbs and corms**

Pot up lachenalia and cyclamen if this was not done last month (*see* August, page 200).

Stop feeding and reduce the watering of achimenes and other flowering bulbs and corms once they have finished blooming.

Start off forced bulbs for Christmas flowering (*see* Bulbs, page 214).

● **Climbers and feature plants**

Remove the growing tips of indoor jasmine (*Jasminum polyanthum*) and keep the plants in a bright position as the flower buds form. Water well and continue to feed fortnightly.

● **Bromeliads**

Reduce watering and stop feeding.

● **Cacti and other succulents**

Give cacti their last feed at the end of September,

and start to reduce watering week by week. Plants such as rebutias and mammillarias will produce more flowers next spring if treated this way.

● **Orchids**

Reduce watering as growth slows down and apply the last feed. From the end of September until next April no feeding is needed.

Bring in any orchids that have been outside for the summer and inspect for pests; clean the pots.

IRISES

In most areas, September is a good month for planting different kinds of irises, but in cold areas leave this planting until the spring.

● **Bearded irises**

Lift and divide any remaining clumps planted four years ago, retaining only the best single rhizomes for replanting in prepared sites (*see* July, page 181).

Soak overnight any new, bare-root plants received from nurseries to plump up the roots.

Plant in groups of three, with the rhizomes about 20 cm (8 in) apart. Spread fine soil or potting compost over the roots leaving the top of the rhizome just above ground level, and firm the soil.

Trim all leaves to 10 cm (4 in) to avoid windrock and, in exposed places, secure the rhizomes to the ground with wire hoops. Water after planting and keep them moist until established if the weather is dry. Apply a dressing of sulphate of potash if planting in light soil (*see* Fertilisers, page 390).

● **Beardless irises**

Iris sibirica, I. spuria and similar irises are suitable for mixed borders and thrive in good, deep loam.

I. sibirica must be kept moist when newly planted and also requires more moisture while flowering. It is suitable for pond margins. *I. spuria* prefers soil that is just alkaline.

Leave the planting and transplanting of Pacific Coast irises (Californian Hybrids) until next month (*see* October, page 243), unless you live in a cold area, in which case, plant now.

Plant *I. unguicularis* in a sunny, well-drained site, and keep them moist until established. Lift, divide and replant congested clumps which have lost vigour.

● **Bulbous irises**

Plant bulbs of Dutch, Spanish and English irises 8–15 cm (3–6 in) deep. Dutch and Spanish irises need a sunny, sheltered position and well-drained soil, and produce foliage in autumn and flowers in late spring. English irises or *I. latifolia* (syn. *I. xiphioides*) prefer a good garden soil which does not dry out in summer, and can be left in the ground until the clumps are congested.

● **Controlling diseases**

Remove any leaves that show spots or rust. These are mostly a problem with bearded irises (*see* Diseases, pages 408 and 410).

LAWNS

● **Sowing grass seed**

Grass seed sown now should germinate within two to three weeks (*see* March, pages 84–85). Keep off the young grass as much as possible until spring.

● **Mowing**

When the new grass reaches a height of 5 cm (2 in), cut the lawn back to about 2 cm (¾ in), depending on the type of lawn (*see* April, page 105). Make sure that the mower blades are really sharp. No further cutting should be necessary until next year. Try not to walk on the lawn until the next spring.

As the growth rate of the grass on established lawns slows down, raise the height of the cut to 2.5 cm (1 in) for an ornamental lawn and 3 cm (1½ in) for a wear-tolerant lawn.

● **Scarifying**

Unless you have been scarifying little and often with a spring-tined rake (*see* March, page 72), it is now worth scarifying once really well to remove moss and dead grass before the end of the season. Treat the lawn with mosskiller before scarifying or the moss will simply be spread around (*see* Weed Control, page 419). A powered lawnraker is the easiest option for a medium or large-sized lawn.

SCARIFYING A LAWN

Scarify the lawn in the autumn to remove dead grass and moss. This produces a better, healthier lawn next spring. It is slow and tiring work with a spring-tined rake and it is sensible to hire a powered lawnraker for a large lawn.

● **Spiking and top dressing**

This is the month to start work on your lawn to improve the grass for next year. Spike the whole surface. Spiking loosens compacted soil and helps to improve the drainage, this in turn inhibits the growth of moss and helps the roots of the grass to establish better. Spike small lawns with a garden fork, but use a wheeled aerator or some other kind of mechanical spiker on larger areas (*see* Tools and Equipment, page 439). The best ones remove a core of soil. Brush an equal mixture of sharp sand and sieved garden compost or topsoil into the holes.

● **Applying fertilisers**

It is rarely necessary to apply fertilisers in autumn. In fact, adding too much nitrogen late in the season can make the grass more liable to disease as it promotes soft growth. However, if a lawn is in poor condition and has been well scarified and spiked, apply a proprietary autumn fertiliser to boost root growth. There are a number of combined autumn weed and feed products available.

● **Weeding a new lawn**

Hand weed as much as possible or use a spot weeder (*see* May, page 135). If applying a weedkiller over the whole lawn, choose one suitable for new lawns.

● **Toadstools and fairy rings**

These are a common sight in the autumn and cannot be controlled by fungicides. Fairy rings, rings of lush grass that spread outwards, sometimes with small toadstools, are difficult to control with the chemicals available to amateur gardeners. Regular spiking and flushing the area with diluted washing-up liquid or a solution of sulphate of iron may discourage them. Clumps of toadstools on the lawn can be brushed off and only need treating if you suspect that honey fungus is present (*see* Lawn diseases, page 409).

LILIES

● **Planting bulbs**

September and October are excellent months for planting and transplanting lilies outside. Most lilies which originally grew wild in Europe, and many North American native species, root from the base of the bulbs only. These are best planted now, either in pots or the open ground, as this helps to get a new root system thoroughly established before winter sets in (*see* October, page 244).

Lilies which produce plenty of stem roots as well as roots beneath the bulb can be planted now but can also be planted in the spring (*see* March, page 73).

Begin planting as soon as bulbs are available, giving priority to *Lilium candidum*. Plant this species with not more than 5 cm (2 in) of soil above the bulbs, but cover other kinds of lily bulb with a depth of soil equal to two and a half times the bulb's own height.

When replanting bulbs split from an established clump, cut the stems back by half.

● **Propagating from bulblets**

Stem-rooting lilies often produce bulblets (small new bulbs) on the rooted part of their stems. These bulbs can be removed and planted up on their own this month.

● **Propagating from scales**

Lilies can be easily increased by propagating new bulbs from 'scales' broken off mature bulbs.

● **Transplanting**

Seedlings that are growing well can be transplanted from pots or trays into their permanent quarters outdoors, or into larger pots.

● **Cutting flowers**

Cut the last of the flowers for indoor decoration. When cutting lilies for the house try to leave as much of the stem on the plant as possible, so that

---

LAWNS – SPIKING & TOP DRESSING

A small lawn can be spiked with a garden fork. Make rows of holes about 10 cm (4 in) apart to help air and moisture penetrate.

A wheeled aerator is much quicker, and powered versions are available for large lawns. The best ones remove a core of soil.

Brush in a mixture of equal parts sharp sand and sieved garden compost or topsoil. This helps the drainage and encourages root growth.

LILIES – PROPAGATING FROM SCALES

  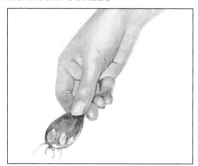 

1 Choose healthy bulbs, then carefully snap off a number of scales as close as possible to the base plate. Each scale has the potential to produce several new bulbs.

2 Fill a pot or seed tray with a mixture of equal parts grit and perlite or vermiculite, and insert the scales two-thirds into the mixture. Cover with a plastic bag.

3 Keep the rooting mixture damp but not wet, and maintain a temperature of 10–15°C (50–60°F). Small bulbs will form along the base in about eight weeks.

4 Do not lift them until tiny leaf blades appear through the surface. Then lift carefully and pot up or grow on in a special bed. They usually take a few years to flower.

the bulb can continue to build up its strength for flowering again next year.

● Saving seed

Continue to collect seed as it ripens and either sow or store (*see* August, page 201). Towards the end of the month or at the beginning of October, cut off with a short length of stem any seed pods that are not ripening fast and bring them under cover. Lay them on a sheet of paper in a dry, airy position to finish ripening.

PELARGONIUMS

● Taking cuttings

Provided you have the facilities for overwintering, it is a good idea to take a few cuttings of your favourite varieties, in case you lose the main plants over the winter (*see* January, page 26).

The regal pelargoniums cut back in July should now have sideshoots that will make excellent cuttings for next year's plants. They will root in four to five weeks, if put on a heated bench or open propagator. Never cover them with a lid or plastic as this will increase the humidity and make them rot. If you cannot provide bottom heat, then put them in the warmest place possible. Never let the compost dry out; regals will wither if they are too dry at the roots.

Take cuttings of zonals, scented-leaved and ivy-leaved varieties in the same way as the regals.

● Specimen plants

Specimen and show pelargoniums taken as cuttings in July should now be in 9 cm (3½ in) pots, and will need to have their first stop as soon as they are about 8 cm (3 in) tall. Pinch or rub out the very top

---

OVERWINTERING PELARGONIUMS

Regal and scented-leaf pelargoniums are always worth overwintering. Mature plants can be overwintered and cuttings taken in spring if you want more plants, but if space is limited you may prefer to take cuttings and overwinter those, especially if you do not have a heated greenhouse and have to keep them indoors.

Zonal pelargonium varieties that cannot be raised from seed, whether grown for flowers or foliage, are always worth trying to keep although it is not economic to heat a greenhouse for just a few plants. In that case it may be more sensible to buy fresh plants each spring. It is usually possible to find space to overwinter a few cuttings indoors even if there is no space for mature plants.

Seed-raised zonal pelargoniums are usually discarded: sow seed now, or in late winter to keep greenhouse heating costs down, for new plants next year.

If you are heating the greenhouse for other plants anyway, and there is sufficient spare space, seed-raised varieties can be overwintered as seedlings or even as cuttings from the summer's plants.

terminal bud. In a week or two new shoots will appear from lower down the stem. The object is to obtain a bushy plant that shoots from low down and starts off with several stems.

● Sowing seeds to overwinter

Sow seeds of pelargoniums now in a frost-free greenhouse or conservatory. Seed sown in September produces plants that come into bloom sooner than those grown from seed sown in January.

Seeds of pelargoniums need to be raised in a warm, sterilised compost, ideally at a constant soil temperature of 20–24°C (70–75°F). Plant the seeds about 5 mm (¼ in) deep in the compost and be sure to move them into the light as soon as they germinate (*see* January, page 27).

RHODODENDRONS & AZALEAS

● Soil preparation

Prepare soil for autumn planting in the same way as for spring planting (*see* February, pages 45–46).

● New plants

September is a good month to purchase both rhododendrons and azaleas from specialist nurseries and, in particular, to obtain specific species or varieties chosen when they were in flower earlier.

Plants ordered from nurseries should be supplied with their rootballs wrapped in sacking or netting to keep the roots intact and to prevent damage. On arrival keep the rootballs moist, but not waterlogged, as drying out can be fatal to both rhododendrons and azaleas at this stage. Plant the shrubs out in well-prepared soil with minimum delay. You will need to keep new plantings well watered until established.

● Layering

Further ground and air layers can be made to increase plant numbers (*see* August, page 202).

● Semi-ripe cuttings

Plant out well-rooted, semi-ripe cuttings taken the previous spring into their final growing positions (*see* May, page 136).

ROCK PLANTS

● Transplanting

Check the list made in the summer of the plants that require repositioning (*see* June, page 159) and transplant now.

Lift the plants carefully, ensuring there is plenty of soil around the roots. Water well both before and after replanting and keep a watch on them afterwards if there is a dry spell.

● Dwarf bulbs

Plant out dwarf bulbs for spring flowering, and pot up some for the greenhouse (*see* Bulbs, page 213).

ROSES

● Planning new plantings

Check on how well the individual roses in the garden have grown, plan new plantings and order selections from a specialist grower well before the 'sold out' lists appear.

● Regular care

Do not feed, but keep pests and diseases in check (*see* Pests and Diseases, pages 395–411). Keep the ground clear of discarded rose heads and foliage.

Deadheading is still important and disbudding will encourage quality blooms on hybrid teas (large-flowered) (*see* June, page 160).

ROSES – TAKING HARDWOOD CUTTINGS

1 Choose a shoot about as thick as a pencil and make the cuttings about 23 cm (9 in) long. Remove the lower leaves and thorns from them.

2 Prepare a slit trench, add sand if the drainage is poor, dip the base of the cutting in rooting hormone and plant to a depth of 15 cm (6 in).

3 Replace and firm the soil, then water well. The plants should root more quickly if covered with a sheet of plastic for a few weeks.

● Tying in shoots

Regularly inspect all climbers and ramblers and tie in new growth as it develops to prevent damage from the autumn storms.

● Cuttings

There are several methods of propagating roses, including budding and grafting, but the simplest method of increasing your stock is by taking hard-wood cuttings. Most varieties can be propagated this way, but the best results are obtained from miniatures, patios and ground-cover roses. Label all cuttings with the name of the parent plant.

Under good conditions, an established plant will be available in about a year's time. This procedure

---

BULB FRAMES FOR ALPINES

A bulb frame provides a most rewarding way of growing alpine bulbs to their very best and makes it possible to grow some of the rarer, 'difficult' bulbs which are more fussy in their requirements.

A base, perhaps the height of two breeze blocks, supports a metal frame with sliding panels of glass in the sides and along the top. This makes access to the plants for repotting and watering easy. The planting medium in the base should be a free-draining mixture of compost and sharp sand. The bulbs can be planted out either directly into the frame or into lattice pots (such as those used for water plants) which are then plunged in a sand mix in the frame. The plunge can be kept moist but the pots are not watered until growth shows through in the spring.

The procedure is simple. Keep the glass on until spring (when a regular feed is beneficial). After flowering remove the glass to allow rain to fall on the bulbs. Once the foliage begins to die down, replace the glass and stop watering. The bulbs will then receive the summer baking they would get in their native habitats.

---

can be accelerated by providing bottom heat for miniature roses grown in pots. Good plants which will flower well the following spring can be obtained in as short a period as four months.

SWEET PEAS

● Choosing seed for autumn sowing

Purchase seed for sowing next month, ordering from a reputable seed company without delay. The colour range of sweet peas is extensive, yellow being the only elusive colour. Include some of the old-fashioned types in your order as they have by far the best perfume. You could also try some of the shorter-growing varieties for the border. 'Snoopea' types are particularly good for ground cover, providing lovely colour and perfume and, not having tendrils, they will not climb.

TREES, SHRUBS & HEDGES

● Soil preparation

Planting in the autumn is beneficial for most trees and shrubs, although spring planting is better for evergreens, conifers and less hardy shrubs. The advantage of autumn planting is that the soil is still warm and this stimulates plants into making root growth before winter. Soil preparation and planting can be carried out from September to March for bare-root plants, longer with container-grown ones.

To prepare individual planting holes for new trees and shrubs, remove grass or other vegetation from the soil surface and watch for roots of perennial weeds such as couch grass, dandelions and docks if a total weedkiller has not been applied earlier. Dig the soil thoroughly and carefully remove as many of the weed roots as you can find.

If you are planting a large area, the soil should be at least single dug; for better results double dig it (*see* The soil in your garden, page 387). Add a generous amount of garden compost or well-rotted manure as this will help get the plants off to a good start.

● Planting

Start planting container-grown trees and shrubs as soon as there has been enough rain to dampen the soil thoroughly. After a dry summer, wait until October. Feed new plants with bonemeal, according to the manufacturer's instructions. Remember to stake and tie newly planted trees and tall shrubs (*see* October, page 247).

Any planting carried out will need watering throughout this month and probably into October; often there is a dry spell at the beginning of both months. Water the foliage as well as the roots.

● Semi-ripe cuttings

As long as the weather is not too dry, take the last few semi-ripe cuttings (*see* Propagation, page 428). However, the success rate will not be as high as earlier in the summer, and some cuttings will not root until the spring. Take semi-ripe cuttings of tender shrubs in particular, as a precaution against any losses in the coming winter.

Pot on any well-rooted semi-ripe cuttings taken in May and June, using a good quality potting compost. Move these to a cold greenhouse or garden frame for the winter, keeping them well ventilated, and water with a light, overhead spray only if they become dry.

● Pruning

Continue to use the one-third pruning method on August-flowering shrubs, established for three years or more, that have now finished flowering (*see* Pruning, page 420).

HEDGES

● Selecting plants for a new hedge

If you want to plant a new hedge this should be planted in October, so the soil needs to be prepared now. Many shrubs and conifers make good hedges, but first decide on what kind of hedge will best suit your garden (*see* February, pages 50–51).

● Preparing the site

Dig a trench a minimum of 1 m (3 ft) wide along the length of the hedge. Remove the top 25 cm (10 in) of soil; put it on boards for easy handling. Fork over the next 25 cm (10 in) layer of soil and dig in a bucketful of garden compost, well-rotted manure or other suitable organic material for every 1 m (3 ft). Infill with the topsoil, mixing in a further bucket of organic material every 1 m (3 ft), so the trench is slightly higher than the adjacent soil.

● Hedge trimming

Give hedges of green and golden privet and *Lonicera nitida* their final trim.

VEGETABLES

This is a busy month for harvesting. Crops will include carrots, potatoes, peas, swedes, turnips and celery. Once the vegetable plot has been cleared, a green manure can be sown to improve the fertility of the soil (*see* The soil in your garden, page 391). Clovers, tares and grazing rye are good choices for late summer or autumn sowing and spring digging. Green manures can either be sown in rows or broadcast and raked in gently. Dig in the green manure with a sharp spade in spring.

Protect overwintering crops from slugs especially during mild, damp spells.

● Beans

Harvest any remaining broad and runner beans before the first frosts. Dwarf French beans may survive early frosts if they are covered with cloches.

● Brassicas

In exposed areas stake late varieties of Brussels sprouts. Tie the plant to a stake just below the leafy head. Early or dwarf varieties do not need staking.

Harvest summer and autumn cabbages and plant out spring cabbages. First water the seed bed well, then lift the seedlings carefully, keeping the roots intact. Protect the young plants from caterpillars and flea beetle (*see* Pests, pages 398 and 400).

Cover spring cabbages and Chinese cabbages with cloches to protect from frost and windrock.

Start to harvest autumn cauliflowers. Break leaves over the curds to keep them white.

● Marrows, courgettes and squashes

Harvest courgettes, marrows, ripe pumpkins and squashes before the first frosts. Pumpkins and squashes can be stored in nets (see August, page 204).

TREES & SHRUBS – PLANTING THOSE GROWN IN CONTAINERS

1 Using a garden fork or spade, dig out a hole about 60–90 cm (2–3 ft) across, removing the soil to a depth of about 25 cm (10 in).

2 Fork over and break up the lower 25 cm (10 in) of subsoil in the hole, and then dig in a large bucketful of garden compost or well-rotted manure.

3 Water the plant thoroughly about an hour before removing it from its pot, and tease out any roots running around the bottom of the pot before planting.

4 Return and firm the soil but leave a slight depression around the base to make watering easier. Mulch to suppress weeds and conserve moisture.

● **Onions**

Complete harvesting and storing onions. Tie them in strings or store them on wooden trays in a cool, but frost-free, well-ventilated place and they should last well into next spring.

● **Other roots and swollen stems**

Harvest Florence fennel if this has not yet been done (*see* August, page 204).

● **Salad crops**

Harvest lettuces and blanch and harvest any remaining curly endive. Make the last sowing of broad-leaved endive (*see* July, page 187). Broad-leaved endive is fairly hardy but, like other winter salads, will need cloche protection from frost.

● **Spinach**

Harvest spinach and spinach beet and sow the last spinach (for a winter crop) if not already done (*see* August, page 205).

● **Tomatoes, peppers and aubergines**

Continue to pick ripe outdoor aubergines and tomatoes before the frost destroys them.

Pick all peppers before the frost. Many will ripen indoors if they are put in a seed tray and placed in a drawer with a couple of ripe apples.

PERENNIAL VEGETABLES

● **Globe artichokes**

Remove any flowers from first year globe artichokes; this will give the roots a chance to build up.

● **Jerusalem artichokes**

When the leaves have blackened after the first frost, cut the stems right down to the ground and mark their position so that the roots can be lifted easily.

WATER PLANTS & POOLS

● **Collecting winter buds**

Gather the turions (winter buds) of plants such as frogbit (*Hydrocharis morsus-ranae*) and bladderwort (*Utricularia vulgaris*) before they sink to the bottom of the pool. Turions may not be obvious until you lift the plants. In the case of frogbit, for example, they look like small swellings on the ends of the submerged roots. Put the turions in a small, unsealed jar of water with a little soil in the bottom and place the jar in a cool place until spring. If the water evaporates, top it up.

● **Bog garden**

Plant waterside primulas and other bog garden plants that were pricked out during May in their permanent positions.

● **Tidying up**

This is a good month to clean and tidy the pool. As marginal plants begin to fade, remove all the old flower heads from them, especially from plants such as water plantain which may seed in the pool and become invasive.

Cut back the top growth of plants that will die back naturally anyway, before they begin to collapse and decay in the water. This may not be practical in the case of a very large pond, but it is not an onerous job for a small one.

Take the opportunity to thin the excessive growth of submerged oxygenators such as elodea.

● **Autumn leaves**

Erect a net over the pool if it is positioned near deciduous trees to prevent leaves from falling into the water and decomposing (*see* October, page 249). Choose a net with a small mesh since some, such as heron nets, have a large mesh through which most leaves can fall. Attach the net securely so that it does not sag under the weight of the leaves.

VEGETABLES – PLANTING SPRING CABBAGE

1 Plant cabbages and spring greens now. Plant spring greens 10 cm (4 in) apart with a gap of 30 cm (12 in) between the rows. Increase the space between the plants to 30 cm (12 in) for spring cabbages.

2 A traditional way to plant spring cabbages is with a dibber: make a hole with the dibber for the plant, then insert the dibber again to one side and press the soil against the roots. Water thoroughly afterwards.

Overwintering Tender Perennials

*A*rgyranthemums, verbenas and other colourful tender perennials used in beds, borders and containers do not have to be discarded at the end of the summer season. With care you can preserve your investment and keep them through the winter to flower again another year.

If you have a frost-free greenhouse or conservatory or can find space on your windowsills indoors, it is well worth saving at least some of the tender perennials in the garden that would otherwise die over the winter. Even your garage, if it has a window and is frost free, may provide a home for a few plants. Totally dormant plants that have shed their leaves and bulbs, corms and tubers can be stored in a windowless shed or garage provided they are kept safe from frost.

When suitable space is short give priority to saving the more expensive plants, such as *Centradenia* 'Cascade', *Scaevola aemula*, lotus, *Bacopa* 'Snowflake', plectranthus, and *Helichrysum petiolare*. These are propagated from cuttings rather than raised from seed and therefore cost more to replace if you have to buy new plants from a nursery or garden centre in the spring.

To overwinter tender perennials from the garden, pot up some of the best plants well before the first frost. Cut back the shoots on established plants to about 10–15 cm (4–6 in) to keep them compact and to save space. To avoid problems with pests and diseases pick off any dying leaves. Some plants, such as *centradenias*, will lose all their leaves over the winter. Remove dead leaves that fall on to the compost. Keep the compost just moist enough to prevent it from drying out completely.

▲ *Argyranthemum foeniculaceum*

▲ *Helichrysum petiolare*

▲ *Bidens ferulifolia*

To guard further against winter losses, you can take cuttings from favourite tender perennials in late summer to overwinter as young plants in a light, warm position.

Bedding plants are normally raised from seed but some varieties, such as Surfinia petunias and the double-flowered lobelia 'Kathleen Mallard', can only be propagated from cuttings so it is worth trying to overwinter a few cuttings of these too.

STANDARDS

Plants trained as standards are always worth saving as they are expensive to buy. Whatever the plant, the method is the same. Shorten the shoots on the head to about half their current length, and remove leaves as they begin to die. Keep the plants in a frost-free greenhouse or conservatory, and take care not to overwater. In spring, once there are signs of new growth, complete any pruning or shaping.

FUCHSIAS

Fuchsias such as *F. magellanica* and *F.* 'Mrs Popple' are hardy enough to survive outdoors over winter, but most showy varieties are tender (if in doubt about the hardiness of a particular variety, check in

▲ *Diascia fetcaniensis*

▲ *Pelargonium* 'Mr Henry Cox'

a specialist fuchsia catalogue). Lift tender fuchsias growing in open ground or containers in late autumn and pot them up individually. Pinch out the green tips and remove the leaves. Place the pots in a frost-free greenhouse, conservatory or on a light windowsill in a cool room. They must be kept cool and almost dry to keep them dormant.

In spring, repot the plants into slightly smaller pots using fresh compost, prune them back hard and keep them moist, misting with water periodically. New shoots will soon grow to provide cuttings. Alternatively, take semi-ripe cuttings in late summer or autumn (*see* page 429) and overwinter them as young plants.

▲ *Verbena* 'Lawrence Johnston'

PELARGONIUMS

Pelargoniums are seldom killed by the first light frost, but take them under cover before a more severe frost can harm them. In most years they are best taken in by the end of September, earlier in cold areas. If space is at a premium, keep those varieties that have to be raised from cuttings in preference to seed-raised plants.

▲ *Fuchsia* 'Leverkusen'

Lift the plants, shake off loose soil and shorten the roots back to 5–8 cm (2–3 in) and the shoots back to about 10 cm (4 in). Pot up the plants individually. Alternatively, place the plants in boxes, at least 15 cm (6 in) deep, and pack compost between the roots. Keep the plants in a light, frost-free place and water them just sufficiently to prevent the compost becoming dust dry. As the weather improves in the spring, start to water them normally again. The new shoots will provide plenty of cuttings.

OCTOBER

This is one of the loveliest
times of the year as the leaves
change colour and the garden
puts on a final show of flowers
before the return of winter.

October

October is one of the loveliest and most colourful months of the year. Many flowers are still in bloom; the autumn-flowering bulbs such as colchicums and nerines are at their best and many shrubs and trees are covered with bright berries and coloured leaves.

At the beginning of the month there is often an unusually fine spell of weather, with warm, clear, sunny days, which shows both countryside and garden at their best.

Night frosts are normal, particularly towards the end of the month, but the mornings are often bright and sunny so things that normally go unnoticed, such as spiders' webs, suddenly become objects of beauty in the autumn garden.

The weather in October

The Indian summer, fortunately common at the beginning of the month, is often followed by a period of wind and rain. October is sometimes the wettest month of the year and the long wet spells can make the soil in the garden difficult to work.

The nights get colder, especially in fine weather when there is no cloud cover, and frosts are much more common than in September. Even mild southern areas can expect some frost this month.

Variations between north and south are becoming more pronounced, with a difference of four to five weeks in the growing season between the extreme south-west of England and the north-east of Scotland.

Making the most of fine weather

If you have time to visit gardens open to the public concentrate on those well known for autumn colour. They may well give you ideas which you can replicate in your own garden.

With the shorter days, gardening in the evening is now impractical, and for many gardeners that leaves just the four or five weekends in the month to do everything that needs to be done. Wet and windy weather may well curtail activity for some of these days, so time and tasks need to be planned carefully.

Give priority to those jobs that won't wait, then try to get winter digging done so that the ground gets the maximum benefit from being left turned and exposed. Weathering during the winter helps to break down heavy soils, and digging also exposes soil-borne pests to hungry predators such as birds.

If you are planning to sow or turf a new lawn in the spring, or plant a new border, try to do the initial digging now. Leave the ground rough – you can hoe and rake off the weed seeds that will inevitably germinate, but postpone the final levelling until spring.

October is a good time to lay turf for a new lawn if you don't want to wait until the spring. There is usually plenty of rain to help the lawn become established before the really hard weather of the winter sets in.

Garden hygiene

Clearing up and tidying around the garden may not be a very exciting job but it certainly makes your garden look more attractive and it will cut down on the problems caused by pests and diseases. October is an excellent month to collect and clear up all the garden rubbish, ranging from fallen leaves and branches to discarded labels and old plant pots. These can all harbour pests and diseases.

Remove fallen leaves from flower beds, the lawn, the rock garden and, if you have not previously netted it, the pond. Leaves in the water may rot during the winter and release toxic gases that can prove harmful to fish if the surface of the pond is frozen for a long time. Leaves left in beds and borders and around plants can encourage slugs and snails which the birds may appreciate but you will not. Use fallen leaves to make leafmould; putting them through a shredder accelerates the process.

Garden canes and stakes used for summer flowers such as dahlias should be tidied away, and the ends that have been in the soil soaked in a wood preservative. Such treatment will make them last far longer, and reduces the risk of them harbouring disease.

Old soil or compost in pots and seed trays should be cleaned off, and the pots and trays washed in a garden disinfectant before storing. Clean and store containers not being used over the winter at the same time. You could leave these cleaning chores later, but washing pots is a more pleasant task on a sunny autumn day than on a cold winter one. Greenhouse staging should also be scrubbed down and disinfected, if this has not been done earlier in the year.

Design and construction

The middle of the autumn is a good time to think about any improvements you would like to make to your garden, and perhaps even to redesign a part of it. Measuring, marking out and the preliminary digging are best done on fine days in October, though most thinking and design planning should take place on paper and indoors.

A start can be made on construction work, but don't lay concrete in frosty weather; wait until there is a frost-free period. The weekly weather forecast for farmers broadcast on the radio is a good guide to the weather you are likely to get in the coming week.

Planting

Autumn is a good time to plant trees, shrubs, herbaceous plants and alpines. Fruit trees and bushes also usually do well if planted now as there is still enough residual warmth in the soil to help them get established. Be wary, however, of planting anything that is not totally hardy; some border plants for example resent cold wet soil. In theory these are better planted in spring when you are less likely to suffer losses. When such plants are well established after a summer's growth they can usually withstand cold, wet and frost more easily than they can if only just planted.

Harvesting and storing

There is still plenty to harvest from the kitchen garden, and it is wise to harvest as much as you can before it is spoilt by the weather. Roots left in the ground, such as carrots and potato tubers, are more likely to succumb to soil pests.

If there are still plants in the garden with seed heads that you want to save, collect them now before the seeds are shed and lost. Dry the seeds off thoroughly before labelling them and storing in airtight containers.

JOBS THAT WON'T WAIT

- Harvest fruit and vegetables. Apples and pears should be picked by the end of the month and maincrop carrots and potatoes should be lifted and stored for the winter.

- Sow hardy annuals, sweet peas and lettuces to overwinter under glass. Sweet peas can also be sown direct in the ground in mild areas and protected with cloches.

- Plant spring-flowering hardy annuals and biennials as soon as possible.

- Plant all evergreens, including conifers, by the end of the month.

- Plant windowboxes and hanging baskets for winter interest.

- Plant spring-flowering bulbs in the garden and in containers.

- Plant lilies for summer flowering.

- Plant garlic, spring cabbages and Japanese onions.

- Lift tender bulbs, corms and tubers, such as dahlias and gladioli, and store in frost-free place.

- Check bowls of bulbs planted for winter flowering indoors. Do not let them dry out.

- Put winter protection in place around vulnerable border perennials and shrubs in cold regions. In milder areas this can wait for another month.

- Bring in pelargoniums and half-hardy fuchsias growing in tubs and pots outdoors.

- Net the pool to protect it from autumn leaves.

- Prepare the garden for winter: clear fallen leaves and other debris, store garden equipment, clean the greenhouse and put insulation in place to conserve heat.

ANNUALS & BIENNIALS

● Sowing hardy annuals

In mild areas you can continue to sow hardy annuals and the hardier bedding plants until the end of the month to overwinter as seedlings (*see* September, page 212). If you want to use only a small section of the greenhouse to overwinter annuals and heat just that portion, erect a plastic bubble 'tent' around the staging (*see* Greenhouses, page 241).

● Planting hardy annuals

Finish planting spring annuals and biennials if this has not already been done (*see* September, page 212). The earlier in the month you do this, the better the display the following year.

BORDER PERENNIALS

● Tidying borders

Later perennials will continue to bloom until killed by frost but may need deadheading. Cut back others and dispose of the dead stalks. Leave all or some of the old stems on less hardy plants as added protection.

Clean and dry any seed you have collected that is not to be sown immediately. Store packages inside a sealed container in a cool place until required.

● Tubers and bulbs

Lift tubers, such as dahlias (*see* Dahlias, page 238) and perennial tropaeolums, and clean and store them for the winter. Frost may have blackened the tops of plants but, unless the weather has been extremely severe, bulbs, corms, tubers and rhizomes of tender and half-hardy plants will still be in good condition. Store them according to their specific needs. Most bulbs need to remain dry in a frost-proof place (*see*

Bulbs, corms and tubers page 235), but dahlias and other tubers require some moisture.

● Ground preparation

Continue clearing the ground for new beds, digging and leaving soil rough for the frost to break it down, especially on clay soils. Add fertilisers, garden compost or well-rotted manure at the same time, and lime if required (*see* The soil in your garden, pages 387–392). Remove the roots of perennial weeds, especially those of couch grass and ground elder.

● Top dressing established borders

In areas with established plants, top dress with well-rotted garden compost or manure. Do not add fertilisers until early spring.

● Planting

Planting can continue this month, provided the weather and the ground remain suitable. Do not plant when the ground is waterlogged, compacted, or when hardened by frost. Check that added fertiliser or manure is well mixed with the soil, to prevent damage to plant roots. Water the plants in, but do this sparingly if the soil is wet. It is now a good time to move plants growing in unsuitable positions (*see* June, page 149).

● Dividing plants

Divide and replant congested or weed-infested clumps of hardy perennials where flowering has deteriorated (*see* March, page 58 and Propagation, page 431–432). Plant weed-free sections from the outside of clumps in fresh soil or replant in the previous site adding manure, garden compost or fertilisers. Discard the central part of the old clump.

● Winter protection

Most popular border perennials survive the winter without problems, but less hardy types and new plantings may require some protection if the weather turns very cold. How much protection borderline

BORDER PERENNIALS – WINTER PROTECTION

1 Border plants, including small shrubs, that are not totally hardy benefit from a covering of bracken held in place by a wigwam of canes.

2 Straw or any insulating material can replace bracken. Wrap a couple of layers of horticultural fleece around the outside of the wigwam.

Slightly tender herbaceous plants can be covered with a thick layer of chipped bark or straw for insulation. Hold in place with a sheet of plastic.

hardy perennials will require depends not only on the temperature, but on the soil and the amount of rain or snow that falls: penstemons, agapanthus, osteospermums, *Lobelia cardinalis* and others can tolerate lower temperatures in a light sandy soil, than in waterlogged heavy clay.

Shrubs, trees, hedges and even dead flowering stems will help provide shelter from biting winds. If sharp frosts are forecast, cover smaller, tender plants with cloches, netting, plastic sheeting, newspaper or horticultural fleece. Dead bracken fronds, straw, mulches and branches can also be used. If available, cover susceptible plant crowns with weathered ashes to deter slugs. Remove damp coverings as soon as the danger of frost has passed.

In cold areas or on heavier soils, it may be safer to lift slightly tender perennials. Pot them up and keep them in a light, frost-free place (*see* September, pages 228–229). Cold frames may need additional protection in very cold spells, but keep them well ventilated to help prevent powdery mildew (*see* Diseases, page 410).

BULBS, CORMS & TUBERS

● Planting bulbs and corms

Plant tulips and hyacinths this month and next and complete planting any bulbs left over from last month. Daffodils should be planted first (*see* September, page 213). Frost-tolerant gladioli can also be planted out now, about 8 cm (3 in) deep. These will flower in early summer, and can be left in the ground from year to year in mild areas.

● Autumn-flowering bulbs

Take pots of amaryllis, crinums and nerines inside if necessary to protect from frost and waterlogging.

● Lifting and storing bulbs and corms

By mid October, as soon as the foliage has been blackened by frost, lift gladioli and other summer-flowering corms, such as ixias and sparaxis, tubers of *Tropaeolum tuberosum* and half-hardy summer-flowering bulbs, such as chincherinchees and tigridias. Lift them with a fork, taking care not to bruise them, and remove any soil sticking to the roots. Cut off all but 1 cm (½ in) of the main stem.

Bulbs, corms and tubers lifted at this time of the year need to be dried off as quickly as possible, as any damp soil, roots or leaves left on will cause the bulbs to rot. Put them in shallow boxes in an airing cupboard or another really warm spot for a few days. This will dry the bulbs and corms completely and make it easy to separate them from the soil and old roots. When absolutely dry, dust them with flowers of sulphur.

CORMS – CLEANING GLADIOLUS CORMS

Clean up gladiolus corms before storing them. Remove the old corm from the base, and save the small cormlets to grow on. They will take a couple of years to reach flowering size. Remove the tough outer skins from the largest corms.

Store bulbs and corms in trays or shallow boxes, in a cool room or greenhouse that is dry and frost-proof, but not too warm or humid as the bulbs will either shrivel or rot.

Clean bulbs and corms at any time between drying-off and replanting them next spring. Break away and discard old, shrivelled corms of gladioli. If the little cormlets are to be kept for propagation, remove these too and store them separately. Remove the tough outer skins from large corms.

Treat gladiolus corms that may be harbouring thrips or if there has been a severe attack of thrips during the growing season (*see* Pests, page 404). Small, pitted lesions indicate dry rot, which can cause serious losses if gladioli are grown on the same plot year after year. Hard rot will produce large, black lesions on the corm, and in some cases the corm shrinks and dies. Fusarium rot, which usually causes the corm to disintegrate in the soil or during storage, shows itself as corrugated surface lesions. Corms affected with grey mould (botrytis) show a black, spongy rot. Discard any diseased corms and plant new corms in a different position in the garden (*see* Diseases, pages 405–411).

● Forced bulbs

Examine the winter bulbs in bowls which are standing in a shed or cool room and water them if the bulb fibre is at all dry. Bowls plunged in the open (*see* September, page 214) should not need much attention, but check to make sure the compost or fibre is neither dry nor waterlogged.

● Winter-flowering arum lilies

Finish repotting winter-flowering arum lilies (*Zantedeschia aethiopica*) if not already done (*see* September, page 214).

● Cannas

Gradually stop watering cannas to dry them off before storing them for the winter in a cool, dry, frost-free place. Do not let the compost become so dried out that it turns to dust.

CARNATIONS & PINKS

● Planting outdoors

Continue to plant border carnations and pinks in prepared beds if the soil and growing conditions are suitable. In cold districts, or if your garden has poorly drained soil, they should be potted on into 10 cm (4 in) pots and overwintered in a cold frame or cold greenhouse until March.

Plant border carnations 38 cm (15 in) apart. Spread out the roots, firm the soil over them and mix in some dry, sifted soil if the ground is wet. Keep the bottom pairs of leaves just clear of the soil, and secure each plant with a 15 cm (6 in) stake and a split ring of thin wire, to hold the plant upright and guard against windrock.

Check that young plants have not been loosened by early frosts, and refirm them if necessary.

● Picking blooms

Modern pinks are likely to continue in flower until the hard frosts. Picking the blooms acts as a natural stop to the plants and encourages them to continue producing bushy sideshoots in readiness for flowering next year. Continue to stop newly planted pinks which are sending out shoots of over ten joints (*see* September, page 214).

● Preparing ground

Continue to dig over any beds that will be used for spring planting (*see* August, page 195).

● Layers

Sever rooted layers of border carnations from the parent plants and pot up those which have been severed for a month.

PERPETUAL-FLOWERING

Keep the greenhouse temperature not less than 7°C (45°F) and maintain some ventilation at all times.

Water and feed the carnations sparingly (*see* April, page 92), cut the flowers and disbud stems as necessary (*see* September, page 214).

Keep watching for pests and diseases and take action as necessary (*see* March, page 60).

CHRYSANTHEMUMS

EARLY-FLOWERING (GARDEN)

As plants stop flowering, decide which method of overwintering is most suitable. Clear away and dispose of unwanted plants.

Overwintering in the ground

Most modern varieties will survive in an average winter in mild areas provided they are in well-drained ground which is not infested with slugs and snails. Clear away rubbish and dead leaves from around them, collect the supporting stakes and store them until spring. Remove dead flowers but do not cut down the top growth until spring. Protect the plants if hard frosts are forecast.

Overwintering in a cold frame

Cut the stems down to about 15 cm (6 in) and cut off all green flowering shoots at ground level. Label the remaining mass of roots and old stems, known as stools, lift them carefully, and wash thoroughly in clean water. Put them in a deep box and cover with 8 cm (3 in) of John Innes No. 1 potting compost or a proprietary soilless compost. Put boxes in a cold frame which should be well drained, protected from frosts by matting and, preferably, facing south.

CHRYSANTHEMUMS – OVERWINTERING IN BOXES

1 Overwinter chrysanthemums in deep boxes in a cold or cool greenhouse, or in a cold frame. Cut the stems down to about 15 cm (6 in).

2 Wash surplus soil off the roots to make them easier to handle. Be careful not to allow the roots to dry out before boxing them up.

3 Place the roots in deep boxes and put potting soil around them until they are at their original depth. Keep them slightly moist.

● Overwintering in the greenhouse

Treat the stools as for overwintering in a cold frame. Then put them in compost-filled boxes on a shelf in an unheated greenhouse where they will get plenty of light and air. Plant the stools at the same depth as they were growing in the garden and water them in, but be careful not to overwater in winter.

LATE-FLOWERING (GREENHOUSE)

The first of the mid-season varieties will come into flower by the middle of the month and will need a dry atmosphere and abundant light. Keep the greenhouse well ventilated at all times, even in cold, wet weather when gentle heat is needed. A cold stagnant atmosphere is very damaging to chrysanthemums in flower.

● Watering and feeding

Water with extra care as early as possible in the day. Be sparing rather than generous, and avoid spilling water on the floor or on the foliage.

Stop feeding late-flowering varieties when they begin to show colour.

● Controlling mildew

If spots of powdery mildew appear on the petals of chrysanthemums in the greenhouse, increase the temperature immediately to 13°C (55°F) and treat (*see* Diseases, page 410).

VERY LATE-FLOWERING VARIETIES

Continue to disbud as necessary (*see* August, page 195). Remove the central bud of spray varieties.

CLIMBERS & WALL SHRUBS

● Planting

October is an ideal month for planting all but tender plants. The soil is still warm and this encourages rapid root growth and allows the plants to develop fully in the coming spring.

● Preventing clematis wilt

To help prevent clematis wilt, plant container-grown clematis 5–8 cm (2–3 in) deeper than the soil level in the container (*see* February, page 38). This will help to protect the lower stem buds from attack, and these will then regrow if the remainder of the plant above the ground becomes infected. New clematis can be replanted in an infected site in the autumn, as the spores of the fungus are only active in May and June.

● Plant supports

Check all ties and replace as necessary where the shoots are rubbing against supports, walls or fences (*see* January, page 20). Overlooking extensive rubbing can have disastrous results for the plant.

● Layering

Dig up any layers that have rooted, cut them free from the parent plant and pot up or plant in their final growing positions. If not planting directly into their final positions, keep the pots in a cold frame or a sheltered part of the garden for the winter.

● Hardwood cuttings

Start to take hardwood cuttings of strong-growing climbers and wall shrubs from now until March (*see* Propagation, page 429).

Plant out young plants which have rooted from hardwood cuttings taken in the spring or last year.

CLIMBERS IN TREES

Training climbing plants to grow through trees is rewarding but not without problems. It is important to choose the right climber for the right tree. Be careful not to plant a strong-growing climber to grow over a tree that is too small for it, or the climber might kill the tree. Avoid planting thorny roses in fruit trees.

A climber needs adequate moisture and a well-prepared planting site, or its growth will be stunted. Plant climbers away from the tree if you can, in as open a position as possible, on the west or weather side, but not against the trunk of the tree as there will not be enough moisture or food.

In the early stages of growth a climber will need support to reach the branches of the host tree. Drive a peg into the soil alongside the planted climber, then stretch a string or plastic chain from the peg into the branches of the tree. Attach the upper end of the support to the tree, using an adjustable tree strap. Pass the strap around a strong branch, allowing for further expansion and ensuring there is no restriction or movement up and down the branch.

Roses and clematis are particularly good flowering climbers to grow through trees, but you will need to choose vigorous varieties. This clematis is C. montana.

CONTAINER GARDENING

● Clearing containers

Once plants in seasonal containers start to look sorry for themselves, clear them out, retrieving any plants that can be overwintered outdoors, such as ivy and creeping jenny (*Lysimachia nummularia*), or indoors, such as pelargoniums, fuchsias and marguerites (*Argyranthemum*). Alternatively, especially if storage space is at a premium, take cuttings (*see* September, pages 228–229 and Propagation, pages 428–429).

● Planting spring bulbs

Continue planting containers for spring, including dwarf bulbs (*see* September, page 215).

Tulips are planted later than other spring bulbs because they can start into growth too soon and then get damaged by frost. Dwarf or species tulips – *Tulipa fosteriana*, *T. greigii*, *T. kaufmanniana* and their hybrids – are excellent small tulips that flower early and are sufficiently compact for containers.

● Winter displays

Continue to plant up winter-interest containers (*see* September, page 216).

DAHLIAS

● Lifting and storing tubers

Once frost has blackened the foliage cut down the top growth, then lift tubers carefully with a fork and remove excess soil. Attach a label to the stem with plastic-covered wire which can be tightened when the stem shrinks as it dries. The fleshy tubers provide the food supply for next year's initial growth, so if any are damaged, cut them off cleanly with a knife and treat the cut with flowers of sulphur to prevent infection entering the tuber. The new growth develops from the crown (the area where the stem joins the tubers).

Stand tubers upside down in a frost-free place for a week to dry out, then trim off the stump and fibrous roots and shake off dried soil. Place them in boxes and cover with slightly damp peat or vermiculite after treating the crowns against fungal attack with a suitable fungicide powder or spray. Store in a frost-free place for the winter.

● Storing seeds

Remove seeds from any dried seed pods you have saved, label and store in sealed containers in a cool place until sowing time in March.

FRUIT

Continue to order any trees, bushes or canes that you want for winter planting (*see* September, page 216).

Check the requirements of the fruit you are planting and prepare the planting sites accordingly; some fruit trees need a large quantity of rubble incorporated in the soil. Add plenty of garden compost and break up the subsoil, not just the topsoil. This will correct any faults in the drainage, something no fruit will tolerate. Avoid replanting fruit where a similar tree or bush stood before as the new plant will find it difficult to get established.

General hygiene is very important in the autumn. Collect and dispose of any diseased fruits and as many diseased leaves as possible. It is unwise to compost them in case any diseases survive and carry the infections on to next year.

DAHLIAS – LIFTING & STORING TUBERS

1 As soon as frost blackens the leaves of dahlias, cut down the top growth then lift them so that the tubers can be stored in a frost-free place. Shake off surplus soil and attach a label to each tuber with a plastic-covered wire.

2 Hang upside down to dry for about a week. Then trim off the stump (do not detach the tubers) and fibrous roots. Place in boxes and cover with slightly damp peat or vermiculite for insulation. Store them in a frost-free place.

APPLE AND PEAR TREES – BANDING

Apply greasebands to apples and pears to control winter moth caterpillars. The bands catch the wingless female moths that climb the trees to lay eggs on the branches. Proprietary bands are the easiest to apply.

BLACKBERRIES – PRUNING CANES

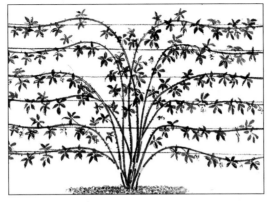

Blackberries are easy to prune, but wear gloves. Untie and cut out back to the base those stems that fruited this autumn. Tie in the new shoots that have grown this year and not yet fruited.

FUCHSIAS

In October the temperature and the intensity of the light drop to the levels preferred by fuchsias so, in areas not yet affected by frosts, outside plants will probably produce their best display.

TENDER AND HALF-HARDY

● **Overwintering half-hardy border fuchsias**

Begin transferring half-hardy fuchsias from borders and large outdoor containers into pots just large enough to accommodate the rootball, ready for housing somewhere frost-free over winter.

● **In the greenhouse**

Continue to maintain strict hygiene, especially as leaves and flowers fall. Debris encourages fungal diseases, particularly grey mould (botrytis), which thrives in damp, unventilated conditions (*see* Diseases, page 407). Keep the greenhouse fully ventilated; close it only if there is danger of frost.

● **Watering and feeding**

Reduce watering, especially of large double varieties and plants with weak root systems, as flowering gradually ceases and the leaves begin to turn yellow. Give plants a final application of high-potash fertiliser to help ripen wood and then let them start resting naturally.

● **Autumn cuttings**

Take semi-ripe cuttings (*see* Propagation, page 428). These will be slower to root than cuttings taken in spring, but bottom heat is not essential. To keep them 'ticking over' through the winter without losing their leaves, keep them at a temperature of about 5–7°C (41–45°F) from now until the spring.

● **Apples and pears**

Continue picking and storing late-maturing varieties (*see* September, page 216). As a general rule, finish picking all apples and pears by the end of the month. Birds, wasps and autumn gales can easily cause the loss of many of the later ones. Apply, or replace last year's, greasebands on trees.

● **Cherries**

Continue to treat cherries to prevent bacterial canker if necessary (*see* Diseases, page 406).

● **Cane fruits**

It often pays to cover autumn raspberry canes with horticultural fleece and leave it there throughout the winter. This provides the ripening fruit with a better chance of reaching maturity.

Cut down any remaining canes of blackberries and hybrid berries that have borne fruit this year. Tie in or bundle up the replacement canes for mutual winter protection.

● **Strawberries**

As the weather becomes colder, cover fruiting strawberries with cloches, tunnels of plastic sheeting or horticultural fleece. This will protect them at night and keep them fruiting by creating a warmer microclimate around them. The only problem is that it can also create conditions suitable for grey mould (botrytis). This can be countered by giving good ventilation on sunny and warm days, and by treating if the problem is severe (*see* Diseases, page 407).

Summer-fruiting strawberries may still be planted, but next year's crop will be light, and any planted after the middle of the month will need some flowers removed; too much fruit may strain the plant.

● Preparing for winter

Trim plants to shape by removing one-third of the growth made during the summer. Standards, other trained shapes and any plants grown for early flowering next year, should not be allowed to become completely dormant. After light shaping and trimming, keep them at a temperature of 5°C (41°F). This will keep them in green leaf.

GARDEN MAINTENANCE

● Soil preparation

As long as the ground is not too wet, start winter digging, incorporating well-rotted farmyard manure, garden or spent mushroom compost to improve the soil. If you garden on clay, adding compost opens up the soil to improve the drainage and provide more oxygen for plant roots; on light land it enables the soil to retain more moisture.

Digging can continue up until Christmas, so spread the task out over the next three months if there is a lot to do, rather than trying to do too much at one time. On heavy land, large clods of earth will be broken down by frost over the winter leaving the soil easier to work the following spring.

● Clearing dead vegetation

Clear up fallen leaves, particularly around ponds, rock gardens and lawns. Erect a net over the pond (*see* page 249) and remove fallen leaves regularly. Check that gutters and drains are free of leaves and other debris.

Different types of tools make collecting up leaves easier (*see* Tools and Equipment, page 440). Recycle leaves by making leafmould, but if there have been problems with apple scab, plum rust or rose black spot, destroy the leaves rather than recycling them.

Tidy up dead vegetation from beds and borders as the debris can harbour overwintering pests and diseases. Add suitable material to the compost heap.

● Summer garden equipment

Clean and dry all garden equipment including pond pumps, barbecues, non-frost-resistant pots, chairs, tables and benches, and store them in a dry place until spring. If it is not possible to store furniture under cover, tilt benches and tables against a wall so that most of their feet are off the ground. Wooden furniture legs are vulnerable to wet and rot, particularly if the endgrain of the wood is left standing on the soil.

● Protecting wooden structures

A dry autumn day is ideal for treating any wooden structures in the garden. Paint-on preservatives will not stop wood from rotting, but they will prevent surface moulds and algae from spoiling the wood's appearance. Many attractive colours are available for use on trellis and fence panels that will greatly improve the look of the garden.

There are three types of woodcare products: creosote, organic solvent-based and water-based. Each has advantages and disadvantages. Creosote has an unpleasant, lingering smell, the fumes may damage seedlings in enclosed places and it is not recommended for wood that supports plants. It is however very useful for sheds and gates, and lasts longer than other treatments. It can also be used to prevent wood rot in new fence posts; soak the ends of the posts in a container of creosote overnight.

Organic solvent-based preservatives also help prevent rot if the endgrain of fence posts or furniture is soaked in them. They improve the appearance of wood and help repel water. Check the instructions, as they may be harmful to plants.

Water-based preservatives are safer and more pleasant to use. Most contain a coloured stain and a fungicide, so they improve the appearance but, as they are water-based, they will not prevent wet rot.

MAKING LEAFMOULD

Leafmould, made from fallen leaves, is of great value to the garden. It can be used as an ingredient if you make your own compost, it can be dug in to heavy soil to make the soil lighter and more workable and it makes a first-class mulch. Shrubs, rhododendrons and azaleas in particular, benefit from a leafmould mulch. It also makes an excellent moisture-retaining mulch on light land. Plants, such as ferns and hardy primulas, which like to have cool, moist roots, can be protected from hot, dry conditions with a leafmould mulch.

The easiest way to make small quantities of leafmould is to pack the leaves tightly into black plastic bin liners and tie up the bags. Store for 18–24 months and the leafmould will be ready for use. Large amounts of leaves can be kept in a wire enclosure. Water them in dry conditions and they will rot down to usable leafmould in a couple of years.

You can use fallen leaves from local parks or from the street but watch out for contamination by dogs. You are not allowed to help yourself to leaves from woodland without the owner's permission. Never collect leaves that may carry disease, such as those from around roses suffering from black spot.

The production of leafmould can be accelerated by putting the leaves through a garden shredder. This breaks down their structure and also enables you to use the tougher leaves such as plane and sycamore which, traditionally, are not included in leafmould.

Gather the leaves as they fall. A rotary mower with a collection box is a quick and efficient way of collecting them.

● Pots, seed trays and labels

The fungi that cause damping off in seedlings are found in dirty pots and seed trays. To prevent problems next spring, use a garden disinfectant when cleaning pots and trays. Also clean plant labels before using them again next year.

GREENHOUSES & FRAMES

● Watering and feeding

As the days get shorter and the nights become colder, progressively reduce damping down and watering in the greenhouse. If it is still necessary, try to do it before midday. Stop feeding plants.

● Heating

Check the greenhouse heating to make sure that it is working properly and that thermostats are operating correctly.

To save heat during the winter, line the greenhouse with plastic sheeting or bubble plastic. There are special clips you can buy to hold this in place. If you are using an oil or gas heater leave the ventilators on the sheltered side of the roof open 5 mm (¼ in) the whole time to allow fumes and moisture vapour, created by the heater, to escape.

● Cold frames

Make sure that the frames are closed each night to protect any overwintering plants in case of a sudden, unexpected frost. Cover with matting as an added precaution. Take any tender plants out of the frames and into the greenhouse without delay.

● Controlling pests

Keep a sharp lookout for damage caused by slugs or other pests (*see* Pests, page 395–405).

GREENHOUSES – CONSERVING HEAT

Clean the glass before fastening plastic lining or bubble plastic inside the greenhouse – dirty glass excludes valuable light. Cover the ventilators separately. If using single plastic sheeting ensure that a gap of about 2 cm (¾ in) is left between the glass and the insulation to maximise the double-glazing effect.

● Sowing

Sow sweet peas without heat (*see* Sweet Peas, page 246) and continue to sow hardy annuals (*see* September, page 218). Sow lettuces to overwinter (*see* Vegetables, page 248).

● Cuttings

Continue to take cuttings of tender perennials and to pot up cuttings that have rooted (*see* September, pages 228–229 and Propagation, pages 428–431).

● Bulbs, corms and tubers

Prepare bulbs, corms and tubers for storage and pot up lilies for early flowering (*see* Lilies, page 244).

● Vines

Continue to pick bunches as they ripen. Treat the vines if red spider mite and mildew have been a problem (*see* Pests and Diseases, pages 402 and 410).

HEATHERS

● Planting new beds

Complete the planting out of new heathers (*see* September, page 219) and mulch to conserve moisture (*see* May, page 131).

● Watering

Water potted-up plants if they are looking dry. Use rainwater if possible (*see* April, page 101).

HERBS

● Harvesting and preparing ground

Gather any remaining soft-leaved culinary herbs. Chervil and parsley which have grown well will be unreliable for a second season as they will only bolt into flower as soon as spring arrives. Pull them up and, before the end of the month, dig over cleared ground, leaving it rough for frost and for birds to reduce the slug and snail population over the winter.

● Tidying up beds

Clear up the herb garden, but leave some attractive old growth, stalks and seed heads. The birds will enjoy the seed heads, and the stalks and dried leaves will provide homes in which natural predators, butterflies and moths can overwinter safely.

● Herbs under glass

Keep herbs in the house or greenhouse fed and watered, but do not wet the foliage. Continue to pick the new shoots when young. Inspect these plants regularly for pests such as aphids, vine weevils, slugs and woodlice and take precautions as necessary (*see* Pests, pages 395–405).

● Garlic

Complete planting of garlic cloves this month (*see* September, page 219).

● New plants

Continue to plant out hardy herbs if the soil is still warm (*see* April, page 101) and divide large clumps of perennial herbs (*see* September, page 220).

HOUSE & CONSERVATORY PLANTS

● Protection from dry air and cold

Keep plants in a warm room, around 18°C (65°F), but keep the humidity around the plants as high as possible by grouping them together to create a humid microclimate. Spray the plants with tepid water or place pots in troughs filled with pea gravel or clay granules and keep these moist.

The area between closed curtains and the window gets very cold at night, so remove plants from the windowsill before drawing the curtains or they could get chilled.

● Regular care

Water and mist sparingly, using water at room temperature rather than cold water straight from the tap. Clean leaves and remove any that are dead (*see* February, page 42).

● Flowering plants

Keep any plants that are in flower, such as azaleas and primulas, in cool, light and airy conditions.

Give chrysanthemums bought in bud a weak feed every two weeks. Stop feeding once flowering starts.

Move clivias to a cooler place, but not below 10°C (50°F), reduce watering and keep nearly dry until the flower buds appear in late winter. Stop feeding so the plants can rest.

Finish the potting of winter-flowering arum lilies (*Zantedeschia aethiopica*) if not already done (*see* September, page 214).

To initiate flower buds in poinsettias, keep the plants in the dark for 14 hours, followed by light for 10 hours and repeat this for two months (*see* September, page 220).

● Indoor bulbs and corms

Once an achimenes has died down, cut back the stems and keep in a frost-free place. Alternatively, dig out the rhizomes, dry and label them and keep them in a frost-free place until next spring.

Keep cyclamen and lachenalia plants in a cool, light and airy place.

Examine forced bulbs to see the compost is not too dry and water sparingly.

● Climbers and feature plants

Continue to water and feed jasmine (*Jasminum polyanthum*) every two weeks. Thin out shoots of plumbagos (*Plumbago auriculata*), passion flowers (*Passiflora caerulea*) and *Tibouchina semidecandra* to let in more light and air during the winter.

● Bromeliads

Continue to water sparingly every two to three weeks, but do not feed.

GROWING YOUR OWN ORANGES AND LEMONS

Oranges and lemons can be grown in pots in a conservatory. During the winter thin out overcrowded branches on well-established plants. They do best if the temperature is kept above 13°C (55°F).

From April to July, feed plants with a balanced liquid feed (with added trace elements) every fortnight. Keep the plants in small, heavy pots in a soil-based compost. Repot mature specimens every three years in the spring.

During the summer, ensure the temperature stays below 32°C (90°F), or the plants will drop their blossoms and fruit. Keep the atmosphere humid, placing pots on trays of moist gravel. Ensure the conservatory is well ventilated and shaded. Pinch back growing shoots and thin any fruit clusters. In August, change to a high-potash feed with trace elements and feed weekly, reducing to fortnightly during September.

In October and November you can harvest the fruit of (non-everbearing) mandarins. Everbearing plants, such as lemons and calamondin oranges (*Citrus mitis*), provide fruit all the time.

● Cacti and other succulents

Stop feeding cacti, if this has not already been done, and reduce watering week by week, stopping completely at the end of this month.

● Orchids

Reduce watering as growth slows down.

IRISES

● Bulbs for winter display

Plant dwarf winter-flowering bulbs, such as *Iris reticulata*, *I. histrioides* and *I. danfordiae*, in pots for display under glass during late winter. Plant bulbs 5 cm (2 in) deep in a soilless compost mixed with an equal volume of pea gravel. Water with a liquid fertiliser and place the pots outside in a sheltered place until late December. Cover with fine mesh netting to protect against mice and squirrels.

● Pacific Coast irises

This is the best month for planting Pacific Coast irises (Californian Hybrid) in all areas, except the very coldest. Soak the roots of new plants in water overnight before planting in soil that is just acid, with added leafmould, peat, peat substitute or humus. After planting keep plants moist if weather is dry. Plants will flower in late April, May and early June.

● Bearded irises

Remove dead leaves of bearded irises by pulling them away from the rhizome and cut back longer leaves to about half. Weed around them carefully, as roots of these irises may be near the surface. Cut off any rotten leaf fans at the rhizome, cleaning the blade after use with a garden disinfectant. Secure any loose rhizomes with a wire hoop.

IRISES – PLANTING PACIFIC COAST IRISES

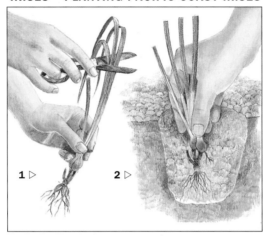

1 ▷   2 ▷

(1) Trim the leaves of Pacific Coast irises before planting, using scissors or secateurs.
(2) Plant at their original level, using the colour change on the stems of bare-root plants to judge the correct depth.

LAWNS

● Mowing

If not done last month, give new lawns a first cut when grass is 5 cm (2 in) high, mowing to a height of about 2 cm (¾ in) (*see* September, page 221).

Established lawns will need mowing less frequently now as the rate of growth slows. Raise the height of the cut slightly. Before mowing brush away wormcasts with a besom (*see* March, page 73).

● Turfing

Turf can be laid all the year round, but for best results you should avoid very hot weather or hard frosts, so October is a good month.

Prepare a weed-free bed for the turf, select and order the type of turf that will give you the lawn you are aiming for and lay it within 24 hours of delivery (*see* March, pages 84–85).

● Improving drainage

Any lawn on heavy soil that gets a lot of use soon becomes compacted and forms an impervious layer which prevents water percolating down. Improve surface drainage by scarifying, spiking and top dressing (*see* September, page 221). If you can, avoid using the lawn during wet weather.

Sub-surface drainage problems occur when the water table is near the surface or water runs down a slope, such as a patio, on to the lawn. This is more difficult to correct and you may have to dig up the lawn and make a soakaway (a gravel-filled pit covered with turf), at the edge of the lawn or install a proper drainage system.

If you think you need to install a drainage system it is advisable to take expert advice before starting. Tile drains (modern ones are plastic) may be installed in a line at 90 degrees to the general flow. It is an expensive and time consuming job, as the drains are laid 45–60 cm (18–24 in) deep, overlaid with 15–25 cm (6–10 in) of a porous material such as stone or gravel. Provided there is an outlet, the water will be carried away. Replace soil and turves carefully or the lawn may become uneven later.

● Clearing autumn leaves

Sweep up fallen leaves from the lawn as they can smother the grass. On a small lawn use a plastic leaf rake and a grabber but for a large lawn consider a wheeled sweeper or powered leaf blower. Rotary mowers with a collection box will remove most of the leaves as you cut the grass. Add these to the compost heap or make leafmould (*see* page 240).

LAWNS – IMPROVING DRAINAGE

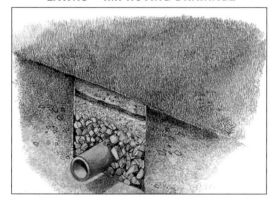

If ground is very poorly drained, it may be worth installing clay or plastic land drains (obtainable from a builders' merchant). They should be on a slight slope leading to a soakaway or drainage ditch.

● **Lawn edges**

Repair any worn lawn edges by cutting and moving forwards a rectangle of grass and making a clean edge (*see* February, page 44). Fill the gap left behind with soil and sow grass seed. Protect the newly sown seed with plastic sheeting.

LILIES

● **Planting bulbs**

This month try to finish the planting of lilies outside. Most lilies like well-drained, fairly rich, moist soil which is neutral or very slightly acid.

When you plant any bulbs that you think will need staking when in flower it is a good idea to insert a small marking stick alongside the bulb. Remove the stick when you want to put in a full-length stake. It is unwise to force a stake down near lily bulbs

without a guide, as the stems do not necessarily grow straight upwards and your stake could go right through the bulb and ruin it.

Plant bulbs at a depth equal to two and a half times their height. This usually means they have 10–15 cm (4–6 in) of soil over their tops. If you are growing lilies for cutting it is best to plant two or three times as many bulbs as the number of stems you hope to cut. Allow the bulbs a season or two to recover after cutting.

● **After flowering**

Allow stems to die down naturally, unless they are diseased. Plants with virus diseases should be destroyed immediately (*see* Diseases, page 411).

Save seed if you have not done this earlier (*see* September, page 223).

● **Forcing bulbs**

You can lift bulbs for forcing in pots once the stems die down. Use 20–25 cm (8–10 in) pots, depending on the eventual size of the plants, and ensure that bulbs have at least 5 cm (2 in) of compost over their tops; more if possible, especially for tall and stem-rooting types. Keep pots moist and frost-free.

The pots should be brought inside into warmth 12 to 13 weeks before flowers are wanted. Keep them at a temperature of 7–10°C (45–50°F) while they start into growth and then increase this to 15–20°C (60–70°F) (*see* January, page 26 and February, page 45). Check that a good root system has been established before introducing too much heat.

PELARGONIUMS

● **Overwintering plants**

Early in the month decide which plants, if any, are

to be kept in for the winter (*see* September, page 223). Throw away all the plants which look sickly or have been disappointing.

The ideal place for pelargoniums in winter is a light, frost-free position where the atmosphere is dry. Temperatures need not be high, but if the plants actually freeze they will not recover. In a greenhouse an electric fan heater is ideal for pelargoniums as it circulates dry air. Plants need some moisture at the roots: this is especially important for regal pelargoniums which do not withstand drought as well as zonals.

It is often necessary to cut back plants in the autumn in order to accommodate them in their winter position. Do this with any that are too large or straggly. Cut just above a node (leaf joint) and dust the stem with a fungicidal powder. Do not cut the plant down to soil level.

PELARGONIUMS – STORING OVER WINTER

If you are short of space you can overwinter pelargoniums by packing them in deep boxes filled with potting compost. Cut back most of the top growth, label them, and cover the roots. Keep barely moist in a frost-free, light place.

Plants brought in from the garden can be potted up or set close together in boxes of compost to save space. If you have a large number of seed-raised plants, you may find it more convenient to discard them and raise fresh plants each year.

● Pricking out and potting on
Prick out seedlings sown last month and pot them on individually, when the second pair of leaves appears, into 5–8 cm (2–3 in) pots, preferably in a good peat-based or peat-substitute compost.

Pot on cuttings taken last month into 9 cm (3½ in) pots and take the last cuttings of the year if wanted. Although regals do not need as much stopping as zonals, it is advisable to remove the top terminal bud when the plant is about 8–10 cm (3–4 in) high. This encourages a bushy plant from the outset.

● Stopping specimen and show plants
Rotate specimen and show plants regularly, and stop any shoots growing faster than others (*see* September, page 223). If regal cuttings are getting too big for their 9 cm (3½ in) pots, move them on to 13 cm (5 in) pots. It is always a good idea to tap a few plants out of the pots to see how the roots are developing and whether the plants need potting on.

RHODODENDRONS & AZALEAS

If you can, visit gardens famous for their rhododendrons to select varieties of azaleas that have good autumn colour to the leaves. Some can be spectacular and are an added bonus in the garden.

● Planting
October is the ideal time to plant rhododendrons, as the soil is still warm from summer sun and moist from autumn rains. Plant growth has stopped and plants find it easy to establish themselves.

● Layering
Many layers propagated on rhododendrons in the previous year will have rooted by now. If they are well rooted, sever the stem from the parent plant and dig up the layer. Plant it in a suitably-sized pot using ericaceous compost and water well using rainwater if possible.

Keep the pots over winter in a sheltered corner of the garden or in a cold frame (*see* August, page 202).

● Semi-ripe cuttings
Pot up any semi-ripe cuttings taken in early summer that have rooted. They should be kept in a cold greenhouse or cold frame for the winter.

Semi-ripe cuttings potted up in March can now be planted in their final growing positions.

ROCK PLANTS

● Planting and transplanting
Planting can continue up to about the third week of the month, but only put out well-established young plants. It is best to do the main planting in spring (*see* March, page 75). Continue transplanting, making sure to dig up plants with a sufficient ball of soil round the roots (*see* September, page 224).

● Winter protection
Start providing protection for tender plants and those with grey woolly foliage. You can cover the plants with a cloche, a pane of glass or rigid plastic supported on bricks.

Remove fallen leaves to prevent susceptible plants from rotting, and remove dying flower stems.

ROSES

● Preparing new beds and sites
To give freshly planted roses a good start, first fork out all perennial weeds, double dig the new site and incorporate a plentiful amount of a good garden compost or, better still, well-rotted farmyard manure. Good rose soil has a pH of 6.5 but this is only an approximate guide. Soil pH can be adjusted within limits (*see* The soil in your garden, page 387).

● Pruning ramblers and climbers
Summer-flowering ramblers and climbers flower on the previous year's growth, so they must be pruned now. The theory is to remove the supporting ties and lay the whole plant down on the ground, then to cut out all the old flowering wood and tie back up the remaining young shoots or canes. In practice, this may not be possible, but at least try to remove the old flowering shoots to within 5 cm (2 in) of the main stems, and space out and tie up the young shoots (*see* January, page 20).

● Pruning hybrid teas and floribundas
Reduce shoots on hybrid tea (large-flowered) and floribunda (cluster-flowered) roses to lessen the risk of damage from windrock (*see* November, page 267). Shorten each shoot by one-third and complete pruning next spring (*see* March, page 75).

● Pruning other roses
Weeping standards, which are ramblers budded on to an upright stem, should be lightly pruned back. Tip back upright standards now and complete the pruning in early spring.

The majority of the old garden roses are better left in their entirety but will benefit from the

ROSES – PRUNING RAMBLERS

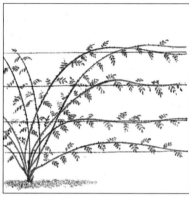

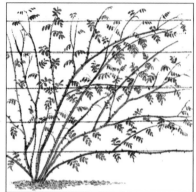

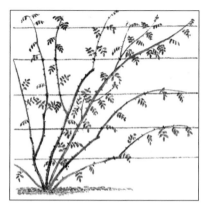

1 Most rambler roses produce new shoots freely from near ground level. This new growth can be easily identified as it is greener than the old wood.

2 Cut out old shoots which have borne flowers this year, taking them back to within about 5 cm (2 in) of their point of origin. Respace and tie in the new shoots.

1 Some rambler roses, such as 'Albertine' and 'New Dawn', do not shoot so freely from the base, and new shoots may arise from higher up the old stems.

2 With this type, just cut the old shoots back to a point where there is a young replacement shoot to take its place. Tie in the new shoots.

occasional removal of whole stems to encourage new growth at the base.

Species (wild roses) must never be pruned except to remove dead or diseased wood.

● **Roses for forcing**

Pot up new plants for early flowering in the greenhouse, and repot old ones, using John Innes No. 3 potting compost.

SWEET PEAS

● **Preparing new sites**

Clear the ground of canes, old stems and any weeds before preparing the new season's growing area next month. Sweet peas do best in an open, well-drained, sunny position, ideally running north to south in very fertile soil.

● **Sowing outdoors**

Lose no time if you wish to sow sweet peas direct in the ground outdoors in mild areas. This method is more suitable for naturally grown plants, rather than cordons, and is successful most years in mild districts under sheltered conditions and on well-drained land. Sow seeds fairly thickly with about 10 cm (4 in) between seeds, and cover them with cloches. The cloches may remain in position until April.

● **Sowing seed under glass**

Sow the seeds in John Innes seed compost, a proprietary compost or a mixture of four parts loam and one part each of sharp sand (or grit) and peat. Make sure that the compost is moist.

Put the pots or trays in a cold frame or cold greenhouse, preferably plunging pots into soil. Cover the containers with newspaper to retain warmth and moisture. From day five onwards check for germination. When the seedlings appear, remove the newspaper immediately and after two more days remove the frame lights entirely. Replace the frame lights only during very wet weather or when a hard frost is imminent; light frost will not harm the young seedlings. When the frame lights are removed, you will need to protect the seedlings against birds, rodents and slugs. Any seeds which are germinated in a cold greenhouse should be put outside in a cold frame straightaway.

Cold frames used for overwintering sweet pea plants should be sited in as open a position in the garden as possible. If you do not have a suitable cold frame available, cloches or even tunnels made from plastic sheeting (*see* Tools and equipment, page 449) should provide sufficient winter protection in most areas.

TREES, SHRUBS & HEDGES

● Planting

Soil conditions this month are ideal for planting hardy deciduous trees, shrubs and conifers. Prepare the planting area well if not already done (*see* September, page 225) and add bonemeal to the soil at the rate recommended by the manufacturer.

● Staking trees and shrubs

Staking plants correctly is as important as good soil preparation. Both are vital for establishment and protection of the fragile root systems of many trees, shrubs and conifers. One school of thought suggests that staking is unnecessary, another that only very short stakes are needed. This may well be the case with robust indigenous trees such as sycamore and ash but with many ornamental trees good early support is important for success and many trees perish without it.

Use a stake as long as the distance from the ground to just below the first branch of the tree, plus 45 cm (18 in). Drive the pointed lower end of the stake firmly into the ground with a sledge hammer, using an old piece of timber held over the top of the stake; this prevents the top of the stake from splitting. Alternatively, a post-hole rammer can be used. Make sure the stake is firmly placed in the ground for, if it is not, both stake and tree will rock, allowing the planting hole to enlarge and fill with water; this may cause the roots of the tree to rot.

For most trees the stake should not be less than 3 cm (1½ in) across, but whether it is square or round is not important. Use stakes that are peeled, unpeeled or pressure treated with a wood preservative but do not use those treated with creosote. This can contaminate the soil and also burn the foliage and new roots of the tree or shrub.

Position the stake on the windward side, so that in a high wind the tree will be blown away from it, which reduces the chances of the stem rubbing.

If you are planting a bare-root tree, fit the stake in between the roots and position it to within 2.5 cm (1 in) or so of the stem.

If the tree is container-grown, push the stake gently into the soil down the side of the pot. If you feel the stake coming up against the roots try pushing it in at another place. It is best to do this probing before removing the tree from the container to avoid breaking up the soil round the roots.

Once the stake is in place, secure the tree to the

TREES – PLANTING & STAKING

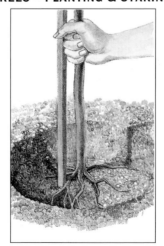

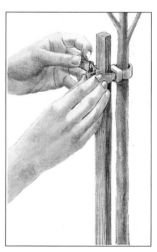

1 If planting a bare-root tree, check the depth of the hole against the soil mark on the trunk to get the planting level right.

2 When the depth of the hole is correct, drive in a stake. There should be at least 45 cm (18 in) of stake under the soil.

3 Position the tree and spread the roots out as evenly as possible. Keep the main stem close to the stake but not touching it.

4 Return the soil to the hole and firm it well, treading to remove large pockets of air. Rake level then water thoroughly.

5 Use an adjustable tree tie, close to the top of the stake. It is important that the tie can be loosened as the tree grows.

stake using two rubber or plastic tree straps. Always use ties that can be adjusted as the tree grows in girth: do not use wire, bailer twine, old tights or nylon string of any sort, as these could restrict the trunk and cause damage.

● Layers and hardwood cuttings

From October through to early December, carefully dig up the layers and hardwood cuttings that have rooted, and plant them out into their final growing positions or pot up for planting next spring (*see* March, page 78). Trim the layers to remove any parts of the layered shoot which have not rooted. Other than good soil preparation they need little aftercare until established.

Bring potted evergreen hardwood cuttings into a cold frame or cold greenhouse before the weather gets too frosty (*see* April, page 111).

● Collecting seeds

Seeds of many shrubs can be collected when they are ripe and saved to sow the following spring. Store dry seeds which do not have a fleshy coat, such as lavender, hebe and conifers, in sealed envelopes. Label the envelopes and keep them in a cool, dark, frost-free place safe from rodents until the following year (*see* February, page 47).

Seeds with fleshy coats, such as cotoneaster, holly and mountain ash, have to be subjected to a period of intense cold to encourage their germination (*see* Propagation, page 424).

● Pruning

Using the one-third method, prune any September-flowering shrubs that have been established for three years or more, once they have finished flowering (*see* Pruning, page 420).

HEDGES

Plant hedges in well-prepared soil (*see* September, page 226), incorporating bonemeal. If the weather is dry, water several times a week, spraying stems and foliage at the same time. Try to complete the planting of all evergreens, including conifers, by the end of the month.

VEGETABLES

Continue to harvest cabbages, carrots, potatoes, turnips and swedes for the winter and start to harvest parsnips. As crops finish dig the ground over. Add plenty of well-rotted organic matter, such as farmyard manure or spent mushroom compost.

● Beans

Harvest any remaining French and runner beans. Covering French beans with cloches may help them survive early frosts.

● Brassicas

Plant spring cabbages if not already done (*see* September, page 226). In cold areas, cover spring cabbages and Chinese cabbages with cloches or plastic sheeting for protection. Harvest early-sown Chinese cabbages, autumn cabbages and cauliflowers.

● Carrots and parsnips

Lift maincrop carrots to store for the winter and begin to harvest parsnips.

● Onions and leeks

Lift and store onions if not done last month. Plant sets of Japanese onions for harvesting in early summer before other onions are ready. Plant them 5 cm (2 in) apart in rows 25 cm (10 in) apart, with

their tops just below the surface.

Harvest the first leeks by lifting them gently out of the soil with a fork. Continue to earth up the stems to blanch them until the end of October.

● Other roots and swollen stems

Lift and store maincrop beetroot. Alternatively cover the rows with a layer of straw or soil for protection, marking the position for later harvesting.

Celeriac can be left in the ground until it is needed, or the 'roots' lifted before severe frosts. Trim off the large leaves and store in boxes indoors.

● Potatoes

Lift and store maincrop potatoes when the weather is dry. Separate any slightly damaged tubers and use these first. Store only sound, dry tubers in paper

---

VEGETABLES – BLANCHING LEEKS

To increase the length of blanched stems, loosely tie black plastic or corrugated paper around them, allowing for expansion. Mound up soil around the sides in stages as the plants grow throughout the winter.

VEGETABLES – SALAD CROPS

Endive is a useful late salad crop, but the leaves are bitter unless blanched first. One way to do this is to use a large pot to cover them, blocking the drainage hole to keep out the light. Blanching may take several weeks.

potato sacks. Keep them somewhere dry, dark and frost-free and they will last all winter.

● Salad crops

Sow lettuces under cloches in mild areas; choose a hardy winter variety, such as 'Arctic King'. If you have an old-fashioned greenhouse with a raised bed, you can grow various varieties of lettuce and other salad crops including radishes or spinach in that over the winter.

Blanch broad-leaved endives some weeks before you want to eat them. The foliage needs to be dry or the plants will rot. Tie the leaves together with soft string or raffia and cover the whole plant with a bucket or pot. Protect from slugs.

PERENNIAL VEGETABLES

● Globe artichokes

In cold areas, protect globe artichoke crowns.

● Jerusalem artichokes

Dig up Jerusalem artichoke tubers as required from October until the spring. Leave a few to produce next year's crop. In cold areas, protect the crowns.

WATER PLANTS & POOLS

● Thinning plants

Continue to thin out congested submerged plants, especially those plants that die back during winter.

● Cutting back marginal plants

Cut marginal plants back, but do not reduce those with hollow stems to beneath the water level (allow for the water level to rise in winter) or they may rot.

● Dividing waterside plants

Divide and replant waterside plants, such as astilbes, rodgersias and trollius, in the bog garden and in boggy areas surrounding the pool.

● Autumn leaves

Net the pool if not already done (*see* September, page 227) and clear falling leaves regularly, to prevent them from building up.

WATER PLANTS & POOLS – NETTING A POND

Temporary netting will keep autumn leaves out of the pond, reducing the risk of water pollution as leaves fall into the pond and decay. Use a fine mesh net otherwise all but the largest leaves will still fall through.

Fix the net securely. Special net pegs can be bought and those pegs used to anchor horticultural fleece are also suitable. If necessary you can make your own pegs from thick wire. Bricks can also be used to help secure the net.

Rock Beds for Alpines

October is a good time to construct a rock garden or raised alpine bed. Contoured rock gardens should resemble rock outcrops, and can look incongruous in flat suburban settings. A simpler and cheaper alternative is to grow your alpines in a specially made raised alpine bed.

A raised alpine bed can be made small enough to fit into most gardens and is easier to maintain than a full-scale rock garden. It is certainly a more economical option than creating a rock outcrop, as buying rocks in quantity is expensive.

An alpine bed is not intended as a natural feature and few, if any, rocks are needed. Planting and maintenance present few difficulties if the bed is raised about 60 cm (2 ft) above ground level. As many as 30 different kinds of alpines can be grown in a bed measuring 3 m² (10 sq ft). Whether you prefer an alpine bed or a full-scale rock garden,

select an open site, preferably sheltered and facing south or south-west, away from overhanging trees.

A rectangular bed works well in most gardens. Walls built of local stone are a good choice, but bricks will work equally well. Dry stone walls are particularly suitable, as plants can be inserted in gaps between the courses. Such niches will provide the cool root run alpines enjoy. If the wall is to be mortared, leave some gaps and fill these with soil so they too can provide a home for alpines.

Good drainage is essential for alpines. On heavy or wet soil, first remove the topsoil, fork over the

subsoil and cover with a layer of broken bricks or other hardcore. On lighter, well-drained soil, place a layer of rubble at ground level. Top the drainage layer of hardcore with some well-rotted compost or with old grass turves placed face down.

SOIL MIXTURE

Fill the bed with a mixture of two parts good-quality loamy topsoil, one part coarse grit and one part well-rotted leafmould, peat or peat substitute. If the soil is heavy, add some extra sand or limestone chippings. Rake in a general-purpose or slow-release fertiliser. If you wish, before beginning planting, carefully position a few large rocks, partly buried in the soil. Try to use local stone and arrange it to resemble a natural outcrop.

A RAISED ALPINE BED

A ROCK GARDEN

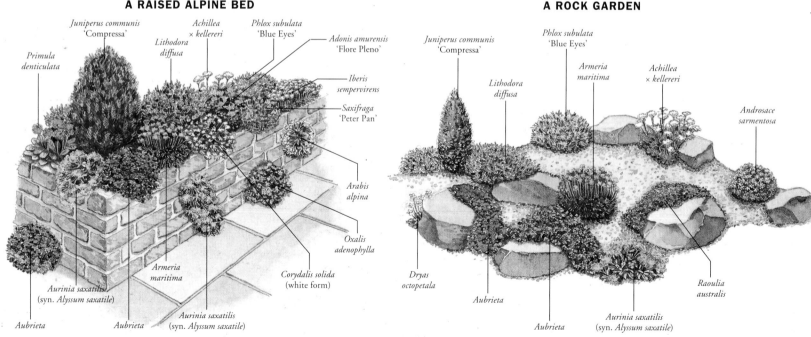

A RAISED ALPINE BED labels: Primula denticulata; Juniperus communis 'Compressa'; Lithodora diffusa; Achillea × kellereri; Phlox subulata 'Blue Eyes'; Adonis amurensis 'Flore Pleno'; Iberis sempervirens; Saxifraga 'Peter Pan'; Arabis alpina; Oxalis adenophylla; Corydalis solida (white form); Armeria maritima; Aurinia saxatilis (syn. Alyssum saxatile); Aubrieta; Aubrieta; Aurinia saxatilis (syn. Alyssum saxatile); Aubrieta

A ROCK GARDEN labels: Juniperus communis 'Compressa'; Lithodora diffusa; Phlox subulata 'Blue Eyes'; Armeria maritima; Achillea × kellereri; Androsace sarmentosa; Dryas octopetala; Aubrieta; Aubrieta; Aurinia saxatilis (syn. Alyssum saxatile); Raoulia australis

Allow a week or two for the soil to settle and top up the bed with more soil mixture before you plant. Finally cover the soil with a 1 cm (½ in) layer of stone chippings. These should blend with any rocks that have been used: limestone chippings with limestone, coarse gravel with sandstone and so on. The chippings help retain soil moisture, protect the necks of rock plants from rotting and prevent rain splashing soil on flowers and foliage.

CHOOSING PLANTS

The flowering season for alpines is from February to October, with a concentration between March and the end of May. Unless you are careful to include some late-flowering plants, the bed may be bereft of colour in late summer and autumn. For helpful ideas, visit gardens and specialist nurseries which feature alpines, or send for their catalogues.

▲ *This beautiful rock garden features Lakeland slate.*

Alpine plants vary in type and habit. There are perennial mat-formers and cushion plants, dwarf bulbous plants, plants that form hummocks and slow-growing dwarf shrubs and conifers. The latter provide interest in winter and will break any tendency to flatness in a raised bed.

Prostrate varieties are not recommended for small areas and should, in any case, be pruned if they start spreading too much. Quick-growing aubrietas, helianthemums or alyssum will also need trimming back as soon as they finish flowering. Other fast-growing mats or rosettes may need lifting, dividing and replanting after their second or third season to promote fresh growth and to curb excessive spread.

Pot-grown alpines can be planted at almost any time, except when the ground is frozen or under snow. It is also better to avoid planting them out during prolonged very dry weather in summer.

ALPINES PLANTED IN A DRY STONE WALL AND IN A TROUGH

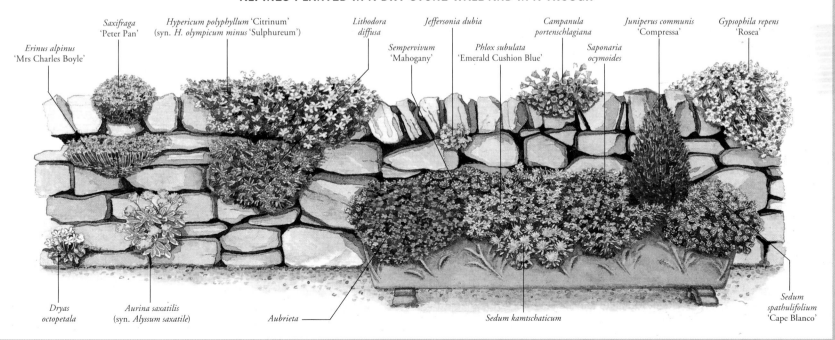

NOVEMBER

As the year draws to an end,
the colour on the trees deepens,
leaves blow down in the wind
and it is time to protect
plants against winter cold.

November

There are pockets of colour in a November garden: the trees still carry their autumn and winter berries, and there are late flowers in bloom in the border – the last roses, the pink nerines and Michaelmas daisies. But November is the month when autumn gives way to the onset of winter and the garden becomes a much less inviting place than earlier in the year.

There are always things to be done but the pace slows down and most jobs will wait a week or two – or even a month or more – if the weather is bad.

It is a month to make the most of your greenhouse and house plants, although, on fine days, visiting other gardens or arboretums can still provide many hours of pleasure, education and inspiration.

The timing of the most spectacular autumn tints varies from year to year, and depends on the weather, but early November is often the best month, when the hedges and woods are gloriously colourful. Berries on trees and shrubs have not yet had time to lose their sparkle and, with a few exceptions, have not yet been eaten by the birds.

The weather in November

There are wide regional variations in the weather at this time of year. Cold regions may already be in the grip of winter, but areas such as south-west England often remain mild and autumnal.

Low cloud, rain and frequent fogs often cause November to be a gloomy month, even though it may not be particularly cold.

The snow will now be on the hills in northern regions, and may even affect low-lying areas. The snow showers are generally short-lived however, and do not normally pose a serious problem for the gardener.

Most plants cease to grow and become dormant when the daily mean temperature is below about 6°C (43°F). This usually occurs by the end of November.

Making the most of fine days

Good gardening days are rare this month, so take full advantage of those that are clement.

Do as much winter digging as possible, for there will be long periods in the winter when the soil will be unworkable. Prepare new beds and borders now for spring planting to give the soil time to settle.

Tidying the garden can transform its appearance at this time of year. Weedy beds or borders or compacted soil beaten down by rain can mar an otherwise attractive garden. Hoeing the weeds off, and loosening the soil with a fork where appropriate, will make everything look much more appealing.

Working indoors

When outdoor gardening is impractical there are always jobs to be done in the greenhouse – not least of which is making sure the glass is clean, the insulation effective, and the heating system working. You can also spend more time grooming your house plants.

November is a good time to look at new gardening books and catch up on your reading of magazines. Very often they are the inspiration for a number of good ideas which you can use in your garden next year.

Send away for a selection of seed catalogues, which are often advertised around November. Tree and shrub catalogues are also available. Many of these include herbaceous border plants, and are well worth studying if you are planning a new border.

Garden hygiene

In some years it is well into November before most of the leaves fall from the trees, usually blown down by strong winds following a sharp frost. Sweep them off the lawn as soon as possible, for if they are allowed to lie there they will block the light; this weakens the grass and encourages the development of diseases. Clear fallen leaves from small container plants and from the rock garden too – they can smother low-growing plants, and provide a haven for slugs and snails.

Leaves can be recycled into leafmould, which is good for the garden in general and excellent for homemade potting composts. They rot down slowly and are best packed into plastic bin liners or kept in an individual wire enclosure, if you have room for one. Leaves may take up to two years to rot down completely, but the wait is worth it (*see* October, page 240).

By clearing debris all around the garden, slugs, snails and other pests will be exposed. Try to kill as many as you can to reduce the population in your garden over the winter – the birds will help you!

Pests such as scale insects on shrubs may become more apparent as the leaves fall, so always be on the lookout for potential problems as you tidy up around the garden and, if pruning, take the opportunity to cut out any diseased or badly pest-infected shoots.

Recycling plant material

With all the tidying that has taken place during the last few months, getting rid of the rubbish and plant material can be a problem, particularly in a small garden.

Put all the material that will rot down easily including stems and leaves from herbaceous plants, grass clippings and soft vegetation in general, on to the compost heap.

Diseased material and hard, twiggy growth and prunings can be burned. Let them dry out first to avoid a slow, smoky fire that will offend your neighbours. Be aware of local bylaws.

Many local authorities offer a disposal service for garden refuse that is large or heavy, but they may charge a fee. In some areas you may have to take garden refuse to the local council tip. A garden shredder is excellent for recycling woody material at home but a shredder is noisy to use and expensive to buy. It is worth asking to see if any of your neighbours are interested in sharing a hired shredder over the busy autumn period. It is also worth checking to see if your local authority offers a shredding facility.

JOBS THAT WON'T WAIT

● Cover vulnerable plants growing outdoors with cloches or horticultural fleece if severe frost is forecast. Protect newly planted and susceptible trees and shrubs over the winter with windbreaks or by wrapping plants in hessian or horticultural fleece.

● Clear out and take under cover decorative containers that are not frost-hardy. Protect pots containing plants of borderline hardiness with insulation and by grouping them together in a sheltered spot.

● Check the pots and bowls of bulbs that are being forced for Christmas and New Year flowering. Ensure they do not dry out or become waterlogged. Move them into a light but cool position indoors when the leaves reach about 2.5 cm (1 in) in height.

● Check bulbs, corms and tubers in store. Any that are becoming soft or are showing signs of disease should be removed and destroyed before they affect the others.

● Plant any remaining tulip and hyacinth bulbs in the garden without delay.

● Plant roses if conditions permit or heel in if the weather is very frosty. Prune climbers and ramblers and cut back hybrid tea roses and floribundas to reduce damage from windrock.

● Cut the lawn for the last time this year and clean and store the lawnmower.

● Prune wisteria to ensure and increase flowering next year.

● Prepare for autumn and winter gales by removing dead or decaying branches on established trees and checking that recently planted trees are well staked and that ties are secure. Also check fences, trellis and other structures supporting plants to make sure they will stand up to high winds.

● Clear fallen leaves and other debris so slugs, snails and other pests have nowhere to overwinter. Use fallen leaves to make leafmould.

● Deal with any pests or diseases left exposed when plants lose their leaves.

● Harvest vegetables including the first Brussels sprouts, kale, cabbages, endives, spinach, turnips, swedes and Jerusalem artichokes.

● Consider installing a pond heater to keep a small area of water ice free if you keep fish.

ANNUALS & BIENNIALS

● Protection of annuals

Keep an eye on the weather forecast and cover rows of hardy annuals growing outdoors with cloches or horticultural fleece if hard frosts threaten.

BORDER PERENNIALS

● Top dressing established borders

Use garden compost or well-rotted manure as a top dressing for borders or for digging in, if not done last month. Leave general application of fertilisers until early spring.

● Tidying borders

Continue cutting back dead foliage and stems unless required for wind shelter; remove stakes. Compost soft material and discard diseased or woody debris. Dig out perennial and evergreen weeds such as brambles and creeping buttercup. Keep beds clear of debris and fallen leaves. Left bare, the ground will be cleared of surface pests by frost.

● Planting

Continue planting new beds (*see* September, page 212) if conditions are suitable. Most hardy plants can be moved this late in the season, but leave anything potentially vulnerable until the spring. Do not move plants if the weather is inclement, or the ground is frozen hard, waterlogged or compacted.

● Ground preparation

Continue clearing ground for new beds, digging and leaving soil rough for the frost to break it down. Add garden compost or well-rotted manure at the same time. Remove any roots of perennial weeds.

BULBS, CORMS & TUBERS

● Preparing gladiolus beds

Select a suitable site for growing gladioli next year. They do best in a medium soil that is neither very light nor very heavy. Gladioli require plenty of moisture, but are not successful in waterlogged soil. Dig the plot evenly, incorporating a moderate dressing of well-rotted manure or garden compost. Also rake some bonemeal into the surface.

● Tulips and hyacinths

Complete the planting of tulips and hyacinths as soon as possible (*see* October, page 235).

● Forced bulbs

Examine bowls and pots of bulbs you are forcing for early flowering. Move them, when the growth has reached about 2.5 cm (1 in) in height, to a cool greenhouse or frame for a few weeks. Alternatively place them on the windowsill of a cool room where frost can be excluded but where the temperature will not exceed 10°C (50°F). Water sufficiently to prevent the fibre or compost from drying out.

As soon as 'Paper White' and 'Soleil d'Or' narcissi start to sprout (*see* August, page 195), bring them into a warmer greenhouse or room. They should then flower by Christmas.

● Begonias

Once begonias have died down in the autumn, lift the tubers before the first frost. Dry them off and store them in dry peat or a peat substitute in a cool frost-free place such as a shed or under the greenhouse staging. Do not allow the compost to become dust dry, but it should not be damp enough to risk causing mould.

● Checking stored bulbs and corms

Continue to clean bulbs and corms, if not already done, and check for rot and thrips (*see* October, page 235).

CARNATIONS & PINKS

● Planting outdoors

If weather and soil conditions permit, continue to plant container-grown border carnations and pinks. Firm the soil around any recently planted that may have been loosened by frost. Keep plants clear of fallen leaves or rotting vegetation. Ensure that stakes and ties of border carnations are secure and keep a watch for pests and diseases (*see* April, page 92).

● Improving growing conditions

Continue to improve the texture of beds by turning the soil with a fork. If a drainage test was made (*see* August, page 195), observe where the water level settles and take appropriate action.

PERPETUAL-FLOWERING

Keep them free from frost, water and feed sparingly (*see* April, page 92). Cut and disbud flower stems as necessary (*see* September, page 214).

Continue to check carefully for aphids and thrips as well as for any signs of rust or rot.

CHRYSANTHEMUMS

EARLY-FLOWERING (GARDEN)
● Preparing borders

If you garden on heavy clay soil now is the time to start digging. Chrysanthemums grow best in soil well supplied with organic matter, such as farmyard manure, spent hops or good garden compost. Add as a 5 cm (2 in) top dressing each year, or dig it in but take care not to bury it more than 15 cm (6 in) deep or the plants will not receive the full benefit. Manure, with a lot of straw in it, is good to use on heavy clay, so apply a more generous amount than on lighter soil.

Chrysanthemums do not like soil which is very acid (below pH 5.0) or very alkaline (above pH 7.5), so pH 6.5 is ideal. Test the pH of soil. Spent mushroom compost, which usually contains chalk, is not suitable for chrysanthemums unless the soil is acid and needs added lime (*see* The soil in your garden, pages 387–392).

● Overwintering

Check the plants outside in the garden for signs of being waterlogged. If any appear to be suffering, deeply pierce the soil around them with a garden fork. Refirm any plants that have been lifted by frost. Keep the beds clear of weeds, such as docks, chickweed and groundsel, which are hosts to the chrysanthemum eelworm.

Keep dormant stools in the greenhouse and cold frame moist, but not wet. Give full ventilation, except in windy or frosty weather, and maintain a maximum temperature of 10°C (50°F).

LATE-FLOWERING (GREENHOUSE)
● Temperature and ventilation

Restrict the temperature to a maximum of 10°C (50°F). Do not close the ventilators completely, except in frosty or very windy weather, or in fog. Open them as soon as conditions improve.

● Greenhouse blooms

The late-flowering varieties will begin to flower this month. They all require a long time to develop their flowers and under no circumstances should any attempt be made to hurry them.

Continue to water as required, but water via the roots and keep the foliage dry.

As the plants finish flowering, cut off all but 15 cm (6 in) of the stems and foliage. This will allow light and air to reach the pots and encourage growth from the base for next season's cuttings (*see* March, page 62).

● Controlling pests

Leaf miners can still be troublesome, but be careful not to spray when there are open flowers as this damages the blooms (*see* Pests, page 401).

CLIMBERS & WALL SHRUBS

● Planting

Complete autumn planting if the ground is not too wet or frozen (*see* October, page 237).

Any plants, except tender ones, raised in the garden from hardwood and semi-ripe cuttings or layering should also be planted out now in their final growing positions. Leave tender plants in pots under cover until the spring.

● Taking hardwood cuttings

Hardy climbers, such as jasmine and honeysuckle, are very easy to propagate from hardwood cuttings.

CLIMBERS & WALL SHRUBS – PRUNING WISTERIA

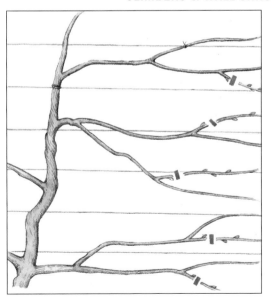

1 Wisterias should be pruned twice a year – in mid summer and again in November. Whether or not you pruned in summer, tie in new extension shoots now, where they are required, then prune back the new shoots.

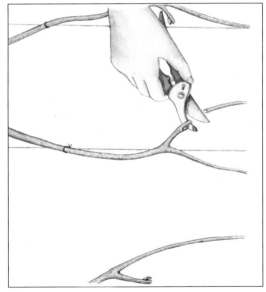

2 Prune any growth not required to extend the framework of branches by cutting back the summer's growth to about 8 cm (3 in) from where it arises from a main stem. Cut it back to a bud.

These can be taken from now until early spring (*see* Propagation, page 429).

● **Pruning wisteria**

Carry out the main pruning of wisterias now after shortening back the new shoots (*see* July, page 174). To ensure and increase flowering next year, search for all this year's growth. Tie in place any shoots you require to extend the area of cover, and then reduce the remaining ones to about 8 cm (3 in) from their point of origin on the main stems, cutting back to a bud. If too many shoots remain, there will be over-crowding and fewer flowers.

This pruning method will bring wisterias into flower within four years of planting; if left un-pruned they may take eight or even ten years.

CONTAINER GARDENING

● **Winter containers**

Finish planting winter containers as soon as possible to give the plants a chance to get established. Finish planting tulips, especially dwarf, early-flowering types, as otherwise flowering will be delayed.

● **Planting deciduous trees and shrubs**

Almost any plant can be grown in a container, including a tree, provided the pot is big enough. Large, wooden half barrels are perfect containers for trees and shrubs. Whatever plant you choose, ensure that the pot is large enough to accommodate the plant easily, with room for the rootball and an inch or two all round, then check that the drainage is adequate (*see* March, page 64). Use a soil-based potting compost; but if you are planting a lime-hating plant, such as an azalea or rhododendron, use a lime-free or a peat-based ericaceous compost.

PROTECTING CONTAINERS

Plants of borderline hardiness grown in containers are more likely to survive the winter if well protected.

Insulating the container, as well as the top growth, will reduce the risk of the roots freezing. Several layers of horticultural fleece wrapped around the plant and container are sometimes sufficient, but bubble plastic or hessian are also suitable. Do not enclose an evergreen in hessian.

Open the covering on warm sunny days, and check that the containers do not dry out completely.

Keep recently planted containers in a sheltered position until established.

● **Protecting plants for winter**

Prepare containers for cold weather by wrapping non-frost-resistant pots, or those containing vulnerable plants, in a 'duvet' of bubble plastic or, more attractively, hessian stuffed with straw.

Grouping containers together in a sheltered spot gives them mutual protection and it also makes it easier to cover them with a sheet of horticultural fleece in severe weather.

● **Cleaning and storing containers**

Pull out dead plants from summer displays, throw them away and retrieve and pot up any plants that can be reused. Tip out spent compost on to the garden or compost heap, checking for vine weevil grubs as you do so (*see* Pests, page 404). Clean out with a brush any compost that remains and store all the containers under cover until needed.

Some wood, plastic and terracotta containers are liable to crack if they are left full of compost for, when it freezes, compost expands and can break weak materials. Their life is extended if they are kept under cover when not in use.

DAHLIAS

Now is a good time to order new plants and tubers for delivery next year.

● **Inspection of tubers**

Examine stored tubers every few weeks during the winter and, if they are shrivelling or rotting, take action as necessary (*see* January, page 21).

FRUIT

● Planting fruit trees and bushes

Start planting bare-root trees and fruit bushes once they are available. This is a good time because the soil is still warm and, usually, not too wet. These conditions encourage quick rooting and help the plants to get established.

If plants arrive from the nursery before you are ready for them, heel them in. Dig a hole large enough to take the roots, put the plants in, shovel back the soil over the roots and firm it down. They can stay like that for many weeks. If winter arrives early and the ground is too hard to dig, leave the plants wrapped in the material they were packed in, and put them in a cool, frost-free outbuilding until conditions improve.

Thorough preparation of the planting sites is most important (*see* October, page 238). When the ground is ready, mark with canes where the trees or bushes are to go and dig the holes, inserting stakes for support before planting. Check the trees are planted at the correct depth and tie trees to their stakes after firming in.

A light dressing of general fertiliser, or bonemeal, mixed with the soil at planting time will encourage new roots to form quickly.

FRUIT CAGES IN WINTER

Check on the condition of the frame and netting and carry out any repairs that are needed. A good design is one with wire netting sides and a removable nylon netting top. The top netting can be taken off now to give birds access to the plants inside where they will clear up late greenfly and caterpillars. The top should be left on the cage only if you need to protect gooseberries from bud removal by bullfinches.

FRUIT – HEELING IN BARE-ROOT TREES

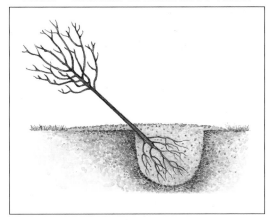

Bare-root fruit trees should be planted without delay, but if this is not possible, dig a shallow trench in a sheltered position and place the roots of the trees in it. Cover the roots with soil to keep them moist and firm down gently.

Always plant fruit trees in cultivated ground. When they are well established, after a few years, they may be grassed around if you prefer, but it will have a negative effect because the grass will rob the trees of much of the summer rain and a fair proportion of the nutrients.

Soft fruit is always grown in cultivated land.

● Apples and pears

Complete all picking as soon as possible. Any remaining fruits are likely to fall victim to birds, squirrels, autumn gales or all three!

Check on the condition of stored fruit and remove any that have rotted or ripened.

Begin pruning once the leaves have fallen. Aim to create an open tree with well-spaced branches that will grow and fruit for many years.

First take out any dead, broken or diseased branches. Badly diseased branches will normally be those attacked by the apple and pear canker. This eats into the wood and, if the infection is allowed to extend round a branch, or even the trunk, the part beyond the canker dies. Where a canker does not reach right round, cut out the dead and diseased tissue down to clean wood and bark, and treat the whole area with a wound paint. This is not always successful but it is well worth trying (*see* Diseases, page 406 and Pruning, pages 420–423).

Finally, take out any branches that are too high, too low, have spread too far or are causing overcrowding in the centre of the tree.

● Peaches and nectarines

When most of the leaves have fallen, treat the trees against infection from peach leaf curl spores (*see* Diseases, pages 408–409).

● Cane fruits

Remove the fruited canes of any blackberries, hybrid cane fruits or summer raspberries that have not yet been attended to, and tie the new ones to the wires in their place. These will fruit next summer.

Cut off the tops of the new canes of tall summer raspberries when they are 15 cm (6 in) above the top wire and tie them to the wire.

In cold and windy gardens, tie the canes of the blackberry hybrids into bundles and secure these to the wires until the spring.

● Gooseberries and currants

By this time it is possible to see whether any blackcurrant bushes have been colonised by the big bud mite (*see* Pests, page 396). These bushes will probably have reversion virus and should be dug up

FRUIT – TAKING HARDWOOD CUTTINGS FROM BLACKCURRANTS

 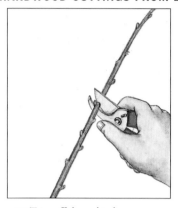 

1 Choose long, straight, healthy shoots from wood produced this year. Cut off a length about 30 cm (12 in) long.

2 Trim off the end to leave a cutting about 25 cm (10 in) long. Do not remove any buds from the cutting; they encourage basal shoots.

3 Insert cuttings in a trench, leaving 5 cm (2 in) above the soil. If the ground is liable to waterlogging put 5 cm (2 in) of sand in the trench first.

and destroyed. There is no cure for the virus; the plant dies and the disease will spread to other bushes.

Propagate currants and gooseberries from hardwood cuttings taken now. For blackcurrants, choose strong, straight, disease-free shoots of this year's growth and make each cutting about 25 cm (10 in) long after trimming. Try not to lose any of the buds. Make a slit in the ground with a spade and push the cutting in so that no more than 5 cm (2 in) is left showing.

Take cuttings of redcurrant and gooseberry 30–40 cm (12–16 in) long, retaining only the top four buds. Remove all the others along with the gooseberry's thorns. Push the cuttings into the ground to half their length. There should be some 15 cm (6 in) between the soil and the lowest bud, giving the future bush a short leg (trunk).

FRUIT – PRUNING CURRANTS AND GOOSEBERRIES

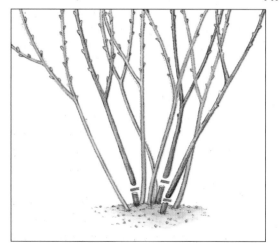 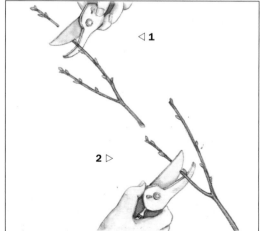 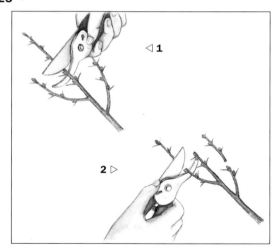

Blackcurrants fruit mainly on the wood produced the previous year and are easy to prune – just cut out up to one-third of the oldest branches close to their point of origin every winter. Do not prune bushes less than three years old.

Redcurrants and white currants are both pruned the same way. (1) Cut back all the current year's growth on the main leading shoots by half to outward-facing buds. (2) Then shorten the sideshoots to about 5 cm (2 in).

Gooseberries fruit on wood that is at least a year old. Established gooseberries are pruned in two steps. (1) Cut back by about half all the main leading shoots that have grown this year. (2) Shorten sideshoots to 5 cm (2 in).

The resulting bushes can be moved to their final growing position in a year's time.

Blackcurrant bushes do not require pruning after the first growing season in their permanent position (*see* January, page 22). After that, you can remove up to a third of the oldest branches on established bushes (over three years old) each winter leaving as much new growth as possible.

Prune established bushes of redcurrants, white currants and gooseberries by shortening the new growth on each leader by half and the sideshoots (laterals) to 5 cm (2 in). Prune cordons by shortening the leaders by one-third and the laterals to 5 cm (2 in). Remove all weak shoots completely on both bushes and cordons.

● **Strawberries**

Autumn strawberries, unlike summer varieties, do not have their foliage and stalks cut back after fruiting. Tidy up existing beds for the winter, remove any ground covering, such as straw or mats, and cloches or tunnels, and cultivate the ground shallowly. Do not feed the plants now; feed in the spring (*see* March, page 66). Plant new beds, if required, as plants become available.

FUCHSIAS

TENDER AND HALF HARDY
● **Overwintering plants**

Half-hardy fuchsias will generally survive a mild frost, but they will need to be brought under cover if they are to survive the winter. Keep their winter quarters, especially greenhouses, well ventilated, as condensation may encourage the onset of grey mould (botrytis) (*see* Diseases, page 407).

A little heat is necessary to maintain some plants and cuttings in green leaf: keep autumn cuttings (*see* October, page 239) at about 5°C (41°F), species and *triphylla* hybrids at around 7°C (45°F). Do not keep plants so warm that they start into growth. Any new shoots at this time of year will be unable to cope with winter temperatures.

● **Defoliation and shaping**

With the exception of autumn cuttings, species and *triphylla* hybrids, let plants continue to defoliate and remove any leaves which are reluctant to fall. Cut back the current season's growth by one-third, if this has not already been done.

● **Watering**

Check the rootball of plants from time to time; the soil should be slightly moist and should never dry out completely. If necessary, give a little tepid water.

● **Overwintering without heat or light**

To overwinter sturdy plants without a heated greenhouse or cool conservatory, strip the plants of foliage, water well then completely bury them – pots, stems, canes and labels – in moist coir or vermiculite, either under or on the staging in a cold greenhouse, or in a shed or outhouse. There they can be left for the winter, without attention, apart from the occasional inspection to check that they are not bone dry.

HARDY

When the first real frosts cut down the foliage and remaining flowers, tidy plants by cutting back one-third of the summer's growth. The remaining bare stems will act as protection. Hardy fuchsias left outside in containers are more vulnerable to frosts which penetrate the container walls; these will need lagging (*see* Container gardening, page 258).

GARDEN MAINTENANCE

While plants are dormant over the winter carry out repairs to trellis, pergolas and any other structures which support plants, but do not apply paints or stains when the weather is wet or frosty (*see* October, page 240). Repairs to outbuildings, such as sheds, can be done at any time of the year, but it is worth checking if anything needs to be done before winter cold, rain and wind causes additional damage. Greenhouse repairs should be done while the weather is still warm and plants can safely be moved outside for a few days (*see* August, page 198).

● **Repairing arches and pergolas**

Wooden arches and pergolas are most vulnerable where the top joins the uprights, so strengthen them with extra nails or screws. Replace any plastic joints on metal arches that are loose or, alternatively, wrap waterproof tape around the metal ends to give a tighter fit. If an arch is rather flimsy, anchor it by lashing the legs to additional vertical supports sunk into the ground.

● **Repairing fences**

On close-board fencing, check the cross pieces for rot. If they are rotten at the ends where they join the posts, fit special galvanised rail brackets. Replace any individual boards nailed vertically to the cross pieces that have rotted.

For overlap panels, where lengths of wood are horizontal and fixed to vertical battens, replace or repair single panels. When repairing a panel, prise off the vertical battens at each end. Then remove the damaged horizontal boards, slide in new ones and fix them with galvanised nails. Replace the vertical battens and secure in position.

TRELLIS

Choose trellis in a material such as timber, plastic or wire that is not only suitable for the character of the building or fence to which it will be attached, but is also strong enough to support a rampant climber.

Fix trellis to a wall or fence with wooden battens to hold the trellis at least 3 cm (1½ in) away from the brick or wood, to allow free circulation of air. This will discourage fungal diseases and also provide a less comfortable refuge for pests.

For easier pointing or painting behind a trellis, fix the bottom of the trellis to a batten, using hinges and a catch at the top. The trellis can then be lowered carefully, with the plant still attached to it, maintenance carried out and the trellis returned to its upright position.

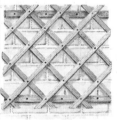

◁ Diamond-shaped trellis looks attractive, but little of it will be visible when the plant is grown.

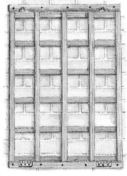

A rectangular ▷ pattern is plain but functional. It is easier to untangle winding plant stems from this than from a diamond-shaped trellis.

For interwoven fences, which have horizontal pieces woven within vertical battens, repairing individual strips is almost impossible and it is easier to replace a damaged panel with a new one.

Once fence and gate posts start to rot at ground level, they need to be replaced or reinforced. There are two ways to put in new or additional posts – either by using a post bolted to a short concrete spur or by inserting a metal post holder.

● **Repairing sheds and outhouses**

Check the roof for leaks and clear the guttering. Check that catches are secure on windows and doors that may get damaged in high winds, and replace as necessary. Use 3 × 3 cm (1½ × 1½ in) wood as diagonal braces between the vertical battens in the wall panels to strengthen a wooden shed. Then screw the braces to the vertical battens.

● **Preventing wind damage**

High winds in autumn and winter can cause much damage and expense, so now is the time to try to minimise any problems. Remove dead or decaying branches from trees, getting outside help if necessary. Support young trees with a stake making sure the tie does not constrict the tree and that the tree does not rub against the stake (*see* October, page 247).

● **Newly planted evergreens**

Erect a temporary windbreak around newly planted evergreens to prevent desiccation. The most effective barrier is one that filters the wind rather than a solid one which causes turbulence on the sheltered side (*see* Trees, shrubs and hedges, page 268).

GREENHOUSES & FRAMES

● **Ventilation and watering plants**

On all sunny days ventilate the greenhouse freely; avoid cold draughts, and close the ventilators fairly early in the afternoon to retain some of the daytime warmth. Dirty glass excludes valuable light, so use warm water containing detergent to wash it.

Keep the greenhouse closed during foggy weather, and cover the plants with newspaper or horticultural fleece if the fog persists.

Water all plants in pots sparingly and keep the atmosphere as dry as possible.

● **Pests and diseases**

Whitefly are often troublesome in the greenhouse at this time of year. Treat at the first signs of an attack (*see* Pests, page 405). It will be too late for natural predators to multiply in sufficient numbers to act as a control. If using a spray, beware of increasing the humidity of the greenhouse too much; fumigation may be more appropriate.

● **Potting up**

Complete any outstanding potting up early in the month. Annuals raised from seed in September will probably be ready for moving into 13 or 15 cm (5 or 6 in) pots. Pot up sweet pea seedlings. Cuttings of pelargoniums, fuchsias and other plants inserted in September should now be rooted and also ready for potting individually into 8 cm (3 in) pots.

● **Overwintering**

Allow pots of begonias, achimenes, heliotropes and hydrangeas, which have flowered during the summer and autumn, to dry off. Store the pots under the staging in a cool greenhouse or in a frost-proof shed, but do not allow the compost to become dust dry. Some fuchsias may also be treated in this way (*see* Fuchsias, page 261). Check dahlias in storage and any bulbs being forced for winter flowering (*see* Bulbs, corms and tubers, page 256).

● **Forcing hardy plants**

Many hardy plants will flower early indoors if lifted

now from the garden and potted into 15–18 cm (6–7 in) pots, depending on the size of the roots. Examples are aquilegia, bleeding heart (*Dicentra spectabilis*), polyanthus, *Primula denticulata* and Christmas rose (*Helleborus niger*) which flowers at Christmas if grown under glass. Move pots into the conservatory or house when they come into flower.

● Vines

Begin pruning vines once the leaves have fallen (*see* December, page 279).

Plant new vines between now and the end of the year. Although the ideal place is in the greenhouse border, the roots will soon take up growing space needed for other plants. An alternative is to plant vines outside and then lead the main shoot through to grow in the greenhouse. Vines succeed with this method, despite the disparity in temperature between the roots and top growth. Dig a hole large enough

GREENHOUSES – PLANTING VINES

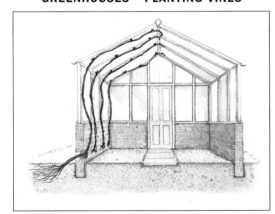

Vines can take up a lot of space in the greenhouse border, but they can be planted outside the greenhouse and the stem taken inside if you have a suitable position. Tape up any gaps in the wall if the greenhouse is heated.

to spread the roots out well, but do not add manure or fertiliser – vines, like figs, grow on poor soil in their native habitat. Cut back the shoot by two-thirds after planting.

HEATHERS

● Pruning

Summer-flowering heathers may be pruned now but leaving the faded flower spikes on will help protect them against frost. If pruning now, cut back to the base of dead flower heads (*see* March, page 68).

● Keeping beds clear

Heather beds need to be sited in sunny, open aspects. Clear away any overhanging vegetation that may have grown over them during the summer months. To minimise the risk of fungal diseases, keep heathers clear of fallen leaves from neighbouring trees, particularly where the leaves pile up against the side of the plants.

HERBS

● Clearing fallen leaves

Remove fallen leaves which will reduce light getting to the plant and encourage disease.

● Protecting container-grown herbs

Terracotta pots are normally frost-resistant, but in prolonged low temperatures the roots inside may freeze. This only shows when the plants start to grow in spring. If the roots are damaged they will no longer be able to sustain the top growth; the plant will look unhappy and may even die. Insulate containers if they cannot be moved to a sheltered place (*see* Container gardening, page 258).

● Sowing sweet cicely

These seeds require frost to germinate. Sow them thinly in gritty compost, cover the seed tray with fine wire mesh to protect it against mice, and place in an exposed situation.

● Growing herbs under glass

Put cloches over September-sown parsley and chervil to encourage winter shoots and keep them clean. Bring in chives and other herbs for forcing (*see* September, page 219). Inspect crops for pests.

HOUSE & CONSERVATORY PLANTS

● Light levels

Place plants near windows during the day or install artificial lights. Ordinary light bulbs give off too much heat and may scorch foliage, instead use cool white or daylight strip lighting and position the lights at least 45 cm (18 in) from the plants.

● Controlling temperature

Many house plants will thrive in living rooms but try to avoid drastic temperature fluctuations and draughts. One solution is to use an enclosed, or partially enclosed, growing case. Don't overwater in cold conditions as this can lead to problems with grey mould (botrytis) (*see* Diseases, page 407).

Aim to keep the conservatory at 7–10°C (45–50°F) by insulating and heating. Monitor the temperature with a minimum/maximum thermometer, as nights can be very cold and days warm.

Central heating makes the air in houses during winter very dry. Plants with leaves that turn brown at the edges or tips need a damper atmosphere. Group plants together to create a more humid microclimate around them or stand the plants on a gravel tray and keep this moist. If you have only a few plants, mist them regularly with tepid water to keep them humid.

Red spider mite thrives in hot, dry conditions so inspect plants for fine webbing and tiny mites (*see* Pests, pages 402–403).

● Watering and feeding
Reduce watering so the compost is allowed to dry on the surface between waterings and only feed plants that are in flower or growing strongly.

● Flowering plants
Place African violets (*Saintpaulia ionantha*) under a table or wall lamp during the evening to encourage winter flowering.

Place winter-flowering primulas, such as *Primula obconica*, in a bright position.

Deadhead chrysanthemums to encourage them to continue flowering.

Pinch back any new growth on the winter cherry (*Solanum pseudocapsicums*) to expose the berries.

● Indoor bulbs and corms
Dry off and store the rhizomes of achimenes if this has not already been done (*see* October, page 242).

Remove spent flowers and yellowing leaves from cyclamen by pulling them gently from the base.

Stop watering gloriosas after flowering, when the stems die back, and let them dry off completely. Vallotas, however, should be kept just moist until growth restarts in spring.

Restart hippeastrums into growth by watering them sparingly (*see* December, page 280).

Check on the condition of any bulbs you are forcing for Christmas or to flower early in the year (*see* Bulbs, corms and tubers, page 256).

● Climbers and feature plants
Keep jasmine (*Jasminum polyanthum*) watered and fed every two weeks.

● Bromeliads
The temperature can drop as low as 7–10°C (45–50°F) without damaging bromeliads, but at low temperatures the plants must be kept dry or they may rot. Water sparingly, especially in cool conditions, and do not feed.

Mist air plants once or twice a week, using a hand-held mister about 30 cm (1 ft) away from the plants.

● Cacti and other succulents
Move plants to a very light position in a cool room for a rest period. Try to keep the plants in a temperature of about 10°C (50°F), though most will be happy in the range 7–13°C (45–55°F). Apart from Christmas cacti, keep them almost dry.

● Orchids
Reduce watering, keeping compost slightly moist, but not soaking wet.

Purchase miniature cymbidiums in flower now. They will flower for about six weeks if kept at 7–15°C (45–60°F) in a well-lit spot. Buy slipper orchids (*Paphiopedilum*) between now and early spring. Keep them in a kitchen or bathroom at 13–18°C (55–65°F) with indirect sunlight.

IRISES

● Controlling pests
Many varieties of *Iris unguicularis* will be in flower. Protect emerging buds from slugs and snails, and cover clumps with pea netting to protect the flowers from birds if necessary.

● Cutting back
Cut down beardless and water irises. Cut out dead leaves from *I. spuria* types and from bearded irises.

LAWNS

● Lawnmower care
When the grass has stopped growing make the final cut for the year and prepare the mower for storage. On petrol-driven models drain off the oil and petrol and clean and adjust the spark plugs. On all mowers remove any grass and mud. Remove rust with a wire brush, and spray a water-repellent, anti-rust product onto exposed metal. Store under cover, preferably on a wooden board, but not on concrete or soil.

LAWN REVIEW

It is worth taking stock at the end of the year and checking to see if there is anything you can do to make cutting the grass less of a chore for next year.

A strip of bricks set just below the level of the lawn where it meets borders, walls or fences will enable you to mow over the bricks and there will be less need to trim the edges – just deal with prostrate stems or leaves if they become troublesome.

Trimming the grass growing around tree bases can be time-consuming, as the bark can get damaged if you don't take care. To make the job easier, lay a sheet of black woven plastic, 1 m (3 ft) in diameter, around the base of the tree. Push the edges into the soil and mow over them.

LILIES

● Planting late bulbs
Although autumn planting of lily bulbs should have been finished by now, many special lily bulbs are not received from the growers until late November

or December. If the weather is still good and the ground workable, plant these late bulbs now (*see* October, page 244). Shrivelled bulbs can be revived by planting them in moist soil, or laying them on a bed of moist peat.

If winter has set in early, preventing outdoor planting, dip bulbs in fungicide and pot them up in a neutral or lime-free (ericaceous) compost. Alternatively, these late-arriving bulbs can be treated with fungicide and set out in trays of slightly damp peat with only the tip of each bulb showing. They can then be planted or potted up when conditions or time allow. If you keep the bulbs frost-proof in slightly moist peat they will remain perfectly healthy. Although the lily is a bulb, it has no outer protective tunic or skin to protect it against damage or drying so needs this additional level of care.

● Protecting bulbs

Protect pots or trays of lilies in the greenhouse, and bulbs stored in a potting shed or garage, from frost, slugs, mice and rats.

● Cutting dead stems

Lily stems left to die back naturally (*see* October, page 244) can now be cut back to 5 cm (2 in).

PELARGONIUMS

● Winter care

All plants should be in the light but out of the frost. They will continue to grow although more slowly than at other times of the year.

Check for signs of grey mould (botrytis), which can be a problem in a cold, damp atmosphere (*see* Diseases, page 407). Try to keep the air as dry as possible, and if the weather is not frosty, open the vents

in the greenhouse to let the atmosphere dry out. A fan, without heat, will keep the air moving which helps to keep down the humidity.

Ensure that these cool, airy conditions do not let the temperature drop below freezing at night.

● Potting up, stopping and shaping

Check on cuttings taken in September or October, and pot up if not already done.

Stop the terminal bud (*see* September, page 223). Look at all the plants, turn them and shape them, and be careful to make sure that they are not crowded together.

RHODODENDRONS & AZALEAS

● Protecting plants from wildlife

Throughout the winter birds, especially bullfinches, will attack the flower buds of azaleas and rhododendrons – dwarf varieties in particular. Bird damage is difficult to control without the help of active cats, but movement and noise in the garden provides some deterrent.

Rhododendrons and azaleas are not as great an attraction to rodents, rabbits and deer as many other trees and shrubs, but these creatures can cause great damage in some areas, so check that any rabbit or deer-proof fencing is sound.

● Planting

As long as the soil is not frozen or waterlogged, planting can continue (*see* October, page 245). Planting in wet soil leads to problems, because when the soil dries it becomes hard, making it impossible for the roots to penetrate beyond the planting hole.

Established rhododendrons and azaleas can also be moved to a new position now.

● Layering

Dig up ground layers, started off about 15 months ago (*see* August, page 202), that are now rooted. Plant them out in their final growing position.

Cut away any new plantlets produced by air layering during the previous summer (*see* August, page 202), and pot them up to grow on for another year before planting. Plant out any plants propagated by air layering last year in their final growing position.

ROCK PLANTS

● Clearing fallen leaves

Continue to clear fallen tree leaves that are covering the rock plants. If not removed, they will keep light off the plants and will encourage slugs and snails as well as diseases.

● Winter protection

Cover vulnerable plants that suffer if their crowns remain wet in winter, with a cloche or an anchored

ROCK PLANTS – WINTER PROTECTION

Vulnerable alpines (mainly those with grey, woolly leaves) will benefit by being protected from the rain in winter. You can improvise with a sheet of glass or clear plastic held in place on four short posts.

sheet of glass or clear plastic. Plants with grey, woolly leaves are often susceptible, and others, such as lewisias, are vulnerable to winter wet. If they are growing in pots, tilt these at an angle to avoid water accumulating around the crowns.

ROSES

● Handling new plants

Plants which were ordered earlier will now be arriving and should be planted out into their permanent positions as soon as possible. If the weather prevents this, then heel them in temporarily. To do this, unpack the plants in frost-free conditions and bury them in a shallow trench. This keeps them in a moist environment. Cut open very large bundles and spread them out so that the plants in the centre also receive moisture. Heel in plants which arrive in very frosty weather, provided they themselves are not frozen. If conditions outside make it difficult even to heel in, wrap the unopened package in sacking or a similar material and store it in a cool, frost-proof shed or garage, but never in a warm place such as a heated greenhouse.

● Moving established plants

This is the time to move roses if you wish to redesign the border. Remember to replace and possibly sterilise the soil if you are replanting where roses have been previously grown (see March, page 75).

All plants, however small a distance they have been moved, must be given every opportunity to re-establish themselves as soon as possible. This can be achieved very quickly by using a good planting mixture. The principal components are about two-thirds peat, or a peat substitute, and one-third well-rotted garden compost or leafmould, with a good

ROSES – PLANTING BARE-ROOT ROSES

1 Bare-root roses, which can be planted now, are just as good as container-grown roses. Trim any dead or damaged shoots before you plant.

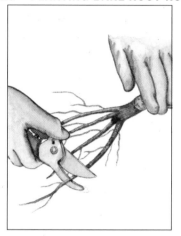

2 Trim off any damaged roots, or shorten any very long, thick roots. Do not cut or damage the other young, spreading roots.

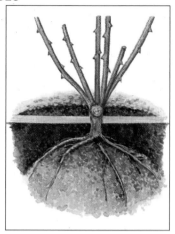

3 Dig a hole large enough for the spread roots. Ideally, plant them over a slight mound. Check the rose is planted at its original depth.

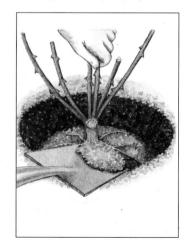

4 Return soil to the hole, trickling it between the roots while holding the plant firmly in position. Keep it at the correct planting depth.

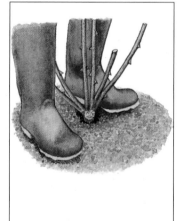

5 Firm the plant in well, using your feet, and particularly your heel, to settle the soil around the roots and to remove any large air pockets.

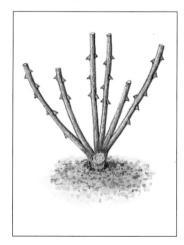

6 Test by pulling the plant gently – it should be firm. Rake the soil so that it is level. Water only in very dry conditions.

handful per plant of bonemeal. This mixture should be prepared well in advance, bearing in mind that a large spadeful will be required for each plant.

Before moving, cut down all bush and shrub roses by at least two-thirds, and climbers and ramblers to a maximum of 1.2 m (4 ft). Dig the plants out cleanly and shake off the soil. Before replanting trim out all thin and dead wood and cut back all roots cleanly to about 25–30 cm (10–12 in).

● Planting a new rose bed

When planting a completely new bed, use a marker to fix the best position for each plant. This simple exercise, although time consuming, can save a lot of frustration later. Bush roses are planted about 60 cm (2 ft) apart, climbing roses on walls give a good coverage about 2.5 m (8 ft) apart and standards must never be planted less than 2 m (6 ft) apart, tree to tree. Shrub roses make a good show when planted in groups of three or five, 1 m (3 ft) apart.

Prepare the first position by digging a hole with a corner of the hole against the marker. Move this soil close to where the final bush is to be planted.

Fill in the first hole with soil obtained when digging the second hole, and so on. Continue with this procedure, using the soil from the first hole to complete the planting of the final rose.

● Planting bare-root roses

Never allow the roots to dry out and, if necessary, soak them in water for half an hour before planting. Dig a hole about 25 cm (10 in) square and as deep. Place the rose in the hole so it is planted at its original depth, and spread out the roots over a small mound of soil. Add a generous spadeful of planting mixture to cover the roots completely, and fill the hole with soil. Firm in well with your feet.

● Planting standards

All standards must be supported with a substantial stake at least 5 × 5 cm (2 × 2 in). The length of the stake should be the same as the stem of the standard plus at least 30 cm (12 in) to drive into the ground. The stake must be properly treated with wood preservative before being used. Having prepared the hole and positioned the plant, drive the stake in while the roots are still visible to avoid damaging them. Check that the top of the stake comes to the height of the lowest branch then fill in the hole, firming the soil well. Secure the stem to the stake with two strong tree ties.

● Planting climbers and ramblers

Although the basic procedure is the same irrespective of the type, planting climbers against walls requires extra attention. The soil in these positions is generally very poor and should be removed completely to a depth of about 60 cm (2 ft) and about 50 × 50 cm (20 × 20 in) wide. Replace this with a mixture combining a quarter well-rotted garden compost, a quarter peat or peat substitute, and half fresh soil taken from a part of the garden where no roses have been grown for at least five years. Add a good handful of bonemeal for every new plant.

● Planting roses in containers

Roses in containers need room for their roots so choose containers with a minimum depth of 30 cm (12 in). Clay or wooden containers are likely to produce better plants than plastic ones as they keep the roots cooler in hot weather. Use a loam-based compost (*see* Container Gardening, page 258).

● Pruning

Hybrid tea (large-flowered) and floribunda (cluster-flowered) roses should be partially pruned to reduce potential winter windrock damage if this was not done last month. Reduce the length of each shoot by one-third and complete the pruning next spring (*see* March, page 75).

Prune climbers and ramblers if this has not already been done (*see* October, page 245).

ROSES – PRUNING TO REDUCE WINDROCK

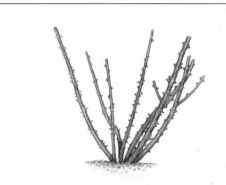

1 Hybrid tea (large-flowered) and floribunda (cluster-flowered) roses are usually pruned in spring but if they are left over winter with tall unpruned stems these may be rocked by strong winds and the plant loosened.

2 To prevent windrock reduce the length of all shoots by about one-third. The shorter stems will then offer less wind resistance and spring pruning can be completed in March.

SWEET PEAS

● Preparing the planting site

Double dig the plot, but do not apply manure if the soil is already in really fertile condition (*see* The soil in your garden, page 387). Otherwise, especially if you are growing for exhibition, dig a trench two spade-depths deep, forking over the subsoil at the base, and incorporate well-rotted manure or compost into the bottom level before returning the topsoil. Manure mixed with the topsoil tends to encourage shallow rooting. Apply two handfuls of bonemeal per m² (sq yd) to the top spit and either fork or hoe it in. Leave the surface rough to obtain the maximum benefit from winter weathering.

● Potting up seedlings

Seedlings raised from last month's sowings in trays should be pricked out and potted up, one or two to an 8 cm (3 in) pot and six or seven to a 13 cm (5 in) pot. The advantage of using the smaller pot is that it helps to keep the soil ball intact when you plant out in the spring. This is particularly advantageous on heavy land. It is essential to grow all autumn-sown plants slowly, and to encourage hardiness with the maximum root production.

TREES, SHRUBS & HEDGES

● Planting

Complete new planting this month if possible (*see* October, page 247). November has always been the traditional planting time for deciduous shrubs, trees and conifers, particularly bare-root ones.

At this time of the year the plants are dormant but the soil is still warm enough for the roots to become established before spring.

● Weather protection

Newly planted shrubs that may suffer in cold winters should be protected through the winter from leaf, stem and root damage.

Strong cold winds in sub-zero temperatures cause more damage to plants than frost on its own. Wind blasts the foliage and stems and also dehydrates them. Roots too can be damaged by the wind as it dries and freezes the soil, which again causes more dehydration. If the soil is frozen solid for longer than four to five days, the roots of the plants cannot replace the lost moisture.

Where no natural protection is present, put up a windbreak of close mesh netting up to 1.2 m (4 ft) high – a solid barrier will create turbulence rather than break the force of the wind. Keep this in place from November through to late March in any part of the garden where wind damage may occur.

Plants can also be wrapped in a thick blanket of straw, plastic or other material. This protects the top growth and, if hessian is used, it retains cool air next to the plants and prevents them starting into growth prematurely during a warm spell in late winter. There is then less likelihood of the plants being damaged by early spring frosts.

● Protection from wildlife

As food in the wild becomes scarcer, birds and mammals will turn to gardens for food. Bird damage is usually no worse than raiding the trees and shrubs for their berries, but squirrels, rabbits and deer can strip the bark from trees and devour and kill small shrubs. Appropriate fencing is the most effective deterrent against rabbits and deer.

● Hardwood cuttings and layers

Take hardwood cuttings of suitable hardy shrubs

(*see* Propagation, page 429). Bring hardwood cuttings in pots into a cold frame or cold greenhouse to protect them over the winter if this was not done last month.

Pot up any layers now rooted or plant them out in their growing position (*see* October, page 248).

● Semi-ripe cuttings

Remove any fallen leaves from semi-ripe cuttings taken in July, to prevent rotting, but do not worry about this leaf loss.

● Pruning

After flowering, use the one-third pruning method on all October-flowering shrubs over three years old (*see* Pruning, page 420).

HEDGES

Continue the planting of new deciduous hedges (*see* October, page 248).

● Hedges from hardwood cuttings

A few hedges can be grown directly in position from hardwood cuttings taken from now through to March (*see* Propagation, page 429). Insert the cuttings into well-prepared soil and they should root and grow to make an inexpensive hedge.

Dig a trench along the line of the proposed hedge and prepare the planting area as you would for any new hedge (*see* September, page 226). Insert prepared cuttings that are about 20–30 cm (8–12 in) long about 30 cm (1 ft) apart, to allow for occasional failures. Planting distances can be adjusted once the cuttings have established.

Hedging plants that root readily from hardwood cuttings include privet, forsythia, *Prunus cerasifera* 'Nigra' and laurel.

VEGETABLES

● Beans

Sow overwintering broad beans, such as 'Aquadulce', but choose a sheltered position and choose a hardy and compact variety small enough to grow under cloches. Beans from this sowing should be ready to harvest in early summer.

● Brassicas

Net winter brassicas if it is necessary to protect them from pigeons and rabbits. Remember to shake the netting after heavy falls of snow.

Harvest the first early Brussels sprouts. Kale can be harvested over a long period by picking young leaves as required. Cut and store Dutch white cabbages as they are not hardy. Savoy and 'January King' cabbages can be left outside until wanted. Cut Chinese cabbages covered in October from now until early spring. Continue to harvest cauliflowers.

● Carrots and parsnips

Store maincrop carrots and parsnips in wooden boxes of sand or sifted, dry soil kept in a cool but frost-free place with easy access, such as a garden shed or garage. Alternatively, cover the rows with a layer of straw and dig up as required. Protect against slugs if these are a problem.

● Onions and leeks

Plant Japanese onion sets if not yet done (*see* October, page 248). Continue to harvest leeks.

● Salad crops

In mild areas you can still sow lettuce to grow under cover in the winter. Complete sowing this month. Cover lettuces sown in August with cloches.

Chicory can be forced in a warm greenhouse. Lift and store the roots in a cool, dark place. Choose unforked roots with a diameter of 3–5 cm (1½–2 in) to force. Cut off the foliage and trim the main roots to 15–20 cm (6–8 in). Pot up in damp compost and cover the pot so that all the light is excluded. It is important to keep them at a temperature of 10–15°C (50–60°F). The heads will be ready for harvesting in four weeks.

Harvest the first broad-leaved endives for fresh salads during the winter.

● Spinach

Pick young spinach leaves from November until spring. Cloches can be put over the plants during winter for extra protection.

● Turnips and swedes

Lift and store maincrop turnips and swedes or cover with straw and use as required.

PERENNIAL VEGETABLES
● Jerusalem artichokes

Continue to harvest Jerusalem artichokes.

To increase stock, or provide replacements for older plants that are past their best, detach suckers from plants that are at least two years old and plant them in pots containing good garden soil. Overwinter them in a cold frame or cold greenhouse, then plant out in April.

● Rhubarb

To propagate rhubarb, lift a mature clump and divide it into fist-sized pieces, each containing one or more buds. Plant the divisions 1 m (3 ft) apart each way in soil that has previously been well manured. Rhubarb can tolerate some shade.

Mature rhubarb (at least three years old) can be forced indoors; the first sticks should be ready in five to seven weeks. Lift the crowns with as much root as possible. Leave outdoors exposed to frost until next month (*see* December, page 283).

WATER PLANTS & POOLS

● Cutting back and removing vegetation

Continue to cut back any remaining faded marginal plants, but do not cut back those with hollow stems to beneath the water level or they may rot. Remove any other vegetation or debris.

● Clearing autumn leaves

Continue to collect up leaves caught by the pool's netting (*see* September, page 227). If the pond has not been netted there will inevitably be a quantity of leaves in the water that could pollute it as they decay. Rake or net out as many as possible, being very careful not to puncture the liner if your pond has one.

● Pump maintenance

Surface pumps and associated pipes must be drained for the winter. It is not essential to remove a submersible pump but if you keep fish it is a good idea to replace it with a pool heater. If the pump is not functioning efficiently now is a good time to send it for an overhaul; otherwise, if you do remove it, clean, dry and grease before storing. It will not matter if the biological filter ceases to function when the pump is removed. Fish feed and excrete very little when the water temperature is low. This means there is little waste to be broken down by the filter; the exceptions are specialist koi ponds and those very heavily stocked, where water quality should be maintained throughout the year.

Latin Lessons

The use of Latin nomenclature for plants is internationally accepted, and helps with identification. Common names, though often appealing and descriptive, vary from one country to another; for example the silver birch of Britain is a European white birch to an American. Even within the same country a plant may have several different common names. More confusingly still, the same common name may be given to different plants in different countries! Latin names are universally recognised and each applies to only one plant.

Latin names are therefore practical. They can also be informative, often providing useful clues to the appearance or natural habitat of a plant. A species called *sagittifolius* will almost certainly have arrow-shaped leaves; *alpinus* suggests that the plant comes from alpine regions. A *fragrans* will probably have a pleasant fragrance, while a *foetidus* is likely to smell unpleasant. Latin names are much more accessible when they impart a meaning. Familiarity with the list of widely used Latin names on the opposite page can make plant names more useful and meaningful.

HOW PLANTS ARE NAMED

Botanical and horticultural nomenclature has rules and guidelines agreed by international committees. These are followed strictly in scientific journals, but most gardening books and magazines, nurseries and garden centres, which cater for gardeners not botanists, tend to take a more relaxed approach.

The basic 'rules' are universally accepted. The first name is the genus and has an initial capital letter and should be printed in italics. The second part of the name is the species. All the species in a genus have common characteristics considered close enough to form a group. Each species has sufficiently different characteristics to make it distinct from others in the genus.

There can be just a single species in a genus, or many hundreds. *Calluna vulgaris*, the ling or Scottish heather, is an example of a genus with just one species – though it has more than 1,000 cultivars (varieties). *Rhododendron simsii*, the Indian azalea from which some popular indoor azaleas derive, is just one of over 700 species in the genus.

This is a simplified explanation, and sometimes there is a third Latin name, also presented in italics, where the plant has sufficient stable minor variations to make it a subspecies or botanical form.

▲ *The umbrella plant* Darmera peltata. *The name* peltata *indicates shield-like leaves.*

WHY NAMES CHANGE

Whether a plant has sufficient common characteristics to place it within a particular genus or enough stable differences to make it distinct from another, is a matter of judgement and botanists do not always agree. Amazingly, from a gardener's viewpoint, plants that look distinct and unlike each other, and which have been regarded as different species in the past, are sometimes grouped together as one species: botanically they may represent extremes of variation within one species, but in gardening terms they are distinct plants!

A common reason for established names changing is the rule that the first published name is the valid one. If a researcher finds an earlier published name for the plant than the one currently in use, then the earlier name becomes the valid one. The reason generations of gardeners familiar with buddleia had to come to terms with buddleja is because the original handwriting had been misread. Once it had been pointed out that 'j' not 'i' was used in the first published record of the plant it became necessary to rewrite our labels.

VARIETIES

In common with many gardening magazines and books, and the horticultural trade in general, the term 'variety' is used in its general sense throughout this book, though botanists and horticulturists distinguish between botanical varieties (those that occur naturally), called varietas and abbreviated 'var.' in written descriptions, and those that have arisen in cultivation, called cultivars and abbreviated 'cv'. Typographically, cultivars have single quotation marks around the name, though new recommendations introduced in 1996 suggest that those used as selling names, which may be registered trademarks, and certain other categories, should not have the quotation marks but be in small and large capital letters instead. As it makes no practical difference in gardening terms, quotation marks have been used for both in this book, for visual consistency and for easier reading.

The strict definition of a cultivar (variety) is that its characteristics should be 'distinct, uniform and stable'. Sometimes, especially with seed-raised plants, there are variations between different plants: these are sometimes referred to by botanists and horticulturists as Groups, though gardeners call them varieties in everyday language.

For most of us, gardening is a pleasurable pursuit not an exercise in taxonomy, and the names used by most garden centres are those everyone is most familiar with, even if they are not strictly up-to-date. So do not worry about using established names until the new ones become widely accepted.

An A–Z of specific names

acaulis stemless
aculeatus prickly, thorny
aestivalis of summer
alatus winged
alba/albus white
alpestris of mountains
alpinus alpine
alternifolius alternate (of leaves)
amabilis lovely
americanus American
angustifolius narrow-leaved
annuus annual
apiculatus pointed at the tip (of leaves)
aquaticus aquatic
arborescens tree-like
argenteus silvery
argutus sharp
armatus armed (with prickles or thorns)
arvensis of fields
asiaticus Asiatic
atro dark (prefix)
aurantiacus orange
auratus, aureus golden
auriculatus ear-shaped, eared
autumnalis autumnal
azureus sky blue
baccus berried
barbatus bearded, barbed
bicolor two-coloured
bicornis two-horned
biflorus two-flowered
borealis northern
bracteatus with bracts
bulbosus bulbous
caeruleus blue
caespitosus tufted
calcareus chalky or limy
campanulatus bell-shaped

▲ *Begonia semperflorens* flowers continuously if kept frost-free.

campestris of fields or plains
candicans whitish
candidissumus pure white
candidus shining white
capensis Cape of Good Hope
cardinalis deep scarlet
chinensis Chinese
cinereus grey, ash-coloured
coccineus scarlet
communis common, growing in company
cordatus heart-shaped
cordifolius heart-shaped (of leaves)
cristatus crested
cruentus blood-red
cyaneus blue
dentatus sharply toothed
edulis edible
elatus tall
elegans elegant
elegantissima very elegant
esculentus edible
fastigiatus erect, close-branched
flavescens becoming yellow, yellowish

flavus yellow
flore pleno double-flowered
foetidus bad-smelling
fragrans fragrant
fulgens glowing, shining
giganteus very large
glaucus covered with a white or bluish-grey bloom
globosus globular (usually of flower heads)
gracilis slender
grandiflorus large-flowered
grandifolius large-leaved
grandis large
hirsutus long-haired
horizontalis horizontal
hortensis of gardens
hyemalis of winter
japonicus Japanese
laevigatus smooth
lanatus woolly
lanceolatus, lancifolius lance-shaped (of leaves)
lutescens becoming yellow
luteus yellow
marco- large (prefix)
major larger
majus great
maritimus of the sea
maximus largest
micro- small (prefix)
minimus smallest
minor smaller
mollis downy, soft
montanus of mountains
mucronatus short, sharp-tipped (of leaves)
multiflorus many-flowered
muralis of walls
nanus dwarf
niger black
nitidus shining
nivalis of snow

▲ *Magnolia stellata* has flowers which look like stars.

novae-angliae of New England
novi-belgii of New Belgium
nutans nodding
obovatus ovate leaves, with the broad end farthest from the stalk
obtusus bluntly rounded (of leaves)
occidentalis western
officinalis medicinal
oppositifolius leaves opposite on each side of the stem
orientalis eastern
ovatus ovate leaves, with broad end at the stalk
palmatus lobed or divided like a hand (of leaves)
palustris of marshes and bogs
peltatus shield-like (leaves) with stalk at or near centre
petiolatus with leaf stalks
plenus full or double flowers
poly- many (of flowers)
praecox very early, precocious
pratensis of meadows
prostratus lying flat
pseudo- false (prefix)

pubescens downy
pumilus dwarf
purpureus purple
radicans rooting
repens, reptans creeping
reticulatus net-veined (leaves)
robustus stout, strong
roseus rose, rosy
rubens red, ruddy
rugosa wrinkled (of leaves)
sagittifolius arrow-like leaves
sanguineus blood-red
scaber rough
scandens climbing
semperflorens ever-flowering
sempervirens evergreen
sessile stalkless
sibiricus Siberian
sino- Chinese (prefix)
speciosus showy
spectabilis spectacular
splendens splendid, brilliant
stellatus starry
suaveolens sweet-scented
sub- nearly or under (prefix)
suffruticosa nearly shrubby
superbus superb, superior
sylvaticus forest-liking
sylvestris of woods or forests
tomentosus densely hairy
tri- three (prefix)
tricolor three-coloured
vagans wandering
variegatus irregularly coloured
veris of spring
vernalis, vernus of spring
virens green
virescens becoming green, greenish
viridiflorus green-flowered
vulgaris common, usual
zebrinus striped
zontaus banded, zoned

DECEMBER

With the onset of winter, planning by the fireside for the next gardening year usually takes the place of working outside.

December

With preparations for Christmas and New Year celebrations in train, gardening usually goes on the back burner in December. For anyone who works away from home during the week, there are few days in which it is possible to get out into the garden. Indeed, with the shortening days and onset of winter weather, there may only be one or two weekends when it is suitable for gardening outdoors.

Fortunately, this is a time when an enormous number of house plants are sold, so your home should be bright and colourful even if there are very few flowers out in the garden. And there are plenty of armchair gardening jobs to be done: looking through the seed and bulb catalogues to select new plants you intend to grow; planning how you are going to redesign or rearrange the garden; or just reading the latest gardening books and magazines.

The weather in December

This is usually a gloomy month, with little sunshine; and both gales and rain are common. Frost is inevitable in all but a few exceptionally favourable locations. It can be very cold, but periods of very low temperatures seldom last for long before Christmas.

Temperature differences over the British Isles show less of a north-south divide now, and the biggest variations are more likely to be between inland and coastal areas. Some coastal parts of Scotland, particularly the warm west coast, can have similar temperatures to inland areas in the Midlands or Home Counties.

Outdoor jobs that you can do

This is an ideal time for winter pruning – especially of apple and pear trees. Don't do all your pruning in winter, however; wait until late winter or early spring to prune your roses. Shrubs that have colourful bark, such as dogwoods, should be left until March. You will not do the shrubs any harm by pruning them now but you will be removing their colourful stems – the very reason for growing them.

It is a good time to check all your shrubs for signs of dead or diseased shoots. It is much easier to spot these shoots and cut them out when there are no leaves to hide them.

Ideally, your garden should already have been tidied, canes and stakes cleaned and put away, and pots and seed trays washed and sterilised. In reality there may not have been enough time or good days to complete these jobs during the previous couple of months, so take advantage of any fine days in December to finish them. You will probably be needing some clean seed trays next month.

Winter digging can continue provided the ground is workable and not frozen. This will expose many soil pests which will be enjoyed by hungry birds – the ideal environmentally friendly way to keep pests under control.

Controlling pests and diseases

Just because it is cold, it doesn't mean that you can forget about controlling pests and diseases. Although diseases are most likely to be a problem in the greenhouse, especially if the atmosphere is too humid, many insects remain active throughout the year. Pests such as greenfly and scale insects are always a potential problem in greenhouses and conservatories, and indoors on house plants. Fortunately, populations are smaller in winter and they breed less rapidly, so control is simpler (you can even remove them by hand if there are just a few), provided you are vigilant.

Slugs and snails may continue to be a problem in the garden, particularly in cold frames and greenhouses. Continue to use slug controls as appropriate.

Greenhouse and conservatory care

You should have already put insulation in place, but if you haven't, it is not too late for your plants to benefit from it. Insulation will reduce your heating bills and increase the temperature that you can achieve. It will also eliminate many damaging, cold draughts. This does not mean you should seal the structure entirely, as some ventilation on mild days is beneficial. Even if you don't use your greenhouse until seed sowing starts from January onwards, insulating it is a useful job to do in advance. As most insulation is fitted on the inside it is a job you can do even if the weather is too wet or windy to work outside.

Stock up on a small amount of seed-sowing compost if you intend to start sowing early. Don't buy bulk stocks yet, as garden centres will not yet have new stock and may be selling old compost which can deteriorate in the bag.

Armchair gardening

When the weather makes physical gardening impractical, it is time to accept the inevitable and do some gardening in your head or on paper instead.

Plan what you are going to grow in the coming season and look through seed and bulb catalogues – this will occupy many a pleasurable hour. Make lists of the plants you want and fill out orders – don't delay if you want to be sure of getting the varieties you want.

If you are interested in a specialist group of plants send off for these catalogues too. Many dahlia, fuchsia and chrysanthemum specialists produce catalogues, and you will have a far wider choice of varieties from these than from your local garden centre. If your interest lies in sweet peas, then send for the catalogues of the seed companies that have a specialist list. There are also specialist clematis and conifer nurseries as well as shrub and rose growers.

Young plants of tender perennials used for summer bedding and containers are offered in some seed and bulb catalogues, but there are also companies that specialise in supplying this type of plant. Catalogues provided by these companies are worth looking at for inspiration but, if you order, bear in mind that the plants will arrive before planting time so you will have to grow them on – ideally in a greenhouse. If you don't have a greenhouse it will be better to buy larger (but therefore more expensive) plants from a garden centre when it is safe to plant them directly into the garden.

Many gardeners like to experiment with a fresh look in the garden each year by using different seasonal plants but they leave the basic structure of the garden the same. This is fine if you are happy with the design of your garden. If, however, you feel the layout could be improved now is a good time to plan changes. These can range from small adjustments to the shape of the lawn or borders to planning new beds or adding a major feature such as a pond or a formal rose garden. Do not just confine your design thoughts to the lawn and flowerbeds. The kitchen garden may well look better with a new potager or raised bed.

JOBS THAT WON'T WAIT

- Order or buy seeds as soon as possible – especially seeds of those plants that should be sown in mid and late winter so that they have a long growing season.

- Check bulbs being forced for Christmas and New Year flowering. Do this regularly to ensure they do not dry out and to make certain they are given light and warmth at the right time.

- Protect any shrubs of borderline hardiness, especially in cold regions. Even if some damage has already been done, it may not be too late to provide protection as the majority of garden shrubs will grow out of limited frost and wind damage.

- Take winter hanging baskets under cover, either into the greenhouse or porch, before very severe weather arrives. Baskets are particularly vulnerable because the compost in them is exposed to cold from all sides and can freeze solid.

- Bring under cover herbs potted up for forcing.

- Check on the condition of stored apples and pears.

- Lift chicory for forcing, pot up and keep in darkness in a warm place. Also lift rhubarb roots for forcing indoors, and start forcing selected crowns outdoors.

- Lag or protect outdoor pipes if not already done. Better still, turn off the supply and drain the pipes.

- Knock snow off branches of shrubs, conifers and hedges to prevent them breaking under the weight.

- Keep an area of the pond ice free if you keep fish.

ANNUALS & BIENNIALS

● Ordering seed

Plan your summer displays now, making notes on which varieties you would like to grow from seed. Order these from seed catalogues as soon as possible, especially if a variety is new or has been heavily promoted, as stocks may run out. Seed catalogues offer a much wider range of varieties than are available as plants from garden centres, and growing your own is much the best way of ensuring you have the more unusual colours or varieties.

If you are looking for new plants it is worth obtaining catalogues from more than one company.

BORDER PERENNIALS

● Ground preparation

Continue clearing ground for new beds, digging out perennial weeds and leaving soil rough for the frost to break it down. Garden compost or well-rotted manure can be added at the same time.

● Clearing trees and shrubs

After the leaves have fallen, cut off the overhanging branches of trees and shrubs that are deflecting sunlight and rain from the underlying plants. This may be a temporary measure only, and you may have to remove the whole bush or tree if you need to open up the site. If you do this, remove tree roots or cut through fibrous roots with a sharp spade.

● Root cuttings

Take root cuttings of appropriate plants, such as acanthus, border phlox, echinops, oriental poppies and verbascum (see Propagation, page 431), and put them in a cold frame or greenhouse.

● Planning ahead

Order seeds and plants for spring sowing and planting, trying out some new varieties and using any plans and notes that you made during the summer.

BULBS, CORMS & TUBERS

● Checking stored bulbs and corms

Check stored bulbs and corms (see October, page 235) and discard any that have become either soft or diseased.

● Forced bulbs

Continue to examine bowls and pots of sprouted bulbs and move them indoors as they are ready or as required (see November, page 256). Bowls moved earlier to a cool greenhouse or room can be taken into the living room when the flower buds are visible among the leaves. If bowls are placed near a window, give them a quarter turn every day to ensure even growth.

● Hippeastrums

Plant hippeastrums for spring flowering in 15 cm (6 in) pots of John Innes No. 2 potting compost. Bury only the lower half of each bulb. Keep pots in a humid atmosphere at about 10–13°C (50–55°F) and water sparingly until flower buds appear.

Restart stored hippeastrums in the same way.

CARNATIONS & PINKS

PERPETUAL-FLOWERING
● Taking cuttings

Select sideshoots from the lower part of the flowering stem of plants that have recently been watered, avoiding any shoots which have begun to lengthen in preparation for flowering. Each cutting should have four or five fully developed pairs of leaves (see Propagation, page 428). Space the cuttings about 2.5 cm (1 in) apart in a tray or pot of sharp sand, and insert them almost up to the bottom pair of leaves. Keep the cuttings at a constant temperature of 13–15°C (55–60°F) in a closed propagator until they show signs of growth.

Between ten days and a fortnight after signs of rooting, pot up the cuttings into 5 cm (2 in) pots.

● Greenhouse conditions

Maintain frost-free, well-ventilated air conditions and check regularly for pests and diseases.

CHRYSANTHEMUMS

EARLY-FLOWERING (GARDEN)

After frost, refirm the ground around plants over-wintering outdoors. Also check that the surrounding soil is not waterlogged; if necessary pierce deeply with a fork to improve the drainage.

Keep dormant stools of early-flowering varieties stored in the greenhouse or cold frame cool and not too wet.

LATE-FLOWERING (GREENHOUSE)

The quality and duration of late flowers depends very much on maintaining an even supply of moisture to the roots, a consistent temperature of 10°C (50°F) and a well-ventilated greenhouse (see November, page 257). Reduce the temperature to 8°C (46°F) during very dull weather.

● Taking cuttings

Take cuttings of late-flowering varieties towards the end of the month (see March, page 61).

CLIMBERS & WALL SHRUBS

● Late planting

Planting should have been completed last month, but if the weather is mild and the soil not too wet, it can be continued into December.

● Frost protection

Tender plants, such as ceanothus, grown against exposed walls, may need protection. Secure a screen of fine mesh netting on the north or east side of each plant or all around them if they are small and space allows. The gap between the shrub and netting can be filled with bracken or straw. If you don't want a covering in place all winter, wrap the plants in horticultural fleece when frost is forecast.

WALL SHRUBS – PROTECTING

Protect vulnerable wall shrubs which are of borderline hardiness with fine mesh netting. You can provide additional protection by filling the gap between the shrub and the netting with straw or bracken.

● Taking hardwood cuttings

Continue to take hardwood cuttings of hardy climbers (*see* November, page 257).

CONTAINER GARDENING

● Planting deciduous shrubs

In good weather continue planting hardy deciduous trees and shrubs, especially any bare-root or root-balled plants. Make sure that all the containers have good drainage and are slightly raised off the ground to allow excess water to drain away.

● Winter hanging baskets

If severe cold weather is forecast, take winter and spring-interest hanging baskets under cover until the weather warms up. An unheated greenhouse, glass porch or conservatory is fine. Hanging baskets tend to suffer more from the cold than other containers because the limited soil volume means that the roots have little protection from the cold and, hanging above ground level, baskets are subjected to greater wind exposure which can be devastating if the roots become frozen. Winter pansies and variegated ivies are especially vulnerable.

● Tidying winter plants

It is important to keep tidying plants in winter containers, as the eye is drawn more strongly to them because of the limited amount of colour elsewhere in the garden.

Cut off yellowing leaves, a common problem on polyanthus and primroses, and remove dead flowers using a pair of scissors. The occasional plant may die and will then need to be replaced. Even in winter, pots may dry out rapidly as a result of the wind, so keep a close eye on watering requirements.

DAHLIAS

● Ordering tubers

To ensure you obtain the varieties you want, order tubers from specialist mail order catalogues.

● Inspection of tubers

Examine the tubers in store and deal with any that are shrivelling or rotting (*see* January, page 21).

FRUIT

Carry on planting trees and bushes if soil and weather conditions are suitable; if this is not possible, heel them in temporarily and they will not deteriorate (*see* November, page 259).

Check all stakes, ties and other supports; this is the time to make any necessary replacements but be sure that they are still needed and that the tree is not holding up the stake!

A winter wash provides protection against many of the worst fruit pests: notably greenfly, apple and pear suckers and winter moth, as it destroys the overwintering larvae and eggs. It also kills moss and algae that have built up on trunks and branches. A wash must be used only when the trees and bushes are completely dormant and leafless. Be aware that it is an indiscriminate weapon and kills as many beneficial insects as pests. It should be used only when appropriate sprays in the spring have failed to control the problem pests (*see* Pests, pages 395–405 and February, page 47).

● Apples and pears

Continue winter pruning apples and pears (*see* November, page 259). Burn or shred the prunings. Shreddings are a valuable raw material and can be used either to aerate the compost heap or kept separately to use as a mulch (*see* November, page 255).

Cut out all cankers when you are pruning and treat the branches with a wound paint. Trained apple and pear trees, cordons, espaliers and fans, are best pruned in the summer but you should prune now the shoots which were not mature then, as well as the branch leaders. Cut back the sideshoots to 2.5 cm (1 in) and branch leaders by a third to a half.

Check on the condition of all stored fruit and remove and throw away any that have rotted or ripened. It will not be necessary to unwrap apples – the paper will be wet and stained if the fruit is diseased. Bring stored fruit indoors a few days before you want to eat or cook it, to allow it to mature properly and develop its full flavour.

● Gooseberries and currants

Finish taking hardwood cuttings. You can still prune gooseberries, and red and black currants if you have not already done so (*see* November, page 261).

FUCHSIAS

TENDER AND HALF-HARDY
● Watering and ventilation

Water fuchsias sparingly in winter; more plants are killed by drought followed by overwatering than by cold conditions.

Keep air circulating whenever possible with perhaps a little heat, but do not allow condensation to form. It is always coldest at floor level, so ensure that any large plants standing at ground level in a greenhouse are not too cold.

Check occasionally on plants packed away in compost for the winter; they should not be allowed to become completely dry (*see* November, page 261).

● Controlling pests and diseases

If pests or disease are still a problem, use smoke cones in the greenhouse in preference to sprays which will raise the humidity at this time of year.

HARDY

In colder areas, protect the crowns of hardy fuchsias with a mulch of peat, garden compost or fine gravel.

GARDEN MAINTENANCE

● Water pipes and taps

Turn off outside water from inside the house and drain the pipes if you can. If this is not possible, lag outdoor taps and water pipes.

● Paths and steps

Consider installing low-voltage lights to highlight garden features. Sold in sets, with a transformer that is kept indoors, they do not need an outdoor power supply and can be moved around the garden. However, low-voltage lights do not give out much light, so for front paths or steps, install permanent, higher voltage lights. These need to be installed by a qualified electrician.

Leave a pile of grit or ash near the front drive and any steps for use if conditions become icy.

GREENHOUSES & FRAMES

● Temperature and ventilation

Plant growth is at its lowest ebb this month, owing to the brief hours of daylight. It is a mistake to try to make plants grow more rapidly by raising the temperature, as the resulting growth will be too soft and sappy. Within reasonable limits temperature must be related to light conditions; a minimum night temperature of 7°C (45°F) is adequate for most plants in the average greenhouse.

Open ventilators a little on sunny days but close them again quite early in the afternoon, before the temperature begins to drop, to retain as much of the heat of the day as possible.

● Watering

Most plants, except those actually in flower, must be kept fairly dry, but do not allow them to dry out to the extent that the soil begins to shrink from the sides of the pot.

In warm greenhouses, if floors and paths need damping down to increase humidity, do this during the early part of the day. This is unlikely to be required where oil or gas heaters are used. Discontinue overhead misting of plants for the time being.

● Taking cuttings

Take cuttings from border perennials, perpetual carnations and late-flowering varieties of chrysanthemums (*see* Border perennials, Carnations & pinks and Chrysanthemums, page 276).

● Overwintering

Check bulbs and tubers in store for signs of fungal diseases and check on resting chrysanthemums and fuchsias to ensure they have not dried out.

● Forcing

Pot up lily bulbs (*see* Lilies, page 281) and prune any roses you are forcing in containers for early flowers (*see* Roses, page 281).

Box up rhubarb and chicory for forcing (*see* Vegetables, page 282). Check on bowls of bulbs being forced for winter flowering (*see* Bulbs, corms and tubers, page 276).

● Vines

Vines should be pruned once the leaves have fallen and the plants are dormant for the winter; if you prune during the growing season, they will 'bleed' (lose sap) copiously when cut.

One of the most convenient and space-saving forms of training for a vine in a small greenhouse is the rod and spur system. Once the main stem or the permanent laterals have reached the length you require, cut back all the shoots each winter to just one plump bud.

Now the vine is dormant this is also a good time to propagate from eye cuttings. Make the cuttings about 3 cm (1½ in) long, each with a single 'eye' or bud. Making sure the bud is facing upwards, remove a strip of bark on the side opposite the bud, making a shallow cut from half way down the stem to the base. Dip the cut surface in a rooting hormone, then insert it vertically in a pot of compost. The bud should be level with, or just above, the surface. Keep in a propagator in a moist atmosphere at a temperature of about 24°C (75°F) until it has rooted, then gradually harden off and plant outdoors or in the greenhouse in late spring.

HEATHERS

● Planning and designing new beds

Heathers look best if planted in beds totally devoted to them, or with conifers or other compatible specimen plants, which will provide a contrast in height, form and foliage texture. If possible, keep summer and winter flowering heathers apart as this makes the maximum use of contrasting flower colour between varieties that are in bloom. If you choose to grow golden-leaved varieties as well, this will provide the bed with colour all the year round.

GREENHOUSES – PRUNING VINES

Greenhouse vines are usually grown on the rod and spur system. On an established plant, prune back this year's growth to one plump bud from its point of origin – whether or not the stem has carried fruit.

Position heather beds in full sun and make the beds with curving rather than straight edges as heathers look more natural in informal drifts.

The species chosen will depend to some extent on whether your soil is acid or alkaline – test the soil if the pH is unknown (*see* The soil in your garden, page 387). If your soil is acid, you can grow any heather. If your soil has a pH greater than 6.5, restrict your choice to those species that will tolerate lime: *Erica carnea*, *E.* × *darleyensis*, *E. erigena*, *E. vagans* and most of the tree heathers except *E. arborea*. Other species can be grown only with difficulty (*see* January, page 23 and May, page 132).

Plant varieties in groups of at least three but the larger the group, the more dramatic the effect. As a general guide, use five heathers per m² (four heathers per sq yd). Heathers can be planted closer together on heavier soils up to 30 cm (12 in) apart, but do not plant closer on light, sandy soils, or on any soil which is prone to drying out in the summer.

● Keeping beds clear

Remove any overhanging vegetation that has grown during summer. To minimise the risk of fungal diseases, keep heathers clear of fallen leaves.

HERBS

● Winter protection

Herbs generally have a long dormant period, and some of them need protection during the winter. Bay grown in tubs can be brought into the greenhouse or put on a sheltered patio away from cold winds. In the coldest districts give French tarragon, myrtle and rosemary a protective layer of leafmould or straw. Rosemary will survive in the open if it is well established and away from north and east winds. Bergamot, chives and mint die down completely until the following spring.

● Culinary herbs for winter use

Bring inside any herbs potted up for forcing (see September, page 219).

● Harvesting

Gather fresh leaves of sage, parsley and thyme needed for the festive season.

● Greenhouse and protected crops

Continue to check any herbs in the greenhouse or under cloches (see October, page 241). They will still require watering periodically.

HOUSE & CONSERVATORY PLANTS

Buying new plants

Avoid buying indoor plants that are displayed out in the cold. Purchase plants at the end of shopping trips and have them carefully wrapped. Check on the correct name of the plant and the instructions for cultivation. Some plants have specific requirements or may have been planted in a container without drainage holes.

Protect all plants from cold and draughts and check on light levels (*see* November, page 263).

Watering and feeding

Water sparingly, but keep compost on the dry side, letting the surface dry out between waterings. Do not overdo this – a finger inserted into the compost should feel some moisture. Yellowing and dropping leaves are signs of over or underwatering. You can check this by taking the plant out of the pot and inspecting the roots. Stop feeding unless the plant is growing actively.

Controlling temperature

Aim to keep the conservatory at 7–10°C (45–50°F) by a combination of insulation, heating and ventilation, and monitor the temperature using a maximum/minimum thermometer.

Flowering plants

Move any plants, such as cinerarias and primulas, that you hope will be in flower at Christmas, to the warmest spot in the house and put any plants that are too advanced in a cooler spot.

Keep African violets (*Saintpaulia ionantha*) that are coming into bud in a light position and supplement daylight with light from a lamp in the evening.

Continue to deadhead chrysanthemums to encourage longer flowering.

Keep hydrangeas that have shed their leaves but are carrying plump buds in a dry atmosphere, and water them just enough to prevent the compost becoming dust dry.

Indoor bulbs and corms

Continue to remove any spent flowers and yellowing leaves from cyclamen corms by pulling them gently away from the base. Move pots of cyclamen that you want to flower at Christmas to the warmest spot in the house, unless they are already too advanced in which case they should be kept in a cooler place.

Plant hippeastrum bulbs for flowering in early spring in 15 cm (6 in) pots containing John Innes No. 2 potting compost. Bury only the lower half of each bulb. Keep them at a temperature of 10–13°C (50–55°F) and maintain a humid atmosphere. Water sparingly until the flower buds appear.

Start bringing bowls of forced bulbs into the warmth and light as the buds start to develop (*see* Bulbs, corms and tubers, page 276).

Climbers and feature plants

Keep jasmine (*Jasminum polyanthum*) watered and fed every two weeks.

Bromeliads

Mist any air plants once or twice a week (*see* November, page 264).

Cacti and other succulents

Keep these at a minimum temperature of 10°C (50°F) in good light during their resting period (*see* November, page 264).

Orchids

Water very sparingly so the compost is barely moist (*see* November, page 264).

IRISES

Dwarf bulbous irises

Bring pots of dwarf bulbs such as *Iris reticulata*, *I. histrioides* and *I. danfordiae* into a cold frame or a well-ventilated unheated greenhouse. Keep the compost just moist and use a combined fungicide and liquid feed at half strength as the leaves appear.

Iris unguicularis

Continue to protect flower buds from slugs and snails in mild weather (*see* Pests, page 403). Pick while still in bud.

Winter protection

In cold areas, protect foliage of Dutch and Spanish irises with bracken or cloches.

LAWNS

Preparing new sites

If weather and ground conditions permit, dig over areas to be seeded in the spring if not done earlier (*see* March, pages 84–85).

Tool maintenance

Clean and service lawnmowers and other tools.

LILIES

Planting bulbs

Bulbs can still be planted if the weather is fine and the soil workable (*see* October, page 244). This will apply in warmer areas. Pot up or store bulbs under glass as an alternative (*see* November, page 265).

● Forcing bulbs

More lily bulbs can be potted up now to give you blooms in late spring. Add a slow-release fertiliser to the potting compost (*see* October, page 244).

PELARGONIUMS

Send for specialist seed catalogues and plan next year's planting.

● Winter care

Pelargoniums thrive in a dry atmosphere so keep them well ventilated over winter (*see* November, page 265). Not much growth takes place this month, but they are never dormant, so keep an eye on the plants and do not let them get dust dry.

● Potting on

Autumn-sown seedlings and cuttings taken in September and October, should now be established. Check the development of their roots and if necessary pot them on into larger pots.

RHODODENDRONS & AZALEAS

● Weather protection

After a heavy snowfall, the weight of snow on branches can break them. Shake off snow as soon as you can before it can do any damage and, for older, cherished specimens, place props under the main branches to support them if snow is expected. Bushes in an exposed position, especially if recently planted, may need the protection of a temporary windbreak of close mesh netting or hessian.

ROCK PLANTS

● Sowing seed

Begin sowing seed as soon as possible this month. Use John Innes seed compost for most seeds or a proprietary nutrient-added peat or peat-substitute compost for acid-loving plants. Most rock plants require good drainage, so ensure that pots or trays have a layer of shards or stones in the bottom, and cover them with a layer of sharp grit, or sand for the finer seeds.

Water from below and leave the pots outside (clearly labelled) on a surface that will discourage both slugs and worms. Cover the pots with a vermin-proof mesh if mice are a problem. Avoid drips from overhanging trees or gutters; the north side of a building is best. Check periodically for

RHODODENDRONS – PROTECTING

Rhododendrons planted in a very exposed and windy position, especially if not yet fully established, will benefit from a temporary windbreak. Fix a fine net or hessian to stout supports on the windy side.

germination and begin to water again in the spring. Some seeds take up to three years to germinate, so do not throw out old pots of seed.

ROSES

● Planting

Planting can continue (*see* November, page 266) provided the weather is clear and mild and the soil is not waterlogged or frozen. If planting in wet conditions do not tread the roots in until it is drier.

● Pruning climbers and ramblers ·

Complete pruning of all climbers and ramblers this month (*see* October, page 245). Check on all wooden structures in the garden, particularly pergolas and the stakes of standard roses.

● Winter protection

Most roses are fully hardy but there are one or two, notably the Banksian roses, the China rose, *Rosa × odorata* 'Mutabilis' and *R.* 'Mermaid', which prefer a sunny, sheltered wall and may need some protection in very hard winters.

● Forcing roses

Roses in pots being forced in the greenhouse should be pruned; late-maturing varieties first. Complete this by the end of the month. Water sparingly and keep all the ventilators open.

SWEET PEAS

● Protecting seedlings

Protect seedlings in a cold frame or unheated greenhouse if severe frost is expected. This type of protection must remain in place until the compost in the pots has thawed out completely – rapid thawing damages the seedlings. Keep a watch for slugs and snails, and ensure that small plants are adequately protected (*see* Pests, page 403).

● Pinching out

At the end of the month, encourage the formation of sideshoots by pinching out the growing tips of any seedlings not showing signs of throwing sideshoots ('breaking') naturally.

● Preparation of site

Complete preparing the ground for next season as soon as possible (*see* November, page 268).

TREES, SHRUBS & HEDGES

● Planting

As long as the soil is not frozen or waterlogged, you can continue planting deciduous trees and shrubs throughout this month. During December, trees used for screens or hedges and many bare-root hedging plants are available for planting. These can be bought by the bundle and are less expensive than container-grown plants.

● Frost protection

Many trees, shrubs and conifers are grown permanently in containers. These need extra protection from winter frosts (*see* Container Gardening, page 277). Keep a length of horticultural fleece handy to throw over plants on frosty nights.

● Pruning

Use the one-third method to prune November-flowering shrubs over three years old after flowering (*see* Pruning, page 420).

● Taking hardwood cuttings

Take hardwood cuttings of suitable shrubs (*see* Propagation, page 429) and plant out rooted hardwood cuttings and layers (*see* October, page 248).

HEDGES

Continue to plant deciduous hedges (*see* October, page 248), as long as the soil is workable.

VEGETABLES

Order vegetable seed from mail order catalogues. These have a greater choice of vegetable varieties than is available in garden centres and shops in the spring. It is worth trying a few new varieties each year, particularly those that claim pest or disease resistance as it could cut down on the need for chemicals. The number of seeds in a packet varies greatly between brands, so it is worth comparing the catalogues to find packet sizes that suit your requirements.

On heavy soils, finish digging over the soil but leave the winter weather to break down any exposed clods of earth. Lighter and sandy soils can be left until spring. This is a good time to add bulky organic matter such as garden compost to the soil.

Plan where crops are to be grown next year.

VEGETABLES – FORCING CHICORY

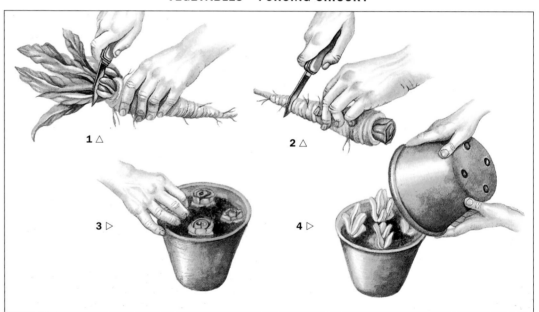

(1) Lift chicory roots grown for forcing and trim the leaves just above the crown. (2) Cut off the bottom so that they will fit in a pot. (3) Put about four roots with the tops just exposed in a 20–25 cm (8–10 in) pot full of garden soil.

(4) Cover the roots with a pot of the same size but with the holes blacked out. Keep slightly moist in an airing cupboard or warm greenhouse. The heads of blanched leaves will be ready to eat in about three to four weeks.

Follow a crop rotation plan, as growing crops in the same soil year after year will build up a reservoir of pests and diseases and the plant yield will decrease.

Continue to harvest Brussels sprouts, cabbages, carrots, cauliflowers, kale, leeks, parsnips, spinach, swedes and turnips.

● **Salad crops**

Lift chicory for forcing if not already done. Take three or four roots, trim the leaves and roots and put them in a 20–25 cm (8–10 in) pot of garden soil with the crowns just visible. Keep them in darkness in an airing cupboard or heated greenhouse with a temperature of 10–13°C (50–55°F). The tight heads of blanched leaves will be ready to harvest in three to four weeks.

PERENNIAL VEGETABLES

● **Jerusalem artichokes**

Continue to harvest Jerusalem artichokes.

● **Rhubarb**

Lift rhubarb for forcing indoors if not yet done (*see* November, page 269). Crowns lifted last month for forcing indoors can now be packed in a strong, wooden box. Fill up the spaces with peat or peat substitute and keep it moist but not wet. Cover the box with black plastic sheeting. Place in a room where the temperature is about 7°C (45°F), such as a spare room indoors or heated greenhouse. The first sticks should be ready to pull in January.

To force rhubarb outdoors, pack straw, leaves or bracken around the clump then cover it with an old bucket, bin or purpose-made pot (*see* January, page 29). Blanched shoots will be ready by early March.

WATER PLANTS & POOLS

● **Keeping areas ice-free**

Keep an area of water ice-free by using a pool heater. This allows noxious gases which build up within the pool to escape, instead of becoming trapped beneath the ice and killing any fish in the pond. If you do not have a pool heater, stand a saucepan of very hot water on the ice and allow the pan to melt through. The pan may need several refills with hot water before the ice melts.

To absorb the pressure and to prevent the ice from fracturing a concrete-lined pool, float rubber or plastic balls on the surface of the water in the winter. However, these will not keep an ice hole open when the weather gets colder. Do not smash thick ice in a pool, as this may concuss or even kill the fish.

PONDS – PROTECTING FROM ICE

The best way to keep an area of water ice-free is with a pond heater, but you can make a temporary hole by standing a pan of hot water on the ice. A ball left in the water will absorb pressure from the ice.

CROP ROTATION

Rotate crops around the plot each year to prevent the build-up of pests and diseases. Here is an example of a three-year rotation.

	Year 1	Year 2	Year 3
Plot A	brassicas	potatoes/roots	legumes/onions
Plot B	legumes/onions	brassicas	potatoes/roots
Plot C	potatoes/roots	legumes/onions	brassicas

Brassicas here include broccoli, Brussels sprouts, cabbages, calabrese, cauliflowers, kale, kohlrabi, swedes, turnips and radishes. Lettuces are often grown with brassicas. Crop rotation helps to control rots and will prevent a build-up of club root. Brassicas need a fertile soil so they should follow legumes (the pea family) and have generous amounts of fertiliser added during the growing season. They also need an alkaline soil (pH 6.5–7.5). Clubroot symptoms are reduced at pH 7–7.5, so check the pH of your soil and adjust with lime.

Legumes include the many types of beans and peas and some green manures. Celery is often grown with this group. Rotating them can help prevent diseases such as foot and root rots, downy mildew and pea thrips. They need a soil with plenty of organic matter but they require little or no fertiliser added.

Onions include shallots and leeks as well as onions. Crop rotation helps to control rots, smuts, downy mildew, stem and bulb eelworm and white rot. These crops like lots of organic matter and fertiliser in the soil before planting or sowing.

Potatoes (and tomatoes) need to be grown on different soil each year as tubers left in the ground can spread blight, scab and eelworm. They need plenty of fertiliser but no lime.

Root crops include carrots, parsnips and beetroot. Spinach is often grown with beetroot. Crop rotation will help to prevent violet root rot, parsnip canker and black rot. These root crops need moderate amounts of fertiliser but they should not have fresh manure added to the soil as this can cause the roots to fork.

Sweetcorn, and squashes, such as courgettes and marrows, can be grown on spare land or used as fill-ins.

Garden Planning & Design

What makes a garden stand out from its neighbours is often not the amount of time or money spent on it, but its design. It may be the pleasing structure and sense of proportion, or it may be the imaginative choice and positioning of plants and ornaments that creates that special impact. When these elements of garden design come together, a garden will be much admired by other gardeners.

The time to plan your garden is before you buy the plants, or start any type of construction work. If you move into a newly built home, the garden will probably have no structure and no mature plants, but it is easier to design your garden without the constraints of existing features.

The advantage of redesigning an established garden is that you can often retain mature features, and it is possible to move border plants and even large shrubs to create a more 'instant' effect. There is less urgency to tackle the whole garden at once, and the design can be improved over several years.

DRAWING A MASTER PLAN

Whether you use a computer or pencil and paper for the final design, you or your landscape designer will need to make an accurate outline of the existing garden, complete with dimensions. This is the starting point for all improvements.

Make a rough freehand sketch of the garden first, then fill in the measurements so that you can transfer the plan to paper afterwards.

Start with a known straight edge or rectangle – your house is ideal – then measure off at right angles from the sides. Once you have the framework of the house, boundaries and permanent structures such as sheds and paths marked, you can measure off at right angles from these to find the position of secondary features such as flower beds.

When all these measurements are on the rough

▲ *This small enclosed town garden has a patio that is enlivened by a raised pool, varied shrubs and large pots.*

sketch, draw a plan of the existing garden on graph paper, using a scale appropriate to the size of the garden (you may need to join several sheets if the garden is very large, or the scale will be too small). A useful scale is 1:50 (2 cm to 1 m or ¼ in to 1 ft) for a small garden. If your garden is large, try 1:100. If you have a graphics or drawing program on your computer, this can be done on screen.

Mark in the fixed points, such as house and boundaries, and any key features, such as trees, that you are sure you will not want to move or alter. Draw in any other features you want to retain, and leave out everything else.

Your design will have a greater sense of structure and will probably work better if you ignore the choice of plants – except perhaps for a few key focal points – when you create the basic plan. If you focus on the plants too soon, the overall structure of the garden may be sacrificed.

The only rule to be followed with garden design is that it should please you and reflect your tastes.

USING A GRID

The simplest way to start your design is to draw a grid over the basic master plan, based on squares perhaps 2 m or 6 ft apart, or maybe to coincide with the spacing of fence posts around your garden. For a large garden, you may need a larger grid.

Next, start to visualise where you might like the lawn, flower beds, a water feature and so on, and sketch them in. Keep the key elements to rectangles as much as possible, but to add interest be prepared to divide the basic grid into smaller units so that the design does not look too rigid. A garden will often look more interesting if the rectangular grid is set at 45 degrees to the house.

For some gardeners, straight edges are incompatible with an attractive garden – they seldom appear in nature. Attractive designs can be created with circles and arcs. With this type of design it is important to remember to make transitional curves gentle, so that they link naturally.

DIFFICULT SHAPES

Long, narrow gardens can often be improved by dividing the area into several smaller sections, using hedges, low walls, raised beds, or shrub borders that extend into the garden and prevent the eye being taken in a straight line to the end.

Each area can be used to create a different type

of garden or an area with a different theme, such as scent, water, herbs or foliage effects, so that the garden becomes a voyage of discovery.

Very small gardens can, paradoxically, be made more interesting by dividing them up into even smaller areas – perhaps a patio separated by a raised bed, or a fragrant area partly screened by a rosemary hedge. The use of a few bold focal points to take the eye across the garden at an angle can also help to overcome the shortcomings of a very tiny space. The important thing is to make sure the whole garden cannot be seen at once.

Sloping sites can be made more interesting, and easier to manage, if you create a series of terraces, linked by steps or slopes. Flat areas make grass easier to mow, and form places to sit out.

FOCAL POINTS AND HEIGHT

Focal points can be large – like a bold tree, a bird-bath or an ornament on a plinth, or a striking plant such as a red hot poker – or small, like an ornament or vase set among the flowers in a border. Their object is the same: to take the eye to a particular part of the garden.

Never overlook the importance of height. The vertical dimension will prevent an otherwise flat area from looking boring. In a large garden, tall trees take the eye upwards, and in a medium-sized garden pergolas, arches and arbours are useful devices. In a small garden use plenty of climbers and shrubs against walls and fences, and consider a patio linked overhead to the house to add height while not encroaching unduly on the garden.

WATER

Most professional designers try to incorporate a water feature. If a pond is inappropriate, try a bubble, pebble or wall fountain.

Ponds should reflect the style of the garden. A

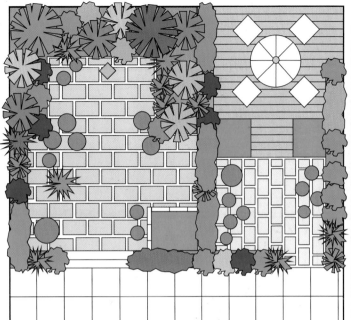

▲ *This is the plan for the small garden shown in the photographs. The red circles indicate movable pots placed on the paving. The orange diamond is a sundial. Blue indicates water features. The decked area has table and chairs.*

▲ *Even a tiny space can be made to work hard: shrubs around the edge screen the fence and the sundial acts as a focal point.*

formal patio demands a rectangular or round pond. A pond in an informal part of the garden usually looks best with an irregular outline.

PRACTICAL POINTS

No matter how pretty a design looks on paper, you won't be satisfied with it in reality if you overlook the practical points, such as where the children will play or how to reach the compost heap in winter.

Unsightly elements such as dustbins, oil storage tanks and tool sheds can be screened, perhaps with plants grown over a trellis, but don't place clothes dryers and dustbins too far from the house.

Finally, consider the type of gardener you are. Do you want a garden which is easy to maintain, or one in which you can potter endlessly? Do you

long to grow all your own fruit and vegetables, or just want somewhere pretty to sit in the summer?

PLANTING PLANS

Once the outline has been drawn, you can start on the planting plans. Consider the effect of different seasons, and what each site offers by way of sun, shade, shelter and soil type. Look at other gardens, as well as books and magazines, for more ideas.

Sketch the border to scale on paper before planting, and if necessary cut out pieces of paper to represent the different plants, colouring them if appropriate, with the likely height and flowering time marked. By moving these around you should be able to achieve interest over a long period with good colour contrasts and harmonies.

SECTION TWO

PLANTS

FOR YOUR GARDEN

Annuals & biennials

BRIGHT AND CHEERFUL annuals and biennials generally prefer a place in full sun. They bloom prolifically because they need to produce plenty of seed to perpetuate themselves. Hardy annuals are the easiest to grow because they are usually sown directly in the ground where they are to flower. Half-hardy annuals are normally raised in warmth and planted out when there is no risk of frost. Some tender perennial plants (such as antirrhinums and impatiens) are generally grown as half-hardy annuals.

▲ **Alyssum maritimum** (syn.Lobularia maritima)
Mounds of small white, highly fragrant flowers, useful as an edging plant or for growing in a drift as a floral carpet. There are also varieties with shades of lavender, violet, pink, purple and apricot, including mixtures. Hardy. Height: 10–13 cm (4–5 in). Spread: 15 cm (6 in).

▲ **Antirrhinum**
Stiff spikes of lipped flowers in many colours. Treated as half-hardy. Height: 15–60 cm (6–24 in). Spread: 23 cm (9 in).

▲ **Ageratum**
Most varieties are blue and compact, and make excellent edging for summer bedding schemes. There are also white and pink varieties, and some taller ones suitable for cutting. Half-hardy. Height: 15–23 cm (6–9 in). Spread: 15–23 cm (6–9 in).

▲ **Amaranthus caudatus**
Long, drooping tassels of red flowers (hence the common name love-lies-bleeding), but there is a green form. An attractive focal point plant dotted among other annuals. Hardy. Height: 90 cm (3 ft). Spread: 45 cm (18 in).

▲ **Arctotis x hybrida**
Bright daisy flowers, mainly orange and red, that open in the sun. Usually seed-raised, but varieties like this ('Flame') are overwintered and propagated from cuttings. Treated as half-hardy annual. Height: 30–45 cm (1–1½ ft). Spread: 30 cm (1 ft).

▲ Annual aster (Callistephus)

Usually grown in one of its compact double forms like this, but there are other flower types. Colours mainly shades of blue, pink, red and white. Half-hardy annual. Height: 15–60 cm (6–24 in). Spread: 23 cm (9 in).

▼ Bellis perennis

The double daisy is a spring-flowering plant, blooming between March and June. Useful for an edging or in containers. Shades of red, pink or white. Treat as hardy biennial. Height: 10–15 cm (4–6 in). Spread: 10 cm (4 in).

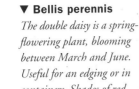

▲ Calendula officinalis

The pot marigold is a cottage-garden plant, and an easy-to-grow cut flower. There are many varieties in shades of orange and yellow, including very compact ones for containers or small beds. Hardy annual. Height: 30–60 cm (1–2 ft). Spread: 23–30 cm (9–12 in).

▲ Cineraria maritima

Silver foliage plant useful as a contrast to the bright flowers of summer bedding. Some have finely divided leaves. Treat as half-hardy annual. Height: 20–30 cm (8–12 in). Spread: 23–30 cm (9–12 in).

▲ Begonia semperflorens

The fibrous-rooted begonia will flower continuously from early summer until the first frost. Flowers are usually in shades of red, pink, or white, and some have bronze or reddish foliage to add variety. Half-hardy. Height: 10–23cm (4–9 in). Spread: 15–20 cm (6–8 in).

▲ Convolvulus tricolor
(syn. C. minor)

An annual, non-climbing and non-invasive convolvulus with blue flowers (some varieties have white or pink flowers). A bright plant that will thrive in poor soil. Hardy annual. Height: 20–30 cm (8–12 in). Spread: 45–60 cm (1½–2 ft).

▲ Cosmos bipinnatus (syn. Cosmea bipinnatus)

Mostly white, pink or red flowers (some varieties have fluted petals), carried above divided, ferny foliage. They perform well in late summer and early autumn, and make good cut flowers. Hardy. Height: 60–90 cm (2–3 ft). Spread: 60–90 cm (2–3 ft).

▼ Dianthus chinensis

Single-flowered annual dianthus. There are many varieties, usually with fringed petals and a contrasting centre. Treat as half-hardy or hardy annual. Height: 10–20 cm (4–8 in). Spread: 10–20 cm (4–8 in).

▲ Eschscholzia californica

The Californian poppy is very easy to grow and will self-seed if you let it. Yellow and orange are the dominant colours, but there are also pinks and whites. Hardy annual. Height: 30 cm (12 in). Spread: 23 cm (9 in).

▼ Foxglove (Digitalis purpurea)

Tall spikes of usually purple, spotted, flowers. There are also whites and pinks. Good in light shade. Biennial, but a few varieties will flower in the first year if sown early. Height: 1.2–1.5 m (4–5 ft).

▼ Gazania hybrida

Brilliant flowers for a sunny spot, excellent in a hot, dry summer. Reds, oranges and yellows are the dominant 'hot' colours. Treat as half-hardy annual. Height: 20–25 cm (8–10 in). Spread: 30 cm (12 in).

▲ Godetia grandiflora

Easy-to-grow colourful flowers for annual borders, and useful gap-fillers in a mixed border. There are single, semi-double and double varieties in a wide range of colours, mainly pinks. Hardy annual. Height: 20–38 cm (8–15 in). Spread: 23–30 cm (9–12 in).

◀ Gypsophila elegans

The small white or pink flowers on long, thin stems make this a popular cut flower. For a garden display it is best grown in a mixed border. Hardy annual. Height: 45–60 cm (1½–2 ft). Spread: 45 cm (1½ ft).

▼ Impatiens (New Guinea hybrid)

Many New Guinea hybrids are propagated from cuttings, but some can be raised from seed. They have large flowers and often variegated or bronze foliage. Better for containers than for massed bedding. Treat as half-hardy annual. Height: 23–30 cm (9–12 in). Spread: 23–30 cm (9–12 in).

▲ Helichrysum bracteatum

An everlasting flower that can be picked before the flowers open fully and dried for indoor arrangements. Yellows and reds are the main colours. Hardy annual. Height: 30–90 cm (1–3 ft). Spread: 30 cm (1 ft).

▲ Honesty (Lunaria annua)

A multi-merit plant with pretty purple or white flowers in early summer, followed by silvery seed heads popular with flower arrangers. There is also a variegated variety (illustrated). Suits shade and dappled shade. Biennial. Height: 75 cm (2½ ft). Spread: 45 cm (1½ ft).

▲ Impatiens

Busy lizzies come in a wide range of colours and bicolours, and flower until the first frost, even in shade. They are great for containers and massed bedding. There are single colours, mixtures and double varieties. Treat as half-hardy annual. Height: 15–30 cm (6–12 in).

▲ Lavatera trimestris

The annual mallow is a large, bushy plant more suitable for a mixed border than formal annual bedding. There are several shades of pink as well as white. Hardy annual. Height: 60–75 cm (2–2½ ft). Spread: 60 cm (2 ft).

▼ Lobelia erinus

Traditional bedding plant. There are trailing varieties for baskets and containers. Blue is the dominant colour but there are purply, white and pink varieties. Half-hardy annual. Height: 10 cm (4 in), or trailing. Spread: 10 cm (4 in).

▲ Limnanthes douglasii

The poached egg plant is a quick-growing plant that self-seeds itself readily. Pretty annual ground cover, and useful for attracting bees and other beneficial insects. Hardy annual. Height: 15 cm (6 in). Spread: 23 cm (9 in).

▼ Mesembryanthemum criniflorum

Livingstone daisies are spectacular in flower, with daisy flowers in a wide range of colours. Unfortunately they need the sun to put on a good display and deadheading is vital. Half-hardy annual. Height: 8 cm (3 in). Spread: 15 cm (6 in).

▲ Marigold, African

The large flowers come in shades of yellow and orange, rarely white. Dwarf varieties are suitable for containers or the front of a border and taller ones are more appropriate for a mixed border. Half-hardy annual. Height: 30–90 cm (1–3 ft). Spread: 23–45 cm (9–18 in).

▲ Marigold, French

These invaluable bedding plants are often in flower even before planting, and continue until the first frost. There are many flower forms, including single, double (illustrated) and crested. Half-hardy annual. Height: 15–45 cm (6–18 in).

▲ Mimulus hybrids

Associated with damp soil, but modern hybrids can be used for bedding and even containers. Tolerant of shade. Reds, oranges and yellows are the dominant colours. Half-hardy annual. Height: 15–30 cm (6–12 in). Spread: 30 cm (1 ft).

▲ Nicotiana

Ornamental tobacco. Modern hybrids are compact and the flowers remain open during the day, but not all are scented. Colours include red, pink, lilac, lime. Good for light shade. Half-hardy annual. Height: 30–60 cm (1–2 ft). Spread: 30–45 cm (1–1½ ft).

▼ Nasturtium (Tropaeolum majus)

The compact non-climbing varieties can be used effectively in beds, borders and containers. The main colours are reds, oranges and yellows. Some have variegated foliage. Hardy annual. Height: 30 cm (1 ft). Spread: 60 cm (2 ft).

▲ Pansy (Viola x wittrockiana)

Pansies can be had in flower most months of the year and are often fragrant. Treat as half-hardy annual or hardy biennial. Height: 15–23 cm (6–9 in). Spread: 15 cm (6 in).

▲ Nemesia

Flowers early. Colours include reds, yellows, oranges, pinks and blues. Half-hardy annual. Height: 20–25 cm (8–10 in). Spread: 10 cm (4 in).

▲ Petunia

These popular plants are fragrant, come in many colours, are ideal for bedding or containers. Half-hardy annual. Height: 23–30 cm (9–12 in). Spread: 60 cm (2 ft).

▼ Poppy, Iceland
(Papaver nudicaule)

Treat as orange, yellow and white hardy biennials or half-hardy annuals. Height: 45–60 cm (1½–2 ft). Spread: 30 cm (1 ft).

▲ Rudbeckia

This bold and cheerful daisy is especially useful for late summer and autumn brightness. There are also double varieties. Perennial, but treat as half-hardy annual. Height: 30–60 cm (1–2 ft). Spread: 30–45 cm (1–1½ ft).

▲ Sunflower (Helianthus annuus)

The easy and reliable sunflower is traditionally single and yellow, but there are double and red varieties, dwarfs as well as the more popular giants. Hardy annual. Height: 60–300 cm (2–10 ft). Spread: 30–60 cm (1–2 ft).

▼ Salvia splendens

One of the best bright red bedding plants, but there are pink, purple, lavender, salmon and white varieties. Grown as an annual. Height: 23–30 cm (9–12 in). Spread: 23 cm (9 in).

◄ Sweet william (Dianthus barbatus)

A cottage-garden plant much admired for its beautiful scent and bright, usually bicoloured, flowers in early summer. It thrives in alkaline soil and comes in pinks and reds, often edged with white. Biennial. Height: 25–45 cm (10–18 in). Spread: 23–30 cm (9–12 in).

▲ **Verbena**

There are many seed-raised verbenas, in a wide range of colours (mauves, pinks, reds and white), for bedding or containers. Half-hardy annual. Height: 15–30 cm (6–12 in). Spread: 30–60 cm (1–2 ft).

▲ **Wallflower (Erysimum cheiri, syn. Cheiranthus cheiri)**

In late spring, wallflowers fill the garden with fragrance as well as colour. There are dwarf and tall varieties, mainly in shades of red, bronze, orange or yellow but also pastels. Height: 30–45 cm (1–1½ ft). Spread: 23–30 cm (9–12 in).

ANNUALS & BIENNIALS

JANUARY   page 18

- Sow under glass half-hardy annuals that are slow to mature.
- Guard seedlings against damping off.
- Prepare new flower beds in fine weather, leaving final raking and levelling until later.

FEBRUARY   page 36

- Continue early sowings of slow-maturing bedding and half-hardy annuals.
- Begin sowing annual climbers.
- Buy seedlings to prick out, especially those which need an early start. Take steps to prevent damping off.
- Prepare seed beds for sowing next month.
- Order young plants by post.

MARCH   page 56

- Complete sowing of annual climbers to allow maximum growing time.
- Continue to prepare seed beds.
- Remove cloches from overwintered hardy annuals and begin transplanting. Water thoroughly and protect from slugs.
- Sow tender bedding plants in heated propagator or on warm windowsill.
- Prick out seedlings from earlier sowings as soon as they produce their first true leaves.
- Sow hardy annuals in a cold frame or unheated greenhouse.

APRIL   page 90

- Continue to sow plants for bedding under

glass (*see* March, page 56).
- Prick out seedlings from earlier sowings providing shelter for the young plants.
- Begin to harden off young plants and overwintered cuttings.
- Start to sow hardy annuals directly into flowering positions.

MAY   page 122

- Sow fast-maturing and late-flowering annuals. Sow additonal plants to fill gaps in the border later in the year.
- Transplant overwintered annuals into final flowering positions.
- Feed seedlings and young plants.
- Clear spring bedding.
- In mild regions, plant out hardened off annuals when all danger of frost is past.
- Begin sowing spring biennials in rows.
- Thin out overcrowded annuals.
- Control pests.

JUNE   page 148

- Continue to sow fast-maturing summer annuals (*see* May, page 122).
- Continue to thin hardy annuals.
- Control weeds in beds and borders.
- Sow spring-flowering biennials.
- Continue to harden off and plant annuals.
- Deadhead plants, paying special attention to those in containers.

JULY   page 170

- Continue to water newly planted and

transplanted annuals regularly.
- Continue to sow biennials for spring-flowering and plant out those sown earlier.
- Deadhead to encourage repeat flowering.

AUGUST   page 194

- Continue deadheading, watering, feeding.
- Pinch out tips of wallflowers.
- Collect and store seed.
- Check for pests and diseases.

SEPTEMBER   page 212

- Plant out spring-flowering annuals and biennials in flowering positions to give plants time to establish before winter.
- Continue routine deadheading and watering. Remove displays spoilt by frost.
- Sow annuals to overwinter.

OCTOBER   page 234

- Finish sowing hardy annuals to overwinter as seedlings.
- Complete planting of spring-flowering annuals and biennials.

NOVEMBER   page 256

- Cover hardy annuals growing outdoors with cloches or horticultural fleece during cold spells.

DECEMBER   page 276

- Order seed from catalogues.

Border perennials

THESE VERSATILE PLANTS are not all herbaceous in the sense that they die down to the ground each year (bergenias are evergreen and ajugas almost so, for example), and the herbaceous border is only one of many potential homes for them. Some make excellent ground cover, most can be used in mixed borders with shrubs and even annuals, and a few can be used successfully in containers. The majority will bring a spectacular or subtle show of flowers to the garden.

▼ Achillea filipendulina

The summer flowers of this striking border plant retain their colour if cut and dried, but it will probably require staking. The variety illustrated is 'Cloth of Gold'. Height: 1.2 m (4 ft). Spread: 60 cm (2 ft).

▼ Ajuga reptans

It is the variegated forms of bugle that are usually grown. The one illustrated is 'Variegata', but there are varieties with leaves in shades of purple, red and bronze. Semi-evergreen. Height: 23 cm (9 in). Spread: 60 cm (2 ft).

▲ Acanthus mollis

Bear's breeches is an imposing border plant when in summer flower, and its deeply cut leaves are semi-evergreen. Height: 1.2 m (4 ft). Spread: 60 cm (2 ft).

▲ Agapanthus

African lilies vary in hardiness, so check which are suitable for your area. Flowers are usually blue and appear in late summer and early autumn. The variety illustrated is 'Midnight Blue'. Height: 90 cm (3 ft). Spread: 60 cm (2 ft).

▲ Alchemilla mollis

Lady's mantle is a multi-merit plant, with mid-summer flowers and foliage both attractive features. The hairy leaves are pleasing whenever they hold droplets of rain or dew. Height: 45 cm (1½ ft). Spread: 45 cm (1½ ft).

▼ **Anemone** x **hybrida** (syn. A. japonica)
Invaluable for early autumn flowering. Colours are mainly shades of pink or white, and there are singles and doubles. The variety illustrated is 'Honorine Jobert'. Good in shade. Height: 1.2–1.5 m (4–5 ft). Spread: 60 cm (2 ft).

▲ **Anthemis tinctoria**
Cheerful flowers for mid-summer, they bloom prolifically. The crinkled, fern-like leaves are evergreen. The variety illustrated is 'E. C. Buxton'. Height: 90 cm (3 ft). Spread: 60 cm (2 ft).

▼ **Aquilegia vulgaris**
Granny's bonnets come in shades of pink, crimson and purple, as well as the white illustrated. Flowering time is early summer. Height: 75 cm (2½ ft). Spread: 45–60 cm (1½–2 ft).

▼ **Astrantia maxima**
Masterwort flowers in summer and into autumn and prefers moist soil. A popular cut flower. Height: 60 cm (2 ft). Spread: 30 cm (1 ft).

▲ **Aster novi-belgii**
A form of compact Michaelmas daisy flowering in autumn. Colours are mainly shades of red, pink and blue. The variety illustrated is 'Little Red Boy'. Height: 45–120 cm (1½–4 ft). Spread: 60 cm (2 ft).

▲ **Astilbe** x **arendsii hybrids**
'Bressingham Beauty' is one of many invaluable astilbe hybrids. They come in shades of red, pink and cream. At their best in moist soil in partial shade, but they will tolerate most conditions, making them a useful border plant. Height: 60–90 cm (2–3 ft). Spread: 60–90 cm (2–3 ft).

▲ **Bergenia**
A useful evergreen, tolerant of shade and flowering in spring. Most have flowers in shades of red, pink or white. This one is 'Silberlicht'. Height: 30–60 cm (1–2 ft). Spread: 30–60 cm (1–2 ft).

▼ Centaurea montana

Cornflower-like blooms appear in early summer. There are white and pink forms. Easy to grow. Height: 45 cm (1½ ft). Spread: 60 cm (2 ft).

▲ Chrysanthemum maximum (syn. Leucanthemum x superbum)

The shasta daisy is easy to grow and has white single or double flowers throughout the summer. This variety is 'Snowcap'. Height: 75–90 cm (2½–3 ft). Spread: 60 cm (2 ft).

▼ Cimicifuga simplex

Eye-catching plants for moist soil and light shade. May need staking. The white fragrant flowers, produced in autumn, will create a pocket of interest in a dull spot. The variety illustrated is 'White Pearl'. Height: 1.2–1.8 m (4–6 ft). Spread: 60 cm (2 ft).

▲ Coreopsis verticillata

A sun-loving, easy and reliable border plant with bright golden flowers throughout the summer. Height: 45–60 cm (1½–2 ft). Spread: 30 cm (1 ft).

▲ Crocosmia hybrids

Although produced from a corm, these late summer and early autumn flowers in fiery colours are usually treated like other border perennials. This variety is 'Golden Fleece'. Height: 60–75 cm (2–2½ ft). Spread: 30–45 cm (1–1½ ft).

▲ Delphinium elatum hybrids

These traditional border plants need staking. They come mainly in shades of blue, but there are both yellow and white varieties. This is 'Lord Butler'. Height: 1.5–2.4 m (5–8 ft). Spread: 75–90 cm (2½–3 ft).

▼ Dicentra

Bleeding hearts are well worth growing, preferably in a sheltered position, for their ferny foliage and pink, red or white flowers in late spring and early summer. Height: 45–75 cm (1½–2½ ft). Spread: 45–60 cm (1½–2 ft).

▼ Doronicum cordatum
(syn. D. columnae)

This is one of several leopard's banes with yellow daisy flowers in spring. May flower again in autumn if deadheaded. They bring colour to the border early, and the flowers cut well too. Height: 75 cm (2½ ft). Spread: 60 cm (2 ft).

▲ Echinacea purpurea

The coneflower is an eye-catching plant at its best in mid and late summer. Reddish-purple is the usual colour for the ray petals, but there are also white varieties. Height: 1.2 m (4 ft). Spread: 45 cm (1½ ft).

▲ Echinops ritro

Globe thistles produce their drumstick thistle-like flower heads in mid and late summer, standing well clear of the prickly divided foliage. The flowers are good for cutting. Height: 1.2 m (4 ft). Spread: 75 cm (2½ ft).

▼ Erigeron

Fleabane hybrids come in shades of violet, pink and blue, of which 'Quakeress' (illustrated) is one. They make good front-of-border plants and flower in summer. Height: 45–60 cm (1½–2 ft). Spread: 60 cm (2 ft).

▲ Epimedium x youngianum

A spring-flowering ground cover which retains its leaves in winter. The variety illustrated is 'Roseum', but there is also an attractive white variety ('Niveum'). Height: 23 cm (9 in). Spread: 30 cm (1 ft).

▲ Eryngium bourgatii

One of the sea hollies, this striking border plant produces its spiky-looking 'thistle' flowers in mid and late summer, well above the grey-green foliage. The variety illustrated is 'Oxford Blue'. Height: 60 cm (2 ft). Spread: 45 cm (1½ ft).

▼ Geranium ibericum

Herbaceous plant which blooms through most of summer. Height: 60 cm (2 ft). Spread: 60 cm (2 ft).

▲ Geum (chiloense hybrid)

Geums make good ground cover for a sunny border. Flowers mainly in shades of red, orange or yellow. 'Mrs J. Bradshaw' is one of the best. Height: 75 cm (2½ ft). Spread: 45 cm (1½ ft).

▲ Euphorbia griffithii

The variety illustrated is 'Fireglow'. Euphorbias are popular garden plants that flower in early summer. Their colour comes from the red bracts that surround the true flowers Height: 90 cm (3 ft). Spread: 45 cm (1½ ft).

▲ Helleborus orientalis

Lenten roses bloom in winter or spring, in purple, pink and white. Best in moist shade. Height: 45 cm (1½ ft). Spread: 45 cm (1½ ft).

▲ Gypsophila paniculata

The airy sprays of white flowers are equally useful in the border or as cut flowers. The variety illustrated is the popular 'Bristol Fairy', but there are also pink varieties as well as other whites. Height: 60–75 cm (2–2½ ft). Spread: 75 cm (2½ ft).

▲ Helenium autumnale

Sneezeweed is a flower of late summer and early autumn, just when the border needs a boost. There are hybrids in shades of orange and red, but yellow is the basic colour. Height: 1.2–1.5 m (4–5 ft). Spread: 60–75 cm (2–2½ ft).

▲ Hemerocallis hybrids

Daylilies flower for most of summer. Many varieties in yellows, pinks and oranges; this is 'Pink Damask'. Height: 75–90 cm (2½–3 ft). Spread: 75 cm (2½ ft).

▼ Hosta undulata var. albomarginata

(syn. H. 'Thomas Hogg')

Invaluable foliage plants for moist shade. Spires of mauvish flowers in summer. Height: 75 cm (2½ ft). Spread: 90 cm (3 ft).

▲ Houttuynia cordata 'Chameleon'

A waterside plant that will also grow in a moist border. Cream bracts in spring. Height: 30 cm (1 ft). Spread: 60 cm (2 ft).

▼ Kniphofia

Red hot pokers vary considerably in height and flowering period, and colours can be red, orange or yellow, or combinations of these. Height: 60–150 cm (2–5 ft). Spread: 45–90 cm (1½–3 ft).

▼ Liatris spicata

Gay feathers is unusual in having spikes that open from the top down. Flowering in late summer and early autumn, it flourishes in a sunny spot. There is also a white form. Height: 60 cm (2 ft). Spread: 30 cm (1 ft).

▼ Monarda didyma

Bergamot attracts bees and butterflies. It may be grown in herb gardens or in borders. There are varieties in shades of pink, red, violet and purple; this is 'Prairie Glow'. Height: 1.2 m (4 ft). Spread: 45 cm (1½ ft).

▲ Liriope muscari

Lilyturf is a tough spreading plant valued for its violet flowers in autumn. Height: 30 cm (1 ft). Spread: 45 cm (1½ ft).

▲ Lysimachia nummularia 'Aurea'

Creeping Jenny is a prostrate plant useful as summer ground cover or as a trailer for the edge of a raised bed. This golden form is brighter than the green species, but both have yellow flowers over a long period in summer. Height: 5 cm (2 in). Spread: 60 cm (2 ft).

▲ Nepeta gigantea

Catmint is a good border plant for early summer colour and its flowers attract bees to your garden. N. x faassenii and N. mussinii (N. racemosa) are also good varieties. Dislikes winter wet. Height: 45–60 cm (1½–2 ft). Spread: 60 cm (2 ft).

▼ Paeonia lactiflora

Peonies come in many varieties, in reds, pinks and white. There are single, double and semi-double flowers, opening in early summer. This is 'Festiva Maxima'. All require deep rich soil and resent disturbance. Height: 90–120 cm (3–4 ft). Spread: 90 cm (3 ft).

▲ Papaver

The Oriental poppy (P. orientale) and its hybrids (such as 'Fireball', the one illustrated) make a superb show in early summer with huge blooms in red, pink or white. Height: 60–90 cm (2–3 ft). Spread: 60–90 cm (2–3 ft).

▼ Polygonum affine
(syn. Persicaria affinis)

A spreading evergreen perennial with poker-like flowers in late summer and early autumn. The leaves usually turn bronze in winter. Height: 15–30 cm (6–12 in). Spread: 45 cm (1½ ft).

▲ Pulmonaria officinalis

Lungworts flower in spring, most with blue or pink, sometimes white flowers, some with spotted leaves. Semi-evergreen. Shade tolerant and ground covering. Height: 30 cm (1 ft). Spread: 45–60 cm (1½–2 ft).

▲ Penstemon

There are dozens of good varieties in shades of red, pink, purple and white (the one illustrated is 'Rich Ruby'), but they may require winter protection in cold areas. Height: 45–60 cm (1½–2 ft). Spread: 45–60 cm (1½–2 ft).

▲ Phlox paniculata

There are many excellent varieties, mostly with bright flower heads in mid and late summer, in pinks, reds and lavenders. 'Norah Leigh' (illustrated) is prized for its variegated foliage. Height: 90 cm (3 ft). Spread: 60 cm (2 ft).

▲ Pyrethrum coccineum
(syn. Tanacetum coccineum)
Excellent plant for a sunny border and a source of cut flowers. Pyrethrums flower in late spring and early summer. The variety illustrated is 'Brenda'. Height: 60 cm (2 ft). Spread: 45–60 cm (1½–2 ft).

▲ Rodgersia aesculifolia
Can be grown in an herbaceous border, but best in moist ground and where they have space to spread. The pinkish-white flowers in mid-summer are less of a feature than the bold foliage. Height: 90 cm (3 ft). Spread: 90 cm (3 ft).

▲ Rudbeckia fulgida
Commonly called black-eyed Susan, this plant will bring a border alive in late summer and early autumn. The variety illustrated is 'Goldsturm'. Double-flowered varieties are also available. Height: 75 cm (2½ ft). Spread: 45–60 cm (1½–2 ft).

▲ Salvia nemorosa
You might find some of these listed as S. x superba *varieties (the one illustrated is 'East Friesland' or 'Ostfriesland'). The flowers are borne profusely in mid and late summer. Height: 60–75 cm (2–2½ ft). Spread: 45–60 cm (1½–2 ft).*

▲ Scabiosa caucasica
A classic border perennial, and popular for cutting too. It flowers for most of summer. 'Clive Greaves' (illustrated) is one of the best varieties. Suits limy soils. Height: 60 cm (2 ft). Spread: 60 cm (2 ft).

▲ Schizostylis coccinea
The kaffir lily is at its best in mid-autumn. There are several good varieties, in shades of red or pink. Needs sun and a moist soil. Height: 60 cm (2 ft). Spread: 30 cm (1 ft).

▲ Sedum spectabile

The ice plant flowers in early and mid autumn, when it attracts bees and butterflies. Best in an open position, it comes in shades of pink and crimson. This is 'September Glow'. Height: 45 cm (1½ ft). Spread: 45 cm (1½ ft).

▲ Solidago

Most varieties of golden rod flower in early and mid autumn, when colour is always appreciated. The variety illustrated is 'Golden Baby'. Height: 60–90 cm (2–3 ft). Spread: 45–60 cm (1½–2 ft).

▼ Stachys byzantina

Although grown primarily for its white, woolly foliage, the mauve-pink flowers in summer are a bonus. An excellent front-of-border plant. Height: 30 cm (1 ft). Spread: 60 cm (2 ft).

▼ Tradescantia

Most of those grown as border plants are varieties or hybrids of T. x andersoniana *or* T. virginiana. *They bloom for most of the summer and will tolerate shade. Height: 60 cm (2 ft). Spread: 45 cm (1½ ft).*

▼ Verbascum

Many of the verbascums grown in gardens, like 'Helen Johnson' illustrated here, are hybrids. Most bear yellow, pink or apricot flowers in mid and late summer, and have grey foliage that is attractive for the whole summer. Height: 90–120 cm (3–4 ft). Spread: 45–60 cm (1½–2 ft).

BORDER PERENNIALS

JANUARY   page 18

- Clear borders of weeds and debris.
- Dig over soil that was left unturned earlier and remove weeds.
- Sow seeds of hardy perennials.
- Protect vulnerable plants from frost and wind damage.

FEBRUARY   page 36

- Begin to feed plants in established borders.
- Continue to sow seeds of hardy perennials.
- Protect vulnerable plants from frost and wind damage.

MARCH   page 57

- Plan replacements for gaps in borders.
- Buy new plants.
- Control weeds, pests and diseases.
- Cut back overhanging trees and shrubs which will cast shade, and rob the soil of nutrients and moisture.
- Divide congested clumps of perennials.
- Plant out cuttings and seedlings after hardening off.

APRIL   page 90

- Plant hardy perennials if weather conditions are suitable.
- Plant out hardened off cuttings and seedlings and protect from frost.
- Stake plants to avoid wind damage.

- Sow annuals, and plant bulbs in pots, for use in the border later in the year.

MAY   page 124

- Continue to plant perennials in the border, watering well in dry weather.
- Fill spaces in borders between perennials with annuals, pots of bulbs and foliage plants in containers.
- Take basal cuttings from plants such as lupins and delphiniums.

JUNE   page 148

- Cut back and deadhead early-flowering plants and feed them.
- Collect seed from plants required for propagating.
- Check stakes around plants.
- Check for pests, mildew and other diseases.
- Continue planting container-grown plants, and established cuttings and seedlings if weather is not too dry.
- Fill gaps in borders and cut back over-vigorous plants.
- Take softwood and semi-ripe cuttings.
- Divide early-flowering plants such as primulas.
- Pot up rooted basal cuttings taken last month and keep well watered.

JULY   page 170

- Plan new beds and begin ground preparation.

- Collect and sow or store seeds from selected plants.
- Cut back flowered stems, remove stakes.
- Water during dry weather, especially if you garden on light soil.
- Feed long-flowering and late perennials.
- Plant out container-grown plants providing conditions are suitable. Water thoroughly and feed.
- Continue to take softwood and semi-ripe cuttings of suitable plants.

AUGUST   page 194

- Clear and dig borders to be replanted.
- Plan new borders for autumn planting.
- Place new plants purchased this month, which are not fully hardy, in a sheltered spot for planting out next spring.
- Take stem cuttings of plants such as penstemons.
- Feed plants, after cutting back old stems, to encourage new growth.
- Deadhead plants or collect seeds if required (see July, page 170).

SEPTEMBER page 212

- Buy new plants from nurseries and garden centres for autumn planting.
- Finish preparing ground and plant hardy perennials. Water in well.
- Plant spring bulbs in the border for early colour next year.
- Protect tender or young plants if frost is forecast.
- Deadhead to keep borders tidy and to

prolong flowering unless you want to collect seeds. Dry seeds before storing.

OCTOBER   page 234

- Cut back old foliage, unless needed as protection, and tidy borders.
- Lift and store tender tubers, bulbs etc.
- Continue to clear ground for planting.
- Top dress established borders.
- Plant hardy perennials if conditions are suitable (see September, page 212).
- Divide and replant congested or weed-infested clumps.
- Protect plants against winter damage.

NOVEMBER   page 256

- Top dress established borders.
- Remove stakes, cut back dying foliage and dig out perennial weeds. Leave ground bare for frost to kill pests.
- Plant out or transplant hardy plants, providing conditions are suitable (see September, page 212).
- Dig over ground for new beds. Remove weeds and add organic material.

DECEMBER   page 276

- Continue to dig and clear ground, adding compost or manure.
- Prune back overhanging branches of trees and shrubs.
- Take root cuttings of plants such as phlox and keep in a cold frame or greenhouse.
- Order seeds and plants for next spring.

Bulbs, corms & tubers

DEPENDABLE AND EASY, bulbs, corms and tubers can be relied upon for a good display provided you buy them from a reputable source. Many will continue to flower for many years with just minimal attention, but others may split into smaller bulbs which may take a season or two to reach flowering size again – when the display will then be more impressive than ever. Frost-tender types have to be lifted in autumn and stored indoors for the winter.

▼ Anemone blanda

A spring-flowering carpeter useful for naturalising, and ideal for the rock garden. Blue is the dominant colour, but there are pinks, magentas and whites. Fern-like divided foliage. Height: 10 cm (4 in). Spread: 15 cm (6 in).

▼ Chionodoxa luciliae

Very easy to grow, these spring-flowering bulbs will multiply readily. They can be naturalised in short grass or interplanted with other low-growing plants. There are also pink and white varieties. Height: 10 cm (4 in). Spread: 8 cm (3 in).

▼ Colchicum autumnale

The flowers resemble large crocuses, but they flower in autumn and the leaves appear separately in spring. There are whites and doubles too. Height in flower: 10 cm (4 in), leaves to 25 cm (10 in). Spread: 15 cm (6 in).

▼ Crinum x powellii

A late-flowering bulb for late summer and early autumn interest. The variety shown is white, but the usual colour is pink. Requires a warm, sheltered position. Height: 60–90 cm (2–3 ft). Spread: 45–60 cm (1½–2 ft).

▲ Allium christophii
(syn. A. albopilosum)
Large, stunning ball-shaped flower heads about 23 cm (9 in) across in early summer. Ideal for the front of an herbaceous border. Can be cut for indoor decoration. Height: 45 cm (1½ ft). Spread: 30 cm (1 ft).

▲ Amaryllis belladonna
In a sheltered spot the Jersey lily will bring colour to the herbaceous border in late summer and into autumn. Do not confuse it with the tender so-called amaryllis (hippeastrum). Height: 60–90 cm (2–3 ft). Spread: 60–75 cm (2–2½ ft).

▼ Crocus, large-flowered

Large-flowered hybrid crocuses, sometimes called Dutch crocuses, are an essential part of spring. You can buy separate colours as well as mixtures. Ideal for naturalising as well as planting in borders. Height: 10 cm (4 in). Spread: 5 cm (2 in).

▲ Crocus chrysanthus

There are many varieties of these small-flowered spring crocuses, mainly in shades of blue, yellow, purple, and white. They are ideal for a rock garden. Height: 8 cm (3 in). Spread: 5 cm (2 in).

▼ Cyclamen coum

Very hardy, flowering in mid and late winter, with about 12 mm (½ in) long red, pink or white flowers; deep carmine is typical. Foliage has silvery markings.
Height: 4 cm (1½ in).
Spread: 15 cm (6 in).

▲ Eranthis hyemalis

The winter aconite, best if left undisturbed to naturalise; flowers between mid-winter and early spring.
Height: 8–10 cm (3–4 in). Spread: 15 cm (6 in).

▲ Fritillaria imperialis

These majestic plants are eye-catching in a border in spring. The usual colour is orange-red, but there are several varieties, including the yellow 'Maxima Lutea'.
Height: 1.2–1.5 m (4–5 ft).
Spread: 60–75 cm (2–2½ ft).

▲ Fritillaria meleagris

The curious flowers in late spring or early summer seldom fail to attract attention. There are named varieties, but they are usually sold as mixtures. Height: 30 cm (1 ft). Spread: 15 cm (6 in).

▲ Galanthus nivalis

Snowdrops need no introduction, but there are numerous varieties, some with larger flowers, a few double. Best left undisturbed to make large clumps. Height: 10 cm (4 in). Spread: 8 cm (3 in).

▲ Galtonia candicans

The summer hyacinth is a distinctive plant for the border, especially if allowed to form a large clump. Lift the bulbs in autumn, however, where frosts penetrate deeply. Height: 1.2 m (4 ft). Spread: 30 cm (1 ft).

▼ **Ipheion uniflorum**

The spring starflower blooms over several weeks in mid and late spring, and looks good in a rock garden or at the front of a border. The species has paler blue flowers than the variety illustrated. Height: 15 cm (6 in). Spread: 10 cm (4 in).

▲ **Gladiolus hybrids**

Gladioli are popular cut flowers, but they are also useful border plants, especially the small-flowered varieties. Height: 1–1.2 m (3–4 ft). Spread: 23–30 cm (9–12 in).

▲ **Hyacinthus orientalis**

This is the common hyacinth popular in bowls indoors. Hyacinths also make an excellent outdoor display too. Height: 23 cm (9 in). Spread: 15 cm (6 in).

▲ **Leucojum vernum**

The spring snowflake resembles a snowdrop at first glance, but the nodding flowers are more bell-like and larger. They usually appear in early spring. Height: 20 cm (8 in). Spread: 15 cm (6 in).

▲ **Muscari armeniacum**

Grape hyacinths are invaluable spring-flowering bulbs that multiply rapidly if left undisturbed. They make an attractive spring edging and suit rock gardens. Height: 23 cm (9 in). Spread: 15 cm (6 in).

▲ **Narcissus, large-cupped daffodil**

There are hundreds of varieties in many shades of yellow, orange, white, even pink, and they can be just as attractive as those with longer trumpets. Best planted in clumps. Height: 30–45 cm (1–1½ ft). Spread: 30 cm (1 ft).

▲ **Narcissus, double daffodil**

Double varieties add interest to any collection of daffodils, and they are available in all the usual daffodil colours. Different varieties vary in their petal formation. Height: 30–45 cm (1–1½ ft). Spread: 30 cm (1 ft).

▼ Narcissus bulbocodium

The hoop petticoat daffodil is one of the daintiest species, suitable for the rock garden or naturalising in short grass. Height: 15 cm (6 in). Spread: 10 cm (4 in).

▲ Nerine bowdenii

An invaluable plant for late colour as it flowers in autumn. It requires a warm, sheltered position preferably by a wall. Height: 60 cm (2 ft). Spread: 30 cm (1 ft).

▲ Scilla sibirica

An easy-to-grow spring-flowering bulb, suitable for the rock garden, in clumps at the front of a border, or in containers. Height: 15 cm (6 in). Spread: 10 cm (4 in).

▲ Sternbergia lutea

These crocus-like flowers bloom in early and mid autumn. Grow in the rock garden or in a drift at the front of a border. Height: 15 cm (6 in). Spread: 10 cm (4 in).

▲ Tigridia pavonia

The distinctive tiger flower seldom has a mass of flowers open at once, but even a single bloom is striking. Colours include reds, yellows, pinks and white. Flowers from mid summer to early autumn. Height: 45 cm (1½ ft). Spread: 23 cm (9 in).

▼ Ornithogalum thyrsoides

Chincherinchees are popular cut flowers from the florist, but they also make excellent garden plants, flowering in summer. Lift the bulbs for the winter. Height: 30–60 cm (1–2 ft). Spread: 23 cm (9 in).

▲ Tulip, Darwin hybrid

These have some of the largest of all tulip flowers, and bloom at the end of April. Although often grown as a mixture, there are individual varieties in different colours and combinations of colours. Height: 45–60 cm (1½–2 ft). Spread: 23 cm (9 in).

▼ Tulipa tarda

This is one of the easiest and most reliable tulip species to grow, and it will usually multiply freely if left undisturbed. The yellow and white flowers are star-like and make a bright splash in early spring. Height: 13 cm (5 in). Spread: 15 cm (6 in).

◄ Tulip, greigii hybrid

The greigii hybrids flower in April and May. The flowers open almost flat in the sun and often there is a striking contrasting centre. Foliage streaked with purple. Height: 15–30 cm (6–12 in). Spread: 23 cm (9 in).

JANUARY	page 19

- Order summer-flowering bulbs and tubers. Unpack immediately on arrival, and store in a dry, frost-free place.
- Check on stored bulbs, corms and tubers and remove any that are soft or diseased.
- Continue to bring forced bulbs in bowls and pots into the warmth and light (*see* November, page 256).
- Water hippeastrums planted last month (*see* December, page 276).

FEBRUARY	page 36

- Prepare soil for planting gladioli, if not already done.
- Sprout gladiolus corms for early flowers.
- Check stored bulbs, corms and tubers and remove any that are soft or diseased.
- Plant begonia tubers.
- Continue to bring forced bulbs into warmth as they come into bud.
- Keep hippeastrums moist and feed occasionally.
- Protect dwarf winter-flowering irises from frost.
- Order or buy summer-flowering bulbs and corms, if not already done.

MARCH	page 58

- Visit flower shows and gardens to see many bulbs at their best.
- Plant hippeastrums for spring flowering.
- Deadhead daffodils as they fade.
- Plant out bulbs grown for indoor use

BULBS, CORMS & TUBERS

which have finished flowering.
- Lift and divide snowdrops and winter aconites.
- Plant 'St Brigid' and 'De Caen' anemones for flowering during the summer.
- Plant lilies in their final positions (*see* Lilies, page 73).
- Divide canna roots and pot up.
- Pot up begonia tubers if not done last month.
- Plant gladiolus corms.

APRIL   page 91

- Remove faded flower heads from any early-flowering bulbs.
- Plant summer-flowering bulbs, such as acidanthera and tigridia.
- Regularly hoe the soil between the emerging shoots of gladioli and continue planting corms.
- Plant out arum lilies in very mild areas (*see* May, page 125).
- Thin shoots on begonias. Take cuttings.
- Water hippeastrums and keep warm.
- Pot up tuberoses and gloriosas for flowering under glass.

MAY   page 124

- Remove faded flowers from daffodils, hyacinths and tulips.
- Lift spring-flowering bulbs if you need the space, and heel in elsewhere.
- Clean bulbs of early tulips and daffodils and store in shallow trays.
- Water thoroughly all plants in dry spells

and feed summer-flowering bulbs.
- Allow hippeastrum foliage to die back after flowering and store bulbs in a cool place until next spring.
- Plant crinum bulbs in a south-facing border or in tubs.
- Plant arum lilies in a pool or open ground.
- Complete planting of gladiolus corms.
- Gradually reduce watering of dwarf alpine bulbs under glass.
- Plant out tubers of *Tropaeolum speciosum* and *T. tuberosum* (*see* Climbers & wall shrubs, page 126).

JUNE   page 149

- Continue to lift spring bulbs as soon as their foliage has died back; dry and store (*see* July, page 171).
- Plant 'De Caen' anemones for autumn and winter flowering.
- Bring greenhouse arum lilies out for their summer rest.
- Plant out rooted stem cuttings of begonias and water freely.
- Water gladioli thoroughly in dry weather.

JULY   page 171

- Lift and divide spring-flowering bulbs when foliage has turned yellow. Spread out bulbs in shallow boxes and store in a well-ventilated shed.
- Treat daffodil pests, such as eelworms and narcissus flies.
- Remove embryo seed pods from begonias when flower buds appear.

- Plant autumn-flowering bulbs in well-prepared soil and feed with a fertiliser containing potash.
- Control thrips on gladioli.
- Order spring-flowering bulbs to plant in the autumn.

AUGUST   page 194

- Order spring-flowering bulbs if not already done.
- Plant daffodil bulbs.
- Plant prepared hyacinths and narcissi in bowls for flowering indoors (*see* September, page 214).
- Cut gladiolus flower spikes regularly, leaving at least four leaves on each plant.
- Control thrips on gladioli.
- Continue to remove embryo seed pods from begonias (*see* July, page 172).

SEPTEMBER   page 213

- Plant spring-flowering bulbs, giving priority to daffodils. Remember to plant up containers as well as putting bulbs in borders and beds.
- Repot arum lilies for winter flowering under glass.
- Cut gladioli as required.

OCTOBER   page 235

- Plant tulips and hyacinths and complete planting of other bulbs for spring flowering.
- Protect autumn-flowering bulbs if weather is frosty or very wet.

- Lift and store summer-flowering corms, *Tropaeolum* tubers and half-hardy summer-flowering bulbs.
- Treat gladiolus corms that may be harbouring thrips. Discard any diseased corms.
- Check that bulbs in pots, being forced for winter display, are not drying out.
- Finish repotting winter-flowering arum lilies (*see* September, page 214).
- Stop watering cannas to allow them to dry off before storing.

NOVEMBER   page 256

- Prepare next year's planting site for gladioli.
- Complete planting tulips and hyacinths (*see* October, page 235).
- Check pots of forced bulbs, water if necessary and bring earliest bulbs starting to sprout into the warmth.
- Lift begonia tubers, dry them off and store in a cool, frost-free place.
- Clean and store bulbs and corms, if not already done, and check for pests and diseases (*see* October, page 235).

DECEMBER   page 276

- Check stored bulbs and corms for disease (*see* October, page 235).
- Continue to bring sprouted forced bulbs in bowls into the warmth and light (*see* November, page 256).
- Plant hippeastrums for early spring, and water sparingly. Restart stored hippeastrums in the same way.

Carnations & pinks

BEAUTY AND FRAGRANCE are characteristic of many carnations and pinks, though not all of them have a strong scent. They are traditional cottage-garden plants, though modern varieties of pinks have made them more versatile all-round garden plants, given a sunny, well-drained spot and a slightly alkaline soil.

Only perennial types suitable for the border are illustrated here. There are also rock-garden types and annuals.

◀ **Dianthus 'Mrs Sinkins'**
A traditional garden pink, sometimes described as one of the Old World garden pinks, and perhaps the best known. It was introduced in 1868, and its strong scent has probably helped to keep it in cultivation. Height: 25 cm (10 in). Spread: 30 cm (1 ft).

▲ **Dianthus 'Doris'**
This is the most famous of the Allwoodii pinks, a race of hardy garden pinks bred by crossing a perpetual-flowering carnation with an old-fashioned pink. They flower through the summer and into autumn. Height: 30 cm (1 ft). Spread: 30 cm (1 ft).

▲ **Dianthus 'Gran's Favourite'**
This variety has all the appearance of the old-fashioned laced pinks, but it was introduced in the 1960s. This is an outstanding variety that combines a strong scent with considerable eye-appeal. Height: 45 cm (1½ ft). Spread: 30 cm (1 ft).

▲ **Dianthus 'Laced Monarch'**
Another variety with the appearance of an old-fashioned pink, but it was introduced in 1972. It has an attractive scent typical of these plants and is very free-flowering. Attractive blue-grey foliage. Height: 45 cm (1½ ft). Spread: 30 cm (1 ft).

▲ **Dianthus 'Hazel Ruth'**
This is one of the best border carnations, but as with all dianthus of this type you should be prepared to stake them to keep the stems upright and the flowers unblemished. Height: 45–60 cm (1½–2 ft). Spread: 30 cm (1 ft).

▲ **Dianthus 'Houndspool Ruby'**
The most famous of the Allwoodii pinks, 'Doris', has spawned many sports (colour variations), and this is one of them. It was noticed and selected over 20 years ago. Height: 30 cm (1 ft). Spread: 30 cm (1 ft).

▲ Dianthus 'Glorious'

Another glorious pink of the Allwoodii type. It flowers throughout the summer, sometimes starting in late spring and continuing into autumn. It has a pleasant scent typical of this type of pink. Height: 30 cm (1 ft). Spread: 30 cm (1 ft).

▲ Dianthus 'Laced Joy'

One of the most popular of the laced pinks. Though introduced in the 1940s, it gives the impression of an old-fashioned, cottage-garden plant. It flowers prolifically, but can be rather straggly without support. Height: 45 cm (1½ ft). Spread: 30 cm (1 ft).

CARNATIONS & PINKS

JANUARY   page 19

- Check soil pH and improve poor drainage.
- Order seeds and plants for spring.
- Sow seeds of annual carnations.

Perpetual-flowering:
- Maintain healthy greenhouse conditions.
- Propagate plants by cuttings and seeds.
- Order new plants for spring planting.

FEBRUARY   page 37

- Continue to sow annual carnations.

Perpetual-flowering:
- Stop young rooted cuttings.
- Continue to take cuttings and sow seed.

MARCH   page 60

- Plant out border carnations and pinks.
- Stop pinks as necessary.
- Control pests and diseases.
- Sow seeds and prick out seedlings.

Perpetual-flowering:
- Maintain healthy greenhouse conditions.
- Pot up and stop rooted cuttings.
- Order new plants for April delivery.

APRIL   page 92

- Continue to plant carnations and pinks.
- Stake tall-growing pinks.
- Watch for slugs, other pests, and diseases.
- Continue to sow and pot up under glass.

Perpetual-flowering:
- Check growing conditions for new plants.
- Pot on young plants as they grow.

MAY   page 125

- Plant out bedding dianthus in mild areas.

Perpetual-flowering:
- Continue to pot on young plants.

JUNE   page 150

- Disbud border carnations for larger blooms.
- Plant out dianthus and border carnations.
- Take cuttings of carnations and pinks.

Perpetual-flowering:
- Continue to pot on young plants.
- Shade glass and damp down.
- Continue to stop plants.
- Cut blooms and disbud.

JULY   page 173

- Propagate border carnations by layering from established plants.
- Disbud, deadhead and cut back leggy plants to encourage flowering.
- Take cuttings of pinks and harden off those which have rooted.

Perpetual-flowering:
- Continue to stop plants.
- Cut flowers and disbud stems.

AUGUST   page 195

- Prepare beds for autumn planting.
- Continue to layer border carnations.
- Take final cuttings from pinks.

- Stop sideshoots as necessary.
- Sow seeds under glass.

Perpetual-flowering:
- Keep greenhouse well ventilated.

SEPTEMBER   page 214

- Plant out well-grown June cuttings.
- Stop shoots to create bushy plants.
- Pot up rooted carnation layers.
- Check on layers and sever rooted ones.
- Prepare beds for planting.

Perpetual-flowering:
- Disbud flower stems for larger blooms.
- Cut first flowers from young plants.

OCTOBER   page 236

- Continue to plant carnations and pinks.
- Pick blooms and continue to stop.
- Prepare beds for spring planting.
- Pot up well-rooted layers of carnations.

Perpetual-flowering:
- Control temperature and ventilate.
- Water and feed sparingly. Disbud stems.
- Check for pests and diseases.

NOVEMBER   page 256

- Continue planting and improve soil.

Perpetual-flowering:
- Maintain frost-free conditions.
- Check for pests and diseases.

DECEMBER   page 276

Perpetual-flowering:
- Take cuttings and keep under glass.
- Maintain frost-free conditions.

Chrysanthemums

THESE INVALUABLE PLANTS for autumn displays are now more correctly called dendranthemas, though they will probably continue to be called chrysanthemums for some time and that is how you will usually find them listed in specialist catalogues. Although the large-flowered show varieties are grown by enthusiasts, there are many excellent chrysanthemums for general garden display. Those illustrated show how versatile these plants are and how much the flowers vary both in shape and colour.

▲ Dendranthema 'My Love'

*Large-flowered single varieties like this are for greenhouse flowering rather than garden decoration. They are useful in mixed flower arrangements.
Height: 1.2 m (4 ft).
Spread: 45 cm (1½ ft).*

▼ Dendranthema 'Christmas Wine'

*Late varieties like this large-flowered intermediate chrysanthemum should be taken into a greenhouse in autumn for protection from the weather.
Height: 1.2 m (4 ft). Spread: 75 cm (2½ ft).*

▲ Dendranthema 'Ringdove'

*Charm varieties, with their masses of small flowers, are for growing in pots, and are 'stopped' when about 15 cm (6 in) tall to induce a well-branched plant covered with bloom like this.
Height: 30–45 cm (1–1½ ft). Spread: 30–60 cm (1–2 ft).*

▲ Dendranthema 'Cassandra'

*Classed as a medium-flowered intermediate variety, this is another example normally grown in the greenhouse. Varieties like this are particularly favoured as cut flowers for the home. Height: 1.2 m (4 ft).
Spread: 60 cm (2 ft).*

▲ Dendranthema 'Dorridge King'

*The medium-flowered reflexed varieties are preferred by some to the more formal-looking incurved varieties. These are greenhouse varieties, but they make excellent cut flowers. Height: 1.2 m (4 ft).
Spread: 60 cm (2 ft).*

▲ Dendranthema 'Pink Gin'

Not yet fully open in this picture, this is a reflexed spray variety for flowering under glass. Spray varieties produce more flowers than disbudded types, and are particularly useful for cutting.
Height: 1.2 m (4 ft). Spread: 60 cm (2 ft).

▲ Dendranthema 'Debonair'

This one is typical of the low-growing outdoor bedding chrysanthemums, useful for a late bedding display or for tubs and troughs, or even suitable for windowboxes.
Height: 30–60 cm (1–2 ft). Spread: 30–45 cm (1–1½ ft).

▼ Dendranthema 'Mei-Kyo'

A hardy semi-pom that flowers late, sometimes into late autumn, and can be left undisturbed like ordinary herbaceous plants to make a large clump.
Height: 60–75 cm (2–2½ ft). Spread: 60–75 cm (2–2½ ft).

▲ Dendranthema 'Bronze Fairy'

The early-flowering outdoor pompons can be in bloom in late summer, but are often at their best in early autumn. Although individual flowers are small, there are plenty of them. Height: 30–60 cm (1–2 ft). Spread: 45 cm (1½ ft).

▲ Dendranthema 'Clara Curtis'

This old favourite is one of the spray varieties deriving from D. rubellum, *which are hardy and are left in a border like most other herbaceous border plants.*
Height: 75 cm (2½ ft). Spread: 45 cm (1½ ft).

▲ Dendranthema 'Crimson Yvonne Arnaud'

This medium-flowered reflexed variety is an outdoor type that will normally flower in early autumn. This type is equally appealing for garden decoration or as a cut flower.
Height: 1.2 m (4 ft). Spread: 60 cm (2 ft).

▼ Dendranthema 'Brown Eyes'

One of the Korean chrysanthemums, which are hardy enough to be left in the border in most areas. They make an eye-catching and colourful autumn display in an herbaceous or mixed border. Height: 60 cm (2 ft). Spread: 60 cm (2 ft).

▲ Dendranthema 'Max Riley'

Outdoor medium-flowered incurved varieties like this can be grown to a high exhibition standard by specialist growers who protect them from the weather. They make impressive cut flowers.
Height: 1.2 m (4 ft). Spread: 60 cm (2 ft).

▲ Dendranthema 'Pennine Jade'

Single outdoor spray varieties are easy to grow and make impressive garden plants for autumn flowering in the border. They do not require disbudding so they are trouble free to grow.
Height: 1.2 m (4 ft). Spread: 60 cm (2 ft).

▲ Dendranthema 'White Allouise'

A medium-flowered intermediate variety bred to bloom outdoors, and one of several with the suffix Allouise. These produce quality flowers if grown with care, but they are also excellent for cutting. Height: 1.2 m (4 ft). Spread: 60 cm (2 ft).

▶ Dendranthema 'Orno'

Spray pompons are most effective in a massed display in a border, where the huge quantities of flowers make up for their small size. They are also very undemanding and easy to grow, and require no 'stopping' or disbudding. Height: 1.2 m (4 ft). Spread: 45 cm (1½ ft).

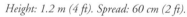

◀ Dendranthema 'Ginger'

This variety does not fall into any of the main classifications, and may be described as a bedding chrysanthemum. It is an outdoor variety, suitable for the front of a border or a large container. Height: 30–60 cm (1–2 ft). Spread: 30 cm (1 ft).

CHRYSANTHEMUMS

JANUARY   page 19

● Order new plants.

Early-flowering (garden):
● Examine plants left in the ground over winter, refirming if necessary.
● Ensure dormant clumps overwintering in a cold frame get sufficient ventilation.
● Continue to prepare beds and borders.

Late-flowering (greenhouse):
● Check for signs of leaf miners and aphids.
● Take cuttings of large exhibition varieties and very late-flowering varieties.
● Pot up any rooted cuttings.

FEBRUARY   page 37

Early-flowering (garden):
● Check on overwintering plants.
● Control weeds and slugs.

Late-flowering (greenhouse):
● Begin to propagate all greenhouse varieties if ready (*see* March, page 61).
● Ensure cuttings are kept moist.
● Pot up cuttings taken last month as they root.

MARCH   page 61

● Take cuttings of most varieties.
● Pot on cuttings when roots have formed.

Early-flowering (garden):
● Continue to prepare beds and borders.
● Pot up plants overwintered under cover, or bed out into cold frames.

Late-flowering (greenhouse):
● Move pots from greenhouse to cold frame.

Very late-flowering:
● Take cuttings to provide suitable shoots for later propagation.

APRIL   page 93

● Start to buy new plants this month.
● Harden off plants.
● Control pests and diseases. Water.
● Stop varieties which require it.

Early-flowering (garden):
● Rake fertiliser into planting sites.

Late-flowering (greenhouse):
● In mild areas, move well-developed plants out to prepared standing ground.
● Continue to pot up cuttings taken last month, once they have rooted.

Very late-flowering:
● Take basal cuttings.

MAY   page 125

● Stop varieties which require it.
● Set up supports before plants grow too tall.

Early-flowering (garden):
● Plant out once danger of frost has passed.
● Check on overwintered plants, discarding damaged stools, and apply fertiliser.
● Take cuttings.

Late-flowering (greenhouse):
● Pot on, moving outside once established.
● Look after stock plants.

JUNE   page 150

● Water weekly and spray with water after hot, sunny days.

● Stop varieties which require it.

Early-flowering (garden):
● Hoe in nitrogenous fertiliser.

Late-flowering (greenhouse):
● Complete potting up and moving outdoors.

Very late-flowering:
● Take cuttings.

JULY   page 173

● Reduce excess stems for large flowers.

Early-flowering (garden):
● Feed with a balanced fertiliser.
● Carry out disbudding if required.

Late-flowering (greenhouse):
● Plant rooted cuttings taken last month.
● Take further cuttings.

AUGUST   page 195

● Water and feed.
● Prevent flower damage from earwigs.
● Disbud for large flowers if required.

Very late-flowering:
● Plant up rooted cuttings.
● Reduce number of shoots on June cuttings.

SEPTEMBER   page 215

Early-flowering (garden):
● Select the best plants and label clearly for propagating later.
● Protect flowers for exhibition.

Late-flowering (greenhouse):
● Return pots to greenhouse before first frosts.
● Check for pests and diseases.
● Continue feeding until buds show colour.

Very late-flowering:
● Disbud if necessary.

OCTOBER   page 236

Early-flowering (garden):
● Decide on method of overwintering.
● Clear away unwanted plants.
● Tidy around plants remaining in ground.
● Prepare plants being overwintered in cold frames, boxes or greenhouse.

Late-flowering (greenhouse):
● Keep greenhouse well ventilated.
● Feed until buds begin to show colour.
● Keep watch for mildew.

Very late-flowering:
● Continue to disbud if necessary.

NOVEMBER   page 256

Early-flowering (garden):
● Prepare borders for next year.
● Check on overwintering plants.

Late-flowering (greenhouse):
● Maintain 10°C (50°F) as flowers develop.
● As flowers finish, cut down.
● Control leaf miners if necessary.

DECEMBER   page 276

Early-flowering (garden):
● Check on overwintering plants.

Late-flowering (greenhouse):
● Maintain ventilation and temperature of greenhouse (*see* November, page 257).
● Take first cuttings of late-flowering varieties towards end of month.

Climbers & wall shrubs

MAKE USE OF VERTICAL SPACE by planting climbers and wall shrubs. These plants make good use of a limited space. Some climbers can also be trained to grow through trees and shrubs, making a feature of these woody plants over a longer period.

The heights and spreads given should be used with caution as it depends on the support. A vigorous clematis may grow to 10 m (30 ft) through a tree, but less when trained horizontally along a 1.2 m (4 ft) fence.

▲ Actinidia kolomikta

An eye-catching climber in late spring and early summer when the variegation is most pronounced. Young foliage is green, white and pink. Needs a warm position in full sun. Height: 6 m (20 ft). Spread: 6 m (20 ft).

▼ Clematis 'Ascotiensis'

One of the Jackmanii group of large-flowered hybrids. Height: 3 m (10 ft). Spread: 1.8 m (6 ft).

▲ Clematis 'Nelly Moser'

One of the most popular large-flowered hybrids. Height: 3 m (10 ft). Spread: 1.8 m (6 ft).

▲ Clematis tangutica

This species looks unlike the more familiar large-flowered hybrids. It produces its yellow flowers in late summer and early autumn. Height: 3 m (10 ft). Spread: 2.5 m (8 ft).

▲ Clematis montana var. rubens

Perhaps the most popular of the vigorous species. It is very versatile and will grow high into a tree or spread along a wall or fence. Can be confined by pruning, but is not suitable for a small space. The species is white-flowered. Height: 9 m (30 ft). Spread: 3 m (10 ft).

▼ Hedera helix 'Goldheart'

All-green ivies can look dull, but the small splash of yellow on this variety makes a big difference. Variegated ivies may also be a little less vigorous, which can be useful in a small garden. Evergreen. Height: 3 m (10 ft). Spread: 3 m (10 ft).

▲ Hedera helix 'Glacier'

This is one of several ivies that are often grown as a pot plant but are hardy enough to be grown outdoors. When grown outside its leaves are usually larger and more irregular than when grown in a pot. Height: 3 m (10 ft). Spread: 3 m (10 ft).

▲ Jasminum officinale

The common jasmine is grown for its sweetly scented white flowers, which are pink in bud. There are also variegated varieties. Height: 6 m (20 ft). Spread: 3 m (10 ft).

▼ Lonicera japonica 'Halliana'

Flowers on the very fragrant Japanese honeysuckle open white but age to pale yellow. Blooms over a long period in summer. Evergreen or semi-evergreen. Height: 6 m (20 ft). Spread: 3 m (10 ft).

▲ Jasminum nudiflorum

The winter jasmine is an invaluable wall shrub for winter colour, flowering throughout the winter. Deciduous, though the green stems suggest an evergreen. Height: 3 m (10 ft). Spread: 2.5 m (8 ft).

▲ Lonicera periclymenum

The popular honeysuckle, widely grown for its intense scent, flowers in summer. The variety 'Belgica' flowers in May and June, 'Serotina' in July and August. Height: 6 m (20 ft). Spread: 3 m (10 ft).

▲ Parthenocissus tricuspidata

The Boston ivy is a vigorous self-clinging climber that will cover an expanse of wall. The autumn colour is a spectacular crimson. Height: 18 m (60 ft). Spread: 9 m (30 ft).

▲ Passiflora caerulea

The blue passion flower blooms over a long period in summer and into early autumn. Egg-shaped orange fruits are sometimes a bonus in autumn. Semi-evergreen. Height: 9 m (30 ft). Spread: 3 m (10 ft).

▼ Pyracantha

Firethorns can be grown as free-standing shrubs, but they look better trained against a wall. Grown mainly for their orange, red or yellow berries they also bear white flowers in early summer. Height: 4 m (13 ft). Spread: 3 m (10 ft).

▼ Vitis vinifera 'Purpurea'

Grape vines can be very decorative, and this purple-leaved form is particularly ornamental. The leaves are claret at first, but turn purplish later, then red creeps in before they fall. Height: 4.5 m (15 ft). Spread: 3 m (10 ft).

▲ Solanum crispum

Called the Chilean potato tree, this scrambler is always eye-catching in flower. It performs best in a warm, sheltered position, in full sun and will need to be tied to a support structure. Height: 4.5 m (15 ft). Spread: 3 m (10 ft).

▲ Wisteria sinensis

Wisterias are usually blue, but this white one is the variety 'Alba'. These are spectacular plants in flower in May and June, but they are very vigorous and demand space and regular pruning. Height: 9 m (30 ft). Spread: 3 m (10 ft).

CLIMBERS & WALL SHRUBS

JANUARY   page 20

- Check on trellis and other supports and repair if necessary.
- Replace rotted ties and secure plants back into position.
- Cut back clinging climbers from windows and doors.
- Take hardwood cuttings of hardy climbers if weather permits (*see* Trees, shrubs & hedges, March, page 63).
- Erect framework for wall shrubs which are to be trained into a fan shape.

FEBRUARY   page 37

- Prepare planting sites.
- Plant hardy climbers, if conditions are suitable.
- Continue to take hardwood cuttings (*see* Trees, shrubs & hedges, March, page 63).
- Sow seed of annual climbers (*see* Annuals and Biennials, page 36).
- Prune overgrown plants by one-third method (*see* Pruning, page 420).
- In sheltered gardens cut back hard any tender climbers and wall shrubs already beginning to put out new growth (*see* April, page 94).
- Prune wisteria if not done in late autumn (*see* November, page 257–258).
- Continue to protect plants from frost (*see* December, page 277).

MARCH   page 62

- Buy new climbers and wall shrubs.

- Add extra plant supports if necessary.
- Feed all plants with a balanced fertiliser.
- Continue to protect vulnerable plants from frost.
- Complete sowing of annual climbers.
- Take hardwood cuttings (*see* Trees, shrubs & hedges, page 78).
- Sever rooted layers taken last summer from parent plant and pot up or plant out.
- Lightly trim summer-flowering clematis and cut back late-flowering clematis hard.
- Cut back golden hop (*Humulus lupulus* 'Aureus') hard.
- Prune tender climbers and wall shrubs if showing signs of strong growth.
- Water plants showing signs of drying out, and mulch to conserve moisture.

APRIL   page 94

- Feed and water plants as necessary.
- Check for pests and diseases and treat.
- Tie in new shoots as plants grow.
- Prick out rooted seedlings of annual climbers (*see* Annuals & biennials, page 90).
- Prune tender climbers and wall shrubs before leaves open fully.

MAY   page 126

- Take cuttings of summer-flowering clematis.
- Take softwood cuttings of suitable plants.
- Plant out annual climbers.
- Plant out tubers of perennial climbers.
- Prune early clematis after flowering.

JUNE   page 151

- Adjust plant supports as growth occurs, to reduce the risk of damage.
- Watch for clematis wilt and treat.
- Continue to take softwood cuttings.
- Prune climbers and wall shrubs after flowering, using the one-third method (*see* Pruning, page 420).

JULY   page 174

- Pot on cuttings taken in June.
- Reduce length of wisteria tendrils by half.
- Prune after flowering, using the one-third method (*see* Pruning, page 420).

AUGUST   page 196

- Check and adjust supports for plants as necessary.
- Propagate by layering (*see* Propagation, page 432).
- Prune after flowering, using the one-third method (*see* Pruning, page 420).

SEPTEMBER page 215

- Choose new hardy climbers and wall shrubs to fill gaps in the garden and prepare new sites for autumn planting.
- Remove any debris built up at the base of plants to discourage pests and diseases.
- Prune after flowering, using the one-third method (*see* Pruning, page 420).
- Plant out rooted clematis cuttings taken in the spring.

OCTOBER   page 237

- Begin autumn planting of new climbers and wall shrubs while soil is still warm, to encourage rapid root growth.
- Plant clematis deeply to prevent clematis wilt (*see* February, page 38).
- Make extra preparations for climbers in trees as the ground beneath trees may be dry and impoverished.
- Check and adjust plant supports as necessary.
- Dig up rooted layers, cut free and pot up or plant in final growing position.
- Take hardwood cuttings of strong plants and plant out rooted cuttings taken in the spring or in the previous year.

NOVEMBER page 257

- Complete autumn planting, if weather is not too wet or cold, including planting out all rooted cuttings and layered plants except those of tender varieties.
- Take hardwood cuttings of hardy climbers.
- Carry out main pruning of wisteria.

DECEMBER page 277

- Finish new planting as soon as possible but only if the weather is mild (*see* October, page 237).
- Protect vulnerable plants from frost and cold winds.
- Continue to take hardwood cuttings (*see* November, page 257).

Container gardening

YEAR-ROUND CONTAINER GARDENING is feasible if you select your plants with care and use frostproof containers. Instead of concentrating all your effort on summer pots, plant up for autumn, winter and spring too. There are plants to bring colour to containers throughout the year. Try to use attractive or interesting containers too, as these can help to make an ordinary planting into a focal point.

▲ Autumn colours

Make good use of long-lasting berries for autumn colour. Pernettya (syn. Gaultheria) mucronata 'Cherry Ripe', will stay like this for months but needs acid soil.

▲ Winter wonders

This container, photographed in January, contains the grass Carex morrowii 'Evergold', a hellebore, Ajuga reptans 'Catlin's Giant', and Euphorbia amygdaloides 'Purpurea'; all plants which retain their attractive foliage through the winter.

▼ Summer spectacular

Favourite flowering plants, like this marguerite, will look even more interesting if placed in an attractive container or surrounded by foliage plants to give a contrasting textured background.

▲ Spring show

An interesting container will give a few plants more impact. These dwarf daffodils might have looked insignificant in an ordinary pot, but by standing them in a shiny watering-can they instantly became a feature.

▲ Permanent planting

A permanent planting of perennials can save labour and money, and there are many attractive plants to try. Houseleeks (Sempervivum) are especially easy as they thrive in dry soil and don't mind if you forget to water them from time to time.

CONTAINER GARDENING

JANUARY page 21

- Move pots and baskets containing vulnerable plants into a greenhouse, conservatory, porch or other shelter during very frosty weather.
- Shake snow from plants in containers to prevent damage.
- If weather is suitable, plant deciduous trees and shrubs in containers.
- Deadhead and tidy winter containers.

FEBRUARY page 38

- Continue to protect containers from frost.
- Tidy winter plantings.
- Prune deciduous shrubs as necessary to maintain shape and size but take care not to jeopardise any spring flowers.
- Buy summer bulbs for containers.

MARCH page 64

- Uncover insulated pots and untie anti-snow damage bindings.
- Complete planting of deciduous trees and shrubs before leaves open.
- Finish pruning deciduous shrubs that should be pruned when dormant.
- Complete purchase of summer-flowering bulbs (*see* February, page 38).
- Bring begonia tubers into growth.
- Top dress or replant overgrown or pot-bound plants adding a slow release fertiliser.
- Buy summer plants to grow on in a frost-free place.

APRIL page 94

- Plant summer hanging baskets and keep under glass.
- Plant up herb pots and baskets (*see* Herbs, page 102).
- Plant evergreen shrubs, especially those that need a long growing period.
- Plant climbers in free-standing pots.
- Apply slow-release fertiliser to containers.
- Mulch pots to conserve moisture.
- Plant summer-flowering bulbs and tubers.
- Trim topiary in pots.
- Check for pests and diseases and remove dead plant material regularly.

MAY page 127

- Complete planting and sowing of permanent containers.
- Harden off hanging baskets and set in position.
- Tidy up frost-damaged evergreens, pruning out damaged growth.
- Remove and replace spring-interest containers with summer plants.
- Begin regular liquid feeding.
- Water containers frequently.
- Protect vulnerable plants from slug and snail damage.

JUNE page 151

- Water baskets daily, check if other containers need water and feed regularly.
- Complete planting of seasonal containers.
- Deadhead regularly to prolong flowering.

- Trim topiary (*see* April, page 96).

JULY page 174

- Continue to water, feed and deadhead plants in containers regularly.
- Trim back over-vigorous or weak, leggy growth.
- Watch for pests, powdery mildew and other diseases.
- Make provision for watering and feeding if you are going on holiday.

AUGUST page 196

- Continue to water daily if necessary and feed and deadhead regularly.
- Trim topiary for last time this year.
- Stop feeding plants in permanent containers.
- Make provision for watering and feeding if you are away (*see* July, page 175).

SEPTEMBER page 215

- Continue to look after summer plantings with regular maintenance and feeding so that they will continue to look attractive until the first frosts.
- Prepare and plant containers and temporary liners with bulbs and other spring-flowering plants.
- Plant winter hanging baskets and containers.
- Consider saving tender perennials by sheltering the pots in a greenhouse or porch (*see* pages 228–229).

OCTOBER page 238

- Clear out containers; retrieve tender plants if you have space to shelter them over the winter, or take cuttings.
- Finish planting spring containers.
- Plant tulips.
- Continue planting winter-interest containers and baskets (*see* September, page 216).

NOVEMBER page 258

- Finish planting winter containers as soon as possible to give the plants time to establish before the coldest weather.
- Finish planting tulips (*see* October, page 238).
- Plant deciduous trees and shrubs but place in a sheltered position until established.
- Wrap up vulnerable plants and containers for winter. Grouping pots gives mutual protection and makes them easier to cover with fleece or similar protection.
- Empty containers not required for winter plantings; clean and store under cover.

DECEMBER page 277

- Continue to plant deciduous trees and shrubs (*see* November, page 258).
- Move winter hanging baskets under cover if necessary.
- Deadhead and tidy plants and keep an eye on watering requirements as pots can dry out rapidly in the wind.

Dahlias

EYE-CATCHING AND FLAMBOYANT, dahlias are at their best in late summer and early autumn, but some of the dwarf bedding types may already be flowering by mid-summer. They look good in the garden and will also give you a regular supply of cut flowers for the home. The display will continue until the first frost brings it to an abrupt end.

The types described here are only examples of the many different kinds on offer, from Lilliput varieties about 30 cm (1 ft) tall to giant decoratives with flowers literally the size of a dinner plate.

The flower sizes given here are approximate; exhibitors must follow the exact dimensions given in the show schedule.

▲ Medium cactus

Cactus varieties have fully double flowers with narrow and pointed rolled-back petals. Mediums are 15–20 cm (6–8 in) across. The variety illustrated is 'Hillcrest Royal'. Height: 1.2 m (4 ft). Spread: 75 cm (2½ ft).

▲ Small semi-cactus

These have petals rolled outwards for up to half their length. Small varieties are 10–15 cm (4–6 in) across. The one illustrated is 'Lemon Elegans'. Height: 1–1.2 m (3–4 ft). Spread: 60 cm (2 ft).

▼ Miniature decorative

Decoratives are fully double with broad petals. Miniatures are up to 10 cm (4 in) across, small decoratives are 10–15 cm (4–6 in) in diameter. This variety is 'David Howard'. Height: 1–1.2 m (3–4 ft). Spread: 60 cm (2 ft).

▲ Peony-flowered

This belongs to a group of dahlias classified officially as 'miscellaneous', which also includes many other flower shapes. The variety illustrated is 'Bishop of Llandaff', a popular old variety. Height: 1 m (3 ft). Spread: 60 cm (2 ft).

▲ Miniature ball

These have fully double, ball-shaped flowers, with distinctive rolled petals. Miniatures are up to 10 cm (4 in) across, small are up to 15 cm (6 in). This one is 'Candy Cupid'. Height: 1–1.2 m (3½–4 ft). Spread: 60 cm (2 ft).

▲ Small waterlily

These attractive flowers with their broad, flat petals resemble waterlilies in appearance. The blooms are usually 10–15 cm (4–6 in) across. The variety illustrated above is 'Porcelain'. Height: 1–1.2 m (3–4 ft). Spread: 60 cm (2 ft).

▲ Collerette

Collerette dahlias have flowers 10–15 cm (4–6 in) across. The variety illustrated is 'Clair de Lune'. Height: 1 m (3 ft). Spread: 60 cm (2 ft).

▲ Orchid flowered

Orchid flowered varieties are uncommon but very distinctive, having a 'spidery' appearance. They make striking border plants. The variety illustrated is 'Jescot Julie'.
Height: 90 cm (3 ft). Spread: 45 cm (1½ ft).

▲ Pompon

These are similar to ball dahlias in shape, but have smaller flowers, up to 5 cm (2 in) across, and the shape is more globular. The petals are rolled for the whole of their length. The one shown is 'Noreen'. Height: 1–1.2 m (3–4 ft). Spread: 60 cm (2 ft).

DAHLIAS

JANUARY page 21

- Examine stored tubers for signs of disease and treat if necessary.
- Start to dig ground for planting dahlias later in the year to allow frost to act on the soil over the winter.

FEBRUARY page 39

- Continue to examine tubers.
- Prepare tubers to produce shoots for cuttings.

MARCH page 64

- Continue digging beds for dahlias and feed with a slow-release fertiliser.
- Prepare further tubers under glass to produce cuttings (see February, page 39).
- Pot up rooted cuttings.
- Sow seed to germinate in gentle heat.
- Prick out seedlings in trays when large enough to handle.
- Examine any tubers left in storage (see January, page 21).

APRIL page 96

- Complete digging of dahlia beds and apply a slow-release fertiliser.
- Divide clumps of tubers to increase stock.
- In mild areas plant out healthy dormant tubers towards the end of the month.
- Pot rooted cuttings and take more as needed (see February, page 39).
- Harden off rooted cuttings and seedlings

in a cold frame. Protect from slugs.
- Sow seed if not already done.

MAY page 128

- Stake the plants of non-bedding varieties.
- Plant out young dahlias when all danger of frost is past. Water thoroughly.
- Keep pots of rooted cuttings fed and watered and watch for pests. Harden off before planting out.

JUNE page 152

- Keep the ground hoed and weed-free.
- Continue to plant out young dahlias when danger of frost is past.
- Pinch out tips to promote bushy plants and tie in new growth.
- Control aphids and other pests and check plants for symptoms of viral disease.

JULY page 174

- Water regularly and feed fortnightly – this is particularly important for any young plants which are slow to grow.
- Restrict number of buds to increase size of flowers for cutting or shows.
- Check for pests and diseases.
- Remove faded flowers.

AUGUST page 196

- Apply a high-potash liquid feed, water regularly and tie in new growth to stakes.
- Disbud for larger flowers and protect

exhibition blooms from sun and rain.
- Continue to spray foliage against pests and to check for signs of viral disease.
- Deadhead regularly to promote further flowering.

SEPTEMBER page 216

- Look out for local dahlia shows and displays to visit.
- Check ties as the plants are now large and autumn gales can cause damage.
- Mark the best plants of each variety for propagating.
- Allow some seed pods to ripen then cut off and leave to dry in a cool place if you want to try to from seed.

OCTOBER page 238

- Cut down the top growth when it is blackened by frost, then lift tubers, dry off and prepare them for storage. Make sure labels are securely attached.
- Remove seeds from seed pods and store in dry containers.

NOVEMBER page 258

- Order new dahlias for next year.
- Examine stored tubers (see January, page 21). Check labels are still attached.

DECEMBER page 277

- Examine stored tubers (see January, page 21). Check labels are still attached.

Fruit

EVEN SMALL GARDENS can accommodate some fruit; trained forms such as cordons take up little space. Dwarfing rootstocks also make it possible to grow a wide range of top fruits on compact trees.

If pests or birds are not to reap the benefits of your efforts, you must take relevant precautions at the appropriate time. Preventative measures are much more important for fruit than for ornamentals.

▲ Red currant 'Rovada'

Although most red currants look similar, especially when seen in isolation, there are many varieties with subtle but significant differences in size, colour and flavour. 'Rovada' is a late variety that crops heavily and has good flavour.

	January	February	March
General	plant, feed, spray	plant, feed	plant, feed
Apples	prune	prune	begin spray programme
Blackberries	cut back new plants	plant	
Cherries			begin spray programm
Currants			
black	prune new plants	prune	prune, feed
red and white	prune new plants	prune	prune, feed
Figs			plant
Gooseberries	prune new plants		prune, feed
Hybrid canes	cut back new plants		tie to supports
Peaches and nectarines	feed established fan-trained plants	prune new plants, spray against peach leaf curl	pollinate, spray
Pears	prune	prune	begin spray programm
Plums			prune large trees, spr
Raspberries	cut back new plants	prune	
summer-fruiting			plant, prune
autumn-fruiting			prune
Strawberries			
summer-fruiting		bring under glass or cover to force	disbud new plants
autumn-fruiting			plant, disbud, feed
Vines (outdoor)			prune

FRUIT

April	May	June	July	August	September	October	November	December
protect blossom from frost, mulch, water	protect blossom if needed, mulch, water	control pests, weed, harvest	harvest, protect from birds and other pests	harvest, destroy fruit affected by rot	harvest, order new plants	prepare new ground, removed diseased leaves and fruit	plant	plant, spray
continue pest and disease control	limit crop on young trees, start biological control, prune	continue pest control	water, continue pest control, thin fruit, prune cordons/espaliers	harvest, water, continue pest control, thin fruit, prune cordons/espaliers	harvest, store, prune cordons/espaliers	harvest, store	harvest, plant, prune	prune, control pests and diseases
	tie in new canes	tie in new canes, control pests and diseases	tie in new canes	harvest	harvest, prune old canes, train new canes	prune old canes, tie in new canes	prune old canes, tie in new canes, plant	
control pests, prune	control pests, prune	harvest, prune	harvest, prune	prune, spray	prune, spray	spray		
			harvest	harvest			take cuttings, prune, plant	take cuttings, prune
			harvest	harvest			take cuttings, prune, plant	take cuttings, prune
feed, prune		stop new shoots	remove fruit formed this year, tie in	remove fruitlets so main fruit will form	harvest overwintered fruit			
spray against sawfly	thin, control pests and diseases	continue spray programme, summer prune, harvest	continue spray programme, harvest	continue spray programme, harvest			take cuttings, prune, plant	take cuttings, prune
	tie in new canes	tie in, spray	harvest, tie in	harvest, prune, train new canes	prune, train new canes	train new canes	plant, prune	
protect fruitlets	thin, control pests and diseases, prune fans	shape, thin	protect fruit, prune	prune after picking	prune, protect		spray after leaf fall	
continue pest and disease control	limit crop on young trees, start biological control, prune	continue pest control	thin, spray, prune cordons/espaliers	harvest, spray, prune cordons/espaliers	harvest, store, prune cordons/espaliers	harvest, store	harvest, prune, plant	prune, control pests and diseases
spray unless in blossom	spray and start biological control	thin fruits, prune	prune	spray, prune	harvest, prune			
	control weeds	spray	control weeds, harvest support canes	prune old canes protect fruit from birds	prune old canes harvest, protect	harvest, protect	plant, prune plant	
feed forced plants	feed forced plants, control mould	propagate protect from birds, harvest	propagate harvest, cutback, feed	plant	plant	plant	plant, tidy leaves	
disbud, feed	disbud			harvest	protect fruits, harvest	spray		
treat against mildew	stop shoots, spray	stop shoots, spray	stop shoots, spray	protect from birds, spray	harvest			

Fuchsias

UNIVERSALLY POPULAR PLANTS, fuchsias are particularly versatile. There are hardy varieties that belong in the shrub border; trained as bushes or standards, they grace garden beds and patio containers; cascaders spill from hanging baskets, while the more delicate ones ornament the greenhouse or conservatory. All are easy to propagate and rewarding to grow. There is even a seed-raised variety – 'Florabelle' – that flowers superbly in the same year as sown.

◄ 'Gartenmeister Bonstedt'
A Fuchsia triphylla hybrid with small flowers but bushy growth and dark foliage, suitable for mixed bedding. Flowers freely. Height: 60 cm (2 ft). Spread: 45 cm (1½ ft).

▲ 'Cascade'
Perhaps the classic choice for a hanging basket, the long pendulous flowers complement the cascading growth. One of the best trailers. Height: trailing to 60 cm (2 ft). Spread: 30–45 cm (1–1½ ft).

▲ 'Florabelle'
This seed-raised fuchsia will put on a show like this in the first season if sown early. The flowers are small, but it is a big performer. Height: 30 cm (1 ft), but cascades. Spread: 60 cm (2 ft).

◄ 'Harry Gray'
Its delicately tinted, medium-sized, double flowers and a cascading habit make this a delightful choice for a hanging basket or the front of a mixed basket. Free flowering all summer. Height: trailing. Spread: 30–45cm (1–1½ ft).

▲ 'Genii'
With its golden foliage this makes an excellent choice for mixed bedding, though the colour will be greener in shade. Sometimes survives outdoors in winter, but best lifted. Height: 30 cm (1 ft). Spread: 30 cm (1 ft).

▲ 'Lena'
A hardy variety with semi-double flowers, useful for a mixed border. A very old variety, but reliable and easy to grow. Height: 90 cm (3 ft). Spread: 60 cm (2 ft).

▲ 'Mrs Popple'
A vigorous and reliable hardy variety that may be grown as a flowering hedge in a sheltered area. Height: 1.5 m (5 ft). Spread: 75 cm (2½ ft).

▲ 'Pacquesa'
A vigorous, upright variety that trains well as a standard but also makes an effective summer bedder. Single to semi-double flowers. Height: 90 cm (3 ft). Spread: 75 cm (2½ ft).

▲ 'Mission Bells'
An attractive scarlet single that looks good as a standard as well as a bush. It flowers prolifically, which makes it a popular choice. Height: 30–60 cm (1–2 ft). Spread: 30–45 cm (1–1½ ft).

◄ 'Paula Jane'
An attractive example of a semi-double with a bushy, upright habit. It makes a good pot plant but is also an excellent bedder. Like most fuchsias, it flowers prolifically all summer. Height: 45 cm (1½ ft). Spread: 45 cm (1½ ft).

▲ 'Rose Winston'
An attractive double that makes a good pot plant but can also be used for bedding. A good choice for a patio container. Height: 60 cm (2 ft). Spread: 30–45 cm (1–1½ ft).

◄ 'Snowcap'
Medium-sized semi-double flowers make this bold free-flowering variety useful in many situations. Can be grown as a pot plant, trained as a standard or planted in a bedding scheme. Height: 60 cm (2 ft). Spread: 45 cm (1½ ft).

▲ 'Swingtime'

A vigorous double with lax growth, making it useful as a standard or in a hanging basket. It is free-flowering and very easy to grow. Height: 90 cm (3 ft). Spread: 60 cm (2 ft).

▼ 'Thalia'

A F. triphylla hybrid sometimes grown as a half-standard, but popular for bedding. Attractive dark foliage. Very free-flowering. Height: 90 cm (3 ft). Spread: 75 cm (2½ ft).

◄ 'Tom Thumb'

You are sure to have space for this hardy and reliable variety, which is small enough to be grown in a rock garden. Despite its small size, it is outstanding when covered in flowers. Height: 45 cm (1½ ft). Spread: 45 cm (1½ ft).

▲ Fuchsia magellanica 'Aurea'

An attractive golden variety of one of the most popular and reliable of the hardy fuchsias. The bright foliage and prolific blooming more than compensate for the small size of the flowers. Height: 1.5 m (5 ft). Spread: 1.2 m (4 ft).

▲ Fuchsia magellanica 'Variegata'

Another variation of this popular hardy species. The foliage is attractive throughout the summer and the small red flowers are a bonus. Height: 1.5 m (5 ft). Spread: 1.2 m (4 ft).

▲ Fuchsia procumbens

A diminutive fuchsia, this carpeter is a curiosity to grow in a rock garden for summer, in a hanging basket, or in a pot in the greenhouse. Height: 10 cm (4 in). Spread: 90 cm (3 ft) or more.

FUCHSIAS

JANUARY   page 22

Tender and half-hardy:
- Check dormant plants are not too dry.
- Maintain sufficient light for plants being overwintered in green leaf.
- Prune when embryo shoots appear.
- Inspect for vine weevil grubs.

Hardy:
- Protect the base of hardy fuchsias with a thick mulch in severe weather.

FEBRUARY   page 40

Tender and half-hardy:
- Prune when embryo shoots appear.
- Pot back established plants into smaller pots.
- Pot up autumn cuttings.
- Spray overwintered plants with tepid water to encourage new growth.
- Unearth plants buried over winter if night temperatures are above freezing.
- Order new plants.

Hardy:
- Firm soil around plants.

MARCH   page 66

Tender and half-hardy:
- Prune when embryo shoots appear.
- Continue to pot back established plants.
- Pot on cuttings.
- Take cuttings.
- Stop shoots to encourage bushy growth.
- Plant up hanging baskets and keep under cover in a light, frost-free place.
- Feed with a weak, nitrogenous fertiliser.

- Provide a lightly shaded, humid atmosphere and spray almost daily.

Hardy:
- Weed carefully round hardy fuchsias and prune if strong new growth is appearing. .

APRIL   page 97

Tender and half-hardy:
- Pot on new and established plants.
- Complete pruning of any plants which have been late starting into growth.
- Take last cuttings for flowering this year.
- Plant up hanging baskets.
- Begin training of special shapes.
- Feed with weak, nitrogenous fertiliser.
- Control pests.

Hardy:
- Prune hardy fuchsias back hard.
- Prepare new planting sites.

MAY   page 129

Tender and half-hardy:
- Feed and water regularly.
- Pot on as necessary.
- Keep the greenhouse well ventilated and all plants shaded from strong sun.
- Complete stopping of *Triphylla* hybrids.
- Pinch out bush plants.
- Stake young standards as necessary. Pinch out to form the head.
- Harden off hanging baskets and half-hardy plants for planting out.

Hardy:
- Feed and weed established hardy fuchsias.
- Plant out new varieties.

JUNE   page 153

Tender and half-hardy:
- Pot on plants into their final pots.
- Water and feed regularly.
- Complete pinching out and stop spraying once flower buds appear.
- Plant out hardened-off plants.
- Train heads of standards.
- Take cuttings for flowering next year.

Hardy:
- Plant out new hardy fuchsias.
- Take softwood or semi-ripe cuttings.

JULY   page 177

Tender and half-hardy:
- Pot on cuttings taken last month.
- Continue training of standards.
- Water regularly and keep air moist.
- Switch to high-potash feed except for plants being trained as standards.
- Check for pests.

Hardy:
- Complete planting and take cuttings.

AUGUST   page 197

Tender and half-hardy:
- Deadhead regularly.
- Feed with high-potash fertiliser.
- Water regularly; shade under glass.
- Pinch out established plants to make new shoots for autumn cuttings.
- Continue training of standards.

Hardy:
- Feed and weed. Water new plantings.

SEPTEMBER page 217

Tender and half-hardy:
- Water and feed.
- Deadhead regularly.
- Control pests and diseases.
- Bring in plants for early flowering.

OCTOBER   page 239

Tender and half-hardy:
- Transfer half-hardy fuchsias into pots.
- Keep greenhouse ventilated and tidy.
- Reduce watering and give a final feed.
- Take semi-ripe cuttings.
- Trim plants to shape.
- Provide standards and plants grown for early flowering with sufficient warmth.

NOVEMBER   page 261

Tender and half-hardy:
- Ensure half-hardy fuchsias are protected.
- Defoliate and cut back as appropriate.
- Keep rootballs moist.
- To overwinter plants without heat or light, bury in moist peat and keep frost free.

Hardy:
- Cut back one-third of summer's growth.

DECEMBER   page 278

Tender and half-hardy:
- Water sparingly. Ventilate greenhouse.
- Check for pests and diseases.

Hardy:
- Protect the crowns of hardy fuchsias.

Garden maintenance

A WELL-MAINTAINED GARDEN is usually a healthy one, with no weeds, damaged flowers or dead foliage to detract from the beauty of the plants. Pests and diseases will certainly be less of a problem if you ensure that any fallen leaves and other debris are tidied away.

Many non-routine maintenance jobs can be done in winter, when there is little else to be done in the garden. In summer, a regular round of weeding and deadheading will save time in the long run.

▲ **Neat and well maintained**
Time spent on maintenance and general garden tidying is always well worth while. It ensures there are fewer refuges for pests and diseases and means your garden always looks smart, and the plants look their best. There's always something to be done.

GARDEN MAINTENANCE

JANUARY   page 22

- Service and sharpen tools and check electrical equipment to save time during the busy spring period.
- Clear out and dispose of any unwanted chemicals carefully. If necessary, take to a local authority waste disposal site.
- Make any necessary repairs to fences, trellises, pergolas and arches while plants growing on them are dormant (*see* November, page 261).

FEBRUARY   page 41

- Clean and service garden tools and equipment, if not already done.
- Dispose of unwanted chemicals.
- Repair wooden structures as necessary (*see* November, page 261).
- Check tree stakes, and firm plants lifted by frost.

MARCH   page 67

- Check all ties securing plants to stakes and loosen as necessary.
- Mulch beds and borders to reduce watering and weeding later in the year.

APRIL   page 99

- Weed patios, paths and drives by hand or with a spot weeder or path weedkiller.
- Clear neglected areas by cutting down and hand pulling weeds or use an appropriate weedkiller.

MAY   page 130

- Clean patios, paths and brickwork by scrubbing or by using a mosskiller.

JUNE   page 154

- Clean patios, paths and brickwork if not already done.
- Take action to conserve water in the garden as much as possible, especially in years with low rainfall.

JULY   page 177

- Prepare and protect the garden before going on holiday.
- Begin a garden diary if you do not already have one.

AUGUST   page 198

- Carry out any necessary repairs to the greenhouse before winter, and clean and disinfect thoroughly.
- Prepare and protect the garden before going on holiday. Check automatic watering systems are working properly.

SEPTEMBER   page 218

- Try to complete any major construction or maintenance jobs before the first frosts.
- Carry out necessary repairs to the greenhouse (*see* August, page 199).
- Drain and clean out water butts and free the downpipes of debris.

OCTOBER   page 240

- Begin winter digging, adding well-rotted organic matter to improve the soil.
- Clear fallen leaves from garden and gutters and recycle leaves to make leafmould.
- Remove dead vegetation from around the garden to prevent pests and diseases from overwintering.
- Clean barbecues, non-frost resistant pots and garden furniture, and store in a dry place until spring.
- Stain or paint wooden structures for protection, when the weather is dry.
- Sterilise pots and seed trays ready for spring sowings and clean and recycle plant labels.

NOVEMBER   page 261

- Prepare for winter storms by removing dead or decaying branches and staking young trees.
- Protect newly planted evergreens with a temporary windbreak until they are established.
- Repair or replace wooden structures such as fences, sheds, trellises and pergolas.

DECEMBER   page 278

- Turn off outside water from inside the house or lag outdoor taps and water pipes.
- Consider installing garden lighting to illuminate dark paths.
- Keep grit or ash to hand for icy conditions.

Greenhouses & frames

GREENHOUSE GARDENING is a year-round activity. Here you will find listed many of the main activities but you will also find more detailed information within the specific plant categories such as carnations, chrysanthemums and fuchsias.

Do not neglect your greenhouse during the depths of winter, even if it is unheated. There are always maintenance jobs to be done, and you can use it to provide shelter for plants of borderline hardiness, especially those in containers.

▲ **Staging a display**
Wooden staging and shelves are invaluable for displaying pot plants, so look after your investment and keep down pests and diseases by cleaning and preserving staging, shelves and the greenhouse itself each winter.

GREENHOUSES & FRAMES

JANUARY   page 23

- Check insulation and heating.
- Water with care and control pests.
- Sow tender and half-hardy plants.

FEBRUARY   page 41

- Bring overwintering plants into growth.
- Move young plants and rooted cuttings into larger pots as necessary.
- Make further sowings, including those of early vegetables and tomatoes.

MARCH   page 68

- Control pests.
- Increase watering and begin feeding.
- Make further sowings and prick out seedlings when large enough to handle.
- Move overwintered plants into larger pots.
- Take cuttings of fuchsias, dahlias etc.
- Sow peppers and aubergines.
- Give space to tomato plants, make further sowings, prepare ring culture system.

APRIL   page 99

- Shade and ventilate young plants.
- Increase watering. Feed established plants.
- Harden off half-hardy plants in frames.
- Control pests and diseases.
- Sow hardy annuals, shrubs, vegetables.
- Pot up rooted cuttings.
- Sow cucumbers and melons.
- Prick out peppers and aubergines.
- Plant tomatoes and train up canes.

MAY   page 130

- Check shade, humidity and ventilation.
- Water and feed regularly.
- Control pests and diseases.
- Sow cinerarias.
- Plant out hardened-off bedding plants, vegetables and hanging baskets.
- Take cuttings of shrubs and perennials.
- Stop lateral shoots on cucumbers.
- Plant out melons in cold frames.
- Plant out peppers and aubergines.
- Tie up tomatoes and feed regularly. Plant those suitable for a cold greenhouse.

JUNE   page 155

- Check shade, humidity and ventilation.
- Stop any artificial heating. Clean heaters.
- Plant out plants when hardened off.
- Take cuttings of perennials, herbs, shrubs.
- Pot up rooted cuttings and seedlings.
- Keep a humid atmosphere for cucumbers.
- Pinch out side shoots on melons.
- Feed tomatoes, peppers and aubergines.

JULY   page 177

- Damp down floors and staging and check if plants need water every day.
- Give attention to shading and ventilation.
- Introduce biological pest controls.
- Take cuttings of flowering pot plants, herbs, shrubs and rock plants.
- Top dress the soil around cucumbers.
- Water and feed peppers and aubergines.
- Pick tomatoes, feed and water regularly.

AUGUST   page 198

- Repair, clean and disinfect greenhouse.
- Take cuttings of hardy plants.
- Pot up seedlings and cuttings.
- Remove the growing tip on tomatoes.

SEPTEMBER page 218

- Check the temperature. Heat if necessary.
- Remove shading from the glass.
- Bring in all tender plants. Take cuttings.
- Sow hardy annuals for spring flowering.
- Harvest last tomatoes.

OCTOBER   page 241

- Reduce watering and stop feeding.
- Insulate greenhouse with plastic sheeting.
- Close cold frames at night.
- Sow lettuces and sweet peas and make further sowings of hardy annuals.
- Take further cuttings of tender perennials.
- Store dahlia tubers and pot up lilies.

NOVEMBER   page 262

- Ventilate on sunny days. Water sparingly.
- Spray or fumigate against whitefly.
- Pot up seedlings and cuttings.
- Pot up hardy plants for early flowers.

DECEMBER   page 278

- Check the temperature. Water with care.
- Take root cuttings of suitable perennials.
- Check resting plants and stored bulbs.

Heathers

HEATHS AND HEATHERS provide year-round colour. By choosing appropriate species and varieties, it is possible to have some in flower almost the year round. Remember that others have attractive coloured foliage or take on rich tints in autumn.

Although some demand an acid soil to perform well, one of the most useful heathers (the winter-flowering *Erica carnea*) will do well on neutral or even slightly alkaline soil. Apart from annual pruning they require very little routine attention.

▲ Erica carnea 'Loughrigg'
Winter heaths are sometimes loosely described as winter heathers. Most flower mid-winter to early spring. This variety is low-growing and spreading, so very useful for carpeting. Height: 15 cm (6 in). Spread: 45 cm (1½ ft).

▲ Erica cinerea 'Glencairn'
Bell heathers flower between early summer and early autumn. They require an acid soil. 'Glencairn' is particularly attractive because the foliage is tipped pink and red, especially noticeable in spring. Height: 30 cm (1 ft). Spread: 45 cm (1½ ft).

▲ Calluna vulgaris 'Sunset'
The Scottish heather or ling will flower in late summer and autumn and demands an acid soil. This variety has pink flowers, and foliage with year-round appeal – golden-yellow in spring, changing to almost fiery red in winter. Height: 30 cm (1 ft). Spread: 45 cm (1½ ft).

▲ Erica arborea
The tree heath is hardy but may be damaged by a combination of frost and cold winds. Its scented white flowers usually appear from late winter to late spring. Useful for adding height to a heather bed. Height: 1.8 m (6 ft). Spread: 75 cm (2½ ft).

▲ Erica x darleyensis
A winter-flowering heather that will tolerate some lime in the soil. The white variety illustrated is 'Silberschmelze', an established favourite for the winter garden. The mauve variety is 'Darley Dale'. Height: 45 cm (1½ ft). Spread: 60 cm (2 ft).

▲ **Erica vagans**
'Valerie Proudley'

*The Cornish heath flowers in late
summer and autumn. This is one of the
most outstanding varieties, grown as
much for its year-round golden foliage as
for its white flowers. Height: 23 cm (9 in).
Spread: 30 cm (1 ft).*

▲ **Daboecia cantabrica**
'Atropurpurea'

*St Daboec's heath flowers in summer and
into autumn, but a lime-free soil is
essential. Daboecias have broader leaves
and larger bell-shaped flowers than ericas.
Height: 60 cm (2 ft). Spread: 60 cm (2 ft).*

HEATHERS

JANUARY   **page 23**

● Dig over new beds during suitable
weather, improving the texture and
acidifying the soil if required.
● Check heathers planted last autumn,
weeding and firming as necessary.

FEBRUARY   **page 42**

● Complete preparation of new beds (*see*
January, page 23) adjusting the pH of
soil if necessary.
● Check heathers planted last autumn,
weeding and firming as necessary.

MARCH   **page 68**

● Prune summer-flowering heathers now
if dead flower spikes have been left over
the winter. Prune young tree heathers.
● Sever last summer's layerings but leave
them undisturbed till April.
● Pot up last summer's cuttings.
● Water potted-up plants frequently, using
rainwater if possible.

APRIL   **page 101**

● Complete pruning of summer-flowering
heathers (*see* March, page 68).
● Prune winter-flowering heathers that
require it, as soon as flowers fade.
● Dig up last summer's layerings and plant
deeply in open ground or in pots placed
outside on a well-drained surface.
● Complete potting up of last summer's

cuttings (*see* March, page 69).
● In dry weather, water young plantings of
heathers and potted-up plants frequently,
using rainwater if possible.

MAY   **page 131**

● Mulch heather beds.
● Eradicate perennial weeds from new beds.
● Complete pruning winter-flowering plants.
● Water and feed.
● Treat any heathers growing on alkaline
soils if they are showing signs of chlorosis.

JUNE   **page 156**

● Weed beds, replacing mulch if necessary.
● Water young plants and plants in pots
regularly and feed all heathers.

JULY   **page 178**

● Choose new plants.
● Propagate by cuttings or layering.
● Deadhead daboecia.
● Keep plants free of weeds.
● Water young plants regularly and feed all
heathers once this month if necessary.
● Treat any heathers growing on alkaline
soils if they are showing signs of chlorosis.

AUGUST   **page 199**

● Hand weed heather beds and replace
mulch if necessary.
● Cut double-flowered *Calluna vulgaris*
to preserve by freezing.

● Deadhead daboecia.
● Buy heathers for new beds.
● Increase stock of heathers by cuttings
or layering.
● Water and feed as required.

SEPTEMBER **page 219**

● Plant out heathers in new beds, first
laying them in position in their pots to
check the overall design.
● Water young plants and plants in pots
regularly, daily if necessary.
● Deadhead daboecia.
● Cut *Calluna vulgaris* for freezing.

OCTOBER   **page 241**

● Complete planting of new beds (*see*
September, page 219) and mulch (*see*
May, page 131).
● Water potted-up plants if they are
looking dry.

NOVEMBER   **page 263**

● Prune summer-flowering heathers if
desired but leaving faded flower spikes
will help to protect plants from frost.
● Cut back any overhanging vegetation
likely to shade heathers and keep plants
free of fallen leaves.

DECEMBER   **page 279**

● Plan and design new beds.
● Clear overhanging vegetation and leaves.

Herbs

A HERB COLLECTION CAN BE BEAUTIFUL as well as practical, as many culinary herbs are ornamental. If you don't have space for a dedicated herb garden, many herbs integrate well among border perennials. Most of them can be grown in containers if necessary, but it makes sense to concentrate on those of modest size.

Only culinary herbs are included here, but there are many medicinal and cosmetic herbs that you can grow in your herb garden.

▲ Angelica
Few gardeners bother to make the crystallised confection from the stems, but this is such an 'architectural' biennial herb that it is worth including it towards the back of a border. It self-seeds freely. Height: 1.8 m (6 ft). Spread: 1.2 m (4 ft).

▶ Basil
This tender annual is grown for its aromatic leaves. The normal form is green but there is a purple-leaved variety which makes a more decorative garden plant. It can also be grown as a pot plant indoors or out. Height: 45 cm (1½ ft). Spread: 30 cm (1 ft).

▶ Borage
An especially decorative hardy annual, it often self-sows so it usually reappears the next year. It can also be sown in the autumn for earlier flowers the following summer. It does not look amiss in the flower border. Height: 60 cm (2 ft). Spread: 60 cm (2 ft).

▲ Chives
Chives are so decorative that they deserve a place in the herbaceous border, and make an appropriate edging in the kitchen garden. They also thrive in containers, so pot some up for winter. Height: 30 cm (1 ft). Spread: 23 cm (9 in).

▲ Fennel
The graceful feathery foliage (there are green and bronze forms) and the delicate-looking heads of yellow flowers make this a highly decorative herb. Deadhead before it sheds its seeds! Height: 1.8 m (6 ft). Spread: 1.2 m (4 ft).

▲ Lemon balm
This is a herb you notice when its scent is released as you brush against the leaves. Try it at the edge of a path where it will overhang slightly. Shear off the flowerheads to keep a bushy shape. Height: 90 cm (3 ft). Spread: 60 cm (2 ft).

▲ Mint, variegated apple

This mint has a delicate flavour and is visually more pleasing and less rampant than most. It is a good choice for containers or at the front of a border. Height: 30 cm (1 ft). Spread: 45 cm (1½ ft).

▲ Marjoram

There are many kinds of marjoram, and this windowbox contains light and dark forms of pot marjoram (Origanum onites) at the back and golden marjoram (O. vulgare 'Aureum') at the front. Height: 30–45 cm (1–1½ ft). Spread: 30–45 cm (1–1½ ft).

▲ Parsley

The curled parsley needs no introduction, though there is a less common plain-leaved or French parsley which has a better flavour but is less decorative. Although a biennial, it is usually grown as an annual. Height: 30 cm (1 ft). Spread: 23 cm (9 in).

◄ Sage

Common sage (Salvia officinalis) is usually grown for culinary use, but there are purple, golden and variegated-leaved varieties that are ornamental. Height: 45–60 cm (1½–2 ft). Spread: 60–90 cm (2–3 ft).

▲ Rosemary

Rosemary is frequently grown as an ornamental shrub, or a flowering hedge. It tolerates clipping to shape. Height: 1.2–1.5 m (4–5 ft). Spread: 60–120 cm (2–4 ft).

▲ Sweet bay

Evergreen Laurus nobilis *can be grown as a very large border shrub, but is more decorative clipped and shaped and growing in a container. It benefits from a sheltered position. Height (contained): 2.5 m (8 ft). Spread: 90 cm (3 ft).*

► Thyme, common

Thymus vulgaris *is usually chosen for culinary use. There are many varieties, some with variegated foliage. Creeping thyme makes an attractive ground cover. Thymes can also be used in the rock garden. Height: 15 cm (6 in). Spread: 30 cm (1 ft).*

◄ Tarragon, French

*This herb is of little ornamental value but invaluable in the kitchen. French tarragon (*Artemisia dracunculus*) is far superior in flavour to the Russian kind (*A. dracunculoides*). Height: 60 cm (2 ft). Spread: 45 cm (1½ ft).*

▲ Thyme, lemon

Thymus × citriodorus *has a strong lemon scent. The one illustrated is 'Bertram Anderson', but there are several variegated and golden varieties. These all look attractive in herb containers. Height: 15 cm (6 in). Spread: 30 cm (1 ft).*

JANUARY   **page 24**

- Plan your new herb garden or alterations to an existing herb garden, and prepare the ground if weather allows.
- Order seeds and plants in readiness for the spring.

FEBRUARY   **page 42**

- Prepare site for a new herb garden.
- Sow parsley in pots under glass.
- Propagate mint by runners. Contain mint by planting in a pot sunk in the ground.

MARCH   **page 70**

- Fork over ground of established beds, scatter bonemeal and mulch.
- Prepare seed beds as soon as soil is warm and make the first outdoor sowings of culinary and salad herbs. Continue to sow at intervals throughout the summer for a succession of fresh leaves and flowers.
- Sow basil in a heated propagator or under glass. Cover till seeds germinate.
- Sow parsley in a damp, shady position.
- Divide and replant large clumps of perennial herbs.
- Plant small hedges of box or evergreen herbs for shelter.
- Prune back shrubby herbs to produce new shoots and leaves.

APRIL   **page 101**

- Sow small amounts of herbs outdoors

HERBS

and thin March-sown seedlings.
- Continue to sow seeds, including basil, under glass. Pot on seedlings.
- Plant out rooted cuttings from previous year of shrubby and perennial herbs.
- Complete planting of hedges for shelter (*see* March, page 70).
- Cut back any weak, straggling shoots on established plants.
- Position stakes to support large plants such as comfrey and lovage.
- Plant herb hanging baskets.
- Start planting of new herb gardens (*see* July, pages 188–189).

MAY   page 132

- Make further sowings of salad herbs and thin out seedlings of herbs sown in April.
- Plant out young herbs from earlier sowings under glass.
- Layer the stems of creeping thymes to propagate, as thyme rarely grows true from seed.
- Take softwood cuttings of shrubby herbs.
- Support the soft-topped growth of large plants as necessary.
- Harvest chives and other salad herbs.
- Position herbs in garden to encourage insect predators.
- Loosen and aerate soil in containers and work in a little fertiliser.
- Complete plantings of herb hanging baskets (*see* April, page 102) and harden off baskets outside.
- Pot on basil plants into larger pots of rich compost to encourage rapid growth.

JUNE   page 156

- Continue sowing salad herbs, also biennial and perennial herbs, in spare ground.
- Thin established seedlings.
- Water plants in dry weather if necessary but remember most herbs come from dry Mediterranean countries so should not be overwatered.
- Harvest non-flowering stems of angelica for preserving.
- Pinch out blossoming shoots of herbs if you want tender leaf growth.
- Take further softwood cuttings.
- Lightly trim herb hedges but leave cotton lavender hedges if flowers are required for drying.
- Position tender herbs in containers in warm, sheltered corners of the garden.

JULY   page 179

- Make further sowings of salad herbs and start sowing winter crops.
- Thin out and hoe between earlier sowings.
- Sow angelica seeds as soon as they ripen on the plant, as they do not store well.
- Take semi-ripe cuttings of perennial herbs and protect with a cloche or in a cold frame until roots form; remember to water.
- Lift garlic bulbs, bunch loosely and hang in an airy place to dry.
- Gather aromatic leaves and flowers to dry for pot-pourri.
- Cut lavender to dry.
- Cut herbs to use fresh or to freeze or dry for later use (*see* page 189).

AUGUST   page 199

- Sow selected herbs in large pots under glass, or outdoors, for winter use.
- Harvest herb seeds as they ripen. Sow or store in a cool, dry place.
- Deadhead flowers to prolong the flowering season if not required for seed.
- Complete lifting and drying of garlic.
- Continue harvesting surplus culinary herbs to freeze or dry for winter (*see* July, page 189).
- Take semi-ripe cuttings of shrubby herbs if not already done.

SEPTEMBER   page 219

- Sow parsley and chervil for winter use.
- Lift clumps of chives, French tarragon, mint and sorrel, and plant in pots to be brought inside later for winter use.
- Complete harvesting of basil leaves for immediate use and for preserving.
- Thin out seedlings of lamb's lettuce, land cress and winter purslane.
- Trim lavender, sage and other aromatic plants to tidy up for winter.
- Cut artemisia stems to bind into circles for festive wreaths.
- Plant garlic cloves in deeply cultivated garden soil.
- Divide and replant large clumps of perennial herbs.
- Remove dead leaves, broken stalks and weeds from around herbs.
- Take further cuttings including those of bay, lavender, sage and thyme.

OCTOBER   page 241

- Harvest any remaining soft-leaved culinary herbs and rough dig where they were planted.
- Tidy herb garden, leaving some old growth for winter protection.
- Check herbs brought inside for winter use.
- Finish planting garlic cloves (*see* September, page 219).
- Continue to divide clumps of perennial herbs (*see* September, page 220).
- Plant hardy herbs if soil is still warm.

NOVEMBER   page 263

- Move containers of herbs to a sheltered place or insulate if they cannot be moved.
- Sow sweet cicely seeds in gritty compost.
- Clear fallen leaves from plants.
- Protect parsley and chervil with cloches.
- Bring indoors for winter use chives and other herbs put in pots (*see* September, page 219).
- Check crops under glass for pests.

DECEMBER   page 279

- Protect plants, as necessary, by moving pots or protect plants in the ground with leafmould or straw.
- Bring herbs for winter use indoors if not yet done (*see* September, page 219).
- Gather fresh leaves of sage, parsley and thyme for use in the kitchen.
- Check the condition of greenhouse and indoor herbs.

House & conservatory plants

Many indoor plants demand more care and attention than those in the garden. With roots confined in a relatively small amount of compost, regular feeding and watering is important. Hot, dry air and lack of light also need to be taken into account. However, your efforts will be rewarded by the pleasure of being able to garden in comfort, whatever the weather.

▲ Flowers and foliage
Foliage plants are usually long-lasting and can be used as a foil for flowering plants which add seasonal interest.

JANUARY   page 24

- Provide as much light as possible but protect plants from cold and wet.
- Feed only if plants are growing strongly or are in flower. Deadhead flowering plants.
- Bring indoors pots of polyanthus.
- Sow seeds of gloxinias and streptocarpus.
- Keep cyclamen and lachenalias cool and deadhead regularly.
- Bring in forced bulbs as they are ready.
- Keep bromeliads in bright light and warmth and mist air plants weekly.
- Keep cacti dry and cool.
- Water orchids very sparingly.

FEBRUARY   page 42

- Provide as much light as possible.
- Water sparingly and only feed plants that are in active growth or in flower.
- Clean leaves, removing dead ones.
- Deadhead flowering plants.
- Buy clivias in bud.
- Sow seeds of gloxinias and streptocarpus.
- Start an early batch of achimenes.
- Give bougainvilleas their first watering and tie in spreading growth.
- Prune plumbago and passion flower.
- Keep bromeliads in bright light and warmth, and mist air plants.
- Maintain cool rest period for cacti.
- Water orchids and buy orchids in flower.

MARCH   page 71

- Increase watering gradually as new growth appears on plants.
- Feed plants if they are actively growing.
- Move suitable plants to west-facing windowsills as light gets stronger.
- Cut back neglected foliage plants to encourage fresh growth.
- Take cuttings of abutilon and *Tibouchina semidecandra*.
- Plant out forced bulbs as soon as they finish flowering.
- Prune and tie in growth of climbers.
- Water bromeliads regularly and feed monthly; mist air plants.
- Move cacti to a warm room and water; pot on or repot in free-draining compost.
- Keep orchids moist to dry.

APRIL   page 102

- Check foliage plants for dead and dying leaves and for pests and diseases.
- Pinch back long or tall shoots.
- Repot overcrowded plants or those starting to deteriorate.
- Increase watering, feeding and humidity once plants start growing.
- Shade and ventilate conservatory.
- Propagate by dividing established plants, detaching offsets or taking cuttings.
- Pot on clivias and gardenias if plants deteriorate.
- Water and spray hydrangeas daily, feed every ten days.
- Pot on gloxinias.
- Pot up tuberoses and gloriosas, and stake.
- Water lachenalias generously as flower spikes appear.

- Move cyclamen to a cool position.
- Pinch out growing tips of trailing plants; insert supports and tie in unruly growth.
- Continue to water and feed bromeliads.
- Move cacti to a warm room and water if not yet done; check for mealy bug; take stem and leaf sections or remove offsets; keep Christmas and Easter cacti humid and in subdued light.
- Water and feed orchids; repot any orchid pushing itself out of the pot.

MAY   page 133

- Increase watering and feed foliage plants as they start to grow more strongly.
- Shade and ventilate the conservatory.
- Move plants outdoors for the summer.
- Clean leaves, remove any dead ones and check for sun scorch.
- Check plant supports.
- Check for pests and diseases.
- Deadhead azaleas, water regularly, repot if necessary and move outside.
- Repot poinsettias and feed.
- Water bulbs less as flowers fade but continue to water lachenalias and vallotas and feed as necessary.
- Support new growth on climbers.
- For bromeliads continue watering, feeding and misting routine.
- Take cuttings from cacti. Water and feed.
- Continue to feed orchids.

JUNE   page 156

- Continue to water, feed, check for pests

HOUSE & CONSERVATORY PLANTS

and diseases and keep leaves clean.
- Keep conservatory ventilated and shaded.
- Increase plants by cuttings or layering.
- Continue to deadhead flowering plants.
- Move azaleas and hydrangeas outdoors.
- Take leaf cuttings of African violets and begonias.
- Pot on streptocarpus and sow more seeds.
- Repot cyclamen that flowered over winter.
- Repot vallotas, water and feed.
- Water tuberoses when shoots appear.
- For bromeliads continue watering, feeding and misting; remove offsets and pot up.
- Feed and water cacti; move desert species outdoors on to sunny patio.
- Increase humidity around orchids that require it; move cymbidiums outdoors.

JULY   page 180

- Continue to water, feed and clean plants.
- Pot up any cuttings taken last month.
- Protect plants indoors from strong direct sunlight and ensure conservatory is well-ventilated and shaded; keep humidity high.
- Inspect plants for pests.
- Deadhead flowering plants regularly.
- Take cuttings of regal pelargoniums and hydrangeas; pot up polyanthus for winter.
- Pinch out growing tips of jasmine.
- For bromeliads continue watering, feeding and misting routine.
- For cacti maintain careful watering and feeding.
- Move cymbidiums outdoors, if not already done; continue to feed; increase humidity around orchids that require it.

AUGUST   page 200

- Continue to water, feed and clean plants.
- Ensure the conservatory is well ventilated and shaded, with humidity kept high.
- Check any plants propagated by layering.
- Keep recently bought gardenias in constant warmth and high humidity.
- Pot up plantlets of African violets once rooted.
- Continue to deadhead plants.
- Feed recently bought cyclamen; restart into growth resting cyclamen.
- Plant lachenalia and prepared bulbs of hyacinths and narcissi.
- Feed jasmine.
- For bromeliads continue watering, feeding and misting routine.
- For cacti maintain careful watering and feeding.
- Increase humidity around orchids that require it; continue to water and feed.

SEPTEMBER   page 220

- Reduce watering and feeding.
- Bring in plants put outside for summer.
- Reposition plants which need lots of light.
- Repot or prune plants that need it, before growth slows down.
- Check plants propagated by layering.
- Adjust temperature and watering for African violets.
- Bring azaleas to a cool position indoors.
- Treat poinsettias for Christmas colour.
- Keep gardenias warm and humid.
- Repot arum lilies for winter flowering.

- Take cuttings of flowering plants.
- Start off forced bulbs.
- Remove growing tips of jasmine: place in a bright position as flower buds form.
- For bromeliads reduce watering and stop feeding.
- Give cacti a last feed and reduce watering.
- Reduce watering for orchids as growth slows down and give last feed of the year; bring in orchids that have been outside.

OCTOBER   page 242

- Protect tender plants from dry air and cold.
- Water sparingly.
- Keep plants in flower, such as azaleas and primulas, in cool, light, airy conditions.
- Move clivias to a cooler place, reduce watering and stop feeding.
- Treat poinsettias for Christmas colour.
- Cut down stems of achimenes, dry off rhizomes and store until spring.
- Keep cyclamens and lachenalias in a cool, light and airy place.
- Check on forced bulbs.
- Continue to water and feed jasmine.
- Thin out shoots of climbing plants.
- Water bromeliads, cacti and orchids sparingly.

NOVEMBER   page 263

- Protect plants from cold and draughts and maintain good light levels.
- Check for pests and diseases, especially red spider mite which thrives in centrally heated rooms.

- Water sparingly and only feed plants in active growth.
- Put African violets coming into bud in light.
- Pinch back new growth on winter cherries to show berries.
- Remove dead flowers and yellowing leaves from cyclamen.
- Stop watering gloriosas after flowering but keep vallotas moist.
- Check on forced bulbs.
- Keep jasmine watered and fed.
- Water bromeliads sparingly; mist air plants once or twice a week.
- Move cacti to a cool, light room to rest.
- Reduce watering for orchids; buy plants.

DECEMBER   page 280

- Take care when buying tender plants; avoid exposing them to cold and draughts.
- Protect all plants from cold and draughts and maintain good light levels.
- Keep compost on the dry side; do not feed plants unless actively growing.
- Monitor the temperature in the conservatory.
- Continue to remove spent flowers and leaves from cyclamen and move to a warmer or cooler area as necessary.
- Bring in first bowls of forced bulbs.
- Keep jasmine watered and feed every two weeks.
- Continue to mist air plants once or twice a week.
- Move cacti to a light, cool room, if not already done.
- Water orchids sparingly.

Irises

THIS VERY VARIED GROUP of plants makes a special contribution to the garden. Many are beautiful border plants, but some belong in a rock garden or alpine house; others, moisture lovers, grow in bog gardens or at the margins of ponds. A few of the dwarf bulbous irises look good in pots and other containers. There are also species that bloom in mid-winter.

Some grow from bulbs, others from rhizomes. Some superficially appear like ordinary herbaceous plants with no well-developed rhizome. This diversity makes irises an interesting group of plants to grow.

▲ Iris ensata
(syn I. kaempferi)
Beautiful iris for a bog garden. Height: 60–90 cm (2–3 ft). Spread: 60 cm (2 ft).

▼ Iris foetidissima
The stinking iris is an evergreen grown more for its bright autumn fruits than its dull yellowish summertime flowers. Height: 45–75 cm (1½–2½ ft). Spread: 60 cm (2 ft) or more.

▲ Iris pseudacorus 'Variegata'
This is a variegated form of the native yellow flag iris. Grow it in shallow water, but be prepared to keep it under control. The yellow flowers appear in June and July. Height: 1.5 m (5 ft). Spread: 1.2 m (4 ft) or more.

▲ Iris, tall bearded
These are popular plants for a herbaceous border. This is 'Jane Phillips'. Height: 90 cm (3 ft). Spread: 60 cm (2 ft) or more.

◀ Iris sibirica
Siberian flags prefer to grow in moist soil or a bog. They bring height and colour to the edge of a pond. The flowers, which appear in late spring and early summer, are mainly in shades of blue. The one illustrated is 'Perry's Blue'. Height: 90–120 cm (3–4 ft). Spread: 90 cm (3 ft) or more.

▲ **Iris reticulata**

Popular for early spring flowering, there are several good varieties in shades of blue or purple. The bulbs are widely available in autumn. Height: 15 cm (6 in). Spread: 5 cm (2 in).

▲ **Iris unguicularis** (syn. I. stylosa)

The Algerian iris is an evergreen. The almost stemless flowers are slightly scented and open in winter. Needs well-drained soil and a warm sheltered position. Height: 30 cm (1 ft). Spread: 60 cm (2 ft) or more.

IRISES

JANUARY — page 25

- Keep compost moist round winter-flowering irises under glass. Feed.
- Protect winter-flowering bulbous irises in the garden from cold weather.
- Remove and destroy bulbs showing signs of virus or fungus attack.

FEBRUARY — page 44

- Protect winter-flowering bulbous irises in the garden from cold or damp weather.

MARCH — page 72

- Check bearded irises for signs of leaf rust and rhizomes for soft rot.
- Check bulbous irises for signs of fungus or virus disease. Destroy those affected.
- Weed and feed irises in beds and borders; mulch and apply a top dressing of sulphate of potash as necessary.
- Protect early-flowering irises from cold weather as necessary.

APRIL — page 104

- Plant herbaceous irises in colder areas if not done last autumn.
- Treat bearded irises for leaf spot, rusts and aphids before flowering.
- Cut off flower stems of bearded irises after flowering; never allow seed pods to form unless needed for propagation.
- Remove bulbs of winter-flowering irises from pots when leaves die down;

replant good-sized bulbs in the garden.

MAY — page 134

- Pinch out flowers as they fade from bearded irises and cut off stems as they finish flowering.
- Check for leaf spots and rusts, ants' nests and aphids.
- Stake tall plants if necessary and tie to canes any single flower stems required for showing. Take care not to damage roots.

JUNE — page 157

- Stake tall irises on windy sites.
- Feed bearded irises after flowering.
- Prepare new beds for bearded irises, digging in plenty of compost or manure.
- Continue to pinch out dead flowers and remove flower stems after flowering unless seed is required.

JULY — page 181

- Order new bulbs now for planting in October.
- Plant new and divided rhizomes of bearded irises.
- Divide and replant congested clumps of winter-flowering bulbous irises.
- Lift and store bulbs of Dutch and Spanish irises in a warm, dry place.
- Remove stems as late irises finish flowering. Cut back leaves on congested clumps.
- Treat waterside irises for sawfly larvae.

AUGUST — page 201

- Continue planting bearded irises provided ground is not too dry.
- Plant dwarf bulbous irises for winter colour in sunny, well-drained sites.

SEPTEMBER — page 221

- Lift and divide clumps of bearded irises.
- Plant bearded, beardless and bulbous irises in prepared sites.
- Remove any leaves showing spots or rusts.

OCTOBER — page 243

- Plant dwarf winter-flowering bulbs in pots for winter display.
- Plant Pacific Coast irises in all but the coldest areas and keep moist.
- Tidy beds of bearded irises.

NOVEMBER — page 264

- Protect flowering *Iris unguicularis* from slugs, snails and birds.
- Cut back beardless, water and bearded irises.

DECEMBER — page 280

- Bring pots of early-flowering dwarf bulbs into a cold frame or unheated greenhouse and feed as leaves appear.
- Renew slug traps round *Iris unguicularis*.
- Cover Dutch and Spanish irises in cold weather with cloches or bracken.

Lilies

ARISTOCRATS OF THE BORDER, lilies come in many colours and with varying flower shapes. Some are excellent in the semi-shade of a woodland area or among shrubs, while many others prefer full sun. There are also dwarf varieties, superb in large pots and other patio containers.

Unless you live in an area troubled by lily beetle, lilies are not difficult to grow, and with care the display will be better each year as the clumps grow larger. Some lilies produce roots on their stems, just above the bulb, as well as basally; cover them with a mulch if seen.

▼ **Lilium martagon**
In early and mid summer the Turk's cap lily makes an impressive display, especially among shrubs in partial shade.
Height: 1.2 m (4 ft). Spread: 45 cm (1½ ft).

▲ **'Pink Perfection'**
One of the trumpet hybrids with large and imposing flowers, it blooms in mid summer. A good plant for the border, it has a delicate fragrance and cuts well for the house too.
Height: 1.5 m (5 ft).
Spread: 45 cm (1½ ft).

▲ **'Imperial Silver'**
An Oriental hybrid with flat flowers, typical of a group of lilies that make excellent border plants. Flowering time is usually late summer. An outstanding variety. Height: 1.5 m (5 ft).
Spread: 45 cm (1½ ft).

▲ **Lilium longiflorum**
The Easter lily actually flowers in early summer in the garden. This variety is 'Gelria'. The elegant white flowers are fragrant and excellent for cutting.
Height: 60–90 cm (2–3 ft).
Spread: 45 cm (1½ ft).

▲ **Lilium speciosum**
Strongly reflexed petals make this a particularly striking species. The scented flowers vary from pink to white according to variety, and usually bloom in late summer.
Height: 1.2 m (4 ft).
Spread: 45 cm (1½ ft).

▲ **'Grand Cru'**
An Asiatic hybrid, typical of the modern varieties with an upward-facing flower that do well in containers. They flower reliably in mid summer and multiply freely.
Height: 1.2 m (4 ft). Spread: 45 cm (1½ ft).

▲ Lilium regale

The regal lily is one of the best for a herbaceous border, forming a large clump in time. The fragrant flowers are produced in mid-summer. There is also a pure white variety. Height: 1.5 m (5 ft). Spread: 45 cm (1½ ft).

▲ 'Mr Sam'

This is an example of one of the very dwarf varieties bred with pots and containers in mind. Although they can be used at the front of a border, they are most effective used in containers. Height: 30 cm (1 ft). Spread: 23 cm (9 in).

LILIES

JANUARY page 25

- Sow lily seeds under glass in pots or in deep boxes.
- Start forcing pots of bulbs for Easter and early summer flowering.
- Plant bulbs outdoors in mild weather (*see* October, page 244) or temporarily pot up until weather improves.

FEBRUARY page 44

- Purchase bulbs, if not done in autumn.
- Continue to plant bulbs outdoors in mild weather (*see* October, page 244).
- Check plants outdoors for early growth which may need protection.
- Check bulbs for any sign of basal rot.
- Pot up bulbs for use as flowering pot plants indoors.
- Make further sowings of seeds under glass (*see* January, page 25).
- Raise temperature for forced bulbs when flower buds are visible, and feed.

MARCH page 73

- Protect young shoots with a light mulch and use cloches or straw to protect them from frost at night.
- Sow seeds in a cold frame in mild areas.
- Move seeds sown earlier to cold frame if space in greenhouse is limited.
- Complete planting outdoor bulbs, especially stem-rooting types.
- Reduce temperature for forced bulbs when flowers are about to open.

APRIL page 106

- Sow remaining seeds and plant all bulbs (potted up bulbs can wait till May).
- Control pests and diseases.
- Water pots under glass as plants grow.
- Plant forced bulbs outdoors after flowering.

MAY page 135

- Plant out bulbs which were temporarily potted up or forced.
- Continue pest and disease control.
- Start to prepare new areas for autumn bulb planting.
- Continue to water pots and containers.

JUNE page 158

- Continue pest and disease control.
- Check for virus-diseased plants and destroy any found.
- Keep pots under glass well watered, and ventilate greenhouse.

JULY page 182

- Deadhead unless you want to keep seeds.
- Pollinate flowers of plants wanted for seed.
- Continue to watch for pests and diseases.
- Water freely in the greenhouse but only in drought outdoors.
- Order bulbs for the autumn.
- Plant Madonna lilies in a sunny spot where they can be left undisturbed.
- Plant lily bulbils in pots or trays to provide new plants.

AUGUST page 201

- Order bulbs, if not already done.
- Sow seed from pollinated plants as soon as ripe or store till next spring.

SEPTEMBER page 222

- Begin to plant new bulbs and move those which need transplanting.
- Plant bulblets.
- Propagate from bulb scales.
- Transplant spring-sown seedlings.
- Collect half-ripe seed pods for ripening.

OCTOBER page 244

- Finish autumn planting of bulbs.
- Allow flowered lily stems to die down naturally unless diseased. Save seed.
- Lift some bulbs to force in pots in the greenhouse for early flowering.

NOVEMBER page 264

- Plant late-delivered bulbs if weather and conditions permit, or pot up or store.
- Protect bulbs stored in pots or trays from frost and from pests.
- Cut back dead lily stems.

DECEMBER page 280

- Plant bulbs outdoors if weather allows or pot up or store.
- Pot up further bulbs for a succession of blooms under glass in late spring.

Pelargoniums

PELARGONIUM ENTHUSIASTS often start growing these plants because of their great diversity. Zonal pelargoniums have a long flowering season and can spend all summer outdoors – they range from bedding 'geraniums' to the cascading, ivy-leaved types that are superb for windowboxes and containers. Regal pelargoniums make excellent pot plants for the conservatory or home; there are coloured-leaf forms whose beauty lies in their foliage as much as the flowers, and scented-leaf kinds which provide a pleasant fragrance.

▲ Zonal pelargoniums
These are popular for bedding and containers. Some varieties can be raised from seed, others only from cuttings. This variety is 'Cardinal' ('Kardinal'). Height: 30–45 cm (1–1½ ft). Spread: 30 cm (1 ft).

▼ Continental trailers
*These may be referred to under a variety of names, such as Continental cascade pelargoniums, Balcon and Decora Series. They flower prolifically.
Height: trailing. Spread: 45 cm (1½ ft).*

▲ Variegated varieties
*Varieties with variegated foliage, often strongly zoned, are sometimes used for bedding as well as pot plants. The variety illustrated is 'Caroline Schmidt'.
Height: 45 cm (1½ ft). Spread: 30 cm (1 ft).*

▲ Miniature zonal
Dwarfs and miniatures are primarily pot plants for home or conservatory. Miniatures will flower for most of the year on a sunny windowsill. Dwarfs are ideal for a windowbox. This variety is 'Fleurette'. Height: 20 cm (8 in). Spread: 15 cm (6 in).

▲ Ivy-leaf
The trailing habit of ivy-leaved pelargoniums makes them popular in hanging baskets and for the front of window-boxes and other containers. The variety illustrated is 'L'Elégante'. Height: trailing. Spread: 30–45 cm (1–1½ ft).

▲ Scented-leaf pelargoniums

These are usually grown in pots indoors, but the more vigorous ones can be used outdoors in summer. The fragrance varies with the species; this is lemon-scented P. graveolens. Height: 60 cm (2 ft). Spread: 60–75 cm (2–2½ ft).

▲ Regal pelargoniums

Regals are at their best from April to June, and are usually grown as pot plants. Dwarf varieties are known as Angel pelargoniums. Height: 45–60 cm (1½–2 ft). Spread: 45–60 cm (1½–2 ft).

PELARGONIUMS

JANUARY page 26

- Take cuttings to root in warmth.
- Pot on into larger pots regals and specimen plants rooted last autumn.
- Sow seeds under glass.

FEBRUARY page 45

- Take cuttings of ivy-leaved varieties for use in hanging baskets and tubs.
- Prick out, or pot individually, seedlings from seeds sown last month; keep on windowsill or in frost-free greenhouse.

MARCH page 73

- Pot up rooted cuttings and young seedlings and place where they will receive good light; feed and water and move to larger pot as soon as roots fill pot.
- Turn plants so they do not grow one-sided and pinch out to encourage a bushy shape.
- Disbud plants for larger blooms.
- Take further cuttings.

APRIL page 107

- Plant up hanging baskets if you have somewhere to keep them in good light and protected from frost.
- Take action against pests.
- Pot up seedlings and cuttings as soon as they are ready. Keep turning once potted so they receive an even amount of light.
- Pot on specimen plants and feed.

MAY page 135

- Harden off plants for planting out towards the end of the month in mild areas.
- Feed plants in small pots regularly.
- Protect coloured-leaved and other vulnerable varieties from strong sunlight.
- Check regularly for pests and diseases.

JUNE page 158

- Plant up tubs. Water and feed.
- Deadhead regals regularly to encourage new buds to open.
- Control pests and diseases, especially whitefly on regals, greenfly on ivy-leaved pelargoniums.
- Prepare any plants grown for showing.

JULY page 183

- Feed and water plants in tubs, window-boxes and hanging baskets regularly.
- Cut back regals after flowering.
- Protect plants under glass from strong sunlight and high temperatures.
- Take cuttings of zonals to grow large specimen plants next year.
- Deadhead zonal and ivy-leaved pelargoniums as necessary.

AUGUST page 201

- Continue to take cuttings of zonal pelargoniums to overwinter for well-grown specimens next year.
- Watch for rust and remove any infected leaves and dispose of them carefully.
- Continue to deadhead.

SEPTEMBER page 223

- Take cuttings to overwinter.
- Pot up and pinch out top terminal bud on specimen zonals so you have a bushy plant that shoots from low down.
- Sow seeds to overwinter if you have a frost-free greenhouse.

OCTOBER page 244

- Before the first frost, bring in plants you want to keep over winter; keep in a light, frost-free place; cut back if necessary.
- Prick out seedlings sown last month.
- Pot up cuttings taken last month and remove the top terminal bud.
- Turn specimen plants regularly and stop any shoots as necessary.

NOVEMBER page 265

- Maintain a winter care programme.
- Pot up cuttings taken in September or October if not already done, and stop terminal bud to make bushy plants.

DECEMBER page 281

- Send for catalogues and plan for next year's plantings.
- Continue to maintain a programme of winter care (see November, page 265).
- Pot on seedlings and cuttings.

Rhododendrons & azaleas

PROVIDED YOU HAVE ACID SOIL, rhododendrons and azaleas should thrive, and you can experiment with the many species and hybrids. The flowering season starts in January and continues well into summer. Some form tall rangy shrubs, while others are compact and grow little more than 30 cm (1 ft) tall. There are species with beautiful leaves, or scented flowers, and some of the deciduous azaleas have wonderful autumn colour. If your soil is too alkaline, you can always grow a few in an acidic compost in containers.

▲ **Rhododendron 'Elizabeth'**
This justifiably popular variety is an example of a compact rhododendron with huge trusses of flowers in April and into May. It is suitable for a small garden. Height: 1.2 m (4 ft). Spread: 1.2 m (4 ft).

▼ **Rhododendron 'Bluebird'**
Low-growing, and eye-catching in April or May, especially in partial shade. This is one of several compact rhododendrons suitable for a small garden. Height: 90 cm (3 ft). Spread: 90 cm (3 ft).

▲ **Rhododendron 'Hino-mayo'**
A famous azalea obtained from the Emperor's Garden in Tokyo in about 1910. An evergreen that looks its best in late spring or early summer. Height: 1.5 m (5 ft). Spread: 1.5 m (5 ft).

▲ **Rhododendron 'Praecox'**
A very popular choice for early flowers, which usually appear in February or March. The blooms are small, but plentiful. Tends to be semi-evergreen in most areas. Height: 1.8 m (6 ft). Spread: 1.5m (5 ft).

▲ **Rhododendron 'Dopey'**
One of the Yakushimanum hybrids, which are useful plants, being compact enough for a small garden, and usually doing well in a large container. They flower in May and early June. Height: 1.2 m (4 ft). Spread: 1.2 m (4 ft).

▲ **Rhododendron 'Fireglow'**
One of the Knap Hill hybrid azaleas, which are deciduous, with autumn leaf colour sometimes a bonus. They flower mid-May to mid-June, but usually lack scent. Height: 2.5 m (8 ft). Spread: 1.8 m (6 ft).

RHODODENDRONS & AZALEAS

JANUARY   page 27

- Protect vulnerable rhododendrons and azaleas in severe weather but remove protection in mild periods.
- Pinch out flower buds damaged by frost to prevent the spread of disease.
- Check for coral spot and cut out any affected wood; destroy the prunings.
- Cut back any suckers at their point of origin as soon as you spot them.

FEBRUARY   page 45

- Start soil preparation for spring planting, taking into account soil acidity and position. If soil conditions in your garden are not ideal, it may be wiser to plant rhododendrons and azaleas in containers (see March, page 74).

MARCH   page 74

- Continue to prepare soil and start planting when weather is warm enough.
- Prepare rhododendrons for layering by pruning lower branches.
- Pot semi-ripe azalea cuttings taken last year into individual pots.

APRIL   page 108

- Complete new planting to give time for plants to establish during the summer.
- Transplant any established plants that need relocating. Make sure that the rootball is not disturbed and that the new planting site is well prepared; water well.
- Water newly planted rhododendrons in dry conditions and feed weekly; spray foliage regularly but not in strong sunlight.
- Remove dead flowers to increase flower bud formation.
- Watch for signs of vine weevil attack and set up a biological predator for control.
- Rejuvenate old plants by pruning after flowering (see Pruning, page 421).

MAY   page 136

- Mulch with lime-free organic material.
- Take semi-ripe cuttings of azaleas.
- Continue rejuvenation pruning as rhododendrons and azaleas finish flowering (see Pruning, page 421).
- Water and spray plants if weather is dry and feed weekly as necessary.
- Continue to deadhead flowers.
- Continue to purchase new container-grown plants while in flower. Take extra care when planting and water well.

JUNE   page 159

- Watch for pests and diseases and treat. In the case of bud blast, remove infected material and destroy immediately.
- In dry conditions continue to water newly planted and established plants, to ensure the rootball is kept moist.
- In very hot weather shade any new plantings with netting.
- Continue to take semi-ripe cuttings.
- Begin to harden off rooted semi-ripe cuttings taken last month.
- Continue rejuvenation pruning.

JULY   page 183

- Stimulate new growth in old plants you are rejuvenating by spraying with growth supplement fortified with iron.
- In hot, dry weather make a regular check on watering, spraying and shading requirements and feed weekly.
- Continue to protect against pests and diseases.

AUGUST   page 202

- Propagate by layering.
- Propagate large-leaved varieties of rhododendrons by air layering.
- Stimulate new growth in ageing rhododendrons and azaleas if necessary.
- Continue to water, spray, shade and feed as necessary.
- Continue to check for pests and diseases.

SEPTEMBER   page 224

- Prepare soil for autumn planting.
- This is a good month to purchase new plants. Keep rootball of new plants moist and plant out in well-prepared soil as soon as possible; continue watering until well established.
- Continue to ground layer and air layer plants to increase your stock of plants.
- Plant out the previous spring's semi-ripe cuttings into their final growing positions.

OCTOBER   page 245

- Visit gardens and nurseries to find azaleas with good autumn colour to the leaves; these are an added bonus in the garden.
- Undertake main autumn planting while soil is still warm and moist.
- Pot up well-rooted layers propagated the previous year; keep the pots over the winter in a sheltered corner or cold frame.
- Pot up well-rooted semi-ripe cuttings and move into a cold greenhouse or cold frame for the winter.
- Plant out last year's semi-ripe cuttings into final growing positions.

NOVEMBER   page 265

- Protect plants from birds and other creatures as necessary.
- If soil is not frozen or waterlogged, continue planting new plants or moving established ones.
- Dig up ground layers that are now rooted and plant out in final growing position.
- Cut away any new plantlets produced by air layering and pot up to be grown on; plant out in final position any plants propagated by air layering last year.

DECEMBER   page 281

- Protect vulnerable plants from wind and snow by putting up temporary windbreaks and shaking off snow; if necessary, place props under main branches of older specimens when snow is forecast.

Rock plants

USE ROCK GARDEN PLANTS IMAGINATIVELY, not only in rock gardens but in other sunny places where the drainage is good. Some are ideal for growing in crevices in paving, in gravel, or in dry-stone walls. Others can be planted at the front of an herbaceous border, or even as ground cover in front of shrubs. Many of them are ideal for raised beds, sink gardens and containers of all kinds.

Many alpines flower in spring, so include some that bloom at other times to ensure your rock garden is bright for many months.

▲ **Achillea tomentosa**
This yarrow produces green filigree mats of foliage, but it is grown primarily for the yellow flowers that appear between June and August. Height: 20 cm (8 in). Spread: 23 cm (9 in).

▼ **Androsace sarmentosa**
An evergreen mat-former flowering in spring. There are deep pink and pale pink forms. A reliable plant except in very wet areas. Height: 10 cm (4 in). Spread: 30 cm (1 ft).

▲ **Aurinia saxatilis**
(syn. Alyssum saxatile)
Although correctly called an aurinia, it is still widely sold as an alyssum. One of the best-known spring-flowering rock plants, the common name of gold dust is apt. Height: 23 cm (9 in). Spread: 30 cm (1 ft).

▲ **Aethionema 'Warley Ruber'**
Evergreen or semi-evergreen, it is smothered with bright flowers in late spring and early summer. Tends to be short-lived. Other varieties are paler. Height: 15 cm (6 in). Spread: 23 cm (9 in).

▲ **Acaena microphylla**
A long-lived carpeting plant which is practically evergreen. The flowers have spiny reddish bracts and appear in summer, followed by the intriguing burs. Height: 5 cm (2 in). Spread: 15 cm (6 in).

▲ Antennaria dioica

A carpeter that makes a good cover for alpine bulbs or between paving. Flowers in late spring and early summer. Height: 2.5 cm (1 in). Spread: 25 cm (10 in).

▼ Arenaria balearica

The sandwort, normally evergreen, is very inconspicuous out of flower, but in late spring and early summer the tiny flowers are surprisingly noticeable. It prefers damp shade. Height: 1 cm (½ in). Spread: 30 cm (1 ft) or more.

▲ Arabis caucasica (syn. A. albida, A. alpina)

A mat-forming evergreen that flowers in late spring and early summer. There are pink forms and white ones, some single, others double, and 'Variegata' has cream-splashed leaves. Height: 15 cm (6 in). Spread: 15 cm (6 in).

▲ Armeria maritima

Thrift has tufts of attractive grass-like foliage the year round. The flowers are pink, red or white, according to variety, and appear in early summer. It is easy to grow and always looks neat. Height: 10 cm (4 in). Spread: 15 cm (6 in).

▲ Aster alpinus

Useful for extending the colour in the rock garden beyond spring, this alpine aster flowers in mid-summer. The flower colour is variable and includes white. Height: 15 cm (6 in). Spread: 30–45 cm (1–1½ ft).

▲ Aubrieta

The popular rock cress is widely grown over walls, and there are many varieties, mainly in shades of blue and purple. The one illustrated is 'Doctor Mules'. Height: 8 cm (3 in). Spread: 30 cm (1 ft).

▼ Corydalis solida

A tuberous plant bearing spurred flowers in spring, it then dies down in summer. The variety 'George Baker' has rose-red flowers. An undemanding yet charming plant to grow. Height: 20 cm (8 in). Spread: 10 cm (4 in).

▲ Campanula cochleariifolia

Fairy thimbles is an apt common name for this dainty but spreading campanula. The pale blue, lavender or white flowers cover the plant in summer, but growth dies back in winter. Height: 8 cm (3 in). Spread: 30 cm (1 ft) or more.

▲ Cerastium tomentosum

Snow-in-summer is a vigorous plant, more suitable for a border than a small rock garden. The flowers appear in late spring and early summer; the silver foliage remains attractive all summer. Height: 8 cm (3 in). Spread: 75 cm (2½ ft) or more.

▲ Dryas octopetala

This prostrate evergreen bears its white flowers in late spring and early summer, followed by attractive feathery seed heads which give the plant a second flush of interest. Height: 5–8 cm (2–3 in). Spread: 30 cm (1 ft) or more.

▶ Erinus alpinus

A short-lived semi-evergreen, blooming in late spring and early summer. Flowers may be pink or purple, and sometimes white. A good choice for planting in crevices. Self-seeds freely. Height: 8 cm (3 in). Spread: 15 cm (6 in).

▲ Erysimum hieraciifolium (syn. E. alpinum)

The nomenclature of these plants can be confusing, and the variety illustrated ('Moonlight') is now considered to be a hybrid. Some varieties have mauve flowers. Height: 15 cm (6 in). Spread: 20 cm (8 in).

▲ Gentiana acaulis

The trumpet gentian is one of the rock garden essentials, and relatively easy to grow. The deep blue flowers appear in late spring and early autumn. There is also a white-flowered form. Height: 8 cm (3 in). Spread: 30 cm (1 ft) or more.

▲ Geum pyrenaicum

An uncommon rhizomatous species but worth growing if you come across it. The yellow flowers bring cheer to the rock garden in summer. Height: 23 cm (9 in). Spread: 30 cm (1 ft).

▼ Gypsophila repens

Useful for a large rock garden but excellent for a dry wall or bank. Flowers may be white, lilac or pink, and may be seen between June and August. Height: 8 cm (3 in). Spread: 30 cm (1 ft) or more.

▲ Geranium cinereum var. subcaulescens

An outstanding plant for a large rock garden. The sprawling growth is studded with purple-red blooms over a long period in summer. The intense colour of the flowers is conspicuous even from a distance. Height: 15 cm (6 in). Spread: 30 cm (1 ft).

▲ Helichrysum bellidioides

A low, spreading evergreen grown for its white flowers with starry petals, attractive for most of the summer. It can be invasive. Height: 8 cm (3 in). Spread: 45 cm (1½ ft).

◄ Hypericum olympicum

Useful for providing late colour in a rock garden or alpine trough. It blooms in mid and late summer and has a dense, tufted habit. Height: 23 cm (9 in). Spread: 15 cm (6 in).

▲ Iberis sempervirens

This perennial candytuft is evergreen, and at its best in late spring when covered with snowy flowers. Varieties differ mainly in compactness; this one is 'Weisser Zwerg'.
Height: 10–30 cm (4–12 in). Spread: 45–60 cm (1½–2 ft).

▲ Linaria origanifolia
(syn. Chaenorhinum origanifolium)

An unusual dwarf toadflax, worth growing if you come across it. The sprays of small violet and white flowers cover the plant in summer. Its small size makes it suitable for an alpine trough. Height: 15 cm (6 in). Spread: 10 cm (4 in).

▼ Leontopodium alpinum

The famous Edelweiss tends to be short-lived unless you can protect it from excessive winter wet.
Height: 15–20 cm (6–8 in).
Spread: 15 cm (6 in).

▲ Lewisia cotyledon hybrid

Evergreen leaf rosettes, with flowers in shades of pink to purple in early summer. Good crevice plant. Height: 30 cm (1 ft). Spread: 23 cm (9 in).

▲ Lithodora diffusa (syn. Lithospermum diffusum)

A semi-prostrate evergreen shrub with a profusion of blue flowers in summer. The variety illustrated is 'Heavenly Blue'. Height: 15–30 cm (6–12 in). Spread: 45 cm (1½ ft).

▲ Lychnis alpina

The alpine catchfly is easy to grow and has conspicuous heads of deep or pale pink flowers (sometimes white) in early summer, often extending into mid-summer.
Height: 10 cm (4 in). Spread: 15 cm (6 in).

▼ Oxalis adenophylla

This tuberous perennial is not as invasive as some oxalis. It is worth growing for its foliage alone. The leaves provide a superb background for the flowers in spring.
Height: 5 cm (2 in).
Spread: 10 cm (4 in).

▲ Phlox subulata

There are many varieties of this ground-hugging evergreen, grown for its carpet of flowers in early summer. Flower colours are mainly shades of red, pink and blue. The variety illustrated is 'Alexander's Surprise'.
Height: 10 cm (4 in). Spread: 20 cm (8 in).

▲ Potentilla eriocarpa

The pale yellow flowers appear over a long period during the summer. It is an easy plant to grow, and a good one for troughs as well as rock gardens and raised beds.
Height: 8 cm (3 in).
Spread: 15 cm (6 in).

▲ Primula 'Wanda'

An old favourite and one of the most reliable of the alpine primulas, regularly producing masses of its crimson-purple flowers each spring.
Height: 10–15 cm (4–6 in).
Spread: 15–20 cm (6–8 in).

▲ Pulsatilla vulgaris

The pasque flower blooms in spring followed by silky seed heads. Colours include shades of purple, red, pink and white. Height: 23 cm (9 in). Spread: 23 cm (9 in).

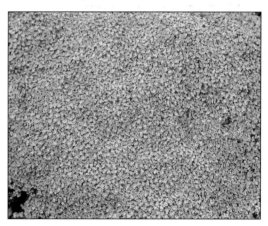

▲ Raoulia australis

The tiny sulphur-yellow flowers in summer go almost unnoticed. The plant itself may be trodden on inadvertently unless you are careful! It is grown for the evergreen film-like carpet of grey-green foliage.
Height: 6 mm (¼ in). Spread: 25 cm (10 in).

▲ Saponaria ocymoides

This soapwort blooms brightly from early summer onwards. A vigorous trailer, it is suitable for sunny walls. Though short-lived, it self-sows freely and may need trimming back. Height: 15 cm (6in). Spread: 45 cm (1½ ft).

▲ Saxifraga cochlearis

One of the encrusted saxifrages, so-called because of the white encrusted edges to the leaves. White flowers, often spotted red, are produced in early summer. Height: 20 cm (8 in). Spread: 25 cm (10 in).

▲ Sedum floriferum

This tough carpeting stonecrop flowers into late summer. The variety illustrated is 'Weihenstephaner Gold', which may be listed as a variety of S. kamschaticum. Height: 15 cm (6 in). Spread: 30 cm (1 ft).

▲ Sedum spathulifolium

The flowers are a bonus, as these evergreens are grown mainly for their foliage. The variety illustrated is 'Cape Blanco', but 'Purpureum' is also recommended. Height: 5 cm (2 in). Spread: 45 cm (1½ ft) or more.

▲ Saxifraga 'Pixie'

There are many mossy-looking saxifrages with dainty flowers in spring, and this is typical of them. They are ideal for a rock garden in semi-shade, and easy to grow, forming cushions of rosettes. Height: 5 cm (2 in). Spread: 23 cm (9 in) or more.

◄ Sempervivum

Houseleeks come in an amazing array of shapes, sizes and colours, and are very collectable. They are good in containers. This is 'Commander Hay'. Height: 5–23 cm (2–9 in). Spread: 15–30 cm (6–12 in).

ROCK PLANTS

JANUARY   page 27

● Keep tidying up beds, removing dead leaves and working the soil between plants with a hand fork.
● Sow any remaining seeds that need frost for germination (see December, page 281).
● Plan new plantings and study catalogues; order plants for the spring.

FEBRUARY   page 46

● Stand plants received through the post in a sheltered place and water carefully; pack damp peat around them if weather is bad and you cannot plant out.
● Add a top dressing of gravel or chippings around plants in rock garden to suppress weeds and ensure free drainage.
● Check for slugs, especially around early-flowering bulbs.
● Take root cuttings.

MARCH   page 75

● Weed carefully, trying not to disturb any bulbs coming through, and replenish top dressing of stone chippings or gravel.
● Check on germination of seeds in trays overwintered outside; once growth appears, move trays to cold frame or unheated greenhouse.
● Plant rock plants as soon as possible after purchase, unless weather is severe.
● Divide carpeting and other suitable plants to increase stock or to improve health of existing plants.

● Plant up rooted cuttings into small pots.
● Water lewisias left dry over the winter.
● Check plants in pots for vine weevil and treat as necessary.

APRIL   page 108

● Check for frost damage and replace plants where damage is severe; if damage is not too severe, divide damaged plants and replant healthy portions.
● Take care not to damage any self-sown seedlings when removing old plants or weeding.
● Pot on root cuttings once they have produced a few leaves.
● Prick out winter-sown seedlings into pots, moving the pots outdoors from the middle of the month onwards.
● Divide earlier flowering plants kept in a cold greenhouse.

MAY   page 136

● Visit gardens and nurseries to see plants in flower and identify new plants you would like to acquire.
● Weed the rock garden thoroughly with a hand fork or small trowel.
● Deadhead as flowers fade and cut back aubrietia to promote strong growth.
● Add fertiliser to rosette-forming rock plants and apply top dressing to the entire rock garden to improve the soil.
● Plant out root cuttings taken in February in their final position when they are sufficiently well developed.

● Feed plants in pots in a cold greenhouse with liquid fertiliser every fortnight.

JUNE   page 159

● Take semi-ripe cuttings and place in compost or sand.
● Continue cutting back plants after flowering.
● Trim trailing and invasive plants, and assess which plants will need transplanting in the autumn.
● Water in the evening during dry spells, but do not overwater; a sprinkler with a fine spray is best as large water droplets will damage the soil structure.
● Take cuttings of plants in pots that have finished flowering and gather seeds of earlier flowering plants.
● Continue feeding plants in pots in the greenhouse with a liquid fertiliser once every two weeks.

JULY   page 183

● Continue with routine tasks, such as weeding, watering, cutting back and deadheading, plus applying a top dressing if necessary.
● Collect and store seed for sowing now or later in the year; label bags and keep in a cool, dry place.

AUGUST   page 202

● Take cuttings, keep shaded and spray daily during hot weather.

● Order dwarf bulbs for spring flowering.

SEPTEMBER   page 224

● Transplant any plants which need to be moved, watering well before and after replanting.
● Plant dwarf bulbs for spring flowering and pot up some for the greenhouse.

OCTOBER   page 245

● Continue planting and transplanting while the weather is not frosty but only put out well-established young plants.
● Prepare for winter by covering tender plants with a cloche, and by removing fallen leaves and dying flower stems to deter pests and prevent diseases.

NOVEMBER   page 265

● Continue to clear fallen leaves from the rock garden. If left they will keep light off the plants and encourage slugs, snails and diseases.
● Cover vulnerable plants with a cloche. Tilt pots at an angle to avoid water accumulating around crowns.

DECEMBER   page 281

● Sow seeds in pots with good drainage and leave outside to overwinter. Water from below. Some seed takes three years to germinate so don't throw away old pots of seed too quickly.

Roses

A FAVOURITE PLANT for most gardeners, the rose is constantly being improved. Varieties are bred for better and better performance as well as scent and good looks, with prolific flowering, compact growth, and even disease resistance evident in many of them. Roses have been developed for new uses too: the ground-cover County roses can be used for long-flowering ground carpeting, others are suitable for growing in containers, and compact 'patio roses' have been bred with the modern small garden in mind. But, of course, the shrub roses – old-fashioned and modern – still have an important role where you have space for them.

There are hundreds of readily available roses, and new ones are introduced every year. The pictures here show only a tiny selection of good varieties, to inspire you to explore the current rose catalogues.

▼ 'Fragrant Cloud'

Hybrid tea. An old-timer which still has a place in the rose garden for its very intense perfume. Unfortunately the colour tends to fade as the bloom ages, and it is prone to black spot and mildew. Height: 90 cm (3 ft). Spread: 60 cm (2 ft).

▲ 'Freedom'

Hybrid tea. The flowers have an intensity of colour retained well even as the bloom ages. Very good disease resistance is another good reason to grow it. Height: 75 cm (2½ ft). Spread: 60 cm (2 ft).

▲ 'Ingrid Bergman'

Hybrid tea. A free-flowering variety of an unfading deep red. Good in beds, and the bushy growth makes it suitable for an informal hedge. Height: 75 cm (2½ ft). Spread: 60 cm (2 ft).

▲ 'Paul Shirville'

Hybrid tea. This vigorous variety has flowers of classic hybrid tea shape, coupled with the outstanding fragrance you would expect from a good rose. Ideal for beds and good for cutting. Height: 90 cm (3 ft). Spread: 75 cm (2½ ft).

▼ 'Loving Memory'

Hybrid tea. Reliable and a good choice for a rose bed, this variety will flower freely to provide plenty of colour. The strong upright stems make it a good cut flower. Height: 75 cm (2½ ft). Spread: 60 cm (2 ft).

▼ 'Peace'

Hybrid tea. There are better roses now, but this veteran is one of the world's best-known roses. It needs plenty of space, and is only slightly fragrant, but the blooms are beautiful. Height: 1.2–1.5 m (4–5 ft). Spread: 90 cm (3 ft).

▲ Peaudouce (syn. 'Elina')

Hybrid tea. Size and quality of bloom are the outstanding features of this variety. Flowering is also prolific and prolonged, so it is a good choice for a bed, or as a contrast to brighter colours. Height: 90 cm (3 ft). Spread: 75 cm (2½ ft).

▼ 'Royal William'

Hybrid tea. Another first-class deep red variety, which combines a strong colour with a delightful scent. Vigorous, healthy foliage is another pleasing feature. Height: 90 cm (3 ft). Spread: 75 cm (2½ ft).

▲ 'Tequila Sunrise'

Hybrid tea. What this variety lacks in classically-shaped blooms, it makes up for amply with its distinctive colouring. It is eye-catching planted in groups and when used as a cut flower. Height: 75 cm (2½ ft). Spread: 60 cm (2 ft).

▼ 'Anna Livia'

Floribunda. An attractive colour and good foliage as a background give this variety its main appeal, though there is a delicate fragrance too. Reliable for a rose bed, or for cutting. Height: 75 cm (2½ ft). Spread: 60 cm (2 ft).

▲ 'Arthur Bell'

Floribunda. Although the colour tends to fade as the blooms age, this variety is worth considering for its strong scent (particularly good for a floribunda) and good disease resistance. Starts early and finishes late. Height: 90 cm (3 ft). Spread: 60 cm (2 ft).

▲ 'Hannah Gordon'

Floribunda. Attractively shaped blooms and striking colouring make this a variety that demands attention. It is an excellent all-round rose for the garden. Height: 75 cm (2½ ft). Spread: 60 cm (2 ft).

▲ 'Korresia'

Floribunda. One of the best yellow floribundas, its unfading blooms are produced over a long period, and it is scented too. It has all the qualities of a first-rate bedding rose. Height: 75 cm (2½ ft). Spread: 45 cm (1½ ft).

▲ 'The Times Rose'

Floribunda. A strong colour and dark green foliage with good disease resistance are its main attractions. It has a light fragrance, and growth is bushy and spreading. Height: 75 cm (2½ ft). Spread: 75 cm (2½ ft).

▲ 'Gentle Touch'
Patio rose. One of the best short, pink floribunda roses. The colour is strong enough to stand out, yet delicate enough not to clash with stronger colours. Height: 60 cm (2 ft). Spread: 45 cm (1½ ft).

▲ 'Baby Masquerade'
Miniature. The multicoloured flowers, just like the full-sized 'Masquerade', are the reason to grow this old favourite. Height: 30 cm (1 ft). Spread: 23 cm (9 in).

▼ 'Top Marks'
Patio rose. Of vivid colour and small size, this outstanding rose is suitable for edging a bed or for growing in tubs. It is compact enough to mix with ordinary bedding plants. Height: 45 cm (1½ ft). Spread: 45 cm (1½ ft).

▲ 'Bantry Bay'
Climber. Beautiful flowers over a long period coupled with restrained growth make this an ideal pillar rose. Height: 2.5–3 m (8–10 ft). Spread: 1.8m (6 ft).

▲ 'Warm Welcome'
Patio climber. This short climber is ideal for a patio or where space is restricted. Flowers all summer. Height: 2.1 m (7 ft). Spread: 1.5 m (5 ft).

▲ 'Climbing Cécile Brünner'
Climbing polyantha. A vigorous climber suitable for a large wall or for growing through a tree. The main flush of flower is in June, with a few flowers later. Height: 4.5 m (15 ft). Spread: 3 m (10 ft).

▼ 'Angela Rippon'
Miniature. A well-established variety with a prettily shaped flower and distinctive colour. It has good repeat flowering and makes a dainty edging for a patio bed. Height: 30 cm (1 ft). Spread: 23 cm (9 in).

▲ 'Climbing Iceberg'
Climber. A climbing form of a famous floribunda. Strong, healthy growth and a mass of white flowers that stand out well against a wall make this a very desirable variety. Height: 4.5 m (15 ft). Spread: 3 m (10 ft).

▼ **'Compassion'**

Climber. This outstanding climber with large hybrid tea flowers is justifiably very popular. A strong scent and vigorous, healthy growth with repeat flowering add to its many qualities. It makes a good pillar rose. Height: 3 m (10 ft). Spread: 1.5 m (5 ft).

▼ **'Dublin Bay'**

Climber. Intense flower colour and well-formed large blooms give this rose strong eye-appeal, and its rather bushy growth with dark, glossy leaves can be a benefit where a compact climber is required. Height: 2.5 m (8 ft). Spread: 1.8 m (6 ft).

▲ **'Wedding Day'**

Rampant rambler. The clusters of fragrant cream-coloured flowers fade to a pinky white and come in a single flush in July or early August. It looks spectacular climbing through a tree or over a wall. Height: 6 m (20 ft). Spread: 3 m (10 ft) or more.

▲ **'Zéphirine Drouhin'**

Climbing Bourbon rose. Also known as the thornless rose, this is still a favourite 130 years after its introduction. It produces a long succession of very fragrant blooms. Height: 3 m (10 ft). Spread: 1.8 m (6 ft).

▲ **'Hampshire'**

Ground cover. Easy to look after and ground-hugging, this variety offers a bright way to cover an area of ground attractively. Good repeat flowering. Height: 30 cm (1 ft). Spread: 75 cm (2½ ft).

▲ **'Kent'**

Ground cover. The flowers are not as bright and colourful as some ground-cover roses, but this variety remains compact and continues flowering over a long period. Height: 45 cm (1½ ft). Spread: 60 cm (2 ft).

▲ **'Nozomi'**

Ground cover. A versatile rose also suitable for container planting. The flowers vary from pearl pink to white and they are borne prolifically on compact plants (the plant illustrated is in a tub). Height: 45 cm (1½ ft). Spread: 60 cm (2 ft).

▲ **'Surrey'**

Ground cover. Taller than some of its County stablemates, this is only suitable where a large area of ground has to be covered. Flowers for a long period, and is slightly fragrant. Height: 90 cm (3 ft). Spread: 1.2 m (4 ft).

▼ **'L. D. Braithwaite'**

Modern shrub rose. One of the best roses of its type for continuity of blooms, and well worth finding space for. The beautiful blooms also have a notable fragrance.
Height: 90–120 cm (3–4 ft).
Spread: 90–120 cm (3–4 ft).

▲ **'Buff Beauty'**

Hybrid musk rose. Many shrub roses lack repeat flowering, but not this one – the autumn display is impressive. Makes a fine flowering hedge.
Height: 1.5 m (5 ft).
Spread: 1.2 m (4 ft).

▲ **'Ballerina'**

Hybrid musk rose. An outstanding variety covered in blooms by mid-summer, with repeat flowering. Grow it as tall ground cover, as a shrub in a border, or even as a flowering hedge. Height: 90 cm (3 ft). Spread: 90 cm (3 ft).

▲ **Rosa xanthina 'Canary Bird'**

Shrub rose. Justifiably popular, this vigorous, easy-care variety has arching stems with fern-like leaves covered with 5 cm (2 in) yellow flowers in late spring. Height: 2.1 m (7 ft). Spread: 2.1 m (7 ft).

▲ **'Charles de Mills'**

Gallica shrub rose. Old-fashioned roses have a special appeal, and the quartered-rosette flowers of this variety have a very strong fragrance. Superb in a mixed border. Height: 1.2 m (4 ft).
Spread: 90 cm (3 ft).

▲ **'Cornelia'**

Hybrid musk rose. Repeat flowering and a strong scent make this a popular shrub rose, but it needs plenty of space. Try it as a flowering hedge.
Height: 1.5 m (5 ft). Spread: 2.1 m (7 ft).

▲ 'Fru Dagmar Hastrup'
(syn. 'Frau Dagmar Hartopp')
Rugosa shrub rose. Its very spiny stems and upright growth make this an excellent choice for a hedge. The large and fragrant flowers are freely produced and followed by red hips. Height: 1.2 m (4 ft). Spread: 90 cm (3 ft).

▼ 'Graham Thomas'
Modern shrub rose. An outstanding variety that has a good scent, bright colour, and the charm of an old-fashioned variety. It blooms continuously from early summer to late autumn. Height: 1.5 m (5 ft). Spread: 1.2 m (4 ft).

▲ 'Nevada'
Modern shrub rose. Given the space to display itself properly, this is an outstanding rose. The large bush may be almost hidden beneath large creamy-white blooms in June. Height: 2.1 m (7 ft). Spread: 2.1 m (7 ft).

▼ Rosa banksiae 'Lutea'
Climber. The yellow banksian rose looks at its best in late spring, and needs a warm, sunny wall to do well. An old rose but worth growing for its early flowers if you have space. Height: 6 m (20 ft). Spread: 3 m (10 ft).

▲ Rosa gallica 'Versicolor'
Gallica shrub rose. The so-called Rosa mundi, *still popular for a shrub border or rose garden more than 700 years after it was introduced! Be prepared to control mildew. Height: 1.2 m (4 ft). Spread: 90 cm (3 ft).*

▲ Rosa glauca (syn. R. rubrifolia)
Species rose. The arching stems are violet-tinged, have few thorns and are clothed with greyish-purple leaves. It produces single flowers in early summer, with red hips by autumn. Suitable for a mixed or shrub border. Height: 1.8 m (6 ft). Spread: 1.5 m (5 ft).

◄ Rosa sericea pteracantha

Species rose. This one is grown not for the beauty of its white flowers, but its young stems and, in particular, the enormous ruby-red translucent thorns. The flowers are followed by red hips in autumn. The small, fern-like foliage is also attractive. Prune out old stems to encourage new young growth.
Height: 2.5 m (8 ft).
Spread: 1.8 m (6 ft).

► Rosa rugosa 'Scabrosa' (syn. R. 'Scabrosa')

Rugosa shrub rose. An impressive rose with single flowers of crimson tinted with violet reaching over 10 cm (4 in) across, followed by large orange-red hips. The typical rugosa foliage acts as an effective backdrop for them. Height: 1.2 m (4 ft). Spread: 1.5 m (5 ft).

► Rosa moyesii

Species rose. The red or pink single flowers that appear in May or June are beautiful, but the 5 cm (2 in) bottle-shaped hips that follow are the main reason why this rose is grown. 'Geranium' is more compact than the species.
Height: 3 m (10 ft).
Spread: 2.5 m (8 ft).

▲ 'Schneezwerg'

Rugosa shrub rose. The small, white, anemone-like flowers are produced on spiny stems over a long period, and the small orange-red hips sometimes overlap with late flowers. Like all rugosas it makes a good hedge and is very healthy. Height: 1.8 m (6 ft). Spread: 1.5 m (5 ft).

▼ Rosa sweginzowii

Species rose. This vigorous shrub demands a large garden. Its flagon-shaped hips are an outstanding autumn feature. The rose pink flowers are rather small and open in summer. Height: 3 m (10 ft).
Spread: 3 m (10 ft).

ROSES

JANUARY   page 27

- Check on roses being forced in the greenhouse; water to keep soil moist.

FEBRUARY   page 46

- Check all wooden structures used for roses to climb up and over; also check standard stakes and rose ties.
- Apply sulphate of potash to encourage greater resistance to disease.
- Start pruning in mild areas.

MARCH   page 76

- Plant bare-root roses as soon as possible, preparing the site well. Tread in plants firmly and also refirm any established plants that have been lifted by frost.
- Most roses should be pruned before the end of March. Remove old, decaying wood and thin, spindly wood.
- After pruning check all stakes and ties, spray plants and mulch soil.

APRIL   page 109

- Finish pruning early in the month (*see* March, page 76).
- Apply the first dressing of rose fertiliser and treat roses for pests and diseases.
- Mulch when ground is moist.
- Plant or repot container-grown roses immediately after purchase.
- Check temperature in greenhouse; water and check for pests.

MAY   page 136

- Container-grown roses can still be planted but keep them well watered.
- Check for pests and diseases.
- Move roses out of the greenhouse immediately after flowering.

JUNE   page 160

- Disbud hybrid teas if you wish to encourage larger blooms.
- Take care not to deadhead roses grown for the colour and profusion of their hips later in the year.
- Remove suckers from the base of plants as soon as they appear.
- Check for pests and diseases.
- Control weeds by hoeing.

JULY   page 184

- Deadhead as blooms fade except for roses grown to display hips in the autumn.
- Give the final feed of the year. Feeding after this will produce late growth prone to frost damage.
- Maintain watering of roses in containers and of recently planted roses.

AUGUST   page 203

- Continue to deadhead as blooms fade except for roses grown for hips.
- Check supports and ties on standards and climbers.
- Watch for rust disease.

SEPTEMBER page 224

- Plan for new plantings and replacements.
- Continue to deadhead and check for pests and diseases; keep the ground clear of discarded rose heads and foliage.
- Tie in new growth on climbers and ramblers.
- Take hardwood cuttings.

OCTOBER   page 245

- Prepare sites for new plantings.
- Prune ramblers and summer-flowering climbers.
- Reduce the length of shoots on hybrid teas and floribundas.
- Lightly prune weeping standards.
- Pot up roses for forcing in the greenhouse.

NOVEMBER   page 266

- Plant newly arrived roses.
- Move any established roses you wish to resite. Use a good planting mixture.
- Prune selected roses if not done last month (*see* October, page 245).

DECEMBER   page 281

- Continue to plant if conditions are suitable.
- Complete pruning of climbers and ramblers and check all wooden structures supporting them.
- Protect frost-prone varieties.
- Prune roses in greenhouse for forcing; water sparingly and ventilate.

Sweet peas

SCENT AND WONDERFUL COLOURS are the attributes that make the sweet pea so popular. Enthusiasts grow exhibition varieties to perfection for shows, but most gardeners grow them simply for scent and colour in the garden and to cut for the house.

There are many varieties of sweet peas available, and the ways in which you can grow them vary. These illustrations show just a small selection and how they can be supported and grown.

▲ 'Bouquet Rose'
The Bouquet series of sweet peas were bred for cutting and garden decoration. The emphasis is on vigour and strong flower stems, but many are scented.
Height: 2.5 m (8 ft). Spread: 30 cm (1 ft).

▶ 'Lady Diana'
Sweet peas grown for garden decoration rather than for cutting look more natural if growth is trained through tall twiggy sticks inserted when the plants are young.
Height: 1.8 m (6 ft). Spread: 30 cm (1 ft).

▶ 'Jet Set'
Useful where a low-growing variety is required for garden decoration, such as near the front of a border.
Height: 90 cm (3 ft). Spread: 30 cm (1 ft).

▲ 'Our Harry'
Sweet peas required for both garden display and cutting can be grown up large-mesh wire or plastic netting. Height: 2.5 m (8 ft). Spread: 30 cm (1 ft).

▲ 'Patio Mixed'
This is one of the really dwarf varieties, intended for use with summer bedding or as an edging to a bed or border. Each stem carries up to four blooms, but they are only lightly scented. Height: 30 cm (1 ft). Spread: 23 cm (9 in).

▲ Mixed sweet peas
Where space is limited, mixtures are often the best choice for general garden display or for cutting. These are growing up wire netting looped around tall canes.
Height: 2.5 m (8 ft). Spread: 30 cm (1 ft).

▲ 'Queen Mother'
Typical of the Spencer type of sweet pea, this variety has well-spaced, sweetly scented flowers. These are being grown inside a mesh column. Height: 2.5 m (8 ft). Spread: 30 cm (1 ft).

▲ **Lathyrus latifolius**

For something different, try the so-called everlasting sweet pea. The flowers do not last longer than normal, but this is a perennial so the plant comes up each year. Height: 1.8 m (6 ft). Spread: 1.2 m (4 ft).

▲ **'Su Pollard'**

Large-mesh wire looped around canes to make a column will produce long, straight stems for cutting, with less effort than plants tied to individual canes. Height: 2.5 m (8 ft). Spread: 30 cm (1 ft).

SWEET PEAS

JANUARY   page 27

- Top dress seedlings sown in October.
- Sow seeds in gentle heat.
- Dress prepared beds with lime or sulphur if necessary.

FEBRUARY   page 46

- Fork over and firm soil on planting site when weather permits and apply a balanced fertiliser.
- Erect supports for cordon-grown plants.
- Sow seeds outdoors in flowering position except in very cold areas, and protect seeds and seedlings against pests.
- Pot on seedlings sown last month and remove growing points of seedlings to encourage sideshoots to develop.

MARCH   page 77

- Plant out autumn-sown seedlings as soon as weather conditions permit; provide support for the growing plants.
- Protect seedlings against pests.
- Sow seeds outdoors in their flowering position if weather permits.
- Make spring sowings under glass as early as possible this month.

APRIL   page 110

- Plant out March-sown seedlings after hardening off.
- Water and feed young plants.
- Remove frost protection from seedlings

sown outdoors in October.
- Start restricting growth if you wish to grow plants on the cordon system.

MAY   page 136

- Complete restricting growth on cordon-grown plants and tie into canes as they grow; pinch out sideshoots and tendrils and first few flower stems.

JUNE   page 160

- Syringe the plants with water in warm weather; if watering is necessary soak the ground at frequent intervals.
- Check for pests and diseases and remove and destroy any unhealthy plants.
- Continue to remove tendrils and side-shoots from cordon-grown plants and tie in shoots as plants grow.
- Layer cordon-grown plants at least two weeks before blooms are required for showing.
- Watch for bud drop.

JULY   page 184

- Liquid feed, if necessary, every fortnight.
- Mist and water copiously in hot, dry conditions and supplement mulch if applied earlier in the season.
- Check for pests and diseases and protect flower buds from birds if necessary.
- Continue to remove tendrils and side-shoots on cordons, tying in and cutting flowers so they cannot set seed.

AUGUST   page 203

- To prolong flowering, water, feed and mulch as necessary. If no mulch has been used, hoe regularly.
- Layer cordon-grown plants for the second time (*see* June, page 160).
- Continue to cut blooms; remove tendrils and sideshoots on cordons regularly; tie in mature stems.

SEPTEMBER   page 225

- Purchase seed and prepare cold frames and greenhouse for next month's sowing.

OCTOBER   page 246

- Clear next year's planting site.
- Sow sweet peas in open ground in areas with mild winters and protect with cloches; also sow seed under glass.

NOVEMBER   page 268

- Prepare next year's planting site.
- Pot on seedlings from October sowing.

DECEMBER   page 281

- Protect seedlings from severe frost and from pests.
- Pinch out growing points of seedlings, if necessary, to encourage the formation of sideshoots.
- Complete preparation of next year's planting site.

Trees, shrubs & hedges

THESE FORM THE BACKBONE OF THE GARDEN, and are the most permanent plants, so choose them with thought and plant with care. Pay particular attention to the likely ultimate size of any trees that you choose. Heights given here are those likely after about 15 years – some may then grow little more, others may continue to grow, though no very tall trees have been included. The height of shrubs can be influenced by pruning as well as soil and site.

▲ Acer platanoides 'Drummondii'
Norway maples grow large, but this is one of the variegated varieties that is more restrained. Nevertheless, it is not one for a very small garden. Height: 6 m (20 ft). Spread: 3 m (10 ft).

▶ Betula pendula 'Youngii'
The silver birch is one of our most common trees, and very quick-growing. Young's weeping birch grows more slowly and less tall. Height: 4.5 m (15 ft). Spread: 4.5 m (15 ft).

▶ Catalpa bignonioides 'Aurea'
The golden form of the Indian bean tree is smaller with brighter foliage than the species, and is more suitable for the garden. Height: 4.5 m (15 ft). Spread: 4.5 m (15 ft).

▼ Crataegus prunifolia
A type of hawthorn that is particularly attractive in autumn, with a display of red fruits and red or orange foliage tints. With flowers in June this is a good all-round well-proportioned garden tree. Height: 4.5 m (15 ft). Spread: 3 m (10 ft).

▼ Cercis siliquastrum
The Judas tree does best in warm areas and may not do well in a cold garden. The pink flowers appear on bare branches in May. Good autumn colour. Height: 4.5 m (15 ft). Spread: 4.5 m (15 ft).

▲ Laburnum x watereri 'Vossii'
Laburnums are popular June-flowering trees, and this is one of the best. The pendent flower chains are long and very few of the poisonous seeds are formed. Height: 4.5 m (15 ft). Spread: 4.5m (15 ft).

▲ Malus floribunda

An ornamental crab apple, though the main feature is the mass of pale pink flowers (darker in bud) in mid and late spring. Height: 4.5 m (15 ft). Spread: 4.5 m (15 ft).

▲ Malus x zumi 'Golden Hornet'

A multi-merit tree with white flowers in late spring and branches laden with yellow crab apples in autumn. A reliable fruiter. Height: 4.5 m (15 ft). Spread: 4.5 m (15 ft).

▲ Prunus 'Kanzan'

This is a good choice for a medium-sized garden. The main appeal is the early spring blossom, but the autumn colour is good. Height: 4.5 m (15 ft). Spread: 4.5 m (15 ft).

▼ Pyrus salicifolia 'Pendula'

The weeping willow-leaved pear makes a dome-shaped tree suitable for a small garden. Delightful silvery foliage, with creamy-white flowers in April. Height: 4.5 m (15 ft). Spread: 3 m (10 ft).

▼ Robinia pseudoacacia 'Frisia'

This golden variety of false acacia is always eye-catching, and an outstanding fast-growing tree for a medium-sized or large garden. Height: 6 m (20 ft). Spread: 3 m (10 ft).

▶ Picea glauca var. albertiana

Popular dwarf conifer, with distinctive cone shape. This variety is 'Alberta Globe'. Height: 1.2 m (4 ft). Spread: 75 cm (2½ ft).

▲ Sambucus racemosa 'Plumosa Aurea'

A bushy, tree-like shrub, this form of red-berried elder is grown for its attractive foliage and clusters of cream flowers. Height: 3 m (10 ft). Spread: 3 m (10 ft).

▲ Sorbus aucuparia 'Fructu Luteo'

The foliage of this mountain ash makes it a desirable garden tree, but its moment of glory comes in late summer and into autumn when the orange-yellow fruits appear. Height: 6 m (20 ft). Spread: 3 m (10 ft).

▲ x Cupressocyparis leylandii

Widely grown as a clipped hedge, but it makes a very tall tree. This is 'Robinson's Gold'. Height: 10 m (33 ft). Spread: 1.5 m (5 ft).

▲ Cupressus macrocarpa

The Monterey cypress eventually grows tall. This variety is 'Goldcrest'. Height: 6 m (20 ft). Spread: 3 m (10 ft).

▲ Juniperus horizontalis 'Blue Chip'

A prostrate ground-hugging juniper useful for ground cover. Height: 45 cm (1½ ft). Spread: 1.8 m (6 ft).

▲ Amelanchier canadensis

Can be grown as a small tree or as a multi-stemmed shrub. White flowers in April, good autumn colour. Height: 3 m (10 ft). Spread: 2.5 m (8 ft).

▲ Caryopteris x clandonensis

An excellent plant for the mixed border or with other shrubs, blooming freely in August and September. The variety illustrated is 'Heavenly Blue'. Height: 90 cm (3 ft). Spread: 90 cm (3 ft).

▼ Berberis thunbergii 'Atropurpurea Nana'

A deciduous berberis is a multi-merit plant, with small flowers in spring and good leaf colour in autumn. This one has reddish purple foliage then becomes redder in autumn. Height: 90 cm (3 ft). Spread: 90 cm (3 ft).

▼ Choisya ternata

The Mexican orange blossom is grown for its fragrant white flowers in May, set off by the aromatic evergreen foliage. Height: 1.8 m (6 ft). Spread: 1.8 m (6 ft).

▲ Buddleja davidii

The butterfly bush is at its best from mid-summer to autumn. This is 'Nanho Blue' but pink, red, white and purple varieties are available. Height: 2.5 m (8 ft). Spread: 1.8 m (6 ft).

▲ Cotinus coggygria 'Royal Purple'

This variety of the smoke tree or Venetian sumach is grown partly for its summer-long purple foliage, but also for the wispy flower heads that look like a haze hovering above the plant. Height: 3 m (10 ft). Spread: 2.5 m (8 ft).

▼ Camellia 'Donation'

Camellias need a sheltered position out of full sun. Evergreen but really only attractive when it flowers in spring. It comes into flower while still young. Height: 3 m (10 ft). Spread: 2.5 m (8 ft).

▲ Cistus x purpureus

Sun roses are vulnerable in winter in cold areas, but spectacular in flower in early summer. This one is 'Betty Taudevin'. Height: 1.5 m (5 ft). Spread: 1.2 m (4 ft).

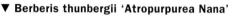

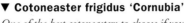

▲ Cornus alba 'Sibirica'
Dogwoods are at their best in winter, when their coloured stems, encouraged by hard pruning, can light up the garden. Autumn leaf colour is a useful bonus. Height: 1.8 m (6 ft). Spread: 1.8 m (6 ft).

▼ Cotoneaster frigidus 'Cornubia'
One of the best cotoneasters to choose if you want a heavy crop of large red berries in autumn. You might find it listed just as C. 'Cornubia'. Height: 3 m (10 ft). Spread: 2.5 m (8 ft).

▲ Cytisus scoparius
Brooms flower prolifically in May and June, but tend to be short-lived shrubs. Prune regularly to prevent them becoming leggy. Height: 2.5 m (8 ft). Spread: 1.5 m (5 ft).

▲ Elaeagnus pungens 'Maculata'
A popular variegated evergreen that looks especially good in winter sunshine. An established plant will provide plenty of foliage for indoor decorations. Height: 2.5 m (8 ft). Spread: 2.5 m (8 ft).

▲ Euonymus fortunei 'Emerald Gaiety'
Invaluable as an evergreen ground cover in front of other shrubs, and it can also be trained to grow up a wall. There are other varieties, some with striking green and gold foliage. Height: 60 cm (2 ft). Spread: 1.5 m (5 ft).

▲ Forsythia 'Beatrix Farrand'
Forsythias are very common, but they bring a splash of vivid colour. This hybrid has particularly large flowers. Also suitable for a hedge. Height: 2.4 m (8 ft). Spread: 1.8 m (6 ft).

▲ Hamamelis x intermedia
The winter-flowering witch hazels are undemanding but need plenty of space. This variety is 'Sunburst'. Height: 3 m (10 ft). Spread: 3 m (10 ft).

▲ Hebe 'Autumn Glory'
Hebes are unsuitable for very cold areas. They are neat foliage shrubs, and some have flowers in white, mauve or pink. This variety may bloom from late summer to November. Height: 90 cm (3 ft). Spread: 75 cm (2½ ft).

▲ Hibiscus syriacus

Useful for colour in a warm, sunny shrub border in late summer and early autumn. This one is 'Woodbridge'. Height: 2.5 m (8 ft). Spread: 1.8 m (6 ft).

▲ Hydrangea macrophylla

Mophead hydrangeas produce pink flowers on acid soil, blue on alkaline. They are at their best in late summer. This is 'Hamburg'. Height: 2.1 m (7 ft). Spread: 1.8 m (6 ft).

▲ Hypericum 'Hidcote'

One of the best of the larger hypericums, blooming for most of the summer. Evergreen or semi-evergreen. Height: 1.8 m (6 ft). Spread: 1.8 m (6 ft).

▲ Kerria japonica

Jew's mallow is a trouble-free spring-flowering shrub that thrives almost anywhere. The variety illustrated is the double 'Pleniflora'. Height: 2.5 m (8 ft). Spread: 1.8m (6 ft).

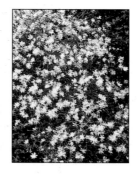

▼ Mahonia x media 'Charity'

Winter-flowering mahonias are especially useful for shade, and this is one of the best. The fragrant flowers usually appear in December and January. Evergreen. Height: 2.5 m (8 ft). Spread: 2.5 m (8 ft).

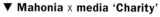

▲ Magnolia stellata

The star magnolia makes a bushy shrub, with slightly fragrant flowers appearing in March and April. There are several varieties, including pinks such as 'Rosea'. An easy and reliable species that is not too large. Height: 2.5 m (8 ft). Spread: 2.5 m (8 ft).

▲ Kolkwitzia amabilis

The beauty bush is covered with flowers in late spring or early summer, but it does not look particularly beautiful for the rest of the year. Easy and undemanding if given sun. Height: 2.5 m (8 ft). Spread: 2.5 m (8 ft).

▲ Leycesteria formosa

Pheasant berry is loved by birds of many kinds – at least when the purple fruits form. The unusual, late-summer flowers always attract comment, and the green cane-like stems look good in winter. Height: 2.1 m (7 ft). Spread: 1.2 m (4 ft).

▼ Philadelphus coronarius 'Aureus'

Like most mock oranges this has fragrant white flowers in summer, but it is grown mainly for its soft yellow spring and early summer foliage. Height: 2.5 m (8 ft). Spread: 1.5 m (5 ft).

▼ Pieris japonica 'Blush'

If you have an acid soil, where rhododendrons thrive, you can try this evergreen. It has pink flowers in spring and copper-red young leaves. Height: 3 m (10 ft). Spread: 2.5 m (8 ft).

▲ Perovskia atriplicifolia

Russian sage, which flowers in late summer and early autumn and resembles a large lavender from a distance, looks at home in either an herbaceous or shrub border. Height: 1.2 m (4 ft). Spread: 90 cm (3 ft).

▲ Potentilla fruticosa

Shrubby potentillas bloom from late spring to late summer. Colours are mainly shades of yellow, pink or white. This variety is 'Abbotswood Silver'. Height: 90 cm (3 ft). Spread: 1.2 m (4 ft).

▼ Salvia officinalis

Sage is grown for its pleasing aromatic foliage, but it can be damaged by a very cold winter. The one shown is 'Purpurascens', but there are variegated varieties. Height: 60 cm (2 ft). Spread: 90 cm (3 ft).

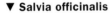

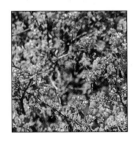

▲ Ribes sanguineum

Flowering currants bring colour to the shrub border in April. There are varieties differing mainly in the depth of flower colour. 'Brocklebankii' has yellow leaves. Height: 2.1 m (7 ft). Spread: 1.8 m (6 ft).

▲ Skimmia japonica

An evergreen shrub grown mainly for its bright red berries that last well into winter. But there are male and female varieties, and you need both to be sure of a good set of berries. Height: 1.5 m (5 ft). Spread: 1.5 m (5 ft).

▲ Spiraea 'Arguta'

Bridal wreath, or foam of May, flowers in late spring and thrives in sun. Its simple white flowers are produced in such profusion that the shrub provides a stunning foil to more colourful flowers. Height: 2.5 m (8 ft). Spread: 1.8 m (6 ft).

TREES, SHRUBS & HEDGES

JANUARY   page 28

- Cut out broken, diseased, dead or rubbing branches on established trees and shrubs, except *Prunus*.
- Plant hardy deciduous shrubs and trees in well-prepared soil if weather permits. If weather is bad, heel in new plants temporarily until conditions improve.
- Ensure stakes of suitable size are inserted properly and that trees and shrubs are attached securely.
- Heel in or store hedging plants in frost-free place if they arrive when soil is frozen or waterlogged.
- Take hardwood cuttings and insert in a trench (see November, page 268).

FEBRUARY   page 47

- Continue to plant trees and shrubs in favourable weather conditions. Mulch, stake and tie new plantings as necessary.
- Spray established trees and large shrubs with a tar oil winter wash if you wish to remove lichen and moss. It will also kill overwintering pests and eggs.
- Remove and plant up rooted suckers in new locations.
- Continue to take hardwood cuttings.
- Now is the right time to sow seeds of many shrubs in a heated propagator. Be prepared for seeds to take a long time to germinate.
- Prune shrubs that have just finished flowering, using the one-third method (see Pruning, page 420).

- To encourage branching, remove end foliage rosettes on young, tall-growing mahonias after flowering.
- Plant bare-root and container-grown hedging plants.
- Clear weeds around base of established hedges and cut back and reshape overgrown deciduous hedges.

MARCH   page 78

- Provided soil is not frozen or waterlogged, continue to plant bare-root specimens this month. Complete bare-root planting this month to give plants time to establish before the summer.
- Apply a general fertiliser to all trees and shrubs.
- Protect new growth on vulnerable trees and shrubs from frost damage.
- Propagate shrubs with low branches by layering into ground or pots.
- Continue to take hardwood cuttings. Insert in trench and leave until autumn.
- Dig up, divide and pot up or replant self-rooted shoots of quick-spreading shrubs to increase areas of ground cover.
- Continue to sow seed in a heated propagator, and pot on seedlings sown last summer and overwintered.
- Pot on semi-ripe cuttings taken last spring and summer even if leaves have dropped off, as new shoots will form from base.
- Increase camellias by leaf bud cuttings.
- Take root cuttings of selected shrubs such as *Romneya coulteri* and plant out last spring's root cuttings in pots.

- Prune spring-flowering shrubs over three years old after flowering, using the one-third method (see Pruning, page 420).
- Hard prune shrubs such as *Buddleja* to encourage vigorous new growth.
- Remove any frost-damaged ends of shoots on shrubs that do not require pruning now, to prevent spread of disease.
- Continue to plant hedging, including evergreens.
- Feed new and established hedges.
- Cut back newly planted deciduous hedges; reshape overgrown laurel and privet hedges.
- Remove bird-sown seedlings from the base of hedges.

APRIL   page 110

- Complete spring planting of container-grown trees and shrubs in well-prepared soil with fertiliser added.
- Water newly planted trees and shrubs, ensuring the rootball of container-grown plants is kept moist.
- Give a balanced feed to all established trees and shrubs if not already done, and apply an additional dressing to any plants that appear undernourished.
- Continue to sow seeds (see February, page 47).
- Propagate suitable shrubs by layering.
- Take hardwood cuttings of evergreens.
- Hard prune selected deciduous shrubs as new growth begins.
- Prune spring-flowering shrubs after they finish flowering, using the one-third

method (see Pruning, page 420).
- Shorten last year's growth on all evergreens by half to encourage bushy habit and new growth.
- Trim upright conifers and remove protruding shoots, tying in larger branches. If there is more than one leader remove the weakest.
- Shorten shoots on spreading conifers.
- Remove whole stems or branches to reduce the size of very large spreading conifers.
- Continue planting hedges, including evergreens and container-grown plants, watering well in dry conditions.
- Check all newly planted hedges are firmly in soil, refirm if necessary and feed.

MAY   page 137

- It is best to stop planting between May and September as the ground is dry, but if you must plant be sure to water well.
- Continue to water newly planted trees and shrubs regularly and spray foliage every evening.
- Take softwood cuttings of selected shrubs and propagate under glass.
- Finish planting container-grown hedging plants and water well.
- Start to clip privet and *Lonicera nitida* and repeat regularly every two months until late summer.

JUNE   page 161

- Weed around border shrubs, and stop

TREES, SHRUBS & HEDGES

grass encroaching on trees and shrubs planted in lawns.

- Clear ground of perennial weeds ready for autumn plantings.
- Continue to water during dry weather and include a high-nitrogen fertiliser during watering for any plants that appear to be establishing poorly.
- Propagate chaenomeles, magnolias and cotinus by layering.
- Take softwood cuttings if not done last month and also semi-ripe cuttings of suitable shrubs.
- Pot up rooted cuttings; plant out strong specimens after a few weeks.
- Prune all May-flowering shrubs over three years old, using the one-third pruning method (*see* Pruning, page 420).
- Remove fast-growing stems or branches that cause overcrowding.
- Deadhead lilac and remove flower buds from grey-leaved shrubs to keep plants bushy and compact.
- Clip fast-growing established hedges.
- Treat hedges, especially beech, for pests if necessary.

JULY　page 184

- Feed any trees and shrubs that appear to be performing badly with a high-nitrogen liquid fertiliser.
- Feed and water newly planted trees and shrubs as necessary.
- Control pests and diseases.
- Take semi-ripe cuttings of suitable shrubs.
- Plant out or pot up softwood cuttings

taken earlier in the year.
- Prune all June-flowering shrubs over three years old, using the one-third method (*see* Pruning, page 420).
- Weed and feed established hedges.
- Water new hedges in dry weather.
- Take semi-ripe cuttings to make a new hedge.
- Reshape overgrown yew hedges.
- Trim and shape hedges as necessary, except conifer hedges.

AUGUST　page 203

- Check on stakes and ties, adding or replacing where necessary.
- During very dry conditions water all trees and shrubs which are vulnerable.
- Take semi-ripe cuttings.
- Pot up rooted leaf bud cuttings of camellias taken in March.
- Put spring-sown seedlings into individual pots.
- Prune July-flowering shrubs over three years old, using the one-third method (*see* Pruning, page 420).
- Check for reversion on variegated shrubs and trees and remove all-green shoots.
- Give conifer hedges their annual trim and reduce the growth on new spring-planted conifers to make a thicker hedge.
- Trim other types of hedge, if necessary.
- Continue to weed base of all hedging.

SEPTEMBER　page 225

- Prepare soil for autumn planting and start

planting if conditions are suitable.
- Complete taking of semi-ripe cuttings especially of tender shrubs to guard against winter loss.
- Pot on rooted semi-ripe cuttings taken earlier and move into a cold greenhouse or cold frame to overwinter.
- Prune all August-flowering shrubs over three years old, using the one-third method (*see* Pruning, page 420).
- For a new hedge, choose plants and prepare ground ready for planting next month.
- Give privet and *Lonicera nitida* a final trim before winter.

OCTOBER　page 247

- Continue soil preparation for new planting and start planting hardy trees and shrubs, staking and tying as necessary.
- Dig up rooted layers and hardwood cuttings and plant out in final growing positions, or overwinter in pots.
- Collect seeds for spring sowing and store in cool, dark, frost-free place.
- Prune all September-flowering shrubs over three years old, using the one-third method (*see* Pruning, page 420).
- Continue planting container-grown hedging plants and complete planting of evergreens by end of month.

NOVEMBER　page 268

- Continue to plant deciduous trees and shrubs if soil is not frozen or waterlogged

(*see* October, page 247).
- In cold areas protect newly planted and susceptible plants from cold winds and frost with windbreaks and by wrapping plants in hessian or similar covering.
- Protect plants from birds and other creatures if necessary.
- Take hardwood cuttings of hardy shrubs.
- Protect hardwood cuttings in pots from cold weather.
- Pot up rooted layers or plant out.
- Remove fallen leaves from semi-ripe cuttings taken in summer to prevent rotting.
- Prune October-flowering shrubs over three years old, using the one-third method (*see* Pruning, page 420).
- Continue to plant new deciduous hedges (*see* October, page 248).
- To create an inexpensive new hedge take hardwood cuttings and insert directly into well-prepared soil in position.

DECEMBER　page 282

- Continue planting deciduous trees and shrubs as long as soil is not frozen or waterlogged (*see* October, page 247).
- Provide extra protection for trees and shrubs permanently planted in containers.
- Prune November-flowering shrubs over three years old, using the one-third method (*see* Pruning, page 420).
- Continue taking hardwood cuttings. Plant out rooted cuttings and layers.
- Continue to plant deciduous hedging as long as soil is not frozen or waterlogged.

Vegetables

AN INTENSIVELY CROPPED KITCHEN GARDEN will provide a succession of fresh vegetables throughout the year. Use this planner to see when to sow or plant for a succession of crops to harvest throughout the year. Where space is limited, concentrate on those crops which are expensive to buy or are particularly tasty when harvested fresh and tender, and wherever possible grow small or compact varieties.

▲ The bed system
The 1.2 m (4 ft) bed system is designed to make it easy to cultivate the vegetables easily from the paths, and to avoid soil compaction for 'no dig' cultivation.

▶ Vegetables on the patio
A small range of vegetables can be grown in containers. Tomatoes and salad crops are a popular choice, but even peas, such as these in a growing bag, can be successful.

	January	February	March
Artichokes			
globe		sow (glass)	
Jerusalem	harvest	plant tubers	plant tubers
Asparagus			
Aubergines			sow (glass)
Beans			
broad		sow (glass)	sow (glass), plant
French			
runner			
Beetroot			sow (mild areas)
Broccoli (sprouting)			harvest
Brussels sprouts	harvest	harvest	sow
Cabbages			
Chinese	harvest	harvest	
spring		harvest	harvest
summer			sow
autumn / winter	harvest		
Calabrese			sow (glass)
Carrots		sow (mild areas)	sow
Cauliflower			
summer			sow
autumn / winter	harvest	harvest	harvest
Celeriac		sow (glass)	sow (glass)
Celery (self-blanching)			sow (glass)
Chicory	harvest forced	harvest forced	sow non-forcing
Endive			sow curly
Florence fennel			
Kale	harvest	harvest	
Kohlrabi			sow
Leeks	harvest		sow
Lettuces		sow (glass)	sow
Marrows, courgettes etc.			
Onions			
English			sow, plant sets
Japanese			
spring		sow	sow
Parsnips	harvest		sow (mild areas)
Peas		sow early varieties	sow
Peppers			sow (glass)
Potatoes			
early	sprout	sprout, plant	plant
maincrop			sprout
Radishes		sow	sow
Rhubarb	force, harvest	harvest	harvest outdoor
Spinach	harvest	harvest	sow
spinach beet	harvest	harvest	sow
Swedes	harvest		sow
Sweetcorn			
Tomatoes (outdoor)			sow (glass)
Turnips			sow

VEGETABLES – SOWING AND HARVESTING PLANNER

April	May	June	July	August	September	October	November	December
sow, plant out	plant out	harvest	harvest	harvest		cover		
						harvest, cover	harvest	harvest
plant crowns, harvest	harvest	harvest						
prick out	plant out (mild areas)	plant out		harvest	harvest			
sow, plant	sow, plant	harvest	harvest	harvest	harvest		sow under cloche	
sow (glass)	sow, plant	sow, plant out	sow, harvest	harvest	cover, harvest	cover, harvest		
sow (glass)	sow, plant	sow, plant out	harvest	harvest	harvest	harvest		
sow	sow	sow	sow, harvest	harvest	harvest	harvest or cover		
sow, harvest	sow	plant out	plant out					
sow	plant out						harvest	harvest
			sow	sow, plant out	cover plants	harvest or cover	harvest	harvest
harvest			sow (cold areas)	sow, plant	plant out, cover	plant and cover		
sow	plant out	plant out	harvest	harvest	harvest			
	sow	plant out	plant out		harvest	harvest	harvest	harvest
sow (glass), plant	sow, plant	sow, plant out	harvest	harvest	harvest	harvest	harvest	harvest
sow	sow	sow, harvest	sow, harvest	harvest	harvest	harvest	harvest or cover	harvest or cover
sow in pots, plant	sow, plant	plant out	harvest	harvest	harvest			
sow	sow, plant	plant out	plant out		harvest	harvest	harvest	harvest
	prick out	plant out				harvest		
sow in pots	prick out, plant	plant out	harvest	harvest	harvest	harvest	force indoors	force indoors
sow, harvest	sow (forcing)	sow (forcing)		sow				
			sow	harvest	sow, cover, harvest	harvest	harvest	
		sow, plant	sow, plant out	harvest	harvest			
sow	sow	sow	sow	sow			harvest	harvest
sow	sow, harvest	sow	sow			harvest	harvest	harvest
		plant	plant			harvest	harvest	harvest
sow, plant	sow, plant	sow, harvest	sow, harvest	sow, harvest	harvest	sow (glass)	sow, harvest, cover	
sow (glass)	sow (glass), plant	sow, plant out	harvest courgettes	harvest	harvest			
plant out	plant			harvest	harvest	harvest		
		harvest	harvest	sow	harvest	plant sets	plant sets	
sow	sow	sow, harvest	sow, harvest	sow, harvest	harvest			
sow	sow					harvest	harvest or cover	harvest
sow	sow	sow, harvest	sow, harvest	harvest	harvest			
prick out	plant out (mild areas)	plant out		harvest	harvest			
earth up	earth up	harvest	harvest	harvest	harvest			
plant out	earth up, plant	earth up		harvest	harvest	harvest	harvest	
sow	sow	sow, harvest	sow, harvest	sow, harvest				
harvest (non-forcing)							force	force indoors
sow	sow	harvest	sow, harvest	sow, harvest	sow, harvest	harvest	harvest or cover	harvest
harvest, sow	sow	sow, harvest	sow, harvest	sow, harvest	harvest	harvest	harvest	harvest
sow	sow	sow			harvest	harvest	harvest or cover	harvest or cover
sow (glass)	plant out, sow (glass)	plant out, sow	harvest	harvest	harvest			
prick out	plant out (mild areas)	plant out		harvest	harvest	harvest		
sow	sow	sow		sow, harvest	harvest	harvest	harvest or cover	harvest or cover

Water plants

PONDS OFFER PLANTING POSSIBILITIES almost as varied as beds and borders. Apart from the floating plants and vital oxygenators, deep-water plants other than waterlilies are relatively few. Fortunately there are many varieties of waterlily to choose from. And there are more marginal plants – those planted in shallow water around the edge of the pond – than you are likely to have space for. The plants illustrated here are just a few of the most readily available pond plants. Remember moisture-loving bog plants can also be grown at the pondside.

▲ Acorus gramineus 'Variegatus'

The sweet flag is grown for its variegated iris-like leaves, and fortunately these are evergreen. The small yellowish flowers in early summer are not a feature. There are other varieties. Height: 30 cm (1 ft). Spread: 30 cm (1 ft). Planting depth to 30 cm (1 ft).

▲ Aponogeton distachyos

Water hawthorn is a 'deep-water' plant, and an amazing performer. It will probably be the first pond plant to flower, and is often still blooming in November. The flowers are fragrant too. Height: surface. Spread: 1.8 m (6 ft). Plant in 15–45 cm (6–18 in) of water.

▲ Butomus umbellatus

Grass-like foliage means the flowering rush will go almost unnoticed out of flower, but in mid and late summer it is transformed by the appearance of pink flowers. In some countries the rhizome is eaten. Height: 90 cm (3 ft). Spread: 60 cm (2 ft). Planting depth to 15 cm (6 in).

▲ Juncus ensifolius

One of several interesting rushes. The stems are semi-persistent, and the globular flower heads, decorative over a long period, are surprisingly attractive despite their brown colour. Height: 30 cm (1 ft). Spread: 30 cm (1 ft). Planting depth to 10 cm (4 in).

◀ Caltha palustris

Marsh marigolds are among the first pondside plants to flower, looking their best in April. They are undemanding and will grow in shallow water or boggy ground. There are double varieties, which tend to be more showy. Height: 30–45 cm (1–1½ ft). Planting depth to 10 cm (4 in).

◀ Mentha aquatica

Water mint can spread rampantly. The foliage tends to turn reddish in full sun. The lavender-lilac flowers appear in mid and late summer. Height: 45 cm (1½ ft). Spread: 90 cm (3 ft) or more. Planting depth to 8 cm (3 in).

▶ Myosotis scorpioides

The water forget-me-not grows in shallow water but will stray into moist soil at the water's edge. Flowers all summer. 'Mermaid' is an improved variety, 'Maytime' has variegated leaves. Height: 23 cm (9 in). Spread: 60 cm (2 ft). Planting depth to 8 cm (3 in).

▶ Menyanthes trifoliata

The bog bean will grow in water or in damp soil at the water's edge. It flowers in late spring and early summer. Height: 23 cm (9 in). Spread: 90 cm (3 ft). Planting depth to 10 cm (4 in) of water.

▶ Nymphaea 'James Brydon'

One of the best red waterlilies for a medium-sized pond. The flowers are freely produced over a long period in summer. Plant in at least 30–45 cm (1–1½ ft) of water. Height: surface. Spread: 90 cm (3 ft).

▲ Nymphaea × helvola

This pale yellow miniature waterlily is suitable for a water feature in a container as well as for a small pond. Once established it will flower for months in summer. Height: surface. Spread: 45 cm (1½ ft). Plant in 15–23 cm (6–9 in) of water.

▲ Myriophyllum aquaticum

Parrot's feather is an oxygenating plant for shallow or deep water with long spreading stems. Leaves can be submerged or aerial. Height: 30 cm (1 ft). Spread: 90 cm (3 ft).

▲ Orontium aquaticum

Golden club is a non-invasive plant. The unusual flower heads appear in April and May. Height: 30 cm (1 ft). Spread: 45 cm (1½ ft). Plant in 15–23 cm (6–9 in) of water.

▲ Pontederia cordata

Pickerel weed is an attractive marginal plant. The blue flowers are at their best in mid and late summer. There is an uncommon white variety. Height: 75 cm (2½ ft). Spread: 75 cm (2½ ft). Planting depth to 15 cm (6 in).

▲ Schoenoplectus lacustris tabernaemontani 'Zebrinus'
(syn. Scirpus tabernaemontani 'Zebrinus')
The zebra rush has suffered many name changes and you may find it is sold simply as Scirpus *'Zebrinus'. Height: 90 cm (3 ft). Spread: 45 cm (1½ ft). Planting depth to 15 cm (6 in) of water.*

◀ Typha laxmannii

This reedmace is modest in size and suitable for a small pond (if space is very limited, choose T. minima*). It flowers from July, but remains attractive into autumn. Height: 1.2 m (4 ft). Spread: 60 cm (2 ft) or more. Planting depth to 10 cm (4 in) of water.*

▶ Veronica beccabunga

Brooklime has tiny blue flowers like forget-me-nots, but this is a rampant plant that will spread quickly, even rooting into border soil. Height: 23 cm (9 in). Spread: 1.5 m (5 ft) or more. Planting depth to 10 cm (4 in) of water.

WATER PLANTS & POOLS

JANUARY   page 29

- Keep an area of water free of ice to release noxious gases (*see* December, page 283); do not break thick ice.
- If you have left the pump in the pond and not replaced it with a pond heater, check its position to make sure it is well below the ice line.

FEBRUARY   page 49

- Continue to keep an area of water free from ice (*see* December, page 283).
- Sow seeds of bog garden plants and allow them to stand in freezing conditions to germinate but protect from heavy rain.
- Have pond pump serviced if necessary.

MARCH   page 82

- Clean the pool if necessary and, while the water has been drained, make any repairs.
- Remove pool heater if used and replace the pump.
- Protect fish from herons.

APRIL   page 114

- Feed fish about three times a week as they begin to become active.
- Plant turions
- Start planting aquatic plants, such as waterlilies and oxygenating plants, in aquatic baskets or on the floor of the pond, using special aquatic soil.
- Purchase waterlilies as established

plants. Only buy bare-root plants from a specialist nursery and choose varieties to suit the size of your pond.
- Plant marginals and oxygenators. Make sure rhizomes are horizontal.
- Move and replant self-sown seedlings.
- Sow seeds of waterside primulas and common mimulus in a cold frame.
- Lift and divide any overcrowded aquatic plants; propagate waterlilies.
- Cover exposed soil and the surface of containers with a top dressing of pea gravel to prevent fish stirring up soil.

MAY   page 140

- Continue planting aquatic plants.
- Feed established aquatic plants with aquatic fertiliser.
- Control algae with an algicide and remove blanketweed with a net or stick to prevent the water from turning green.
- Top up regularly with fresh water to replace water lost by evaporation.
- Propagate waterlilies from eyes or by dividing (*see* April, page 115).
- Propagate marginal plants from cuttings or by dividing.
- Place new and overwintered hardy floating plants on the surface of the water.
- Prick out seedlings of spring-sown bog plants.
- Weed the bog garden regularly.

JUNE   page 163

- Complete the main planting of aquatics

this month, including tender varieties, if you want a display this season.
- Continue to top up regularly with fresh water to replace water lost by evaporation.

JULY   page 187

- Continue to top up pool with fresh water; use a spray attachment to aerate.
- Remove faded flowers from marginal aquatic plants and cut back any excess growth.
- Continue to weed the bog garden regularly.
- Thin leaves on waterlilies and any excess growth of submerged oxygenating plants.

AUGUST   page 205

- Plant out waterside primulas and other bog plants raised from seed.
- Continue topping up the pool with fresh water. Aerate with a spray.
- Remove faded flowers from marginal aquatic plants. Pull away any excess growth.
- Thin waterlilies and excess growth of submerged oxygenating plants.

SEPTEMBER   page 227

- Gather turions (winter buds of floating plants such as frogbit and bladderwort) and keep until spring in a cool place.
- Plant spring-sown bog plants in their permanent positions.
- Clean and tidy the pool. Remove any

plants likely to rot in the water.
- Net the pool (*see* October, page 249) to prevent leaves from falling into the water and decomposing.

OCTOBER   page 249

- Thin out congested submerged aquatic plants, especially ones that will die back during the winter.
- Cut back marginal plants but do not reduce those with hollow stems to beneath water level or they may rot.
- Divide and replant waterside plants.
- Net the pool if not already done and clear out dead leaves so that they do not decay in the water.

NOVEMBER   page 269

- Continue to cut back any remaining faded marginal plants and remove any other vegetation or debris.
- Continue to clear leaves from the pool netting (*see* October, page 249).
- Consider removing submersible pump and replacing with a pool heater for the winter. Dry, clean and grease pump before storing for winter.

DECEMBER   page 283

- Keep an area of water free of ice by using a pool heater. If you do not have a pool heater use other methods to keep an area ice-free. Do not break thick ice as this may kill fish.

SECTION THREE

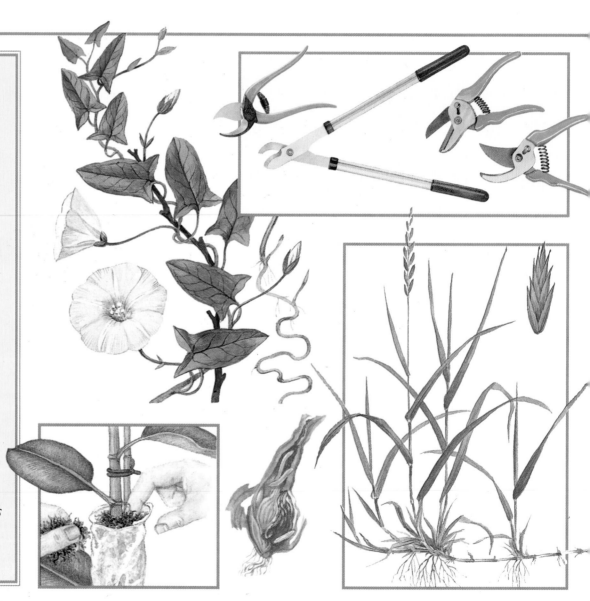

GARDEN BASICS

The soil in your garden

The first thing all gardeners should assess is the type of soil they are gardening on. What determines soil type are the proportions of sand, silt and clay particles it contains. The main soil types are loam, clay and sand, with additional types described as stony, peaty or chalky. Regardless of the type, soil is also acid, alkaline or neutral, which describes its chemical make-up. Soil fertility depends on a combination of the physical properties of the soil and the nutrients it derives from materials and organic matter; these interact and can be affected by acidity and alkalinity. The fertilisers and manures that will help the plants in your garden flourish depend on the soil in your garden.

THE TYPES OF SOIL

LOAM

The easiest soils to work with are those containing a mixture of sand and clay particles, as well as humus (the organic residue of decayed vegetable matter), in proportions that make the soil easy to dig while retaining plenty of nutrients. Such soils are usually described as loam. A loamy soil has 8–25 per cent clay with sand forming the major part of it. This combination creates conditions that suit the majority of plants. The gardener who gardens on good medium loam is extremely lucky.

CLAY

Clay particles are very tiny and therefore cling together easily and form a dense, poorly draining mass. This makes soils containing more than 25 per cent clay particles physically heavy to dig, and sticky to work after rain. Clay soils do not warm up quickly in spring, and in hot, dry weather the clay shrinks as the moisture is lost, so the soil becomes very hard with large cracks and fissures appearing on the surface.

There are some plants which will not tolerate such cold, wet soils in winter, and the structure makes a clay soil unsuitable for certain crops such as carrots. However, its density means it has good nutrient-holding capacity, and, if plants can tolerate the soil, they will often grow very well in clay.

SAND

Sandy soils are seldom waterlogged, and they warm up more quickly in spring. Digging is usually easily carried out at any time throughout the year.

The main problem with sandy soils is that nutrients wash out easily through their loose structure and therefore they are seldom very fertile. You will usually have to use more fertilisers than on a clay or loam soil.

STONY, PEATY AND CHALKY SOILS

In addition to the main types, soil is often described as stony, peaty or chalky. Stony soil usually occurs where the rock outcrop is close to the surface and may be clay, loamy or sandy. Peaty soils are acidic and occur naturally in moorland areas. Peaty soils are often very fertile but may require drainage and liming to improve the alkalinity of the soil. Chalky soils are usually alkaline, and while they suit a

SOIL COMPOSITION

Stony soil may be clay, loamy or sandy; it is often shallow and difficult to cultivate but is generally free-draining.

Peaty soil is likely to be acid and ideal for plants such as rhododendrons, azaleas and many heathers, but other plants may not grow so well.

Chalky soil is too alkaline for many plants; it may have only a thin layer of topsoil and plants will require feeding.

Sandy soil is easy to work and seldom waterlogged but it is usually dry in summer and generally needs feeding, as nutrients are easily washed out.

Loamy soil will suit a very wide range of plants and is easy to work. It is easy to dig and is usually fertile.

Clay soil is often poorly drained in winter and bakes hard in summer as it dries out. It is heavy and difficult to dig but is often very fertile.

STONY

PEATY

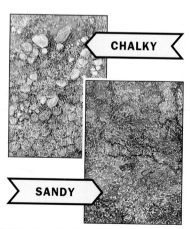

CHALKY

SANDY

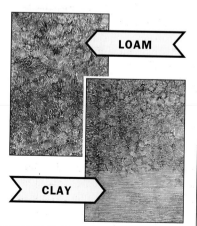

LOAM

CLAY

number of flowering plants they can be difficult to manage. In wet weather they are sticky, the layer of topsoil may be thin, and they have to be improved by adding plenty of humus.

THE pH FACTOR

Soil pH is a measure of the acidity or alkalinity of your soil. It is measured on a scale of 1 (very acid) to 14 (very alkaline). In practice, most soils are between pH 4 and 8. Most plants grow best at pH 6.5, as at this level most of the nutrients they need are available to them.

It is worth measuring the pH of your soil every two years. You can do this yourself using a simple soil-testing kit or you can send a sample away to a specialist laboratory. If you do it yourself take a representative sample from various parts of your garden or border. Follow the instructions on the kit carefully. Similar test kits are available to test the levels of the main nutrients necessary for plant growth – nitrogen, phosphates and potassium (potash) – although the results may not be so accurate.

Alkaline, or limy, soils, which have a pH above 7, usually occur in chalky or limestone areas. Many plants grow well on chalk (the beautiful flowers associated with chalky downland like a slight alkalinity best) but it can pose a particular problem for some plants. Acid-loving plants will require supplementary feeding with trace elements in a form which will not become 'locked in' by the high pH. Alkaline soils tend to be deficient in manganese, boron and phosphorus.

Soils with a low pH (below about 6) are described as acid. These are usually found in peaty or woodland areas. They too support a wide range of plants, but some groups – rhododendrons, gaultherias

and many heathers, for example – only really thrive if the soil is acid. Acid soils tend to be deficient in phosphorus.

MAKING THE BEST OF YOUR SOIL

The pH of a soil can be adjusted by the addition of peat or flowers of sulphur (to increase acidity) or lime (to increase alkalinity), but this is best limited to a localised area where you want to grow a few 'contrary' plants. The best advice for any gardener is to grow those plants that will thrive in the soil conditions available to them. Rather than attempt to grow a garden full of acid-loving plants on a chalky soil, it is better to concentrate on those plants that thrive in soil with a high pH.

IMPROVING YOUR SOIL

Most soils contain plant nutrients in varying concentrations, but as plants grow these are used up and some are leached out of the soil by rain. Because gardens support a wide range of plants, growing close together, the soil becomes short of nutrients and the plants need extra food in the form of fertiliser if they are to reach their potential.

Manures and fertilisers are vital elements of a fertile soil. Some manures, such as stable manure, return nutrients to the ground, but the levels are likely to be much lower than those provided by fertilisers. The best results often come from a combination: bulky organic manures to improve the soil structure and assist in the retention of nutrients and moisture, and concentrated fertilisers, which generally do little to improve the soil structure but provide the nutrients essential for plant growth.

DRAINAGE AND DIGGING

If you have wet soil you should try to improve the drainage of your garden. Conversely, if you have very light, dry soil you should try to adjust the texture so that it retains more moisture.

If you have extremely wet soil then you might have to consider installing an artificial tile or rubble drainage system, or you can usually improve the drainage

by improving the structure of your soil. On clay soils digging helps, and in particular double digging to break up the 'pan' of the soil. If the pan is very hard this may require a pickaxe. Dig in the autumn and leave the soil in clods over the winter, exposing as much surface to the weather as possible. Frost and rain help to break down the particles.

You can improve the structure of both

DOUBLE DIGGING

Double digging is used to break up newly cultivated ground or improve the depth of fertile soil in established gardens. It enables a compacted subsoil, or pan, to be broken up which improves drainage, and humus can be incorporated at a greater depth. It is best done in autumn, leaving the soil in clods to be broken down by frost and rain over the winter.

(1) Divide the area to be dug lengthways into two rows with a garden line, then divide it into 60 cm (2 ft) strips. Remove soil from the first strip (A) to the depth of about 25 cm (10 in). Heap the excavated soil to one side, at the end of the second row. This will be used to fill in the final trench H (see 4).

(2) Fork over the subsoil at the bottom of trench A, working in plenty of garden compost or well-rotted manure.

(3) Remove the topsoil from strip B and use it to fill in trench A. Fork over subsoil of trench B and work in garden compost or well-rotted manure.

(4) Use the topsoil from strip C to fill in trench B, and so on. When the plot has been dug, fill in trench H with the soil from trench A.

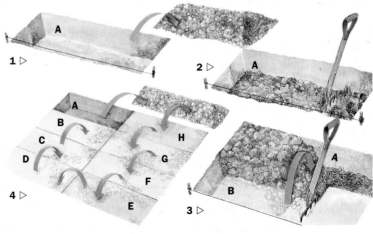

SOIL CULTIVATION

Tap-rooted plants, such as carrots and parsnips, need deeply cultivated soil to produce long, straight roots. Carrots should not be grown in recently manured soil.

If soil is cultivated shallowly to the same depth for many years, for instance with a rotovator, a hard 'pan' forms through which roots are unable to penetrate.

heavy and light soils by adding copious quantities of humus, in the form of manure or garden compost. You should also add lime to clay soils (*see* Soil Improvers, pages 391–392).

FERTILISERS

The main chemical nutrients required for plant growth are nitrogen, phosphorus and potassium. The secondary, intermediate nutrients are magnesium, calcium and sulphur. Of these, nitrogen is the one most gardeners need to supply each year, as it is necessary for strong leafy growth and is prone to being leached out of the soil during winter rains.

There are also elements such as iron, boron, zinc, manganese, copper, chlorine and molybdenum that are only needed in very small quantities. These are known as trace elements. Although they are important for growth, you do not usually need to worry about adding these as they occur naturally in soil or are present as impurities in other fertilisers.

Fertilisers may be organic or inorganic in origin but all will eventually be broken down into a soluble form and then taken up by the root hairs of the plant.

Organic fertilisers will not release their nitrogen until they have been broken down by micro-organisms in the soil. The rate at which nitrogen is released depends on the soil conditions. In late spring, summer and early autumn the soil will be warm and moist, the micro-organisms will be active and so nitrogen will be released quickly. In a cold, water-logged soil, typical of many clay soils in winter and early spring, the micro-organisms slow down and very little nitrogen will be released.

One advantage of organic fertilisers is that there is little risk of nitrogen scorching the plants or being leached away by heavy rain. This makes them useful for light, sandy and chalky soils. However, using organic fertilisers is more expensive than using inorganic fertilisers.

Inorganic fertilisers are sometimes called 'artificial' or 'chemical' because they are often manufactured, but some are naturally occurring minerals that are mined. The nutrients are usually in a readily soluble form and do not need micro-organisms to release them to the plants. As inorganic fertilisers are quick-acting they are useful for fast-growing crops and for treating deficiencies. They need to be applied carefully, according to the directions on the packaging, as many contain large amounts of nutrients which can scorch seedlings and plants, especially if not watered in well.

If you prefer to avoid the inorganic chemicals, such as sulphate of ammonia and superphosphate, you can use 'organic' alternatives, such as dried blood, hoof and horn or bonemeal.

Never use fertilisers if they are not necessary – it is a waste of money.

STRAIGHT FERTILISERS

These contain significant proportions of one major nutrient only. They can be useful when growing crops with a high demand for a particular element – you can just add the lacking nutrient as a top dressing rather than waste the other elements by adding a general fertiliser. Nitrogen fertilisers are the most useful but it is possible to get straight potash and phosphate fertilisers.

NITROGEN

Nitrogen promotes healthy, green growth of leaves and stems. Symptoms of lack of nitrogen include stunted growth and pale green foliage. Too much nitrogen can cause sappy, soft growth which is susceptible to pests and diseases. Excess nitrogen can also prevent fruiting or delay ripening.

Sulphate of ammonia

A cheap, inorganic fertiliser containing 21 per cent nitrogen. The nitrogen is released quickly, making it a useful top dressing on neutral or alkaline soils. A typical application rate would be 35 g per m² (1 oz per sq yd) for soft fruit and as a base-dressing for brassicas and potatoes. Repeated applications can make the soil more acid, so on acid soils you should use Nitrochalk. Sulphate of ammonia keeps well if kept dry.

Nitrochalk

An inorganic fertiliser containing 26 per cent nitrogen; it is used as a top dressing on acid soils. The nitrogen is released very quickly. It is particularly useful if you

THE CYCLE OF DECAY

Soil fertility is maintained, and fewer fertilisers needed, if as much vegetable matter as possible is returned to the soil. Nutrients taken from the soil are locked into plants during growth and released again to be recycled by the process of decay. Natural decomposition occurs when leaves and stems fall to the ground and are carried down into the soil by worms and other insects. There they are broken down by soil creatures, fungi and bacteria. Gardeners usually use a compost heap to accelerate this process of decay and return the nutrients to the soil as garden compost.

are a keen vegetable grower of leafy brassicas and salad crops. It does not keep well so only buy what you think you will use in a season.

Nitrate of soda

A very fast-acting inorganic fertiliser containing 16 per cent nitrogen. It can be used as a top dressing, and is useful for beetroot and celery which benefit from the sodium. Apply 35–70 g per m^2 (1–2 oz per sq yd).

Dried blood

A fast-acting, organic fertiliser to be used sparingly and only on actively growing plants. It contains about 13 per cent nitrogen and is a useful tonic for plants suffering from nitrogen deficiency. Use as a top dressing at 35–50 g per m^2 (1–1½ oz per sq yd) for vegetables, such as brassicas and potatoes.

Hoof and horn

A slow to fast-acting organic fertiliser, depending on the size of the particles, it contains about 13 per cent nitrogen and is usually used as a base-dressing at a rate of 35 g per m^2 (1 oz per sq yd).

PHOSPHATE

Phosphate – phosphorus – is essential for the healthy development of roots. It also has a role in maturing and ripening fruits and seeds. Phosphate deficiency is rare, but is occasionally found on acid or heavy clay soils, or in areas of very high rainfall. The symptoms are stunted growth, dull green or purple foliage and poor fruit quality. Phosphate fertilisers are slow-acting and treating a deficiency is difficult, but superphosphate or bonemeal worked into soil close to the roots can be beneficial and is worth trying.

Superphosphate

This is an inorganic fertiliser supplying 17 per cent phosphate. The phosphate is not available to plants for some time after application, so it is best to apply 35 g per m^2 (1 oz per sq yd) in winter or early spring. This allows the phosphate to be released into the soil and washed down towards the roots in time for the start of the growing season. It tends to make soils more acidic.

Bonemeal

This is an organic form of phosphate obtained by grinding up and crushing bones. Although it is sterilised, it is nevertheless a wise precaution to use gloves when handling it and this applies to all fertilisers. Bonemeal releases its nutrients slowly but much depends on the size of the particles – the very fine grades are faster-acting. Once applied, bonemeal will remain in the soil for three to four years, so it is not needed annually. Its slow, steady release makes it ideal for slow-growing plants such as shrubs and herbaceous perennials – put a handful in the planting hole. It can be used as a base-dressing for vegetables at a rate of 35 g per m^2 (1 oz per sq yd).

POTASH

Potash – potassium – is an essential nutrient for flower production and for fruiting crops. Plants, particularly fruit on light or chalky soils, can suffer from lack of potassium. The symptoms are reduced growth, thin shoots and soft growth which is vulnerable to pest and disease attack. The leaves may appear discoloured or have brown, yellow or purple patches. Rock potash is acceptable to those gardening organically, while most other sources of potash are not.

COMPOST HEAPS

A free-standing compost heap should be large: aim for 1.8 m (6 ft) square if you have the room. Build it up in layers, sprinkling soil between each layer.

Proprietary plastic compost bins come in many shapes. They do not necessarily make better compost but they are tidier and more pleasing visually.

A homemade bin can be inexpensive to make. This one uses old planks sawn to measure and nailed to posts but you can use corrugated iron or plastic sheets.

The compost material can be contained in a ring of wire mesh attached to supporting timber posts. Cover the top with old carpet cut to shape to retain warmth.

Sulphate of potash

This is an inorganic fertiliser that contains about 50 per cent potassium. It is quick-acting and soluble but is prone to leach out of soils, so it is best applied in early spring. Too much sulphate of potash can cause a calcium deficiency in the soil. Apply it at the rate of 15–35 g per m² (½–1 oz per sq yd).

Rock potash

This provides about 11 per cent potash and as it comes from a naturally occurring rock it can be used by organic gardeners. You may not find it in garden centres but you can order it from mail order companies. The potash is released very slowly so it is best to give an annual application of 70 g per m² (2 oz per sq yd) in autumn or winter. Wood ash is another organic source of potash and can be applied in the autumn.

GENERAL FERTILISERS

A fertiliser with the three main elements, nitrogen (N), phosphate (P) and potash (K), incorporated together in roughly equal amounts, is convenient for use all around the garden, rather than applying the individual elements separately. Containers of pre-mixed fertilisers show the main ingredients as proportions: so NPK 5:5:5 would be a balanced general fertiliser, and NPK 5:6:10 would be one with a higher proportion of potash, making it suitable, for example, for tomatoes.

Growmore (NPK 7:7:7) is a particular formula, not a brand name, that is widely available, cheap and has stood the test of time. It is ideal for most purposes; the only drawback is that all the nitrogen is released quickly and there may be circumstances where some slow-release nitrogen would be beneficial. The amount of Growmore you apply depends on the plants and the fertility of the soil. Most packets come with application rates, but as a guide lawns, trees, shrubs, flowers and soft fruit need about 35–70 g per m² (1–2 oz per sq yd), the slightly higher range for less fertile soils.

The organic version of Growmore is blood, fish and bone. Unlike Growmore, it is not made to a standard formula, so the proportions of NPK depend on the manufacturer. Some are balanced and contain proportions very similar to Growmore, others may contain hardly any potash so check the label.

General-purpose liquid feeds also have roughly equal proportions of nitrogen, phosphate and potash. They are sold either as liquid concentrates or soluble powders and are usually applied to the whole garden at every watering or once or twice a week.

Other proprietary general fertilisers are available. Those that contain some slow-release nitrogen are worth considering on sandy, free-draining soils or where rainfall is high.

SPECIFIC FERTILISERS

There are many proprietary fertilisers available that are promoted for specific plants such as house plants, flowering plants, roses or lawns. In most cases, they are likely to be more expensive than using a general fertiliser or straight fertiliser but they may be more convenient to apply. When growing plants in containers, liquid feeds, or controlled-release granules or plugs, are worth considering.

The high potash content of tomato feeds makes them useful for other fruiting plants such as peppers and cucumbers, as well as for flowers. Tomato fertilisers often include iron and magnesium as deficiencies of these can lead to problems with the fruit. Watering with sequestered iron helps acid-loving plants.

Epsom salts

Epsom salts (magnesium sulphate) is a useful standby if you have an alkaline soil and have problems with magnesium deficiency. All plants can be affected but tomatoes, roses and fruits are particularly susceptible. The leaves yellow in a very distinctive way between the leaf veins, and they may drop prematurely. As well as occurring on alkaline soils, it can also be a result of heavy rain leaching out magnesium or excess potash. Apply Epsom salts at 25 g per m² (¾ oz per sq yd) or make up a foliar spray of 20 g per litre of water (3½ oz per gallon).

SOIL IMPROVERS

Adding fertilisers to the soil helps your plants to reach their full potential but does nothing for the structure of the soil. Adding well-rotted organic matter to the soil primarily helps improve its physical structure. It also eventually makes the soil more fertile, as some improvers also contain nutrients, but these can vary and are best not looked upon as the only source of fertiliser.

Earthworms and insects break down the organic matter, then micro-organisms break it down further into humus. Humus combines with the mineral parts of the soil, such as clay and sand particles, producing a stable soil structure which plant roots can penetrate easily and which contains variously sized spaces for holding air, water and oxygen.

A good soil structure not only helps plant growth but also makes working the soil easier. Heavy soil into which copious amounts of organic material have been incorporated should be able to be dug without the soil sticking to the spade, and it should also retain water without becoming waterlogged.

Improving the soil structure is a long-term job. It might be several years before you reap the benefits, although if you apply a layer of organic material on top of the soil, you will get the benefits of it as a mulch within a single season. Apply the soil improver to heavy soils in the autumn but to light, sandy soils in late winter or early spring.

Farmyard manure, leafmould and garden compost are the traditional soil improvers. They cost next to nothing, but may be difficult to obtain or to make in sufficient quantities in some areas. There are now many more proprietary soil improvers available, but they vary in their cost, application rate and claims. A realistic application rate is 25–40 litres per m² (5½–9 gallons per sq yd) or a layer at least 5 cm (2 in) deep over the surface. If you have a large area that needs improving, concentrate on a different bed each year.

MANURES

If you have access to manure, it is a cheap and valuable soil improver. Farmyard manure contains the dung and urine of farm animals mixed with their bedding, so when handling it wear gloves and wash your hands afterwards. It may be fresh, partly composted or fully composted.

Fully composted manure will have an earthy smell and be brown with very little straw or bedding material visible. Fresh manure will be smelly and not uniform in colour or composition. Uncomposted manure needs to be heaped up, covered and left to stand for several months before it is used.

Poultry manure is more concentrated than other manures and more like a fertiliser. Unfortunately, much of its nitrogen is in the form of ammonia which has a strong smell and can increase the pH of the soil and scorch seedlings. This can be overcome by composting before use, or it can be added to the compost heap where it will act as a compost activator.

Most animal waste is worth recycling whenever a quantity is available. Rabbit and guinea-pig bedding and waste should be added to the garden compost heap. It is always better to compost any bedding before use, especially if wood shavings or newspaper have been used.

Green manures are quick-growing grasses or leafy crops which are sown specifically to be dug into the soil. They are only practical on vacant ground or in the vegetable garden, where they provide a useful source of nutrients as well as improving the texture of the soil (*see* September, page 226).

GARDEN COMPOST

Any plant material from the garden or kitchen can be added to a compost heap where it will rot down and can then be returned to the garden.

Recycling waste vegetation from the house and garden keeps the garden tidy, reduces problems with pests and diseases and puts goodness back into the soil.

You can buy plastic or wooden bins or make your own with second-hand timber. Make sure the bin is at least 1 m (3 ft) square and high – bigger if possible – as garden waste will rot down more effectively in bulk. Slatted sides are useful, so the compost can be removed easily when ready. The composting material should be kept moist but not sodden, so cover the bin with a lid when it is raining heavily. In cold weather put a piece of old carpet over the top; this helps to keep the heat in.

Most plant material is suitable for composting, but aim for a balance of green and woody material and do not add too many grass clippings or prunings at one go. Thick woody stalks or shrub prunings are best put through a shredder before composting. There are a few things it is best not to add, such as weeds that have set seed, roots of perennial weeds, potato peelings as these may root, and plants with soil-borne diseases.

Once a compost heap starts to generate heat many pests and diseases will be destroyed, but root-feeding pests and diseases can survive, so destroy any roots suffering from club root, foot and root rots, or carrot and cabbage root fly (*see* Pests and Diseases, pages 395–411).

Garden compost should be ready in 3–18 months. Turning the heap, although hard work, will speed up the process and help the compost to rot evenly. An activator, such as dried blood or sulphate of ammonia, will help woody material rot down more quickly.

LEAFMOULD

Composted leaves, like other garden waste, make a useful mulch or soil improver (*see* October, page 240).

SPENT MUSHROOM COMPOST

This is ready-composted and sterilised by the mushroom grower so is cleaner to handle than manures. Use it for improving a sandy soil and where you are planning to grow brassicas, but remember it does contain lime so do not use it around acid-loving plants.

SPENT HOPS

Small local breweries can often provide spent hops, or you may find them with added fertiliser and sold as hop manure.

STRAW

Straw bales are usually available from farmers. Straw is high in carbon, so can rob the soil of valuable nitrogen, and may also contain weedkillers. For these reasons it is best to compost it before use with a compost activator such as chicken manure or sulphate of ammonia.

PEAT

Peat used to be recommended as a soil improver but this use is now considered by many to be a waste of a valuable resource as harvesting leads to a loss of precious habitats. It still makes sense to use any spent peat-based composts, such as the contents of old growing bags, as a soil improver.

SEAWEED

Where seaweed is available and free from oil, it may be collected and used on the garden. It contains nitrogen, potash and trace elements but in variable amounts. It does not need to be composted but the salt needs to be removed by hosing it off or by leaving the seaweed outside in the rain for a week or so.

PROPRIETARY SOIL IMPROVERS

These come ready-composted or processed in bags and can be bought from garden centres or by mail order. They are more expensive than loose products but they are often easier and more pleasant to handle. Many are alkaline, so if you apply large amounts, it would be worth checking the pH of your soil before you add extra lime.

LIME

If the pH of your soil is less than 6.5 (see page 387), you may want to add lime, particularly if you want to grow vegetables such as brassicas. Using lime has many benefits. It sweetens the soil, encourages earthworms and beneficial bacteria, lightens heavy clay soil, provides calcium, frees the other elements in the soil to promote healthy plant growth and discourages pests and diseases such as slugs and club root. Many gardeners lime in rotation every three years. However always test the pH of your soil before adding lime. If the pH is above 6.5 the soil doesn't need it.

Use ground chalk or limestone, which can be applied at any time of year but is best used well in advance of planting. Autumn is a convenient time. Apply on a still day and wear goggles to protect your eyes. Follow instructions carefully. Do not apply lime at the same time as manure or a nitrogenous fertiliser and do not lime every year as a matter of course.

MULCHES

A mulch is a layer of material spread over the soil surface to conserve moisture beneath and to suppress weeds. Some mulches, such as chipped bark, also have a role in insulating plant roots from the air temperature, and some improve the soil structure and fertility. A wide range of mulching materials is now available, ranging from organic materials that are applied loose, to sheet mulches made of anything from plastics to old carpet. The

TYPES OF MULCHES

Chipped bark only decomposes slowly. It makes an attractive, semi-permanent mulch for shrub borders. The size of the chips affects the appearance.

Garden compost should cost nothing, and unlike the other mulches illustrated, actually contributes useful nutrients to the soil. Apply a layer at least 5 cm (2 in) thick.

Gravel comes in different sizes and colours and looks attractive. Lay down a sheet of plastic and cover with gravel. This prevents the gravel being worked into the soil.

Cocoa shells have an attractive colour and a pleasant smell when wet. They may blow about in windy weather when first laid but, once wetted, the shells bond together.

SHEET MULCHES

Sheet mulches are useful for warming up the soil before sowing seeds, but it is also possible to plant vegetables, such as cabbages and sweetcorn, through the sheet by cutting a crossed slit large enough to insert a trowel. Use a knife to cut the cross and anchor the edges of the sheet by inserting in a narrow trench and covering with soil.

only drawback to using mulches is that they encourage slugs, so you may want to put down slug deterrents.

ORGANIC MULCHES

These are applied loose. The layer needs to be at least 5 cm (2 in) thick to be effective at suppressing weeds, so an 80 litre bag will cover only about 1.5 m² (15 sq ft). The area you have to cover, and the money you have budgeted for mulches, may influence your choice. You can save money by combining a sheet mulch such as layers of old newspaper with a thinner layer of loose mulch.

Mulches should be applied to wet soil and March is the best time. Most rain falls between October and March.

CHIPPED BARK

This is the best long-term solution for keeping the soil moist and it doesn't blow away like composted bark. Various types of bark are available – pine bark is one of the best but is expensive. Some of the cheaper barks contain a high proportion of wood shavings; these rot down more quickly than bark and do not look very attractive, so inspect a sample before buying. Chipped bark is worth using on large shrub borders or rose beds.

In the process of rotting down, bark and wood shavings can take nitrogen from the soil. This is unlikely to be a problem for established shrubs, but look out for signs of nitrogen deficiency if you use chipped bark extensively round the garden. Compensate by giving plants a nitrogenous foliar feed or a top dressing of Nitrochalk.

GRASS CLIPPINGS

These make a cheap, useful mulch, but never use grass from lawns that have recently been treated with weedkiller, or where there might be a lot of weed seeds. Do not overdo the grass clippings, uncomposted grass clippings get very hot very quickly as they decompose and prolonged use can be detrimental.

PEAT AND COIR

These can improve the soil structure once dug into the soil, but they are not good mulches, as they tend to be poor at retaining water, weed seeds germinate readily in them, and in windy gardens they get blown away. It is a good idea to reduce the use of peat whenever possible.

STRAW

Straw is a traditional mulch, but in its raw state (uncomposted) it needs to be applied at least 10 cm (4 in) thick. It can get blown about, and if herbicides have been used on it, sensitive plants may well be damaged. It is traditional to mulch strawberry beds with straw to keep the fruit sound and dry.

COCOA SHELLS

These are a by-product of chocolate production. The shells are an attractive rich brown and are pleasant and easy to apply. When wet the shells form a gum which bonds them together, preventing the mulch from blowing away. During very wet weather they can become slimy. Cocoa shells are expensive but worth considering for beds with bulbs, bedding or other small plants, where chipped bark would be too large.

INORGANIC MULCHES

SHEET MULCHES

Sheet mulches such as black plastic sheeting keep moisture in and weeds at bay, and also warm the soil slightly, so they are ideal when growing vegetables. Lay them over the area and anchor them to the soil by sinking the edges into slits dug in the soil (or use special pegs). The drawback compared to loose mulches is that it is harder to add fertiliser to the soil once they have been laid.

The newer sheet mulches are perforated or woven to allow water through them, and these are a better choice for long-term crops or plants.

Floating mulches are sheets of transparent plastic or fleece that are laid over planted crops. They warm the soil, act as a physical barrier against pests, keep birds and cats away from young plants and seed beds but they do not control weeds. As the crop grows the sheet 'floats' up and acts like a cloche.

If you just want to stop weeds growing over an area of vacant land, old carpet is perhaps the least expensive solution. A carpet-like mulch made from waste wool can be bought off the roll. This acts like a normal mulching sheet. It lets water penetrate easily, but will eventually decompose and be worked into the soil by worms and other soil life.

GRAVEL

Gravel and stone chippings can make attractive weed-suppressing mulches if applied at least 5 cm (2 in) thick. Small stone chippings look attractive as a mulch for the rock garden, and larger gravel for gravel beds – but make sure the gravel does not spill on to the lawn and damage mower blades.

Pests, diseases & disorders

Opinions vary on the best way to treat many of the pests and diseases that you will encounter in the garden. Whether to use chemicals, and which ones, must be largely a matter of conscience but in many cases a combined approach is often the most effective – use cultural and non-chemical methods to keep the problems to a minimum, and resort to chemical control only where alternative methods are not working satisfactorily. Good gardening practice combined with growing disease-resistant varieties will avoid a lot of problems.

Some of the chemical sprays and dusts are generally regarded as kinder to the environment than others. These are the natural plant products such as derris and pyrethrum, along with modern equivalents of the old soap sprays described as 'fatty acids' on the label.

New chemicals are being developed all the time, and existing ones – sometimes long-established – are occasionally withdrawn for a variety of reasons. Seek advice from a good garden centre and read the labels carefully. The label will list the major pests or diseases for which the pesticide has been approved.

Follow the advice on the label and treat safety warnings seriously; certain plants may be damaged by some chemicals. Don't attempt to make up your own and never mix two chemicals together. Sometimes insects become resistant to one formula, so if a product does not appear to be working, try a different one based on an alternative chemical.

BIOLOGICAL CONTROL

Biological controls are bacteria, insects or nematodes that either eat or parasitise and kill specific pests. They are usually sent by post and, as they are living creatures, most should be used without delay. Some may be kept for a number of weeks, often in a refrigerator; always check the packet for the expiry date.

Biological controls work well, and are environmentally friendly, but they are living creatures that have to be released at the right time and in suitable conditions.

The temperature may have to be above a minimum level, the soil may have to be moist, and in the case of nematodes it is best to water them on in the evening so that they are not desiccated in hot sunshine. Some will only thrive in green-houses, others can be used outdoors only when it is warm enough.

It is a waste of money to apply biological controls if there are no appropriate pests. Timing can be crucial so always check the best time to apply, and the conditions needed, before you order.

COMPANION PLANTING

French marigolds are often planted among brassicas to deter cabbage white butterflies.

The principles of companion planting are well rooted in gardening folklore. A scientific explanation of why it works is less easy to come by but it is a fact that certain plants, when grown together, flourish: either common pests are repelled or predators and parasites that prey on those pests are attracted. The crops grow better and are generally healthy and disease free.

There are various possible explanations of this phenomenon: the companion crop may conceal the main crop from its pests; it may produce a scent that deters predators; it may act as a trap, drawing pests from other plants; it may provide food for beneficial insects or act as a welcome habitat in which they flourish.

Whatever the reason there are a number of plants which are commonly grown together with benefit. French marigolds (*Tagetes patula*) are thought to mask the smell of brassicas which attracts cabbage white butterflies. The butterflies lay eggs that turn into caterpillars which eat the brassicas. The marigolds also attract hoverflies which feed on aphids, and their roots give off a substance which repels any nematodes in their immediate area.

Other strong-smelling plants, such as mint (*Mentha*) and catmint (*Nepeta*), are thought to confuse moths and butterflies, and tomato plants grown among the vegetables also help to keep off cabbage white butterflies and flea beetles. A chemical in tomatoes is toxic to some weevils.

Onions can be grown alongside carrots as this helps to deter carrot root flies, and parsley can be grown near asparagus if you are afflicted with asparagus beetle. Nasturtiums attract aphids so, if you want, they can be grown as a trap around fruit trees and any other plants which are prone to aphid damage.

Beware of using biological controls and chemical sprays or dusts at the same time: always read the instructions that come with the biological control carefully, as they should contain advice on which chemicals you can use when, without upsetting the biological balance. An inappropriate chemical used at the wrong time may wipe out your predator.

ATTRACTING NATURAL PREDATORS
Natural predators can be encouraged to visit the garden by planting flowers that attract them. Plants such as chives, French marigolds, marjoram and the poached-egg plant (*Limnanthes douglasii*) (particularly useful because it flowers early) will encourage hoverflies and lacewings, which will help to control the aphid population.

Frogs will help to control slugs, and many birds eat aphids. It is difficult to entice ladybirds to your garden as it is usually the presence of aphids, such as greenfly, that brings them in, but never destroy ladybirds as they are particularly effective at controlling greenfly. Planting to attract predators may be ineffective if you use pesticides heavily.

SYSTEMIC OR CONTACT?
You will sometimes see the terms 'systemic' and 'contact' used on containers. Systemic means that the chemical is capable of passing through the surface of the leaf and into the tissue within the plant. Most fungicides are systemic to some extent because the fungus usually grows within the leaf, but some only pass into the leaves – they are not moved around the whole plant.

Systemic pesticides are usually carried round the plant in the sap, which means these are particularly useful as a protection against sap-sucking insects such as aphids and mealy bugs.

Contact insecticides remain largely on the surface of the plant, where they affect chewing insects such as caterpillars. When applying a contact pesticide you must make sure all vulnerable parts of the plant are wetted (although a few do also produce some vapour which helps to protect parts of the plant that the spray does not actually contact). Control is mainly by physical contact with the pest when spraying or dusting and works best for crawling or chewing insects such as caterpillars and earwigs.

A contact insecticide with a very short toxic life may also be preferable to a systemic insecticide, if spraying edible crops. When asking advice on the control of a particular pest, always make it clear if it is needed for fruit or vegetables. Some are safe to use provided you allow sufficient time between spraying and harvesting. Always read the instructions.

METHODS OF APPLICATION
Some garden chemicals are available as liquids, powders or dusts, so choose the most appropriate formulation for the job. Sprays are less obtrusive on foliage than powders, which are usually more suitable for application to the soil.

For the greenhouse, smoke cones are available for fumigation. These provide more effective control than spraying, and also have the advantage in winter of not raising the level of humidity.

Winter washes are a type of spray formulated for use on deciduous trees in winter; they are mostly used on fruit trees, such as apples, pears and plums, as a protection against disease and winter moths. Greasebands are another good way of controlling these pests.

Ants farming aphids

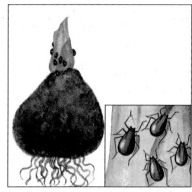
Aphids – tulip bulb aphid

PESTS

ANTS
These small insects are often a nuisance in the garden because they swarm over plants infested with aphids, searching for the honeydew excreted by the aphids. They may even 'farm' the aphids by carrying them bodily to another plant.

They can also damage the roots of herbaceous and annual plants when tunnelling underground to build nests in the soil. In a severe case the damage and exposure of the roots to the drying air can kill the plant. Ants can be a problem in cold frames and greenhouses, where they feed on newly sown seeds. Ripe fruit can also be spoilt.

CONTROL Dust the nest and areas where they run with a recommended insecticide. In the greenhouse treat surfaces around propagators and places where they enter the greenhouse with a residual product that will form a long-lasting barrier. It should not be necessary to spray the plants if you treat the surrounding surfaces. Try to destroy nests by exposing them and pouring boiling water over the nests.

APHIDS
There are many kinds of aphids, including the ubiquitous greenfly and blackfly. Some of the less common kinds feed on roots or around the base of a plant – the tulip bulb aphid attacks various bulbs and corms. All are sap-suckers and endanger the plant, weakening it and causing direct damage, such as distorted leaves, and by spreading virus diseases from plant to plant. They also look unsightly and in some cases the sweet 'honeydew' excrement may encourage the growth of black sooty moulds.

Aphids are usually up to 5 mm (¼ in) long, and may be green, yellow, grey, black or brown; certain types are covered with a fluffy white wax. There are both winged and wingless generations.

Apple aphids, of which there are several species, attack apples and pears. They all look similar to greenfly, but vary in colour from green or yellowish green to pink or grey. The small, shiny black eggs are sometimes visible on twigs and branches in the autumn, and if these are noticed it is important to use a winter treatment to prevent them hatching.

Aphids – blackfly

Aphids – woolly

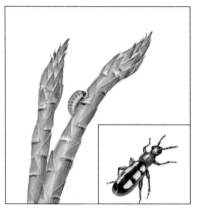

Asparagus beetle

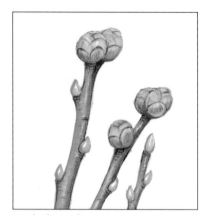

Big bud mite damage

Blackfly, resembling black versions of the common greenfly, are familiar to all gardeners. Many plants are particularly prone to them, especially broad beans, cherries, nasturtiums and dahlias.

Greenfly are a problem in all gardens. These small green pests are especially troublesome after a mild winter and feed on a huge range of plants; roses are particularly susceptible

Mealy cabbage aphids are grey-green and usually covered in a white mealy wax. They can attack a variety of plants but cabbages and Brussels sprouts are particularly prone to them.

Root aphids are usually found as wingless insects, normally yellowish white or grey, clustered around the roots or the crown of the plant, especially on autumn and winter lettuces. As they feed at root level, the first indication of their presence may be the collapse of a plant. The aphids will be obvious when you pull up an affected plant.

Woolly aphids are small, greyish black insects, but what you normally see is the white waxy secretion with which they cover themselves. This sometimes looks like a white mould growing on the plants' stem. Apple trees are the plants mainly affected, although their ornamental relations, cotoneasters and pyracanthas, are also susceptible.

CONTROL Pinch out the growing tips from broad beans and other similar plants when they have set four trusses of flowers. This removes the blackfly that cluster at the tips of the shoots and makes the plants less attractive to aphids. This also makes bushier plants which will produce a heavier crop of beans.

In a greenhouse or indoors, you can use a biological control. A parasite called *Aphidius* will kill young aphids, but should be introduced at the first sign of adult aphids.

Most common aphids, such as greenfly and blackfly, can be controlled by spraying with a suitable systemic or contact insecticide. An environmentally friendly control, such as spraying with a solution of washing-up liquid, can be effective and will not harm beneficial insects such as bees and ladybirds. Apple aphids are best controlled by spraying with a winter wash while the trees are dormant, and root aphids require a soil drench.

ASPARAGUS BEETLE

Asparagus beetles eat the leaves of this vegetable crop, but also attack the stems, which in turn causes the growth above to die. The beetles, about 5mm (¼ in) long, are a distinctive yellow and black, the larvae are greyish yellow.

CONTROL Spray with a suitable insecticide. Small infestations can sometimes be controlled by removing them by hand.

BIG BUD MITE (BLACKCURRANT GALL MITE)

This tiny mite lives in blackcurrant leaf buds, which swell to an abnormal size, then eventually wither and fall off. Red and white currants may also be affected, but the buds do not swell before they die off. Some ornamentals, such as brooms, may also be affected. It is important to control these mites, as besides reducing the crop, they spread a serious virus disease known as reversion.

CONTROL Pick off and destroy affected buds. Normal insecticides are not effective, but you can try spraying with a recommended fungicide at 14 day intervals. If the infestation is severe, dig up and burn the plant.

BIRDS

Birds add much beauty and interest to the garden, but at some times of the year they can cause as much damage as insect pests. Bullfinches are a serious pest in winter and early spring when they take leaf and flower buds from fruit and ornamental trees and shrubs. Wood pigeons and collared doves can devastate a vegetable garden in winter when they tear and shred the leaves of brassicas, and in spring when they scratch up and eat seeds and young vegetables. Sparrows and bluetits sometimes cause damage to flowers and buds. Winter and spring flowers are most at risk, and crocuses and primroses are a common target for sparrows. However, birds such as these do as much good as harm. Tits, for example, eat greenfly and caterpillars.

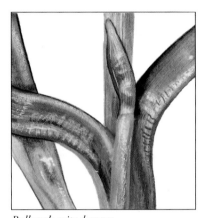
Bulb scale mite damage

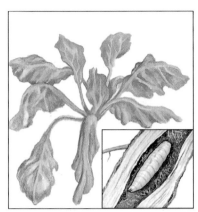
Cabbage root fly

CONTROL Netting is the most effective protection for vulnerable crops and the best solution for soft fruit. Choose an appropriate mesh size: a 12 cm (5 in) mesh is suitable for pigeon protection, but a 2 cm (¾ in) mesh will be necessary to keep out small birds such as tits. If they are hung on a frame the nets can be removed when they are not required. Horticultural fleece provides good protection for young crops in spring.

In other parts of the garden you need a more flexible approach. Scaring devices, such as humming lines, aluminium foil strips and model birds of prey, all have some short-term effect. Within a fairly short time, however, most birds start to ignore them. The best approach is to use a range of different scarers, and to change their position frequently. Black cotton stretched just above the ground will sometimes help but, as with most deterrents, many birds get used to it, and some people prefer not to use it because of the risk of the birds getting tangled in it. Repellent sprays must be used frequently if they are to be effective.

BLACKFLY *see* Aphids

BULB SCALE MITE
These tiny mites infest the scales and young leaves of bulbous plants such as daffodils and amaryllis. Plants being forced or stored in warm conditions are particularly vulnerable.

Brown patches may be seen between the scales when the bulbs are lifted; other symptoms of attack are rust-coloured streaks on foliage and flower stalks, poor blooms and weak growth.
CONTROL There is no practical chemical control available to amateurs. Destroy affected bulbs, and avoid growing others in the same ground.

CABBAGE ROOT FLY
The white larvae of these flies, which look like small maggots, tunnel into many root vegetables, such as turnips, swedes and radishes. The larvae also attack the roots of newly planted cabbage and other brassica seedlings, such as cauliflowers. Affected plants turn bluish, wilt and often die.

CONTROLLING PESTS IN THE HOME AND CONSERVATORY

Pesticides that can be used safely in the open garden may be unsuitable for use indoors where food is prepared or served, or where fabrics and furniture could be marked or damaged by inaccurately aimed sprays.

Fumigation – an option for the greenhouse – is also clearly inappropriate, and some pesticides designed for outdoor use also have an unpleasant smell that would not be acceptable indoors. For all these reasons, a different approach to pest control is sometimes necessary for the home or conservatory. If pot plants are inspected regularly, perhaps at watering time, much can be achieved by picking off the first few affected leaves, or removing individual pests such as caterpillars. This is a sensible first line of defence for many insect pests and some leaf diseases.

Insects that do not multiply rapidly and are easy to spot, such as mealy bugs and scale insects, can be dealt with by dabbing them individually with a cotton bud or small paintbrush dipped into an insecticide (traditionally, alcohol or methylated spirits have been used). This is a very easy and satisfactory method of control for some pests if used at the beginning of an outbreak.

On plants with large, shiny leaves, it may be possible to control pests simply by wiping them over with a damp cloth or a leafshine wipe.

Insecticidal plant pins (small pieces of card impregnated with a systemic insecticide) will control many sap-sucking pests such as aphids. They are pushed into the compost, where they release a chemical absorbed by the roots.

Vine weevil grubs are best controlled with a nematode bought as a biological control and watered onto the compost. Aphids, such as a heavy infestation of greenfly or whitefly, or any fungus disease that affects more than just a few leaves that can be picked off and destroyed, may require more drastic chemical treatment. Low-toxicity sprays and aerosols are available for house plants, but before spraying move the plants where the spray will not affect food or furniture (outside in summer). Do not use an aerosol too close to the plant – it can damage the leaves.

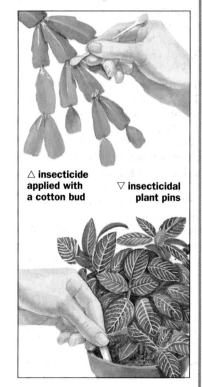
△ insecticide applied with a cotton bud
▽ insecticidal plant pins

Capsid bug

Carrot fly

Caterpillar damage on rose leaf

Caterpillar damage on chrysanthemum bloom

CONTROL Brassica collars are an effective non-chemical control. Buy them or make your own from carpet underlay or roofing felt: cut out circles about 15 cm (6 in) across and make a slit to the centre. Placed around the base of a plant, a collar deters the female flies from laying their eggs there (*see* April, page 112). Dust seed drills and the soil around transplanted seedlings with a suitable soil insecticide.

CAPSID BUG

There are several species commonly grouped together as far as the gardener is concerned. The small wingless nymphs do most of the damage, making holes in the leaves of most soft fruit bushes, as well as those of peaches and pears. They are green or brown insects about 5 mm (¼ in) long, but you will often notice the damage before you see the insects. They suck the sap, especially from the tips of shoots, and destroy the plant tissue, causing it to tear.

In June and July they often migrate to feed on herbaceous plants or weeds. Chrysanthemums, dahlias and fuchsias are particularly affected. The flower petals often grow unevenly, and on fuchsias the buds may fail to develop.
CONTROL Clear up all plant debris in winter to reduce the overwintering population. On fruit trees, a winter wash will also help, or spray plants with a recommended pesticide.

CARROT FLY

The larvae of these flies tunnel into carrot roots. The symptoms of damage are reddening and wilting of the foliage. In dry weather, seedlings may be killed. Parsnips, celery and parsley are also sometimes affected.
CONTROL Build a plastic sheeting barrier at least 60 cm (2 ft) tall around the bed. The females fly low above the ground and this may be enough to minimise the problem (*see* April, page 113). Do not leave carrot thinnings on the ground, as the smell may attract the flies. Water the soil after thinning, and refirm it around the remaining roots. As a further precaution, dust along the rows of emerging seedlings with a soil insecticide.

CATERPILLARS

Caterpillars are the soft-bodied larvae of butterflies and moths, which themselves cause no damage to plant life. Some caterpillars, such as those of the peacock and small tortoiseshell butterflies, feed mainly on weeds such as nettles. Others, such as those of the cabbage white butterfly, can devastate crops.

The caterpillars that pose the most serious problem to gardeners are three species that attack cabbages and related plants, such as cauliflowers, as well as some ornamentals (perhaps the most vulnerable of which is the nasturtium). Holes are eaten in the leaves and the caterpillars are clearly visible.

The large cabbage white caterpillars (*Pieris brassicae*) are yellow and black and hairy, those of the small cabbage white butterfly (*Pieris rapae*) are pale green and also slightly hairy. The cabbage moth (*Mamestra brassicae*) caterpillar varies from brown to yellowish green, and has few hairs.

Most caterpillars hatch out from eggs in spring and early summer and begin to feed immediately. They often pupate in a tiny cavity in the soil or suspended from a sheltered wall. The following spring the adults break out of the chrysalis to mate. Always deal with them as soon as you notice them.
CONTROL For a small number of plants, regular inspection and the removal of the eggs (usually yellow and clustered together on the leaves), followed by hand picking of any caterpillars, may be enough if you want to avoid the use of chemicals. For treatment on a larger scale, there is a biological alternative, *Bacillus thuringiensis,* which is available in a form that is mixed into a spray and applied to the plants; the bacteria infect and kill most of the caterpillars. Pesticides will help to control them, but need to be used as soon as caterpillars are noticed and before the damage is done.

CATS AND DOGS

Cats and dogs are often a nuisance in the garden. Dogs dig holes, bitches' urine makes yellow patches on lawns and cats are irresistibly attracted to finely tilled

Rose chafer beetle

Codling moth

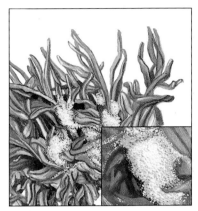

Cuckoo spit

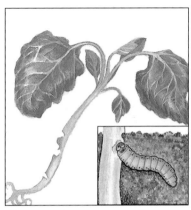

Cutworm

seedbeds where they scratch up the seeds and young plants. Cats are also a threat to fish if you have a garden pond.

CONTROL If your garden is invaded by other people's dogs try to make it dog proof. If you own a bitch, water the lawn well as necessary.

If you are invaded by neighbours' cats try chemical repellents, though they are only likely to be of short-term benefit, and some animals seem untroubled by them except perhaps at very close range.

Electronic deterrents that emit a high-pitched sound at a frequency inaudible to humans but disturbing to cats can be very effective. The range and direction of the sound can be adjusted so that you can protect vulnerable parts of the garden without deterring cats from other areas; useful if you have a cat yourself. Seed beds have to be netted.

CELERY FLY *see* Leaf miner

CHAFERS

The larvae of the cockchafer (*Melolontha melolontha*), the rose chafer (*Cetonia*

aurata) and the garden chafer (*Phyllopertha horticola*) cause extensive damage to many plants. The adult beetles attack the leaves of trees and shrubs, and the larvae feed on the roots of herbaceous plants, annuals and bulbous plants.

The fat, white, curved larvae, 3–4 cm (about 1½ in) long, have three pairs of legs and a brown head. They live in the soil, eat cavities in root vegetables, sever stems at the base, and often cause small plants to wilt and die. They also cause problems on lawns as birds and animals will dig holes to find and eat them.

CONTROL Dust with a recommended insecticide. If you want to avoid chemicals, destroy the ones you find by hand, and expose them by hoeing and cultivation, so that the birds can eat them.

CODLING MOTH

These small, pale pinkish caterpillars are a serious pest to apples, boring into the fruits. They leave the fruit in the autumn and pupate on the bark of the tree.

CONTROL Use pheromone traps in trees between late spring and mid summer.

This reduces the number of males and helps to control the population. It also helps you to choose the right time to spray. Spray the trees with an insecticide in mid June and mid July, when there are a lot of males on the wing, and repeat the process three weeks later.

Another good idea is to trap the cocoons by tying sacking or corrugated cardboard round the tree trunk. Do this before mid July, so the caterpillars will pupate in it. Remove and destroy the sacking and cocoons before spring.

CUCKOO SPIT

Cuckoo spit is the frothy or spittle-like covering that the pale green or yellow nymphs of the froghopper produce. Many herbaceous plants, shrubs and annuals are attacked, but they seldom cause much harm unless young growth is affected, when it may become distorted.

CONTROL Pesticide sprays are effective, but it is usually possible to control a low-level infestation by hand, especially as the consequence of missing a few is unlikely to cause a serious problem.

CUTWORM

These fat caterpillars belong to various moths and may be green or mud-coloured. They inhabit the soil and come to the surface at night to feed on the stems and leaves of many herbaceous plants and vegetables, as well as eating the roots. Root vegetables such as beet, carrots and onions can be badly damaged. Affected plants may wilt and die.

CONTROL Regular hoeing will help to expose the cutworms to be eaten by birds. Dust the soil with an insecticide.

DEER

Deer can be very troublesome in rural areas. Most damage is done in spring when they browse on new shoots and emerging leaves. They may also strip bark from trees during winter.

CONTROL The only practical solution is to erect a high fence or hedge at least 1.8 m (6 ft) tall. If you can't do that, protect vulnerable young trees with tree guards. Audible deterrents may help initially.

DOGS *see* Cats and dogs

Earwig

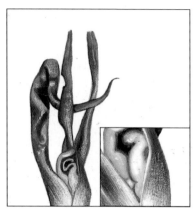

Eelworm in onion

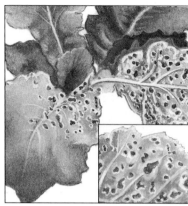

Flea beetle

Leaf hopper

EARWIGS

These brown insects are generally 2 cm (¾ in) long, with curved pincers at the rear end. They feed at night and are seldom discovered until the damage is done. In damp, warm weather they will sometimes attack the leaves of dwarf beans, cauliflowers, cucumbers and tomatoes, and the flower heads of chrysanthemums, dahlias and French marigolds. In the garden they seldom do severe damage, though they occasionally strip the foliage and spoil flower petals.

CONTROL Pack upturned flower pots with straw or hay and place them on canes among affected plants. Many of the earwigs will shelter in these during the day, when they can be tipped out and killed. Keep debris and rubbish to a minimum. Apply a pesticide spray or dust at dusk when they become active.

EELWORMS

Eelworms, or nematodes, can be a serious pest, and control is extremely difficult. These minute, worm-like creatures are invisible to the naked eye, but are widely distributed in the soil and attack a wide variety of food crops and herbaceous plants. An attack may show as stunted growth, with yellow leaves, and any tubers may be severely reduced. Some types of eelworm produce cysts or galls (containing the minute eggs), but do not confuse these with the nitrogen-fixing nodules that occur on plants such as peas and lupins. Chrysanthemums and dahlias suffer from an eelworm that causes dark patches on the lower leaves. This is followed by drooping leaves and flowers that do not form properly.

Some bulbs, daffodils, tulips, irises and hyacinths, may suffer from eelworm. The symptoms are deformed leaves or flowers, and there are sometimes small swellings on the leaves. Infested bulbs are often soft to the touch and may have a white woolly substance on the base – when a bulb is cut across it usually has dark rings in the flesh.

CONTROL There is no effective control available for amateurs. Destroy affected plants, and do not replant similar crops in the same place again. You will reduce the chances of eelworm becoming a problem on vegetables by regular crop rotation (*see* December, page 283).

FLEA BEETLE

There are numerous species of these small black or metallic blue beetles, sometimes with yellow marks. The beetles are about 2 mm (¹⁄₁₆ in) long, and often appear to jump when disturbed. They attack mainly brassica seedlings (such as cabbages), radishes and turnips. Related ornamentals such as stocks and wallflowers can also be infested. The leaves of the seedlings are often peppered with holes, and they can also chew off small seedlings at the base.

CONTROL Keep plant debris on which flea beetles (and other pests) can overwinter to a minimum. A small population is unlikely to affect a crop seriously, and the plants normally soon outgrow the damage. Where the pest is troublesome, dust with a pesticide powder as soon as the seedlings emerge.

GREENFLY *see* Aphids

LEAF-CUTTING BEE

These resemble hive bees. They damage the foliage of roses, and sometimes laburnums, lilacs and rhododendrons as well, by cutting small pieces from the leaves and using them to line their nests. The damage is seldom severe.

CONTROL Seldom necessary as they are unlikely to be a serious pest and do some good as pollinating insects. If the damage is serious, kill them if you see them.

LEAF HOPPER

There are several different leaf hoppers that you may find in the garden and greenhouse. They are green or yellow insects about 2–3 mm (¹⁄₁₆–¹⁄₈ in) long, and characteristically leap when disturbed. Roses are commonly affected, and they may be a problem on rhododendrons and tomatoes. Many other trees and plants, including vegetables and fruit, can also be attacked. They are more likely to be a problem in hot weather, and are usually found on the underside of the leaves, which become mottled where the sap has been sucked.

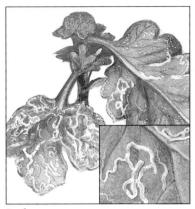

Leaf miner

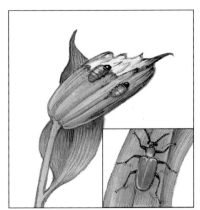

Lily beetle

Mealy bug

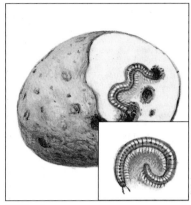

Millipede

CONTROL Spray affected plants with a recommended pesticide.

LEAF MINER

The larvae of several species of insect feed on the tissues between the leaf surfaces of vegetables such as beet, celery and parsnips. Tomatoes in the greenhouse may also be affected, and chrysanthemums, cinerarias, hollies and lilacs are particularly prone to these pests. The larvae or grubs mine or tunnel between the upper and lower surfaces of the leaf, causing white wavy marks on the foliage. Eventually the whole leaf may be destroyed.

CONTROL Removing and destroying tunnelled leaves by hand can be very effective if the plant is not badly affected. Spray with a recommended pesticide as soon as the damage is seen. In severe cases it may be necessary to repeat the treatment at fortnightly intervals.

LEATHERJACKETS

These large, earth-coloured grubs are the larvae of the cranefly, or daddy-long-legs.

They feed on the roots of grasses, particularly in lawns, causing whole areas to grow weak and thin. Many plants in herbaceous and vegetable gardens are also attacked by leatherjackets, especially after a wet autumn, as they thrive in damp conditions. The leatherjackets often sever the stems at ground level and the plant wilts and dies.

CONTROL Dust the soil around affected or vulnerable plants with a soil insecticide. If you want to avoid chemicals, dig or hoe the soil and destroy weeds.

If leatherjackets are troublesome in a lawn, try soaking the grass with water then covering it with black plastic sheeting or sacking for about a day; this will bring many of them to the surface where they can be gathered up and killed.

LILY BEETLE

Lilies are the most likely plants to be attacked by these attractive-looking bright red beetles, but fritillaries are also vulnerable (*see* June, page 158).

The beetles are about 8 mm (⅜ in) long and their bright colour makes them

conspicuous and attractive. The larvae are reddish brown, but they are usually covered with ugly black excrement.

CONTROL If just a few plants are affected, try picking off the beetles and larvae by hand, but you must remain vigilant.

Systemic insectides will help foil beetles and larvae.

MEALY BUGS

These pink or yellow insects, covered in a white wax, are common in the greenhouse and are often found on house plants, including cacti. Outdoors they may infest flowering currants, ceanothus and laburnums. They feed on a wide range of plants, sucking the sap.

CONTROL A ladybird (*Cryptolaemus montrouzieri*) can be used as a biological control in the greenhouse or indoors. Mealy bugs can also be controlled indoors by washing with an insecticidal soap, and outdoors by washing or spraying with pesticide. On house plants that cannot easily be moved outdoors to be sprayed, use a small brush to paint on spray-strength pesticide.

MICE AND VOLES

Small rodents are only likely to be a problem if they gain access to stored seeds or bulbs, or where bulbs or large seeds such as peas have just been planted. Stored fruit is also vulnerable.

CONTROL Store bulbs, seeds and fruit in mouse-proof containers. It is always a good idea to store seeds in an airtight tin or jar anyway.

Sown seeds and planted bulbs can be protected by covering the soil with small-mesh netting, though this is only practical for a small area.

Poison baits and traps are an effective means of control but take great care to prevent pets, birds or children from getting access to them. Put baits and traps under floorboards, or in cloches that can be closed off to stop unwanted access. Cats are good deterrents.

MILLIPEDES

There are several species of these multi-legged creatures, all long, black, grey, brown or white, and slow-moving. They live in the soil and feed on vegetable

New Zealand flatworm on earthworm

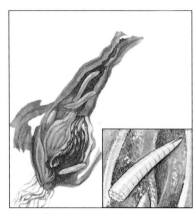

Onion fly

Raspberry beetle

Red spider mite damage

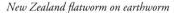

matter, both dead and living, and can tunnel into seeds, gnaw roots and chew into tubers and bulbs. Lilies and young seedlings are particularly at risk.

CONTROL Chemical control is difficult but slug pellets can work. Frequent hoeing to keep the soil disturbed will help.

NEW ZEALAND FLATWORMS

These worm-shaped creatures from New Zealand threaten our native earthworms, and therefore the ecological balance of our gardens. Earthworms are very beneficial and help to recycle organic material.

The New Zealand flatworm grows to about 15 cm (6 in) long, sometimes a little more, but young ones will be much smaller. They have dark, flat, sticky bodies, with a tell-tale pale edge along each side. When they make contact with earthworms they release a paralysing chemical and an enzyme that dissolves the earthworm's body.

They are most likely to be found in Scotland, Ireland and the north and west of England. However, they may be spreading to other areas.

CONTROL Kill them by treading on them or dropping them into a bucket of salty water. Handle them wearing gloves.

ONION FLY

Onion fly larvae look like small white maggots, and are found in the bulbs or roots of onions and shallots, and sometimes in garlic and leeks. Growth is poor and the leaves turn yellow and wilt. The bulb may be reduced to pulp.

CONTROL Lift and burn affected plants. As a precaution for plants not yet affected, treat the soil with a suitable pesticide; this can also be useful when sowing seeds or planting sets.

PEA MOTH

The 'maggots' found in the pods of peas are the caterpillars of the pea moth.

CONTROL The pea moth is most active in mid summer and early and late-sown peas (those sown in February–March and after mid June) often escape. Pheromone traps will reduce the population or spraying with a pesticide 7–10 days after the plants start flowering will help.

RABBITS AND HARES

In some areas these animals can have a devastating effect, especially in the vegetable garden. Entire rows of seedlings can be devoured in a day, and even quite tall plants such as sweetcorn can be toppled where they are chewed through at the base. They can also kill young trees by gnawing away the bark.

CONTROL The most effective control is a rabbit-proof fence. Strong wire netting with a 2–3 cm (1–1¼ in) mesh is suitable, but make sure the base is buried 30 cm (1 ft) below the soil to reduce the risk of penetration by burrowing. The fence should also be at least 1 m (3 ft) high, or they will jump over.

If fencing off the area is not practical, protect vulnerable young trees and shrubs with a bark guard.

Chemical repellents may have some short-term effect.

RASPBERRY BEETLE

The adult beetles appear in May, and feed on the flower buds of raspberries, blackberries and hybrid cane fruits. They

also lay their eggs on these plants in early and mid summer, and the larvae feed on the developing fruit causing damage and making them maggoty.

CONTROL Spray or dust with a recommended pesticide – at dusk if possible to reduce the risk to bees. Treat raspberries when the first fruits are turning pink, loganberries as soon as most of the petals have fallen. Blackberries are best sprayed when the flowers begin to open. It may be necessary to repeat the application.

RED SPIDER MITE

All these mites, of which there are several species, are tiny (about 1 mm (¹⁄₃₂ in) across), orange-red to yellowish green, sometimes with black markings, and have eight legs. A fine web may be spun among the leaves, which become pale or bronzed and mottled. These are serious pests to many plants grown in the greenhouse and in the home. Melons, grapes, tomatoes, chrysanthemums, carnations, orchids and pot plants are particularly vulnerable. Outdoor plants can also be affected, including fruit trees.

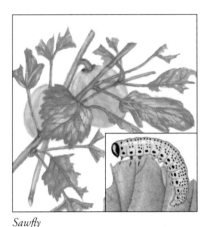
Sawfly

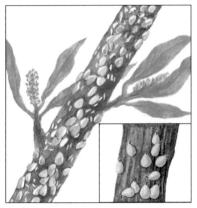
Scale insects

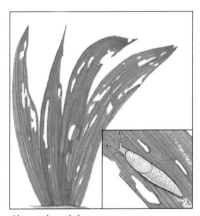
Slug and snail damage

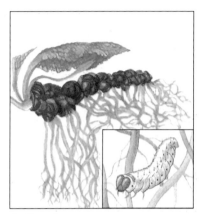
Swift moth

CONTROL Much can be done to control indoor red spider mites by keeping the atmosphere moist and humid. There is also an effective biological control for indoor red spider mites: *Phytoseiulus persimilis*. This parasite can also be used outdoors on crops such as strawberries, apples and pears, from May to August, but conditions must be warm. Insecticidal soaps or pesticide sprays can be effective if repeated as instructed. Be prepared to try a different chemical if the first does not work as some red spider mites show resistance to pesticides.

SAWFLY

The larvae or caterpillars of these small insects cause serious damage to fruit, vegetables and flowers. Apples, gooseberries, pears and cherries are all prone to attack. Roses are attacked by the rose-leaf-rolling sawfly, which, as its name implies, causes the leaflets to roll into small tubes (the pale green caterpillars feed inside them). Species that attack fruit usually cause blemishes, tunnels and scars on the fruit itself, where the white caterpillar-like larvae, up to about 1 cm (½ in) long, have been feeding.
CONTROL On roses, affected leaves can easily be picked off and destroyed. Spray affected fruit trees with a recommended pesticide about a week after petal-fall at dusk. This reduces the risk to bees that are still actively pollinating other flowers.

SCALE INSECTS

There are several species of scale insects that might be encountered in the garden, greenhouse or home. They are small, hard-coated insects that suck the sap of ornamental and fruit trees, shrubs, herbaceous and greenhouse plants. Usually brown, grey, yellowish or white, they are practically immobile and resemble blisters on the bark, stems and leaves. All can be disfiguring and may also cause the plant to wilt. Many species excrete honeydew, leading to sooty mould (*see* Aphids, pages 395–396). You might also find white deposits that contain eggs.
CONTROL In the greenhouse or indoors, a small parasitic wasp, *Metaphycus helvolus*, can be used as a biological control.

Chemicals to control scale are most effective on newly hatched nymphs and repeated applications may be necessary.

SLUGS AND SNAILS

These creatures cause immense damage. Field and garden slugs and snails eat their way through the soft foliage and flowers of numerous plants, often climbing to surprising heights. They also enjoy vegetables and strawberries. Keeled slugs, which are small and black and live underground, feed off bulbs, roots and tubers, causing widespread damage.

Slugs and snails are nocturnal feeders, and they usually hide beneath stones, leaves and rubbish during the day.
CONTROL Pick off as many as you can by hand, preferably in the evening when they are more likely to be seen. Encouraging frogs, toads and birds into your garden will also help to control them. Cultivate the soil to expose the eggs.

Physical barriers such as plastic collars around seedlings (cut from plastic bottles, for example) are good deterrents, and irritant substances like sharp sand, grit or lime sprinkled around vulnerable plants may also help. Slug traps, baited with beer, to drown them may be useful over a limited area.

Use slug pellets or bait among plants attractive to slugs and snails, or spray a liquid slug killer over badly affected soil; some preparations are promoted as less likely to be harmful to animals and birds. You can also use a tiny nematode called *Phasmarhabditis hermaphrodita* to achieve biological control. If slugs and snails are a severe problem, avoid organic mulches as these provide useful shelter.

SQUIRRELS

Squirrels dig up and eat bulbs, denude shrubs of fruit and berries, and cause severe damage to young trees by stripping the bark off stems and branches.
CONTROL Fruit cages and netting will keep them off vulnerable plants and crops, and planted bulbs can be protected by covering the area with small-mesh wire netting until they begin to grow. Young and newly planted trees are best protected with spiral stem-protectors.

Thrips

Tortrix moth

Wasps

Weevils

Squirrel traps are available, but may not be totally effective if there are large numbers in the surrounding area.

SWIFT MOTH

Swift moths (species of *Hepialus*) are usually active at dusk during summer and unlikely to be noticed. It is the caterpillars, which live in the soil and feed on roots, that cause the damage. These white caterpillars, often 2–3 cm (1–1¼ in) or more in length with a shiny brown head, will continue to feed on roots, tubers, bulbs and corms throughout autumn and winter. They usually move backwards if disturbed.

CONTROL Regular hoeing may expose the caterpillars for killing by hand or to be eaten by birds. Dust the soil with a recommended pesticide.

THRIPS

These tiny elongated insects (also called thunder flies) infest greenhouse plants, and also attack herbaceous plants outdoors. There are several types of thrip, but most puncture and tear minute holes in leaves, which then assume a silvery appearance. At a later stage they pierce flower petals, producing white spots. Peas, gladioli, cyclamen, fuchsias and roses are among the plants often attacked. Pea pods may turn a silvery brown. Thrips are also a hazard because they transmit virus diseases.

CONTROL Thrips are less likely to be a problem if you keep the plants well watered, and keep the temperature down in the greenhouse by shading, ventilating and maintaining a moist atmosphere. Predatory mites (*Amblyseius* spp.) can be used as a biological control, or there is a range of suitable pesticides.

TORTRIX MOTH

The caterpillars of the various tortrix moths have brown heads and characteristically wriggle backwards when disturbed. They are up to 2 cm (¾ in) long. They feed on the foliage of ornamental trees, shrubs and roses, fastening the leaves together with a cobweb-like substance, making it difficult to penetrate with a contact spray. Dry skeletal patches on the leaves are another characteristic sign of these pests.

CONTROL Spray with recommended insecticide. Alternatively, kill them by hand, squeezing them inside their folded leaves.

WASPS

Wasps feed on most top fruits, such as apples, pears and plums, gnawing holes in them. The spoilt fruit is then likely to be attacked by fungal diseases, especially brown rot (*see* page 406).

CONTROL If possible, locate and destroy their nest, or have them dealt with professionally. Wasp traps will help to reduce the population around a particular tree, or use a recommended pesticide if they are a real problem.

WEEVILS

Weevils form a large family of small, active beetles, distinguished by elongated snouts. The adult beetles can spoil plants by eating the leaves, while their larvae can destroy a plant from beneath by eating the roots. Weevil larvae are small, rather wrinkled grubs about 8 mm (⅜ in) long with curved white bodies and brown heads. A wide range of plants can be affected, from shrubs to annuals, both indoors and out. The vine weevil is one of the most destructive, and is a major pest in some areas.

CONTROL Biological controls are available using parasitic nematodes such as *Heterorhabditis megidis*. These can be used for pots indoors and for outdoors if applied according to instructions. Good garden hygiene, removing debris and hiding places for the weevils, will also help to reduce the population.

As a mechanical trap for protecting plants in containers, try using double-sided adhesive tape around the rim. This may be enough to prevent the adult weevils crawling over to lay their eggs in the compost.

To control adults that are eating the foliage, spray the leaves with a suitable pesticide, or hand pick at dusk when the pests become active. Dusting the soil or potting compost with a pesticide powder in mid summer, and again in late summer, gives limited control of the larvae.

Whitefly

Wireworms

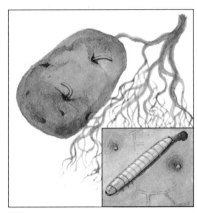
Woodlice

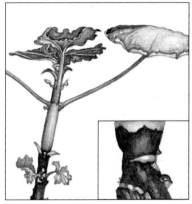
Blackleg

WHITEFLY

Adult whitefly are like very small white moths, and often rise up in a cloud if the plant is moved. The nymphs are scale-like, immobile and greenish. One species is common in the greenhouse and in-doors, where they are often found in dense clusters on the backs of leaves. Another species attacks members of the cabbage family outdoors.

CONTROL A parasitic wasp called *Encarsia formosa* is a very effective bio-logical control for use in the greenhouse or conservatory.

If spraying, be prepared to try out dif-ferent formulae, as resistant strains occur; if one chemical does not work, experi-ment with another. Repeat the treatment as instructed. In a greenhouse fumigation with a recommended formula will give good control.

WINTER MOTH

The pale green caterpillars of the winter moth are about 2–3 cm (1–1¼ in) long. They affect many deciduous trees and shrubs such as roses, and fruit trees are

also vulnerable. The emerging leaves are eaten and blossom or young fruit may also be damaged.

CONTROL Apply greasebands to the trunks of trees in autumn to prevent the wingless female moths from climbing up to lay their eggs on the branches. The biological control *Bacillus thuringiensis* can also be effective. Spraying with a rec-ommended pesticide should be done as the buds begin to open.

WIREWORMS

These yellow, thread-like grubs are the larvae of the click beetle. They feed on the underground parts of many plants. The symptoms of wireworm damage are yellowing and wilting foliage, and young plants may die.

CONTROL As this pest is usually a prob-lem of newly cultivated land, frequent digging and cultivation will do much to reduce the population. If they are ex-posed, they will be eaten by birds. If they are a major problem use one of the soil insecticides recommended for wire-worm control.

WOODLICE

These grey, hard-skinned creatures can be found in damp and shady parts of the garden, where they feed on decaying or dead vegetable material. They feed on stems, leaves and roots, but are normally only a problem on seedlings, especially in the greenhouse (holes in the leaves may indicate treatment is necessary).

Woodlice generally feed at night and hide in dark places during the day. Another common name is pill bug, be-cause of their habit of rolling into a ball for protection.

CONTROL Good garden hygiene, with the removal of rubbish and hiding places will help to control the population – they seldom justify chemical control. If it is necessary, use an insecticidal dust.

WOOLLY APHIDS *see* Aphids

WORMS *see* New Zealand flatworms

Normal earthworms are not pests but are extremely beneficial as they help to aerate the soil and break down compost.

BLACKLEG

Blackleg affects cuttings, particularly of pelargoniums. The base of the stem turns black and soft, and the plant collapses. It is caused by several fungi.

Potato blackleg is a bacterial disease that causes the stem to rot at the base, accompanied by discoloured foliage and eventually total collapse of the plant. Usually the crop remains healthy.

CONTROL Blackleg on cuttings can be controlled by using a rooting powder that contains a fungicide. When taking cuttings, always use clean, preferably sterilised, compost, and keep tools and containers scrupulously clean. Remove any cuttings that are affected without delay. Bacterial blackleg of potatoes is best controlled by destroying affected plants then applying strict crop rotation.

BLACK SPOT

This prevalent disease causes dark brown spots on rose leaves, often leading to de-foliation and general loss of vigour. The

Black spot

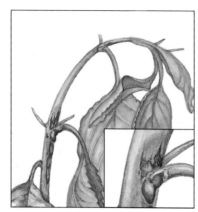

Canker (bacterial)

Clematis wilt

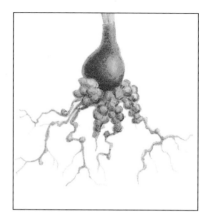

Club root

disease is not easy to control, especially during wet weather, and is usually worst in clean air areas.

CONTROL Pick off affected leaves, and take care to clear up fallen leaves and prunings in autumn. Spray with a suitable fungicide. Where black spot is a severe problem, choose varieties that show a resistance to the disease (rose catalogues usually list varieties that are black spot and mildew resistant).

BLIGHT *see* Potato blight, Tomato blight

BOTRYTIS *see* Grey mould

BROWN ROT

This common fungus can damage most tree fruit but is most often found on apples. The fruit rots, turns brown at the top and develops concentric rings of pale whitish or yellow pustules. It may mummify on the tree.

CONTROL Spraying is unlikely to be effective. You can reduce the risk of infection in future years by picking up and burn-

ing affected fruit and any branches that are dead and diseased. Spray the tree with Bordeaux mixture just before leaf-fall, halfway through leaf-fall and at budburst. Reduce the risk of injury to the fruit by controlling wasps and other insects that may damage the fruit (*see* Wasps, page 404).

CANKER

Cankers, caused either by bacteria or fungi, are sunken, often wrinkled, areas on the shoots of woody plants, particularly trees. Apples, cherries and plums, as well as ornamental *Prunus*, are especially prone to some forms of canker.

Bacterial canker sometimes causes brown spots on the leaves in summer, which later become small holes, but the most obvious symptoms are the sunken scars on the branches.

CONTROL Cut out the diseased wood as soon as noticed, cutting back into unaffected wood. Paint the wound with a fungicidal wound paint. As a precaution, if there has been an infection, spray the whole tree with an appropriate fungicide,

in August and September. Ornamental *Prunus* are usually sprayed in spring. Where bacterial canker is severe on a plum or cherry tree, it may be best to remove the tree. When planting a new tree, choose a more resistant variety. Some apples are more likely to be attacked than others ('Cox's Orange Pippin' is vulnerable, for example, but 'Bramley's Seedling' is more resistant).

CLEMATIS WILT

The first sign of this serious disease is when the tops of healthy shoots begin to wither and the plant wilts. It progressively dies back, often alarmingly quickly. CONTROL Cut back affected stems to healthy growth (to ground level if necessary), then spray the crown and new growth with a recommended fungicide. Healthy new growth may appear from ground level. Spray as a precaution in spring if the disease has been troublesome previously. Planting all new clematis deeply, so that a couple of buds are below ground level, is a wise precaution which may help the plant to survive.

CLUB ROOT

This very serious disease affects members of the Cruciferae or Brassicaceae family, especially vegetables such as cabbages and swedes, and ornamentals such as candytuft and wallflowers. The roots become swollen and distorted, and there are few of the fine roots normally found. The leaves wilt in dry or hot weather, and the plants are generally stunted.

CONTROL The fungus which causes this disease is more prevalent in moist, acid soil, so improving the drainage and adding lime may help. Lift and burn any plants showing symptoms, and practise regular crop rotation. This alone will not eliminate the problem, as the spores can remain active in the soil for over 20 years. Plants suffer less if they get off to a good start so if you want to try plants in club root-infested ground, start them off in pots of sterilised compost, and plant them out with an intact rootball of compost. Immerse the roots in a proprietary dip when planting. Be sure to eliminate weeds that can carry the disease, such as charlock and shepherd's purse.

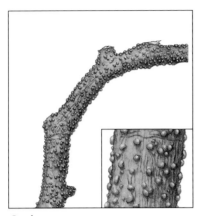

Coral spot

Downy mildew

Fireblight

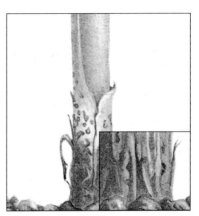

Foot and root rots

CORAL SPOT

Orange-pink spots are the conspicuous sign of this disease, but these only appear after the fungus has killed the shoot. It commonly affects dead wood but it can also attack living tissue. Plants that are particularly susceptible include apples, beeches, currants, elaeagnus, gooseberries, horse chestnuts, limes, magnolias, maples and pyracanthas, though most trees and shrubs can also be affected.

CONTROL Cut back affected shoots to healthy wood. Burn old prunings and dead wood that may spread the disease.

DAMPING OFF

This is a disease of seedlings, which causes them to collapse and die. The problem usually starts in one part of the seed tray, then spreads. If left, fluffy white fungus growth may appear on the dead seedlings or the compost. Several different fungi cause damping off, which is encouraged by wet, cold compost, and by overcrowded seedlings.

CONTROL Water seedlings occasionally with a suitable fungicide, as a precaution.

There is nothing that can be done to save seedlings already affected. Ensure that you always use clean containers sterilised with a garden disinfectant and fresh seed compost. This will reduce the risk of getting the disease.

DOWNY MILDEW

Downy mildew is caused by various species of fungi, which are not the same as those that produce powdery mildews (*see* page 410). The fungal threads grow deep into the tissues, especially on seedlings. They are encouraged by damp weather, and produce white, mealy growths on the underside of the foliage. The upper surface may become blotched or discoloured yellow or brown. Many border perennials, annuals, bulbous plants and vegetables such as lettuce, onions and spinach can be affected.

CONTROL The disease is difficult to control, but may be prevented by giving adequate moisture to the roots and improving ventilation if the plants are grown in a greenhouse. Try to avoid overcrowding and overhead watering.

FIREBLIGHT

This serious bacterial disease of the Rosaceae family used to be notifiable but it no longer has to be reported. The plants most often affected are apples, pears, cotoneasters and pyracanthas.

The leaves turn black or brown then shrivel and die. Often the blossom dies too. The affected part of the tree can look as though it has been scorched with a flame. Dark greenish brown cankers form on the branches, from which a slime oozes. The symptoms spread rapidly and the plant can be killed in a season.

CONTROL If just a small part of the plant is affected, and the problem is identified quickly, cut back to healthy wood, at least 60 cm (2 ft) beyond the infection (be sure to disinfect the saw before using elsewhere). If the disease already has a firm hold, dig up and destroy the plant. Always burn affected wood.

FOOT AND ROOT ROTS

Several fungi can cause the base of a stem to shrivel and turn brown or black, leading to total collapse. When dug up,

the roots have usually rotted or turned black. Many plants can be affected, from bedding plants such as petunias to vegetables like peas, beans and tomatoes. Some shrubs and trees are also affected by root rots: the roots gradually die back from the stem, and usually turn black.

CONTROL Sprays will not help, so lift and destroy affected plants (and remove and discard the soil from the area directly around the roots). In future, rotate vegetable crops regularly (*see* December, page 283), and use sterilised compost if the problem is in the greenhouse.

GREY MOULD (BOTRYTIS)

Grey mould fungi can attack practically any flower, vegetable or fruit in the garden, covering stems, foliage and fruit with a soft, grey fluff, and seriously damaging crops. Soft-leaved plants are the most vulnerable. On unripe tomato fruit the disease causes pale green rings (ghost spots). The fungi are particularly active in the greenhouse, where they may destroy whole trays of seedlings.

The disease is encouraged by cold,

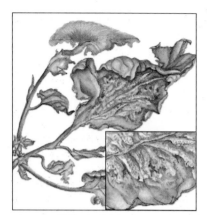

Grey mould (botrytis)

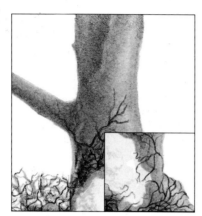

Honey fungus

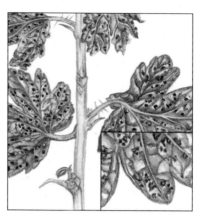

Leaf spots

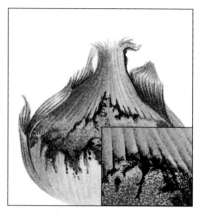

Onion neck rot

wet conditions. It spreads rapidly on dead and rotting vegetation and weak plants. CONTROL Grey mould (botrytis) can be combated with fungicide, but to avoid creating the conditions in which it thrives, observe strict garden hygiene: pick up all dead leaves and deadhead flowers unless you are growing fruit or wanting seed. Ventilate the greenhouse as much as possible, and try to reduce the humidity. Remove and burn affected material.

HONEY FUNGUS

This extremely serious disease affects a wide range of woody plants, and even some herbaceous ones. Once established, it can spread through the soil to affect nearby plants, so it should always be taken seriously.

The fungus responsible is usually *Armillaria mellea*, though other species can be involved. Diagnosis is not always easy, especially at the early stages, but be suspicious of toadstools growing in clusters, usually between late summer and mid autumn, at the base of the stem or trunk of a tree or shrub that is already ailing.

These are usually yellowish or tawny and can have a cap up to 15 cm (6 in) across. Pull back some bark at the base of the trunk or the stem: if there is a mass of white thread-like mycelium, this is an ominous sign. Toadstools and mycelium may not always be obvious, even on a badly affected plant, so if a tree or shrub appears to die gradually with no obvious explanation, and especially if several die in close proximity, explore the soil around the roots. If tough black 'bootlace' strands, called rhizomorphs, are found, these strongly suggest honey fungus, though they can be produced by other fungi. CONTROL Chemical controls are sometimes used, but these are best employed as an additional precaution to help disinfect the area after the affected plant has been removed. The best way to deal with honey fungus is to dig up the plant, and if possible burn or otherwise safely dispose of it. Dig out the roots (employing a contractor, if necessary, to remove the stump, which may otherwise remain as a source of infection). Try to dig up and

safely dispose of the soil around the root area if that is practical. If possible, do not plant trees or shrubs in the area for a couple of years, and if the soil in a neighbouring garden close to your boundary is affected, try mechanical barriers such as sheets of metal or plastic sunk at least 60 cm (2 ft) deep into the soil.

Some plants are more susceptible than others, especially apples, birches, cedars, cypresses, lilacs, pines, privets, rhododendrons, willows and wisteria. Avoid replanting with these.

LEAF SPOTS

A number of different fungi and bacteria cause spots and blotches on leaves. Almost any kind of plant can be affected. The spots or blotches may be round, angular, or even have a yellow halo (ring spot). In a severe infection the spots may merge until the leaf is covered and eventually drops. In the case of those caused by fungi, a fluff or down may appear on the leaves. (*See* Black spot, page 405.) CONTROL Use an appropriate fungicidal spray and follow instructions carefully.

MILDEW *see* Downy mildew, Powdery mildew

ONION NECK ROT

Onions and shallots may be affected with this disease when they are growing, but often it is not noticed until the bulbs are stored. The neck becomes soft and discoloured, often appearing black. Grey fungal growth may also be noticed. CONTROL There is little to be done at this stage. Aim at prevention – buy seed or sets from a reputable source, do not over-feed the plants with nitrogen, ripen the bulbs well, see they are properly dried off when they are harvested and store them in a cool, dry place.

ONION WHITE ROT

This white fluffy rot affects onions, shallots, leeks, garlic, and sometimes chives. CONTROL Fungicides are of limited use. Maintain crop rotation.

PEACH LEAF CURL

Reddish blisters develop on the leaves of peaches, almonds, nectarines and orna-

Peach leaf curl

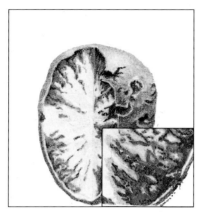

Potato blight

mental forms of these trees causing premature defoliation and reduced vigour.

CONTROL Once the blisters are present there is little that can be done for the current season, but pick off affected leaves to reduce the risk of the disease spreading. In future spray the leaves with a suitable fungicide in February, as the buds start to swell, and again a fortnight later. Repeat at leaf-fall in the autumn. Wall-trained plants can be covered by thick plastic sheeting on an open-sided wooden frame during the winter to reduce the risk of infection from air-borne spores (*see* February, page 39).

POTATO BLACKLEG *see* Blackleg

POTATO BLIGHT

Blight is a very serious disease of potatoes. The first signs are brown spots or blotches on the margins and tips of the leaves. As these spots spread, the affected foliage dies, and the stems turn black. Eventually, the entire plant becomes a rotten, evil-smelling mass.

Warm, wet weather favours the disease

and, if untreated, the spores are washed down into the soil and infect the tubers, which then rot. The disease can also spread to other tubers in store.

CONTROL Spray with a suitable fungicide preventatively. This needs to be done at regular intervals as advised by the manufacturer, from about the end of June (earlier in wet areas). If plants are already affected, cut off the stems at ground level and burn, then harvest and use the tubers early. If you are regularly troubled by the disease, avoid overhead watering, which will encourage the disease and, if possible, grow varieties that show some resistance, such as 'Cara', 'Romano' and 'Wilja'.

POTATO SCAB

Scab is actually the damage caused by various fungi. Normally, the flesh itself is undamaged, but the disease looks unsightly. Potatoes can be infected with both common scab and powdery scab. The symptoms of common scab are raised spots and patches on the skins of the tubers which crack, leaving the

---

LAWN DISEASES

Lawn diseases can often be difficult to identify in the early stages, and it is only when a large area has become affected that the symptoms are obvious.

The most common lawn diseases are described here. In all cases treatment with an appropriate fungicide, applied according to the manufacturer's instructions, should control the disease if it has not been allowed to infect too large an area. Apply at the correct time and required rate to eradicate the disease. Improved drainage and aeration often reduce the incidence of lawn diseases.

Dollar spot is caused by the fungus *Sclerotinia homeocarpa*. The symptoms are round yellow or brown patches about 5–8 cm (2–3 in) in diameter, though they may form larger patches. It is most common in mild, damp weather in late summer and usually only affects fine grasses.

Fairy rings are cause by various fungi, but they all make the same characteristic rings. For a short while a circle of toadstools or puffballs is the most conspicuous symptom, but when these

are absent a ring of darker grass may be the tell-tale sign. The grass within the ring may die, but sometimes it recovers.

Chemical control is seldom satisfactory, but preventing the fungus producing spores by knocking off the toadstools while small will reduce the risk of it spreading. It may be necessary to resow or returf the area, removing any soil that might contain the fungus.

Fusarium patch (snow mould) is a common disease caused by the fungus *Fusarium nivale*. Brown or reddish brown patches up to 30 cm (1 ft) across are the normal sign, and most often appear in autumn. In moist conditions patches of white mould can be seen. The top growth dies but fresh grass sometimes comes from the roots.

Red thread is caused by the fungus *Corticium fuciforme*. The lawn appears to have yellow or brown patches of grass and close examination shows the tips of the leaves are brown or dying, with reddish fungus threads. It is most serious in summer and early autumn. Feeding the lawn in summer will help.

Fusarium patch

Red thread

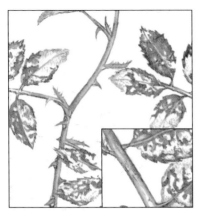

Powdery mildew

Rusts

Scab

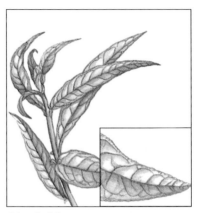

Silver leaf disease

whole surface covered in ragged edges. Powdery scab, which is less common, may distort the tubers so badly that they are inedible, and when the scabs burst they release a dry powder (the spores).

CONTROL Chemicals are not the solution to scab diseases. Instead, add plenty of organic material to the soil before planting, and avoid liming the ground unless absolutely necessary. Regular watering to keep the plants growing rapidly will also help. Where common scab is an annual problem, the choice of variety is important. Some popular varieties such as 'Desirée' and 'Maris Piper' are particularly susceptible.

POWDERY MILDEW

This common fungal disease affects many garden plants, producing a white powdery coating on the foliage and stems. Later the coating turns brown and appears as a kind of felt, studded with minute black dots. These are the fruiting bodies that overwinter in the soil to release spores the following year. Border plants may be affected, but it is a particular prob-

lem on roses and peas. Gooseberries are also prone to powdery mildew. Annuals, bulbous plants, trees and even pot plants are vulnerable.

CONTROL Pick off affected leaves and shoots, keep the plants well watered and mulched, and avoid placing susceptible plants in a dry position. Spray with a recommended fungicide.

REVERSION *see* Viruses

RING SPOT *see* Leaf spots

ROOT ROT *see* Foot and root rots

RUSTS

Rusts are fungal diseases easily recognised by yellow, brown or orange pustules on the foliage, which assumes a rusty appearance. Stems may also be affected. Many different rust fungi attack garden plants, but the damage is seldom fatal. Rust can be a serious disease on roses. Some rust fungi have a complicated life cycle that involves a second host plant, so to achieve good control it may be necessary to

identify and treat the alternative host at the same time.

CONTROL Removing affected stems and leaves will reduce the risk of the disease spreading. Spraying the plants with a recommended fungicide will help, as will ensuring good air circulation by avoiding overcrowding.

SCAB

Scab is a disfiguring problem caused by several fungi that affects fruits such as apples and pears, as well as some other plants like gladioli. Potatoes also suffer from various forms of scab, which is often worse on well-limed soils (*see* Potato scab, page 409). Corky scab is a disease which affects cacti. Infection on apples and pears appears as black spots on the young foliage and blisters on the bark of young shoots. The disease spreads to the fruit, causing raised areas and blotches that eventually crack. This makes the fruit unsuitable for storage.

CONTROL Spray with a recommended fungicide. Rake up and destroy any affected leaves or fruits that fall.

SILVER LEAF DISEASE

This fungal infection appears as a silvery sheen on the foliage of many fruit and ornamental trees, especially plums and cherries. Silvered leaves alone are not sufficient to identify the disease positively. Cut across a suspect branch or shoot – if the tree is infected there will be dark brown stains. A severely infected tree will die, then bracket-like fungus growths may appear on the dead wood.

CONTROL Cut out affected parts of the plant to a point at least 15 cm (6 in) beyond the stained wood. This may save a tree only mildly infected, but a badly infected one is best dug up and destroyed. To avoid the risk of infection for highly susceptible plants, prune them in summer when infection is less likely than at other times.

SOOTY MOULDS *see* Aphids

TOMATO BLIGHT

A very serious disease of potatoes, blight can also affect tomatoes, especially those grown outdoors. The leaves are affected

Tomato blight and leaf mould

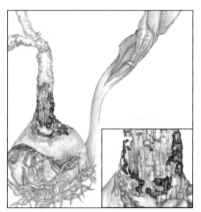
Tulip fire

Stunt virus – chrysanthemum

Leaf curl virus – pelargonium

in a similar way to potatoes (brown spots and blotches at the margins and tips), and brown mottled spots appear on the ripening fruit. Affected areas on the fruit then shrink and start to rot.

CONTROL Spray with a recommended fungicide as soon as possible after the first signs are noticed, or as a precaution in areas where it is a common problem.

TOMATO LEAF MOULD

This can be a serious disease of tomatoes grown under glass, with all the foliage affected and the crop severely reduced. The symptoms are yellow spots on the upper leaf surface and browny green or purple-grey patches of fungal growth on the undersides.

CONTROL Remove affected leaves as soon as the disease is noticed, then spray with insecticide, although if the season is well advanced it will not be worth spraying. Some tomato varieties, such as 'Grenadier' and 'Shirley', show some resistance to the disease and should be chosen if this is a disease which affects your crops frequently.

TULIP FIRE

A common disease of tulips, the symptoms are distorted leaves and shoots, which may be covered in brown patches and become withered and covered with a grey mould (botrytis) bearing black fruiting bodies (sclerotia). Flower buds may fail to open or be spotted or blistered. Small black sclerotia develop on the outer scales of the bulb, which may also have sunken brown lesions.

CONTROL Dig up and burn the affected plants. When bulbs are lifted at the end of the season, discard any with black sclerotia, and dip the bulbs in a fungicidal solution. Do not replant tulips in the same soil the following year.

VIRUSES

Viruses consist of minute particles that live in the sap of plants, and are thus distributed throughout the tissues of a plant. Viruses affect many plants, and although a few can live with the virus without significant deterioration, most suffer serious consequences. Just a few viruses are described here but similar symptoms are

likely to occur with other plants and viruses. Viruses cause the fruitfulness of all plants, especially raspberries, to decline.

Blackcurrant reversion is a disease spread by big bud mites (*see* Pests, page 396). The leaves on reverted shoots are coarse and have fewer serrations than normal around the leaf edge.

Chrysanthemum stunt is caused by a virus-like organism. The plant and its flowers are smaller than normal.

Pelargonium leaf curl virus causes puckered leaves with small pale spots.

Raspberry mosaic shows itself as mottled and often curled or distorted leaves.

Spotted wilt is a serious virus disease of tomatoes and sometimes ornamentals such as dahlias, begonias and zantedeschias. It causes bronzing of lower leaves and sometimes circular brown spots on the foliage, which then droops and becomes oily-looking.

Tomato mosaic virus shows as bright yellow blotches on the leaves with alternate areas of light and dark green. Other viruses cause streaks and stripes on the leaves and sunken pits on the fruits.

Yellow edge in strawberries causes dwarfing of young leaves, which turn yellow and curl at the edges; the foliage becomes yellow-spotted and wrinkled.

Flowers of many kinds show signs of viral damage in their mottled or streaked foliage and streaked or distorted flowers. The plants are usually stunted in comparison with healthy plants, and generally perform poorly.

CONTROL Pull up and burn all affected plants immediately, to minimise the likelihood of the virus being transmitted to other plants. The best way to control virus diseases is by vigilant control of pests and the use of healthy plants initially – there is no effective chemical control. Don't replant the same species in the same place, and rotate crops in the vegetable garden.

Wherever possible (with strawberries and raspberries, for instance) buy certified virus-free stock. Then keep the plants virus-free by controlling sap-sucking insects, such as aphids, by spraying or other forms of control. This is important and should be practised assiduously.

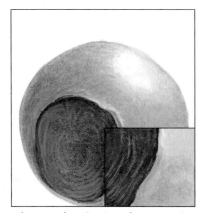

Blossom end rot (see Irregular watering)

Chlorosis

Drought

Fasciation

DISORDERS & DEFICIENCIES

If there are no obvious signs of pest damage on the top growth or at the roots, and the symptoms do not correspond with any of the widespread diseases, ailing plants may be suffering from a physiological or deficiency problem.

BITTER PIT *see* **Calcium deficiency**

BLOSSOM END ROT *see* **Irregular watering**

CALCIUM DEFICIENCY

Calcium deficiency contributes to blossom end rot of tomatoes and sweet peppers (*see* Irregular watering, page 413) and bitter pit of apples. Fruit affected with bitter pit has brown spots and flecks in the flesh, which may taste bitter, and the skin is usually pitted. If bitter pit is a regular problem, spray the trees with calcium nitrate at 10 g per litre of water (1½ oz per gallon) every 10–14 days from early summer until harvest time.

CHLOROSIS

Yellowing of the foliage may be due to a common disorder known as chlorosis. Chlorosis is caused by the inability of a plant to produce sufficient chlorophyll (which is what enables plants to photosynthesise and gives them their green colour), a problem that is usually induced by too much lime or too little iron in the soil (*see* Iron deficiency). The iron may be present in the soil but unavailable, because the high pH caused by the lime locks it into an unavailable form. You can make the soil more acid by adding peat or flowers of sulphur, or by treating plants with sequestered iron or fritted trace elements. Better still, avoid growing acid-loving plants in a limy soil, or grow them in containers filled with an ericaceous compost if practicable.

DROUGHT

Wilting is an obvious sign of water shortage among soft-leaved plants, but with trees and shrubs the foliage may turn brown and begin to shrivel, almost as if autumn had arrived prematurely. If the drought is prolonged, the foliage may be shed. Thorough watering is the obvious solution, but if water shortages mean water rationing, mulching and shading may help – especially if you can water thoroughly first. If the area is regularly short of water in summer, choose plants that can cope with dry conditions.

FASCIATION

Fasciation is a form of abnormal growth, usually with a flattened and distorted stem. It can be caused by several factors, such as insect or frost damage to the growing tip, or a genetic quirk. No action is required and usually only one or two stems are affected. They can be left or simply be cut out.

INSECTICIDE/FUNGICIDE DAMAGE

Bleached or scorched (brown) areas on the foliage, perhaps on just one part of the plant, could be caused by insecticides or fungicides incorrectly applied. Suspect this cause if the damage is noticed shortly after spraying. If garden chemicals are used according to the instructions, this should not be a problem. Remember that aerosols applied too close to the plant may also cause this kind of problem.

IRON DEFICIENCY

The symptoms of iron deficiency and manganese deficiency are very similar, and the solution is the same, so they are grouped together here. Yellowing between the veins is common to both, and in each case the veins themselves usually stand out as conspicuously green. In the case of iron deficiency, the affected areas can be almost white. The actual symptoms and colouring will vary according to the plant. With iron deficiency the problem is often most pronounced on young leaves, with manganese deficiency the older leaves are often the first to be affected. Acid-loving plants growing in alkaline soil or compost are generally the most severely affected, as the high pH can make the elements unavailable.

The use of chelated or fritted trace elements and sequestered iron is the best way to treat affected plants, but whenever possible avoid growing plants

Magnesium deficiency

Manganese deficiency

Nitrogen deficiency

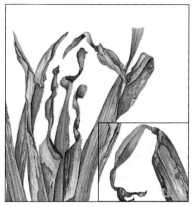

Scorch

that prefer acid soil on chalky ground or where the pH is high.

IRREGULAR WATERING

Irregular watering should be avoided, but it is most likely to affect the fruit of tomatoes. Try to ensure that tomatoes receive a regular amount of water because drought followed by a surplus of water causes the skins to split and crack with the sudden expansion.

Blossom end rot is due partly to calcium deficiency aggravated by an irregular supply of water. Dark, blackish brown areas develop at the bottom of the fruit.

MAGNESIUM DEFICIENCY

Typical symptoms are yellow or pale green areas between the veins, with darker green close to the veins. Sometimes the affected areas may be reddish brown instead of pale green. The easiest way to control the deficiency is by applying Epsom salts – as a foliar feed for quick results or to the soil for convenience but slower results. Apply to the soil at 25 g per m² (¾ oz per sq yd), or for a foliar

feed dilute 20 g per litre of water (3½ oz per gallon).

MANGANESE DEFICIENCY *see* Iron deficiency

MOLYBDENUM DEFICIENCY

The only plants likely to show obvious signs of this deficiency are brassicas, in particular sprouting broccoli and cauliflowers. In a condition known as whiptail, the leaves appear narrow and ribbon-like, and if heads develop at all they are usually very small. This deficiency is most common on acid soils. Treatment with a balanced fertiliser containing molybdenum as one of the trace elements will rectify the problem, and liming to raise the pH will usually help.

NITROGEN DEFICIENCY

Pale green or yellowing leaves coupled with thin or weak growth suggest nitrogen deficiency. This particularly affects plants in pots and containers. Yellowing leaves might also be caused by lime-induced chlorosis (*see* Chlorosis, page

412), but that is usually only evident on lime-hating plants. Increase the nitrogen content of the soil or compost (*see* Fertilisers, page 388).

PHOSPHATE DEFICIENCY

Phosphate deficiency can be difficult to diagnose, as the overall result is slow growth that is not as vigorous as it would otherwise be. Young leaves may appear pale and dull. Increase the phosphate content of the soil or compost (*see* Fertilisers, page 389).

POTASSIUM DEFICIENCY

Potassium (potash) deficiency often results in small or poor quality fruits and flowers. The leaves may also have brown blotches or edges, possibly blue, yellow or purple in colour. Increase the potassium content of the soil or compost (*see* Fertilisers, page 389).

SCORCH

Brown marks on the leaves, or at the edges, that do not look as if they are caused by a disease, and especially if just

on those parts of the plant exposed to strong sunlight, may be the result of sun scorch. Plants under glass are especially prone to this, as the glass acts like a magnifying glass. Water droplets on outdoor plants can have the same effect and cause scorch marks – so water or spray when the sun is off them. Similar scorch marks can be caused by frost and cold winds in winter.

WEEDKILLER DAMAGE

Pale white or yellow streaks or bleached leaves can be caused by contact weedkiller damage, and distorted growth could be a sign of contamination from a hormone (selective) weedkiller of the type used for lawn weeds. Suspect weedkiller if the problem is confined to plants near an area recently treated. The damage may not be terminal, but be careful to avoid spray drift or run-off from paths. Don't mulch with grass clippings from a lawn treated with a weedkiller.

YELLOWING FOLIAGE *see* Chlorosis, Nitrogen deficiency

Weed control

Most gardeners like to keep weeds under control because weedy lawns, flower beds and paths look unsightly. There are also practical reasons for keeping down weeds: they compete with cultivated plants for available light, moisture and nutrients. Weeds also encourage pests and diseases. Shepherd's purse, for example, harbours the flea beetle and cabbage root fly, which attack many types of green vegetables; thistles serve as a host for the beet leaf miner and the bean aphid. When the ground around cultivated plants is congested with weeds, air circulates less freely, which can lead to diseases such as grey mould (botrytis).

Controlling weeds need not be an onerous chore. Modern chemicals make weed control relatively simple, but there are plenty of practical alternatives if you want to control them by cultural methods, such as hoeing and mulching.

HOEING

A Dutch hoe can be very effective at controlling weeds, but choose a dry day and slice off the weeds just below the surface.

MECHANICAL & CULTURAL METHODS

Hoeing is a good form of weed control for a small area, and recently hoed ground also looks better than soil that is capped with a firm crust. To be effective, hoeing must be repeated frequently. Try to hoe in dry weather (to reduce the chances of severed weeds rerooting) and slice off the weeds just below the surface to discourage them from resprouting.

Digging can increase the problem of weeds by bringing more weed seeds to the surface. No-dig systems leave the soil undisturbed and depend on organic mulches being worked into the ground by earthworms and other creatures. Gardening this way makes weed-free conditions relatively easy to maintain once deep-rooted problem weeds, such as bindweed, have been eliminated. You must prevent new weeds from seeding.

GROUND COVER

Any form of ground cover thick enough to keep light off germinating seedlings and emerging shoots will help to suppress them. A thick organic mulch of chipped bark or a sheet mulch of black plastic will provide effective weed control (*see* The soil in your garden, pages 392–393).

Living blankets, using ground-cover plants such as *Pachysandra terminalis* and heathers, will also suppress weeds provided the ground is relatively weed-free initially and the plants are well established. Ground-cover plants can be visually pleasing, and a practical alternative to chemicals and hoeing for a large area. However, not all plants sold as ground cover make effective weed suppressants, especially when young.

In the vegetable garden, crops such as potatoes will often suppress most of the weeds provided the ground is kept weed-free during the early stages of growth.

CHEMICAL CONTROL

It is important to understand the ways in which different weedkillers work, so that you choose the one most appropriate.

Some weedkillers will destroy plants of all types, others kill only specific weeds. There are formulae that have long-lasting effects, and those that are neutralised by contact with the soil. Different weeds respond to different chemicals, and the same weed may need different treatment depending on where it is growing. For example, a dandelion in the lawn would need to be treated with a selective weedkiller so that the grass is not harmed, but in an area to be planted with annuals or border plants, a short-lived total weedkiller may be more appropriate, and to keep them out of your paths and drives

a long-lasting residual total weedkiller would be best.

Always study the labels – including the small print – very carefully. It is essential to know what a weedkiller is designed to do and how long it will remain active.

BE SENSIBLE AND SAFE

Weedkillers are very useful aids, but bear in mind that they can do considerable damage if instructions are not followed exactly.

- Do not apply liquids on a windy day, as the spray may drift on to desirable plants and kill them.

- Only use for the purpose recommended by the manufacturer – do not use a path weedkiller on flower beds, for example.

- Use only at the recommended rate; do not increase the concentration or application rate in the hope of faster or better results.

- Do not store any unused diluted weedkillers.

- Use a dribble bar rather than a rose on a watering can as this will reduce the risk of spray drift and will help you to apply the weedkiller safely and evenly.

- Keep a special watering can just for weedkillers, and mark it accordingly, as traces left in the can could harm your plants if used for ordinary watering.

- As with all garden chemicals, use protective clothing, such as rubber gloves, when mixing and applying.

TOTAL WEEDKILLERS

Total weedkillers can be divided broadly into those chemicals that render the ground unsuitable for sowing or planting for many weeks or months, and those that leave the ground ready for rapid replanting. Never use total weedkillers on the lawn, except where you can apply non-persistent kinds to the individual leaves of a few problem plants. They will kill the grass as effectively as they kill the weeds in the lawn.

For quick replanting choose a weedkiller that is quickly inactivated by contact with the soil or the environment. Some contact weedkillers act like chemical hoes and kill the top growth but leave the soil ready for planting within a day or so. These have no effect on the roots of many deep-rooted perennials.

For dealing with well-established perennial weeds a systemic weedkiller is necessary. These are designed to move through a plant's vascular system into the roots. Although some of these leave the soil safe for planting soon after application, it may be necessary to allow time, possibly up to a fortnight, for the roots to be killed before cultivation, otherwise regrowth is more likely.

For paths there are weedkillers specifically formulated for the job. These often contain a cocktail of weedkillers, some to kill the established weeds and others to prevent new ones from germinating or emerging. Some weedkillers have a tendency to creep sideways through the soil, so use with care on paths that are close to flower beds.

For around established trees and shrubs weedkillers have been formulated that remain in the surface layer of the soil to help prevent seedlings germinating for many months. The ground usually has to be cleared first, and these treatments are only suitable for certain trees and shrubs, and selected fruits. Always check the label very carefully before using this type of weedkiller.

For vacant ground choose a systemic weedkiller which allows quick replanting if you want to cultivate the ground soon after application. Some are good for dealing with woody-stemmed plants, including tree seedlings, small shrubs and brambles, but you may not be able to plant for two or three months.

Long-lasting weedkillers that remain active for six months or more may be a better choice to clear an area that you do not intend to cultivate in the short term.

SELECTIVE WEEDKILLERS

Selective weedkillers (sometimes called hormone weedkillers) overstimulate the growth of certain types of plant while not being harmful to others. These can be used to eliminate one kind of plant or weed from among a desirable crop.

Usually they act on broad-leaved weeds, such as daisies and dandelions, among narrow-leaved plants such as grasses in a lawn. Some work in reverse and kill most grasses among non-grassy perennials. This makes them particularly useful for difficult-to-eradicate grasses, such as couch, among border perennials and in the rock garden.

TOUCH WEEDERS

It is not always convenient to apply weedkillers with a watering can. In rock gardens or walls, and for isolated weeds in a lawn, touch weeders can be useful. There are various types, including impregnated sticks and sponge applicators, all designed to apply the weedkiller to individual weeds.

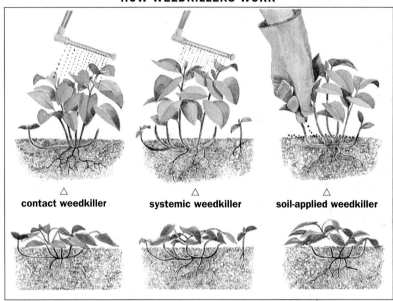

HOW WEEDKILLERS WORK

△ **contact weedkiller**   △ **systemic weedkiller**   △ **soil-applied weedkiller**

Contact weedkillers are absorbed by the leaves and stems. They kill the top growth but not necessarily all the roots or the leaves that are not wetted. Translocated weedkillers travel through the plant via the sap; systemic weedkillers are absorbed through the leaves, and granular, soil-applied weedkillers through the roots.

EFFECTIVENESS

Although a range of weedkillers can usually be used to control a particular weed, some may work more effectively. If one doesn't work, an alternative may be more satisfactory. Manufacturers often include several weedkillers in one product, as the combination may achieve better control than a single chemical. However, don't mix weedkillers yourself, or apply more than one at a time.

Although developed resistance is much less common in plants than in insects, it can occur. The solution is to try a different chemical if the first one is not successful (after repeated applications if recommended). Some weeds, such as bindweed and clover, may need repeated applications before they are eradicated, but this is nothing to do with developed resistance.

Heed any advice about timing. Many weedkillers work most efficiently when the weeds are young and growing actively, and applying in winter may have minimal effect. Some may be inactivated if it rains too soon after application.

ORGANIC WEEDKILLERS

If you do not wish to use chemical weedkillers, and prefer to confine sprays to milder 'organic' products, there are

bindweed ▷

annual
meadow grass
▽

bramble
▽

buttercup
▽

goosegrass ▷

weedkillers based on fatty acids. The weeds must be covered with the soap-type substance, and this approach is best suited to the control of a small number of individual weeds. These weedkillers are not suitable for weeds in lawns.

Do not expect good control of difficult-to-eradicate weeds, although repeated applications will help.

COMMON PROBLEM WEEDS

Details of the methods of control for weeds listed here are given on the previous pages.

ANNUAL MEADOW GRASS (*Poa annua*)

Low-growing tufted grass, 5–20 cm (2–8 in) tall, that flowers while still young, and almost throughout the year. It is easily controlled by hand weeding or hoeing, or with a non-persistent contact weedkiller suitable for beds and borders.

BINDWEED

This common and tenacious weed has pretty funnel-shaped white or pale pink flowers on long, twining stems. The stems of field bindweed (*Convolvulus arvensis*) grow to about 60 cm (2 ft), but the roots spread horizontally and have been known to grow downwards for over 6 m (20 ft)! Fortunately the roots of hedge or great bindweed (*Calystegia sepium*) do not travel down as far, but its stems can exceed 2.5 m (8 ft), twining through other plants. Hedge bindweed is recognisable by its larger flowers, often 5 cm (2 in) across.

Hoeing is useless and may even stimulate more growth. Digging out may work for a few young plants of field bindweed,

or for hedge bindweed growing in an open area. If it is growing at the base of shrubs, pulling off emerging stems at ground level every few days in spring may be effective but will need to be carried out regularly for at least a second year. Fragments of the brittle roots are likely to grow into new plants so digging is not very effective. Repeated applications of a systemic weedkiller give the best chance of killing it. If it is growing among other plants, unwind the stems, then paint the exposed leaves on the ground with weedkiller.

BRAMBLE (*Rubus fruticosa*)

The bramble, or wild blackberry, needs no introduction. Its fruits are attractive in autumn but the long arching and spiny stems, which root readily at the tips, can be a major problem on neglected ground. Old plants also have deep, woody roots. Cut back the top growth in winter, then dig out the roots before new growth occurs in spring, or use a strong weedkiller, often described as a brushwood killer. Other systemic weedkillers can be used, but brambles are persistent so you need to be prepared to re-treat fresh growth next spring.

BUTTERCUP (*Ranunculus* spp.)

Several buttercups can be a problem in the garden, but the far-ranging stems of creeping buttercup (*Ranunculus repens*) are a particular nuisance. They run along the surface of the soil, rooting as they go, and a large area can be covered in a season. Hoeing is inappropriate, but you can dig them out where practical; the roots are shallow. Otherwise treat with a non-persistent systemic weedkiller. Do not allow the plants to flower as the seeds are very long-lived.

CLEAVERS/GOOSEGRASS (*Galium aparine*)

This weed of hedgerows and cultivated ground has tiny down-turned prickles on its fruits, stems and leaves, which it uses to cling to other plants for support. It has leaves in whorls of six or eight, and inconspicuous white flowers. The dry fruits, covered with hooked bristles, readily catch on clothing. Hand weeding can be difficult because the stems are brittle, but hoeing is very effective. Use a weedkiller that prevents seedling germination around established shrubs, preferably before the new growth appears. In an open position, any weedkiller designed for beds and borders is suitable.

COMMON CHICKWEED (*Stellaria media*)

Chickweed, with its small fleshy leaves on floppy stems and little white flowers, is a very common weed of cultivated ground. The plants are easily pulled up by hand, and hoeing is very effective. Most non-persistent total weedkillers will control chickweed.

CONVOLVULUS *see* Bindweed

COUCH GRASS (*Elymus repens*, syn. *Agropyron repens*)

A tenacious, coarse grass with hairless stems 30–60 cm (1–2 ft) tall, easily recognised by gardeners from the underground creeping stems with sharp points. These can extend underground for a considerable distance in all directions, producing new plants along their length. Digging couch grass out is difficult, and hoeing useless unless you persevere over a very long period, as bits left in the ground will soon grow into new plants. Systemic weedkillers will achieve control if they

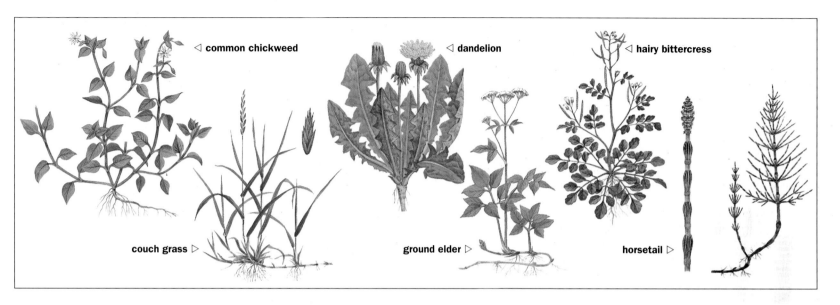

common chickweed ◁
◁ dandelion
◁ hairy bittercress
couch grass ▷
ground elder ▷
horsetail ▷

are applied several times as new growth appears. A selective weedkiller is available to control couch grass among cultivated plants and in the rock garden, where the roots may extend beneath the rocks.

DANDELION (*Taraxacum officinale*)

The dandelion, with its cheerful yellow flowers and drumstick seed heads, needs no introduction. Hoeing is inappropriate, as the sliced-off root will regrow and probably produce more heads. Young plants can be dug out easily, but older ones are much more difficult to remove without leaving part of the root in the ground. Do not allow the plants to set seed. If hand digging is not practical, any of the weedkillers designed for beds and borders will control dandelions, and a selective weedkiller suitable for lawns is normally effective when dandelions appear in the grass.

GOOSEGRASS *see* Cleavers

GROUND ELDER (*Aegopodium podagraria*)

This perennial with hollow grooved stems and trifoliate leaves grows to approximately 30–60 cm (1–2 ft) tall, but often forms extensive patches. Its white underground stems can extend to 1 m (3 ft) or more in all directions, and each piece left behind may produce a new plant. The white flower heads appear from early to late summer.

The best way to control ground elder is to dig out as much as possible, then treat with a systemic weedkiller as new growth appears in April or May. Repeat the application on any regrowth.

GROUNDSEL (*Senecio vulgaris*)

This variable annual weed is usually 8–20 cm (3–8 in) tall, with narrow, lobed leaves and small yellow flowers. It can be found in flower every month of the year. Hand weeding and hoeing will keep the weed down easily once the

population is under control. Always pull up or hoe off while the plants are small, as flowering occurs very quickly and the seeds are soon spread. All the weedkillers suitable for beds and borders control it.

HAIRY BITTERCRESS (*Cardamine hirsuta*)

A common low-growing annual, with a rosette of slender, hairy, lobed leaves and small white flowers. The conspicuous cylindrical seed pods are held erect and explode violently to eject their seeds. Regular hoeing will control bittercress, especially if this is done before the plants set seed (they flower through spring and summer). All the weedkillers suitable for beds and borders will control it, and if there is only bittercress plus other annual weeds to be killed, choose a nonpersistent contact weedkiller.

HORSETAIL (*Equisetum arvense*)

Horsetails have their leaves in whorls

around stiff, upright stems. They do not flower, but chocolate-coloured 'cones' about 2–3 cm (1-1¼ in) long are produced at the tips of fertile stems. The thin, black underground stems can creep sideways and downwards for a long way in the soil, and fragments of these can produce new plants. Constant hoeing and digging out will have some effect, but eradication is unlikely. Treat with a systemic weedkiller, but crush the stems lightly first otherwise the weedkiller will not easily penetrate, as there are no flat leaves to absorb it. Be prepared to repeat the treatment monthly during the growing season and often for several years after that.

JAPANESE KNOTWEED (*Polygonum japonicum*, syn. *P. cuspidatum*, *Fallopia japonica*)

This stout perennial will form a bamboo-like thicket about 1–1.8 m (3–6 ft) high if not controlled. Broad, pointed leaves,

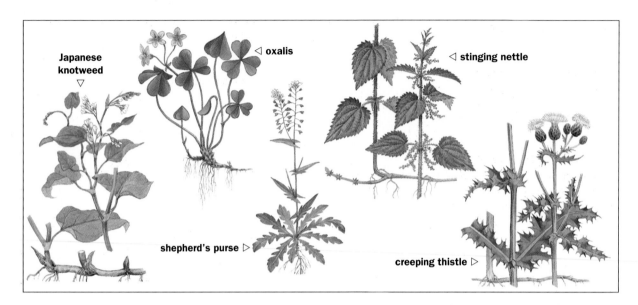

Japanese knotweed ▽
◁ oxalis
◁ stinging nettle
shepherd's purse ▷
creeping thistle ▷

Many of the weeds which spring up in flower beds and borders also thrive in the lawn, but often become ground-hugging from constant mowing. Creeping stems can usually be seen growing among the grass. Hand weeding with a daisy grubber is effective for a small area; otherwise selective lawn weedkillers will achieve good control of all common lawn weeds listed below. There are several 'weed and feed' products available which combine a weedkiller with a lawn fertiliser – promoting a healthy, dense lawn will allow fewer weeds to germinate and survive.

abruptly truncated at the base, are borne on reddish brown stems that appear to zig-zag. It spreads by tough creeping stems that radiate vast distances below ground level. It is extremely difficult to control, and digging it out requires considerable effort and dedication. In a wild part of the garden, it may be easier to keep cutting it back, and digging out roots around the edge of the clump. A systemic weedkiller will help, but you must expect to repeat the treatment monthly in the growing season.

NETTLE (*Urtica* spp.)

Annual stinging nettles (*Urtica dioica*) spread easily by seed, which female plants produce prolifically. Perennial types spread by stems that creep along the surface. Neither type roots deeply and digging out the roots is an effective method of control. Any weedkiller suitable for beds and borders will also control them, and around trees and shrubs an application of one designed to prevent weeds from germinating or emerging will deter new growth. A small patch of nettles left in a wild part of the garden will attract butterflies.

OXALIS

Some pink-flowered oxalis, such as *O. corymbosa* and *O. latifolia*, produce dozens of fleshy brown bulbils just below the surface. These break off easily and start new colonies.

Treat the plants with a systemic weedkiller as they begin to grow in spring, and repeat the procedure at monthly intervals throughout the summer as regrowth occurs. Avoid cultivation around the plants. If any regrowth appears the following spring, try lifting these out with a trowel, taking as much soil as possible with the roots, and throw them away on a skip or dispose of them in a part of the garden where the bulbils will not be a problem.

SHEPHERD'S PURSE (*Capsella bursa-pastoris*)

An ubiquitous weed, with distinctive triangular seed pods, flattened and notched, which give it its common name. Hoeing will control this weed effectively provided it is done before the seeds develop. Any weedkiller that is recommended for beds and borders will also control it, but a non-persistent contact weedkiller is a good choice if the other weeds are annuals or easily controlled perennials.

THISTLE (*Cirsium* spp.)

Creeping thistle (*Cirsium arvense*) has pale lilac flower heads. It will reach 1.5 m (5 ft) in field conditions, but is more likely to be 30–60 cm (1–2 ft) tall as a garden weed. Young plants can be dug up, but with older ones the roots are difficult to remove in one piece. If digging them out is not practical, a non-persistent systemic weedkiller can be used, but be prepared to re-treat any regrowth.

BROAD-LEAVED PLANTAIN/ RATSTAIL PLANTAIN (*Plantago major*)

The rosette of broad, flat leaves tends to hug the ground, but the greenish flower spikes, up to 15 cm (6 in) long, are more upright and make it a prominent lawn weed. Hand weeding with a daisy grubber is effective for a small area.

BUTTERCUP (*Ranunculus repens*)

In the lawn the creeping buttercup (*see* page 416) becomes ground-hugging through constant mowing. Its creeping stems are usually visible growing among the grass.

CLOVER (*Trifolium* spp.)

Clover, with its three-lobed leaves and white or mauve flowers which are so popular with bees, is known to most gardeners. The species most commonly found in garden lawns is the white clover (*Trifolium repens*).

COMMON MOUSE-EAR CHICKWEED (*Cerastium fontanum,* syn. *C. vulgatum*)

An ubiquitous weed resembling a coarse chickweed but with thicker and coarser stems and leaves. The small white flowers appear from April onwards.

DAISY (*Bellis perennis*)

The white rayed flowers above a rosette of flattened foliage are known to everyone. Hand weeding with a daisy grubber is sufficient control for a small area.

DANDELION (*Taraxacum officinale*)

In lawns the dandelion is always ground-hugging through constant mowing.

LESSER YELLOW TREFOIL (*Trifolium dubium*)

The foliage resembles a small clover, but the growth is wiry and the small insignificant flowers are yellow on sparse stems.

MOUSE-EAR HAWKWEED (*Hieracium pilosella*)

The basal rosette has untoothed elliptical pale green leaves covered with long white hairs above. There are often long, creeping, leafy runners. The dandelion-like yellow flowers are produced on stems up to 30 cm (12 in) high.

PEARLWORT (*Sagina procumbens*)

This prostrate and hairless little plant resembles a moss, but has small greenish white flowers. The stems root as they spread, and can form small colonies where the grass is weak.

SELF-HEAL (*Prunella vulgaris*)

Short, squarish heads of purple and violet, or occasionally pink, flowers rise to about 20 cm (8 in) in open ground, but in the lawn, they nestle among the prostrate, leafy stems.

SPEEDWELL (*Veronica filiformis*)

A prostrate, mat-forming plant with small round kidney-shaped leaves, and small, solitary, mauvish blue, four-petalled flowers on thread-like stalks.

YARROW (*Achillea millefolium*)

In open ground this plant will grow to about 45 cm (18 in), but as a lawn weed the heads of small white flowers nestle among the ground-hugging foliage.

MOSS

Mosskillers will help to control lawn moss in the short term, but it is better to do all you can to eliminate the conditions in which moss thrives.

Moss prefers shade and damp, so cut back overhanging trees and shrubs where possible and try to improve the drainage. Aerating the lawn with a hollow-tined aerator, brushing sand or a lawn dressing into the holes may improve a heavy soil, but it would be worth considering proper drainage if the problem is serious (*see* September, page 222).

Low soil fertility is another possible cause. Use a combined lawn feed and mosskiller in spring and summer to encourage grass and do not mow too closely as this also encourages moss. In autumn apply a mosskiller, then scarify or rake to remove as much as possible. Do not do this before the moss is dead otherwise you could spread it. Check the label for the best application time for mosskillers, as some are only suitable for certain times of the year. The best way to tackle moss is to use a combination of chemical and cultural methods.

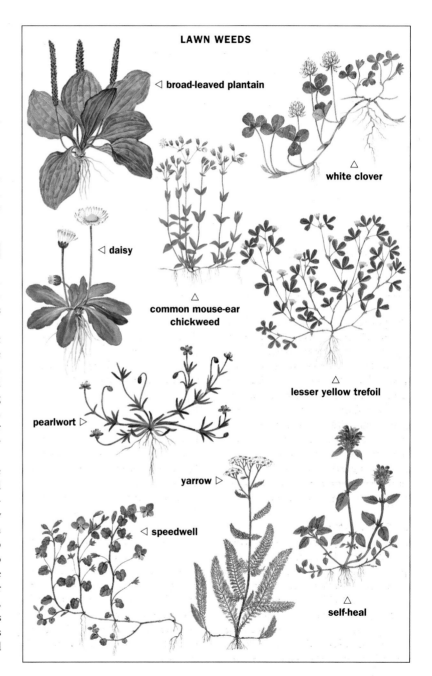

LAWN WEEDS

◁ broad-leaved plantain

△ white clover

◁ daisy

△ common mouse-ear chickweed

△ lesser yellow trefoil

pearlwort ▷

yarrow ▷

◁ speedwell

△ self-heal

Pruning

Pruning is used to regulate and shape growth, to improve the quality of flowers and fruits, and to remove damaged, diseased or dead wood.

The pruning of mature trees is a job for a qualified tree surgeon, who will be able to carry out any remedial work safely, but shrubs and small trees are well within the scope of most gardeners.

Do not be afraid to prune – shrubs can usually withstand quite drastic treatment. If, for example, you cut back in spring a plant which flowers on one-year-old shoots, you may cut out this year's flowers, but the bush is unlikely to be harmed in the long term and may give an even better show the following season. Although pruning bush roses by conventional methods is explained on pages 75–77, they are surprisingly resilient to casual and sometimes crude pruning methods – simply cutting them to an appropriate height with a hedge trimmer or with secateurs, without paying careful attention to the position of buds, is likely to produce a crop of roses just as good for garden display as on plants pruned by more traditional methods.

There are often several ways to prune the same shrub, with each method having its pros and cons. Generally, the advice given in this book has been kept simple and easy to follow, with the objective of producing a general garden display rather than exhibition-quality flowers or the special shaping of shrubs.

Outlined here are the basic principles of pruning, with a few typical examples. Detailed advice on dealing with plants with more specific requirements, such as fruit trees, roses and some climbers, is covered in the relevant section of Gardening Month by Month.

THE ONE-THIRD METHOD

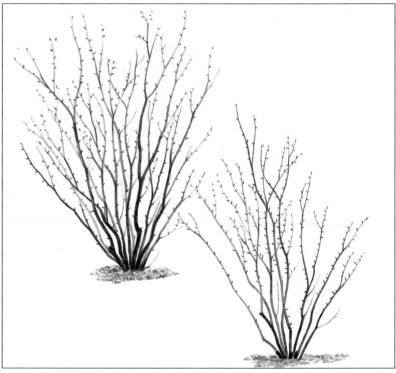

This is a simple pruning method suitable for a wide range of shrubs. It ensures tidy plants and many flowers. Do not prune until the shrub is at least three years old.

Start pruning when flowering has finished. Count the number of main stems, then aim to remove about one-third, taking out the oldest branches.

PRUNING FOR SHAPE & FLOWERS

CLIPPING

Many evergreen shrubs simply require clipping to shape to keep them small and compact. This can be done with hand shears, which is suitable for small-leaved plants like box (*Buxus sempervirens*) and privet (*Ligustrum ovalifolium* varieties), but large-leaved shrubs, such as spotted laurel (*Aucuba japonica*) and also conifers, should be cut with secateurs as the large leaves or sprays look unattractive and often turn brown if they are cut in half at random.

Clipping or trimming to a neat outline does not have to be confined to evergreens, but in all cases it should be done only if a formal shape suits the situation.

Mid summer is a good time to clip or shape, cutting the youngest growth and trying not to cut back into old wood (*see* August, page 203).

THE ONE-THIRD METHOD

This is a suitable pruning method for a wide range of shrubs, and you are unlikely to do any long-term harm even if you do it to the wrong kind of shrub, as there will always be some flowering shoots on the plant. The principle is to cut out the oldest stems each year, so that new shoots replace the old and keep the shrub compact and vigorous.

Do not begin this type of pruning until the shrub has been established for at least three years. Then prune annually by removing the oldest third of the stems – these will be the thickest and darkest.

Cut them right back to just above the ground. It may be necessary to remove some newer and weaker shoots instead if the plant is becoming congested or badly placed branches are crossing and rubbing against each other. Climbers can also be pruned using this method although extra care must be taken (see June, page 151).

The technique is particularly useful for shrubs that flower early on shoots produced the previous year, such as flowering currants (*Ribes sanguineum*) and forsythia, but it can also be used for many other shrubs, including those which are grown for ornamental foliage effect. The timing will depend on the shrub being pruned, but an easy rule of thumb is to prune immediately after the shrub has finished flowering.

REJUVENATION PRUNING

The one-third method can be used to rejuvenate shrubs which have been allowed to become shapeless and bare-legged through neglect.

Begin the rejuvenation of deciduous shrubs by cutting out the oldest third of the stems in December, while the shrubs are dormant. Miss out the usual spring or summer pruning in the year that follows, but in the second and subsequent years revert to pruning as soon as flowering is over.

Leggy climbers can be improved in the same way, but in this case carry out the first year's pruning in February.

The renovation of old evergreen shrubs such as rhododendrons should begin immediately after flowering. In the first year, cut out the oldest third of the branches. There may be only one or two of them. Over the next two years, a number of new stems will grow to replace the old branches.

In the third year, remove another third of the old branches and in the fifth year the final third. If you do this the plant will be rejuvenated yet stay in flower throughout the five-year process.

HARD PRUNING

A few shrubs benefit from very hard pruning each spring.

Shrubs that are grown for their brightly coloured winter stems will produce many more young shoots, which are usually the most colourful, if they are pruned severely every March. Cut back dogwoods, particularly *Cornus alba* 'Sibirica', and varieties with coloured stems, to an outward-facing bud about 5 cm (2 in) from the old stump that will build up through annual pruning.

Such hard pruning keeps shrubs more compact than usual and on a few has the additional effect of enhancing the leaf size enormously. The foxglove tree (*Paulownia tomentosa*) is one of these, producing leaves 60–90 cm (2–3 ft) across, while the lacy foliage of *Sambucus racemosa* 'Plumosa Aurea' develops into huge fronds. Eucalyptus can be pruned in this way. They then produce charming juvenile foliage and turn into attractive compact shrubs.

Shrubs such as *Buddleja davidii* and *Hydrangea paniculata* flower most freely on stems produced in the current year and will soon become tall and leggy if not kept pruned. Cut back all the previous year's growth to about two buds from the stump of old, darker and thicker wood. This pruning is best carried out early in spring just as the leaves begin to open (see March, page 79).

REDUCING GROWTH BY HALF

Plants such as brooms (*Cytisus*) become bare and leggy at the base if they are not pruned regularly and the same applies to heathers and lavenders. Shrubs of this type should not be pruned hard in the spring and are best pruned immediately after flowering, starting within a couple of years of planting.

Cut the young, green growth back by about half its length. Do not cut back into dark, old wood as this does not produce new shoots readily. Heathers can be pruned simply by clipping off the dead heads with hand shears (see March, pages 68–69 and April, page 101). Lavender should have the flower stalks trimmed off in the autumn and should be pruned again in spring to within 2.5 cm (1 in) of the previous year's growth.

STIMULATING FLOWERS ON SUMMER SHRUBS

A number of summer-flowering shrubs which flower on shoots produced the previous year will generally remain shapely and bloom reliably without any regular routine pruning. These are often the less hardy shrubs, such as cistus, ceanothus and *Convolvulus cneorum*. But you can encourage more prolific flowering the following summer if you shorten the new growth on shoots that have flowered by about two-thirds just after flowering has finished.

This kind of pruning is not severe, and afterwards the bush may not look very different, but it keeps the growth compact and encourages the production of more flowering shoots.

HARD PRUNING

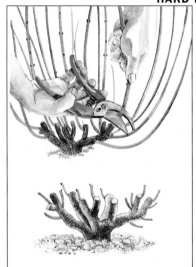

Prune Cornus alba *varieties hard in early March to within 5 cm (2 in) of the old stump. This encourages more colourful young shoots for the following winter.*

Buddleja davidii *and its varieties flower on the new wood produced in the current year. Cut them back hard in early spring to within two buds of the stump.*

REVERSION

Variegated shrubs sometimes produce shoots with normal green leaves – a process known as reversion, because the shoots have reverted to their original form.

These will grow stronger than the original shoots and may eventually dominate the plant. Remove any green shoot by cutting back to its point of origin.

PRUNING OUT PROBLEMS

Once a year it is worth going round the garden to check all shrubs – even those that do not require routine pruning – to spot any problems.

DEAD, DAMAGED AND DISEASED WOOD

Cut back dead or damaged shoots to an outward-facing bud on healthy, undamaged wood. A new shoot will replace the pruned stem and will grow in the direction the bud is pointing, so cutting to an outward-facing bud will help to create a bushy, open-centred shrub; too many inward-facing shoots will make it congested in the centre.

Eliminate crossing branches or shoots that are starting to rub against each other. If you do not do this while the shoots are young, the friction will cause injury, through which disease may enter.

Spring is a good time for this operation, as you can then see whether any shoots have been killed or injured by winter cold, and it is easier to study the condition and placing of the branches if the plant is not yet in full leaf.

REVERSION

All-green shoots on variegated plants should be cut out as soon as they are noticed, but a specific yearly check is worthwhile. This can be carried out at any time on evergreens, but for deciduous plants it is best done in spring or

summer. Cut these shoots back to their point of origin. If you do not do this the more vigorous, all-green shoots will take over and dominate the plant. This also happens on varieties of some flowering shrubs such as lavateras.

SUCKERS

Shoots seen growing from below the point of a graft (when a variety is not grown on its own roots) should be removed while still young. If you leave them untouched, they may eventually dominate the plant at the expense of the grafted variety. You can usually identify suckers by their different foliage and flowers (if you allow them to reach flowering stage). They usually arise from the base of the plant or beneath the soil. Cut them back to their point of origin, even if this means scraping back some of the soil to expose the base.

FORMATIVE PRUNING

By pruning a young plant in a certain pattern, its future shape can be determined. Most shrubs and trees bought from garden centres and nurseries will already have had most of the formative pruning done. Retaining or removing the growing tip will determine whether a birch or a catalpa, for example, grows with a single tall trunk or with multiple stems. Pruning out sideshoots will create an upright plant, while pinching out the growing tip will encourage low branching, so a pyracantha, for instance, could be trained into a shape suitable for either a wall shrub or a free-standing shrub.

This early training normally applies only if you have planted a cutting or seedling, but even then the majority of trees and shrubs will grow into attractive and natural-looking plants without

REMOVING SUCKERS AND WATER SHOOTS

Suckers sometimes appear from the rootstock of trees and shrubs. Expose the base of them and then simply pull them off at source, wearing gloves if necessary.

Clusters of thin shoots that appear on trunks where branches have been removed are called water shoots. Cut them off in the winter using secateurs.

formative pruning. However, this is important in young fruit trees and many techniques have been developed to provide a wide range of sizes and shapes to suit different growing requirements and garden sizes.

Although you can train cordons, espaliers, fans and other shapes from a single stem, this is a complicated process unless you are used to this type of pruning, and it takes several years to produce the desired shape. It is much easier to buy bushes and trees ready-trained which is how you usually buy them from garden centres. The higher cost will save you several years of time and effort.

REMOVING LARGE BRANCHES

Do not remove very thick or heavy branches from a tree unless you are competent and properly equipped – this is really a job for a tree surgeon (but make sure he is well qualified and insured).

If you have to remove a large branch, make some preliminary cuts so that the weight does not cause a damaging tear to the main trunk as it falls.

First make an upward cut about halfway through and about 30 cm (1 ft) from the trunk. Next, cut downwards on the outside of this, to remove the branch. Finally, remove the stump that remains. Avoid cutting flush with the trunk or main stem – leaving a small raised 'collar' will encourage rapid healing. Smooth off any jagged edges with a pruning knife. If you are uncomfortable using a knife try using a rasp instead.

Wound paints can be used on large cuts, but should not be necessary for normal shrub pruning. On most large cuts, paint around the outside of the wound, but leave the centre open. However, with some fruit trees such as

REMOVING LARGE BRANCHES

1 First make a short upward cut on the branch about 30 cm (1 ft) away from the trunk to prevent a damaging tear. Then saw through the branch from above.

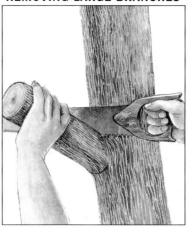

2 Saw off the stump close to the trunk but not flush with it, first making a small upward cut to reduce the risk of tearing the bark if the branch breaks.

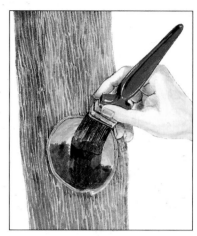

3 Treat the cut surface with wound paint without delay to help prevent disease spores entering. Paint the centre of the cut surface, or leave open, according to tree type.

cherries, pears and plums and their ornamental relatives, it is best to paint over the whole cut surface, as they are particularly prone to serious diseases that can enter through wounds.

SPECIAL TECHNIQUES

ROOT PRUNING

Pruning the roots to control the vigour of a tree, and to induce fruit such as plums to crop more prolifically, should be carried out only as a last resort. In the case of fruit trees a better solution is to plant a variety grafted on to a dwarfing rootstock. Ornamental fruit trees are seldom root pruned – use normal pruning techniques.

A deep trench is dug around the tree, at about the same distance from the trunk as the edge of the branches. The thick roots uncovered are sawn through and the soil replaced. Because of the impact this has on the tree (and because it is a very tiring job!), the work is usually carried out over two years.

POLLARDING

This is a technique of severe pruning similar to the hard annual pruning method described above, but with the branches cut back to a taller trunk. After pruning, only the trunk and stubs of the main branches are left. The method is sometimes used on trees that are causing an obstruction, sometimes as a decorative feature, and sometimes to stimulate lots of new shoots, for instance on willows and poplars, to provide material for basket making. Pollarding is not used routinely in the garden except for special effect on some willows with

brightly coloured young stems and occasionally on lime trees.

LOPPING

Severe cutting back of the upper large branches of a tree is best left to a tree surgeon. This should only be done if it is really necessary, for instance when a branch has died.

HEADING BACK

On large trees and overgrown shrubs all or some of the main branches can be shortened to just above well-developed dormant buds to stop the plant growing too large. This should not be necessary on shrubs that have been pruned regularly, and only a tree surgeon should tackle this kind of pruning on a large tree.

For description and details of pruning tools, see pages 437–439.

Propagation

Propagation – the increase of plants – is one of the most satisfying jobs in the garden. There is often more than one way in which a particular plant can be propagated, but some methods are more suited to certain types of plant than others.

Annuals are always grown from seed, and this is sometimes the preferred method for perennials where a large number of plants is required and the offspring will grow true to type. Raising shrubs and even trees from seed can be a satisfying test of skill, but it is a slow and uncertain process. Vegetative propagation (cuttings and layers of various kinds) is usually quicker and more rewarding, and sometimes the only method that ensures the offspring will be identical to the parent. However, specialist techniques such as grafting and budding are not discussed here as they are used mainly by professional nurserymen.

The advice and techniques given here apply to a wide range of plants and often have to be general over details such as cutting lengths and optimum temperatures. Adapt the advice to suit the plant – the length of a cutting of an alpine is obviously going to be less than that of a large shrub. Wherever possible, follow the advice given in Section one: Gardening Month by Month section for specific plants.

PROPAGATORS

PROPAGATING BENCH

If you do a lot of propagating and have a greenhouse, you may want to make a propagating bench. This is like a small cold frame with a sand base, with soil-warming cables buried in sand to provide bottom heat and more cables attached to the sides to warm the air. To keep in the warmth and create a humid environment, a close-fitting lid is important, but there should be a means of ventilation. Thermostatically controlled, this provides a suitable environment for germinating seeds and rooting cuttings without the cost of heating a large space.

If you propagate a large number of cuttings, especially woody plants that are difficult to root, a mist unit should improve your success rate. A sensor detects when the air is drying out and turns on mist heads which saturate the air with fine water droplets. You need a plumbed-in water supply as well as an electrical power source.

You can buy heating and misting components from a number of companies who specialise in supplying greenhouse equipment.

PROPRIETARY PROPAGATORS

Many gardeners who raise rooted cuttings and seedlings mainly for their own use prefer to buy a ready-made propagator. These are generally smaller than one you might make yourself, but are more convenient to install and use.

Unheated propagators are inexpensive but limited in their usefulness. They have a similar effect to that of enclosing cuttings or a tray of seeds in a plastic bag, but are more convenient. They usually have a simple form of ventilation. Warmth for this type of propagator has to come mainly from ambient heat, so they are most useful indoors, especially on a windowsill. In summer they can be used in the greenhouse to provide a humid atmosphere for cuttings.

Heated bases, and trays with a self-contained heating element, provide vital bottom heat that encourages quick germination and speedy rooting of cuttings. They should be used with a plastic dome over the seed tray to conserve warmth and increase humidity.

Windowsill propagators usually hold two to four standard seed trays, and contain a heating element in the base. A plastic dome increases the humidity and conserves warmth. These are very versatile propagators. Although the capacity is limited it is possible to raise a large number of seedlings or cuttings in these propagators over a period of time. Move the seedlings and rooted cuttings on to make room for others.

They can be used in the greenhouse and the plants benefit from the better light, but in cold weather the heating element works more efficiently indoors where the temperature differential is less. They are also useful if you do not have a power supply in the greenhouse.

Mist propagators are expensive but ideal if you want to propagate lots of cuttings, especially the more difficult ones, such as conifers. They are often too large to fit on a windowsill, and are more suitable for a greenhouse. If you wish only to germinate seeds, mist propagators are an unnecessary luxury.

SOWING SEED

This is the most basic form of propagation. Most seed packets and catalogues give practical advice for sowing depth, light requirement and target temperature. If the advice appears to vary from one brand to another, this simply reflects the fact that there is often no precise and universally accepted ideal. If results are disappointing with one method, try an alternative the next time, but bear in mind that the germination of some seeds can be low, slow or simply erratic.

Pre-sowing treatment

Check whether any pre-sowing treatment is required. Some seeds require a cold period (stratification), which can be achieved by sowing in pots of compost or sand in an unheated cold frame for the winter. This process can be accelerated by mixing the seeds with moist peat and sand, or scattering them on moist filter paper, and then sealing them in a plastic bag or container. Put this in the refrigerator at 1–5°C (34–41°F) for four to twelve weeks, according to the plant (rinse seeds off the paper before sowing).

Some hard seeds, such as cyclamen and sweet peas, may benefit from soaking overnight, or gentle abrasion to break the tough coat. This allows moisture to penetrate more easily. Seed packets should give appropriate advice.

TREATED SEEDS

Seeds that are small and difficult to handle, or that do not germinate reliably, are sometimes treated to make the results more predictable. The names for these treatments may vary, but there are three main types.

Coated or pelleted seeds are coated with a material that makes them larger and therefore easier to handle. You can space them out more evenly and pricking out becomes unnecessary. Take the precaution of sowing a couple of seeds in each position and thinning to one if both germinate. This is a more certain way of ensuring there are no gaps.

Chitted or pre-germinated seeds are less common, and usually used for popular plants that are difficult to germinate unless you are able to maintain a suitable temperature. Cucumber seeds are sometimes sold this way.

There are strict order-by dates for pre-germinated seeds and delivery is made within a specified period. When the seeds are received, the root will already have emerged from the seed, so prompt planting is essential. Instructions come with the chitted seed.

Primed seeds have been specially stored and treated to bring them to the point where they are ready to germinate. Any inbuilt dormancy will have been broken, so you should have seeds that germinate faster and more evenly. Primed seeds are usually more expensive than untreated seeds. You have to order from a specialist seedsman by specified dates (which may vary according to the type of plant), and they are sent to you within a particular period.

SOWING SEED UNDER GLASS

Seeds are usually sown under glass because they require high temperatures to germinate, or because the seedlings are not frost-hardy. Some hardy annual flowers, and frost-hardy vegetables such as cabbages, are sometimes sown under glass to advance their growth and provide an earlier display or crop.

Summer annuals are usually sown in a greenhouse or on a light windowsill in late winter or early spring, but a heated propagator will save on heating in a greenhouse. Once the seeds have germinated they will usually tolerate cooler conditions, and then the greenhouse can be kept at a more economic temperature.

The seeds of many rock plants, shrubs and border perennials do not require high temperatures, but they benefit from the shelter and protection provided by a cold frame. Some of these seeds take time to

---

SOWING VERY FINE SEED

Some plants, such as lobelias, *Begonia semperflorens* and busy lizzies, produce dust-like seed which is very difficult to sow thinly enough. Use a flat piece of wood which fits inside the seed tray and press it down to make an even, firm surface on which to sow. In order to see where you have sown, carefully mix the seed in the packet with a little sieved silver sand – do not shake the contents or they will separate out. Do not cover seed with compost. Watering from overhead with a rose can disturb the seeds, so if you need to water the compost after sowing, stand the tray in shallow water in a sink until the surface has darkened, and allow it to drain. To prevent surface-sown seed from drying out, cover the tray with cling wrap or a sheet of glass and shade from direct sunlight, which can cause overheating. Remove the cover as soon as the seedlings emerge.

SOWING SEED IN A TRAY

1 The majority of seeds will germinate readily in loam-based or a soilless compost, but choose one that is specifically recommended for sowing seeds.

Space out large seeds individually and sprinkle small ones as evenly as possible on the surface of the compost. It may help to mix very fine seeds with silver sand.

2 Cover the seeds thinly with moist compost unless the packet advises otherwise, or you know that the seeds germinate better in the light. Mist to moisten the compost thoroughly – a watering can may wash fine seeds to one side. If the seeds are very fine, water from beneath by standing the tray or pot in shallow water.

3 Allow the compost to drain, then put the container in a propagator. If a propagator is not being used, cover the top of the tray or pot with cling wrap or a sheet of glass to keep the compost moist. Make sure it is not in contact with the compost. Keep in a warm place for quick germination. Remove the covering when the first seeds germinate.

4 Prick the seedlings out into individual pots, or space them further apart in trays of potting compost, as soon as they are large enough to handle and before they become congested. Always lift a seedling by its seed leaves (the first ones to appear), which usually have a different appearance from the true leaves that follow.

germinate, and a cold frame is a convenient place to keep them provided you never neglect the watering.

SOWING SEED OUTDOORS

Careful preparation of the seed bed is essential for reliable results. Always break down large clumps of soil into small pieces, so that the surface is level and the structure of the soil fine and crumbly. If necessary, work sand and peat or a peat-substitute into the top of the soil to improve the structure. For a seed bed, soil structure, moisture and temperature are more important than fertility, and it should not be necessary to add fertilisers unless the soil is very impoverished. Fertilisers can be applied once the seedlings are growing.

Sowing in drills

Vegetables and other plants sown in a seed bed to be transplanted later, such as wallflowers and cabbages, are usually sown in straight rows (drills). This makes jobs such as weeding and thinning much easier. Hardy annuals sown in the position where they are to flower are usually broadcast but, to help identify seedlings from weeds, can be sown in drills at varying angles (*see* April, page 90).

Continue to keep the soil moist until the seeds have germinated. This will make all the difference to the speed and rate of germination.

Do not sow too early. Plants sown later, when the soil is warm, often overtake earlier sowings that may have suffered a severe check to their growth from cold soil or unfavourable weather. For vegetables, the use of cloches and horticultural fleece to raise the soil temperature will enable most sowings to be advanced by several weeks. (For further guidance, *see* February, pages 47–48 and March, page 80.)

Thinning and transplanting

Thinning is best done in two stages, first to half the final spacing then, a week or two later, to the final spacing. This increases the chances of an even row of mature plants, for you won't be left with such large gaps if some plants later fail to survive the first thinning or succumb to pests and diseases.

Thin the seedlings while they are still small, preferably on a damp day, and water afterwards if the weather is dry.

When thinning, try to hold down the soil around the seedling with your fingers, to cause as little root disturbance as possible to the adjacent plants.

Seedlings being raised in seed beds for transplanting to spare 'nursery' beds (wallflowers and double daisies are often grown this way because their final planting position is usually occupied by summer flowers) should still be thinned in the rows first. This produces larger plants with better root systems for lifting.

Space them out in a position so that they can be grown on for the summer without becoming overcrowded (the seed packet will usually advise). Vegetables, such as cabbages and leeks, are often transplanted straight to their growing positions, but should still have been thinned in their seed rows first.

Always water the seedlings thoroughly about an hour before you lift them, as well as after planting.

RAISING PLANTS INDOORS

If you don't have a greenhouse, or do not want to heat yours too early in the season, most seeds can be germinated indoors if you have enough room.

The airing cupboard is an ideal place for most seeds, unless the seed packet indicates that they will benefit from light. Cover the pots or trays with a sheet of glass or plastic to help keep the compost moist and check them daily to see that the compost has not dried out and whether germination has started.

Always bring the container into the best possible light as soon as the roots start to emerge from the seeds. If you leave them in the dark until the leaves open, the seedlings will grow thin and elongated, and may not recover.

If you can't check progress once or twice a day, keep your seeds on a light windowsill, even if it is cooler there and they take longer to germinate.

Do not be tempted to sow too many kinds unless you have adequate space where they can be grown on. Every pot or tray of sown seeds may represent half a dozen trays of seedlings if you prick them all out.

Sow as late as possible in the recommended period, so that the seedlings spend the shortest time indoors.

Trays of seedlings on your windowsill will not do the woodwork much good, so be sure to place them on drip trays raised a little above the sill's surface.

If simply left on the windowsill, very few seedlings will grow into plants that you will be proud of. Turn the containers daily to even up the light source, and if possible use supplementary electric lights. Special growing lights will greatly

SOWING SEED IN DRILLS

1 Always sow in well-prepared ground. Dig the soil, break it down and consolidate it, then rake it level to provide a fine surface for sowing.

2 Make every effort to sow in straight lines. Use a garden line as a guide, and take the seed drill out with the corner of a hoe or rake.

3 Space seeds as evenly as possible to avoid waste and reduce thinning. Hold the seeds in a cupped hand and sprinkle them thinly.

improve the quality of the plants. These lights must be used carefully; follow the manufacturer's instructions regarding the distance between lights and plants.

Plants started off indoors are unlikely to be as sturdy as those raised in the better light of a greenhouse, but if you give them more space than normal, turn them regularly so that they don't grow lop-sided towards the light and move them into a greenhouse or cold frame as soon as it is safe to do so, then the results can be very successful.

Growing on

Prick out the seedlings into individual pots or space out into seed trays as soon as they are large enough to handle. Always handle them by their leaves, not the fragile stems, preferably the seed leaves (the first two to open) if they have not fallen off by this stage.

After pricking out into seed trays, modules or individual pots, water the seedlings thoroughly and shade from direct sunlight for about a week. If they show signs of wilting during the first few days, spray them with a fine mist of water a couple of times a day. Avoid overwetting the plants or compost.

Grow them on in good light until the seedlings are ready to be moved outdoors, preferably to a cold frame initially, which will acclimatise the plants to outdoor conditions.

Seedlings intended for planting in the garden sometimes become overcrowded if they have to spend many weeks or months in their containers waiting for the weather to improve. Spacing out the pots will help. Spacing seed trays will not benefit those in the centre of the tray, but it will help those around the edge and encourage a better circulation of air around the plants. This makes better plants and reduces the risk of disease.

The amount of compost in a seed tray is limited and it is often quickly exhausted of nutrients. If the seedlings begin to look stunted, yellow, or generally unhealthy, and they have to remain in the trays for any period of time, start to feed them regularly with a suitable diluted liquid fertiliser.

PRICKING OUT SEEDLINGS

1 First loosen the compost around the seedling's roots with a plant label or small dibber, then lift it out carefully.

2 Hold it by the seed leaves (the first to emerge), and place it into a spaced hole made with a dibber, pencil or label.

SAVING SEEDS FROM YOUR GARDEN

Raising plants from home-saved seed can be fun, and makes economic sense too. But choose the plants carefully, otherwise you will waste valuable time and have many disappointments when the plants flower.

Avoid saving seed from any variety described as an F1 or F2. These have been bred from specially selected varieties with parents that breed pure to type, but that are different from each other. The hybrid variety may be totally different, or combine recognisable qualities of both parents, but the seed saved from these varieties is often inferior as the genetic material becomes scrambled again. The problem is you will not know whether an F1 hybrid is going to break down into something worthwhile or not. The chances of raising good plants from seed saved from an F2 plant are even smaller.

The most rewarding plants to grow from your own seed are annuals that have not been highly bred, such as the poached-egg plant (*Limnanthes douglasii*) and blazing star (*Bartonia aurea*). Mixtures of annuals, such as pot marigolds (calendulas) and poppies can usually be relied upon to give a good show, but don't be surprised if they are slightly different from the parent plants. Salvias are among the highly bred plants that usually provide good plants from self-saved seed.

Among the border perennials, rock plants, trees and shrubs, most of the true species will produce offspring like the parent plant, though growing trees and shrubs from seed takes many years

and is usually left to specialists.

Highly bred species with many varieties and hybrids, such as aquilegias, dahlias, delphiniums, gladioli, roses and rhododendrons, will usually produce unpredictable results. Growing varieties of these from your own seed is best regarded as an entertaining way to try to raise a worthwhile new variety, rather than as a means of propagation.

When collecting seed, allow the seed heads to ripen on the plant for as long as possible. Collect the seed as soon as the pods or capsules start to split and the seeds are about to be shed.

Ripe seed can often be collected directly in envelopes or small containers by pressing the seed head between the fingers to release the seeds. Otherwise cut the stems, and leave them on a tray in a warm, airy place, perhaps on a windowsill, until the seeds fall out.

Separate the seeds from the pieces of stem and seed pod by shaking or blowing on them gently.

Seeds embedded in berries have to be extracted in a different way. Squash the berries between the fingers and thumb when they become soft, then rinse the seeds free in warm water.

A few seeds, such as many primulas and meconopsis, are best sown soon after collection, but many can be stored for a year or two if they are kept in a suitable container. For short-term storage, paper bags kept in an airtight tin are adequate, but if you have a lot of seeds, screw-top jars are better.

TAKING CUTTINGS

This is the most common method of propagating woody-stemmed plants and perennials. The various techniques reflect the ripeness of the wood at different times of the year.

ROOTING HORMONES

Most cuttings benefit from the use of a rooting hormone, which will often increase the speed of rooting or the percentage that root. It is not necessary for all plants, however, and many, such as ivies, busy lizzies and pelargoniums, root easily without using a rooting compound. Do not use rooting hormones on leaf cuttings or root cuttings, only on stem cuttings.

Rooting hormones are usually formulated as a powder, but liquids and gels are also available. They are likely to have a fungicide added to reduce the risk of losses through rotting.

Gels adhere easily to all cuttings, but if you are using powders it is best to dip the end of the cutting in water first so that the powder sticks to the cut surface more readily.

Only the cut end of the stem should be treated. The important place where you need the hormone is on the cut surface; it is not beneficial to have lots of powder or gel on the outside of the stem.

As formulations and strengths vary, always read and follow the instructions on the container.

SOFTWOOD CUTTINGS

Softwood cuttings are taken from the tips of shoots that are still soft and sappy, usually before mid summer with outdoor plants. These generally root easily provided you can maintain a humid atmosphere, but being soft they quickly wilt and will collapse in dry air. Keep the cuttings in a closed plastic bag when you collect them so that they do not wilt before you can prepare them.

The optimum size of the cutting depends on the plant, 5–8 cm (2–3 in) is normal for most garden shrubs.

Trim just below a leaf joint, and remove lower leaves that would otherwise

ROOTING WITHOUT COMPOST

Because most cuttings need moisture and oxygen but not nutrients in order to root, there are a number of alternatives to proprietary cuttings composts which can be made up and used by all gardeners.

Sand alone is often used commercially, but perlite or horticultural vermiculite are usually more convenient. These are both light to handle, trap air (so are relatively warm) and hold plenty of water while being free-draining. Both can be mixed with peat to make a good rooting medium. Adding sand or perlite to a loam-based compost will lighten its structure to suit cuttings.

Some cuttings that root quickly and easily, like busy lizzies and ivies, will form roots in water. You can buy specially designed containers to support the cuttings while they root, but a jam jar is quite adequate. There are also proprietary water-retaining gels on the market.

Cuttings rooted in a medium with minimal nutrients must be potted up before they begin to show signs of starvation. Those rooted in water or gel should be handled particularly carefully as their roots will be brittle and easily damaged. Keep newly potted cuttings in a humid atmosphere (cover with a plastic bag if necessary) until they appear to be growing well.

be below the level of the compost. Remove the soft tip of the shoot to cut down on the chance of attack from fungal diseases such as grey mould (botrytis). Insert the cuttings in trays in a propagator, or a pot that you can cover with a plastic bag or cut-down plastic bottle. Make sure the cuttings do not touch each other, and are not in contact with the side of the propagator or the plastic bag. Keep out of direct sunlight, shading if necessary with newspaper.

Check progress periodically, and as soon as a mass of white roots has been produced, pot up the cuttings individually into a potting compost.

Smaller cuttings, using only the tips of the shoots with a few leaves, are called tip cuttings. These make sturdy plants readily, but are more difficult to handle. Tip cuttings of carnations and pinks are known as pipings (*see* June, page 150).

SEMI-RIPE CUTTINGS (half-ripe or semi-mature)

These are cuttings from shoots that have grown in the current season but have started to harden and darken at the base. They are usually taken in late summer,

SOFTWOOD CUTTINGS

1 Choose the ends of non-flowering shoots that are still soft and pliable, and then remove them, making sure that they each have four or five pairs of leaves.

2 Trim off the lowest pair of leaves on each cutting, then cut out the top pair of leaves at the tip to reduce both moisture loss and the risk of disease.

3 Insert the cuttings in a rooting compost, ensuring that they do not touch. Keep in a warm, humid environment until they have rooted.

and 5–10 cm (2–4 in) is a typical length, though this will depend on the shrub. Prepare and root semi-ripe cuttings in the same way as softwood cuttings.

For a few plants, such as clematis, semi-ripe cuttings are trimmed between the leaf joints rather than just below a joint. These are called internodal cuttings (*see* May, page 126).

HEEL CUTTINGS

A heel is a small piece of wood and bark that remains attached if you pull away a sideshoot from its supporting stem. It is at this point that growth hormones are often concentrated, so some cuttings root more successfully if taken with a heel of older wood. The technique is usually used for semi-ripe and hardwood cuttings. It is especially effective if the shrub has a pithy or hollow stem.

Carefully pull away the cutting with a downward movement so that a small strip of bark comes away with it, but avoid tearing the bark more than necessary. Trim the heel with a sharp knife or blade to shorten and neaten it.

HARDWOOD CUTTINGS

Hardwood cuttings are taken from mature shoots that have grown in the current season. These cuttings should be taken when the plant is dormant, and are usually longer than other kinds – a common length would be 25–30 cm (10–12 in). They are normally rooted outdoors, generally in a trench in the kitchen garden or in a cold frame.

Prepare a V-shaped or slit trench about 10 cm (4 in) deep, and sprinkle coarse sand or grit in the bottom to ensure good drainage. Strip the leaves, if any remain, from the lowest part of the stem that will be beneath the soil, dip the end in a rooting hormone, and insert the cutting in the trench. Return the soil and firm it around the cuttings. Some fruiting and ornamental shrubs that are grown on a short trunk, such as gooseberries and roses, should have all but the top three or four buds rubbed out.

Hardwood cuttings will remain dormant during the winter, but with many kinds you can expect to see signs of rooting and growth the following spring. Leave all hardwood cuttings undisturbed until autumn, apart from the occasional watering in dry weather.

OTHER TYPES OF CUTTINGS

STEM CUTTINGS OF PERENNIALS
Because herbaceous border perennials and some rock plants do not produce woody growth, softwood cuttings can be taken throughout spring and summer. Take cuttings from plants of borderline hardiness, such as penstemons, in late summer or early autumn in case the parent does not survive a cold winter. Overwinter in a cold frame.

BASAL CUTTINGS
Many perennials, such as delphiniums, chrysanthemums and lupins, have stems

HARDWOOD CUTTINGS

1 Take hardwood cuttings when the plant is dormant, and for cuttings, select only shoots that have just completed their first year's growth.

2 The length of the cutting will depend on the type of plant, but for most trees and shrubs about 25–30 cm (10–12 in) is about right.

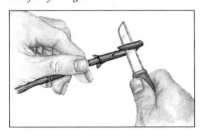

3 To aid rooting, remove a thin sliver of wood from near the base of each cutting. Dipping the end of the cutting in a rooting hormone will also aid rooting.

4 Insert the cuttings to at least half their length in a shallow trench with coarse sand or grit in the bottom to aid drainage. Space them 8–10 cm (3–4 in) apart.

BASAL CUTTINGS

1 Cuttings of herbaceous plants without branching growth, such as lupins, are taken in late winter and early spring from new shoots at the base of the plant.

2 Dig away the soil from around the base of the plant and then cut off the young growth from the outside of the plant before the shoots have become hollow.

3 Pot them up in the same way as any other cuttings, although a rooting hormone is not usually necessary if they are given a warm and humid environment.

LEAF BUD CUTTINGS

This method is sometimes used for camellias and a few other shrubs, particularly when a large number of plants is required. To raise a few plants it is usually more convenient to take stem cuttings or to layer the plants.

Choose semi-ripened shoots and cut them into sections, each with a leaf attached. Cut the stems just above a leaf, and make the other cut about 2 cm (¾ in) below the leaf stalk (the exact distance will depend on the space between the leaves). Remove a small sliver of bark at the base to stimulate rooting (a rooting hormone is not normally necessary), then insert the cuttings in pots of compost so that the base of the leaf stalk sits just above the surface.

that do not branch but grow in a clump directly out of the plant's base (crown). Basal cuttings should be taken in late winter or early in spring while the stems are still young and have not yet become hollow – the ideal stage is when the first leaves have just unfurled. If possible include part of the woody basal tissue when taking the cutting. They normally root easily without the need for hormone rooting powder.

Sometimes you will see outer shoots which have already begun to develop independent roots. These can be gently pulled from the main crown and potted up to develop into individual plants. A halfway house between basal cuttings and division (*see page 431*), these are sometimes called Irishman's cuttings.

LEAF CUTTINGS

PETIOLE CUTTINGS

Petiole is the technical name for a leaf stalk, and African violets (*Saintpaulia ionanthe*) and peperomias are often propagated from petiole cuttings.

Bend a mature leaf of the parent plant sideways so that the entire stem comes away, leaving no part attached to the plant. Shorten the stalk to 5 cm (2 in) with a sharp knife. Make a small hole in the compost, insert the cutting and firm down.

Rooting usually takes about six to eight weeks, when new leaves start to grow around the stalk. Pot up into individual pots when well rooted and large enough to handle conveniently.

PETIOLE CUTTINGS

1 African violets and peperomias are the plants most often propagated from leaf petiole (stalk) cuttings. Break off healthy, mature leaves without leaving a stump.

2 Make a hole with a small dibber or pencil, and insert the leaf stalk into rooting compost so the base of the leaf just sits on the surface. Gently firm the compost.

LEAF SECTION CUTTINGS

1 Mother-in-law's tongues can be propagated by cutting their leaves into 3–5 cm (1–2 in) sections. However, cuttings from variegated Sansevieria produce all-green plants.

2 Insert the cuttings, lower side down, into pots of gritty compost, burying the bottom halves. Keep them warm and humid until new growth forms in a month or so.

LEAF SECTION CUTTINGS

Leaves with a pronounced keel, such as mother-in-law's tongues (*Sansevieria*), can be cut into sections. Insert these, lower side down, in gritty compost.

LEAF BLADE CUTTINGS

For some popular house plants, such as *Begonia rex*, the blade of the leaf is used for cuttings. Once the cuttings are large enough, pot them up in individual pots.

LEAF BLADE CUTTINGS

1 Begonia rex and some other begonias can be grown from leaf blade cuttings. Select a mature, healthy leaf and trim the stalk to leave a 12 mm (½ in) stump.

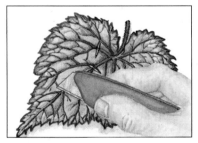

2 Cut through the underside of the leaf at intervals where the main veins intersect using a sharp knife or blade. New plants should form at these points.

3 Lay the leaf, cut side down, on a gritty compost, keeping it in position with small stones or pieces of bent wire. Pot up the plants individually when well rooted.

ROOT CUTTINGS

◁1   2▷   ◁3   4▽

Root cuttings are not widely used, and success rates can be disappointing unless you take them at the right time, usually in autumn or winter; relatively few plants are suitable for propagation by this method.

Californian poppies (Romneya coulteri) are often propagated by root cuttings, but these are usually taken in late February or March.
(1) For plants with reasonably thick roots, such as acanthus, oriental poppies and Primula denticulata, choose roots about pencil thickness and cut them into pieces 5–8 cm (2–3 in) long.

(2) Cut the top of each piece (the part nearest the soil surface) horizontally and the lower end diagonally, so you will not be confused when you come to insert them.
(3) Plant several root cuttings in a pot of multi-purpose or cutting compost, with the top of the root flush with the surface. Cover with a layer of grit or sand.

If the plants have thin roots, such as those of border phlox, they are best laid horizontally in seed trays of compost, then covered with a thin layer of compost.
(4) When new plants begin to appear, usually in spring, pot them up individually.

PLANTLETS AND RUNNERS

Some plants produce plantlets on arching or trailing stems called runners. The spider plant (*Chlorophytum comosum*), mother of thousands (*Saxifraga stolonifera*, syn. *S. sarmentosa*) and strawberries are well-known examples.

Peg these plantlets, still attached to the parent plant, down into small individual pots of moist compost and keep watered. They will root after a couple of weeks and can then be severed from the parent plant (*see* June, page 153).

DIVISION

FIBROUS-ROOTED DIVISION

This is one of the easiest and most instant forms of propagation. Border plants and rock plants with a fibrous root system, such as Michaelmas daisies, geraniums and heleniums, are easily divided into a number of smaller pieces.

Lift the clump on to the surface, then prise the roots apart. Small plants can often be divided by fingers or hand forks; larger ones will need to be levered apart with two forks back to back. The larger the pieces that you break off, the more quickly you will have an established clump again, but if you want a large number of plants, break the crown up into small pieces, making sure each one has some roots and shoots.

Replant large pieces immediately, but grow on small divisions in a nursery bed for a year, before planting them out in their final positions.

Some pot plants, such as aspidistras and many ferns, can be divided in this way. Pot the divisions up individually, water them, then keep out of direct sun until they have established. Mist them frequently to help recovery.

FIBROUS-ROOTED DIVISION

1 This is the easiest form of propagation for large border plants. Dig up the plant then place two forks back to back in the middle of the clump.

2 Split the clump in half using the forks with a to-and-fro levering movement. If the clump that you are dividing is large it can be split again if necessary.

3 If the clump was old and large, discard the oldest, inner section and replant only the younger, outer pieces. Replant without delay.

DIVIDING OFFSETS

1 Plants such as bromeliads produce offsets (young plants) around the original plant. First remove the plant and its offsets from its pot.

2 Carefully pull the new plants apart, using a knife to separate them if necessary. Finally, pot the plants up, disturbing the roots as little as possible.

DIVISION OF OFFSETS

There are various kinds of offset. Bulb offsets, the small bulbs that form at the sides of larger ones, can simply be removed and grown on separately.

Small plants that grow around the crown of the parent and can be detached easily are also called offsets. This is the normal form of propagation for bromeliads, as the flowering part of the plant dies and the offsets that form around it take over. Remove bromeliad offsets when they are about one-third the size of their

SIMPLE LAYERING

1 Select a healthy, flexible stem and strip the leaves where it will be in contact with the ground once it has been pegged down. Leave the other leaves on.

2 Wound the stem to stimulate rooting – a small slit made with a sharp knife where it will be pegged down is a convenient method of doing this.

3 Peg the layer into a shallow depression made close to the parent plant, using a piece of bent wire. Return the soil and secure the plant to an upright cane.

parent. Some can be pulled away, others have to be cut with a knife. Even if they have no roots, these should soon form.

Offsets removed from other types of plant, including the popular African violet (*Saintpaulia ionanthe*), can usually just be pulled away from their parent, and potted up.

LAYERING

SIMPLE LAYERING

Simple ground layering is a useful way to propagate shrubs with low-growing branches that can be pegged to the ground, such as rhododendrons. This method can be carried out at any time of the year.

Choose a young, flexible shoot that can easily be bent down to soil level. Make a shallow depression in the soil just below it with a spade or trowel. Because of their situation at the base of a shrub, the greatest danger to rooting layers is

lack of water, so work some moisture-retaining material into the soil.

Strip the leaves from the area of stem to be layered and peg the shoot down with pieces of bent wire. Secure the growing tip to an upright cane. The stem should bend easily, but be careful not to snap it off. Cover with compost and water in well.

With many species wounding the stem will aid rooting. Before pegging the layer down, remove a very thin layer of bark from the underside of one of the buds on the shoot and apply a little rooting hormone to the cut.

Most layers will have rooted by the following autumn, when they can be severed from the parent plant and grown on in pots or a nursery bed until large enough to plant in their final positions.

Serpentine layering is a technique similar to simple layering, but multiple layers are made from the one stem. It is used mainly for climbers with long,

DIVISION OF RHIZOMES   ## DIVISION OF TUBERS

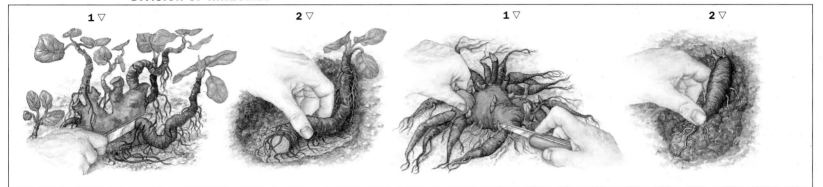

1 ▽   2 ▽   1 ▽   2 ▽

Rhizomes are underground stems, usually beneath the soil but sometimes, as with border or flag irises, clearly visible on the surface. Old clumps are often divided because they become congested, but it is also a practical form of propagation.
(1) Lift the plants when flowering has finished, shake off surplus soil, then cut off small pieces of rhizome which include a

clump of leaves: choose the younger pieces from the edge of the clump and discard the toughest, oldest pieces.
(2) Dust the cut ends with a fungicide and replant so that the leaves are upright and the rhizome is half buried in the soil. Firm in, then water well. Trim iris leaves back to about 15 cm (6 in) before replanting, to reduce windrock while plants are rerooting.

Stem tubers form either below ground, potatoes and Jerusalem artichokes being examples, or on the surface of the soil like tuberous-rooted begonias.
(1) Using a sharp knife, cut a stem tuber into sections, each with an 'eye' (bud). Each division should grow into an individual plant. Alternatively, basal shoots can be grown on and used for cuttings.

(2) Dust the cut surface with a fungicide, then pot these up at the depth the tubers normally grow.
    Root tubers, such as dahlias, are treated in the same way but, unlike stem tubers, they must contain a piece of stem with a bud. Start the tubers into growth and when shoots develop, divide the tuber with a piece of shoot or a bud on to each section.

---

supple stems, such as honeysuckles and clematis, and can be used for house plants such as ivies and *Ficus pumila*.
    Lay the trailing shoot along the ground, and strip the leaves and sideshoots from every second or third leaf cluster. Wound the stem close to the points where the leaves have been stripped, and apply a rooting hormone before pegging these sections down in shallow depressions in well-prepared soil. Leave the intermediate leaf clusters above the ground, so that the stem snakes in and out of the ground. In due course the pegged-down sections should root and produce shoots. When growing strongly the new plants can be severed and grown on independently.

AIR LAYERING

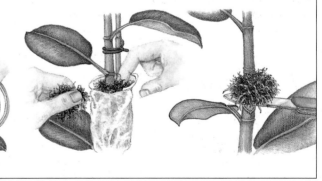

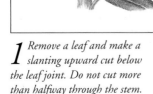

1 Remove a leaf and make a slanting upward cut below the leaf joint. Do not cut more than halfway through the stem.

2 Brush with rooting hormone and wedge a match into the cut. Then tape a sleeve of plastic around the bottom of the cut.

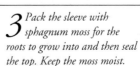

3 Pack the sleeve with sphagnum moss for the roots to grow into and then seal the top. Keep the moss moist.

4 When plenty of new roots have formed, sever with secateurs or a sharp knife and pot up. Be careful not to damage the roots.

Tools & equipment

The majority of gardening tools should be seen as long-term investments. Tools that are well designed and kept in good condition really do make a difference. Often a job is easier and completed more quickly with less effort. Good tools sometimes cost a lot more than cheaper versions, but they are almost always worth it. Once you have used a stainless steel spade or trowel, for example, you will almost certainly never want to go back to a traditional one. A really good pair of secateurs will probably outlast two or three pairs of cheaper ones – and be easier and more efficient to use. Cleaning your tools after use will protect your investment and often keep the blades sharper too (*see* January, page 22). Most metals will rust, so don't put digging tools away that are caked with soil, or cutting or pruning tools with sap left on the blades. Wipe them clean with a damp cloth or rinse under running water, then dry thoroughly with a cloth. Finally, wipe over with an oily rag, or spray with a rust-proofing product.

Tools have been grouped here according to use. Although many tools have more than one use – the humble garden rake is often used for drawing out a seed drill, raking water weeds out of the pond or leaves from the lawn, as well as for levelling ground – this makes it easier to weigh up the pros and cons of different tools intended for similar jobs.

Sharp blades make pruning and cutting easier and they will do less damage to the plants. Most blades can be kept sharp with a sharpening stone, but blades that need special sharpening techniques, such as mowers and some secateurs, are best serviced by a professional unless you are familiar with the methods used.

Tools take up space in your garden shed, and large ones can be expensive to buy. Consider hiring those that you use only occasionally. A hired cultivator will probably do all the turning over of soil that you would want in a day. A post-hole borer will make erecting a fence easier but, unless you are putting up a lot of fencing, it is much better to hire one rather than have it taking up valuable space. A shredder is another example of a bulky and expensive item that you may prefer to hire rather than buy.

The condition of hired tools can vary enormously, and powered tools that are not well maintained are a potential hazard. Always satisfy yourself about the condition of tools that you hire – and never leave the shop without receiving instructions or advice if you don't know how to use the tool. This applies especially to potentially dangerous tools, such as chainsaws, hedge trimmers and cultivators.

Protective clothing may be necessary for the safe operation of some tools (goggles, ear protectors and gloves, for example). A good hire shop will be able to advise and should supply these with the tools.

DIGGING TOOLS

SPADES

A most basic garden tool, usually intended for digging and planting – though there are specialist kinds for digging out post holes and drainage trenches, for example, that are used mainly by professionals.

Of all the gardening tools that you will buy, this is the one that will cause you the most physical stress if you make the wrong choice. If you can afford it, a stainless steel blade will make digging easier: it slides through the soil more efficiently and soil falls off the blade more readily (especially important for clay soils).

Blades coated with a non-stick finish are also useful, but the coating will wear off in time with regular or heavy use. Ordinary carbon steel is perfectly satisfactory if you don't use a spade often and if you clean it after use.

If you have an allotment, or regularly dig a large area of ground, the normal blade, which is about 28 × 19 cm (11 × 7 in) is best. If you don't mind lifting heavy loads, it might be worth considering one with a larger 'heavy' blade – usually about 30 × 20 cm (12 × 8 in) – to speed up the job.

For occasional use in a small area, and for planting or digging among established plants, one with a smaller blade, about 23 × 13 cm (9 × 5 in), is likely to be more useful. These are usually called border spades, but if you find bending and lifting difficult they may be the best option for all your digging jobs.

A long-handled spade makes digging less hard on the back and anyone over 1.75 m (5 ft 7 in) tall is likely to find a long-handled version of benefit.

Where infirmity or disability make the use of an ordinary spade impossible, an 'automatic' spade that works on the spring and lever principle may be the answer. This throws the soil forward as you pull back on the handle – the weight of the soil does not have to be supported and the height of the handle can be adjusted. They are, however, more expensive, difficult to use in a confined area, and not very good for digging holes.

The length of the spade is more important than the material from which it is made or coated, or the shape of the hilt (handle). Historically, hilt shape often reflected regional preferences, but nowadays most spades have a D-shaped hilt. These are perfectly satisfactory for most people, but if you have large hands and wear gloves for gardening, make sure the space is large enough for comfort.

A 'tread' (a flattened area on the top of the blade, on which the foot is placed) can make digging more comfortable over a long period. The benefits are less obvious if you wear tough boots or Wellingtons for digging, and some types of spade – stainless steel, for example – don't have them because of manufacturing difficulties.

FORKS

Forks are sometimes used instead of spades on heavy clay soils. They are lighter to use and easier to push through hard or sticky ground. Forks are versatile tools, however, and are widely used for lifting bulky material such as manure and garden compost as well as harvesting root crops which might be damaged by the blade of a spade. Special potato-lifting forks, with broad flat tines on a larger head, are available, but these are only really a worthwhile investment if you grow a large amount of potatoes or other root crops.

The standard fork head has four tines (prongs) and measures about 30 × 20 cm (12 × 8 in), but border forks for light work or confined areas are available, with heads about 23 × 13 cm (9 × 5 in).

POWERED CULTIVATORS

If you have a large area of ground that has to be cultivated annually – an allotment, for example – or need to bring a neglected or new garden into a good condition for planting, cultivators can save an enormous amount of effort.

Electric cultivators are adequate for a small area near to a power supply. They are less expensive to buy, not so noisy, and quite easy to manoeuvre (be careful of the trailing cable). Petrol cultivators are generally much more powerful, and the only practical option where there is no convenient power supply.

Front-engined cultivators have the digging rotors behind the engine and driving wheels. They are not so good for deep cultivation, but steering them is relatively easy. Mid-engined cultivators don't have wheels but instead are propelled by the rotors as they turn to cultivate the soil. The weight of the engine above makes deep cultivation easy, but control and manoeuvring is a skill that has to be acquired. Rear-engined cultivators have the rotors on a boom in front of the engine and wheels. Although they can be tiring to operate, deep cultivation is easy and they are more manageable in difficult-to-reach areas.

With a good cultivator it should be easy to adjust the depth of cultivation. A wide range of attachments (such as a potato lifter) is available, but a more useful feature to look for is a handle that can be adjusted for angle as well as height. If it can be pivoted sideways it will enable you to walk along behind the machine without walking over the area you have just cultivated.

WEEDING & CULTIVATING TOOLS

Many of the tools described here serve more than one function.

HOES

Hoes come in many shapes and sizes. Choose one with a handle long enough to be able to use without stooping too much. Some have a shaped or angled handle, which helps to position the blade at the right angle so that you don't have to bend excessively.

A **Dutch hoe** (with an angled, roughly D-shaped head) is the most versatile all-round type. It is used with a pushing motion, while walking forwards or backwards. This chops off weeds just below the surface. It also helps to aerate the soil.

A **draw hoe** is used with a chopping motion. It is more difficult and tiring to use for general weeding but the curved neck may make it easier to use among growing plants. Its major advantage is the ease with which soil can be drawn up around plants (to earth up potatoes, for example). It is a useful tool for making a seed drill, which can easily be drawn out by holding the hoe at an angle with one corner of the blade in the soil.

CULTIVATING TOOLS

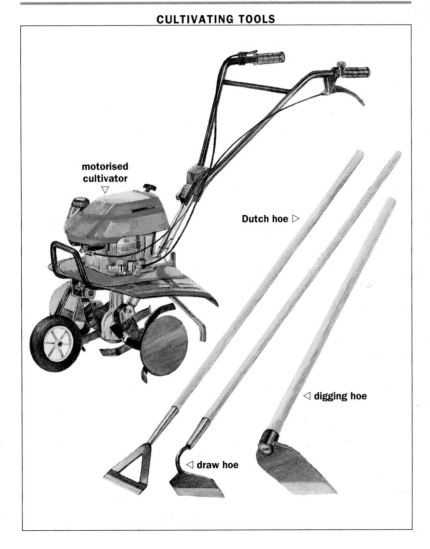

motorised cultivator ▽

Dutch hoe ▷

◁ digging hoe

◁ draw hoe

An **onion hoe** looks like a small draw hoe on a short handle – it is used while crouching or bending. It is useful when working in confined spaces, such as in a rock garden or herbaceous border, not just between rows of onions!

Digging hoes are less popular, but very effective in some situations. They have a chisel-like blade set at an angle to the head, and are used with a swinging action (like a pickaxe). They are sometimes used instead of a spade, but can also be used to loosen difficult weeds that need deeper penetration than is provided by a Dutch hoe. This type of hoe is also handy for drawing up earth around plants. A variation has a prong on the opposite side from the chopping blade, designed to break up hard soil. These are usually known as **combination hoes**.

Proprietary hoes usually have blades with a distinctive shape. The Swoe, for example, has a small blade that cuts on three sides, convenient when working among crops or plants growing close together. Proprietary hoes vary in their usefulness as much as in their designs.

MANUAL CULTIVATORS

Manual cultivators come in many shapes and sizes. They are mostly used for weeding and loosening the earth, or for breaking down large lumps of soil left after digging. Most have three or five angled prongs which dig into the soil as you pull on the handle. The weight of the head, the angle of the prongs and the design of the points all contribute to ease of use. The central prongs of some hand cultivators can be removed, so that the tool can be used to loosen the soil and weeds, while leaving a row of seedlings in the centre untouched.

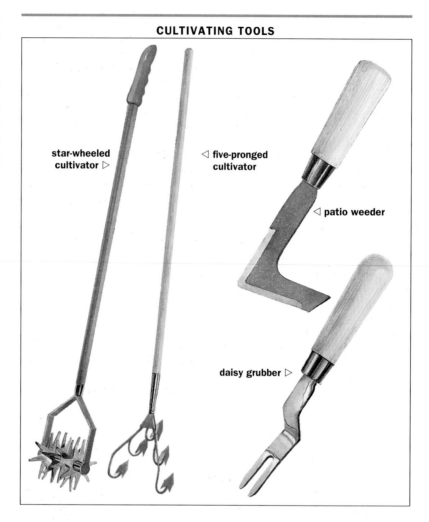

CULTIVATING TOOLS

star-wheeled cultivator ▷

◁ five-pronged cultivator

◁ patio weeder

daisy grubber ▷

Alternative designs of head include a star-wheeled cultivator, intended for breaking down soil into a finer structure, suitable for seed sowing.

RAKES

There are several kinds of rakes for specific jobs (*see* Lawncare tools, page 439), but ordinary garden rakes are used for levelling the ground, removing large stones and other debris, breaking down lumps of soil into a tilth, and preparing the ground for sowing or planting.

Inexpensive rakes sometimes have nail-like teeth, but these are now uncommon, and the best rakes are those with a one-piece head. The ideal number of teeth and their spacing, along with the width of the head, will depend on the use for which it is intended. A standard head with about 12 teeth is adequate for most garden jobs, but if you have a large area of ground to rake regularly, a wide head with perhaps 16 teeth should do the job more quickly. The bigger and heavier the head, however, the more tiring the tool is to use.

A long handle will make the work less tiring, and should be better for your back. Handle length and the overall balance of the tool are likely to be more important than the material from which the handle is made.

HAND FORKS

For loosening soil and levering up weeds, and also for planting, a small fork is ideal. If there are many weeds, a long-handled version, with a handle about 90–120 cm (3–4 ft) long, will reduce the amount of bending and give better leverage.

DAISY GRUBBERS

These little tools can be handy not only for removing daisies and dandelions from a lawn, but for removing individual weeds from an area of cultivated ground. The forked blade is long and narrow, and is used with a levering action.

PATIO OR PAVING WEEDERS

Designed for use in the narrow gaps between paving, these weeders have a narrow pointed or hooked blade.

BRUSHWOOD CUTTERS

Similar to nylon line trimmers (*see* Lawn-care tools, page 439), brushwood cutters are designed for rougher work, slashing through tough weeds and undergrowth. Many have a metal rotating blade, though nylon lines can also be used with some.

Electric versions are not as tough and powerful as petrol versions.

PLANTING TOOLS

Although trees, shrubs and large perennials are usually planted with a spade, bedding plants, bulbs and small border plants are usually planted with a trowel. A bulb planter can also be useful if you have a lot of bulbs to plant.

TROWELS

A simple planting tool, but trowels vary considerably in design. Carbon and coated (chrome-plated) trowels are relatively inexpensive, but cheap ones soon begin to rust if not cleaned properly after use. Stainless steel trowels will give many years of use, and you don't have to be so methodical about cleaning them (although it is very easy as you need only to wash or wipe the blade).

A wide blade is an advantage for general planting, but a narrow-bladed trowel is particularly useful if you are working among plants in a confined space, such as in a rock garden.

The quality of a trowel is often shown in the handle. Cheap wooden ones may soon split or come free from the blade if not adequately maintained. High-quality wood, well secured to the handle, will last for years. Plastic and plastic-coated handles can be comfortable to use; they are often brightly coloured, which is an advantage as it makes the tool easier to spot if left lying among plants. Metal handles are uncommon, and tend to be cold to use in winter.

Long-handled trowels – the handle is usually about 30 cm (12 in) long – are useful for planting where you have to reach across other plants, or if you want to reduce the amount of bending that

you do. The long handle also produces more leverage if you have difficulty making a hole in hard ground.

BULB PLANTERS

These are worth considering if you plant a lot of bulbs. They are designed to remove a core of soil – even the compacted earth of a lawn – which is replaced over the planted bulb. Some have a planting depth guide to assist you in making holes of the appropriate depth.

DIBBERS

Dibbers make a narrow hole, suitable for planting vegetables such as leeks and cabbages. Although they compress the soil, the earth can be firmed against the roots by inserting the tool again slightly to one side and pressing it into contact with the roots. Sometimes the soil is washed in around the roots by filling the hole with water after planting.

Traditional dibbers resemble a cut-

down spade handle with a T-shaped top, but pointed at the end. Some are steel-tipped to make penetration easier and to prolong the useful life of the tool. A few are all metal.

Small pencil-sized dibbers are sometimes used to make small holes for seedlings when pricking them out.

WIDGERS

These simple spatula-shaped tools are helpful when pricking out seedlings or planting very small plants.

PRUNING & CUTTING TOOLS

SECATEURS

The most important of the pruning tools, secateurs will cope with most routine pruning jobs around the garden. Most secateurs are only intended for branches up to about 1 cm (½ in) thick, so thicker branches need loppers (long-handled

pruners) or one of the pruning saws (*see* page 438).

There are two main types of secateurs, by-pass and anvil:

By-pass secateurs, the most common, have two cutting blades, as scissors do, and make a clean cut provided the blades are sharp.

Anvil secateurs cut with one sharp blade moving against a blunt anvil. Because the anvil is made of a softer metal it does not blunt the blade, as you might imagine, but the blade must be kept sharp to avoid crushing the stem rather than cutting it cleanly.

A third type, **parrot-beak**, is less common: these have a scissor-like action like the by-pass but the two blades curve towards each other.

Flower gatherers are like secateurs but grip the flower stem after cutting.

Quality counts. Cheap secateurs probably won't last long, an expensive pair will probably last a decade or more,

PRUNING AND CUTTING TOOLS

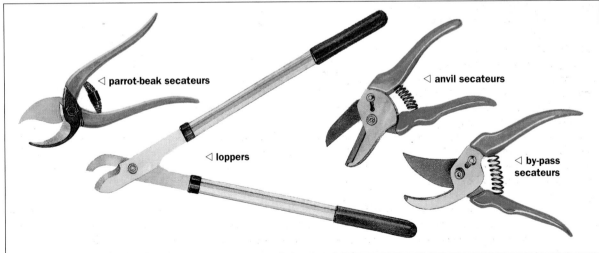

◁ **parrot-beak secateurs**

◁ **loppers**

◁ **anvil secateurs**

◁ **by-pass secateurs**

PRUNING AND CUTTING TOOLS

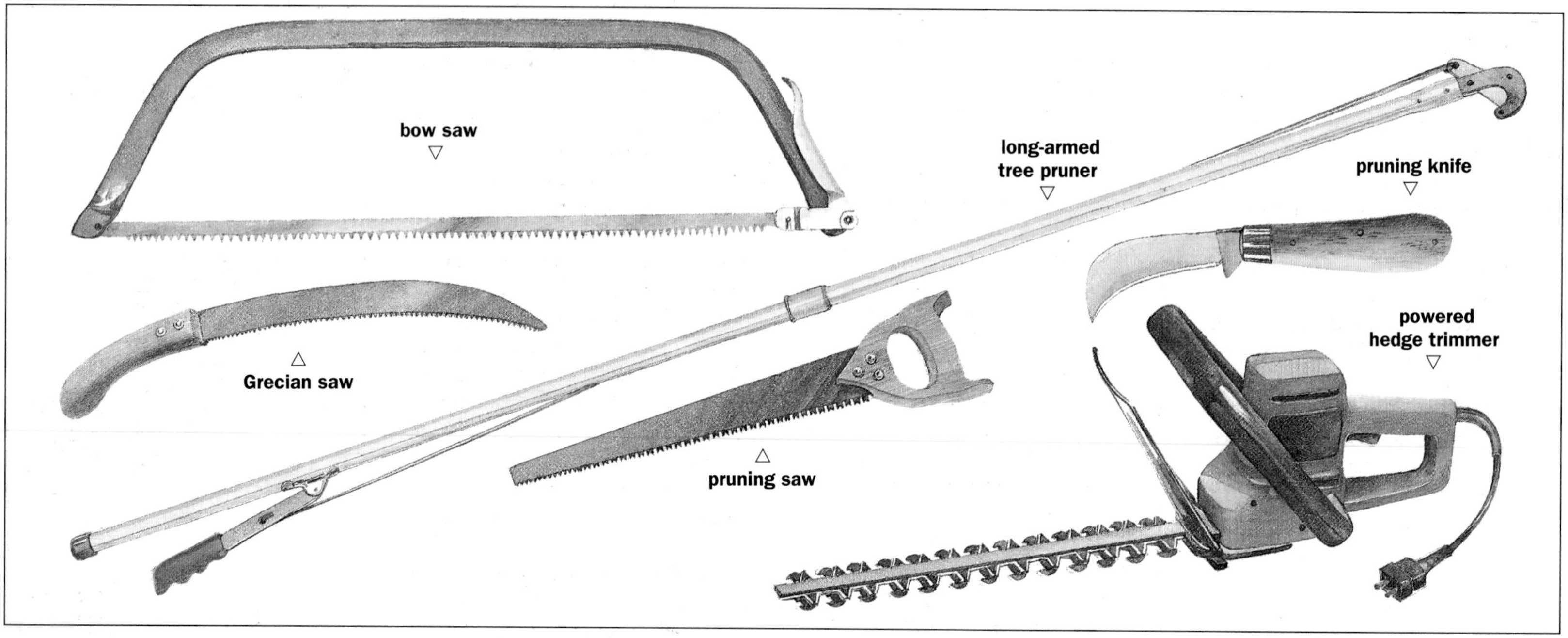

bow saw
▽

Grecian saw
△

long-armed
tree pruner
▽

pruning knife
▽

powered
hedge trimmer
▽

pruning saw
△

and spare parts will be available to keep them working well. If you want them only for occasional pruning, or perhaps cutting back herbaceous plants, you may be quite happy with a cheap pair.

LOPPERS (LONG-HANDLED PRUNERS)
Use loppers for cutting through thicker branches, about 1–2 cm (½–1 in) thick. As with secateurs there are both by-pass and anvil types. Their larger blades and the leverage of the long handles make the job relatively effortless, and some have a ratchet mechanism to make it easier to deal with thick stems.

Weight and balance are important, as you will probably have to use them on branches above head height.

LONG-ARMED TREE PRUNERS
These are designed to cut through branches – usually up to 2–3 cm (½–1 in) thick – that are too high for loppers or secateurs. They have a long reach and may have an extension mechanism. The blade is operated by a lever or rope.

PRUNING SAWS
For any branches more than 2–3 cm (½–1 in) thick you will need a pruning saw. A straight-edged single-sided type with its handle set at an angle is the best general-purpose saw for pruning. A Grecian saw (with a curved blade) is for working in a confined space. Although a bow saw is useful for cutting up pieces that have already been removed, the large handle makes it difficult to use in

a restricted space, and double-edged saws with tapering blades are difficult to use without the other edge damaging parts of the plant that you want to retain.

PRUNING KNIVES
Unlike an ordinary knife, the blade of a pruning knife is curved to control the cut more easily. They are popular with some professionals, but are potentially dangerous if used carelessly.

Some pruning knives also have a special blade for budding.

GARDEN SHEARS
Shears are intended primarily for hedge trimming but are useful for deadheading plants such as heathers and for cutting down the dead stems of herbaceous

plants. They are also used sometimes for trimming the overhanging grass on lawn edges (though long-handled shears are better for this).

Wavy-edged blades are designed to make it less easy for stems to slip out as the blades are closed, and may be better for cutting thicker stems.

There is often a notch towards the handle end of the blade. This is intended for cutting the odd shoot that would otherwise be too thick to cut.

Single-handed shears are intended only for light work and are not suitable for cutting a hedge although they can be very useful for tidying up grass verges.

POWERED HEDGE TRIMMERS
After a powered lawnmower, these are

one of the best investments if you have a lot of hedging to cut. They save both time and effort.

If the hedge is not too high or long and within easy reach of an electricity supply, an electric hedge trimmer is relatively inexpensive, reliable and easy to use. Great care must be taken with the trailing cable (take it over your shoulder and through a belt, with the cable always behind you), and the supply must always have an RCD in the circuit to reduce the risk of an electric shock in the event of an accident. For a small hedge, a battery-powered version may be adequate – and less hazardous.

Petrol models are usually more powerful, have longer blades, and will deal with tougher stems. They are usually heavy and extremely tiring to use, however, if you are not used to working with this kind of trimmer regularly.

Irrespective of power supply, safety features such as blade guards, shields and quick stopping are very important.

Some cut on only one edge, others on both. Although in theory you can use two-sided blades to save time by cutting with a back and forth sweeping motion, many gardeners find it more natural to cut in just one direction.

Double-action or reciprocating blades (in which both blades move) are generally considered less tiring to use as they vibrate less than single-action blades (in which only one blade moves).

CHAINSAWS

Use with great caution. Chainsaws are useful for cutting down a small tree, but are best not regarded as a pruning tool in the hands of amateurs. Unless you are familiar with all the safety precautions, it is best to have a professional remove

ELECTRICAL SAFETY

Electrically powered tools – even those operating at mains voltage – are used safely by gardeners everywhere and tragedies are fortunately rare. However, deaths and serious injuries do occur, and it will be no consolation to know that the odds are remote if you or a member of your family is a victim. Don't take chances, then you are much less likely to become a tragic statistic.

Always follow the specific advice given by the manufacturer carefully, especially regarding the safe positioning of cables while in use, and always use a residual current device (RCD) in the circuit. This will almost instantly detect any change in the current caused by an accident and disconnect the supply before any potentially lethal shock is received.

Do not clean equipment while it is still connected to the power source.

branches thick enough to demand the use of a chainsaw.

LAWNCARE TOOLS

LAWNMOWERS

The lawnmower is perhaps the most important tool in the garden. Powered mowers have made hand-pushed models almost obsolete, but they are still available and for a very small lawn they can be useful. Some people welcome the exercise that they provide.

Side-wheeled hand mowers are light, easy to push, and perfectly adequate for a simple utility or play lawn. Mowing up

to the edge of the lawn is difficult unless there is a level mowing edge to support the wheel. Rear-roller models produce the striped effect so often sought, but are generally heavier to push.

There are many types of powered mowers, from the most basic to ride-on petrol versions. Choice depends on lawn size, lawn type and budget.

For most small gardens, electric mowers are adequate and convenient, as well as less expensive. The trailing cable is a potential hazard, so mow in such a way that the cable never lies across your route over the lawn. The electrical supply must always have an RCD to reduce the risk of electrocution in the event of an accident.

Petrol mowers are the only practical alternative for a larger garden, or where there is no power supply available. They are generally more powerful than electric versions and, although heavier, the engine takes the effort out of pushing. They are impractical on steep banks, however, since as well as being awkward and heavy, the carburettor is liable to flood.

Cylinder mowers have a rotating cylinder of blades that cut against a fixed blade; this gives a high-quality cut and is suitable for formal lawns. They have a large rear roller which flattens the cut grass in the direction of travel and leaves a striped effect.

Wheeled rotary mowers cut with a slashing action from a fast-rotating blade, carried at the cutting height by wheels in front and behind. These produce a striped effect only if they are fitted with a roller for this purpose. They are usually better at coping with long grass than a cylinder mower, and although the quality of cut is generally inferior, most do a satisfactory job.

LAWNCARE TOOLS

◁ powered lawn rake

◁ hand lawn rake

long-handled shears ▽

△ hollow-tined aerator

Rotary mowers have either metal or plastic blades, and on some models there is a choice. The main advantage of a plastic blade is safety.

Hover mowers also work on a rotating blade principle, but the blade is suspended above the ground by a cushion of air which is created within its hood-like protection. As there is minimal friction between the mower and the lawn, these machines are light and easy to handle.

Originally many wheeled rotary and hover mowers did not have a grass box, and the finely chopped grass clippings were simply left on the surface (where they soon become inconspicuous), but many models now collect the clippings in a box or bag. The capacity is important if you have a large lawn, as you could spend a lot of time emptying a small grass collector.

The greater the cutting width, usually the more quickly any given area will be cut. But wide mowers are more difficult to manoeuvre and sometimes physically more demanding to use.

LAWN RAKES AND SCARIFIERS

Lawn rakes are intended for raking out moss and dead grass (thatch) from around the grass roots, and for gathering leaves and debris. Hand lawn rakes come in many designs, one of the most popular (spring-tined) having wire-like tines that are springy and act like a penetrating comb. Others have flat tines, which may be made of metal or plastic.

Scarifiers or scarifying rakes cut more heavily into the grass to remove thatch more effectively, but are not intended for jobs like leaf gathering.

Lawn rakes and scarifiers are tiring to use on a large lawn. A powered lawn rake will do both jobs quickly and easily.

AERATORS

Opening up compacted soil and introducing air into the soil around the grass roots helps to stimulate lawn growth. Hollow-tined aerators (which take out a core of soil) are best for this, and there are both hand and powered versions. Slitters are also available, but these only cut slits into the turf and penetration may not be good if the soil is hard.

NYLON LINE TRIMMERS

These are valuable tools that earlier generations of gardeners would not have imagined. They are used to trim grass in awkward areas than cannot easily be reached by a mower, and for trimming a lawn edge. They are also useful for cutting down weeds, especially those growing close up to a fence or other inaccessible places.

Like mowers, trimmers can be either electric or petrol-driven. Petrol models tend to be heavier, noisier, and possibly more difficult to handle, but will usually cope with tougher growth and there is no cable to worry about. Electric models may be more convenient for light use in a small garden.

Always try holding a selection of trimmers before you buy. Make sure the balance and height feel right. A second and adjustable handle will make the trimmer easier to hold and balance.

Some come with refinements such as automatic line feed, cutting guide and a swivel head for trimming lawn edges.

LAWN EDGERS

Trimming the edges of a lawn is a cosmetic rather than an essential task. It can be done with hand shears if you don't mind the bending, or there are several tools specially designed for the job.

Long-handled edging shears allow you to work from a standing position, but they are still tiring to use. Powered trimmers produce a very neat edge quickly and for little effort. A few electric mowers also have an edging attachment that will do the job for you. Nylon line trimmers can also be used as lawn edgers by turning them on their side; some have a special swivel head to adapt them for this purpose.

HALF-MOON EDGERS (edging irons)

To produce a neat, straight edge to a lawn the crescent-shaped blade is pushed into the turf with a slight rocking movement. Use a straight-edged piece of wood, held firmly with the feet, for a cutting guide. If you cut back the edges too often, the flower beds will become larger and the lawn smaller, so use this tool sparingly. It may be better to repair the edges from time to time, rather than constantly slice off slivers of grass (see February, page 44).

LEAF SWEEPERS

For a small lawn a leaf rake is sufficient to keep it relatively free of leaves in the autumn, but for a large garden surrounded by lots of deciduous trees, a leaf sweeper could be an investment. Most work on the principle of picking up the leaves as the tool is pushed along, with a bag or box collecting them ready to put on the compost or leaf heap. There are also powered versions which work like outdoor vacuum cleaners.

CARRYING TOOLS

WHEELBARROWS

Invaluable if your garden is large, wheelbarrows can be used not only for moving garden debris, but for carrying tools, manures and fertilisers, and most of the heavy or awkward items that you will need to use around the garden. Many come in a simple kit form that is easy to bolt together.

Traditional wheelbarrows have a conventional wheel in front, which is fine on a hard surface, but a problem if you have to push the barrow over loose soil or rough ground. For this a barrow with a plastic ball instead of a wheel is likely to be easier to push.

CARTS AND TROLLEYS

For some jobs garden carts (with two wheels and pram-type handles) are more stable and easier to load and unload than a single-wheeled barrow. However, they are less manoeuvrable, especially on uneven ground. Trolleys, with four wheels and a low platform for loading, are useful if you have to move heavy loads, such as bricks or paving slabs. They sometimes have places for stacking garden tools as well.

BAGS AND SHEETS

A large wide-mouthed bag or a strong plastic garden sheet with handles is extremely useful for moving lightweight garden waste, such as hedge trimmings or leaves. These weigh little, fold away flat when not in use, and can be lifted, carried or pulled over any kind of ground.

TRUGS

Traditionally wooden, but nowadays often plastic, trugs are shallow baskets with a single arched handle across the centre. They are intended for gathering cut flowers or when picking fruit or harvesting vegetables, but they are also good for collecting weeds.

SOWING AIDS

GARDEN LINES

You can improvise with string and a couple of sticks, but for sowing straight rows outdoors a proper garden line is most helpful; it is not expensive and will last for years.

SEED SOWERS

These are designed to space out seeds evenly, and are usually intended for use in drills outdoors. Wheeled ones with a long handle reduce the need to bend when sowing. Seed sowers for trays have protrusions that make depressions for the seeds when pressed into the compost.

You may need to shake some hand sowers to operate them. This shaking or vibrating motion may require practice to perfect, but all seed sowers should help you to sow more evenly.

POTS, TRAYS & MODULES

POTS

Plastic pots are popular commercially because they are cheap and light to handle and transport. Clay pots are still used, however, for their aesthetic and decorative qualities, and some gardeners prefer the porosity of clay. The majority of plants are equally happy in either.

Normal plant pots are about as deep as they are broad, but a variety of differently proportioned pots are available. Seed pans are shallow pots which can be used for seed and shallow-rooting plants such as some cacti. Deeper than usual pots (long Toms) are useful for plants with deep roots that will remain in their pot for a long time.

Ring culture pots are large bottomless

pots made from whalehide (a kind of bituminised paper), used for growing tomatoes and certain other plants above gravel beds where the garden or greenhouse border soil is not suitable (*see* April, page 101).

Whalehide is also used to form sweet pea tubes, and for other seedlings that produce long root systems quickly.

Biodegradable peat pots are sometimes used for plants that will eventually be planted out into the garden, such as sweetcorn seedlings, but they require careful watering to maintain the right moisture content. Expandable compressed peat pots are used for a variety of purposes, but mainly for plants which will be planted out in the garden later, or to start off rooted cuttings of house or greenhouse plants that will then be moved into ordinary pots. As the pots

rot down, the young plants can be transplanted pot and all, without the disturbance of knocking them out.

SEED TRAYS

Like pots, these come in a variety of sizes. They are almost always made of plastic, and the quality varies considerably: some will last only one or two seasons, others last for many years. Trays with drainage holes are more useful.

MODULAR SYSTEMS

These comprise individual cells (often held in a more rigid outer seed tray) in which either only a very few seeds are sown, or a single seedling or cutting inserted. This makes thinning easier and ensures that each plant receives adequate compost and space. Root damage is minimised when the seedlings are planted out

as the roots will not have become entangled as they do in a normal seed tray of shared compost.

WATERING EQUIPMENT

Water is a precious commodity and all responsible gardeners should take steps to minimise the amount of water they need to use in their garden. The two most obvious steps are to mulch beds when they are moist, with a thick layer of compost, and to collect rainwater. There are water butts available for this which can be linked to the guttering.

WATERING CANS

Cans come in many shapes and sizes, but consider ease of use before style or appearance. For general garden watering,

MODULAR/CELL SYSTEMS

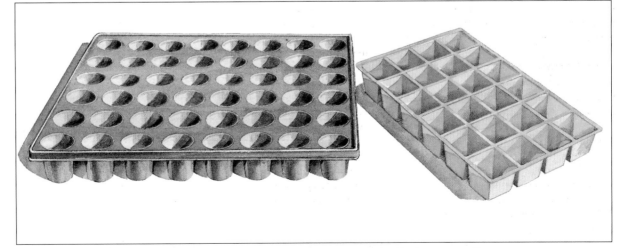

Seedlings usually transplant better from a modular system of cells like these, as their roots are not damaged when they are separated from other seedlings in the tray. Some systems, such as the one on the left, require less compost than a tray of the same size, but most seedlings will suffer if there is insufficient compost to sustain growth. There are many proprietary modular and cell systems for seedlings and most of them require an outer tray to hold them rigid; some are designed to fit a standard or half-size seed tray.

a 9 litre (2 gallon) can is a good compromise between adequate capacity and weight. Plastic is the most widely used material, but galvanised metal will usually outlast many of the cheap plastic versions. Plastic cans come in a wider range of designs, however, and you may find some of these better balanced and easier to carry. For the greenhouse and indoors, a special design with a long spout will make watering much easier. These usually hold less than the normal outdoor can because they often need to be lifted up high to water plants and seedlings on the greenhouse staging. Make sure you can fit your hand around the handle of a small can easily.

Interchangeable roses are desirable: a coarse one for general watering, and a fine one for seed beds and seedlings. A sprinkler bar attachment enables more precise watering which is very useful when applying weedkillers.

Watering cans are not expensive and it is worth keeping a separate one just for weedkillers, to avoid any accidental contamination when watering.

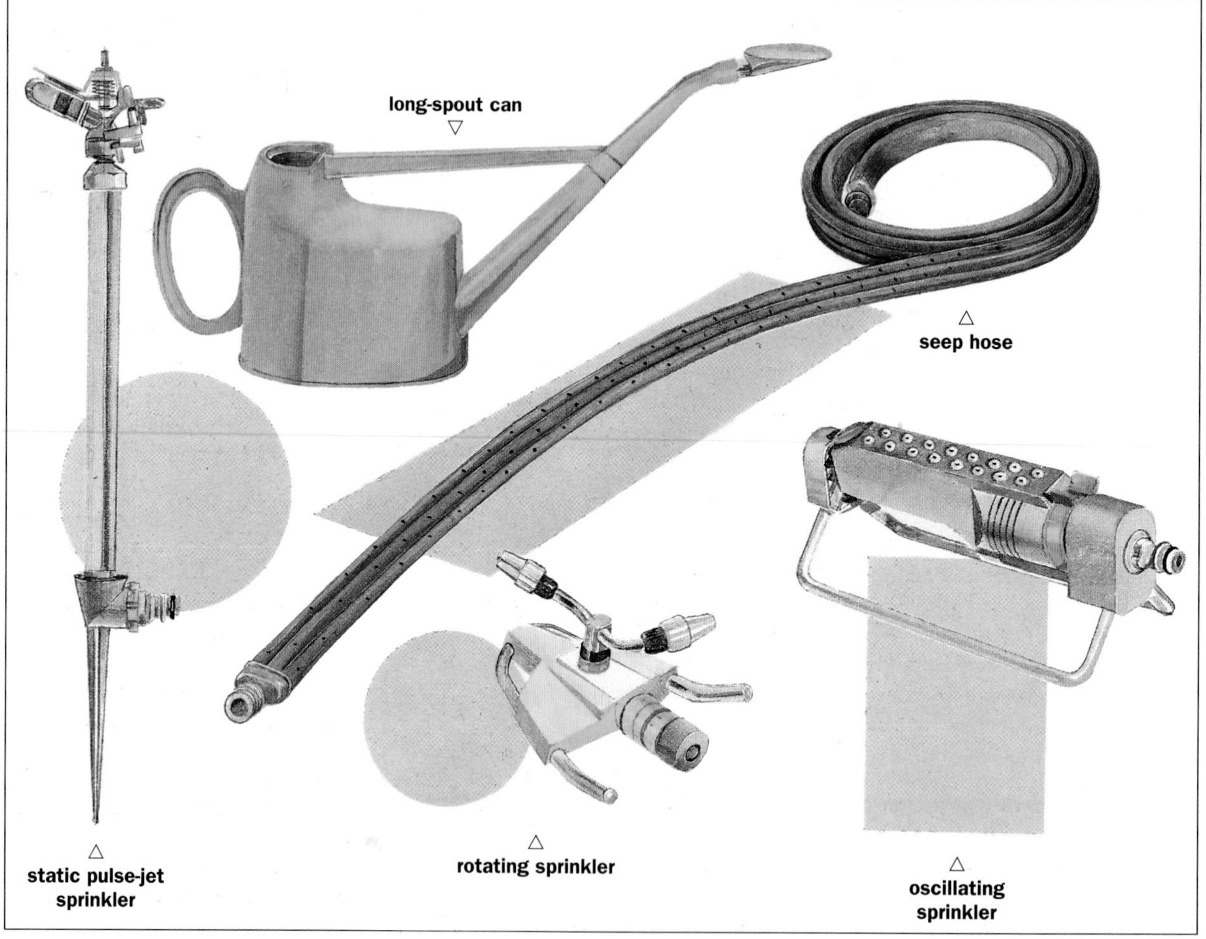

HOSEPIPES

A hose takes most of the physical work out of watering. Most are made from PVC, but the design and degree of the reinforcement varies. Double-walled and reinforced hoses are less likely to kink. Fold-flat hoses are easy to store, but can be troublesome to wind up as the water must be drained out, and they are prone to kinks while in use.

A hose reel will eliminate most of the frustrations associated with hosepipes.

SEEP & SPRINKLER HOSES

Laid along rows of vegetables, or in beds and borders, these provide a gentle flow

WATERING EQUIPMENT – SHOWING SPRAY PATTERNS

long-spout can

seep hose

static pulse-jet sprinkler

rotating sprinkler

oscillating sprinkler

of water to the base of plants. Sprinkler hoses have rows of fine holes on one side; turned upwards, they act as fine sprinklers, turned downwards the water goes directly into the soil.

Seep hoses have small holes which allow the water to seep out. Some can be buried in the soil, others are for surface use only; some can be used either way.

SPRINKLERS

Sprinklers are widely used for lawns, but are also suitable for beds and borders.

The simplest type of sprinkler is static with a head on a short spike pushed into the ground; this commonly waters in a circular pattern. They are used mainly for small lawns. Rotating sprinklers, which deliver the spray through rotating arms,

also cover a circular area, but larger than that normally achieved by static sprinklers. Oscillating sprinklers have a perforated bar that sweeps from side to side. The area covered by any spray will depend on the pressure of the water.

There are many refinements to these basic sprays, including stems to raise the head above the surrounding foliage,

DRIP-FEED SYSTEM

Drip feeds are a satisfactory method of watering individual plants in pots in the garden or in the greenhouse. For just a few plants, a manually topped-up reservoir like the one illustrated above is adequate. However, if you have a lot of plants that need watering it is advisable to choose a reservoir that is connected to the mains.

CAPILLARY SYSTEM

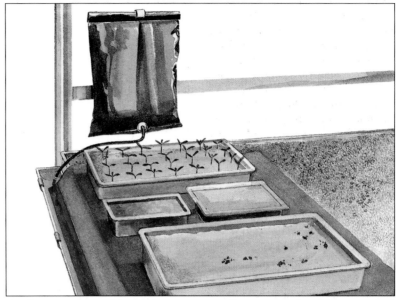

Capillary systems are widely used for watering plants kept on a greenhouse staging. Kits can be purchased, but they are easy to improvise using readily available capillary matting. If possible, connect them to a mains-fed reservoir, but a hand-filled one is adequate if you have just a few plants that need watering.

which is useful for beds, and multi-heads which give a choice of spray shapes.

TRICKLE & DRIP-FEED SYSTEMS

Because of the cost, these are generally reserved for watering in the greenhouse or for containers outdoors. Some systems can be fed from reservoirs topped up manually, but most are connected to a mains supply through a hosepipe. A flow reducer is usually part of a mains system.

There are many proprietary systems, but most work on the principle of a network of small hoses, connected by T-pieces and other fittings, so that each container or plant has its own small hose delivering a periodic drip of water. The individual flow can usually be adjusted.

TIMERS

Timers can be used to control the length of time an ordinary sprinkler is connected, or form part of a more sophisticated automatic watering system. These devices vary widely in price and complexity: the more expensive ones have more timing programmes available to them.

Bear in mind that timer-controlled systems will also water when the ground doesn't need it unless you use manual override or have them connected to a system that detects moisture levels in the soil. Such systems control the flow by sensors in the soil or compost, or by special cones fitted to the delivery nozzles that open or close the supply of water according to the moisture content.

CAPILLARY SYSTEMS

Capillary action can provide a simple way of watering plants on solid staging in the greenhouse. It is also a useful temporary solution for the care of house plants or small potted plants during periods when they have to be left unattended, such as when you are away on holiday.

Commercial growers sometimes use sand beds, but the simplest method is to buy proprietary capillary mats, which can be cut to size. Pots (without crocks in the bottom) are placed on the mat, one end of which is immersed in a reservoir. As long as both compost and mat are moist initially, the water in the reservoir is drawn up into the compost through the mat, where the mat and compost come into contact.

Special reservoirs and control tanks can be bought for the purpose, but a length of guttering in front or at the end of the bench makes an acceptable improvisation. The reservoir must be kept topped up by hand or by an automatic system connected to a mains water supply.

Greenhouses, frames & cloches

Greenhouses and frames (cold or heated) enable a much wider range of plants to be grown than would be possible without the protection they afford. They also enable you to extend the growing season, to benefit from the luxury of early strawberries or late lettuces for example. Cloches also provide useful protection, mainly in the vegetable plot, but they can be used to help vulnerable rock and border plants through the winter, or to protect blooms on low-growing flowers from adverse weather.

There are many types however, and for the best results it is important to choose one suited to your specific needs.

GREENHOUSES

When choosing a greenhouse, always buy the biggest you can afford and accommodate. You will always be able to fill the space, and a small one will soon make you frustrated with its limitations in busy times, such as the spring. To economise on fuel costs, partition off a section for heating in the winter leaving the rest of the greenhouse to provide welcome shelter for the wide range of plants that benefit from winter protection, especially if it is insulated.

Any greenhouse is better than no greenhouse, and a small one, even a mini-greenhouse, will increase the range of plants that you can raise and grow.

The main shapes and their advantages are set out below, but there are some general points to be considered.

MATERIALS

Aluminium alloy is the most popular choice for the framework, combining strength and low weight with a narrow profile (which allows more light to penetrate). Erection is simple – usually the components just bolt together, and the glass is held in position with special clips.

Timber is still frequently chosen on aesthetic grounds. Wood requires more maintenance, however, and regular painting is essential to keep the greenhouse looking good and to extend its life. This applies especially to the less durable timbers. Cedar is a popular choice of wood because it has a natural resistance to rot and does not require regular painting, but it should be treated every year or two with a cedar preparation to help retain its colour.

Galvanised steel is strong, but seldom used. Exposed areas must be painted to prevent rust.

For the glazing, glass is still much the best all-round material and is more commonly used than anything else. The light transmission is good and it does not scratch or discolour with age, unlike plastic. Plastics are useful for a curved profile, or where safety is important.

POSITION

When most greenhouses were made of timber, with thick glazing bars that could cut down the light, much thought was given to positioning to give the best light penetration. The principle was to orientate the greenhouse with its long axis running north to south if it was used mainly in the summer, but east to west if good light in spring (for raising seedlings for example) was the most important factor.

In most small modern gardens, there often is not much choice of position, but most modern greenhouses are made of aluminium alloy which has a small profile and the panes of glass are usually large, so light loss is marginal.

A more important consideration, if you are heating the greenhouse in winter, is to avoid a windy, exposed position, as wind lowers the temperature and thus increases the fuel bills. Try to position the door on the leeward side of the prevailing wind. Try, also, to avoid shade from trees and tall hedges.

The greenhouse will also work better if it is positioned where you can provide a power source for heating, lighting and propagators. Supplementary lighting on dark days can then make up for any slight loss of light penetration.

VENTILATION

Adequate ventilation is essential. When choosing a greenhouse, always consider the number and type of opening windows, or 'lights', that it has – many are sold with an inadequate number of ventilators. You can usually buy additional ones as optional extras, and it is easier to install these when you erect the greenhouse. Install plenty of louvre vents in the sides and low down at the end, and if possible have hinged ventilators along half the length of the roof. This combination creates a better movement and exchange of air, which will help to keep the greenhouse atmosphere healthy and easier to cool on hot days.

Automatic vent openers work on the principle of metal or wax expanding or contracting according to temperature changes, and it is well worth investing in at least one or two. The temperature can sometimes rise rapidly early in the morning, and a couple of vents which open automatically will prevent excessive temperatures building up before you can open the rest of them manually.

If you have a power supply, a ventilation or extractor fan is a useful accessory.

INSULATION

This should be your first priority. You could recoup the cost of installing insulation within a few seasons if you attempt to keep the greenhouse more than just frost-free over winter.

Double-glazing is one of the most efficient methods of insulation, but adds considerably to the cost, and is normally only used where the initial cost is not a significant consideration.

Bubble plastic or even just plastic sheeting is inexpensive enough to replace after a few seasons, and makes a significant reduction to heating costs; for most small greenhouses it is the most efficient form of insulation. It is quite easy to fit (see October, page 241) although it does reduce the amount of light available during the winter.

There are also various proprietary insulation systems available on the market, such as thermal screens, but these are more appropriate to commercial than domestic use.

TRADITIONAL GREENHOUSE

Blinds will help to control shading, but choose ones that are easy to adjust. This type can be controlled by cords which enable the blinds to be unrolled partly or completely, as necessary. When fully unrolled the blinds should provide some protection for the sides as well as the roof.

An extractor fan fitted with a thermostat will also prevent the heat building up and will assist in the movement of air.

A propagator, ideally with a mist unit, will enable a much wider range of seeds and cuttings to be propagated. Using a propagator may avoid the need to heat the whole greenhouse to a high temperature.

Louvre ventilators must be close-fitting to avoid cold draughts in winter, but they are a useful way to control air flow in summer. Ordinary ventilators can be used instead, but side ventilators of any kind are best placed low down to create good circulation of air.

Roof ventilators are essential. It is a good idea to add extra ones. Fit an automatic opener on at least some of them to prevent heat building up when you are not around to adjust the ventilation manually.

A power supply with its own greenhouse control panel will make greenhouse gardening less of a chore. Thermostatically controlled electric heaters and propagators can be run efficiently and you can even add supplementary lighting for better plant growth during the dull months.

A water butt is useful even if you have a mains supply for an automatic watering system. Some plants benefit from the use of rainwater rather than tap water and it will reduce the amount of water you have to take from the mains.

Automatic watering systems are invaluable and may help to prevent plant losses in hot weather or if you are away for a few days. A capillary bench is useful for pot plants, while plants in the greenhouse border can be watered by a drip-feed system.

Greenhouse space is valuable, so make the most of it by adding extra shelves or staging when they are most needed – during spring if you raise a lot of plants from seed, for example. Automate the greenhouse as much as possible using thermostatically controlled heaters, some automatic ventilators and a suitable watering system. Then disaster will not strike if you go away and cannot attend to your greenhouse for a day or two.

An electric fan heater is particularly efficient because it also creates air movement, which helps to distribute the heat quickly. If fitted with a thermostat an electric heater may not cost much more to run than heaters using other types of fuel.

HEATING

There is no ideal heating system for everyone, as much depends on the temperature you want to achieve, whether the greenhouse is well insulated, and the cost and availability of fuel.

Electricity is the most convenient way to heat your greenhouse, and if close to the house it may be easy to provide a power supply without much expense. If it is a long way away, you will need to have a supply installed and connected by a qualified electrician. This could make installation expensive.

With thermostatic control and good insulation, running costs of an electric heater may not be any higher than other forms of heating. And there is the big bonus of convenience.

Electric tubular heaters are usually positioned at the sides of a greenhouse, just above the floor, but fan heaters have many advantages. They distribute the heat quickly and efficiently, and you can use them as cooling fans with the heating element switched off in warm weather.

Paraffin heaters are relatively inexpensive to buy and install, but running costs can be high if you need to maintain a high temperature. You also have to carry and replenish the paraffin. They may produce toxic fumes and excessive condensation if care is not taken to ventilate the greenhouse adequately.

Gas systems can sometimes be run off the mains supply, but usually the position of the greenhouse means using bottled gas. Propane gas releases fumes and water vapour as it burns so, as with paraffin, you must ensure that ventilation is adequate. Bottled gas is useful for achieving a high temperature if mains electricity is not available, but running costs can be high, and you will have to manhandle heavy gas cylinders regularly. You must have at least two bottles connected by an automatic switching device in case one runs out.

FLOORING & STAGING

A central path of some kind is essential for easy access to the plants, but it will take up valuable growing space. Path space, greenhouse width and the type of plants that you wish to grow have a bearing on each other.

Paving slabs are the most practical form of path and they can simply be bedded on to sand. If the greenhouse is placed close to an area paved with bricks or clay pavers, you may prefer to use the same material for aesthetic reasons.

Preformed wooden paving panels can look pleasing but are more likely to harbour debris and pests, so you should be prepared to remove and clean them occasionally. Bed them on gravel to ensure free drainage.

If you are tall, and the ridge of the greenhouse is low, consider sinking the path by 15 cm (6 in) or so – you can build a low retaining wall of bricks to contain the border soil.

In all but the tiniest greenhouse, staging (slatted or solid shelving) will provide a home for plants in pots and a surface on which to work.

Slatted and mesh staging is particularly useful for plants that like fairly dry air and compost and good ventilation, such as cacti and alpines. For most pot plants, solid benching is often more practical and can be covered with a layer of sand or capillary matting if extra humidity is required. If you are using a sand system a lipped edge is helpful, but a flush surface is suitable for capillary matting. Some systems can be reversed to suit the particular need.

If storing dormant plants below staging, slats can provide extra light, but beware of drips from above.

For many gardeners, fixed staging along one side supplemented by free-standing staging along the other, offers flexibility to suit various needs throughout the year.

MAKING THE MOST OF SPACE

Think about the way in which you will use your greenhouse.

If you are mainly going to grow pot plants on staging, then a greenhouse wider than 1.8 m (6 ft) may be a waste. Most proprietary staging for a small amateur greenhouse is about 60 cm (2 ft) deep (anything wider is difficult to reach across) and a central path 60 cm (2 ft) wide is usually adequate.

If the greenhouse is to be used mainly for border crops, such as tomatoes, chrysanthemums or winter lettuces, then a greenhouse 2.5 m (8 ft) wide will increase the growing area by about 50 per cent – at much less than a 50 per cent increase in cost.

Rather than running a path the entire length of the greenhouse, leave 60 cm (2 ft) at the end for more staging or for

GREENHOUSE SHAPES

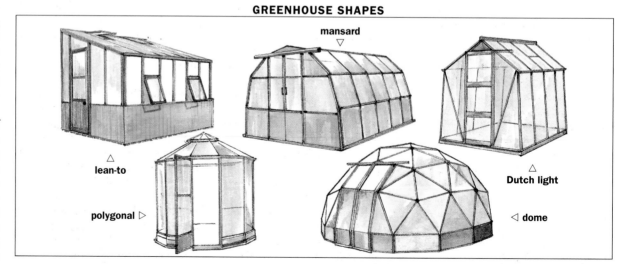

mansard ▽

lean-to △

polygonal ▷

Dutch light △

◁ dome

growing crops in the border. This gives you the maximum growing space with the minimum area taken up by the path.

In a very large or wide greenhouse, you can run the path around the outside edge with a large bench in the centre. This is more appropriate for ornamental displays of pot plants than for a mixed-use amateur greenhouse.

To make maximum use of space, dormant plants can 'rest' below the staging.

SHAPES

TRADITIONAL SPAN

Most greenhouses are this shape, and the design generally offers a large amount of usable growing space for relatively modest cost, and is suitable for many crops.

The smaller sizes may have limited headroom. Look for a good height to the eaves if you are likely to want to grow tall pot plants on staging, and if you are tall yourself, check that the ridge is high enough so that you can work comfortably standing up.

If you plan to grow mainly pot plants and seedlings, choose a design with a solid base up to staging level (the insulation is usually better). Choose a design with glass to the base if you plan to grow crops in the greenhouse border, or to stand tall plants (such as tomatoes and chrysanthemums) in pots or growing bags on the ground.

DUTCH LIGHT

This design is superficially similar to a normal span greenhouse, but the sides slope, and the panes of glass are much larger. The sloping sides help to make the most use of available light, and the glass-to-ground design makes it well suited for tall crops in the border.

Bear in mind that, if there is an accident, the large panes of glass will be more expensive to replace than the traditional, smaller ones.

MANSARD (curvilinear)

The curved shape, created by angling the rows of glass, is intended to make the maximum use of available light. The additional light penetration may be minimal in most small gardens unless the greenhouse can be sited in an open, sunny position, but some people find this type of design visually more pleasing than the traditional span greenhouse.

LEAN-TO

A lean-to is effectively half a greenhouse with the ridge supported against a wall. The distinction between some of the larger modern ones and a conservatory or garden room is blurred. Some can be used primarily for people or for plants, but they are obviously less ornate than a proper conservatory. The true lean-to greenhouse will also have its door at the end, and is not intended for positioning against patio doors.

A lean-to has many advantages. It is usually comparatively easy to run heating and light from the house, the back wall is ideal for training tender climbers against, and with suitable staging the entire height from floor to ridge can be used for an ornamental display. Warmth is generally retained by the bricks and a lean-to should not lose heat as rapidly as an equivalent size glazed all round.

Light is more likely to be a problem than with a free-standing greenhouse. If the wall is south-facing it may be difficult to keep the greenhouse sufficiently cool on hot days, so an effective shading and ventilating system is essential. If

positioned on a north wall, the lack of direct sunlight may limit the types of plants that can be grown successfully.

A variation on the normal lean-to is the three-quarter span, which has a normal ridge and a short extra span of roof sloping down towards the wall against which it is fixed. Light penetration may be marginally better, but this design is now very uncommon.

DOME

Dome-shaped greenhouses have multi-angled panes that create a shape with very little wind resistance (good for an exposed site), and they can look very stylish. Headroom and growing height may be limited around the edges, however, and you will probably have to use the manufacturer's staging and fittings.

POLYGONAL

Octagons and other polygonal shapes usually provide only limited growing space, and ventilation can sometimes be a problem, but this type of greenhouse is usually chosen for its visual appeal. A greenhouse of this type can look appropriate in a small garden or even on a patio, where a traditional shape may appear out of place.

CONSERVATION GREENHOUSE

The few greenhouses with this label are generally much more expensive for a given growing area. Their advantage lies in reduced running costs and low energy consumption for heating. Plants may also benefit from high light levels created within the greenhouse by the angled roof and side panels and reflecting mirrored surfaces inside. Double-glazing and a high level of built-in insulation are features of this type of greenhouse.

MINI-GREENHOUSE

These are usually small lean-tos, but a range of small, free-standing pyramidal shapes is now available. All the space is intended for plants, and you must work from outside. Mini-greenhouses have low running costs and take up little space.

It is important to choose a design with adequate ventilation and to site your mini-greenhouse so that it receives good light but is not in direct sunlight for most of the day.

THE ALPINE HOUSE

A useful addition to a rock garden is an alpine house. This differs from the conventional greenhouse in that there must be continuous ventilation along the eaves of the house and vents at bench level, with, ideally, a door at both ends. Here alpine plants that require controlled conditions to achieve their full potential, such as those which will not tolerate winter wet, can be cultivated, although some of the commoner species can be grown in here too. No heat is necessary, although some growers keep their houses at a minimum of 1°C (34°F).

FRAMES

Cold frames are perhaps most widely used for relieving the pressure on space in the greenhouse in spring, and for acclimatising plants raised in the greenhouse to the colder temperatures outdoors. With or without a greenhouse they are invaluable in summer for growing vegetables, in winter for protecting slightly tender plants, and throughout the year for the propagation and protection of seedlings and cuttings.

Most cold frames follow the traditional design of a low front and high

MAKE YOUR OWN FRAME

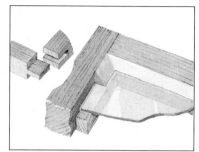

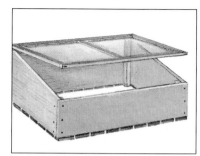

1 A frame can be made quite easily from 19 mm (¾ in) exterior-grade ply and planed softwood battens. Adjust the sizes to suit your need.

2 Glue and screw the battens to the basic frame, then attach the sides. Cut recesses for two strong hinges at the back for securing the 'light' or top.

3 Joint and glue the top of the frame together, then fix the glass using glazing battens glued and nailed into place. Bed the glass on putty.

4 Hinge the top of the frame so that it opens easily for access and ventilation. It can be held open with a window opener or small blocks of wood.

back, with a sloping top (called a 'light'). The purpose of the slope is to catch as much light as possible, and to discourage rain and snow from lying on the top.

The most commonly used material for ready-built or ready-to-assemble cold frames is aluminium alloy. Frames that come as a kit can be easily assembled simply by bolting the pieces together. Aluminium alloy frames are often glazed to the ground. These let in plenty of light, which is a significant advantage for many crops, such as lettuces and seedlings, and the sides can be insulated against excessive heat loss in winter with pieces of expanded polystyrene.

A frame is not difficult to construct from scratch. A brick framework offers particularly good insulation while timber also offers reasonable insulation and is easier to work with. You can also buy timber-sided frames, though they are likely to be more expensive than the home-made variety.

Glass is the best glazing material, but clear plastic is adequate.

CLOCHES

Cloches are usually used to warm up the soil for early sowing of vegetables and to protect and advance them for early cropping. Those with tall sides or removable tops can remain in position around those crops that benefit from extra protection, such as aubergines and peppers. To get the most from them, use cloches to extend the season at the end of the year by protecting late sowings of crops such as lettuces and for overwintering plants such as parsley.

Choose a cloche type that suits the purpose for which it is likely to be used. Some of the least expensive ones are perfectly adequate for soil-warming and encouraging early growth, but may have only limited use beyond that.

BARN

The extra height of most barn cloches, and the greater usable height close to the edges, because of the almost vertical sides, make the barn cloche the most

useful and versatile design, although they are more expensive than simpler designs such as tent cloches. A removable top will make watering and weeding easier.

TENT

The simple inverted V shape of the tent cloche makes it an inexpensive choice. The angle of the glazing where it meets the soil, and the overall low clearance,

make tent cloches most suited to soil-warming, germinating seeds and for early protection of young crops until they become too tall.

DOME

These short tunnel-like, one-piece cloches are easy to move around. Although the height may be little more than some tent cloches, the curved profile enables crops

TYPICAL FRAME

to be grown much closer to the edge than in some other cloche types. They are likely to be more expensive than tent cloches, however.

TUNNEL

Continuous tunnel cloches are generally used in the vegetable plot, for advancing crops such as carrots and for general soil-warming prior to sowing. They are also widely used to cover early strawberries, to encourage an early crop and to protect the fruit from birds. Both ventilation and access for weeding and harvesting is achieved by ravelling up the sides.

The cloches are sold as kits, with hoops to push into the ground, a length of plastic sheet and tensioning wires to hold the sheet in place. The covering is only likely to last for a couple of seasons, but is inexpensive to replace. Always use heavy-duty plastic treated to resist the destructive effects of UV light. The hoops and wires will last for many years.

Semi-rigid plastic tunnel cloches are also available. These come in short lengths with the plastic held in place in a wire frame. A series of cloches can be placed end to end to make a longer tunnel. Use special end pieces to prevent the cloche becoming a wind tunnel.

FLOATING CLOCHES

These do not look elegant, and are really only practical in the vegetable plot, but they are very effective. Within limits, they stretch or expand as the crop grows, so you can leave them over carrots and even cabbages, to provide protection from pests, such as butterflies and moths.

They consist of a sheet, usually made from perforated plastic or horticultural fleece, weighted or pegged down around the edge of the bed with special plastic

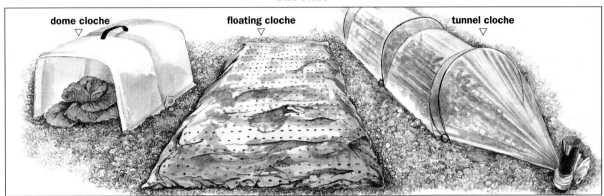

CLOCHES

dome cloche ▽　　floating cloche ▽　　tunnel cloche ▽

pegs. Some environmental meshes can be used in a similar way. The sheet has to be removed for weeding, but water will penetrate through the small holes.

There is some natural stretch that allows space for the growing crop, and further growth can be accommodated by loosening the edges of the sheet as it becomes necessary. Low-growing crops can be protected until ready for harvesting, but the sheet must be removed from taller crops once the early protection is no longer needed.

Frost protection will not be as good as with most other types of cloche, but a floating cloche will help to warm the soil, will aid germination, and almost certainly produce better yields than crops which are unprotected.

INDIVIDUAL CLOCHES

Small individual cloches are useful for putting over single plants that require a little protection. Some are made from waxed paper, others from plastic. Large plastic drinks bottles with the bottoms

cut off are excellent, but leave the top off for good ventilation.

POLYTUNNELS

Plastic tunnels, shaped over special curved frames, are widely used commercially, where appearance is unimportant but cost is crucial. If you have a large garden, however, it is worth considering a polytunnel for an unobtrusive area.

Polytunnels are not usually heated, so the main benefit is derived from wind and weather protection, but the plants within them are almost always more advanced than those in the open garden. Many bedding plants can be grown on without additional heat, once the period for frosts has passed.

Although you can use staging in polytunnels, crops are usually grown in the ground or in containers on a weed-suppressing groundsheet.

The plastic covering will stay in good condition for only a couple of seasons, but is relatively inexpensive to replace.

Ventilation is often a problem, so a door at each end that can be opened or rolled up is an advantage.

WATERING AND WEEDING

If the cloches are to be used just for short-term soil-warming and early protection, the weeding can be done once the cloches have been removed. If cloches are to remain in place for a long period, however, choose a design that allows easy access, or one where the whole cloche can be lifted and replaced without too much effort.

Sideways penetration of water in the soil will provide some moisture for the roots of established plants but for rapid and full germination the soil must be kept moist as well as warm. Many growing crops, such as carrots, also require regular watering in dry weather. Some cloches are designed to allow water to penetrate through small holes, and a few have a built-in hose watering system, but for most you will have to remove the cloches temporarily for watering, or run a seep hose beneath the cloches (see Tools & equipment, page 442).

Glossary of gardening terms

Use this glossary to find an explanation of any horticultural term used in the main part of the book that you are not familiar with. You will also find many technical terms that are not used elsewhere in this book but which have been included to make the glossary a useful aid whenever you encounter unfamiliar words in other books and magazines.

A

ACARICIDE
A pesticide used to control mites, such as red spider mites.

ACCELERATOR
A fertiliser, often nitrogenous, added to the compost heap to hasten rotting. Some proprietary compost accelerators also contain bacteria to speed up decomposition.

ACCLIMATISATION
The process of accustoming plants to different (usually cooler and less protected) conditions from those under which they have previously been grown (*see* HARDENING OFF).

ACID SOIL
One with a pH of less than 7.

ADVENTITIOUS
Applied to a root or shoot that forms where it would not normally be expected, usually the result of cutting back the stem or root.

AERIAL ROOT
A root that grows from the stem above ground level. Plants such as ivies use them to assist climbing, and some plants, such as philodendrons, use them for support and to absorb moisture and nutrients from moist air.

AIR LAYERING
Method of propagation in which the 'layer' is made by packing damp moss around the stem of the plant (*see* page 433).

ALGAE
Primitive green plants that form a green scum on damp rocks, paths and flower pots. Free-floating algae cause green water in ponds, and filamentous aquatic algae produce blanketweed in ponds.

ALGICIDE
Chemical for controlling algae.

ALGINATE
Chemical soil conditioner made from seaweed. It is used to bind fine particles in heavy soil to produce a more crumbly texture.

ALKALINE SOIL
One with a pH value above 7.

ALPINE
Strictly a plant that grows naturally in the Alps or similar mountains. Alpines are adapted to mountainous environments by their dwarf, compact habit and deep, extensive root systems. The term usually refers to any plant suitable for growing in rock gardens, and includes dwarf forms of shrubs and conifers.

ALTERNATE
Term applied to leaves that are placed singly at different heights and on alternative sides of the stem. Leaves which grow in pairs up a stem are called **opposite**.

ANNUAL
A plant that grows, flowers, sets seed and dies within the space of one growing season.
Hardy annuals, such as cornflowers and larkspur, are usually sown outdoors in March or April. They will tolerate frost; some may be sown outdoors in September or October and overwintered in favourable areas of the country.
Half-hardy annuals will not withstand frost and must either be raised from seed under glass and planted out when danger of frost is past, or sown outdoors in late May or early June when frosts are unlikely. Some plants grown as half-hardy annuals are perennials, for example antirrhinums and fibrous-rooted begonias, but are best treated as half-hardy annuals.
Tender annuals, such as celosias and schizanthus, are best grown in a greenhouse or conservatory. Some tender annuals are sometimes grown outdoors as summer bedding plants in favourable areas of the country.

ANTHER
The pollen-bearing terminal point of the stalk or filament that forms the flower's male organ, the stamen.

APEX
The tip of a shoot or branch. A shoot situated at the apex of a plant is termed **apical**.

AQUATIC
A plant that lives in water. It may float on the surface and root in the mud at the bottom of a pond or stream, like waterlilies, or be free-floating like water hyacinths (*Eichhornia*). Some are completely submerged, such as Canadian pondweed (*Elodea*), or have both submerged and aerial parts, like parrot's feather (*Myriophyllum*) (*see* MARGINAL PLANTS).

ARBORETUM
A collection of trees and shrubs grown for botanical rather than decorative interest, though many are decorative as well.

AREOLE
A small depression or raised, cushion-like area on a cactus that bears spines or wool.

AROID
A member of the Araceae family, which includes anthuriums, philodendrons and monsteras among the house plants, and lords-and-ladies (*Arum maculatum*) among the hardy plants.

AUXIN
Naturally occurring or synthetically produced plant growth substance, affecting root formation, shoot growth and other processes.

AXIL
The angle between a leaf stalk and the stem to which it is joined. It often contains a shoot or flower bud.

AXILLARY BUD: *see* BUD

B

BACK-BULB
A dormant old pseudobulb on an orchid, without leaves.

BACKFILL
To refill a planting hole settling the soil around the roots of the plant.

BALL: *see* ROOTBALL

BALLED
A plant lifted from the field and sold with a ball of soil around the roots secured in place with a piece of hessian or plastic material (which must be removed when planting).

BARK RINGING
The removal of a partial or complete ring of bark from a tree – often an apple or pear if the aim is to encourage a reluctant fruiter with over-vigorous growth to produce a crop. This is seldom necessary with modern dwarfing rootstocks.

BASAL
Applied to a shoot or bud arising from the base of a plant.

BASAL-ROOTING
A bulb that roots from the base only. Most European and American species of lilies are basal-rooting (*see* STEM-ROOTING).

BASE-DRESSING
Fertiliser or manure dug into the soil before sowing or planting.

BEARD
Dense growth of long hairs, usually yellow, which occurs at the upper end of the falls of flag irises.

BED
Any clearly defined plot of cultivated ground within a garden.
Island beds are usually surrounded by lawn or paving, and are generally of an informal, curved shape. Tall plants are placed in the centre and low-growing plants near the edge.

BEDDING PLANTS
Any plants raised in quantity for a temporary garden display. A wide range of hardy and half-hardy annuals, biennials and perennials, and some tender species, can be used. Planting or bedding out is traditionally done twice a year: in late spring or early summer for a summer and early autumn display, and in autumn for a spring display.

BERRY
Stoneless fruit, in which the seeds are protected by a fleshy outer covering, such as gooseberries.

BIENNIAL
A plant that completes its life-cycle in two growing seasons. Foxgloves,

for example, germinate and form a rosette of leaves in the first season, then flower, set seed and die in the second year.

BIENNIAL BEARING
The habit of bearing alternately light and heavy fruit crops. The habit may start if frosts kill the blossoms one year, resulting in a heavy crop the following year if the weather is more favourable.

BIGENERIC
A hybrid that combines the genetic factors of two different genera. Most hybrids are the result of crossing plants of different species but of the same genus. For instance, X *Fatshedera lizei* is a bigeneric hybrid between *Hedera helix* (ivy) and *Fatsia japonica* (false castor oil plant) – different genera but both members of the same plant family Araliaceae. The large multiplication sign before the name indicates that it is a bigeneric cross – in common usage this symbol is often omitted.

BISEXUAL
A plant that has both stamens and pistils in the same flower.

BLANCHING
Excluding light from the stems and leaves of vegetables to make them more palatable and tender by preventing the formation of chlorophyll. The parts to be blanched can be earthed up, wrapped in thick paper, or covered with a flower pot or proprietary cover sold for the purpose. Celery, leeks, chicory and seakale are commonly blanched.

BLEEDING
Excessive loss of sap from a tree or plant after being cut. This is more apparent in spring when the sap is rising; vines should not be pruned then. Beetroots whose skin is damaged during lifting will also bleed, and lose their red pigment.

BLIND
A term applied to a plant without a terminal growth or flower bud. This is usually due to physical damage or disease and often results in cessation of growth.

BLOOM
1. The whitish or bluish powdery or waxy coating on a leaf or fruit. This is easily removed by rubbing or handling.
2. An alternative name for a flower.

BOG GARDEN
Garden constructed in association with a stream or water garden. The marshy soil, which must be permanently wet, is suitable for growing **bog plants** such as water irises and rushes.

BOLTING
Running to seed, particularly prematurely. Lettuce may bolt in hot, dry weather, either before or as soon as the hearts have formed.

BONEMEAL
A natural, slow-acting fertiliser, containing phosphate and a little nitrogen. Bonemeal is sterilised but gloves should be worn when handling it (and other chemicals) as a precaution (*see* page 389).

BONSAI
An artificially dwarfed tree. The dwarfing technique consists of severe root restriction, and pruning and pinching back of growing shoots. The gnarled appearance of a bonsai tree, which should be grown in a shallow container to restrict root growth, is achieved by cutting back the main stem repeatedly over a number of years. The shape is induced by careful training on wires.

BORDEAUX MIXTURE
General-purpose copper-based protective fungicide which will prevent a number of fungal diseases such as potato blight and leaf spots.

BORDER
A cultivated area of garden running beside a path, boundary fence or wall. Borders are chiefly planted with herbaceous subjects, but roses, fruit bushes (with fruit trees trained against the boundary wall) and annual flowers are equally effective. Shrub and mixed borders (those containing both herbaceous shrubs and perennials, and sometimes annuals) are also popular.

BRACT
A modified leaf, often brightly coloured and petal-like, associated with flowers that themselves lack size or colour. The colourful parts of a poinsettia are its bracts. Some bracts are small and scale-like, however, and serve mainly to protect the buds.

BRASSICA
Generic term for members of the cabbage family, such as broccoli, Brussels sprouts, cabbages, cauliflowers, kales, savoys, swedes and turnips.

BREAK
Side growth or shoot formed from the main stem of a plant. Formation of these shoots occurs naturally in such plants as chrysanthemums. Artificially stopping or pinching out the growing tips encourages new shoots earlier than when the plant is left to grow naturally.

BROADCAST
Seeds sown broadcast are spread evenly over an area of ground, rather than in drills. Grass seed is sown in this way, as are annuals where the desired effect is irregular groups.

BROMELIAD
A member of the Bromeliaceae family. Most are epiphytic, and the leaves usually form a rosette. Most are stemless or short-stemmed plants with stiff, channelled leaves that direct water inwards to the crown, which may form a 'vase' to hold the water.

BUD
Embryo growing point from which leaves, stems or flowers will develop. **Axillary buds** are situated in the axil of a leaf.
Crown buds are flower buds at the tip of a shoot and surrounded by other flower buds.
Fruit buds (a term used in connection with fruit pruning) are larger than **growth buds**.
Terminal buds are the ones found at the end of a shoot, from which further growth will continue.

BUD STAGES
Different stages of fruit-tree growth, from late winter through early spring, are often used as a guide for when to apply certain sprays. It is therefore important to recognise these various stages which are listed here as they occur.
Swelling: when the dormant – apparently inactive – buds start to increase in size and the outer scales begin to loosen.
Breaking: when green leaves can be seen at the apex of the buds.
Bud burst: when these leaves begin to separate.
Green cluster: the bud scales have dropped off and a tight cluster of green flower buds can be seen within each leaf rosette.
Pink-bud: flower buds are not open, but display a trace of pink or white.
Petal fall occurs after full blossom and before the formation of fruitlets.

BULB
Although the term is often used to include corms and tubers, a bulb is strictly a structure consisting of modified leaves that protect the next season's embryo shoot and flowers.

BULBIL
A small bulb that forms above ground on a few plants. Bulbils can be removed and potted up to grow into normal bulbs.

BULB FIBRE
Medium in which bulbs are grown for indoor decoration, consisting of peat, oyster shell and charcoal. Bulbs grown in this mixture live on the food stored within themselves, and are exhausted after flowering. Its main use is in containers without drainage holes, but watering must still be done with great care.

BUSH
Low shrub with no definite leader, and with branches all arising near ground level.

C

CALCICOLE
Lime-loving plants that thrive in alkaline (limy) soils, such as lilacs and most dianthus.

CALCIFUGE
Lime-hating plants which will not grow in alkaline (limy) soils. Examples are rhododendrons and many heathers.

CALLUS
A growth of corky tissue that forms over a wound, sealing and healing it. A callus forms at the base of a cutting to heal the wound before the roots are produced.

CALYX (PL. CALYCES)
The outer green ring or whorl of a flower, consisting of a number of sepals which enclose the petals. The tubular calyx of a vigorous carnation or pink bloom may burst and produce a shapeless flower. This can be overcome by placing an elastic band or similar round the calyx at an early stage in its development.

CAMBIUM
The narrow layer of bright-green growing tissue between the bark and

the wood of most plants. This moist tissue forms the callus and roots on cuttings, heals wounds and causes grafts and inserted buds to unite.

CAPILLARY MAT
An absorbent mat that holds a lot of water. Plants placed on it can draw up moisture by capillary action.

CAPSULE
Seed case with divisions that give it a number of compartments. The seed heads of irises and poppies are well-known examples.

CARPEL
One of the divisions of a pistil.

CATKIN
Flower spike, often pendulous, which is composed of stalkless, unisexual flowers. Birch, hazel and willow bear catkins.

CERTIFIED STOCK
Stock certified by the appropriate official department as being free of certain diseases and pests. Used for plants such as strawberries, raspberries and seed potatoes.

CHELATED AND FRITTED TRACE ELEMENTS
Trace elements are sometimes sold in special forms to make them more available to plants. Chelates, which are a compound of metallic salt and organic acid, are complex substances. They remain available to plants even in soil conditions where elements become unavailable to some plants. Iron is the most common chelated element and is used to help acid-loving plants grow on alkaline soil. Manganese, zinc, copper and boron are also available in this form. Fritted trace elements are fused into glassy beads and being insoluble are not leached away; root hairs are able to absorb them.

CHESHUNT COMPOUND
A soluble copper compound to control damping-off disease.

CHIMAERA
Botanically, a plant in which two separate kinds of tissue exist. There are several kinds of chimaera, but the most visible ones cause variegation on some popular plants.

CHIPPING
Nicking the outer coating of a seed. Germination of hard seeds, such as sweet peas, is speeded up by chipping the seed coat with a sharp knife.

CHITTING
1. Allowing a potato tuber to produce shoots before planting.
2. The sprouting or germination of seeds before sowing.

CHLOROPHYLL
The green colouring pigment in plants which enables them to manufacture food from sunlight (*see* PHOTOSYNTHESIS).

CHLOROSIS
An unhealthy yellowing of foliage, usually caused by a deficiency of iron or other trace elements. Most common in lime-hating plants growing in alkaline medium.

CHRYSALIS
The stage in the life of an insect between the larva (or caterpillar) and the winged insect. It is a papery capsule within which the larva completes its growth before becoming an adult insect.

CLADOPHYLL
Also called **cladode**. A modified stem that simulates a leaf in appearance and function: butcher's broom (*Ruscus aculeatus*) and *Asparagus densiflorus* are examples of plants with cladophylls.

CLAMP
Old-fashioned method of storing root crops in the open. A potato clamp is formed by heaping the potatoes into a pyramid and covering them with a 30 cm (1 ft) thatch of straw, topped with 23 cm

(9 in) of soil, to keep out frost. A 'chimney' of straw is left in the top of the clamp for ventilation.

CLAY: *see* SOIL TYPES

CLIMBER
A plant that ascends towards the light. Climbers may attach themselves to such supports as walls, fences and trellis by aerial roots, leaf stalks and tendrils. Other plants twine their stems round the supports, or may be self-clinging by means of sticky pads.

CLOCHE
A small, portable structure, usually glazed with glass or a plastic material, used to warm the soil and provide protection from the weather. **Floating cloches** are plastic sheets designed to cover the soil or crops, which are perforated to let some moisture through and flexible enough to allow crops to grow beneath them (*see* pages 448–449).

CLONE
The collective term for plants which have originated from one individual plant by vegetative means. 'Bramley's Seedling' apple trees, for example, form a clone, since they are the result of grafting material of the original specimen on to rootstocks.

CLOVE
1. A type of border carnation which is strongly scented.
2. A small bulb in a cluster of shallots or garlic.

COMPOSITE
Member of the Compositae family of plants, better known as the daisy family. The apparently single flowers are made up of many smaller **florets**, either neuter or each with petals and stamens or stigma.

COMPOST (POTTING SOIL)
The medium in which pot plants are grown. Traditionally loam-based composts were used and these were

standardised with the John Innes formulae. Lack of good quality loam and the light weight and clean handling of peat made peat-based composts popular. In turn this put a strain on the ecology of peat bogs and now peat-substitute composts have become more important. These are based on a variety of waste products such as coir and bark. Most composts are intended for potting up established plants.
Ericaceous compost has a lower pH than other types and is intended for lime-hating plants that require a more acid compost.
Hanging-basket compost may have superabsorbent polymers (water-retaining crystals) added to reduce the risk of the soil drying out.
Multi-purpose compost is suitable for a variety of purposes.
Special composts are also formulated for **seeds** and **cuttings**.

COMPOST, GARDEN
The substance produced from organic waste material that has decomposed on a compost heap or in a WORMERY (see page 459).

COMPOST BIN
Wood, plastic or wire mesh holder, in which garden compost is made.

COMPOST HEAP
A mound of vegetable material such as garden and kitchen waste, left to decompose into garden compost.

COMPOUND
Applied to a leaf, flower or fruit composed of several similar parts, such as a rose leaf, a daisy flower, or a strawberry fruit.

CONIFER
Tree or shrub, usually evergreen, which bears its seeds in cones. Pines, firs and cedars are conifers. The cluster of flowers or fruit is a cone.

CONTROLLED-RELEASE FERTILISER
One in which the nutrients are

released only when the soil temperature is warm enough for them to be used.

COPPICING
Annual pruning back of trees and shrubs close to the ground to produce vigorous young shoots.

CORDON
A trained tree or bush where the growth of the main stem is restricted and grown at an angle, and lateral shoots are induced to form fruit spurs. This produces a high yield for a fruit tree of modest size. The stems may be erect, but are usually trained obliquely. A double cordon has two trained stems. It is mainly used for apples and pears, but gooseberries and redcurrants can also be trained.

CORM
A swollen stem base that usually remains underground and stores food during the dormant season. If cut across, no distinct layers of leaves can be seen, unlike in a bulb.

CORMLET
A young corm which forms around the parent corm; gladioli and crocuses produce cormlets. They are easily detached and will usually flower after being grown on for a year or two.

COROLLA
The interior petals of a flower, or at least the inner ring of petals. These can be separate as in an anemone flower, or fused like a daffodil.

COTYLEDON
Seed leaf (the first to emerge upon germination, which often looks very different from the normal leaves). Plants that are monocotyledons produce seedlings with one seed leaf, dicotyledons produce two.

CROCKS
Pieces of broken clay pot placed over the drainage hole inside a pot to prevent the compost from being washed through the hole. If pieces

of broken clay pots are not available, coarse chipped bark or gravel will serve a similar purpose.

CROP ROTATION
System whereby vegetable crops are grown on different parts of the plot in successive years. This reduces the risk of diseases building up in the soil, and makes the best use of available nutrients (*see* page 283).

CROSS: *see* HYBRID

CROTCH (OR CRUTCH)
The angle where the main branch joins the stem or trunk of a tree.

CROWN
The point at which the stem and roots meet at soil level.

CROWN BUD: *see* BUD

CULTIVAR
The correct name for a variety raised in cultivation, as opposed to a naturally occurring variety. The juniper *Juniperus communis depressa* is a naturally occurring variety, but *J. c.* 'Depressa Aurea' is a cultivar. Note the difference in typographical presentation. In a practical gardening sense the cultivation is the same for both. For that reason, in this book we have used the word 'variety' in a loose sense to cover both cultivars and botanical varieties. This makes the text simpler and avoids distracting the reader from the main, practical purpose of the book.

CUTTING
A short length of stem used for propagation (*see* pages 428–431).

D

DAMPING DOWN
Watering the floor and staging of a greenhouse to increase the humidity.

DAMPING OFF
A disease, caused by fungi, responsible for losses among very young seedlings (*see* page 407).

DEADHEADING
The removal of dead flower heads from plants.

DECIDUOUS
A term applied to plants, usually trees and shrubs, that shed their foliage in winter. This contrasts with **evergreen** plants, which retain their foliage throughout the year.

DECUMBENT
A botanical term used to describe plant stems which are prostrate for part of their length but which turn upwards at the tips.

DICOTYLEDON: *see* COTYLEDON

DIEBACK
The death of the tip of a shoot due to disease.

DIGGING
Cultivation by turning over the soil to improve its structure, especially if manure or compost is incorporated at the same time. It also controls weeds, and prepares the ground for later sowing or planting. Single or plain digging and double digging refer to the depth to which the soil is cultivated (*see* page 387).

DISBUDDING
Removing unwanted buds to direct a plant's energies into a few buds. It is done to produce exhibition-sized blooms on plants such as carnations, chrysanthemums, dahlias and roses. It is also carried out on young shoots to help shape fruit trees.

DISK
The compact centre of a flower of the daisy family. It consists of many disk florets, each a small tube containing a stamen.

DIVISION
Method of dividing a large plant into a number of smaller pieces to increase the number of plants or to improve the vigour of an old plant (*see* pages 431–432).

DORMANT BUD: *see* BUD STAGES

DORMANT PERIOD
The time when growth slows down and the plant needs less warmth and water. Some plants have no discernible dormant period, but with others it is pronounced. Deciduous trees and shrubs are usually dormant during the winter.

DOT PLANT
Tall-growing plant used as a single specimen in a formal flower bed to provide contrast in height, colour and texture with smaller plants.

DOUBLE
A flower with more than the usual number of petals.

DRAWN
Plants or seedlings that are crowded, or have been grown in poor light, causing the shoots to become thin and weak. To prevent this, sow seeds thinly, and give seedlings and mature plants as much light as possible.

DRIED BLOOD
A quick-acting nitrogenous fertiliser (*see* page 389).

DRILL
A straight, shallow furrow in which seeds are sown outdoors.

DROUGHT
A period of dry weather during which plants are stressed by lack of water. Technically a drought is a period of 15 days during which there has been no measurable rain.

DRUPE
A stone fruit. The seed or seeds (stones) are surrounded by fleshy tissue, as in cherries and plums.

DUTCH LIGHT
A type of greenhouse with large panes of glass and sloping sides (*see* pages 446–447).

DWARF PYRAMID
A trained fruit tree, usually apple or pear, of restricted height, which branches from a central trunk. They are useful for small gardens.

E

EARTHING-UP
Drawing soil up and around plants so that they are covered more deeply than if the soil was level. Potatoes are earthed up to prevent the tubers from turning green through exposure to light. It also protects the plants from frost damage and from blight spores which may fall from the haulm (stems and foliage of the plant) or from the atmosphere.

Celery and leeks may be earthed up to blanch them, and earthing-up the stems of Brussels sprouts and broccoli helps to reinforce them and reduce the risk of wind damage. The soil is drawn around the plants with a draw hoe or spade and left with sloping sides so that surplus water drains away freely.

EPICORMIC
Shoots that develop from latent buds or from the trunk of a tree or shrub. Also called water shoots.

EPIPHYTE
A plant that grows above ground level, usually in trees. Epiphytes are not parasites and only use their host for physical support.

ERICACEOUS
1. A member of the Ericaceae family – the term is sometimes applied to other acid-loving plants.
2. A potting soil or compost specially formulated with a low pH to suit acid-loving plants.

ESPALIER
1. A support of upright posts and horizontal wires upon which espalier trees are trained.
2. A method of training used for fruit trees and ornamental shrubs, such as pyracanthas. Growth is stopped at the appropriate height and branches are trained horizontally at intervals.

EVERGREEN
Trees and shrubs that are always clothed in foliage. The leaves are shed, but not all at once as with deciduous trees and shrubs.

EVERLASTING
Flowers with papery petals that retain their colours after being cut and dried. Helichrysum and statice are among the best-known examples, but there are many more that are suitable for drying. Pick the flowers just before full bloom, in dry weather, and hang them upside down in a dark, cool and airy shed or loft until dry.

EXHIBITION
Term used of highly developed flowers, such as chrysanthemums, dahlias and roses, grown for exhibition purposes.

EYE
1. The centre of a flower bloom when it is a different colour from the rest of the flower.
2. A stem cutting with a single lateral bud.
3. A tuber with a dormant (undeveloped) bud on its surface.

F

FALLS
The lower, pendulous petals of flag irises. Often different in colour from the ordinary upright petals.

FAMILY
A group of related genera.

FAN
A tree, usually a fruit tree, trained against a wall in a fan shape. Plums, peaches, cherries and apricots are all trained this way.

FANCY
Applied to some flowers, particularly exhibition carnations, which have variegated blooms. **Selfs** have blooms of one colour.

FASCIATION

Abnormal plant growth in which several stems become fused together. The flattened and swollen stems may be found on a wide range of flowers, including delphiniums and lilies. It does not do the plant any lasting harm and affected stems can simply be cut out.

FASTIGIATE

Trees and shrubs with narrow, erect growth. Lombardy poplars, flagpole cherries and upright yews are among the common fastigiate trees.

FEATHER

A lateral shoot produced on the current year's growth of a maiden (one-year-old) tree.

FEMALE FLOWER

A flower bearing only the female reproductive organs, the pistils. Many plants bear bisexual flowers with both pistils and stamens, but in other species these occur separately.

FERN

A non-flowering plant which reproduces by spores carried on the undersides of the fronds.

FERTILE

1. A plant which produces flowers and fruit.
2. Soil with a high nutrient level that will yield good crops or plants.

FERTILISATION

The process whereby the male and female reproductive cells fuse.
Pollination – the natural or artificial transference of pollen from anther to pistil – is necessary to effect fertilisation, whereby flowering plants reproduce and set fruit.

FILAMENT

The stalk at the point of which is the anther in a male flower.

FIMBRIATE

Petals with fringed margins.

FLAKED

Bicoloured carnations, in which the ground colour is streaked with broad bands of a second colour.

FLOATING CLOCHE: *see* CLOCHE

FLORET

An individual flower in a compound inflorescence. The flower of a daisy, for example, is composed of central disk florets and outer ray florets.

FOLIAR FEED

A quick-acting liquid fertiliser that can be absorbed through the leaves as well as the roots.

FORCING

Hastening plants into growth, flower or fruit before their time. This can be done by placing them in darkness and applying heat under glass. Narcissus bulbs cooled for a period of several weeks and then forced will flower more quickly than untreated bulbs.

FORMATIVE PRUNING

A method of pruning carried out on young trees and shrubs to establish a basic shape.

FRAME

Usually described as a cold frame, a frame is a glazed wooden or brick structure used to protect or harden off plants. It may be heated.

FRIABLE

Soil of good, crumbly structure, suitable for sowing and planting.

FRITTED: *see* CHELATED

FROND

The leaf-like organ of a fern, which often carries spores.

FROST

Frost occurs when the temperature falls below 0°C (32°F). Ground frost is more frequent than air frost; some plants that would be killed by an air frost will survive a slight ground frost.

FRUIT

Seed-bearing organ of any plant, for example a bean pod or an apricot.

FRUIT BUD: *see* BUD

FUMIGATION

The exposure of pests and disease-carrying organisms in the greenhouse to fumes (usually from a special smoke cone) that will kill them.

FUNGICIDE

Chemical that kills fungi, especially those responsible for diseases.

F1 HYBRID: *see* HYBRID

G

GENES

The hereditary units in each plant chromosome.

GENUS (PL. GENERA)

A group of closely related species that have enough characteristics in common to group them together like a 'family'.

GERMINATION

The process by which a fertilised seed starts to grow into a seedling, following various internal chemical and physical changes.

GLAUCOUS

Having a blue-green, blue-grey or white bloom.

GLOCHID

A tiny, barbed spine or bristle, usually occurring in tufts on the areoles of some cacti. These penetrate the skin easily and can often set up irritation, making some cacti hazardous to handle.

GRAFTING

The practice of joining two living parts of plants so that they form a permanent union. There are various forms of grafting and the technique is widely used commercially for roses, shrubs and fruit trees. It is not often used by amateurs.

Grafting is carried out to control vigour and size, to enable the plant to grow in a wider variety of soils than it would by nature, to create a special shape, such as a standard, and occasionally because the plant is difficult to propagate from cuttings.

GRAFTING TAPE

Tape used to protect a graft while the wound heals.

GRAFTING WAX

A special wax used to seal the wound after grafting or budding, to prevent the tissue drying out or becoming infected by disease spores.

GREASEBAND

A paper band about 10 cm (4 in) wide coated with a sticky substance, applied in late summer around the trunk of a fruit tree about 90 cm (3 ft) above ground level. The band traps female winter moth caterpillars as they crawl up the trunk to lay their eggs in early autumn. Remove and burn the bands the following March.

GREEN CLUSTER: *see* BUD STAGES

GREEN MANURE

A fast-growing leafy crop, such as mustard or ryegrass, grown to absorb and recycle nutrients on vacant ground, and to add humus to the soil, when the crop is dug in before it flowers.

GROUND COVER

Plants that cover the ground with dense growth, suppressing weeds. Most ground-cover plants are low-growing evergreens with carpeting or spreading growth, but plants that die down in winter, such as hostas and some geraniums, are also used for summer ground cover.

GROWING BAG

Plastic bag filled with a nutrient-enriched growing medium, traditionally peat-based but now often a peat substitute such as coir fibre. It is intended primarily for single-season crops, additional feeding is normally required.

GROWING POINT

The tip of a shoot or branch, from which further growth takes place.

H

HALF-HARDY

A term used to describe plants that are unable to withstand frost. Such plants require the protection of a heated greenhouse or frame during the winter months.

HALF-STANDARD: *see* STANDARD

HARDENING OFF

The practice of gradually acclimatising plants raised indoors or under glass to outside conditions, often in a cold frame. This avoids a sudden check in their growth.

HARDWOOD CUTTING

One taken at the end of the growing season, when the shoot has matured and hardened (*see* page 429).

HARDY

Frost-tolerant. Hardy plants tolerate frost but vary in the extent to which they will survive low temperatures, and in particular prolonged cold.

HAULM

The stems and foliage of some plants, particularly peas, potatoes, runner beans and sweet peas.

HEAD

1. A group or cluster of flowers crowded together at the end of, or along, a stalk.
2. The network of branches on a tree or shrub grown on a single stem, that forms on top of the trunk.
3. A fully developed cauliflower or cabbage ready for harvesting.

HEART-WOOD

The hard wood at the centre of the trunk or main branch of a tree.

HEAVY

A term which, when applied to soil, means it contains a high proportion of clay particles.

HEEL

A small piece of bark attached to a cutting when it has been pulled away from its main stem.

HEELING IN

The temporary planting of trees, shrubs or other plants, until they can be planted permanently. This is sometimes necessary if plants arrive when the ground is frozen or waterlogged, or if the area has not been prepared to receive them.

HERBACEOUS

Plants that produce soft, non-woody growth. Herbaceous plants usually die down in the winter, but grow again the following spring from basal shoots.

HIP

The fleshy fruit of a rose.

HOOF AND HORN

An organic nitrogenous fertiliser (*see* page 389).

HORMONES

Growth: chemicals, usually artificially synthesised, to imitate naturally occurring hormones. They are used in powder or liquid forms to promote plant development.
Rooting: an organic compound used to stimulate a cutting into forming roots.

HOSE-IN-HOSE

An abnormal arrangement of the flowers in some primroses and cowslips. The flowers grow in pairs, one from the centre of the other.

HUMIDIFIER

A device for raising the humidity in a room or greenhouse.

HUMIDITY

The amount of moisture in the atmosphere. It is often expressed as 'relative humidity', a percentage of the maximum that would be present if the air were saturated.

HUMUS

The organic residue of decayed vegetable matter.

HYBRID

A plant which has resulted from crossing two different species, often of the same genus, and which contains some of the characteristics of each. Plants raised from the seeds of hybrids often do not breed true to type (will not be like the parent).
F1 hybrids are plants raised from seed produced by crossing two perfectly true parent strains. Pollination is often by hand. F1 hybrids are vigorous and uniform. Seeds from these hybrids do not breed true to type (*see* BIGENERIC).

HYDROPONICS

A method of growing plants in nutrient solutions without using compost (potting soil).

I

IMMUNE

Plants which by their nature are unaffected by certain pests or diseases. Immune varieties resistant to some pests or diseases may be vulnerable to others.

INCINERATOR

Receptacle for burning garden and other waste. Usually designed with good ventilation to create a draught for rapid burning.

INCURVED

The flower heads of certain chrysanthemums where the florets curve inwards to form a firm globe are described as incurved.

INFLORESCENCE

The flowering part of a plant.

INORGANIC

The term is applied to any chemical compound that does not contain carbon. Inorganic fertilisers are artificially synthesised, in contrast to organic fertilisers, which are produced from bones, blood, feathers or other natural matter that was formerly alive.

INSECTICIDE

Any substance or chemical compound that will destroy garden pests. Insecticides, in liquid, powder, smoke or vapour form, fall into two categories – contact poisons and systemic poisons. Some chemicals combine both types of action (*see* SYSTEMIC INSECTICIDE).

INSECTIVOROUS

Insect-eating: the native wild plant sundew (*Drosera*), for example, traps insects between its toothed leaves. These plants generally dissolve their prey in special secretions and absorb the result as food.

INTERCROP

A crop which is grown between the rows of another crop, particularly while the latter is in the early stages of its growth and not taking up much space.

IRRIGATION

The artificial application of water to stimulate growth.

J

JOHN INNES COMPOSTS

Term used to describe loam-based composts made to particular formulae; not a trade name.

JOINT: *see* NODE

K

KEY

The winged seed pods of the ash, lime and sycamore.

L

LATERAL SHOOT

Shoot branching off from the leader or a main branch.

LAYERING

Method of propagation, in which a suitable low-growing branch is laid down and pegged in contact with the soil (*see* pages 432–433).

LEADER

The main shoot extending the branch framework of a tree.

LEAF MOULD

A foliage disease caused by a range of fungi.

LEAFMOULD

Leaves that have decomposed; usually used as garden compost.

LEGUME

A botanical term for the type of seed pod found in plants of the pea family. Also loosely applied to a plant which is a member of the pea family, especially to food plants.

LEVELLING

Cultivating an area of ground to give an even, smooth surface that is level or gently sloping.

LICHEN

Primitive growth often found on rocks or old trees. The grey-green encrustation is formed of algae and fungi which live together.

LIFTING

Digging up all types of plants, including trees and shrubs, for planting elsewhere, especially of bulbs and root crops for storing.

LIGHT

1. The glass top of a cold frame which can be opened and shut.
2. Sandy soil that is easily dug.
3. An essential ingredient for plant growth. Energy from sunlight is used by plants to convert water and atmospheric carbon dioxide into simple sugars, which form the basis of the plant's tissues. Length of daylight also influences plants and it controls flowering and bulb formation in many species.

LIMB

A large branch of a mature tree.

LIME

Alkaline soil conditioner, generally used to raise the pH of a soil.

LOAM: *see* SOIL TYPES

M

MAIDEN TREE

A tree in its first year after grafting or budding. It consists of a single, unbranched stem.

MAIN CROP

Vegetables and fruit that produce their crop in the main season, and over a longer period than early or late varieties.

MALE FLOWER

A flower bearing only the male, pollen-bearing organs, the stamens. The female flowers may occur on the same plant or on a separate female plant.

MANURE

Bulky organic animal waste used to improve soil condition and add essential nutrients.

MARGINAL PLANT

One adapted to growing in wet soil and the margins of ponds. Many, such as the marsh marigold (*Caltha palustris*), will grow in damp soil in a bog garden or with the crown submerged in shallow water.

MICROCLIMATE

The climate in a very local area, surrounding a group of plants or a small part of the garden.

MICROPROPAGATION

A form of tissue culture where the minute growing tips of stems are grown and divided under sterile conditions to provide a large number of healthy plants. The technique requires sterile conditions, special nutrient solutions to sustain growth, and growing chambers to produce warmth and light. It is widely used in commercial propagation.

MIXED BORDER

One in which shrubs and herbaceous perennials, and sometimes annuals, are grown.

MODULE

A container for seeds, seedlings or cuttings, usually with multiple cells, one for each plant.

MONOCARPIC

Plant that flowers and fruits just once – often after several years of growth – then dies.

MONOCOTYLEDON: *see* COTYLEDON

MORAINE

The tumbled deposit of rocks and grit found at the end of glaciers. Certain alpine plants will grow only in such conditions, which combine moisture with sharp drainage. A simulated moraine bed of small, stone chippings fed with water from below can be constructed as part of a rock garden.

MOSS

A non-flowering group of plants. Moss can be a serious problem on lawns, where it grows in damp, stagnant and acid conditions, and is difficult to eradicate.

Sphagnum moss is used in air layering to retain moisture round newly forming roots.

MULCH

Any top-dressing of organic material: farmyard manure, straw, compost, pulverised bark or cocoa shells. It is spread generously, several centimetres thick, usually in spring or early summer, over the surface of the soil to conserve moisture and supply the roots with nutrients as it decomposes.

MUTATION

A chance-occurring variation of a plant. A chrysanthemum, for example, may produce a shoot with flowers of a colour different from its type. This is also known as a 'sport' and if it is thought valuable, it may be perpetuated by cuttings or by budding or grafting on to a suitable rootstock.

N

NATURALISE

To establish bulbs or other plants in the garden, usually in grass, so that they appear to be growing there naturally. Daffodils, crocuses and snowdrops are frequently naturalised.

NECTAR

A sweet liquid secreted by some flowers to attract pollinating insects. Bees make honey from the nectar they collect from flowers, and in the process carry pollen from the anthers of one flower to the stigma of another.

NEMATODES

Microscopic worm-like creatures, some of which cause serious plant diseases. Others can be beneficial, and many are neutral in their effect.

NICKING

Cutting off a small crescent of bark from beneath a bud (usually on a fruit tree), to retard its development.

NITRATE OF SODA

A fast-acting nitrogenous fertiliser (*see* page 389).

NITROCHALK

A fast-acting nitrogenous fertiliser, useful on acid soils (*see* page 388).

NODE

The joint on a stem from which leaves or axillary buds arise.

NOMENCLATURE

The method by which plants are named. This is decided by botanists, and the name changes that can be so irritating to gardeners are because the rules of nomenclature state that the oldest valid name found is the one that should be used (though at the time of writing it has been proposed that the rules be changed so that long-forgotten names do not have to be reintroduced to displace familiar and well-established ones). New research also finds differences between plants that justify some being put into new genera.

Names evolve in the light of research, though the horticultural trade and gardeners often take many years to accept a new name or spelling. In this book we have used the names under which we think you are most likely to find plants sold at the time of publication, but have also given the synonyms under which they may also be found. Old synonyms now rarely used are not included.

NOTCHING

Cutting off a small crescent of bark from above a bud to stimulate its growth.

NURSERY BED

Area of ground in which young plants are grown on until large enough to be planted in their final positions.

O

OPPOSITE

Leaves arranged in pairs on opposite sides of a stem.

ORGANIC

Any chemical compound containing carbon. Organic fertilisers, such as bonemeal, dried blood and hoof and horn, are of animal rather than artificial origin.

OVULE

The part of a seed-bearing plant containing the egg which develops into a seed after fertilisation.

OXYGENATOR

An aquatic plant, such as water violet (*Hottonia*), which releases oxygen through its leaves.

P

PANICLE

A compound flower cluster consisting of several branches, each with numerous stalked flowers. Lilac flower heads are panicles.

PARASITE

Any living organism growing on and taking nourishment from another living organism. Fungi and other living organisms growing on dead organisms are known as **saprophytes**.

PATHOGEN

Micro-organism that causes disease.

PEAT

Dead vegetable matter in a partially decomposed state. It is formed when plant remains from bogs (sphagnum peat) or heath land (sedge peat) are prevented from decaying beyond a certain point through lack of oxygen. It has many uses in the garden. As a result of concern over the depletion of peat reserves and the destruction of wildlife habitats, alternatives to peat are used wherever possible.

PEAT SUBSTITUTES

Natural waste organic products used in the garden in place of peat. These include ground and composted bark, coconut fibre (coir) and cocoa bean shells.

PERENNIAL

Any plant that lives for an indefinite period. Usually applied to non-woody plants.

PERIANTH

Botanical term for the corolla and calyx which surround the sexual organs of many flowers.

PERLITE

A compost additive or rooting medium, made by heating a volcanic rock. It has exceptionally good water- and air-holding capacity.

PERPETUAL

Flowering plants which bloom intermittently throughout the year.

PESTICIDE

Chemical used to kill insects, mites, nematodes and other such pests.

PETALS

The separate, brightly coloured leaves of the corolla. Their main function is to attract insects.

PETALOID

Flower parts, notably the stamens, which have become modified to resemble petals.

PHOTOSYNTHESIS

The process by which, in the presence of chlorophyll, energy from sunlight is used by plants to convert water and atmospheric carbon dioxide into simple sugars, which form the basis of plant tissues.

pH SCALE

A measure of the degree of acidity or alkalinity of the soil. 0 is most acid and 14 most alkaline. Soils below 7 are acid, above 7 alkaline. As it is a logarithmic scale, with 1 point on the scale being ten times more acid or alkaline than the next, a soil with a pH of 8 is very alkaline by horticultural standards.

PICOTEE

A type of carnation whose petals are narrowly edged with a colour on a white or yellow ground.

PILLAR

A trained apple tree, grown in a limited space. A pillar tree has an upright, centre trunk, which produces a succession of young fruit-bearing lateral shoots. The shoots are one or two years old, and are replaced by a system of renewal pruning.

Pillar roses, such as 'American Pillar', are so called because they are frequently trained up pergolas.

PINCHING

Removing the tips of unwanted growing shoots (*see* BREAK).

PINK BUD: *see* BUD STAGES

PISTIL

The total female reproductive organs of a flower.

PLUNGING

Burying pot-grown plants to the rims in soil or a special plunge bed of peat, sand or similar. This prevents them from drying out and reduces the need for watering during summer. Bulbs for indoor cultivation placed in their bowls in the plunge bed will make a strong root system before being taken indoors in late autumn.

POD

A non-fleshing fruit containing several seeds, which splits open when ripe. The fruits of peas, beans and wallflowers are pods.

POLLEN

The dust-like grains produced by the anther of the male flower.

POLLINATION

The transference of pollen from the anthers to the pistil to fertilise the same or another flower.

POTTING

The general term used to describe the act of putting a plant in a pot.

Potting up: the initial act of putting a plant (such as a cutting or seedling) in its own individual pot.

Potting on: moving a plant into a larger pot than it is in already.

Repotting: either loosely used to describe moving to a larger pot (potting on), or, specifically, replanting in the same-sized pot with fresh compost.

PRICK OUT

To transfer small seedlings from the trays in which they have germinated to trays or individual pots where they have more space to grow.

PROPAGATOR

1. Person who propagates plants.
2. Enclosed case or frame, usually heated, where a warm and humid environment can be created to facilitate rapid germination of seeds and rooting of cuttings.

PSEUDOBULB

Thickened, bulb-like stem arising from the rhizome of an orchid.

R

RACEME

A compound flower head consisting of a central, often pendulous, stem with numerous, stalked flowers arranged regularly along it. The flower heads of wisteria and laburnum are racemes.

RECURVED

Petals which are curved backwards from the face of the flower. Many lilies have recurved petals.

REFLEXED

Flower petals which curve sharply backwards and downwards. The term is used particularly of lilies and of certain types of chrysanthemums.

REPOTTING: see POTTING

REVERSION

1. Virus disease of blackcurrants.
2. The change of a hybrid or highly selected plant to its prototype. A grafted tree may produce suckers, which, if not removed, supersede the choice variety grafted on to it.

RHIZOME

Thickened underground stem with roots and leaf buds. The stem, which is the plant's storage organ during the dormant season, grows horizontally, and is sometimes partly above ground.

RING CULTURE

A method of (usually) greenhouse cultivation, mainly for tomatoes and chrysanthemums, in which the bottomless pots (the 'rings') containing the compost are placed on a bed of aggregate such as fine gravel or coarse sand. The plants develop two root systems – those for feeding remain mainly in the ring (through which feeding takes place) and those for absorbing water

penetrate the aggregate below. The system was devised as a method of growing plants in greenhouses where the borders had become impoverished or a source of disease. It is less popular nowadays as growing bags perform a similar function with less work.

ROCK POTASH

A naturally occurring fertiliser that releases potash very slowly. Rock potash is acceptable to organic gardeners (see page 390).

ROOTBALL

The roots and compost visible when a plant is removed from its pot or container.

ROOT PRUNING

Method of controlling vigorous growth, or a way to attempt to produce better flowering and fruiting in a reluctant tree (see page 423).

ROOTSTOCK

The roots onto which a more desirable variety of tree or shrub is grafted or budded.

ROTATION: see CROP ROTATION

RUNNER

A horizontally extending shoot or stolon. Strawberries, for example, produce runners which form new plants where they touch the soil. The new plants can be severed from the parent and planted out when they have rooted.

S

SAPROPHYTE

Any living organism growing on a dead organism. Fungi in the soil are beneficial to the decay of dead matter. (See PARASITE.)

SCALE

The individual segment of a bulb. These segments are sometimes used for the propagation of certain bulbous plants, especially lilies.

SCARIFICATION

1. Abrasion (sometimes chemical treatment) of hard seed coat to facilitate quicker germination.
2. The removal of moss and dead grass from lawns with a lawn rake or scarifier.

SCION

The shoot or bud removed from a plant to be grafted or budded onto the roots (rootstock) of another.

SCREE

Alternative name for MORAINE.

SEAWEED

Seaweed can be used as a fertiliser, providing nitrogen, potash and some trace elements (see page 392).

SEED

A fertilised plant ovule containing a dormant embryo within a seed coat.

SEED LEAF

The first leaf, or pair of leaves, produced by germinating seed (see COTYLEDON).

SEED PAN

Similar to a pot, but shallower, used for sowing seeds, which generally require less depth of compost.

SEED TRAY

Shallow trays (nowadays always plastic) designed to hold the compost for seeds or young plants.

SEEDLING

A young plant with a single, soft and unbranched stem. The term is also used to distinguish a plant raised from fertilised seed from one that has been raised vegetatively.

SELF-COLOURED

A flower of a single colour. Self carnations have one colour only, in contrast to fancy carnations.

SELF-FERTILE

A plant that will set seed when fertilised with its own pollen. Self-fertile fruit trees are suitable for the small garden, as no pollinating partner is needed.

SELF-STERILE

Applied to a plant, especially sweet cherry and many varieties of apple, that needs a pollinating partner to produce seeds and fruits.

SEMI-DOUBLE

Applied to a flower with more than the normal number of petals. Some but not all of the stamens and pistils have developed into petals, as in a double flower.

SEPAL

One of the leaf-like growths that form the calyx of a flower.

SEQUESTRENE

Organic chemical compound used to correct iron or other mineral deficiencies in the soil.

SERPENTINE LAYERING

Technique used for layering climbers where a long stem can be pegged down in several places to make more than one layer from a single stem (see pages 432–433).

SET

1. Small onions, shallot bulbs or potato tubers, which are planted out early in the season.
2. Fruit blossom that has been fertilised (pollinated).

SHADE

Although light is essential to all green plants, some plants require less than others. Some plants prefer shade and many plants need to be shaded from strong sunlight, particularly young seedlings raised under glass.

SHELTER BELT

One or more rows of trees left to grow unhindered to their full height and spread. The effectiveness of a shelter belt as a windbreak depends on its height, thickness and length.

SHRUB

A plant with woody stems and branches, and with no central trunk. Shrubs may vary in height from a few centimetres to over 4.5 m (15 ft).

SIDESHOOT: *see* LATERAL SHOOT

SINGLE

Applied to a flower with the normal number of petals.

SLOW-RELEASE FERTILISER

A fertiliser that releases nutrients steadily over a long period, but not necessarily according to the temperature of the soil.

SOIL TESTING

This is usually carried out to discover the level of alkalinity or acidity (the pH) of the soil (*see* page 387).

SOIL TYPES

Soil texture is determined by the proportions of sand, silt and clay particles that it contains.

Clay soils are heavy to dig, slow to warm up in spring, and become hard and often crack in hot, dry weather. They hold nutrients well and plants seldom suffer from deficiency problems.

Loamy soils fall between the extremes of clay and sand, and are the most desirable for the majority of crops and flowers.

Sandy soils are light and easy to work, warm up quickly in spring and drain freely, but are usually very low in nutrients and organic matter. Soil is also defined by its alkalinity or acidity (*see* pages 386–387).

SPECIES

A group of plants with the same or very similar characteristics within a genus. In *Geranium pratense*, for example, *pratense* is the species and identifies it from all other types of geraniums. Within a species there may be slight botanical variations, which if fixed and well established are called varieties. If these are naturally occurring varieties then they appear in italic type after the species name, for example *G. pratense roseum*; if they have

been raised in cultivation (known technically as cultivars) then they appear in roman type within parenthesis, for example *G. pratense* 'Mrs Kendall Clark'.

SPECIMEN PLANT

A plant which is grown so that it can be seen from all angles. An example is a tree planted in the centre of a lawn.

SPHAGNUM MOSS: *see* MOSS

SPIKE

A compound flower head that consists of a central stem along which are arranged numerous stalkless florets.

SPIT

One spade's depth, which is about 25–30 cm (10–12 in).

SPORE

1. The minute reproductive bodies of ferns and mosses. Fern spores appear on the backs of the leaves; moss spores appear in fruiting bodies which are borne on stalks above the plant.
2. The reproductive cells of fungi.

SPORT: *see* MUTATION

SPROUT

A young shoot, particularly on a germinating seed or tuber. Potato tubers are encouraged to form sprouts in a light, cool and frost-free place, before they are planted.

SPUR

1. A short lateral branch bearing clusters of fruit buds. On old fruit trees such spurs may become large and unwieldy and need thinning out when autumn or winter pruning is undertaken.
2. Tubular appendage in some flowers, such as aquilegias, in which nectar is produced.

STAGING

A bench used in a greenhouse or conservatory, on which plants are grown or displayed.

STAMEN

The male reproductive organ of a flower. It consists of the pollen-bearing anther at the end of the filament or stalk.

STANDARD

1. A plant grown with a bushy head on top of a long stem that is free of sideshoots.
2. Upright petal of the bearded iris, in contrast to one of the falls.

STARTING

Encouraging plants into growth, particularly tubers, such as begonias, after the dormant period.

STEM

That part of a plant above the root system, which carries leaves, buds and shoots.

STEM-ROOTING

Applied to a bulb which roots from the base, but later produces roots from the stem above the bulb. Most Asiatic species of lilies are stem rooting and require deeper planting than basal-rooting species.

STERILE

1. Unable to breed; the term is often applied to plants that produce fertile pollen but no seed. Many double flowers are sterile, as the necessary reproductive organs have become petaloid. Other plants, such as sweet cherries, cannot set fruit without a pollinating partner.
2. Potting composts which have been partially sterilised by heat or chemical means to destroy weed seeds, fungi and other soil organisms that may harm seedlings.

STERILISATION

The act of destroying fungi, weed seeds and harmful bacteria in the soil. Sterilisation, either by heat or by chemical treatment, is only partial: complete sterilisation would render the soil completely lifeless and infertile.

STIGMA

The tip of the female reproductive organ of a flower. It becomes sticky when the ovules are ready for fertilisation, so that pollen adheres to it readily.

STIPULE

Leaf-like or scale-like organ at the base of the leaf stalk, on some plants only. Pelargoniums have stipules.

STOLON

A rooting stem, or runner, on the surface of the soil. Strawberries and mint both produce stolons.

STOOL

Botanically, any plant used solely for propagating purposes. A chrysanthemum stool consists of the old roots and basal shoots, which are taken as cuttings.

STOPPING

Removing or pinching out the growing tips, especially of chrysanthemums and carnations. This encourages the formation of breaks, or sideshoots, and controls the flowering.

STRAIN

A variation or a plant variety raised from seed. Seedsmen select their seed plants for certain desirable characteristics, and a particular flower variety bought from two different seedsmen may be of different strains.

STRATIFICATION

Storage of seeds in warm or cold conditions to overcome dormancy and aid germination.

STYLE

The stem that joins the stigma to the ovary in a female flower.

SUB-SHRUB

An intermediate between a shrub and a herbaceous plant. It produces some woody growth at the base, but the herbaceous top growth dies back annually.

SUCCULENT

Any plant with thick, fleshy leaves or stems. The foliage and stems retain large amounts of moisture, and are adaptations to the arid climates in which succulent plants grow naturally. Cacti and sempervivums are succulents.

SUCKER

1. A shoot which arises from below ground, at the base of a plant.
2. A shoot growing from the rootstock on grafted plants. These suckers must be removed to prevent the stock taking over the plant from the choice variety grafted on to it. Roses frequently produce suckers.

SULPHATE OF AMMONIA

A fast-acting inorganic nitrogenous fertiliser (*see* page 388).

SULPHATE OF POTASH

A widely used inorganic fertiliser high in potash (*see* page 390).

SUPERPHOSPHATE

Sometimes called superphosphate of lime, this inorganic fertiliser contains phosphate that is released fairly slowly (*see* page 389).

SWARD

Area of turf or lawn.

SYMBIOSIS

A state in which two different organisms live together, each contributing something to the other's nutrition. Lichen, which is formed of algae and fungi living together, is one such example. Mycorrhizal fungi, which are often found in association with the roots of beech trees and conifers, also live symbiotically with their host plants.

SYSTEMIC INSECTICIDE

Chemical compound, which when watered on the soil or sprayed on plants enters the sap of the plant. Sap-sucking insects are consequently destroyed, and beneficial insects are generally left unharmed.

T

TAP ROOT

A long anchoring root, which grows downwards into the soil. Vegetables such as carrots and parsnips form tap roots.

TENDER

Plants which are liable to frost damage when grown outdoors. In winter, tender plants, for example pelargoniums and begonias, should be removed to a frost-free room or greenhouse. Some plants are tender in their young stages, but are moderately hardy as they mature and become woody.

TENDRIL

A thin, stem-like, curling outgrowth arising from the stem or leaf stalk of a climbing plant. Members of the pea family climb by twining their tendrils round convenient supports.

TERMINAL

Applied to a shoot or bud at the end of the extending plant growth.

THATCH

Dead organic material mingled with living grass stems on a lawn.

THINNING

1. Reducing the number of seedlings in a drill or tray so that the remaining young plants have room to develop. Thinning is best done in two stages: first, as soon as the seedlings can be handled, leaving twice as many seedlings as are finally required; then thinning to the eventual spacing a few weeks later.
2. Reducing the number of flowers or fruit buds to prevent overcrowding and to improve the quality of fruit and flowers.

TILL

To cultivate the soil by digging, forking, raking or hoeing, or with a mechanically powered plough or a rotary or tined cultivator.

TILTH

Fine crumbly structure to the surface of the soil.

TINE

One of the prongs of a garden fork or rake, or of a mechanical cultivator.

TIP-BEARING

Applied to fruit trees which produce fruit buds at the tips of shoots. These can arrest the growth of the tree, and such buds should be removed while the tree is immature. 'Worcester Pearmain' is a tip bearer.

TOPIARY

The art of clipping and training trees and shrubs into intricate shapes.

TOPSOIL

The most fertile upper layer of the soil, containing most of the nutrients and humus. The subsoil beneath lacks these, and is generally less well aerated.

TRACE ELEMENTS

Certain chemical elements, such as iron, manganese, boron, copper and zinc, are required in minute quantities, but are essential for plant growth. Lack of any of these chemicals, which are present in fertile soil in small quantities, can lead to deficiency diseases (*see* pages 412–413).

TRANSPLANTING

Moving plants from one place to another to provide them with more growing space, or to check their root growth. Plants such as cabbages and wallflowers are transplanted for both reasons. Shrubs and trees raised in nurseries are transplanted annually to keep their roots compact, so that they will establish more readily after lifting for sale.

TREADING

Firming recently cultivated soil by walking heavily on it, before preparing it for sowing or planting. In firm soil, plant roots are in close contact with the soil particles and are able to take up water and nutrients in solution. Transplanted trees and shrubs should always be firmed in by treading carefully round them to eliminate air pockets.

TREE

Any plant with a central woody trunk or main stem.

TRUE BREEDING

Plants whose flowers, after being fertilised with their own pollen, set seeds which germinate into seedlings that are indistinguishable from the parent plant.

TRUMPET

The name given to Division I of the 12 Divisions of the narcissus family (those known as daffodils), in which the tubular, trumpet-like corolla is as long as, or longer than, the perianth segments.

TRUNK

The main stem of a mature tree.

TRUSS

A loose cluster of flowers or fruits at the end of a stem.

TUBER

Swollen underground root or stem used for the storage of food and producing shoots. These shoots produce new plants, which in turn develop underground branches that swell and become tubers. Potatoes are tubers; dahlias and begonias are tuberous plants.

TUFA

Porous type of limestone.

TUNIC

The thin outer skin or membrane surrounding corms and most bulbs.

TURF

1. A grass sward maintained for ornamental purposes.
2. Pieces of turf cut and lifted for laying a lawn.

TURION

Winter bud or resting shoot of certain aquatic plants, such as frogbit (*Hydrocharis*). The shoots become detached from the parent plant, and spend the winter either resting on the bottom of the pool or floating. In spring, turions form individual roots and develop into independent plants.

TYPE

That specimen of a species which was first described and accepted for the purpose of botanical classification. Species which differ from the type are considered to be variants of it.

U

UMBEL

A flower cluster in which the stalked flowers all arise from the same point on the plant's stem, as in polyanthus.

V

VARIEGATED

Applied to leaves (and occasionally flowers) of two or more colours.

VARIETY

A variant of a species which has arisen either naturally or as a result of selection. (*See* NOMENCLATURE and SPECIES.)

VERMICULITE

A natural substance, allied to mica, which, when heated, expands and produces air-filled granules. This light and absorbent material is used as a rooting medium for cuttings and seeds.

VERNALISATION

Keeping seeds or bulbs for a period at a particular temperature – low temperature for temperate plants, particularly alpines, and high temperature for tropical plants. This causes them to pass more quickly from their vegetative to their reproductive phase, so that when seeds are sown or bulbs planted they will grow or flower more quickly, or out of season. This practice is used by nurserymen in preparing bulbs sold for forcing.

W

WATER SHOOT: *see* EPICORMIC

WHORL

Three or more organs arising from the same point on a plant.

WILT

Plants in full growth may flag or droop for a number of reasons. Wilting may be caused by lack of moisture in the soil, by physical damage to the roots, or by pest or disease damage, especially fungal diseases, which attack the water-conducting tissues in the plant stems.

WINDBREAK

A hedge, fence or wall which lessens the force of strong winds.

WINTER WASH

Any insecticide or fungicide applied to plants during the dormant season. The term is chiefly applied to tar oils and other chemicals that are sprayed on fruit trees in late winter to destroy overwintering insects and their eggs.

WOOD BUD

Alternative name for a growth bud (*see* BUD).

WORMERY

A container in which vegetable matter is decomposed by the action of suitable worms (such as brandlings), producing humus like that from a compost heap.

WORMS

In the cultivated parts of the garden worms are beneficial, as they aerate the soil and help to produce humus. Worms should be discouraged from lawns, as they produce unsightly, slippery casts that spoil the turf.

Index

Page numbers in *italic* refer to illustrations.

C